D0857738

IMPRINTING

BEHAVIORAL SCIENCE SERIES

IMPRINTING

EARLY EXPERIENCE AND THE
DEVELOPMENTAL PSYCHOBIOLOGY OF ATTACHMENT

Eckhard H. Hess

FOREWORD BY KONRAD LORENZ

BEHAVIORAL SCIENCE SERIES

Van Nostrand Reinhold Company
New York Cincinnati Toronto London Melbourne

Van Nostrand Reinhold Company Regional Offices:
New York   Cincinnati   Chicago   Millbrae   Dallas

Van Nostrand Reinhold Company International Offices:
London   Toronto   Melbourne

Copyright © 1973 by Litton Educational Publishing, Inc.

Library of Congress Catalog Card Number: 72-14437
ISBN: 0-442-23391-4

Manufactured in the United States of America

Published by Van Nostrand Reinhold Company
450 West 33rd Street, New York, N.Y. 10001

Published simultaneously in Canada by Van Nostrand Reinhold Ltd.

15   14   13   12   11   10   9   8   7   6   5   4   3   2   1

Library of Congress Cataloging in Publication Data

Hess, Eckhard Heinrich, 1916-
  Imprinting.

  (Behavioral science series)
  Includes bibliographies.
    1. Imprinting (Psychology)   2. Animals, Habits and behavior of. I. Title.
  QL763.2.H47   156   72-14437
  ISBN: 0-442-23391-4

For Dorle

BEHAVIORAL SCIENCE SERIES

The Van Nostrand Reinhold Behavioral Science Series will publish a broad range of books on animal and human behavior from an ethological perspective. Although presently observable behavior is the focus of this series, the development of behavior in individuals, as well as the evolutionary history in various species, will also be considered. It is felt that such an holistic approach is needed to come to a fuller understanding of behavior in general. This series is a contribution toward this goal.

Erich Klinghammer, Consulting Editor
Purdue University

Foreword

My old friend Eckhard Hess has asked me to write a Foreword to his book on imprinting. I feel very honored indeed, though my claim to this honor is a rather tenuous one: I happen to be one of the numerous people who, independently of each other, have made the discovery that certain species-specific behavior patterns of birds become fixated on their object by a process which is different, in many ways, from all other kinds of learning. But even this claim is doubtful, as my "discovery" was more or less thrust upon me at a very early and sensitive period of *my own* ontogeny. At the age of five I wanted to have a duckling of my own, and I yearned for its possession with all the obstinate singleness of purpose which is characteristic of the true scientist. I got my wish, notwithstanding the dark predictions which my father uttered concerning the life expectancy of that duckling. He was proved wrong. The duckling grew into a fat female Rouen duck which lived to a ripe old age, seldom attained by organisms of equal edibility. It is my honest belief that I learned, from that bird, quite as much as I did from most of my human teachers.

Among other things, this duck taught me quite a lot about imprinting. At five, I pardonably failed to grasp the importance of the phenomenon, but, like St. Cuthbert (see p. 67), I *did* realize that it could be used to render birds permanently tame and attached to their human keeper. I have, in fact, never ceased to make use of imprinting for this purpose and I am still doing so.

Fate ordained that I should learn quite a lot more about imprinting, still not in concerted effort to elucidate the phenomenon, but in research directed at altogether different goals. For instance, when I tried to settle a colony of free-flying jackdaws (Coloeus monedula spermologus) in the garret rooms of our house in Altenberg, I tried, at first, to get the birds as tame as possible, and, for that purpose, took them under my care when they were only a few days old. By doing so, I got their sexual responses imprinted on humans, so that they were useless as objects of an investigation concerned with the social life of their species. When I took jackdaws that were already in the act of fledging, I failed to get them tolerably tame at all, and consequently they refused to follow me and were lost. In experimenting with different ways of rearing, taking the birds at different ages, I discovered that the sexual responses of jackdaws become fixated on their object much earlier than do the infantile responses of following the parent bird. There is but a narrow temporal margin between both processes and it is not too easy to rear a jackdaw in such a way that it will follow its human keeper without simultaneously "humanizing" its normal sexual behavior. One of the main reasons why all kinds of geese are such opportune objects for sociological investigation lies in the fact that it is extremely easy to imprint their infantile attachment and, with it, many of their social responses, to human beings without affecting the bird's sexual reactions. The latter are imprinted more by the siblings than by the parents, which accounts for the fact that, contrary to the experience of Mascall (see p. 68), waterfowl fostered by hens do not usually become sexually imprinted on chickens.

The irreversibility of imprinting also was impressed on me very early in my life, long before I studied jackdaws. I did not actively strive to gain that knowledge; it literally flew in by the window. I was sitting at breakfast near an open window in the Vienna flat of my parents when there was a flutter of wings and a lovely fully adult-plumaged female hawfinch (Coccothraustes Coccothraustes L.) landed close to my coffee cup. As the bird was between the window and myself, there was little chance of getting around it, so I prepared to risk grabbing the bird. I am very good at making a swift grab, but the bird forestalled my intentions by casually hopping on to my hand as it slowly crept closer. I realized that the bird had been hand-reared and I conscientously advertised its arrival in a newspaper. When none answered, I gladly added the bird to my collection. I was lucky in being able to procure a male hawfinch almost at once, but my hope of seeing these birds breed remained unfulfilled. For many years—the larger finches are long-lived—the female persisted in courting myself and other people while remaining absolutely unresponsive to the advances of the male which, being a wild-caught bird, courted her assiduously.

By telling these anecdotes, to which I could add many analogous ones, I want to impress upon the reader that we came upon the phenomenon of imprinting quite unexpectedly, in the day's work of the aviculturist. At first we regarded it as a welcome means to make birds permanently tame, and, simultaneously, as a most unwelcome obstacle to their breeding. We did not expect the results of imprinting to be irreversible and we most persistently did our best to reverse them, hoping against hope.

I am not denying, however, that I did, at an early stage, realize that imprinting is indeed a very remarkable process. What struck me was its similarity to the process which, in experimental embryology, is termed *induction*. At that period, like most of my contemporaries and indeed like most present-day behaviorists, I more or less equated all learning with the process of classical conditioning by reinforcement. From that point of view, imprinting does indeed seem very different from learning. However, as my views on learning in general changed and developed, I gradually came to understand how closely akin *all* learning processes really are to embryogenetic induction, although the affinity is, of course, particularly striking in the case of imprinting.

Most of what I have said hitherto is contained in my old "Kumpan" paper published in 1935. It will be evident that I myself have only been making some observations about imprinting and giving some thought to the phenomenon. I am admittedly a poor experimenter and our knowledge about imprinting would have remained, for the time being, at a more or less prescientific stage. Hardnosed scientists would have dismissed everything I knew as "anecdotal." What was needed was an experimenter who had a knack for the "nonobstrusive" experiments that alone could furnish the base for any analytical understanding of imprinting. The man who succeeded in putting some hard, incontrovertible facts under the noses of scientists was Eckhard Hess. It was he who put imprinting "on the map." I had heard and read about his work after I came home from Russia in 1949 and when he visited me In Germany in 1951. I learned more about it in 1954. When I came to the States in that year, Eckhard Hess was on the pier at my arrival to give me a warm welcome. We talked about imprinting and we have been personal friends and allies ever since in respect to science as well as to philosophy of science.

The greatest gift one scientist can give to another and particularly a younger man to an older one, is the continuance of a line of research initiated by the other. Eckhard Hess has made that gift to me, and much more than that. He not only has confirmed hypotheses which were hardly more than conjectures, but he has offered a really constructive critique of my ideas, changed many of them, and he has gone on building up on whatever was sound in my early ideas of imprinting.

In this book, Eckhard Hess has given an unsurpassable representation of imprinting, viewed from all its sides, and giving a really comprehensive statement of its problems. The historical development, not only of our ideas concerning imprinting, but of the whole science of animal behavior, is stated in a way which is a real achievement.

It is an arduous and demanding task to represent the opinions and attitudes of other scientists, and that is exactly why it is so difficult to write an impartial and just history of science. In fact, very few authors are sufficiently conscientious in restating other scientists' opinions. I myself, in particular, may be pardoned for saying so. As I wrote my first, and, as I think, most important papers in German, many English-speaking students of animal behavior have read more of what has been written about me than of what I have written myself. I have become resigned to having my opinions grossly distorted and these distortions criticized. Thus I have rejoiced all the more in finding, in Eckhard Hess' book, an absolutely correct rendering of my work, not only as far as it concerns imprinting, but equally in respect to all fundamental questions of ethology in general. As an old man, I feel particularly gratified by his analysis of the historical background out of which our science has grown.

I feel convinced that many other students of animal and human behavior will feel, as I do myself, that their scientific opinions and philosophical attitudes have been correctly restated by Eckhard Hess. This conviction raises my hope that his book will do a lot to eliminate semantic and other misunderstandings as well as antagonisms born out of misunderstanding. It may do a lot to create a better mutual understanding of ethologists and psychologists.

Konrad Lorenz

Preface

This volume is an account of my personal view of that early experience effect known as *imprinting*. The book reflects the study and work I have done in this area over a period of 25 years. Consequently, I have emphasized those studies that are reasonably consistent with my methodology, findings, and conclusions, although opposite findings and interpretations receive considerable attention. Chapter 3 and 4 are particularly comprehensive in reporting on the representative studies on imprinting from every viewpoint.

When I completed the manuscript for this book, well-meaning friends cautioned me about my insistence on dealing with such topics as "nature versus nurture" and the problem of innate behavior. I decided, however, to retain this material. This was partly because it seemed important in order to gain a historical perspective and also because there appears to be a reemergence of these problems resulting from the advances being made in behavioral genetics. For example, in one of the most recent books in this area, *Gene Organization and Behavior* by Delbert D. Thiessen (1972), the point is made, in regard to the use of highly inbred strains of animals, that it allows "partitioning phenotypic variance into genetic and environmental components." This is a far cry from the views expressed by many psychologists and some ethologists. Robert A. Hinde, for example, in his second edition of *Animal Behaviour*, has gone so far as to declare that the distinction between innate and learned behavior is "not only *false* but *sterile*" (italics mine). The statement is, of course, somewhat redundant, but it is important as a typical example from the current mainstream of scholarly thinking and writing upon animal and human behavior. Fortunately, there is a minority position, held not just by some European ethologists, but also by workers in other areas of the world, that there is no compelling evidence that would lead to the complete rejection of innate behavior. R. F. Ewer of Ghana, for example, has written that "it seems a bit silly to object to the term 'innate' . . . (my preference [is] for 'endogenous') when in fact the class of phenomena which it is supposed to cover is one with which both ethologists and comparative psychologists deal" (Ewer, 1971, p. 803). This points to the fact that innate behavior is actually being studied, but with a refusal to recognize it as such, by many researchers, presumably because they regard the issue as passé.

It is clear to me that with the growth of knowledge relating to genetic determination of behavior our approach to the total analysis of behavior will have to include the contribution of the genotype. Whether we use the now-popular term "genotype-dependent ontogenetic process" or something else is not of much concern to me as long as the genetic contribution to behavior is studied and its importance and effects are being clarified. Only by knowing the genetic potential will it be possible to assess accurately the influence of the environment and particularly of learning during the ontogenetic process.

Furthermore, the phenomenon of innate behavior is still very much alive. In the literature of the very same people who disdain the usefulness of the innate behavior concept, one can find references to such things as "movements whose form is not determined by 'practice' or 'example'" (Hinde, 1970, p. 435) or to repertoires of behavior patterns which appear in complete form at the first appropriate situation without previous relevant experiences.

The rise of epigenesis, which I describe in Chapter 1, has been the principal means by which the environmentalists have tried to explain away innate behavior as being an unnecessary concept. The emphasis upon the effects of environment upon animal behavior has continued to dominate such students of animal behavior and has prevented them from perceiving the actual primary importance of innate behavior as the foundation for all behavior. Certainly I have not always been immune from the overemphasis upon learned behavior.

In fact, when I first started studying the imprinting phenomenon I was struck by the fact that it appeared to be a perfectly beautiful case of learning from scratch. I saw the brains of hatchling chicks and ducklings as complete "tabulae rasae" upon which the first social experiences made indelible marks. Because the animals were treated so soon after hatching, I thought that all the experimental variables could be so beautifully controlled. In the early years of my imprinting research, the title of the project was "The Experimental Analysis of Imprinting—A Form of Learning."

I soon began to find out, however, that the learning situation was not all that pure. Chicks and ducklings treated in an identical fashion responded differently to the same experimental situation, and different breeds of chicks and ducklings also reacted differently. I soon realized that this could be only because the genetic substrates of these different species and breeds were not identical with each other. I also began to find that predictions of experimental outcomes on the basis of laws of learning had a persistent tendency to miss the mark. By 1962 I was compelled to admit that if imprinting were indeed learning it had to be a special kind of learning, and one that was genetically programmed into the behavior repertoire of the hatchling. Konrad Lorenz's 1965 proposal that all animal species are innately programmed to learn specific kinds of things buttressed my conclusion.

Then, only a few years later more evidence compelled me to recognize even more the extremely strong role played by innate factors in the imprinting process. For example, I discovered that ducklings would imprint so much more decidedly to a simulated duck than to a human being. I then began looking at real imprinting events occurring out in nature between newly hatched ducklings and their own parent. As a result of doing this I found that in nature there are a whole host of innate factors which work together to guarantee the formation of an optimal parent-young bond. I found that the situation was extremely different from that which is usually found in experimental laboratory studies of imprinting where animals are given completely abnormal social and sensory experiences and are tested in unnatural situations. In these laboratory situations the introduction of abnormal variables into the life of hatchling ducklings and chicks had led to widely differing results and theoretical formulations upon the nature of imprinting.

So, after 25 years of doing research on imprinting, I have become convinced that much of the imprinting process, particularly in the natural situation, has a complex innate substrate. I have concluded, in fact, to paraphrase a statement I quoted above, that the study of imprinting solely from a learning viewpoint is "not only *false*, but *sterile*."

It would have been very difficult to conduct intensive research on imprinting over these many years without the help of a great number of people whose efforts were indispensable to my study of the imprinting phenomenon.

Professor John E. Cushing at Johns Hopkins University in Baltimore got me started on the whole thing by advising me to read Konrad Z.

Lorenz's classic 1935 article on the subject. Inspired by this article, I asked Cushing to arrange for me to meet A. Ogden Ramsay, who had worked with him on parent-offspring relationships in birds and who had done independent imprinting research at nearby McDonogh, Maryland. Ramsay and I then decided to collaborate and I have been "in imprinting" ever since.

Not only was Lorenz's article instrumental in the early days of my research work, but so were the writings of Uli Weidmann, also from Germany.

In addition to Ramsay, many people have worked directly with me in the conduct of the research. My wife, Dorle, has been a real help to me in this respect. She has performed beyond the call of duty by pitching in with everything from the unglamorous job of animal caretaking to testing animals and publishing with me. Several additional people at Maryland were closely connected with the imprinting research. Samuel O. Bowers and Woodrow Wilson Harper worked faithfully as animal caretakers during the early years, Elihu S. Abbott has now been my highly talented technical assistant for several years, and his wife, Doris Marie Abbott has spent many hours imprinting ducklings to herself.

At The University of Chicago Earl Gartley has worked very compentently for over ten years as my animal caretaker and general assistant. Students at Chicago have, of course, been many. Among the ones that have spent the most time on the project, James M. Polt, Erich Klinghammer, and Slobodan B. Petrovich were virtual right-hand men who expended vast amounts of time, talent, and energy to keep things moving. An additional student who conducted outstanding imprinting research for his doctoral dissertation was Joseph K. Kovach.

The United States Public Health Service of the National Institutes of Mental Health will be giving financial support to the research project for the twentieth year during 1973, so it is appropriate that this volume should appear during this anniversary. The research grant has been given the designation #776, with variations in prefixes and suffixes during the years. I am grateful for USPHS's recognition of this work and for their confidence in continuing to support the project. The University of Chicago, of course, has provided many facilities and many different forms of indirect aid to the project.

Lastly, and in particular, I want to express my gratitude to Elizabeth Goodwin, my research associate, whose editorial skills are apparent in most of my writing but particularly in this volume. Betty's association with me covers a span of fifteen years, from student to colleague.

Erich Klinghammer and Slobodan B. Petrovich have read the manuscript and made many helpful suggestions. Any errors or inconsistencies left in this book are, of course, mine.

Eckhard H. Hess

Contents

1

The Problem of Behavior Origins

The central problem in the study of behavior—whether of animals or of men—is not only what it is but also what are the factors that bring behavior about. Actually, the problem of the origins of behavior is just as old as history: the question of why one behaves as one does has an ever-enduring fascination for man, the "thinking animal." There is an almost universal fascination in *psychology* or "what makes people tick." All of us are continually concerned with the causes and prediction of behavior: the mother teaches her children manners; schools attempt to help us to reach the highest level of scholastic achievement that our abilities will permit; Madison Avenue puts strenuous efforts in its constant striving to influence us to buy particular wares; pollsters attempt to determine in advance the outcome of elections; religious leaders inculcate ideals of behavior and belief; and so on. We are influenced by the behavior of others and in turn we influence their behavior. Everywhere in our contemporary American culture we may see an intense focus of attention on the problems of human behavior and human relationships. What, then, causes behavior of a particular kind in general or specific situations?

While the forms that this basic question has taken are many, and the various answers that have been proposed are also legion, in general, there have been two main factors considered as primal sources of behavior: *nature* and *nurture,* sometimes called *heredity* and *environment,* or *instinct* and *learning.* Furthermore, the issue has been considerably complicated by the fact that not everyone in discussing this question has meant exactly the same things by these terms, nor has the line of demarcation between the two categories always been clear. Nevertheless, such polarizing has actually persisted for centuries, having been reflected in the dualism of many philosophers since antiquity, and it has been only fairly recently that there has been recognition of the fact that even though there are these two broad categories, simple dualism is grossly inadequate to encompass the whole range of behavioral causes. We may find an interplay of various particulate causal factors in any instance of behavior which is being scrutinized.

In any event, the philosophical implications of the origins of behavior have not been limited to scholars, for in common speech we can see reflected the idea that character traits or behavior tendencies are inherited just as are bodily features. "Bad blood" is a well-known expression which implies that good or bad character is directly inherited in toto. We may hear a mother say of her child that he has his father's temper, cleverness, or stubborness, although, to be sure, she may see the father as a model which the child has imitated, so that the child's similar behavior can also be regarded as learned under the father's influence.

The persistent dichotomizing of causes of behavior always has been a factor causing confusion in the whole issue. Although the Ionic philosopher Anaxagoras (500–428 B.C.), the founder of dualism, made a basic distinction betwen mind and matter, the bipolar division of which we are most aware is that between *living* and *non-living* (and we do not know to what degree viruses are living organisms), but when we consider the matter from the point of view of the *living,* the distinction becomes *organism* and *environment.* In other words, we have at hand living matter, which not only consists of a mass of interrelated forces within itself, as seen in the controlled division of labor in multicellular organisms and in the intricate interaction of molecules or particles in single cells, but also is subject to influences emanating from sources outside it. If we study the behavior of living matter, we will easily see that it is a product of both internal and external influences. Seeing light, for example, may make an organism move toward its source, but there must also be a disposition, originating from within, to approach light sources. If an animal needs food, it will attempt to obtain it. The environment usually offers certain opportunities, which the animal may act upon, to fulfill this physiological need. The animal may learn to perform new adaptive behavior or in some way to modify its previous behavior in order to obtain the food it needs, in accordance with the environmental conditions. In spite of all this, it has been shown that simple dualism between the internal and external environment is a gross oversimplification of the true situation.

HISTORY OF THE CONCEPT OF INSTINCT

What we have just stated is not a simple series of facts but really a philosophical way of looking at the nature of the world. The concept of instinct, for example, did not arise as the idea of inherited behavior originating within the organism and providing for a response to a specific situation and not resulting from adaptation resulting from the trial-and-error behavior of the individual. The philosophers of antiquity did not have the benefit of present-day scientific knowledge or of the number-less experiments that have been carried out since their time, especially recently. While specific aspects of their concepts of the nature of the world and of the universe sometimes do appear ludicrous in comparison with today's more sophisticated scientific theories (which means that today's theories may also appear ludicrous to the man of years hence), they were a necessary beginning, and sometimes did steer in the right direction.

Wilm (1925), Langfeld (1951), Beach (1955), and Fletcher (1957) have traced the concept of instinct from antiquity to Darwin and beyond. It is clear that before Darwin's time instinct was purely a philosophical concept. It was not a scientific concept, for practically no experiments were actually carried out to determine the origins of behavior. After Darwin's theory of evolution became current, the concept of instinctive behavior could be subjected to scientific inquiry.

Ancient Philosophical Views on Instinct

While most of the philosophers of antiquity subscribed to ideas of the evolution of life from non-living matter and saw a relationship between man and animal (as reflected in the prohibition of the eating of meat by the Epicureans and Neoplatonists on the ground of this relationship), they did distinguish between man and animals on the basis of reasoning ability, which they supposed to be absent in animals. Heraclitus (c. 536–470 B.C.), whose ideas were enlarged upon by the later Stoics, saw men and gods as products of rational creation and animals and plants as products of irrational creation. Plato (427–347 B.C.) also denied rational abilities to animals, and regarded them as governed only by vegetative and organic impulses. Thus, according to the Platonic view, reason could direct the actions of man, while only appetites or emotion could influence the actions of animals. The great Greek philosopher, Aristotle

(358–322 B.C.) had similar ideas regarding the distinct division between animal and human behavior on the basis of the supposed presence and absence, respectively, of reason in man and animals; nevertheless, he did conceive of the animal kingdom as a gradual and continuous progression from the lowest to the highest, the acme being represented by man, above the Indian elephant, in his "Scala Natura" (in *Historia Animalium*). Thus difference betwen human and animal behavior was really one of degree rather than of kind in the Aristotelian system. But there were some scholars who went further and refused to differentiate between man and animal on the basis of the presence or absence of rational capabilities. Theophrastus (372–286 B.C.), the Aristotelian Greek philosopher, his follower Straton (d. 270–268 B.C.), and the Greek biographer Plutarch (c. 45–c. 125 A.D.) emphasized the relationship between men and animals not only in physical characteristics but also in feelings and intelligence. Such differences as existed between man and animal were regarded as being only in degree. Plutarch, for example, attributed to animals a widsom equal to the acquisition of complex purposive and adapative behavior. Moreover, he regarded animals as having a moral sense and capable of having fits of insanity. Two Romans, Pliny (23–79 A.D.) and Porphyry (233–305 A.D.), similarly had views expressing a close intellectual and behavorial relationship between man and animal. Porphyry postulated that animals possess all human faculties, including memory, imitation, speech, logical inference, aesthetic appreciation, and regular sense.

Stoicism, however, continued the Aristotelian tradition. The Stoics believed that animal behavior—instincts—was implanted in animals by the Creator. These instincts, conceived of as being unconscious, had, according to their viewpoint, the characteristics of being present at birth, independent of experience, having adaptive function or utility, and of being uniform in their performance, as opposed to the variable nature of learned activities. These concepts regarding the nature of animal behavior, in particular, the notion of the absence of reason in animal behavior, have persisted up to modern times and were particularly stereotyped during medieval times by Saint Albertus the Great (d. 1280) and his pupil Saint Thomas Aquinas (1224–1275). Aristotle's ideas regarding continuity between man and animals were completely disregarded by Albertus, even though he used Aristotle's other ideas as source material in his *De Animalibus*, for he removed man from the "Natural Scale" in order to conform to the Scholastic theology. He wrote that animals, bereft of reason, "are directed by their natural instincts and therefore cannot act freely." Saint Thomas Aquinas, the medieval churchman, also used the concept of the instinctive control of animal behavior, as opposed to the rational control of man's behavior by a divinely implanted soul. Aquinas' writings on this topic, even though devoid of empirical support, still have considerable influence on popular thinking today. It is to be particularly noted that instinctive behavior as well as rational behavior were regarded as implanted by the Creator. Such an explanation of behavior origins, of course, did not lead to any further analysis.

More Recent Philosophers: The Role of Experience in Behavior

Although during the Renaissance, the French essayist Michel Fyquem Montaigne (1533–1592) had popularized the notion of animal intelligence, the famous French philosopher René Descartes (1596–1650) carried the distinction between men and animals to an extreme in his *Discours de la Méthode* (1637) where he said: "Were there such machines exactly resembling in organs and outward form an ape or any other irrational animal, we could have no means of knowing that they were in any respect of a different nature from these animals; but if there were machines bearing the image of our bodies and capable of imitating our actions as far as it is morally possible, there would still remain two most certain tests whereby to know that they were not therefore really men." These two tests were the inability of animals to use or understand language and their failing to show action based on knowledge, but acting "solely from the disposition of their organs." In *Traité des Passions de l'Ame* (1649), Descartes revealed a strongly emotional reason for his opposition to the notion of the minds of animals resembling those of men: it would mean that "we have no greater right to future life than have gnats and ants."

A contemporary of Descartes, the English philosopher Thomas Hobbes (1588–1679) did not conceive of such rigid differentiation in kind between man and animal; he considered both as having essentially similar faculties, with man having the capacity to develop them to a higher level than animals could, especially through the use of language (*De Corpore*, 1655). One of Hobbes' philosophical contributions was an analysis of the relationship between mental operations and environmental conditions. He pointed out that thoughts occur in connected series, and that thoughts were derived from sensations. Sensation was defined as the reception of motions produced by objects external to the individual, with memory and imagination being what remained in the mind after the sensation had ceased (*Leviathan*, 1651). Hobbes postulated a very firm connection between sense experience and mental activities by proposing that the order of sense experiences determined the order of corresponding ideas in the mind.

Seeing the succession of conceptions in the mind are caused (as hath been said before) by the succession they had one to another when they were produced by the senses; and that there is no conception that hath not been produced immediately before or after innumerable others, by the innumerable acts of sense; it must needs follow, the one conception followeth not another, according to our election, and the needs we have of them, but as it chanceth us to hear or see such things as shall bring them to our mind (*Elements of Law,* 1650).

It is clear that the process of the association of ideas was regarded as purely mechanical in nature by Hobbes.

John Locke (1632–1704) then popularized this notion that knowledge was completely determined by the experience of the individual. Locke asserted that in the beginning of existence a mind is blank, or a *tabula rasa,* a clean slate—it contains nothing. Locke made it clear that he rejected the notion of "native ideas and original characters stamped upon their minds in their very first being," but also pointed out that though children had no innate ideas, they apparently acquire ideas while still in the womb (*Essay concerning Human Understanding,* 1690). In this famous passage, Locke declared: "Let us then suppose the mind to be, as we say, white paper, void of all characters, without any ideas; how comes it to be furnished? . . . To this I answer, in one word, from experience. In that all our knowledge is founded, from that it ultimately derives itself." Locke's emphasis on the importance of sense experiences for the attainment of knowledge is illustrated by his prediction that a blind man suddenly given sight for the first time would not be able to tell which of two visually perceived objects of the same size was a cube and which a ball, even though he knew these shapes perfectly by touch.

Associationism

The empirical philosophy associationism had an extremely important and permanent influence on subsequent philosophical and psychological thinking on the origin of behavior. In particular, the concept of the association of ideas which Locke and Hobbes had stated was subsequently greatly elaborated upon. Étienne Bonnot, Abbé de Condillac (1715–1780), for example, extended it to animal behavior. In *Traité des Sensations* (1754) and *Traité de Animaux* (1755), he attributed to animals a mentality akin to man and denied that they had either innate ideas or congenital instincts. Condillac's famous marble statute, which had a soul but which was unable to acquire knowledge until the various senses, first smell, then taste, then hearing, then sight, and finally touch, were supplied, shows how completely he believed that the whole of mental life, and therefore behavior, was the product of experience; not even reflection was regarded as a source of knowledge. Condillac averred that animals have souls just as men do, and are capable of sense perception, ideas, memory, judgment, and even language, thus taking a position which was almost diametrically opposed to that of Descartes. Condillac attributed the animals' lower achievement level in comparison with man only to their lack of experience resulting from their supposedly inferior bodily equipment and sense organs. All their so called instincts were regarded as not innate in origin, but as having been derived from sense experiences.

Subsequent philosophers theorized in increasing detail upon the mechanism of the association of ideas. Hobbes and Locke had not gone so far as to dogmatize that the association of ideas influenced the nature of man's thoughts and his thinking process, and, ultimately, his behavior, but such notions were taken up by David Hartley (1705–1804), a contemporary of Condillac. Hartley theorized that mental structure was complicated by sensation, ideas of sensation, and association processes. His Latin treatise *Various Conjectures on the Perception, Motion, and Generation of Ideas* (1746, but probably composed in 1736) and his book *Observations on Man* (1748) explained the mechanism involved in the association of ideas on the notion of vibratory impulses of nerves in response to vibratory impressions from the environment, with memory consisting of miniature vibrations remaining from past sensations. Hartley extended his theory to behavioral as well as mental phenomena, for he regarded man as living almost entirely by habits which were formed by the constant compounding and recompounding of elementary sensations until the original natural state in which he had been born simply vanished. However, he recognized only one principle of the process of the association of ideas—that is, contiguity in time of sensations or ideas, or simultaneity in the succession of sense experiences.

Philosophers who followed Hartley described other principles of association. Three governing the connections between different ideas succeding each other, "resemblance, contiguity in time or place, and cause and effect," were postulated by David Hume (1711–1776), Scottish philosopher and historian. He considered the effect of contrast to be a mixture of causation and rememblance. As with the other associationists, Hume regarded the role of sense experience in determining man's mental activity to be of the utmost importance: "All this creative power of the mind amounts to no more than the faculty of compounding, transposing, augmenting, or diminishing the materials afforded us by the senses and experience" *Essay concerning Human Understanding,* 1751, a popular rewording of *Treatise of Human Nature,* 1739). Thus it is obvious that in Hume's system ideas were derived strictly from sensations. However, he did not feel that experience was the sole determinant of animal knowledge, as he considered to be the case with man.

> But though animals learn many parts of their knowledge from observation, there are also many parts of it, which they derive from the original hand of nature, which much exceed the share of capacity they possess in ordinary occasions, and in which they improve, little or nothing, by the longest practice and experience. These we denominate *instincts,* and are so apt to admire as something very extraordinary, and inexplicable by all the disquisitions of human understanding. But our wonder will, perhaps, cease or diminish when we consider, that the experimental reasoning itself, which we possess in common with beasts, on which the whole conduct of life depends, is nothing but a species of instinct or mechanical power, that acts in us unknown to ourselves. . . . it is an instinct, which teaches a man to avoid the fire. . . .

Hume stated in no uncertain terms that differences between man and animal were of exactly the same nature as the differences between man and man.

Following Hartley's lead, another Scotsman, James Mill (1773–1836), attempted, in his *Analysis of the Phenomena of the Human Mind* (1829), to construct a complete and consistent account of experience in terms of the theory of the association of ideas. He began by considering "that when our sensations cease, by the absence of their objects, something remains in our mind. This trace is denoted by the name IDEA. The idea is the representative of the sensation." Then he went on to postulate, like Hobbes, that "our ideas spring up, or exist, in the order in which the sensations existed, of which they are the copies. This is the general law of the 'Association of Ideas'; by which term, let it be remembered, nothing here is meant to be expressed, but the order of occurrence." According to Mill, ideas came to be associated when the sensations which they represented had occurred either simultaneously or successively, with succession being the preponderantly more numerous occurrence. But associations—the connections between ideas—varied in strength, as reflected by the length of time they persist and by the certainty or facility with which they are performed. Mill suggested that there were two causes for this variation in the strength of association: the vividness of the associated emotions and ideas, and the frequency of the association. He regarded frequency, or repetition, to be the most important cause of the association of ideas. Other principles, such as resemblance, contrast, causation, contiguity of time and place, he preferred to regard as subspecies or combinations of his two principles of vividness and frequency.

However, Mill did not regard the human mind as enslaved to its particular sense experiences, for he emphasized that while the foundation of mental life lay in experience and the mind could not go beyond its sense data, it was free to make up whatever components it had experienced into arbitrary combinations. Mill also described another important mental phenomenon, one in which individual ideas did not retain a discrete identity but fused together into a single idea which appeared to be just as simple as any one of its original components. As an example of this, Mill mentioned the concept *gold*, which could be broken down into the idea of a specific color, hardness, extension, and weight. *Weight* itself is a complex idea, involving an idea of resistance or force (gravity) in a given direction, extension, and so on.

A different set of basic principles for the association of ideas was devised by the Scotch psychologist Alexander Bain (1818–1903). First of all, he postulated that past impressions received from an agent fuse with the present sensation of it. Thus there may be multiple associations, with a particular idea, and the more of these that operated in a particular instance, the more strongly the associated idea would be called forth. This brought him to the principle of similarity or resemblance in association, which Mill had tried to discount. He also gave far more emphasis to the influence of recency on the strength of the association than Mill had, pointing out that "the difference between transient and permanent recollections turns entirely upon the strength of the association. . . . It is difficult to estimate with precision the influence of recency; we know it to be very considerable. A thing distinctly remembered for a few hours will be forgotten, or else held as a mere fragment, at the end of a month; while anything that persists for two or three months may be considered as independent of the power of recency, and may last for years." (Critical notes in the 2nd edition of J. Mill's *Analysis of the Phenomena of the Human Mind*, 1878.) Bain also specified the intensity of concomitant emotions such as pleasure and pain as a factor in determining the strength of association. Two remaining principles were postulated to govern the strength of association: frequency of repetition, and "mental concentration." Bain considered animals to have the same learning powers as humans but to be limited by a relative lack in power of mental concentration. Finally, the kinds of ideas that were associated were those that occurred contiguously (either temporally or spatially), those that were similar, and those that contrasted with each other, usually by being at opposite ends of a scale of qualities or by mutual definition (as in north versus south).

The associationists undeniably made a very important and influential contribution to the analysis of experience and behavior. The notion of mental connections between components in the stream of mental activity eventually became a fundamental law of thinking and learning. While there had always been an awareness of learning, this appears to be the first that the process of learning was subjected to analysis. Together with the expounding of the associationist doctrine was the emphasis on the role of experience in shaping mental capacity and, after Hartley, behavior.

The Influence of Biology: Darwin

In the meantime, biology was well on its way as a science. Earlier, Erasmus Darwin (1731–1802), the grandfather of Charles Darwin, had expressed agreement with Locke that all knowledge is derived from experience and generally subscribed to Condillac's ideas regarding the sensorial foundation of the acquisition of knowledge and generation of ideas. At the same time, he emphasized the relationship between man and animals in morphology and physiology, saying, "The whole is family of one parent" (*Zoonomia*, 1794). Darwin also expressed the viewpoint that the process of experience in providing for the foundation of all knowledge did not begin at birth but started in the womb.

As an example of prenatal learning, Darwin cited the swallowing of amniotic fluid by the embryo: "The celebrated Harvey [the English physician, 1578–1657] observes, that the foetus in the womb must have sucked in a part of its nourishment because it knows how to suck the minute it is born, as any one may experience by putting a finger between its lips, and because in a few days it forgets this art of sucking, and cannot without some difficulty again acquire it. The same observation is made by Hippocrates."

While the elder Darwin regarded "sensations and desires" as a part of the organic system just as much as muscles and bones, he emphasized that *actions* did not have the same origin: "By a due attention to these circumstances many of the actions of young animals, which at first sight seemed only referable to an inexplicable instinct, will appear to have been qualified like all animal actions, that are attended with consciousness, by the repeated efforts of our muscles under the conduct of our sensations or desires." In fact, he derided the notion of instinctive causation itself, for it was, in his words, "explained to be a *divine something*, a kind of inspiration; whilst the poor animal, that possesses it has been thought little better than a *machine*!"

A completely different viewpoint on instinct was held by the younger Charles Darwin, (1809–1882). While building supporting pillars for his theory of evolution, he described much of man's behavior, especially with respect to the movements involved, as having been descended from similar behavior in animals, just as man's arms and legs descended from similar limbs which his ancestors had. Thus human and animal behavior was regarded for the first time as subject to *hereditary* influences. A prime example of evolved behavior in man was the expression of emotion, which Darwin treated extensively in *The Expression of Emotion in Man and Animals* (1872). In a chapter written for *The Origin of Species,* but first published posthumously as a separate essay in a book by Romanes (1885), Darwin discussed the topic of instinct and stressed that similarity of behavior between related species meant inheritance of that behavior from common progenitors. Darwin had travelled all over the globe, observing minutely not only animal morphology but also animal behavior.

If we suppose any habitual action to become inherited—and it can be shown that this does sometimes happen—then the resemblance between what originally was a habit and an instinct becomes so close as not to be distinguished. ... It would be a serious error to suppose that the greater number of instincts have been acquired by habit in one generation, and then transmitted by inheritance to succeeding generations. It can be clearly shown that the most wonderful instincts with which we are acquainted, namely, those of the hive-bee and of many ants, could not possibly have been acquired by habit. ... It will be universally admitted that instincts are as important as corporeal structures for the welfare of each species, under its present conditions of life. Under changed conditions of life, it is at least possible that slight modifications of instinct might be profitable to a species; and if it can be shown that instincts do vary ever so little, then I can see no difficulty in natural selection preserving and continually accumulating variations of instinct to any extent that was profitable. It is thus, I believe, that all the more complex and wonderful instincts have originated. As modifications of corporeal structures arise from, and are increased by, use or habit, and are diminished or lost by disuse, I do not doubt it has been with instincts. But I believe that the effects of habit are, in many cases, of subordinate importance to the effects of natural selection of what may be called spontaneous variations of instincts; that is, of variations produced by the same unknown causes which produce slight deviation of bodily structure.

Darwin expressed similar views in *The Descent of Man,* (1871) and added, "In the case of the many instincts which, as I believe, have not at all originated in hereditary habit, I do not doubt that they have been strengthened and perfected by habit; just as in the same manner as we may select corporeal structures conducing to fleetness of pace, but likewise improve this quality by training in each generation."

Exactly the same principles of morphological evolution, convergent evolution, divergent evolution, natural selection pressure, and variation between individuals were applied to the evolution of instinctive behavior. It is clear that with Charles Darwin we have a true turning point in the history of the concept of instinctive behavior. Before Darwin, it was generally believed that the "knowledge" displayed in the instinctive behavior of animals was implanted in them by the Creator. But with

Darwin's theory came the idea of the transmission of such instinctive behavior from one generation to another through heredity and being subject to the influence of natural selection. Since then, the dualism in behavior theory has been not of the instinct versus reason but of the inherited or innate (not merely congenital) versus the acquired or learned. Eventually, the problem became how to determine the inherited and acquired bases of behavior and how these are mediated. But that approach was not to be immediately carried out. After Darwin there was a period of acceptance and extension of his views followed by a time of indiscriminate use of the instinct concept, as we shall see, which eventually led to its complete rejection in favor of the influence of experience and learning in the determination of behavior. The Darwinian viewpoint was continued only on the European continent, while for several decades United States psychologists made an all-inclusive and indiscriminate use of learning processes as determinants of behavior. Only now does it appear that this tendency is definitely on the way to being corrected in the United States and that we are returning to a more balanced view of behavior origins. In the fields of genetics, neurology, and physiology, important studies are now being made in an attempt to determine the relationship between the organism's structure and heredity, as well as between its behavior and its experience.

Post-Darwinian Views on Behavior Origins

The old idea that instinct was an extremely rigid behavior mechanism which rendered animals practically into machines acting on an all-or-none fashion, a view which reached a zenith with Descartes, gave way, with Darwin, to a more flexible notion of instinct which regarded it as much the product of evolutionary forces as bodily forms and therefore subject to the same degree of plasticity and modification.

The English naturalist, D. A. Spalding (1840–1877), for example, declared in 1875 his views that there are individual variations in both physical structure and instincts. According to his theory, learning could replace instincts, and instincts could be adapted in accordance with environmental requirements. For example, a hen sitting on duck eggs will incubate them for the week longer it takes to hatch duck eggs than it does for chicken eggs. Spalding also pointed out that behaviors do not have to be manifested at birth in order to merit classification as inherited actions. To him it was an "unwarranted assumption" by the celebrated German scientist Ludwig Ferdinand Helmholtz (1821–1894) that all the actions of which animals are incapable at birth are due to pure learning, and reported his famous experiment with nestling swallows to prove this point. In this experiment, Spalding found that even though the swallows he had isolated in dark boxes from the time of hatching had no opportunity to practice flying during their period of isolation, they were perfectly able to fly when he released them from confinement at an age when normally reared swallows are flying freely. Furthermore, Spalding emphasized that instincts can deteriorate through disuse even when they have never been brought into play, a point which has been made by several modern-day proponents of instinctive behavior.

Other views which are currently receiving emphasis in the consideration of innate behavior were held by another Englishman, C. Lloyd Morgan (1852–1936). Morgan pointed out, in his *Habit and Instinct* (1896), that individual experience can modify the object to which instinctive behavior is directed. For example, he noted, chicks have a "congenital and instinctive tendency to nestle in any warm place," but, he went on, there was considerable doubt that there was any innate recognition of the hen, since chicks that he had reared by hand refused to associate with their own mother or to pay any attention to her when she was made available, even when she tried to entice them to her. Morgan pointed out that there were behaviors which appeared even though the animal had never had relevant experience. He gave as an example a story of hand-reared squirrels which had always lived indoors and never had had any experience with earth or any loose material which could be dug into. Nevertheless, when given nuts for the first time these squirrels "buried" them in the carpet and made patting movements in the air above the nuts as if tamping down loose earth.

Both learning and instinct often coexist and interact in the same behavior of an animal, according to Morgan.

> The final products of individual development may be, and no doubt generally are, of two-fold origin, partly instinctive and partly due to acquisitions; but this, I repeat, does not in any way serve to annul the distinction between the two several elements in the final product. If we add water to our whiskey, there is no longer pure whiskey . . . the whiskey has been more or less modified, but the spirit is still there, none the less, and we cannot neglect its presence.

The spread of Darwinism was certainly intensified by George John Romanes (1848–1894), an English zoologist who was one of Darwin's disciples. An avid observer of animals, as shown by his book *Animal Intelligence* (1881), he took up Darwin's theories as a framework for his *Mental Evolution in Animals* (1883) and *Mental Evolution in Man* (1888). In these books, he made a rather comprehensive attempt to outline the probable sequence of the evolution of abilities and emotional expression in animals and children. He was careful to emphasize that his theoretical scheme was subject to revision and change in the future as more knowledge on animal and human behavior came to light.

While Romanes has been commonly dismissed as "anthropomorphic," a careful study of his writings shows that his terminology (including words such as "animal mind") does appear highly anthropomorphic when quoted out of context; nevertheless, it must be pointed out that the esteemed Charles Darwin could certainly also be accused of this, for he once called an earthworm "timid" when it "jumped like a rabbit" into its burrow. In fact, Darwin and Romanes never claimed the emotions and mental faculties they attributed to animals to be exactly like those in humans but to be highly analogous. Both Darwin and Romanes affirmed that reason, as they defined it, was not a special prerogative of man: Darwin cited an instance of reason in a lowly shore crab, and Romanes (1883) argued that there was no difference in kind between this crab's act of reason and any act of reason performed by man, especially since he did not regard reason as merely self-conscious thought. Scrupulously avoiding any attempt to draw hard and fast lines between different mental faculties, Romanes insisted that the various categories he used in his scheme were only a convenience for analysis, not a reflection of the actual structure of mental activity. Furthermore, the gradual evolution of these various faculties prevents them from being discrete factors; just as one cannot say when an acorn has become an oak, one cannot draw a line and say, "here feeling, choice, etc., begin." For example, differential reaction, or discrimination between different stimuli, occurs even in plants, as seen in the Venus flytrap's differential response to different types of tactile stimulation.

A keystone of Romanes' theoretical system was set forth when he said: "Instinct is reflex action into which there is imported the element of consciousness," consciousness being regarded as simple awareness, not necessarily self-awareness. He went on to say: "The term [instinct] is therefore a generic one, comprising all those faculties of mind which are concerned in conscious and adaptive action, antecedent to individual experience, without necessarily knowledge of the relations between means employed and ends attained." Like Darwin, Romanes saw instinct as not rigid or inflexible but as having many variations between and within individuals of the same species. What is more, Romanes pointed out that instinct can be interwoven with learning in the same instance of behavior—for example, while nest building by birds is an instinctive activity, the use of man-made fibers in the nest may be learned.

The notion of continuity between man and animal was also supported by the Canadian physiology professor Wesley Mills when he declared (1898): "The great distinction between man's faculties and those of animals lower in the scale is difference in degree and not in kind; certainly in so far as they run parallel," especially if man is to be regarded as the outcome of development through lower forms. He went on to say:

"Such a view does not prevent our conceiving of additional forms of psychic (ie., mental) activity not represented in man as in the possession of the brutes. . . . Nor does such a view imply that there may not be avenues of knowledge of a special kind open to man which are closed to those lower in the scale." Today we do know that bees can see ultraviolet light, dogs can hear higher pitches than we do, many insects see polarized light with far greater facility than man does, and most other mammals have much greater olfactory acuity than we do.

One of Mill's favorite themes was that the behavior of animals must be closely observed under natural conditions before any behavior theorizing can be done. He declared "Mere closet psychology is of little value. Comparative psychology will, I fear, continue to suffer till those who assume to deal with it authoritatively spend more time among animals and less in their studies. A few observations or experiments do not give them insight into the psychic (mental) nature of animals." He warned against "assuming the validity of explanations which are not true solutions at all, but mere assumptions."

The evolutionary view of animal behavior was continued and expanded by the American zoologist C. W. Whitman (1842–1910). In an 1898 paper, he propounded the view that unlearned behaviors have the same origin as reflex action and digestion, and are due to organic features or structural-physiological systems. The evolution and genetic variability of instinctive behavior were reemphasized and elaborated upon by Whitman as a mechanism promoting survival of the species. What is more, Whitman discovered that instinctive movements actually could be used as taxonomic characteristics of species, and in some cases could more thoroughly characterize a particular species than could any morphological character. Whitman felt very strongly that it was not enough to merely enumerate, describe, and explain the utility of instincts, but their development and relation to each other and other behaviors should also be explored along phylogenetic lines. Whitman's emphasis on the phylogenetic importance of instinctive behaviors was one of the most important influences in the modern-day study of innate behavior in Europe, the school of ethology.

Contemporaneously, Edward L. Thorndike (1874–1949), well known to psychologists in this country for his pioneer work on association learning processes in animals, expressed thorough agreement with Whitman's position (Thorndike, 1899a, b). It is interesting that his views on innate behavior came to be totally ignored by disciples of the laws of association learning, who eventually claimed practical exclusiveness of association learning in all animal and human behavior. Thorndike had always argued for the previously unrecognized existence of instinct in some behaviors. He also made some observations supporting the biogenetic basis of some behaviors. For example, he noted: "The frog, lizard, chick, and cat all react to irritation of the head by scratching with the hind leg with a quick, repetitive motion that is startlingly alike in the last three. Here we have an instinct which apparently ranges over a sub-kingdom" (Thorndike, 1899b). This scratching movement, made by the hind leg raised over the front limb in the majority of vertebrate species, was subsequently discussed in some detail by Heinroth, another founder of European ethology, in 1930, according to Lorenz (1958b).

Thorndike concurred with Spalding that instinctive behavior may be manifested sometime after the organism is born, and also showed that an instinctive movement may be apparent long before its normal use when he recorded his observation that 6-day old chicks engage in a rudimentary form of the combat behavior of sexually mature roosters. Thorndike emphasized the great variability in instincts between individuals and even in the same individual, as had Darwin, Romanes, and Whitman. Like Morgan, he pointed out that an instinct does not need to be complete in every respect, for the chick, while it has an instinct to follow, does not absolutely require a hen as the object to be followed.

> Instinctive reactions are not necessarily definite, perfectly appropriate and unvarying responses to accurately sensed, and, so to speak, estimated stimuli. The old notion that instinct was a God-given substitute for reason left us an unhappy legacy in the shape of the tendency to think of all inherited powers of reaction as definite particular acts invariably done in the presence of certain equally definite situations . . . our experiments show that there are acts just as truly instinctive [as, for example, the web spinning of the spider], depending in just the same way on inherited brain-structures, but characterized by being vague, irregular, and, to some extent, dissimilar reactions to vague, complex situations.

Almost half a century later, when the concept of instincts had come under severe atack, Thorndike (1942) defended their existence, averring that the human child gets movements such as those of walking, grasping, sucking, and sitting up, "from the same source and with much the same regularity that it gets teeth."

Indiscriminate Use of Instinct

But at the turn of the century the concept of instinct in human behavior was so uncritically accepted that some psychologists began to use it promicuously, apply it to practically every instance of behavior. It probably all started when William James (1842–1910), the philosopher-psychologist, wrote his *Principles of Psychology* (1890). While he regarded instinct as being compound reflexes, he was, nevertheless, more concerned with them as *impulses* in the same sense as today's notions of *motive* and *drive*.

Man has a far greater variety of *impulses* than any lower animal and any one of these impulses, taken in itself is as "blind" as the lowest instinct can be; but, owing to man's memory, power of reflection, and power of inference, they come each one to be felt by him, after he has once yielded to them and experienced their results, in connection with a *foresight* of those results. ... It is obvious that every instinctive act, in an animal with memory, must cease to be "blind" after being once repeated. ...

Thus in such animals practically all behavior would become modified in its mere exercise, and all, according to James, compete on the same basis, regardless of origin.

James was correct in saying, "Every instinct is an impulse," in the sense that every instance of innate behavior is, of necessity, impelled by some motive; but, unfortunately, he came to assume the converse when he wrote:

Nature implants contrary impulses to act on many classes of things, and leaves it to slight alterations in the conditions of the individual case to decide which impulse shall carry the day. ... Each one of them, then, is an instinct, as instincts are commonly defined. But they contradict each other—"experience" in each particular opportunity of application usually deciding the issue. The animal that exhibits them loses the "instinctive" demeanor and appears to lead a life of hesitation and choice, an intellectual life; not, however, because he has no instincts—rather because he has so many that they block each other's path.

James' overextended application of the term *instinct*, without regard as to whether specific impulses have an inherited or acquired basis, had unfortunate results. As we shall see, there came a reaction to this carelessness in using the concept of instinct, a reaction which eventually came to deny the very existence of inborn behavior patterns. This reaction lasted for several decades and still has its effects on present-day scientific thinking in the United States.

REVOLT AGAINST INSTINCT

After James, practically every writer on human psychology, including Thorndike and Woodworth, made lengthy lists of human instincts. For example, McDougall's highly influential *Social Psychology* (1908) had its list, including flight, repulsion, parental feeling, self-abasement. All of these supposed instincts were seriously discussed in detail as such. It appears that after McDougall's book was published feelings that the concept of instinct had far overstepped its boundaries of usefulness began to come to the surface. W. S. Hunter declared many years later (1947), "I believe that the prime basis for the origin of the anti-heredity movement was the violent reaction against the topic of instinct in William McDougall's (1908) *Introduction to Social Psychology.*" Nevertheless, such an indictment is hardly fair, for McDougall was no more extreme than James had been, and it appears a more accurate diagnosis of the situation to say that the accumulation of discontent with the promiscuous use of the instinct concept finally turned into a violent reaction, much as it is the last straw that breaks the camel's back. What is more, the reaction was against what people *thought* McDougall's instinct theory was, while in fact he was far less dogmatic than was believed, and cautioned care in the use of the instinct concept lest it become a "cloak for our ignorance." He regarded the central impulse as the only factor which was really innately specific, while he regarded the actions resulting from such impulses or drives as quite variable. This is an important point, whether an instinct theorist is referring to motivation or to actual movements when he speaks of instinctive behavior (Maze, 1952).

While McDougall should be exonerated, it is true, as was charged, that many of the popular instinct writers of that time had come dangerously close to the notion that, having called certain behaviors instinctive, they had explained them, and no experimental analysis was made of them to determine their actual origins. What is more, this use of the instinct concept had no consistency among the instinct writers, and was likely to be used in a self-contradictory manner, as Holt (1931) pointed out: "Man is impelled, it is said, by his instincts. If he goes with his fellows it is the 'herd instinct' which actuates him; if he walks alone, it is the instinct of pugnacity; if he defers to another, it is the instinct of 'self-abasement'; if he twiddles his thumbs, it is the thumb-twiddling instinct. Thus everything is explained with the faculty of magic—word magic." So it was that, just before the 1920s, the so-called anti-instinct revolt came into being, and not only denied instincts in man, essentially going back to Locke's empiricism, but some of its extremists eventually declared that there were no instincts in animals either, as Condillac had.

Watson's Behaviorism and Emphasis on Experience

John B. Watson (1879–1958), the father of behaviorism, expressed deep dissatisfaction with the psychology current during his young manhood which concentrated primarily on the study of states of consciousness. He made an emphatic call for the study of behavior using only carefully gathered objective facts which could be observed or replicated by anyone. He pleaded very strongly for the causal analysis of all behaviors engaged in by humans and animals in terms of the environmental course of these behaviors. Watson, it is to be noted, never denied the existence of innate behavior patterns in animals; in fact, he had made naturalistic studies of the behavior of noddy and sooty terns (1908). His famed excision of the word *instinct* from psychology was really only in reference to human behavior. He initially supported James' definition of instinct as compound reflexes (Watson, 1919); regarded instinctive behavior in animals and men as phylogenetic modes of response having conceptionally determined neural connections as their basis (Watson, 1914); and classified human emotions and many neonate behaviors as hereditary modes of response (Watson, 1919). However, his longitudinal study of human neonate behavior and the general reaction to the promiscuous application of the term *instinct* to details of human activities such as thriftiness which exploded after Dunlap's 1919 article "Are There Any Instincts?" led Watson to abandon that term in favor of the notion of *unlimited plasticity* of the human child (Watson, 1922). Another reason was that many of the behaviors which had been generally regarded as instinctive, often on the basis of their automatic character, not on the basis of origin, turned out on the basis of cross-cultural studies and close observation, to be largely influenced by the environment. Nevertheless, Watson (1922) always adhered to the notion that emotions had unlearned beginnings, so that his views bore several resemblances to those of Erasmus Darwin. Watson regarded all human emotions as being complex forms of three unlearned primal emotions present in the newborn baby: love (in the same sense as sex in Freud), fear, and rage, all elicited by precise situations. Watson postulated that such responses, as the individual grew, were eventually, transferred to a multitude of objects through conditioning, so that a large number of objects or situations could elicit emotional responses in the experienced person that could not be elicited in the neonate.

The notion of conditioning, which became very popular in the behavioristic movement, had some similarities to that of the concept of association of ideas which refers to mental connections, but differed in that it referred to a process whereby an originally neutral stimulus, or aspect of the environment, could be made to elicit a specific response by associating it with a stimulus which aroused this response. Here the connection is between a stimulus and a response. This process of conditioning was first extensively experimented with and described in detail by the great Russian physiologist Ivan Pavlov (1849–1936). The most widely known example of Pavlov's demonstration of conditioning is the salivary response of a dog to the ringing of a bell. This was done by presenting the animal with meat powder at the ringing of the bell for several times. Eventually, the animal would come to salivate when the bell rang, even though there was no meat powder present. It was this type of behavior acquisition that Watson and other behavorists came to emphasize greatly. Conditioning and association came to be relied upon more and more in the explanation of behavior, and usage eventually gave the two concepts almost synonymous meanings. Such emphasis on the stimulus-response connections eventually resulted in behaviorism being called a stimulus-response (S-R) psychology.

It must be noted that Watson particularly stressed the childhood years as of utmost importance in the formation of personality: "In a way the whole of behaviorism is but an expression of the fact that infancy and childhood slant our adult personalities." (Watson, 1922.) Furthermore, as the individual grows older, Watson points out, changeability through reconditioning or other methods steadily declines, and after the age of 25 to 30, little personality change usually takes place. In fact, Watson averred, the first two years of life are the most important in setting the direction of a person's characteristics. "I have an undying respect for what we can do with that squirming mass of protoplasm we call the human infant," Watson (1928) declared. However, this did not mean that he considered the human neonate as completely formless, for he suggested (Watson, 1922) that there probably was habit formation even in embryonic life. Yet, the childhood period had so much importance to Watson that he made a bold promise that he could take any healthy baby chosen at random and have it follow any profession he chose, from thief to lawyer, provided he was allowed to place the child in the environment he specified. It is interesting to note that Watson's words echoed what Bishop Francis Atterbury (1622–1732) had said more than two hundred years earlier: "The force of education is so great that we may mould the minds and manners of the young into what shapes we please, and give them the impressions of such habits as shall ever after remain."

Nevertheless, Watson (1922) did stress that there are heritable differences in organic form and structure which determine behavior and its limits, and not *instinct*, in the same way that a boomerang's shape makes it return to the thrower. Since the greater emphasis was on learning as the primal source of behavior, the contribution of hereditarily determined response tendencies came to be largely ignored as psychologists began to devote more and more of their attention to learning processes, especially since Watson (1914) had always considered the study of animal learning to have the most relevance for the understanding of human psychology, even though he also said that the study of the behavior of even amoebae was important in its own right. As time passed, some followers of Watson's behaviorism began to deny instincts, even in animals, and became more extreme in their own direction than the most rhapsodic of the instinct theorists had ever been.

Extreme Anti-Instinct Theorists

Undoubtedly, the most radical of the anti-instinct theorists was Kuo (1921, 1922, 1924), who tried to "abolish" instincts entirely as a factor in either human or animal behavior, unlike Watson or Dunlap, who merely sought to end the overextended application of the concept and to confine it to certain areas of behavior. Kuo's objections to the entire concept of instinct were based on several points, the main one being that its use as an explanatory device retarded progress in the scientific study of the origins of behavior. If behavior is inherited, he pointed out, then the inheritance itself has to be explained. A psychology that used heredity to explain behavior, he declared, was a finished psychology, especially since the then current views on instinct as a causative factor in behavior did not offer any means for anyone to discover that a certain manifestation or failure of occurrence of a specific behavior was due to learning not to heredity, making hypotheses on the heredity of behavior "unexperimentable." If responses are to be deemed hereditary, as Kuo correctly pointed out, it is necessary to determine how they are correlated to neuromuscular organization and how these, in turn, are related to germinal organization or heredity. Cytological analyses and physiological studies of development were necessary to do this, and up to that time none of these had been attempted. In sum, Kuo felt that the heredity concept was, in effect, a "lazy substitute for energetic and painstaking work in the laboratory." The only cure for this state of affairs, Kuo decided, was to abolish the concept of instinct entirely, so that psychology could go on with its true task of determining the origins of behavior.

Other points Kuo cited against the instinct concept were that there was no agreement on the number and kind of instincts in existence and that there was lack of due recognition of the importance of environmental stimuli in eliciting behavior. He proposed that the sharp distinction between the inherited and the acquired should be abolished, since, in his view, all behavior consisted entirely of responses to stimuli and reflected an interaction between the organism and its environment.

Also, Kuo felt that assuming a prior relationship between the organism and aspects of its environment was no less objectionable than the notion of innate ideas; just as one cannot have an idea of a tree before having seen one, one cannot have any food trends before having experience with food, he insisted. Kuo furthermore maintained that the idea that instincts could appear later than birth was false, for if certain activities are not capable of being manifested at least shortly after birth, later on they must, by definition, be acquired activities. Walking, for example, he felt to be integrated out of gradually acquired coordination of several parts of the body, so that he was reluctant to consider it an innate activity.

Originally, Kuo had been willing to include in the human endowment a large number of reflex-like *units of reaction*, out of which were supposedly integrated an endless number of coordinated activities manifested in later life. Later, however, Kuo (1932a, b, c, d) denied even these as innate equipment and maintained that reflexes were learned in pre-natal life. He went even further than any of his predecessors in denying the existence of instinct even in the emotions; he did not regard emotional feelings and expressions as inherited responses. Kuo (1924) attempted to explain all behavior on the basis of physiological mechanisms, and defined psychology "as the science which deals with the physiology of bodily mechanisms involved in the organismic adjustment to environment," with special emphasis on the effect, or result, of the response.

Then, in a series of papers (Kuo, 1932a, b, c, d) devoted to the ontogeny of behavior in the chick embryo from a physiological point of view, Kuo reported his observation that the embryonic heart beat caused the chick's head to move up and down. On the basis of this observation, Kuo concluded that the heart beat taught the chick how to peck before it hatched, a view reminiscent of William Harvey's and Erasmus Darwin's suggestions that swallowing was learned during the embryonic life period and of Helmholtz's contention (Spalding, 1875) that chicks learn how to peck before hatching.

Other anti-instinct writers agreed with several of Kuo's points and centered their attacks principally on what they considered to be logical flaws in the use of the instinct concept. Josey (1922), for example, reiterated the behavioristic emphasis on the importance of the environment, or external factors, in eliciting man's behavior: if a ball rolls down hill, we do not need the past history of the ball to explain what happened, but merely need to describe the contemporary situation causing the ball to roll down hill. Josey's particular dragon was the Lamarckian view of instincts: "Man does not inherit a mass of impulses as the result of the experiences of his ancestors." The behavior of remote ancestors he felt to be totally unnecessary as an explanation of the behavior of a contemporary individual, for if a particular behavior had been called forth in our ancestors by the same conditions as in our case, then no appeal to phylogeny is needed; but if the conditions were different, then there is no connection between the two situations and no explanation can be made on the basis of ancestral behavior.

Like Kuo, Josey denied the inheritance of drives and emotions, calling them "acquisitions of the individual that are determined largely by the nature of the society in which he is reared." Not even sexual drives were regarded as innate, but were considered as growing out of experience, for, in his opinion, if abnormal sex results from abnormal environment, then normal sex must be considered as coming from a normal environment.

Another anti-instinct writer was Bernard (1924), who objected to the instinct concept because it had been used, by Romanes and others, to designate acquired habits. Furthermore, he felt that it was wrong to regard activity complexes as inherited, for he felt that it was not really the activities as such but the structures underlying them that were really inherited. He proposed that units of activities be called *instinct*, since they were the basic material out of which an individual's behavior repertory grows. Bernard's instinctive activity units were not the same as Kuo's *unlearned reaction units* because they did not have to be present at birth in order to be considered unlearned, as Kuo had insisted. "The actual instincts," Bernard declared, "are at once much simpler and more elemental than those set forth in the classification of such writers as McDougall, Thorndike, and other psychologists. There are probably hundreds or even thousands . . . of these inherited mechanisms mainly overlooked by the casual observer because they do not ordinarily function as independent units in adjustment processes but rather as constituent elements in larger habit complexes developed in response to environmental pressures." These ideas may seem reminiscent of James, but it must be pointed out that James placed the instinct concept at the level of particulate *impulses* (or what we would term drives or submotives), and Bernard referred to the particulate motor elements themselves as the instincts.

Return to Notion of Innate Origins of Behavior

However, in spite of the anti-instinct revolutionaries' strenuous efforts to expunge the concept, it did not die because even these people found themselves assuming the existence of organismically derived influences of behavior in the form of either underlying structures or of drives or motives, such as hunger and thirst, upon which biological survival could depend. It was Wyatt (1927) who aptly remarked, "The S-R psychologist, having publicly denied Instinct, lets him in at the back door in disguise," since the new lists of *desires, drives,* and so on, that were being drawn up by behaviorists so closely resembled the discredited instinct lists "as to suggest distinction without a difference." McDougall made a similar remark in 1924, charging the anti-instinct theorists with having rejected instincts in name only.

Enthusiasm for the study of learning processes as all-inclusive determinants of behavior reached a height in the 1940s with the construction of learning theories. Such theorizing reached its zenith with the work of Clark L. Hull, Robert Guthrie, Edward Tolman, and others; the so-called stimulus-response (S-R) formula proposed by Watson became the gospel of many psychologists.

Whatever extremism was committed and whatever useless experiments performed, it must be said that the "anti-instinct revolt" made some positive contributions to the study of behavior, the most important being to point out the need for experimental observation rather than armchair disputes concerning the origins of behavior and to argue for the use of objective facts in order to arrive at the truth. Naturally, not all the experiments which the behavioristic movement called for supported the naïve idea of conditioning or association as the sole learning processes. There has been experimental work proving that not all behavior changes are due to conditioning, association, or trial-and-error learning. Various workers, for example, have demonstrated the maturation of behavior patterns independent from learning.

One of these experiments is that of Carmichael (1927), who anesthetized salamander tadpoles (*Amblystoma punctatum*) with chloretone long before any locomotor movements ever appeared. When the anesthetized tadpoles had shown a morphological development in advance of the stage at which the unanesthetized control ones of the same age had become free swimmers, they were removed from the drug's influence. They swam just as well as the normal controls. Similarly, McGraw (1946) has shown that motor skills in children arise as a result of maturation rather than specific practice.

Today there is due recognition that no amount of training can overcome limitations imposed by heredity. For example, environment determines whether a child learns English or Swahili or some other language as his native tongue. But there are no means by which an ape can be taught to speak any human language, as Hayes and Hayes (1951) have shown by their failure to teach an infant ape, which they had raised in their home just as one would a human child, how to speak. And it has become clear that differences in heredity cause differences in behavior in similar environments, as shown by Schooland (1942), who reared chicks and ducklings in the same environment; these animals still had clear-cut differences in their behaviors, just as children reared on exactly the same diet do not grow up to have identical body features.

PRESENT-DAY VIEWS ON ORIGINS OF BEHAVIOR

In the United States: Emphasis on Experience

Even though no extreme polemic against the idea of inborn capabilities is heard today, the influence of behaviorism is still strong in current experimental psychology in the United States. Many researchers who devote their energies exclusively to problems of learning have practically no knowledge of the inherited repertoire of their experimental animals, contrary to Watson's original injunction in 1914 that systematic knowledge of the habitual and distinctive behaviors of animals under natural conditions is indispensable for the proper interpretation of laboratory results. Moreover, the tendency has been to favor learning interpretations of behavior, just as the earlier psychologists had favored instinct interpretations of behavior.

But today there are several psychologists in the United States who have what is called an *epigenetic view*, with its main proponents being Schneirla (1946, 1956, and 1957; with Rosenblatt, 1961), Hebb (1953), Lehrman (1953, 1956), and Moltz (1965). The epigenetic viewpoint, according to a recent exponent, Moltz (1965), "considers gene effects to be contingent on environmental conditions and regards the genotype as capable of entering into different classes of relationships depending on the prevailing environmental context."

Essentially, the epigenetic viewpoint appears to be one that arose out of a conviction that the traditional heredity-environment dualism served only to obscure the problem of the origins of behavior. Although Kuo (1924) had suggested abolishing the dichotomy, this conviction was first set forth in detail in Carmichael's classic 1925 paper entitled "Heredity and Environment: Are They Antithetical?" In this paper, Carmichael pointed out that the main differences between instinct proponents and opponents appeared to lie in the degree of complexity in behavior which each was willing to regard as having come into existence without intervention of learning. Carmichael felt that, on the basis of current knowledge, it was not possible to differentiate betwen that which is native and that which is acquired, once the fertilized egg has begun to develop, and especially since there was no agreement between supporters of the instinct concept as to what human behaviors should be considered instinctive, thus reflecting the fact that there was no true criterion for separating the two elements in adult behavior. "The so-called hereditary factors can only be acquired in response to an environment and likewise the so-called acquired factors can only be secured by a modification of already existing structure, which in the last analysis is hereditary structure," Carmichael declared.

Schneirla (1946, 1956, 1957; and Rosenblatt, 1961) seems to be the first to call this trend in thought *epigenetic*. In his 1956 paper, Schneirla discussed several factors which suggested to him "the unwisdom of attempts to distinguish what is 'innate' from what is 'acquired' or to estimate the proportionate effects of these or to judge what kinds of effects they might produce separately. There exist no separate entities of this sort. . . ." In his opinion, all cases of development "come about through continuous interactions between intraorganic developmental processes (maturation) and the effects of extrinsic conditions (experience)." The term *instinct*, he felt, did not refer to "a real and demonstrated agency in the causation of behavior, but a word for the problem of species-typical behavior at all phyletic levels." In other words, the term should "designate a developmental process resulting in species-typical behavior." Schneirla allows the existence of nonlearned behavior, but at the same time his concept of instinct does not necessarily imply that all species-typical behaviors are invariably inherited and nonlearned. This way of looking at species-typical behavior appears to be shared by Beach in an excellent 1960 paper. Finally, Schneirla postulates that "the phyla, and the vertebrate classes, differ in their respective capacities for reaching higher orders in maturation, in experience, and in the relationships of these (Schneirla, 1956)." This, of course, is not to be construed as an appeal to discontinuity between the species, but as a recognition that there do exist inherent species differences which are ultimately reflected in behavior.

Lehrman, while differing from Schneirla in several respects, began with similar ideas on heredity and environment as determinants of behavior (Lehrman, 1956). For example, he has spoken of the "somewhat artificial dichotomy between innate and acquired," in discussing Schneirla's 1956 paper. Lehrman, in 1956, exemplified the resistance toward conceding that nonlearned behavior may be hereditary. While he admitted that an animal's inherited body structures and physiological characteristics determine its potential behavior, he felt that "this is not to say that the behavior is already contained in, or given by, the structure of the animal. The characteristic assumption of the instinct theorists that some elements of the observed behavior are innate as such, is just as likely to lead us astray as is the naive assumption that everything is learned," for he felt that the involvements of learning and of structure were too complex to permit a satisfactory analysis through a distinction between innate and learned components in behavior patterns. Finally, Lehrman insisted that all actual behavior of an animal could be more profitably regarded as the result of experience or of peripheral physiological characteristics. Like Kuo, he believed that behaviors present at birth or hatching were prenatally learned through physiological channels.

In later years, however, Lehrman's viewpoint became distinctly broader. In a report by Lehrman and Wortis (1967) on breeding behavior in the ring dove, Lehrman stated:

> The data reported here represent one kind of experiential influence on the development of species-specific behavior patterns. There are undoubtedly many others, acting at different loci, in different directions, and in different ways. Analysis of such effects does not, by any means, imply that the behavior patterns concerned are simply "learned," or that non-experimental developmental processes play no role in the organization of the behavior. Data like ours should be regarded rather as a very preliminary step in the analysis of the complex and varying roles of different aspects of experience,

and of growth processes, in the development and interpretation of behaviour patterns of many different levels and kinds of organization.

While in 1949, Hebb was willing to call instinct "behavior in which innate factors are predominant," he later (1953) decided that there were logical grounds for considering the dichotomy of innate and learned to be false, for the two were often defined in mutually exclusive fashion, that is, *innate* was often conceived as "not learned" and *learned* as "not innate." The problem is, as Beach (1954) has also pointed out, that a factor which is identified by the exclusion of something cannot be considered unitary. As we shall find, the ethologists agree completely with this particular point. Hebb argued: "There are not two kinds of control of behavior and that the term 'instinct,' implying a mechanism or neural process independent of environmental factors, and distinct from the neural processes into which learning enters, is a completely misleading term." He believed, like the other writers we have just discussed, that any bit of behavior is fully dependent on both heredity and environment for its expression. Hebb (1949) constructed a theory that perceptual capabilities are built up in neural organization as a result of experience with environmental stimuli impinging on the organism, especially during the earliest life period.

European Emphasis on Organismic Factors

While the anti-instinct feeling at times reached a fever pitch in the United States, little of this occurred in Europe, perhaps because the sciences there tended to be guided by tradition and to evolve gradually, whereas Americans tended to have an idealistic faith in radical changeability (Pear, 1942–3). Thus, the European concept of the instinct tended to remain at the Darwinian level, and the over-application that had occurred in the United States through James and McDougall did not come into being in Europe, and therefore, neither did the revolt.

Ethology, the science of the phylogenetic study of the behavior of animals, arose in Europe some sixty years ago as a result of Whitman's (1899) and Heinroth's (1910) independent discoveries that specific behavior patterns or actions could be used as taxonomic characters. This led to an interest in the intensive study of species-typical behavior in all animals. Ethology has grown considerably over the years, and today is a highly respectable science in Europe. It has emphasized, first of all, as the first step in behavior analysis, the gathering of all data on what animals of the different species do, when and how these behaviors arise, how they change during the life cycle, and how they are related to ecological factors. Then, certain of these behaviors are compared between species and phylogenetic levels, to determine their possible course of evolution in response to species-survival requirements in specific environments. After this, the genetic transmission and genetic influences on these specific behaviors may be studied as well as their physiological bases, including the role of neural functions and structures. Ethology first came to the attention of psychologists in the United States about two decades ago, through the publication of a paper by Lehrman in 1953, and two books, one by Tinbergen in 1951 and one by Thorpe in 1956.

Since the ethologists have concentrated most of their research on the typical behavior repertoire—that is, the species-specific behavior of animals—they have been led to stress the innate features of many animal behaviors in the course of the study of the survival value and evolution of such behaviors. However, this does not mean that they have totally ignored the mechanisms of learning or that they deny the existence of learning. While they have not worked on learning processes to the extensive degree that United States psychologists have, they certainly have always recognized that learning exists. For example, there have been observations, similar to Romanes', that birds make innate nest-building movements but have to learn which materials are suitable for nest construction. Although ethologists have contrasted the *innate* and the *learned*, thus apparently implying a dichotomy, they really have gone much deeper than this, and have not conceived of two completely separate, parallel behavior-determining neural mechanisms, as Hebb has charged (1953). In reality, as Lorenz (1960, 1961) has recently pointed out, there are many neural mechanisms which have been postulated by ethologists to determine behavior, and learning is only one of them. Ethologists have not postulated just *one* physiological or neurological process which "innately" determines behavior, but *several* of them, and to group them together by the exclusion of learning would be, in Lorenz's opinion, as meaningless as an anatomic group composed of eyes, ears, and knees which was defined by the lack of dental enamel. According to the ethologists, bits of these different processes, including those of learning, interweave with each other in any instance of behavior.

We have already mentioned the coexistence of different elements in the nest building of birds, but shall mention another example to illustrate how, even when a behavior is apparently an indivisible unit, it can be constituted of components having different causal bases. This instance is that of the greylag goose rolling back into its nest an egg which has been taken out and placed some distance away. According to Tinbergen (1951), there are two separate components in the bird's action of rolling the egg back: a straight motion of the bill toward the nest, and the little side-to-side movements which serve to balance the asymmetrical egg in its course. The existence of these two separate components is shown by the fact that if the egg is suddenly removed while the bird is rolling it back, the action will continue to be performed, right up to the nest. However, the bill is moved directly, without the little balancing movements. The straight movement of the bill is considered by the ethologists to have been released, but not guided, by the egg's presence outside the nest, while the balancing movements are considered to be guided by continuous external stimulation from the egg. Tinbergen (1951) has compared these two behavioral determinants with the propulsory and steering mechanisms of a ship, respectively. The concept of behavior units welded out of causally different components is fundamental to ethological theory.

Ethology is far from considering species-typical behaviors as being "preformed" by the genetic constitution or as all having the same kind of determinants. There is indeed a wide difference among phyla in the degree of rigidity of species-typical behavior, in the role of learning, afferent stimulation, and central control. All these vary for different species and for different behaviors.

The concept of instinct in ethological theory is limited in scope, and is very different from what it was formerly. The ethologists have restricted the term *instinctive* to the so-called *fixed-action patterns* of the kind discovered as taxonomic characters by Whitman and by Heinroth and exemplified by the straight movement of the greylag goose's bill toward the nest. These fixed action patterns are highly stereotyped movements, usually released or triggered off by some kind of definite stimulus. Such movements are often known as *consummatory actions* by the ethologists. They resemble reflexes in some respects, but are subject to rather different laws regarding the conditions of their elicitation. These fixed action patterns are not modifiable with regard to the mode of execution, but, in some cases, there can be modification with respect to the object toward which they are directed, as in the case of the chick's following the hen, wherein the following action itself is a highly specific action, and the hen is acquired as an object eliciting such action, as has been shown by research in the laboratory imprinting process.

While ethologists give due recognition, as we have said, to the effect of the environment in stimulating the organism by providing the conditions under which certain behaviors will be performed, and, in some cases, by promoting learning processes, they insist that there are certain behavior elements which must be regarded at least as innate as morphological characters, as reflected in Lorenz's (1956) declaration:

> There is absolutely nothing in any organism's body or behavior that is not dependent on environment and, to a certain extent, subject to modification through environment. Even the most direct and rigid effect of genes is

dependent on environment in so far as it cannot appear if the organism's milieu is changed to such an extent, that an animal sickens and dies. What is inherited, is not the character itself, but the range of its modifiability.

This concept of the role of genes in behavior certainly cannot be quarreled with, as others have made similar comments. E. G. Conklin (as quoted in Carmichael, 1925), pointed out that genes "are not the characters in miniature, nor are they the 'representatives' or carriers of the characters, but they are the differential causes of the characters." Montagu (1950) put the matter this way: "Genes determine, not characters nor traits, but the responses of the developing organism to the environment." All these statements are equally true for morphological features and innately fixed behavior patterns.

Some psychologists have regarded the ethological concept of congenitally fixed behavior patterns with resistance born out of complete mistrust of the concept of instinct. Lehrman (1953), for example, contended that congenitally present fixed behavior patterns, such as pecking by the chick, are prenatally learned. Lorenz (1958), while admitting that such a possibility should not be excluded from consideration, nevertheless felt that it was well to pause at the fact that behavior of this type is extremely well adapted to the environmental requirements with which the young animal is faced.

Further aspects of the concept of instinct as used by ethologists and the scientific bases for the study of instinct have been detailed in two papers by Lorenz, "The establishment of the instinct concept" (1937) and "Inductive and teleological psychology" (1942). Both have recently become available in English (Lorenz, 1970) and show that the ethological use of the concept is based upon physiologically oriented causal analysis of behavior, and is far removed from vitalistic and finalistic methods. In these papers it becomes clear that ethologists have a much greater foundation of objective facts than they were initially credited with having by behavioristically oriented psychologists in the United States.

MEETING OF S-R PSYCHOLOGY AND ETHOLOGY

In past years, however, the antagonism between the proponents of ethology and of learning has materially lessened, and they have been coming into greater contact with each other through the attendance of international ethology conferences by United States psychologists and through lecture tours of this country by prominent European ethologists. This has had a salutary effect on theoretical concepts and research efforts, in that it has brought about increased mutual understanding of each other's concepts, where they are similar, where they differ, the reasons for the differences, and the gradual development of a mutually agreed upon vocabulary. As of now, it is universally agreed that there is such a thing as species-specific behavior and that there are nonlearned aspects of behavior. It is also generally agreed that every species is innately endowed with sense receptors, neural functions, and motor capabilities which set the limits of behavior. When the organism is maintained in environmental conditions which are characteristic of its species, then it will, in the course of maturation and in continuous interaction with this environment, develop species-typical behavior patterns. Some of these behavior patterns tend to safeguard the survival of the individual and/or of the species.

As an example of the spreading acceptance of the concept of species-specific behaviors in the United States, we may cite Beach's excellent 1960 paper, which urged the greater use of species-specific behaviors in different species for psychological research rather than the exclusive use of learning problems which use, primarily, rats as subjects. Such behaviors, Beach maintains, should be studied to determine the historical, environmental, and organismic determinants. These include the effects of maturation, experience, releasers, neural organization, and physiological conditions. Beach proposes that man's own species-specific behaviors are the use of language, not only for immediate communication but also for storage of information, and the capacity to form a wide variety of complex social interrelationships; Beach further proposes that these can be studied just as animals' species-typical behaviors are.

It is clear that, thanks to scientific research, behavior will never again be considered as "simple," or completely explicable on the basis of just one or a few principles. No one considers learning as the sole cause of behavior, and the concept of inherited behavior has come into its own again, through ethology, but now as a respectable, empirical, and testable scientific concept. No longer is a simple dualism considered adequate to account for the origins of behavior, though we can consider some behaviors to be traceable to genetic transmission and others to learning. However, there are other causes, including physiological disturbances induced by illness or drugs, special environmental exigencies, and so forth. Just as not all noninherited behavior is due to learning, so not all species-typical inherited behaviors are due to the same determining mechanisms. Some of these mechanisms, for example, are morphological structure, different physiological processes, and different neurological structures and processes. Furthermore, hereditarily determined factors can also influence the character of the specific experiences received by the organism, with this screening effect ultimately influencing behavior characteristics. A simple example of this is color blindness and behavior toward traffic lights.

We cannot know, of course, what the controversies of the future will be, in regard to the origins of behavior, except that they will exist; but it is becoming highly evident that research on the origins of behavior will focus more and more upon two specific areas which are currently generating a great deal of excitement and interest. These are the role of brain structure and function and the role of ontogenetic or developmental factors in both inherent and acquired behaviors.

The latter can be called the "effects of early experience"—that is, the interplay of experience and developmental processes. Ever since 1950, but having its roots around the turn of the century as far back as James (1890), there has been a growing amount of evidence that organisms, both human and animal, often show "sensitive periods" which appear to be related to morphological and physiological development. During these periods, which have been found to have a fairly high degree of predictableness, the organism shows extreme sensitiveness to particular aspects of the environment, with the result that a relatively strong effect on behavior ensues and may persist even when the sensitive period in question has passed. The majority of the sensitive periods which have been discovered are in early life. We shall explore this topic in the next chapter.

REFERENCES

ARISTOTLE. *History of Animals*. Trans. by R. Cresswell. London: G. Bell, 1891.

BEACH, FRANK A. Ontogeny and living systems. In *Group Processes*, B. Schaffner, editor. New York: Macy Foundation, 1954. 9–74.

BEACH, FRANK A. The descent of instinct. *Psychological Review*, 1955, **62,** 401–410.

BEACH, FRANK A. Experimental investigations of species-specific behavior. *American Psychologist*, 1960, **15,** 1–18.

BERNARD, LUTHER LEE. *Instinct*. New York: Holt & Co., 1924.

CARMICHAEL, LEONARD B. Heredity and environment: Are they antithetical? *Journal of Abnormal & Social Psychology*, 1925, **20,** 245–260.

CARMICHAEL, LEONARD B. The development of behavior in vertebrates experimentally removed from the influence of external stimulation. *Psychological Review*, 1927, **34,** 34–47.

DARWIN, CHARLES. Instinct: A posthumous essay. In: *Mental Evolution in Animals,* by G. J. Romanes. London: Kegan Paul, Trench, & Co. 1883.

DUNLAP, KNIGHT L. Are there any instincts? *Journal of Abnormal Psychology*, 1919, **14,** 307–311.

FLETCHER, RONALD. *Instinct in Man: In the Light of Recent Work in Comparative Psychology*. New York: International Universities Press, 1957.

HAYES, CATHERINE. *The Ape in Our House*. New York: Harper, 1951.

HAYES, KEITH J., and HAYES, CATHERINE. The intellectual development of a home-raised chimpanzee. *Proceedings of the American Philosophical Society*, 1951, **95,** 105–109.

HEBB, D. O. *The Organization of Behavior*. New York: Wiley, 1949.

HEBB, D. O. Heredity and environment in mammalian behaviour. *British Journal of Animal Behaviour*, 1953, **1**, 43–47.

HEINROTH, O. Beitrage zur Biologie, namentlich Ethologie und Psychologie der Anatiden. *Verhandlungen 5th International Ornithologie Kongress, 1910*, **5**, 589–702.

HESS, ECKHARD H. Imprinting. *Science, 1959*, **130**, 133–141.

HOLT, E. B. *Animal Drive and the Learning Process*. New York: Holt & Co., 1931.

HUNTER, W. S. Summary comments on the heredity-environment symposium. *Psychological Review*, 1947, **54**, 348–352.

JAMES, WILLIAM. *Principles of Psychology*. New York: Holt, 1890.

JOSEY, CHARLES CONANT. *The Social Philosophy of Instinct*. New York and Boston: Scribners' Sons, 1922.

KUO, ZING YANG. Giving up instincts in psychology. *Journal of Philosophy*, 1921, **18**, 645–664.

KUO, ZING YANG. How are our instincts acquired? *Psychological Review*, 1922, **29**, 344–365.

KUO, ZING YANG. A psychology without heredity. *Psychological Review*, 1924, **31**, 427–447.

KUO, ZING YANG. Ontogeny of embryonic behavior in *Aves*. I. The chronology and general nature of the behavior of the chick embryo. *Journal of Experimental Zoology*, 1932, **61**, 395–430. (a).

KUO, ZING YANG. Ontogeny of embryonic behavior in *Aves*. II. The mechanical factors in the various stages leading to hatching. *Journal of Experimental Zoology*, 1932, **62**, 453–489. (b).

KUO, ZING YANG. Ontogeny of embryonic behavior in *Aves*. III. The structures and environmental factors in embryonic behavior. *Journal of Comparative Psychology*, 1932, **13**, 245–272. (c).

KUO, ZING YANG. Ontogeny of embryonic behavior in *Aves*. IV. The influence of embryonic movements upon the behavior after hatching. *Journal of Comparative Psychology*, 1932, **14**, 109–122. (d).

LANGFELD, HERBERT S. Heredity and experience. *Anneé Psychologique*, 1951, **50**, 11–25.

LEHRMAN, DANIEL S. A critique of Konrad Lorenz's theory of instinctive behavior. *Quarterly Review of Biology*, 1953, **28**, 337–363.

LEHRMAN, DANIEL S. On the organization of maternal behavior and the problem of instinct. In *L'instinct dans le comportement des animaux et de l'homme*. P. P. Grassé, editor. Paris: Masson et Cie., 1956. 475–514. Discussion, 514–520.

LEHRMAN, DANIEL S., and WORTIS, ROCHELLE P. Breeding experience and breeding efficiency in the ring dove. *Animal Behavior*, 1967, **15**, 223–228.

LORENZ, KONRAD Z. The objectivistic theory of instinct. In *L'instinct dans le comportement des animaux et de l'homme*. P. P. Grassé, editor. Paris: Masson et Cie., 1956. 51–64. Discussion, 64–76.

LORENZ, KONRAD Z. The deprivation experiment: its limitations and its value as a means to separate learned and unlearned elements of behavior. Paper presented at the Downey Hospital, Illinois, 1958. (a).

LORENZ, KONRAD Z. The evolution of behavior. *Scientific American*, 1958, **199**, No. 6, 67–78. (b).

LORENZ, KONRAD Z. Prinzipien der vergleichenden Verhaltensforschung. *Fortschritte der Zoologie*, 1960, **12**, 265–294.

LORENZ, KONRAD Z. Phylogenetische Anpassung und adaptive Modifikation des Verhalten. *Zeitschrift für Tierpsychologie,* 1961, **18,** 139–187. Trans. *Evolution and Modification of Behavior.* Chicago: University of Chicago Press, 1965.

LORENZ, KONRAD Z. *Studies in Human and Animal Behaviour.* Volume 1. Translated by R. Martin. Cambridge, Mass.: Harvard University Press, 1970.

McDOUGALL, WILLIAM. *An Introduction to Social Psychology.* 1908. (23rd edition of 1927 available in paperback form from Barnes & Noble, New York).

McGRAW, MYRTLE B. Maturation of behavior. In *Manual of Child Psychology,* L. Carmichael, editor. New York: Wiley & Son 1946. 332–269.

MAZE, J. R. Instincts and impulses. *Australian Journal of Psychology,* 1952, **4,** 77–93.

MILLS, T. W. *The Nature and Development of Animal Intelligence.* New York: Macmillan, 1898.

MOLTZ, HOWARD. Contemporary instinct theory and the fixed action pattern. *Psychological Review,* 1965, **72,** 27–47.

MONTAGU, M. F. ASHLEY. Constitutional and prenatal factors in infant and child health. In *Symposium on the Healthy Personality,* Milton J. E. Senn, editor. Transactions of special meetings of Conference on Infancy and Childhood June 8–9 and July 3–4, 1950, New York, N.Y. Supplement II: Conference on Problems of Infancy and Childhood. Transactions of Fourth Conference, March, 1950. New York: Macy Foundation. 148–175.

MORGAN, CONWAY LLOYD. *Habit and Instinct.* London: Edward Arnold, 1896.

PEAR, T. H. Are there human instincts? *Bulletin of the John Rylands Library,* 1942–43, **27,** 137–167.

ROMANES, GEORGE JOHN. *Animal Intelligence.* London: 1881.

ROMANES, GEORGE JOHN. *Mental Evolution in Animals.* London: Kegan Paul, Trench, & Co., 1883.

ROMANES, GEORGE JOHN. *Mental Evolution in Man.* London: 1888.

SCHNEIRLA, T. C. Problems in the biopsychology of social organization. *Journal of Abnormal and Social Psychology,* 1946, **41,** 385–402.

SCHNEIRLA, T. C. Interrelationships of the "innate" and the "acquired" in instinctive behavior. In *L'instinct dans le comportment des animaux et de l'homme.* P. P. Grassé, editor. Paris: Masson et Cie., 1956. 387–439. Discussion, 439–452.

SCHNEIRLA, T C. The concept of development in comparative psychology. In *The Concept of Development: An Issue in the Study of Human Behavior,* D. B. Harris, editor. Minneapolis: University of Minnesota Press, 1957. 78–108.

SCHNEIRLA, T. C., and ROSENBLATT, J. Behavioral organization and genesis of the social bond in insects and mammals. *American Journal of Orthopsychiatry,* 1961, **31,** 223–253.

SCHOOLAND, J. B. Are there any innate behavior tendencies? *Genetic Psychology Monographs,* 1942, **25,** 219–287.

SPALDING, D. A. Instinct, with original observations on young animals. *MacMillan's Magazine,* 1873, **27,** 282–293. Reprinted in *British Journal of Animal Behaviour,* 1954, **2,** 3–11.

SPALDING, D. A. Instinct and acquisition. *Nature,* 1875, **12,** 507–508.

THORNDIKE, EDWARD L. Instinct. *Biological Lectures, Marine Biological Laboratory, Wood's Hole Massachusetts, 1898,* 1899. **7,** 57–68. (a).

THORNIKE, EDWARD L. The instinctive reaction of young chicks. *Psychological Review,* 1899, **6,** 282–291. (b).

THORNDIKE, EDWARD L. Human instincts and doctrines about them. *British Journal of Educational Psychology,* 1942, **12,** 85–87.

THORPE, WILLIAM H. *Learning and Instinct in Animals.* London: Methuen, 1956.

TINBERGEN, N. *The Study of Instinct.* Oxford: Oxford University Press, 1951.

WATSON, JOHN B. The behavior of noddy and sooty terns. *Papers Marine Biological Laboratory Tortugas, Carnegie Institute of Washington,* 1908, **2,** 187–255.

WATSON, JOHN B. *Behavior: An Introduction to Comparative Psychology.* New York: Holt, 1914.

WATSON, JOHN B. *Psychology from the Standpoint of a Behaviorist.* Philadelphia & London: Lippincott Co., 1919.

WATSON, JOHN B. *Behaviorism.* New York: The People's Institute Publishing Co., Inc., 1922.

WATSON, JOHN B. *The Ways of Behaviorism.* New York: Harper & Bros., 1928.

WHITMAN, CHARLES OTIS. Animal Behavior. *Biological Lectures, Marine Biological Laboratory, Wood's Hole, Massachusetts, 1898.* 1899, **7,** 285–338.

WILM, F. C. *Theories of Instinct. A Study in the History of Psychology.* New Haven: Yale University Press, 1925.

WYATT, H. G. The recent anti-instinctive attitude in social psychology. *Psychological Review,* 1927, **34,** 126–132.

2

Early Experience and Sensitive Periods

THE NATURE OF EARLY EXPERIENCES

Our main concern in this chapter is to examine the effects of certain early experiences of animals and human beings on their later behavior. Early experiences by definition begin at the onset of an organism's life history, that is, at fertilization of an ovum by a sperm in the case of most species. Early experiences are thus *first experiences* and may occur either prenatally or postnatally. In general early experiences are regarded as those taking place during an organism's immaturity. We all know that past experiences definitely have an important influence on the characteristics of behavior. But do early experiences have any special qualities which differentiate them from simple past experiences? No one would quarrel with the statement that past experiences are of great importance in determining what we know and what we do. The aggregate massiveness of our educational institutions, in fact, is substantial testimony to our belief in this importance of past experiences. Every civilized culture has devoted a great deal of time and energy to preparing young people for adult life. The more complex the civilization, the more important and elaborate is the educational system. In contemporary Western culture of today, the amount of training necessary for optimal functioning as an adult has increased to the point where schooling usually lasts to early adulthood. Furthermore, the growing complexity of our society has resulted in enlarging the amount of education that must be accomplished during childhood. It is only natural that the best means of education should be sought for by any highly civilized society.

Does a child (or a young animal) actually have a special plasticity which renders him particularly impressionable to the experiences he receives? Or is he merely a miniature adult, differing from grown-ups only in body size and amount of past experience? The most common tendency is to see the child as a small adult. He is, after all, in the process of growing up, and there is a continuity between the child and the adult he becomes. Much classical art, for example, has pictured children as having adult proportions. There is no question that children have less past experience than do adults.

But there is also plenty of evidence that since the beginning of man's self-awareness there has been a recognition of the fact that what a child learns has a rather persisting influence throughout life. In the Bible, for example, a saying in Proverbs 22 admonishes: "Train up a child in the way he should go: and when he is old, he will not depart from it." The effects of early experiences were of interest to the Greek and Roman civilizations. In these civilizations, we find a strong emphasis on the education of children, as it was believed that their training must begin very early in order for them to become adults having the virtues desired. Euripides, the Greek dramatist of the 5th century B.C., advised: "What one learns, one carries to old age; so, give good education to your boys."

John Locke (1635–1704), the father of associationism, believed firmly in the great importance of first education:

> The little and almost insensible impressions in our tender infancies have very important and lasting consequences and there 'tis, as in the fountains of some rivers, where a gentle application of the hand turns the flexible waters in channels that make them take quite contrary courses; and by this direction given them at first in the sources they receive different tendencies and arrive at last at very remote and distant places (Locke, 1699).

There has also been the idea that childhood experiences have a profound effect because of special characteristics of the child and not merely because they are the first experiences that he has. Saadi (c. 1258) reflected this notion when he said: "Wood, while 'tis green, thou mayst at pleasure bend; when dry, thou canst not change it save by fire." So also Alexander Pope (1688–1744) wrote, "As the twig is bent so the tree's inclined" (*Moral Essays*, c. 1733). It may thus be said that the adult is shaped during childhood, or, as William Wordsworth (1770–1850), the poet laureate of the nineteenth century, wrote: "The child is father of the man."

One of the most interesting comments expressing fundamental differences between childhood and adulthood education are those made by Richard Whately (1787–1863), English theologician and logician, when he was commenting on Bacon's *Essay of Education and Custom*:

> Education may be compared to the grafting of a tree. Every gardener knows that the *younger* the wilding stock is that is to be grafted, the easier and more effective is the operation, because then, one scion put on just above the root will become the main stem of the tree and all the branches it puts forth will be of the right sort. When, on the other hand, a tree is to be grafted at a very considerable age (which may be very successfully done), you have to put on 20 or 30 grafts on the several branches; and afterwards you will have to be watching from time to time for the wilding-shoots which the stock will be putting forth and pruning them off. And even so, one whose character is to be *reformed* at a mature age will find it necessary not merely to implant a right principle but also to bestow a distinct attention on the correction of this, that, and the other bad habit. . . . But it must not be forgotten that education resembles the grafting of a tree in this point also, that there must be some affinity between the stock and the graft, though a very important practical difference may exist; for example, between a worthless crab and a fine apple. Even so, the new nature, as it may be called, superinduced by education, must always retain some relation to the original one, though differing in most important points. You cannot, by any kind of artificial training, make *any*thing of *any*one, and obliterate all traces of the natural character.

It may be noted that Whately's analogy points out several facets regarding the nature of the effects of early experience. One is that greater and more general changes can be made more easily earlier in life than later. But this is because there are specific capacities for only certain types of changes at different developmental stages.

PRIMACY

We can discern two major types of propositions attempting to explain the existence of the prepotent effects of some early experiences on the nature of later behavior. The first type regards early experience deriving its ascendancy from being the *first* experience in life history. Habits are more often easier to form than to break, and the existence of previously formed habits can prevent the acquisition of new ones that compete with them. Thus, the early habits may form a selective disposition in the young animal or child to react to new situations in the same way, so that there is a transfer effect between first experiences and later ones. This would result in making early experiences "foundational" (Sluckin, 1964). Thus the primary framework or organization of behavior formed by the early experiences, even though it is built upon and perhaps even completely overlaid by subsequent experiences, could nevertheless control the pattern of later behavior development. Hence behavioral organizations may be easily formed but decomposed only with difficulty.

By and large, the transfer or primacy theory regarding the effects of early experience has been most commonly assumed. This notion is congenial to the followers of behaviorism in their stress on the importance of learning per se as a determinant of behavior in animals and man. Traditional learning theory, as developed in the 1940s and 1950s, did not accord any particular emphasis to the effects of early learning experiences, but chose to stress the effects of *past experience.*

When early experiences are considered "foundational," this implies that the organism is initially relatively undifferentiated and extremely plastic. According to this view, behavioral organization becomes, as time goes on, structured and resistant to further change. As a result, the young animal or child becomes less and less susceptible to the effects of the experiences it has. This notion of an inverse ratio between the age of an animal and the effect of a given experience thus recognizes no clear line of demarcation between early and late experiences, just as there is no definite point in time at which an acorn has turned into a tree, even though the two are very different.

The Canadian psychologist D. O. Hebb, of McGill University, is the most influential present-day exponent of the foundational view of early experiences. In his 1949 book, *The Organization of Behavior*, Hebb propounded his theory of the development of perceptual functioning, particularly in the visual modality, through experience. In his theory, the development and differentiation of behavior are postulated to be built up in neural structures via the sensory data accumulated by the organism from its sense experiences. The frequent stimulation from, say, triangles, will set off a particular firing sequence among a set of brain cells. Eventually, proposed Hebb, this particular firing sequence is so facilitated that it is automatically and extremely rapidly executed whenever any portion of a triangle is seen. The brain cells of particular importance, according to Hebb, in organizing perceptual capacities are those of the cortex and diencephalon. This theory, with appropriate elaborations, is extended by Hebb to other sensory modalities, so that the whole construct of behavioral organization is seen as being formed by the slow acquisition of such systems of nerve cells and firing sequences.

Unfortunately, this theoretical proposition has had to be reconsidered in the light of research by Salapatek and Kessen (1966) and by Bower (1971). Salapatek and Kessen found that patterned visual stimulation in the form of a large equilateral triangle 8 inches on a side has the effect of *decreasing* total scanning by infants who are less than 8 days old. The decrease in scanning is in comparison with that performed when only homogenous visual stimulation is available. Bower's work, in addition, shows that human infants very early have considerable perceptual organization in the visual modality with respect to shape and solidity attributes, with the principal difference between infant and adult perception due, in part, to the infant's failure to identify a moving object as being the same object as when it is stationary. In addition, perceptual development is currently regarded as occurring independently of the development of learning during life history (e.g., Hinde, 1970).

However, even if Hebb's scheme does not account for perceptual development, there remains a possibility that some learning processes in general undergo a process of development similar to that proposed by Hebb. The research currently being conducted with respect to memory engram in neural processes will, it is hoped, eventually answer this question.

"The nature of the learning process changes significantly with development," Hebb declared in his book. He proposed "that the characteristics of learning undergo an important change as the animal grows, particularly in the higher mammals; that all learning tends to utilize and build on any earlier learning, instead of replacing it, so that much early learning tends to be permanent; and finally that the learning of the mature animal owes its efficiency to the slow and inefficient learning that has gone before, but may also be limited and canalized by it." Hebb emphasized in particular that "the first learning of primates is extremely slow, and very different from that of maturity." Hebb regarded the transfer effects of early learning experiences on later behavior as very broad and general. He also postulated that the differences in the ratio of associative and sensory cortices in the brain were factors in determining the length of the first learning period. For example, the rat is thought to complete its visual learning in only 15 minutes, while primates take from weeks to months to accomplish the same thing, according to Hebb's system.

There is a great deal of evidence that learning capacity changes significantly with age. There is even neurological evidence which suggests this, according to Russell (1959). In human beings, for example, outgrowths of cortical cell dendrites, also known as spikes or gemmuli, continue to develop during the first two years of life, with the consequence that nerve cell interconnections also continue to develop during that time. As for direct behavioral evidence, it has been found that, among other things, classical conditioning becomes easier for both animals and human infants as they grow older, depending on the response conditioned (Munn, 1954; Scott, 1958; Fuller and Waller, 1962; Stanley, Cornwell, Poggiani, and Trattner, 1963). Maze learning ability also improves with age in rats, according to Munn (1950), and Vince (1961) has made an extensive review of the literature on age-related differences in learning ability.

However, other aspects of age-related changes in sensitivity are reflected by the fact that homeostatic control is less efficient in young animals than in adults. This may result in drive states and drive reduction being far more potent forces for young animals than they are for older ones. Similarly, susceptibility to physiological and psychological trauma can be greater in younger than in older animals. For example, it is commonly known that resistance to certain viral and bacterial diseases increases with age.

DEVELOPMENTALLY SCHEDULED SENSITIVITIES

Thus, we arrive at the second major type of propositions endeavoring to account for the effects of early experiences on later behavior. This type does not regard the young animal as a "blank," but as definitely structured and ready to react to and absorb the features of its environment in certain highly specific ways. The effects of early experiences are regarded as being due, therefore, to special characteristics of the young animal or infant. These special characteristics do not arise from its being a relatively inexperienced organism, but from its particular developmental condition—that is, its biological situation. A young organism differs from the not so young not only in amount of experience but also in neurological and physiological structure and functioning. This means that its susceptibility to different types of experiences can differ radically from the susceptibility of an older organism to the same experiences. It can be more sensitive to certain types of events and less sensitive to other classes of events because of *biological*, not just experiential, differences. Since a young organism is constantly changing as its development progresses, this means also that its specific susceptibilities to various classes of stimuli change. Furthermore, development has long been known to be more than accretion in size or piling up of experiences: there are changes in form and organization of both body and behavior. At any point in time, the development of various body regions and of different physiological or neurological functions progresses at different rates. Furthermore, the various parts themselves develop at different rates at different times, so that there is no permanence in their relationship with each other. This means, then, that at any time the organism may have a selective sensibility to its environment; certain things may be reacted to very strongly at some times and not at all at other times.

Thus, while organization of body or behavior is seen to be inhibited when prior organization has taken place, as in the primacy theory, the theory of developmentally timed sensibilities postulates that initial organization is most likely to occur during *specific* developmental epochs. Within the sensitive phase itself, the first relevant experience may possibly have greater influence than do subsequent ones.

The sensitivity of the child to his environment has long been noted, as we have seen in various observations made since antiquity. While the child is obviously not ready for many kinds of learning at birth, he grows and develops, both mentally and physically. The concept of development —the various series of changes, stages, and processes—has been with us for a long time.

Biological Phenomena

The fact of changes and stages of physical growth long ago laid the foundation for the concept of *sensitive periods*, during which morphological features can be deeply influenced by abnormal environmental conditions. About one hundred years ago, research in embryological teratology by the French biologist Camille Dareste (1822–1899) disclosed that by far the largest majority of congenital physical abnormalities were the result of developmental arrest (Dareste, 1869, 1877), an idea which had been suggested several decades before, in 1822, by Étienne Geoffroy Saint-Hilaire (1772–1844), the founder of the recapitulation theory in embryology. According to Dareste, Saint-Hilaire believed that the resemblance between certain physical anomalies and specific embryonic states showed that these anomalies were due to developmental retardation and not to hereditary defects or to pathology of orginally well-formed organs. It was Dareste who was able to take advantage of the newly invented methods of artificial incubation of fowl eggs and experimentally to demonstrate the truth of Saint-Hilaire's contention, for he found that small changes in incubator temperature affected the growth rate of chick embryos and produced specific physical defects according to the specific stage during which developmental arrest was imposed. In other words, the anomalies of certain organs and even of certain bodily regions were the result of their more or less completely remaining in the anatomical condition which they had at certain periods of embryonic life. Most important, the teratogenic effects were usually found to have their origin *before* the organs concerned had even been formed out of the homogenous primordial material. Dareste's work was confirmed by many others, and it was then found that a variety of agents applied at the same embryological stage could produce the same defect and that the same agent applied at different times could produce very different defects.

For example, another Frenchman, Charles Féré (d. 1906), in 1894 reported experiments on the effects of mechanical vibration and toxic mercury vapors at different stages of chick embryos. At earlier stages, monsters were produced by these treatments, but at later stages, the embryos died. In an 1899 paper, Féré emphasized his contention: "We will not see any particular monstrosity in connection with a special influence [for] the influences capable of disturbing the development of the embryo have variable effects according to the stage at which they come into play. . . . The same harmful influence is able, according to the stage at which it acts, to determine infertility, monstrosity, abortion, still birth, developmental arrest, or congenital weakness." He concluded that "the specilization of the anomaly is determined, perhaps by special susceptibility of the embryo, perhaps by the developmental stage at which its development is disturbed."

While Dareste believed that *all* congenital defects not of hereditary origin were due to developmental arrest of the embryo, he did not have the means to prove this. It was in our own century that an American, Charles Stockard (1879–1939), proved that this was indeed the case. His extensive research (Stockard, 1909, 1910), beginning in 1907, with eggs of the common sea minnow (*Fundulus heteroclitus*) subjected to lowered temperature or oxygen deficit conditions, as well as different chemicals, demonstrated beyond a doubt that "the primary action of all the treatments is to inhibit the rate of development, and the type of deformity that results depends simply upon the developmental moment at which the interruption occurs." (Stockard, 1921.) He noted that any deformity reported in the literature could be produced by stopping development at the appropriate time. That is, "several developmental moments have been located at which rather definite defects of particular organs may be induced. These are the moments during which the organs are in their most rapidly proliferating conditions. Arresting the rate at such a moment gives decidedly injurious results. When an organ is developing at a slow rate the arrest fails to affect it." What is more, "the earlier the arrest the more numerous will be the type of defects found and the later the arrest the more limited the variety of deformities, since there are fewer organs to be affected during their rapidly proliferating primary stages." The period during which a certain organ's development was progressing at its highest rate was called a *critical stage* by Stockard. Finally, he expressed a belief that critical stages still exist after birth, since several important organs and tissues still have a considerable degree of growth and differentiation to accomplish. Since then, the work of the German zoologist Hans Spemann (1869–1941) on embryonic induction and organization and that of countless other researchers have demonstrated repeatedly and enlarged on the sensitive stage-developmental period concept in ever-increasing detail.

Spemann's research (1938) on transplants of embryonic tissue is particularly interesting in this connection. If prospective spinal cord, for example, is transplanted on the prospective belly areas before a particular stage, then this tissue becomes completely part of the new location and develops in accordance with it; but if the transplant is effected after this particular stage, then this tissue will continue to develop exactly as it would have if it had been left in its original location. That is, it becomes a piece of spinal cord even though located on the belly. When tissue transplants are made between different individuals, the stage of development of the host area, as well as that of the transplant, plays a role in determining the results.

In botany also, there arose the notion of transient periods of sensitivity to external conditions. The Dutch botanist Hugo De Vries (1848–1935), at the turn of this century, while studying the factors influencing the growth and development of unusual plant forms, discovered an extremely interesting fact. With a particular variety of poppy, *Papaver somniferum polycephalum s. monstruosum*, which turns stamens into superfluous pistils, the number of secondary pistils diminishes if the plant has been subjected to even the slightest disturbance before its sixth week. De Vries (1899, 1905) noted that at the age of 7 weeks not even microscopic examination could differentiate between the buds that would produce stamens or pistils. Nevertheless, at that time the "decision" had already been made. No matter what was done to 7-week old plants—shading out sun, cutting off leaves, thus making them very weak—the number of pistils could not be changed. In complete contrast, the smallest adverse influence, particularly in the area of nutrition, before the sixth week, would reliably reduce the numbers of pistils even though the whole plant appeared very sturdy and healthy. The time during which this effect could take place was called the *sensitive period* by De Vries. Sometimes he called it the *critical stage* or *susceptible period*. De Vries (1899) stressed the tremendous importance of the sensitive period principle, declaring that it extended beyond the usual domain of biology as such; this prediction has certainly turned out to be correct. De Vries also observed sensitive period phenomena in other unusual plant forms, such as those with twisted stems and in several ordinary plants such as clover, oats, and wheat. For example, with oats or wheat, the amount of water in the soil during the time of shooting determines the number of internodes along the stem as well as in the ears themselves; thus, much water at this time increases not only the amount of straw but also the amount of grain produced.

DeVries was very careful to point out that the sensitive period was strictly limited in time: "External influences exert their effect on the development of organs during their youth, that is to say, during the so-called susceptible period. After the character of the organ has been definitely established in this period, further development cannot affect it" (1910). The sensitive period, he cautioned, was not the same during the entire lifetime; one can observe the existence of transient periods of stronger and of weaker responses to specific conditions. "One must take into account the susceptible period. One organ will pass through this period earlier, another later" (1909).

Behavioral Phenomena

During the very time that these biologically based ideas of development-ally determined sensitivities influencing the course of morphological development were forming, similar ideas were also arising in the area of human behavior. One of the earliest writers in which we can see evidence of this trend of thought was Friedrich Froebel (1782–1852), a German educator. Since he was also a contemporary of Saint-Hilaire, it is clear that the intellectual climate was then favorable for the development of such notions. In his *Die Menschenerziehung (Education of Man)*, Froebel wrote of the great sensitivity of the child and of the necessity for proper development at each stage in order to have optimal development at the next stage.

> The child, the boy, man, indeed, should know no other endeavor but to be at every stage of development wholly what this stage calls for. Then will each successive stage spring like a new shoot from a healthy bud; and, at each successive stage, he will with the same endeavor again accomplish the requirements of this stage; for only the adequate development of man in each preceding stage can effect and bring about adequate development at each succeeding later stage.... [Otherwise,] whatever of human education and development has been neglected in boyhood will never be retrieved.

Later, the English educator Herbert Spencer (1820–1903) pointed out the existence of transient periods in child development in which the child shows an intense interest in certain intellectual activities. "The rise of an appetite for any kind of knowledge implies that the unfolding mind has become fit to assimilate it and needs it for the purposes of growth," Spencer wrote in 1861. Furthermore, "there is a certain sequence in which the faculties spontaneously develop and [there is] a certain kind of knowledge, which each requires during its development." In fact, "the genesis of knowledge in the individual must follow the same course as the genesis of knowledge in the race," thus showing Spencer's belief in the biological determination, through inherited action tendencies, of the stages which he had observed in individual development.

Similar ideas were developed by the American psychologist William James (1842–1910), with reference not only to human behavior but also to animal behavior. James (1887, 1890) observed the importance of sequences of experiences in determining the character of later behavior, and gave several instances of this phenomenon.

> I am told by farmers in the Adirondack wilderness that it is a very serious matter if a cow wanders off and calves in the woods and is not found for a week or more. The calf, by that time, is wild, and almost as fleet as a deer, and hard to capture without violence. But calves rarely show any particular wildness to the men who have been in contact with them during the first days of their life, when the instinct to attach themselves is uppermost, nor do they dread strangers as they would if brought up wild.

Noting several instances in human behavior in which first-formed preferences appeared to prevent the formation of new ones, James concluded that "a habit, once grafted on an instinctive tendency, restricts the range of the tendency itself, and keeps us from reacting on any but the habitual object, although other objects might just as well have been chosen had they been the first-coming." He then drew up the first of his "two principles of non-uniformity in instincts."

The first of these was expressed in the statement, "When objects of a certain class elicit from an animal a certain sort of reaction, it often happens that the animal becomes partial to the first specimen of the class on which it has reacted, and will not afterward react on any other specimen." This principle closely resembles the first major type of proposition on the effects of early experience which we discussed earlier. It may be recalled that this viewpoint regards primacy of experience and transfer of effects from first to subsequent experiences as the primary factors involved. But James did not stop there; he went on to set up his second principle of non-uniformity in instincts:

> Many instincts ripen at a certain age and then fade away. A consequence of this law is that if, during the time of such an instinct's variety, objects adequate to arouse it are met with, a *habit* of acting on them is formed, which remains when the original instinct has passed away; but that if no such objects are met with, then no habit will be formed; and later on in life, when the animal meets the objects, he will altogether fail to react, as at the earlier epoch he would instinctively have done.

James noted, as an instance of this second law, the loss of sucking behavior in mammalian young, including human babies, if not activated during the first few days of life, and the difficulty of resurrecting it after that time.

> The instinct of sucking is ripe in all mammals at birth.... But the instinct itself is transient, in the sense that if, for any reason, the child be fed by spoon during the first few days of life and not put to the breast, it may be no easy matter after that to make it suck at all. So of calves. If the mother die, or be dry, or refuse to let them suck at all for a day or two, so that they are

fed by hand, it becomes hard to get them to suck at all when a new nurse is provided.

James felt that similar phenomena were at work in cases where a child does not have the opportunity to perform certain sports activities early in life. Practically no motivation to learn these is present in adulthood, even though the opportunities are then available. The refusal of Spalding's hand-reared chick (Spalding, 1873) to follow its own mother when it finally met her was cited as another instance of this law of transiency of instincts. Naturally, James pointed out, not all instances of behavior follow these laws. Some behaviors come and go, while others never fade away.

Soon afterward, Sigmund Freud (1856–1939), the Viennese psychiatrist, began to spread the psychoanalytic gospel of the effects of events during infantile life on adult behavior. Freud took up the notion that there were specific periods in the child's development during which certain aspects of the environment made a particularly strong impact. His observations of neurotics led him to the conclusion that their behavior toward their fellow men and themselves was infantile in character. The behavior was infantile because it either had never progressed beyond a certain level of development or had gone back to an immature stage. Thus, Freud drew the further conclusions that events during very early childhood were etiological in the formation of neurotic behavior, and that young children were particularly susceptible to psychological trauma. "The very impressions which we have forgotten have nevertheless left the deepest traces in our psychic life, and acted as determinants for our whole future development," Freud declared (1905).

Physical development in the child was described by Freud as the sequential appearance of different psychic functions, all of which are present in the adult, but which in the child have different degrees of intensity according to the developmental stage which he is undergoing. The child also progresses from relative undifferentiation to fully structured functions in the course of his personality development. According to Freud (1927), the infant is born having only an *id* which is able to react only with pleasure or displeasure at any given state of affairs. But it is not long after that, perhaps at the age of five or six months, that the *ego* develops out of the id by means of the direct influence of the environment. The ego acts in the service of the id by developing instrumental behavior sequences, the goal of which is to bring about pleasurable states and to avoid unpleasurable ones, in accordance with actual environmental possibilities. Thus, while the id can only wish for pleasure, the ego acts on the *reality principle*, and works directly on the environment to bring pleasure about. It can postpone immediate gratification in order to achieve greater later pleasure.

Then, as time goes on, the child develops strong attachments to certain aspects of his environment, in particular the parents. The approval and disapproval of the parents and of society in general become important factors in the control of the child's behavior, since they involve the giving and withholding of love from the parents. Thus, the *super-ego* evolves from the ego. Freud described the super-ego as an internalized form of the child's relations with his parents. The child identifies with the parents; by internalizing them and their attitudes, he feels that he is like them. A sense of security is thus maintained, since the internalized portion of the parents remains with him. Furthermore, the child can love this part of himself which he has modeled on the parents; this forms the basis of self-estem and promotes the development of independent functioning.

Parallel with the sequential development of these different personality functions, Freud postulated three different stages during which the child is sensitive to different aspects of the environment. The stages of sensitivity were described in terms of *erogenous zones*, which had an intensified cutaneous sensitivity and formed the principal centers of pleasurable sensations. The first such stage was called the *oral stage*. At this time, the mouth region is the principal erogenous zone, and feeding activities are the most important ones for the child, except for breathing. It is a fact that during the earliest months of life, sensations from oral activity can override those from other parts of the infant's body, and parents can often calm a fussy baby who is not hungry by sticking a pacifier in its mouth.

At first, the child's orientation toward the environment is passive as he takes in food and visual, auditory, and tactual experiences. Then he becomes more active, around the age of six months, when he begins to show goal-oriented activities as he reaches for objects and puts them in his mouth. He no longer merely receives stimulation but actively seeks it. Later on, when the child is walking and the parents begin to use disciplinary measures and to toilet-train him, he enters the so-called *anal stage* of the second and third years of life. In this stage, there are pleasurable sensations in the withholding and expulsion of excretory matter. It is during this period that the child develops control over opposing impulsive tendencies.

Finally, in the Freudian system, there is a *phallic stage* in the 4th and 5th years, during which the child becomes aware of sensations from the primary sexual organs. This is the time of the so-called *Oedipus complex*, in which the child, developing a role as male or female, engages in affectional rivalry with the same-sex parent in regard to the opposite-sex parent. According to Freud, the normal outcome of the Oedipus complex in our culture is identification with the same-sex parent, the assumption of the super-ego, and the onset of what Freud termed the *latency period*, in which erogenous cutaneous sensations assume a minor role in the experiences of the child as he sets out to acquire competence in the social and intellectual environment. The beginning of adulthood, puberty, ushers in the final *genital stage*, when mature sexual drives arise and must be dealt with.

Freud's theory of sequential stages in personality development has been very influential, and even today there are several personality theories which are enlargements or modifications of Freud's. Erikson (1950, 1963), for example, emphasizes the fact that "the oral stages form in the infant the spring of the basic sense of trust and the basic sense of evil," since the manner in which the parents handle the feeding situation is often typical of the degree to which they are willing to meet the child's needs. In the *muscular-anal stage*, according to Erikson, the child is attempting to develop autonomy, the ability to function independently. Similarly, in the *locomotor-genital (phallic) stage*, the child develops aggressiveness, and models himself on adults so as to develop effective means of dealing with his environment. Erikson emphasizes that adequate development in each of the postulated eight life stages, three of which we have just described, is a necessary preparation for optimal performance in the following stage. Thus we see that certain events in specific life periods are considered to be highly important in determining the character of later behavior.

White (1960) has also described personality development as a series of stages, each of which is relevant to the development of different personality functions. While White believes the Freudian model of personality, in terms of gratification of erogenous zones, is valid, he believes also that it is vastly incomplete and fails to account sufficiently for many of the stage-dependent phenomena of emotional and intellectual development during childhood. He postulates the development of a "sense of competence" in the child as he copes for mastery with different aspects of his environment. White regards theories based only on physiological drives to be inadequate because they emphasize the reduction of drive states, whereas children are often intensely interested in increasing sensory stimulation, as shown by their exploratory and manipulatory tendencies.

In the meantime, beginning in the early 1920s, the Swiss psychologist Jean Piaget, in his studies of the development of intellectual capacities in the individual from birth to maturity, found this development to consist of a series of periods, subperiods, stages, and substages. However, just as in biology, description and classification of phenomena must be carried out before they can be studied and explained, Piaget has regarded his principal task to be the description and structural analysis of ontogenetic changes in intellectual functioning. This task alone has been found to be an extremely monumental undertaking, as can be discovered by examining Flavell's 1963 book on Piaget's theory and methods. As Piaget has made no study of the many factors which can facilitate or hinder the appearance of the successive stages, his theoretical system, while definitely developmental, does not include the effects of early experience. Nevertheless, it may be noted that each of Piaget's periods and stages can be regarded as "critical," since he postulates that development in each must occur in order for the succeeding period or stage to occur. Thus, for example, a child must perform concrete operations before he is able to perform symbolic ones.

Furthermore, the ages which Piaget has given for the periods and stages of intellectual growth are not absolute, but represent average ages during which they appear in normal development. It is only the *sequence* of these stages which is absolutely invariant. Thus while there might well be maturational determinants of the stages which Piaget has studied, there is so far no attempt in Piaget's system to point them out. This task will probably have to be carried out by others.

The absence of maturational determinants in Piaget's theory does not mean that Piaget conceives of the role of experience in the same way as theorists of learning via association do. He conceives of the newborn infant's brain not as a completely passive, homogeneous entity but as clearly structured so as to promote selective, not indiscriminate, responses to environmental data. That is, at each stage, the child responds to some stimuli and not to others. This is a premise which we have seen, and will continue to see, in theories of the effects of early experience. Furthermore, the child is considered not to behave randomly but from a repertoire of available actions. These actions frequently are performed for their own sake, and not solely in the service of the traditional physiological drives of hunger and thirst which have been the favorites of association theorists. Thus, given a normally structured child and a normal environment, we have the development which has been described by Piaget. If either of these is abnormal, then development will also be abnormal.

Finally, there is a great deal of congruence between some of Piaget's concepts and those found in biologically based theories of behavioral development, an example being the overlap between Piaget's *schema* and ethology's *fixed action pattern*. It thus appears likely that further study of the phenomena described by Piaget will lead to the confirmation of the existence of maturationally determined sensitive periods in mental development.

The concept of maturationally determined sequences of sensitive periods in personality development has also been developed by Maria Montessori (1870–1952), an Italian physician who created an educational method specifically based upon age-related sensibilities of children between the ages of 3 and 9 years. She observed the development of children to be a series of transitory sensitive periods. In each sensitive period, according to Motessori, children are highly susceptible to certain aspects of their environment, and this susceptibility is related to the acquisition of a specific characteristic. "Once this characteristic has evolved, the corresponding sensibility disappears. Thus, every characteristic is established by the help of an impulse, of a transient sensibility which lasts over a limited period of growth" (1936). She emphasized that "psychic development does not come about by hazard, and does not originate [solely] in stimuli from the outer world; it is guided by transient sensibilities, temporary instincts connected with the acquisition of certain characteristics" (1936). She went on to say:

> The inner sensibilities we have mentioned determine the selection of necessary things from a many-faceted environment, and of circumstances favorable to development. This guidance is exercised by making the child sensitive only toward certain things, leaving him indifferent toward others. . . . But it is not a question only of an intense desire to find himself in given situations, or to absorb given elements. The child has a special, unique capacity for profiting by these in order to grow, for it is during the sensitive period that he acquires certain psychological faculties.

Montessori enumerated several sensitive periods in the development of children. Those periods were not necessarily absolutely sequential, but could overlap to some degree. The longest sensitive period, beginning at 6 months of age and lasting almost to 5 years, was described by her as one in which children can have a prodigious capacity to imprint the features of their environment on themselves. During this period, for example, the child may acquire unshakable emotional attachments to the features of the climate and geographical location in which he lives. She declared: "What the child has absorbed remains a final ingredient of his personality. And the same thing happens with his limbs and organs, so that every grown-up person has an individuality indelibly stamped upon him in this early period of life" (1949). Montessori's concept of children absorbing the features of their environment bears a marked resemblance to Lorenz's (1935) concept of imprinting, which we shall discuss later.

The importance of proper development at each stage, in order for optimal development to be able to take place at the following stage, has a cardinal place in Montessori's theory. "Although, as I have hinted, each period is basically different from the other two (before and after), nevertheless, each lays the foundation for the one following it. . . . The more fully the needs of one period are met, the greater will be the success of the next" (Montessori, 1949). In her opinion, defects in one period can sometimes be corrected in the following period, but after that stage is over, it is impossible to do any correction. Like Freud, she felt that incomplete development at one level caused either fixation at that level or regression to it.

It was Montessori's contention that physical growth—in particular, brain development—is correlated with the child's mental evolution. For example, at the age of 6 months, a turning point in development that has been noted by many investigators, the cerebellum begins to develop very rapidly, slowing down somewhat at the age of 14 to 15 months and continuing until the age of 4½ years. Montessori noted that after the age of 6 months, children are in need of environmental stimulation as offered by being picked up, rocked, and cuddled, citing the fact that institutionalized children usually thrive until that age, and then begin to do poorly unless given intensive individual attention. This phenomenon has been widely studied by many researchers.

It is of interest that some of Montessori's ideas and findings regarding child development have recently been confirmed independently by Glenn Doman, Robert Doman, and Carl Delacato of the United States. These workers and their colleagues at the Institute for the Achievement of Human Potential at Chestnut Hill, Pennsylvania, have discovered the amazing fact that certain physical activities are apparently essential for proper neurological functioning involved in intellectual processes (Delacato, 1963). One of the most important of these physical activities is the baby's cross-pattern crawling which normally occurs from the age of 6 months to 12 or 14 months. The function of the crawling, in addition to locomotion, is to develop the synergistic action of the two halves of the brain. If this neurological development fails to occur because of child-rearing practices which inhibit crawling experiences, then the child may appear to be mentally deficient or, in borderline cases, to have reading and speech difficulties. The same basic problem—incompleteness of neurological organization—is reflected in a whole continuum, ranging from aphasia, delayed speech, stuttering, retarded reading, poor spelling and handwriting, to reading which falls within normal range but is below mathematical performance. Therapy in which the child is made to perform the cross-pattern crawling has produced spectacular improvement in these areas of intellectual functioning.

Crawling, of course, is not the only physical activity important in the development of intellectual and emotional capacities. Actually, there is a whole series of developmental activities involved as the infant progresses from neurological organization at the medulla, pons, mid-brain, early cortex levels, and, finally, cortical hemispheric dominance. Correspondingly, the infant progresses from homolateral movements, bilateral movements, crawling, and unilateral dominance, as reflected by right-handedness, right-footedness, and right-eyedness, in the majority of cases (Delacato, 1963). The performance of the activities of each stage of neurological development is essential for optimal completion of each of these—a concept foreshadowed in Montessori's statement, "If a child is prevented from using his powers of movement as soon as they are ready, the child's mental development is obstructed" (1949).

Bronson (1962) has also pointed out recently some of the same principles that Montessori had emphasized. Noting a congruence between ethological observations such as those made by Lorenz (1935) and human phenomena, Bronson observed:

> The principle of the critical period recognizes the role of maturational factors in predisposing the organism to acquire certain basic orientations to the world at certain critical stages of its development. The quality of experiences during these early developmental phases, in interaction with the constitutional predisposition of the individual, will affect the fundamental nature of the individual's later involvement with the world; experience beyond the critical periods act only to influence the modes and the areas in which these orientations will find expression.

Bronson went on to propose:

> The explanation for these processes is found in a theory of emerging motivational systems. At each critical developmental stage the dominant motivation engenders a selective responsiveness to pertinent characteristics of the environment and dictates the significant dimensions of learning. One would also expect a significant constitutional difference in the strength of these various motivational systems to first become manifest during the appropriate critical periods.

It is clear that the notion of sensitive periods, even of critical stages, is assuming greater and greater importance in the realm of human behavior. Money, Hampson and Hampson (1957), Green and Money, (1960), and Hampson and Hampson (1961) suggest that the child forms its gender role during the first two or three years of life. Any attempts to change the sex in which the child is being reared after the age of 2½ years generally fail, and permanent emotional damage may result. Another instance of critical stages is the finding of Barry and Lindemann (1960) that the death of the mother before the child is 5 years old is a significantly more frequent occurrence among psychoneurotics than among the general population. The most sensitive time for little girls in this respect is during the first 2 years of life.

While we have up to now concentrated principally on human behavior, the area of animal behavior is certainly not without its pioneers, who have, in increasing numbers, discovered the existence of sensitive or critical periods in the development of behavior characteristics. We have already discussed William James' (1887) awareness of these periods, but it was an Austrian zoologist and ethologist, Konrad Lorenz, who was responsible for bringing these notions more fully to the attention of present-day students of behavior. In a classic 1935 paper, Lorenz postulated a critical period for the formation of the affective bond between young ducks and goslings and their mothers, for he found that if they were exposed to him, instead of to the mother, soon after hatching, they would regard him as their mother and pay no attention to their real mother. Likewise, if they stayed with their own mother after hatching, they would pay no attention to him. Thus it appeared to Lorenz that there was a crucial period shortly after hatching for the formation of the filial bond. This process of bond formation Lorenz called *Prägung* or, *stamping-in*, of the features of the mother. This term has been translated into English as *imprinting*, and so it is called today. Imprinting will be discussed in considerable detail in later chapters of this book.

Just as James (1887, 1890) had postulated, Lorenz indicated that the critical period for imprinting are irreversible in their effects. Lorenz pointed out that before imprinting has occurred, the animal has the potentiality of learning almost any object as its parent; but after imprinting has occurred, the range of objects to which the animal will respond filially has become extremely delimited, so that the specific object which had been experienced during the imprinting process is the one which will reliably elicit positive responses. This principle of irreversibility is not absolute but only relative.* Nevertheless, it certainly exists in imprinting phenomena, and is of value since it is essential for the survival of the species that there be a high degree of stability in the class of objects which an animal considers to be own-species members. Thus irreversibility of the effects of critical periods and the strong permanence of the effects of experiences during sensitive periods are related phenomena.

Since 1950, research reports have been published at ever-increasing rates each year on the effects of early experiences of animals of many types. Many of these papers have demonstrated the existence of critical periods and sensitive periods of many varieties. In actuality, we have many more empirical findings of sensitive periods in the development

---

*See Chapter 7 for discussion of reversibility in imprinting.

of animal behavior than we do in the case of human behavior, as we shall discover in Chapter 6.

THE FUNCTION OF DEVELOPMENTAL STAGES

It is by now obvious that the notion of sequences of developmental stages is a fundamental one in psychology today. The fact of physical growth and development, wherein certain phenomena and processes occur at particular times, is a familiar one. It is of utmost importance to appreciate the fact that the process of development entails a change from one state to another, that it is more than just an increase in size. The laws governing the processes of development may differ at the various stages, and thus we must regard the processes of the different stages as perhaps conforming to different laws, if only because different things are in the process of development at each of these stages.

Nevertheless, it is possible to make some broad genearlizations regarding development from the beginning to maturity. If the process of development is interrupted at any time, then whatever was in the state of most rapid change or organization is affected. This has been found to be true in both embryology and growth processes in general. It is now obvious that this is also the case in the growth of the intellect and personality. Certain learning processes are evidently more easily and rapidly accomplished at certain age periods than at others. That is, the child is much more sensitive to particular aspects of his environment at certain ages that at earlier or later ages. During the 3rd year of life, for example, as Montessori (1949) and Delacato (1963) have pointed out, the child picks up the structure of his mother tongue—without being taught—and from them on to the age of 6, a tremendous vocabulary development takes place, one which adults rarely duplicate. To return to our original statement, then, if conditions are adverse to the full realization of whatever is in the process of development during a particular stage—whether an eye, vocabulary acquisition, or the ability to discriminate finely the sounds of a spoken language—it will be stunted. Hence the idea of special sensitivity at particular stages is extremely important, not only in embryology but also in child development and animal behavior.

In nearly all theoretical accounts of development, there is an emphasis on the fact that proper development at one stage is absolutely essential for optimal development to be able to take place during the succeeding stage. Each stage lays the foundation for proper development at the next one. This principle is most evident in mental development, and now it appears that one of the reasons that it is so important in mental development is that neurological development, which underlies mental functioning, is itself subject to the laws of staged development (Delacato, 1963).

CLASSES OF SENSITIVE PERIODS

These notions regarding stages and sensitive periods of development have been derived from a wealth of observational and experimental data. However, it is well to realize that not all sensitive periods obey the same laws; nor do they all have the same character. There are varying degrees of absoluteness in the length of the sensitive period and in the crucialness of stimulation during that time. As Sluckin (1964) has pointed out, all critical periods are sensitive periods, but not all sensitive periods are critical.

There are at least three different ways in which the idea of sensitive periods in behavioral development can be regarded. The first of these is the notion of the *critical period*, a very brief period of time in the development of an animal during which certain experiences must be undergone. The effects of such experiences are permanent. But if these experiences are not undergone, then the animal will show abnormal behavior for the rest of his life. This concept is held by Konrad Lorenz and others in regard to the imprinting of the filial bond between young birds and their parents. It is beyond a doubt, that in social imprinting there is such a thing as a critical period which does not begin until a short time after birth and which lasts for only a short time, after which it disappears and is no longer retrievable (see Chapter 4). The effects are extremely long-lasting, and laboratory research has demonstrated that the consequences of social imprinting can last at least as long as 10 years and probably for a lifetime in fowl. It is possible that such strictly limited critical periods exist only for imprinting.

The second way of regarding sensitive periods is the concept of *susceptible period*, corresponding to what several workers have called the *sensitive period* or *sensible phase*. According to this concept, there is a period of time during which the animal is extremely susceptible to certain types of stimuli and during which it makes innate responses to these stimuli. Whatever stimuli the animal makes such responses to will continue to elicit these responses after the susceptible period has passed. In other words, the susceptible period is the time during which the animal acquires specific objects to which certain innately rooted behavior is thenceforth directed. For example, it is known that chickens must exercise pecking behavior sometime during the first 2 weeks of life or they will never be able to eat properly (Poulsen, 1951). Chickens which have been dark-reared and hand-fed for more than two weeks, even though they show pecking movements in the air, are totally unable to use these movements to eat food and will starve to death, even in the midst of plenty of grain (Padilla, 1935). Hence the function of the susceptible period is to call forth behavior which is then maintained for the rest of the animal's life and to link this behavior to certain specific stimuli. If such behavior is not called forth during this time, the animal will never be able to perform it for an adaptive purpose. Thus again, abnormal behavior can result if certain conditions are not met.

The third sensitive period concept is that of the *optimal period*. It has been observed that there are periods of time during which the animal or child has the greatest sensitivity to certain aspects of the enviornment and thus can respond most readily to certain kinds of learning situations. This sensitivity remains in the animal or child for an extended period of time. It has also been observed that such learning can, of course, also take place at some other time, but less easily and less effectively or completely (Riesen, 1961). Furthermore, the effects of the learning during the optimal period are not necessarily permanent. But there are definitely specific periods during which the child or animal is most highly susceptible to certain kinds of experience, and these periods come and go. An example at the human level is the acquisition of language. The child is obviously not ready at birth to begin learning a language, but after the age of 9 years it is progressively harder for a person to acquire perfect pronunciation and usage of a new language (Penfield and Roberts, 1959), although, of course, people beyond that age can and do learn new languages. The principal fact here is that the majority can never, after the age of 9, learn a new language as well as they did their mother tongue. Another example is crawling activity. If a child does not crawl sufficiently during his infancy, most of the defects created by the lack of this kind of exercise can be eliminated by later practice. Dramatic improvements are accomplished by this course of therapy when undertaken in children under the age of 8 years. But after the age of 16 years, comparatively very little change can be brought about, and great effort is required to bring about any improvement in individuals over that age (Delacato, personal communication, 1965).

Each of these three concepts—critical period, susceptible period, and optimal period—represents a different grade of sensitive periods in behavioral development. Considering them all together gives some idea of the dimensions along which sensitive periods can vary in character. Furthermore, these three periods represent only convenient categories expressing the extreme and medium levels, rather than ultimate classifications, for there are most likely many instances which are actually intergrades between two of these types. All these classes of sensitive periods are relevant to various types of organisms, plants, animals, or humans, and to various types of behavior. The terminology is by no means a standard one, for different persons have used the same term to express different kinds of sensitive periods. This has resulted in much discussion and confusion regarding the nature of sensitive period phenomena, especially whenever an attempt has been made to consider all sensitive periods as having the same character with regard to temporal limitations and permanence of effects. This has been particularly the case with the term *critical period*. It is hoped that the terminology proposed here will help to clear up some of this confusion.

Furthermore, there are several instances of sensitive periods and of very rapid attachment which do not occur during early life periods. For example, life-long pair-formation in foxes occurs extremely rapidly—as a result of a single night's cohabitation, in fact—as soon as maturity is reached (Enders, 1945); Eskimo dogs learn territorial boundaries during a similar life period (Tinbergen, 1951); mother sheep and goats form the attachment to their own offspring during the critical first few minutes after parturition (Collias, 1956; Hersher, Moore, and Richmond, 1958; Klopfer, 1964; Klopfer, Adams, and Klopfer, 1964). However, it still appears that by far the majority of sensitive periods exist very early in life rather than later, for it is plainly advantageous to the organism to form early the bulk of its behavioral adjustments necessary for survival in its environment.

Even though the idea of crucial stages or sensitive periods in behavioral development has come to assume more and more importance as we have accumulated additional evidence concerning the nature of the effects of early experiences, the primacy principle still retains considerable relevance. Many sensitive periods, especially critical periods, occur extremely early in the life of the animal or child. Furthermore, in some of these sensitive periods, the first relevant experience is the most effective one in determing the animal's behavior or the object to which such behavior is thenceforth directed. Hence, the primacy principle can operate within the sensitive period, just as James (1887, 1890) postulated. Imprinting is an especially clear illustration of this phenomenon.

DIFFERENCES BETWEEN SENSITIVE PERIOD LEARNING AND ORDINARY LEARNING

The existence of unique biological phases differentiates learning processes occurring during sensitive periods from those occurring outside the sensitive periods. This distinction is of supreme importance in giving early experience a special status apart from past experience in general. The imprinting phenomenon, involving the most extreme form of sensitive periods, the critical period, illustrates this fact perfectly. The imprinting phenomenon also illustrates the fact that the processes occurring during the critical period are fundamentally different from the processes that occur when the critical period has passed, in terms of both the laws governing the effects of specific experiences and the long-range effects of these experiences. In imprinting, the distinction is particularly important, for it has been found that the effects produced by specific experiences during the critical period for imprinting can be nearly duplicated by a long period of association learning experience when that critical period has passed. The behavioral results of the critical period events are, however, only superficially similar to the behavioral results of the more tedious association learning or training experiences which can occur later, particularly because the effects of imprinting during the critical period are far more complete and permanent than the effects of the later taming experiences (Hess, 1964; Klopfer, 1964). In Chapter 7 and elsewhere in this book the association learning processes that bring about effects which resemble those of imprinting proper will be called the *association learning counterparts* of the respective specific imprinting processes which they resemble. The imprinting processes are characterized by critical periods whereas the association learning counterparts are not.

The short-term similarity between the behavioral effects of sensitive period and association learning phenomena and an ignorance of the very basic underlying differences between these two phenomena are some of the major factors which have led to disputes between investigators regarding the effects of specific early experiences. For example, if an experimenter applies a particular experience reasonably early in the life of an animal and then finds that its effects were not very permanent, he might conclude that early experience of the sort he applied was not appreciably different from past experiences in general, and that there was no effect of the age of the animal on the consequences of these early experiences. However, his conclusion may not be justified if he has happened to miss the sensitive period entirely, for, in some cases, it may be so early as to escape the notice of the investigator. Hence, his finding that the particular experience which he administered at a certain age was not permanent would not necessarily be incompatible with another investigator's report that this experience, administered at a different age falling within the sensitive period, had effects which were not easily eradicable.

Differences between sensitive period and association learning phenomena have been recently pointed out by the research of Hess (1959, 1962, 1964), Riesen (1961), and Klopfer, (1964). It has become highly important for experimenters to be vigilant of the two different processes of sensitive period learning and association learning in view of their different causal bases and ultimate long-range effects. The task is not an easy one, for effects from these two processes can exist side by side in the same animal or person. For example, an animal may be imprinted to its own mother and tamed by association learning to man; the taming to man does not replace or reverse the imprinting to the mother, but coexists. In the same way, animals handled both during and after the critical period for handling effects will show coexisting results from these experiences. Nevertheless, it is a grave error to consider the behaviors resultant from these two different types of experiences as similar in their underyling causes just because their manifestations may appear similar.

BIOLOGICAL BASES OF SENSITIVE PERIODS

Concommitant physiological or maturational processes certainly appear to be a primary causal difference between sensitive period phenomena and association learning processes. But what exactly are those specific physiological or maturational processes?

This question is one of those explored by J. P. Scott in a paper (1962) on critical periods in behavioral development or what we have called sensitive periods. In his view, the basic timing mechanisms for developmental periods are the biological ones of growth and differentiation rather than chronological age periods. In some specific cases, Scott believes that the development of the nervous system forms the bases of the developmental phases during which sensitive periods occur. However, it is his belief that the common underlying principle in all sensitive period phenomena is the process of growth. He declared:

> Both growth and behavioral differentiation are based on organizing processes. This suggests a general principle of organization: that once a system becomes organized, whether it is the cells of the embryo multiplying and differentiating or the behavior patterns of a young animal becoming organized through learning, it becomes progressively more difficult to reorganize the system. That is, organization inhibits reorganization. Further, organization can be strongly modified only at the times when active processes of organization are going on, and this accounts for critical periods of development.

Thus, Scott's theory is a combination of both the primacy and sensitivity propositions since he postulates a temporally limited special sensitivity which determines the period of primary organization. As with the primacy viewpoint, once the organization has taken place, new organization is relatively difficult to accomplish, and may in some cases be impossible.

Thus the problem for future research is to identify the specific maturational processes which promote sensitive period phenomena. One approach in attempting to determine the mechanisms which open and close sensitive periods is to correlate the sensitive period with different behaviors of the animal, as Hess (1959) has done in the case of imprinting and as Bronson (1962) has attempted with children. Another approach is to establish the specific physiological processes which occur during the onset and ending of the sensitive periods. This is an extremely difficult task, and will require many decades to accomplish through patient and imaginative research efforts. There is so much that we do not know.

But this much we do know: that sensitive periods play a role in many early experience phenomena—early perceptual learning in rats; social learning in many animals, even ants; early handling of rats, with effects on emotionality and curiosity; song learning in various bird species; (Hinde, 1970). In all these, it is evident that the relevant experiences have important effects on later behavior. As a result of such evidence as we now have, the concept of sensitive periods is acquiring increasing importance for theories of and research on the genesis of animal and human behavior. We shall see that this is the case as we explore various aspects of the imprinting phenomenon in the remainder of this book.

REFERENCES

BARRY, HERBERT, JR., and LINDEMANN, ERICH. Critical ages for maternal bereavement in psychoneuroses. *Psychosomatic Medicine*, 1960, **22,** 166–181.
BRONSON, GORDON. Critical periods in human development. *British Journal of Medical Psychology*, 1962, **35,** 127–133.
BOWER, T. G. R. The object in the world of the infant. *Scientific American,* 1971, **225,** No. 4, 30–38.
COLLIAS, NICHOLAS E. The analysis of socialization in sheep and goats. *Ecology,* 1956, **37,** 228–239.
DARESTE, CAMILLE. Sur l'arrêt de développement considére comme la cause prochaine de la plupart des monstruosités simples. *Comptes-Rendus hebdomadaires des séances, de l'Académie des Sciences Paris,* 1869, **69,** 963–966.
DARESTE, CAMILLE. *Recherches sur la Production Artificiélle des Monstruosités.* Paris: C. Reinwald, 1891 (1st ed., 1877).
DELACATO, CARL H. *The Diagnosis and Treatment of Speech and Reading Problems.* Springfield, Illinois: Thomas, 1963.
DELACATO, CARL H. Personal communication, January 4, 1965.
DE VRIES, HUGO. Alimentation et sélection. In: *Cinquantenaire de la Société de Biologie.* vol. jubilaire. Paris: Masson, 1899. 17–38.
DE VRIES, HUGO. *Species and Varieties.* Chicago: Open Court Publishing Co., 1905.
DE VRIES, HUGO. *The Mutation Theory.* Transl. by J. B. Farmer and A. D. Darbishire (from *Die Mutationstheorie,* 1901). Vol. 1. *The Origin of Species by Mutation.* Chicago: Open Court Publishing Co., 1909.
DE VRIES, HUGO. *The Mutation Theory.* Transl. by J. B. Farmer & A. D. Darbishire. Vol. 2. *The Origin of Varieties by Mutation.* Chicago: Open Court Publishing Co., 1910.
ENDERS, ROBERT K. Induced changes in the breeding habits of foxes. *Sociometry,* 1945, **8,** 53–55.

ERIKSON, ERIK. *Childhood and Society.* New York: Norton, 1950. (2nd edition, 1963).

FÉRÉ, CHARLES. Note sur les différences des effets des agents toxiques et des vibration mécaniques sur l'evolution de l'embryon de poulet suivant l'époque où elles agissent. *Comptes-Rendus hebdomadaires des seances et mémoires de la Société de Biologie, Paris,* 1894, **46,** 462–465.

FÉRÉ, CHARLES. Tératogénie expérimentale et pathologie générale. In: *Cinquantenaire de la Société de Biologie.* vol. jubilaire. Paris: Masson et Cie, 1899. 363–369.

FLAVELL, JOHN H. *The Developmental Psychology of Piaget.* Princeton, New Jersey: Van Nostrand, 1963.

FREUD, SIGMUND. Three essays on the theory of sexuality. In: *The Standard Edition of the Complete Psychological Works of Sigmund Freud.* London: Hogarth, 1953. Vol. 7, 125–248. (Article originally published in 1905).

FREUD, SIGMUND. The Ego and the Id. Transl. Joan Riviere. London: L. and Virginia Woolf at The Hogarth Press and The Institute of Psychoanalysis, 1927.

FROEBEL, FRIEDRICH. *Die Menschenerziehung.* Leipzig: Reclam. 1826. (transl. into English as *Education of Man* by J. Jarvis. New York: Lovell, 1885).

FULLER, JOHN L., and WALLER, MARCUS B. Is early experience different? In: Bliss, E. L., *Roots of Behavior.* New York: Hoeber, 1962.

GEOFFROY ST.-HILAIRE, ÉTIENNE. *Philosophie anatomique des monstruosités humains.* Paris: J. B. Baillière, 1818–1822.

GREEN, RICHARD, and MONEY, JOHN. Incongruous gender role: Nongenital manifestations in prepubertal boys. *Journal of Nervous and Mental Diseases,* 1960, **131,** 160–168.

HAMPSON, JOHN L., and HAMPSON, JOAN C. The ontogenesis of sexual behavior in man. In: Young, W. C., editor, *Sex and Internal Secretions.* Baltimore, Maryland: Williams & Wilkins Co., 1961. Vol. 2. 1401–1432.

HEBB, D. O. *The Organization of Behavior.* New York: Wiley, 1949.

HERSHER, L., MOORE, A. U., & RICHMOND, J. B. Effect of post partum separation of mother and kid on maternal care in the goat. *Science,* 1958, **128,** 1342–1343.

HESS, ECKHARD H. Imprinting. *Science,* 1959, **130,** 133–141.

HESS, ECKHARD H. Imprinting and the critical period concept. In: Bliss, E. L., editor, *Roots of Behavior.* New York: Hoeber, 1962. 254–263.

HESS, ECKHARD H. Imprinting in birds. *Science,* 1964, **146,** 1128–1139.

HINDE, ROBERT A. *Animal Behaviour.* Second Edition. New York: McGraw-Hill, 1970.

JAMES, WILLIAM. What is an instinct? *Scribner's Magazine, 1887,* **1,** 355–365. Reprinted in James, William. *The Principles of Psychology.* New York: Holt, 1890.

KLOPFER, PETER. Parameters of imprinting. *American Naturalist,* 1964, **98,** 173–182.

KLOPFER, PETER H., ADAMS, DONALD K., and KLOPFER, MARTHA S. Maternal "imprinting" in goats. *Proceedings of the National Academy of Sciences, Washington,* 1964, **52,** 911–914.

LOCKE, JOHN. *Some Thoughts Concerning Education.* 4th edition, London, 1699. (1st edition, 1693).

LORENZ, KONRAD Z. Der Kumpan in der Umwelt des Vogels. *Journal für Ornithologie,* 1935, **83,** 137–214, 289–413. Transl. by Robert Martin in Lorenz,

Konrad Z. *Studies in Human and Animal Behaviour.* vol. 1. Cambridge, Mass.: Harvard University Press, 1970. 101–258.

MONEY, JOHN, HAMPSON, JOAN G., and HAMPSON, JOHN L. Imprinting and the establishment of gender role. *Archives of Neurology and Psychiatry*, 1957, **77**, 333–336.

MONTESSORI, MARIA. *The Secret of Childhood.* Transl. by B. B. Carter. New York: Longmans, Green, 1936.

MONTESSORI, MARIA. *The Absorbent Mind.* Adyar & Madras: Theosophical Publishing House, 1949.

MUNN, NORMAN L. *Handbook of Psychological Research on the Rat.* Boston: Houghton Mifflin, 1950

MUNN, NORMAN L. Learning in children. In: Carmichael, L., editor, *Manual of Child Psychology.* New York: Wiley, 1954.

PADILLA, SINFOROSO G. Further studies on the delayed pecking of chicks. *Journal of Comparative Psychology*, 1935, **20**, 413–443.

PENFIELD, WILDER, and ROBERTS, LAMAR. *Speech and Brain Mechanism.* Princeton, New Jersey: Princeton University Press, 1959.

POULSEN, HOLGAR. Maturation and learning in the improvement of some instinctive activities. *Videnskabelige Meddelser fra Dansk Naturhistorisk Forening*, Copenhagen, 1951, **113**, 155–170.

RIESEN, AUSTIN H. Critical stimulation and optimal periods. Paper presented at 1961 meeting of the American Psychological Association.

RUSSELL, W. R. *Brain, Memory, Learning.* Oxford: Clarendon Press, 1959.

SALAPATEK, PHILIP, and KESSEN, WILLIAM. Visual scanning of triangles by the human newborn. *Journal of Experimental Child Psychology*, 1966, **3**, 155–167.

SCOTT, J. P. Critical periods in the development of social behavior in puppies. *Psychosomatic Medicine*, 1958, **20**, 42–54.

SCOTT, J. P. Critical periods in behavioral development. *Science*, 1962, **138**, 949–957.

SLUCKIN, WLADYSLAW. *Imprinting and Early Learning.* London: Methuen, 1964.

SPALDING, D. A. Instinct, with original observations on young animals. *McMillan's Magazine*, 1873, **27**, 282–293. Reprinted in *British Journal of Animal Behavior*, 1959, **2**, 2–11.

SPEMANN, HANS. *Embryonic Development and Induction.* New Haven: Yale University Press, 1938.

SPENCER, HERBERT. *Education, Intellectual, Moral, and Physical.* New York: Appleton, 1861

STANLEY, W. C., CORNWELL, A. C., POGGIANI, C. and TRAINER, A. Conditioning in the neonatal puppy. *Journal of Comparative and Physiological Psychology*, 1963, **56**, 211–214.

STOCKARD, CHARLES R. The origin of certain types of monsters. *American Journal of Obstetrics*, 1909, **59**, 582–593.

STOCKARD, CHARLES R. The influence of alcohol and other anesthetics on embryonic development. *American Journal of Anatomy*, 1910, **10**, 369–392.

STOCKARD, CHARLES R. Developmental rate and structural expression: an experimental study of twins, "double monsters" and single deformities, and the interaction among embryonic organs during their origin and development. *American Journal of Anatomy*, 1921, **28**, 115–277.

TINBERGEN, NICHOLAS. *The Study of Instinct.* Oxford: Oxford University Press, 1951.

VINCE, MARGARET A. Developmental changes in learning capacity. In: Thorpe, W. H., and Zangwill, O. L., editors, *Current Problems in Animal Behavior.* Cambridge: Cambridge University Press, 1961.

WHITE, ROBERT W. Competence and the psychosexual stages of development. In: Jones, M. editor, *Nebraska Symposium on Motivation,* 1960 (vol. 8). Lincoln: University of Nebraska Press. 97–144.

3

Early Social Experience and Laboratory Imprinting In Birds

Imprinting is not synonymous with *socialization.* There are many cases of early socialization which are clearly not carried out by the imprinting process, and the imprinting process occurs in cases other than socialization (Hess, 1964).

In our view, imprinting is a type of process in which there is an extremely rapid attachment, during a specific critical period, of an innate behavior pattern to specific objects which thereafter become important elicitors of that behavior pattern. This innate behavior pattern may, in turn, influence the choice of objects selected as targets for a limited number of other, related, behaviors, Innate or not, when it has been thusly imprinted, even when the original innate behavior pattern in question drops out of the individual animal's repertoire during the course of ontogeny. Thus, while certainly the innate behavior pattern of pecking, when imprinted to a certain class of objects, remains as an extremely important component of feeding behavior, the innate behavior pattern of following the mother object may drop out after the young animal has achieved a certain age. Nevertheless, the influence of the initial social imprinting experience will remain in the same direction, so that either learned or later-appearing innate social behaviors of that animal may come to be directed toward the same class of objects to which the following behavior had been directed. However, it must be kept in mind that only the original specific innate behavior pattern may be said to be imprinted to the class of objects, since the later-appearing behaviors, even though belonging to a similar motivational system, may be strongly influenced by factors additional to the imprinting experience.

Furthermore, it should be made clear that we regard imprinting as a distinct genetically programmed learning mechanism. This mechanism can be independently involved in the attachment of different innate or species-typical behavior patterns to specific objects involved in different situations. Thus we find pecking behavior involved in relation to food imprinting; locomotion and other behaviors in social imprinting. Food imprinting, social imprinting, and other types of imprinting are, of course, separate events from each other. In all these cases the genetically programmed imprinting is regarded as a genotype-dependent ontogenetic process and as not involving conventional learning processes. In the closing sections of Chapter 2 we have already distinguished between imprinting processes and their association learning counterparts. Thus social imprinting is a socialization process which is achieved through an imprinting mechanism during ontogeny. Social imprinting is distinguished from its association learning counterpart, taming, because the former involves critical period processes while the latter does not.

In Chapter 7, we will state further our views regarding the nature of the imprinting process, particularly with respect to its differentiation from the type of association learning problems which have conventionally been studied in laboratories. For example, we believe that imprinting, to be regarded as such, must occur during a fairly well-defined brief period. We also maintain that this brief period is a critical period in distinction to the other types of sensitive periods which may be found in other processes. And, most important, we assert that the processes promoting the imprinting process are different from those promoting conventional association learning processes.

Thus, it is perfectly apparent that we do not consider everything imprinting that other researchers do. We consider true social imprinting to be much more sharply restricted than the general phenomenon of socialization, and we are more reluctant to use this term than are other writers. For our purposes, then, we distinguish between social imprinting proper and socialization in general. Certainly, we are willing to concede that there may be several other specific socialization processes besides that of social imprinting. Possibly such other processes may be those that involve susceptible periods, optimal periods, or no sensitive period at all, thus making the total possible quantity of fairly different socialization processes at least four.

However, we ourselves feel much more capable of discussing differences between social imprinting and other socialization processes than we do of distinguishing sharply between all four kinds. Thus, we will be much more vague about the nature of socialization mechanisms other than those involved in imprinting than we will be about social imprinting itself. We will, however, be fairly specific about our distinctions between social imprinting and conventional association learning paradigms, even though we must leave to future research the task of delineating the nature of the socialization processes which are not those of social imprinting. We will therefore not pretend to be highly specific about those socialization mechanisms, simply because we do not have the information to do so.

HISTORY: BEFORE LORENZ

The Austrian zoologist Konrad Lorenz certainly is to be given the major credit for initiating the current widespread interest in the imprinting phenomenon. It is not at all surprising, however, that the phenomenon had in fact been part of the folklore for a number of centuries before Lorenz. What Lorenz did was to bring the phenomenon out of the realm of pure anecdote and into that of respectable scientific investigation.

The Greeks, as might be very well expected, recorded the existence of unusually strong attachments between certain birds and people. In A.D. 27, Pliny the elder, for example, wrote of a goose that followed his friend Lacydes faithfully.

The use of this phenomenon in the domestication and taming of birds has cropped up again and again in various writings since then. Saint Cuthbert (635–687), the protector of birds and other wildlife, for example, indubitably domesticated wild eider ducks by means of imprinting young ducklings on himself. According to the monk Reginald, who wrote of Cuthbert's life five centuries later, Cuthbert lived alone with the young of these birds on a cliff of one of the Farne Islands off the coast of northern England, with the result that "he thoroughly tamed these flying and swimming creatures, since their members freely submitted to him as if they were his slaves. He was responsible for a place for them to build their nests and he fixed a certain terminus for their comings and goings. Thus they came even in settled times, and they fled to him [Cuthbert] when they were attacked or in the face of danger. They returned again and again to St. Cuthbert's home." Cuthbert's domestication of these birds was considered by his successors to have a long-lasting effect on the behavior of this duck species on the islands, for Reginald wrote that they showed strong sociability toward people: "If you call them with a nod of your head, they walk forth following your footsteps. They flee, fluttering their wings, toward the hands of those who coax them" (Reginald, 1165–1175).

Not only extraordinary social attachments to people but also interspecies social fixations have been noted for several centuries in birds. In 1581, Mascall wrote a handbook on the rearing and care of different kinds of fowl. In this book he noted, "Those Ducks that haue bene brought up under a henne, the Drakes of that broode will desire to tread the hennes." Since country people of centuries ago and even today often did incubate duck eggs by using a hen, mutual interspecies attachments have been noted for a long time indeed. However, the extent to which ducks do form such interspecies attachments to hens has been lately doubted by Fabricius (1962b), who has stated that thousands of ducks and geese have been reared with foster parent hens at the Wild Fowl Trust at Slimbridge, England, and yet very few of them have ever been observed to court domestic hens. Possibly the resolution of this apparent discrepancy may lie in the relative availability of female conspecifics; however, it is obvious that research is necessary in order to determine what factors will preclude sexual attachments to hens on the part of drakes.

Sir Thomas More, in his *Utopia* (1517), described the imprinting phenomenon in artificially incubated chicks:

> They rear a very large number of chicks, by an amazing device. For the hens do not sit on the eggs. Instead they keep a great number of eggs warm with an even heat and so hatch them. As soon as the chicks come out of the eggs, they follow the men and recognize them as if they were their mothers.

Around the turn of this century, there were a number of observations regarding the nature of the early socialization process of young birds, particularly those of precocial nidifugous species. These were all naturaltistic and relatively informal reports. What most of these authors noted was the transfer of filial responses by young birds to a human caretaker who had fostered them in the absence of their natural parents. In many cases, the persistence of these responses was rather remarkable, since the experiences often could cause the young birds to actively forsake parents of their own species.

Douglas Spalding (1873) seems to have been one of the first of this group of observers and was more of an experimentalist in his approach than some of the rest. He hooded chicks, thus preventing their use of vision, for a time after hatching, beginning as soon as they emerged from the shell. When the hoods were removed, Spalding observed the reactions of the chicks toward the hen and toward him. Spalding found that when the chicks were unhooded at a very early age, they would quickly follow his hands. But if the chicks were kept hooded past the age of 3 days, they showed extreme fear of him. Since the change in behavior was so marked, Spalding concluded that it "could not have been the effect of experience; it must have resulted wholly from changes in their own organization." Spalding further found that chicks which he himself had raised from an early age, when first presented with their own mother hen at a later age, would refuse to have anything to do with her, no matter how hard she attempted to attract them to her. One such chicken at the age of 10 days persisted in running to any person it saw and trying to be with him in spite of being "cruelly maltreated" by the person concerned, who "repeatedly beat the chick back with a small branch, but without succeeding in driving it away."

The failure of hand-reared chickens to show social tendencies toward hens or other chicks was also observed by Morgan (1896) and by Hunt (1898). At the same time, Mills (1898) and Kline (1899) observed the very strong tendency of chicks to follow objects during the first days of their life. While Mills came to the opinion that warmth was a necessary factor in eliciting following, Kline decided that it was not necessary at all. Morgan (1896) found that newly hatched birds of several species— chicks, pheasants, partridges, plovers, moorhens, and others—would all run to his hands and, after a very short time, nestle down between them. Like Mills, Morgan stressed warmth as an attractive stimulus to chicks.

Another report of the effects of hand rearing on the social behavior of young birds was given in 1892 by W. H. Hudson, who told the story of how he himself had raised two rhea birds in South America and how they followed him around, rushing to his call as if he were their own parent. Since they were clearly independent in foraging for their food themselves, their attachment to him had no connection at all with feeding activities.

J. B. Watson (1908), the originator of the behaviorism we discussed in Chapter 1, noted the ease with which newly hatched noddy and sooty terns could be induced to follow him as if he were their natural parent, provided they were taken from the first day of life; otherwise, it would be impossible to cause them to manifest such an attachment.

The effect of early rearing experience on the later social behavior of nidicolous birds—that is, species in which the young must remain in the nest and be fed by the parents for some time after hatching—in contrast to the nidifugous species which we have just now mentioned, was discovered by an American zoologist, Charles Whitman, and his student, Wallace Craig. Whitman (in Riddle and Carr, 1919; Craig, 1908) took the eggs or young of different wild doves and pigeon species and gave them to the domestic ring dove to foster. Such foster young, when they grew up, were found to remain in association with ring doves and to attempt to mate with them. For example,

A male passenger-pigeon that was reared with ring-doves and had remained with that species was ever ready, when fully grown, to mate with any ring-dove, but could never be induced to mate with one of his own species. I kept him away from ring-doves a whole season in order to see what could be accomplished in the way of getting him mated finally with his own species, but he would never make any advances to the females and whenever a ring-dove was seen or heard in the yard he was at once attentive. (In Riddle and Carr, 1919.)

Whitman therefore used this technique of cross-species fostering in order to produce hybrid offspring of two species of pigeons. Craig (1913, 1914) noted the effect of early hand rearing on the later sexual behavior of ring doves, who directed this behavior to humans.

In Europe, Heinroth and his first wife (Heinroth, 1910; Heinroth and Heinroth, 1924–1933) observed the development of social behavior in several species of European birds, particularly in ones they hand reared. Heinroth (1910) wrote that it was so easy for incubator-hatched greylag goslings to become attached to human beings and follow them about religiously that if he wanted them to become attached to a family of geese with goslings, he had to put them in a sack immediately upon removal from the incubator so that they could not even see a human being. Those goslings that he permitted to follow him about could not be shaken off and would, when presented to a goose and gander, have no notion of considering them as parent objects and run away from them, peeping loudly, preferring to look upon humans as parents. Other hand-reared birds—eagle owls, a corncrake, a female European partridge, and a male pheasant—were found to have transferred their adult sexual behavior toward their human caretaker (Heinroth and Heinroth, 1924–1933).

A further example of the extent to which adult sexual behaviors could be diverted from fellow species members by hand-kept birds was provided by Portielje (1921, 1927, 1930), who wrote of a South American bittern (tiger heron) who, although eventually induced to mate with a female of its own species, would forcibly expel its mate from the nest and invite its keeper to "sit on the nest" whenever he appeared in view. Bierens de Haan (1926) reported sexual courtship directed to objects other than conspecifics in an argus pheasant.

KONRAD LORENZ: INITIAL THEORIES

All these observations showed that while young chicks, ducklings, or goslings apparently have an innate disposition to follow moving objects soon after hatching, it is not at all necessary that the natural parent be the object followed. This fact was recognized by Spalding (1873), James (1890), Morgan (1896, 1900), and Thorndike (1899).

But it was Lorenz who, on the basis of these observations and several that he had made himself, first gave the phenomenon a definite name and set up several very explicit theoretical postulations regarding the nature of the processes of social attachment during an early age in the various species of young birds he had observed. While Lorenz certainly has evolved his conceptualizations regarding the nature of social imprinting further since his pioneering 1935 paper, his earliest theories had an extremely strong influence not only in instigating experimental research but also in channeling the nature of the specific aspects of imprinting that were investigated by subsequent researchers.

Lorenz chose the term *Prägung*, later translated as *imprinting* (Lorenz, 1937), similar to the term *Einzuprägung* used earlier by Heinroth. According to Lorenz (1935):

> The most important result of this investigation of instinctive behaviour patterns oriented towards conspecifics [is] the fact that *not all acquired behaviour can be equated with experience and that not all processes of acquisition can be equated with learning.* We have seen that in many cases the object appropriate to innately-determined instinctive behaviour patterns is not instinctively recognized as such, but that recognition of the object is acquired through a quite specific process, *which has nothing to do with learning.*

> With very many instinctive behaviour patterns oriented towards conspecifics, the motor component is itself innate, but the recognition of the object of the pattern is not. This is the case with many other behavioural chains, in which instinct-conditioning intercalation occurs in the course of ontogeny. However, there is a difference from the latter in the *manner of acquisition* of the elicitatory component.

> An instinctive behaviour pattern adapted towards a conspecific, yet initially incorporated without an object, is fixated upon an object in the environment at a quite specific time, at a quite specific developmental stage of the young bird. This specification of the object can take place hand-in-hand with the emergence of the motor component of the instinctive behaviour pattern, but it can also precede the latter by a matter of months or even years. In the normal free-living existence of the species, the conditions are so organized that the choice of object of the instinctive behaviour patterns is reliably limited to a conspecific which represents the biologically-appropriate object. If the young bird is *not* surrounded by conspecifics at the psychological period for object-selection, the responses concerned are oriented towards some other environmental object, but usually towards a living organism (as long as such is available), but otherwise towards some inanimate object.

> The process of object-acquisition is separated from any genuine learning process by two factors, and rendered parallel to another process of acquisition which is known from the mechanics of embryogeny and is referred to in that context as inductive determination. In the first place, this process is *irreversible*, whereas the concept of learning necessarily incorporates the condition that the acquired element can be both forgotten and revised.

Secondly, the process is bound to a sharply-demarcated developmental condition of the individual, which often exists for only a few hours.

The process of acquisition of the objective of instinctive behaviour patterns oriented toward conspecifics, which are initially incorporated without the object, has been termed *imprinting*. Imprinting involves a peculiar and extremely puzzling selection of the characters of the object: *only supraindividual* characters are fixated. (Translation by R. Martin, in Lorenz, 1970, Vol 1. pp. 245–246.)

There were many factors which led Lorenz to take this particular theoretical position. One was clearly the current status of theories of learning at the time that Lorenz formulated his conceptual notions regarding the nature of the social imprinting phenomenon that he had observed so many times in his hand-reared birds. Thus, it was that particular aspects of Lorenz's theory of social imprinting presented a vivid challenge to investigators who were influenced by behavioristic theories of learning.

To appreciate the nature of the challenge presented by Lorenz's theory, we must recall some of the background factors involved in the scientific orientation of students of behavior in this country, which have been discussed in some detail in Chapter 1. Behaviorism, as we have noted, had two basic tenets: the problem of behavior should be studied through pragmatic, empirical, and experimental methods, rather than by philosophical, speculative methods; behaviors are learned. Behaviorism did bring about considerable progress in psychology through its insistence on the use of measurable, public, and operationally definable behavior. The popularity of the belief that behavior is learned was derived from the cultural idealism of an equal chance for everyone from the first moment of life. The hope for a single, unifying theory of behavior, however, was, as time passed, shown to be rather naïve, so that today the concept of learning is rather different from what it was at the time Lorenz first described the phenomenon of social imprinting.

We must also keep in mind, in assessing the imprinting phenomenon, that Lorenz drew his examples of social imprinting from several different species. This fact shows that he did not even regard the process of social imprinting as exactly identical in every one of the bird species he had observed. He was highly aware of the fact that social bonds become attached in different ways in different species. The criteria of social imprinting which he enunciated in his 1935 paper, therefore, were not intended to be applied rigidly to all species.

The major point which Lorenz made was that social imprinting was an instance of behavior which did not conform to the classical characteristics of learning through conventional association or conditioning processes. In the first place, the learning of the parent object in the cases of social imprinting observed by Lorenz obviously was not that of slow conditioning—that is, a trial-by-trial incremental process during a period of time, or trial-and-error learning. Only *one* experience, lasting but a few minutes, was sufficient for the young bird of precocial species to attach its filial behavior to a specific parental surrogate.

The transfer of a response away from a specific object, usually by means of training to a new object and extinction with respect to the first object, was another major tenet of learning that Lorenz specifically postulated did not apply to social imprinting. Lorenz (1935) said, regarding this point:

> The imprinted recognition of the object of instinctive behaviour patterns directed towards conspecifics, following the *expiration* of the physiological imprinting period determined for the species, has *exactly the same appearance of corresponding innate behaviour—the recognition response cannot be "forgotten"!* The possibility of "forgetting" is, as Bühler particularly points out, *a basic feature of all learning processes.* Of course, it is not yet permissible, in the light of the relative novelty of all observations on this process, to make a final statement about the permanence of these acquired objects. The justification for such a pronouncement is based upon the fact, observed in many cases, that birds which have been hand-reared by a human being and have come to direct their conspecific-oriented instinctive patterns towards the human frame do not alter their behaviour in the slightest, even when kept together with conspecifics and away from human beings for many years. (Translation by R. Martin, in Lorenz, 1970, Vol. 1, p. 127.)

Thus did Lorenz point out that considerable training, much longer in time than the original social imprinting experience, normally does not offset the effects of the social imprinting. This is an observation which has been repeatedly made for a number of species by several investigators since Lorenz (e.g., Hess, 1964; Kruijt, 1964, Schein, 1963b).

Another important impliction of classical learning theory is the notion that external stimuli in themselves form the necessary conditions for learning to take place. Thus, provided that certain operations and procedures are carried out, the animal will learn. However, in the case of social imprinting, Lorenz asserted, "A very specific physiological state in the young animal's development is required to accomplish it" (Lorenz, 1937). This physiological state, according to Lorenz, causes the young bird to be in a particular sensitive period, in fact a critical period, for the social imprinting to take place. This physiologically determined critical period, Lorenz maintained, "is confined to a very definite period of individual life, a period which in many cases is of extremely short duration" (Lorenz, 1937).

Still another important distinction between social imprinting and other learning processes which Lorenz pointed out was the fact that the young birds were not induced by conventional reward or punishment to direct their filial actions toward a specific object. What was necessary, Lorenz asserted, provided that the animal was undergoing its maturationally determined sensitive period for social imprinting, was that the animal be *exposed* to the relevant stimuli.

Furthermore, Lorenz emphasized that in social imprinting there is an effect of the experiences during this early life period on sexual preferences manifested in later life. He pointed out that this did not fit the contemporary proposition of learning theorists that during learning a specific response is attached to a specific stimulus. In many instances, the same feelings may be signified by different behaviors at different ages by the same animal. For example, affection is expressed by the young puppy by jumping and licking, while the older and less vigorous dog may express the same sentiment by means of the classical faithful look. There is thus no rigidity of the stimulus-response pattern that forms an essential postulate of the classical conditioning paradigm but, rather, a rigidity of the bond formed. Thus the change in the form of the behavior shown by the imprinted animal from following during the infantile stage and sexual behavior during the mature adult stage cannot by itself be taken as evidence of a learned change in its social behavior.

Since 1935, there have been tremendous changes in the breadth and complexity of learning theory. Many of the paradigms current in 1935 have been shown to be inadequate to cover situations of learning. Reinforcement theory, in particular, has undergone considerable alteration, as have also drive concepts. We certainly cannot detail here all the changes which have taken place. We will, however, mention that the concept of *latent learning* illustrates the present willingness of learning theorists to hypothesize changes in behavior which are not consequences of conventional reinforcement or drive reduction mechanisms. This is related to another current concept, that of *perceptual learning*, which is often understood to mean the learning of associations between stimuli which are present either contiguously or simultaneously, or of stimuli qua stimuli, and without any obvious reward. In such cases, there is some kind of learning which occurs before the performance of a particular response in connection with a specific stimulus. While there is still a great deal of controversy between the so-called cognitive and S-R theorists about the nature of the learning processes in such cases, it is noteworthy that at least the roles of reinforcement mechanisms or of stimulus-response connections are no longer as integral parts of learning theory as they once had been. Furthermore, learning is not usually regarded as a homogeneous process.

Of considerable importance in the evolution of learning theory, as we have already pointed out in Chapter 2, is the increasing readiness to accept the notion of sensitive periods in the development of behavior. These sensitive periods, as we have asserted, vary a great deal in their temporal duration and in the degree of criticality of events occurring during them. Certainly, it can no longer be asserted that any type of learning can occur with equal facility at all stages of life cycle. In some instances of learning, the optimal phase for learning is sufficiently limited so that it may be termed a sensitive period. The most marked instance of a sensitive period in the determination of behavior we believe to be evident in the imprinting phenomenon. In this case, the type of sensitive period involved is the temporally very brief critical period.

HISTORY: AFTER LORENZ, TO 1954

After Lorenz's statement of the problem of the nature of early socialization processes in certain species of young birds, there was little other research, primarily because of the interruptive effects of World War II. Lorenz's presentation, of course, did not go entirely without notice. Lack (1941) discussed Lorenz's paradigm, noting that absolute limitation of the effects of early social experience to specific objects only as sexual objects during adulthood was not the case in every bird species, as shown by Portielje's (1921) South American bittern, who would mate with a female of his own species so long as he did not see his keeper, to whom he had been socially imprinted, and by the research of Craig (1914), Whitman (in Riddle and Carr, 1919), and others, who found that social responses could be made to other than the very first social object and that sexual responses might be made to more than one object. Lack did, however, agree that, while social imprinting was not actually absolutely immutable in all birds, it certainly was much less capable of alteration than an ordinary conditioned reflex. Lack also noted that the process of imprinting might possibly occur in other than social situations.

Thorpe (1944, 1951) was another writer who gave some treatment to Lorenz's theoretical position on social imprinting. While he reviewed it relatively briefly, he noted that it did not appear to "fall neatly into any of the categories of learning already discussed, although it has affinities with both habituation and latent learning." Thorpe strongly suggested the possibility that the imprinting process might play a role in habitat preferences, especially in some insect species. In his 1951 paper, Thorpe also suggested that the imprinting process might occur also in song learning in some bird species, in particular the chaffinch.

In addition to these theoretical considerations made by Lack and by Thorpe, there were several reports, mostly of informal studies of early social experiences in young birds, particularly hand-reared ones. These often were made without any specific reference to Lorenz's theoretical position. A few were the result of laboratory experimentation: these included reports of Brückner (1933; as reported in Katz, 1937), Pattie (1936), and Howells and Vine (1940). Brückner noted that partial social isolation of domestic chicks, even for only a week, producd highly aberrant behavior, as manifested by hyperactivity, phantom fly chasing, stereotypy, and nervous eccentricity. When confronted with other chicks for the first time, at 7 weeks of age, they were in a state of fear and "bewilderment"; fighting broke out and continued until some sort of dominance hierarchy had been established.

Another laboratory study of the effects of early social experience in domestic chicks was performed by Pattie (1936). He kept 42 chicks in isolation and 42 others in social groups. Beginning at the age of 4 days, each subject was tested daily for 3 minutes for social preference between an age mate and a mouse. The socially reared chicks consistently preferred to be with the chick stimulus, while the isolated chicks showed a decreasing preference for their own kind and by the 8th day of age actually preferred to be with the mouse stimulus.

However, another laboratory investigation, by Howells and Vine (1940) indicated that there was readier socialization by chicks to fellow species members or to others of the same breed than to those of other species or breeds when both had been present during rearing. Howells and Vine reared Seabright bantams and white leghorn chicks in mixed groups. When the animals were 3 weeks old, they were trained in a discrimination box with their companions as cues. All learned at a much faster rate to go to their own breed members rather than to those of the other breed. Differential size factors between the breeds, of course, may have served to enhance this discrimination. Nevertheless, the more recent investigations by Kilham, Klopfer, and Oelke (1968) and Kilham and Klopfer (1968) do show that chicks have a perceptual bias in favor of the characteristics of the breed to which they belong.

The remainder of the literature during the immediate post-Lorenz period dealt with changes in the social behavior of birds as a result of hand rearing. Cruikshank (1939), for example, noted that a young American crow, raised in his house after the age of 2 weeks, would, from then on, have nothing to do with local wild crows that lived in the vicinity. It likewise paid no attention to humans other than Cruikshank and his wife, but acquired a great liking for herring gulls, which became his secondary companions. In the same year, Lorenz (1939) reported that ravens he had hand reared would mate with their own species and also accept man as a member of the social group.

Darling (1940) gave a touching account of his experience in raising two very young goslings. He noted, as Lorenz had, that "geese have a faculty for becoming 'fixed' on a foster mother in a very complete manner. All [the people there] were kind to the goslings, but they [the goslings] took little notice of anyone but myself." When one gosling died, he noted that "this placed an even greater responsibility of companionship towards Lily on my shoulders, for I was beginning to realize that if you rear a gosling in this way you make it human and deprive it of kinship with others of its tribe. As time has passed this has become the more plain; Lily is a personal person, not a goose anymore."

Ivor (1944) noted that the age at which hand rearing was instituted had a marked effect on whether the birds were tamed or showed fear reactions to him. Räber (1948) reported on a turkey cock which courted humans; however, if a turkey hen crouching on the ground were met, he would copulate with her, thus showing the existence of two different schemas—one innate, the other acquired—which influenced his courtship and copulation behavior, since he never courted a turkey hen. Hediger (1950) wrote of an emu that attempted to mate with its caretaker during the breeding season.

Social attachments to birds of other species as a result of being reared with them were noted by Nice (1950) and by Goodwin (1948). Goodwin asserted that merely seeing members of other species could influence the direction of later adult behavior, even when no physical contact took place during the early experience.

Alley and Boyd (1950) made the observation that the ability of newly hatched coots to show social responsiveness to new objects lasted only to the age of 8 hours after hatching, since up to that time they would follow men, accept food from them, and respond to calls made by them. It appeared to Alley and Boyd that under natural conditions the formation of social bonds to the parents by the young coots occurred most readily during this period and that the process was complete by the time the young had reached the age of 48 hours. Collias (1950a, b, c) reported a series of observations on the early social behavior of chicks from the moment of hatching. He noted an initially increasing responsiveness to social stimuli, particularly as the walking ability developed in the young chicks. It also appeared to him that not only did responsiveness increase from the time of hatching but also that the need for social stimuli increased, as shown by the increasingly greater frequency of distress calls between the stimulus presentation periods. He observed differences in social behavior between normally reared chicks and ones that had been socially isolated for 11 days or more. As Brückner had reported in 1933, Collias observed that the isolated chicks behaved aggressively toward age mates when they met them. At the age of 2 months, the socially reared and isolated chicks were all turned loose together in a courtyard. It was found in observing the chicks that the ones that had been isolated early in life had a somewhat greater tendency to keep apart from the group.

Then in 1951, two specific and systematic researches on the social imprinting phenomenon in newly hatched birds—those of Ramsay (1951) and of Fabricius (1951a, b)—conducted independently in the United States and in Europe, respectively, were published.

Ramsay's study was an extension of an earlier one in which he had participated (Cushing and Ramsay, 1949). The 1949 study dealt with the development of family unity in various families of mixed species of nidifugous birds—Rhode Island red, bantam, and barred rock chickens; mallard, black, muscovy, and pekin ducks; quail; and Canada geese. Cushing and Ramsay noted that the development of family bonds in these species appeared to be established through experience acting at the time of hatching rather than primarily through genetic factors. They showed that interspecies family groups could be maintained in spite of placement in artificial situations designed in an attempt to disorganize and regroup them. Earlier, Cushing (1941) had suggested that the imprinting phenomenon was of potentially great importance in evolution, particularly with respect to mating preference, in which case it could, under certain conditions, work toward reproductive isolation of subspecies.

In his 1951 study, Ramsay investigated the various factors influencing the formation of parent-young bonds in families in which he had exchanged young. Again, it was apparent that the attachment of the young toward the foster mother, even when of a different species, was formed during the course of early social experience with the foster mother, and remained highly persistent. By means of various experiments concerned with the recognition of the rearing parent by the young, Ramsay found that auditory cues were far more predominant and more accurately used by the young animals than were those of form, color, or size.

The effects of the early social experience soon after hatching in directing social behavior in these young birds was further emphasized by a series of experiments which Ramsay performed. In the first, he presented isolation-hatched chicks and ducklings with an adult hen or female duck. While some individuals showed preference for a particular parent-object, the results of all the animals taken together indicated that there was no highly specific innate parental preference in young ducklings of either the muscovy or mallard species or in the domestic chick. In the second experiment, Ramsay hatched 6 young chicks in an incubator, with a small green box containing a ticking alarm clock also present. For the next 12 days, the chicks were brooded with this box in such a way that the young chicks could form contact with it while it hovered. At 2-day intervals during this period, Ramsay took the 6 chicks outside the brooder and confronted them with the box hung on a cable between two trees for 30 minutes and then with a hen for the same period of time. The box could be pulled by the cable, so that the tendencies of the chicks to follow it could be observed. While at the age of 1 and 2 days the chicks showed responsiveness to both the box and the hen, the attachment to the box persisted over the passage of time, while practically none was eventually shown to the hen. These results are reminiscent of those of Pattie (1936), which was discussed above.

The behavior of young of several other species was tested in a similar manner, using a football hung from the cable between the two trees as well as the green box. Canada goslings were able to accept the football or the green box-alarm clock as parent substitutes, while mallard ducklings showed a disinclination to respond to either of these objects. Chicks responded to the box-clock but not the football, and muscovy ducklings responded to the football but not to the box-clock.

Fabricius' (1951a, b) report of a two-year research study carried out in 1945 and 1946 provided evidence that reinforced many of Ramsay's observations, and also gave notice to several other aspects of the social imprinting phenomenon. For example, Fabricius found that in the tufted, the shoveler, and the mallard ducks, auditory stimuli from the parent object appeared to have considerably stronger attractive effect on the young animal than did visual ones. However, the heterogenous summation of stimuli impinging on both sensory modalities brought about the enhancement of the filial responses of the young birds. Like Lorenz, Fabricius noted that the age of the young birds in hours after hatching had a tremendous influence on their readiness to attach filial responses to a potential parental object. The first 12 hours, in fact, seemed to be the age of the strongest susceptibility to imprinting in tufted ducks, whereas after the age of 36 to 38 hours, Fabricius could not get ducklings to follow him as a potential parent object. This phenomenon was attributed to a decrease in the *internal motivation* to follow and to an increase in escape tendencies.

While Fabricius recognized that newly hatched ducklings do not have a highly specific innate conception of the parent object, he emphasized that there were considerable differences between various types of visual stimuli in their ability to evoke the filial response of following in the ducklings he studied. For example, he was unable to induce young tufted ducks to approach an immobile stuffed adult female mounted in a standing position or to follow a stuffed adult female mounted in the swimming position and drawn along the surface of water. On the other hand, young naïve ducklings were observed to immediately go to ducklings of other species which were several weeks older and to follow them in spite of harassment and violent nipping by the older ducklings. Also, Fabricius found that he could readily induce naïve ducklings to approach him so long as he stretched his hands toward them or walked away from them. If he was sitting motionless, they paid no attention to him.

From these results, Fabricius concluded that, in releasing following reactions in young ducks, shape or size, within limits, was not of great importance, while qualities of movement were—these probably being movements of limbs and other articulated parts of the body moving in relation to each other, since forward movements in a stuffed model did not appear to have any attractive value to naïve ducklings.

With respect to auditory stimuli, Fabricius found that it was not at all necessary for him to quack like the female parent, but that the repetition of monosyllabic sounds, when uttered in rapid succession, could release the following reaction. This result, and the ones with respect to visual stimuli, formed the basis for Fabricius' conclusion that young naïve birds of the species he studied were not entirely without an *innate schema* of the parent object. The releasing mechanisms for the instinctive reaction to follow a potential parent, Fabricius asserted, respond to several visual and auditory sign stimuli which work together in a cumulative way. Nevertheless, the *sign stimuli* involved are so simple that the innate releasing mechanism is very unselective. During the first reaction, however, the mechanism becomes completed with conditioned elements, which makes it more selective. "Thus the duckling in imprinting does not attain a 'releasing schema' for its reaction to follow a parent bird, but it only completes an already existing innate releasing mechanism," Fabricius concluded. The imprinting experience was thus considered to have resulted in a future greater selectivity in favor of objects of the kind that had released the first filial response. This was the basis for the so-called *irreversibility* in imprinting, since after the sensitive period had passed, the young animal's reactivity to innate sign stimuli alone was found to be very low: only those experienced during imprinting were found to elicit the response in question.

There were several other points that Fabricius reported. One was that imprinting was preferentially directed by newly hatched ducklings to parent objects rather than to siblings, since, in a choice test, the ducklings would, in a conflict between the impulse to flock with age mates and following of the parent, choose the parent, even though the tendency to join siblings of the same age was of considerable strength. Ducklings that were not imprinted on him could subsequently show tameness to him, but they never followed him as they would have had they been socially imprinted to him. Imprinted ducklings would continue following him faithfully until about 3 weeks of age. Isolation-reared ducklings past the age of 4 days would not immediately show any attention to age mate siblings when first introduced to them. In some cases in which ducklings were kept isolated in the incubator for an extremely long time, an incomplete imprinting was manifested when they were exposed to Fabricius. In these instances, the ducklings would follow but show escape reactions at Fabricius' every sudden or rapid movement.

Unlike Lorenz, Fabricius did not feel that there were essential differences between social imprinting and learning. "It is not possible to draw a sharp line between imprinting and ordinary learning," he stated.

Fabricius' research inspired Nice (1953) to informally demonstrate imprinting by offering herself as a parent companion to twelve recently hatched ducklings of different species, and found the techniques of social imprinting to be easy and simple, as Lorenz had stated in 1935.

Later, Fabricius and Boyd (1954) reported on the results of two more years of investigation on imprinting with additional duck species, including pintails, gadwalls, Carolinas, and—with particular attention—mallards. There were some differences from the previous research reported. For example, though the diving ducks of the 1951 report refused to have anything to do with a stuffed duck model, it was found in the 1954 report that simple models such as flat boxes and balloons, although devoid of articulated movements characteristic of living vertebrates, could release following. This is a finding which was later paralleled by Schaefer (1958) and Hess (1959a, c), who found that hatchling chicks would readily follow simple balls or a duck decoy but would have nothing to do with a stuffed adult chicken. Collias (1950b) also reported that newly hatched chicks did not pay any attention to a mounted hen.

A further difference from earlier research that was reported by Fabricius and Boyd (1954) was the fact that maximal following tendencies were observed at a later age for mallard ducklings than had earlier been found for tufted ducklings. With mallards, the highest proportion of followers was obtained at the age of 25 to 50 hours, with 80 percent following, while at the ages of 3 to 25 hours and 65 to 72 hours, 60 percent were observed to follow. Furthermore, exposure and testing of animals were found to be more effective when subjects were run separately rather than in small groups. This was because the ducklings, when in groups, would respond to each other as well as to the model, thus producing misleading results. The strength of the flocking reaction to age mate siblings was again noted, for it was found that even birds that had been kept in individual isolation for ten days before testing were able to show responsiveness to siblings within a few hours of exposure to them.

LABORATORY APPROACH TO IMPRINTING

In 1954 Ramsay and Hess published their paper on the laboratory study of imprinting. In this paper it was shown how the imprinting process could be studied objectively and quantified through laboratory techniques. They reported that there were age-related differences in the imprintability of chicks and ducklings, and that the age period of 13–16 hours was one of peak sensitivity to laboratory imprinting exposure in both species. This was on the basis of differential positive responses shown by the subjects upon testing at a time after the laboratory imprinting experience. They also showed that ducklings older than the age of 24 hours could be partially imprinted to an artificial parent by having well-imprinted ducklings present during the exposure to the imprinting object.

Ramsay and Hess (1954) also made comparative study of the relative effectiveness of different imprinting objects and different sounds. They reported that cochin bantam chicks showed considerably less imprinting than did the mallard ducklings.

Soon after, Jaynes (1956, 1957, 1958a, b) published a series of papers utilizing the laboratory analysis of imprinting. Subsequently, and up to the present, there have been many scientific investigations of early imprinting in chicks and ducklings. As Kessen (1968) has put it,

> A paper on imprinting by Ramsay and Hess (1954) and a series of papers by Jaynes (1956, 1957, 1958a, b) opened the way to a flood of American studies on patterns of following in precocial birds. Hess and his colleagues have published papers reporting studies on thousands of animals and a variety of species have been examined although most studies have been on domesticated mallards (Peking ducks) and on domestic chicks.

Many studies on the imprinting phenomenon have also been conducted in several European countries as well, particularly in England and Germany.

GROWTH OF RESEARCH AND DEBATE

From this time on, the social imprinting phenomenon attracted ever-widening interest, both in its own right and as a point of attention for behavioristic psychologists who sought to determine whether imprinting could be regarded as following the laws of learning rather than as a different process, in contraposition to Lorenz's conceptualization of the nature of the processes involved. In particular, the notion of its irreversibility was extensively examined. Most of these studies were laboratory investigations, and therefore somewhat divorced from the natural context of social imprinting. A wide number of bird species and a great variety of experimental procedures were used, with the result that the findings so far established have not yet been fitted into a comprehensive framework. Different species have been found to differ with respect to the manipulation of almost any particular variable. Consequently, there have been attempts to completely standardize laboratory procedures.

Completely automated imprinting apparatus, such as proposed by Kovach, Callies and Hartzell (1969), and Shapiro (1970), only partially solve the problem, because experimental animals are maintained and studied in environments which are completely unnatural, with the result that the animals are very different behaviorally from the way they are when raised in natural conditions by their own parents.

Thus, as we will come to see, we are not in any position to make detailed generalizations regarding the nature of the social imprinting process. The principal conclusions which we ourselves have been able to make, as we have stated, are that the social imprinting process is of fundamentally different nature from any other, more conventional, learning processes, and that it is a socialization process which is limited to a particular period in the young animal's life. Thus, socialization processes which occur outside this limited time are not, in our opinion, social imprinting processes. Hence, many of the researchers which we will proceed to review, although the authors believed they were dealing with social imprinting phenomena, were actually, in our view, dealing with the wider area of socialization and not with imprinting at all. Since, as we have earlier proposed, there may be several coexisting types of early socialization processes, according to the nature of the sensitive period involved—critical, susceptible, optimal, or, indeed, none at all—the picture becomes highly complex. The diversity of findings on early socialization in birds attests to this fact.

In a wide sense, then, many of the questions ostensibly asked about the imprinting process were really directed to the effects of early socialization experiences in birds. For example, the principal center of controversy has always been whether the learning of the mother and fellow species members is merely association learning and therefore extinguishable. On the one side there is the position that the appropriate responses to the mother object and species members depend on specific experiences at a particular life period for their formation, and are forever directed only to the class of objects met at that time. On the other side, the position is that social learning of this type need not be formed during such specific life periods, and may at a later time be superseded, so that social responses may be directed to other objects as well. While theoretical views often have tended to be placed on one or the other of these two sides, the actual situation is not that simple.

This is because there *is,* in our view, a social imprinting process which depends upon experiences at a specific life period—a critical period— for the determination of which objects are to be recipients of a certain class of social responses. *In addition,* there are other socialization processes which certainly are extinguishable or reversible, in the conventional sense of the term, and which obviously are not confined to any *critical* period, but perhaps to other sensitive periods, or to no sensitive period at all. This is apparent on the basis of simple everyday observation of the social behavior of animals. It can be easily seen that animals that have been normally reared in infancy by their own species members do not behave in the same way toward humans or members of other species as they do toward each other. If an animal is tamed by means of a conditioning process after it has been reared by its parents, it is possible to elicit some types of social responses to humans or other non-species members, as desired. Obviously, taming can result in the reduction of the fear responses of an adult animal, even to the extent that it follows or approaches, or even mates with, an extra-species object, particularly when fellow species members are unavailable. Such behavioral changes could be classified as imprinting by undiscriminating observers, and be considered as evidence that imprinting is extinguishable. In contrast, however, we feel that this does not constitute such evidence, but, in actuality, shows that some phases of socialization can be extended to new classes of objects at later periods in life. It does not show that social imprinting is reversible.

Undeniably, much of the confusion between social imprinting and the larger area of socialization has been caused by the prior assumption of some experimenters that social imprinting is a form of classical association learning. This assumption has led them to design their experiments on socialization in birds on the association learning model: several "practice trials" are given past the critical age period, food is placed under the imprinting model, and so on. Such procedures are contrary to the very concept of social imprinting as a process which occurs during a single brief exposure to an object and which is independent of ordinary biological drives that operate in the course of most association learning situations. If various socialization processes are superimposed in addition to social imprinting, then it becomes manifestly difficult to assess the effects of social imprinting itself.

Still another difficulty arises when the normal imprinting process has been interfered with. There appears, in many bird species, to be an innate disposition to learn in a certain direction, as shown by variations in responsiveness to various types of objects or stimuli which may be offered as parental objects (e.g., Howells and Vine, 1940; Hess and Hess, 1969; Kilham and Klopfer, 1968). There appears, in other words, to be limitations or certain bounds, within which objects may vary and still be acceptable as parent objects, even though there is very little specificity in the class of objects which initially have the potential capacity to elicit social responsiveness in the young birds. Mallard ducklings, for example, may not respond to certain objects when young of other species do, as shown by Ramsay (1951) and others. This leads to the possibility that if the proffered social object is less than optimal, true imprinting may not occur. If imprinting to the "correct" object is prevented, the whole social behavior pattern may be disrupted, with the result that one sector of the total behavior process becomes attached to one imperfect object, another to another, and the various social and mating behaviors may become attached to almost any object except the correct one. This was implied by Lorenz in his 1935 paper when he spoke of the various types of "companions" in the social life of the bird. Many cases of abnormal sexual fixations in birds have in fact shown that this is the case.

The various aspects of early socialization in birds that have been examined are virtually legion. Because of the wide variation due to species differences and differences in methods of social exposure and testing, it is not possible to make any precise generalizations regarding the nature of early socialization of birds. Analysis of the findings in the literature is also rendered difficult by the fact that researchers and writers have differing concepts regarding the significance of the early social experiences to which young birds may be exposed. For example, the term "imprinting" itself was, in Lorenz's original conceptualization, a referent to a *type* of socialization process. However, because of the prominence of following behavior in response to the parent in nidifugous (precocial) birds, more and more writers came to focus their attention primarily upon following behavior, assuming that all cases of following behavior were subsumed by imprinting or socialization concepts. Or, alternately, "imprinting" came to designate, in many reports, an experimental *procedure,* one of "visually presenting to an animal a large moving object during the first several hours of its life under conditions that insure that the object is not associated with such conventional reinforcing agents as food and water" (Moltz, 1960). Imprinting has also been thought of as early socialization in general. Sluckin (1964) has stated that "the term, in its empirical sense, refers to the formation by young precocial birds of relatively specific attachments"—a definition which leaves to the discretion of the reader to decide what are, and what are not, "relatively specific attachments." Furthermore, such a definition does not differentiate between social imprinting and socialization in general.

Therefore, we will first review studies in which following behavior is the principal focus of interest as an indicator of social behavior, after which we will review those in which the exposure did not involve any manifest following behavior and in which subsequent social behavior was not measured by means of following behavior. Such a division, of course, cannot always be absolute, since not every study can handily fall into one or the other category.

Because of the theoretical biases we have, we will deal with the findings of our own research on imprinting and early socialization in birds in the next chapter, and for the present confine our attention primarily to the investigations of others on early socialization. In Chapter 7, we will conclude our considerations of the theoretical aspects of the imprinting phenomenon.

THE FOLLOWING RESPONSE: ONTOGENY, ELICITATION, PREVENTION, AND EFFECTS

Following behavior, as performed by nidifugous birds, has been taken by many investigators to indicate that imprinting has taken or is taking, place. This, in actuality, may or may not be the case, depending on the conditions under which following takes place. For example, it is well known that newly hatched precocial birds do follow the parent object consistently. However, as the individuals get older, such following of the parent is no longer essential for survival, since with age, an increasing number of factors promote the ability of the individual to be independent of the mother. Thus the amount of following eventually will decrease to a nearly zero level. However, this does not necessarily mean that the individual that no longer follows has lost social responsiveness to the species to which the parent belongs, even though some investigators have assumed that decreased following implies that imprinting is not irreversible or inextinguishable. This certainly is not necessarily so. Furthermore, even retention of following behavior does not necessarily imply that social imprinting has taken place.

The act of following is by no means a simple behavior. As Fabricius (1962a, b) has pointed out, there are many gradations of following behavior, "from close following without any signs of fear, through hesitant following mixed with fear responses, to strong escape behaviour in which only slight indications of following can be observed. Moreover, following can also alternate with aggressive behaviour, and the actual behaviour of the young bird is largely determined by the balance between these competing tendencies." Fabricius was of the opinion that escape tendencies may possibly be present in young precocial birds from the very outset and that these persist through the entire life span, particularly since in many instances he observed that naïve ducklings, upon their first encounter with a moving model, show ambivalent behavior—that is, an unexpected movement elicited escape movements, followed by approach, in turn followed by alternation between the two behaviors, until following behavior was predominant.

There are strong differences in the factors influencing following behavior in different bird species. Even within the same species, domestication apparently influences the manner in which following behavior is affected by different factors.

Now we shall review studies of following behavior—which may sometimes involve social imprinting—according to the species of experimental subjects. In all species, it appears that the first following response of naïve young birds is brought about by an innate releasing mechanism which reacts to certain sign stimuli, which are so few and simple that it appears almost as if naïve young nidifugous birds tend to follow the very first moving object they encounter. Nevertheless, there are specific limits in the nature of the objects followed. Although there are investigators (such as Moltz, 1960, 1963) who are disinclined toward the notion of the releaser function of stimuli in the elicitation of following behavior, there is ample evidence in many research reports that different types of stimuli have varying effectiveness in promoting the occurrence of following behavior. This fact in itself indicates that there is a releaser function of stimuli eliciting following behavior, as the following discussion will show.

Surface-Nesting Wild and Domestic Ducks

Eliciting Stimuli.   Stimuli releasing following behavior are usually visual and acoustic. There are inter- and intra-modality differences in the effectiveness of stimuli. Among visual stimuli, moving ones are normally much more effective than stationary ones for eliciting approach (e.g., Klopfer, 1971). Furthermore, Fabricius (1951a, b), as we have earlier mentioned, concluded that complex articulated movements of living creatures were more effective than were simple gliding motions of stuffed models. However, when decoys or other non-living models have been used, simple motion has been found effective in eliciting following in ducklings by several investigators. Nevertheless, such models are often relatively less effective when silent than when they are vocal.

For example, Collias and Collias (1956) found that hatchling redhead ducklings would begin to follow a vocalizing model much sooner than they did when it was silent, and, furthermore, followed it farther and more regularly. Boyd and Fabricius (1965) observed that the facilitating effect of adequate sound stimulation is such that, even after it is removed, naïve mallard ducklings will continue to follow the associated visual stimulus—the model.

Most investigators have concluded that rapid, rhythmic, short sounds are highly effective in eliciting following behavior. It is not necessary that the female parent's call be closely imitated. Collias and Collias (1956), while not studying following behavior specifically, assessed the relative attractive value of various auditory stimuli for canvasback, redhead, and mallard ducklings during their 1st day after hatching by placing them individually in a 3-foot runway and presenting the sound at the end of the runway opposite to the duckling so that no visual concomitant was present. Both canvasback and redhead ducklings were found to move toward parental attraction notes and to move away from alarm notes. Mallard ducklings, on the day of hatching, were found to go much more readily under these conditions to brief low-pitched notes than to high-pitched or long notes. This is congruent with a later observation of theirs that redhead and canvasback ducklings, 15 to 30 hours old, moved more readily toward contentment notes than toward distress calls of other ducklings. These ducklings also went more readily to high (3/sec) rates of contentment notes than toward lower rates.

Weidmann (1955, 1956) made similar findings, observing that long notes, even if repeated, do not ordinarily have any releasing effect on following behavior. However, most rhythmic, repetitive signals are attractive to several of the surface-nesting duck species, according to Klopfer (1959a), who found that there were no *exclusive* preferences, in terms of following behavior, among different sound signals used. These sounds included recorded calls of female mallards, geese, human renditions of "pip-pip," "hel–lo," and "kom, kom, kom," although there was certainly a stronger attraction for some of the sounds than for others. The newly hatched isolation-reared young included many species: Canada and emperor goose, pintail, mallard, gadwall, redhead, blue-winged teal, and chloe widgeon ducks. Half or more of the subjects gave a positive response to "pip-pip," "kom-kom," and emperor goose sounds.

When models are moving and auditory, variations in size, shape, and color apparently are well tolerated, as there is an extremely wide range which is effective in eliciting following behavior at an early age: boxes or balls of different colors (the most popular among investigators being green or blue), duck decoys, dolls, and others have been used with success. Klopfer and Hailman (1964a) have reported that a highly variegated duck decoy which had been painted with blotches of different colors elicited the same proportion of followers among 12 to 20-hour-old pekin hatchlings as did a plain white one. There was also no significant difference in the amount of following of the two models among those that did follow.

James (1959) has found that while different strains of domestic chicks will approach a flickering light, wild mallard and blue-winged teal ducklings could not be induced to do so. However, in one of the few published flicker experiments using wild mallards as subjects, Bateson and Reese (1968) reported that nearly all of their day-old wild mallard hatchlings learned to go on a pedal in order to light up a 45-watt bulb that flickered at the rate of 85/min, or at the rate of 2.83/sec, not very different from the .25/.25 on/off rate used by James.

Klopfer (1962), on the other hand, has reported differences, even within the same species, with respect to the role of auditory and visual stimulation. Pekin ducks are regarded as a highly domesticated form of the wild mallard *Anas platyrhynchos,* and are certainly different in appearance even from domesticated mallards. They are sometimes called *Anas platyrhynchos domesticus.* It is not known when they were differentiated from the wild progenitor. What Klopfer observed was that when a repetitive sound signal was emitted by a previously silent moving duck decoy, the proportion of subjects that followed the model was increased much more among wild mallard ducklings than among pekins. Apparently, the pekins responded at a level maximum for them in the absence of sound stimulation, whereas the mallards required simultaneous visual and auditory stimulation to evoke maximal following. In other words, the wild mallards were more selective regarding what they would respond to in the exposure situation than the pekins were.

Consonant with Klopfer's findings, Gottlieb (1961b) exposed wild mallards, domesticated mallards, and pekins to a silent moving male duck decoy, and found that 33 of the 65 pekins followed the model during the 20-minute exposure session, while only 20 of the 65 wild mallards and 11 of the 65 domestic mallards followed. However, the wild mallards which did follow spent more time in following the model than did the pekins that followed, particularly at the age of 3 to 12 hours, where the difference was statistically significant. The domestic mallards showed a lower persistence of following at both ages than did the other two groups. In another experiment, Gottlieb added the sound of a metronome ticking at a rate of 3/sec to the models and found no change in the results obtained. However, it may be that this type of acoustic stimulus is ineffective, since Gottlieb did not obtain as high a level of following in his mallard ducklings as other investigators have obtained with the same species. Nevertheless, it is still rather clear that there are species differences between ducks. Moltz and Rosenblum (1958) have claimed another point of difference between duck species in following behavior: they state that in pekins, following behavior decreases rapidly after having been established, whereas in mallards and muscovies, following remains at a high level.

Gottlieb (1965a) has found that there is an innate preference for the conspecific call in the elicitation of following behavior in pekin ducks. Of his pekin ducks, 85 percent followed a rendition of mallard female calls; 63 percent followed the wood duck female call; 40 percent followed the chicken calls; and only 4 percent were observed to "follow" silence. In another report published the same year, Gottlieb (1965b) pointed out that mallard ducklings are more likely to follow a sound if it is connected with a visual object.

Age Parameters in First Elicitation. Differences in following responsiveness to stimuli according to the age of the animal has been studied by several investigators. This aspect of following behavior has attracted a great deal of attention on the part of investigators, since some of the experimental data have suggested the notion of developmentally timed periods of "sensitivity" with respect to the elicitation of following behavior.

In the first place, there appears to be a decreasing readiness to follow in naïve ducklings as they become increasingly older. There have been reports of the elicitation of following in naïve young ducks as late as the age of 10 days after hatching (Fabricius and Boyd, 1954; Boyd and Fabricius, 1965; Asdourian, 1967; Smith and Nott, 1970), although it certainly seems possible that older individuals could occasionally be found to follow for the first time at even later ages. However, most of the studies on the relationship between age and elicitation of following behavior have utilized ages up to 80 hours, or less than 4 days. Weidmann (1956) reported that mallard ducklings past the age of 40 hours would not react when called, even when they showed no signs of fear. In 1958, Weidmann reasserted this finding, observing that ducklings isolated socially for more than 50 hours would remain passive or flee when approached by other ducklings as social objects for the first time.

Fabricius (1955) exposed incubator-hatched mallards with either a box or a balloon at different ages. While there was no sharply limited age period for the elicitation of following behavior, he found that the highest proportion of followers was in the age group of 25 to 50 hours after hatching. This was congruent with the finding of Fabricius and Boyd (1954), earlier mentioned, that there seemed to be a comparatively low readiness to follow in their mallard ducklings during the first few hours after hatching, then an increasing readiness to a maximum level, after which the ease with which following behavior could be elicited gradually fell off, finally approaching zero. The initial increase in readiness to follow after hatching has also been found in wild mallard ducklings by Gottlieb (1961b). Fabricius (1964) reported that 58 percent of naïve mallard ducklings could be induced to follow a moving silent model at the age range of 10 to 20 hours after hatching. No significant decrease in the proportion of followers of the same age period was found until a post-hatch age of 40 to 50 hours.

Fabricius pointed out the adaptive value in maintaining potential responsiveness to moving objects up to the age of 50 hours in ducklings, since there are several species which do not perform the exodus from the nest until the young are 24 to 36 hours old. This notion was felt to be further supported by the finding that when acoustic stimuli alone (i.e., motionless vocal model) were used, there was a rapid increase in the ease with which following behavior could be elicited by "kom–kom" calls after the post-hatch age of 10 to 20 hours, with a maximal level of following responsiveness evident at the age of 25 to 50 hours, after which it became progressively more difficult at later ages, to induce following responses with such acoustic stimuli, although even at the age of 240 hours—that is, 10 days—it remained easier to elicit following with acoustic stimuli from a motionless model than with a visual stimulus alone. Fabricius suggested that in natural conditions the value of acoustic sensitivity over such a long period might lie in enabling the young to follow the mother by means of her calls, even when it is difficult to see her because of having to travel through relatively dense vegetation.

Subsequently, Boyd and Fabricius (1965) published a detailed account of the proportion of naïve isolated wild mallard ducklings that could be induced to follow for the first time at different ages. Up to the age of 35 hours, more than half of the ducklings followed a silent model (58.5 percent of those 10 to 20 hours old, 51.2 percent of those 20 to 25 hours old, and 56.0 percent of those 25 to 35 hours old). In the age range 40 to 50 hours, exactly half of the ducklings followed the model; in the age range 65 to 80 hours, 23.3 percent did. Those that were exposed to the silent model for the first time at the age of 240 hours showed a rather low following response disposition, as only 14.3 percent followed when presented with the model.

Again, the higher responsiveness to auditory stimuli, as reflected in the higher proportion of wild mallard subjects following, was demonstrated by Boyd and Fabricius. During the first 15 hours after hatching, 50 percent of the subjects followed a rapidly repeated monosyllabic "kom," 63 percent of those in the 15 to 25-hour age group did so; while increasing responsiveness was reflected by the fact that 80 percent of the 25- to 35-hour-old subjects followed, 85 percent of the 40- to 50-hour-old naïve ducklings did so. After this age, auditory responsiveness in the form of following decreased to 71 percent at the age of 65 to 80 hours and 45 percent at the ages of 90 to 100 hours. However, fully 50 percent of the mallard subjects were found to follow the acoustic stimulus when it was first heard at the age of 240 hours.

Gottlieb (1961a) has studied the relationship between post-hatch age, developmental age, and the incidence of following behavior to a model by naïve pekin ducklings. Of 35 naïve pekin ducklings 3 to 17 hours old, 57 percent followed a silent duck decoy, while 80 percent of 25 hatchling pekins 18 to 27 hours old followed. Gottlieb compared this increase in following responsiveness according to post-hatch age with the incidence of following behavior in naïve ducklings according to developmental age. He had chilled the eggs of *all* subjects at 37 to 42°F for at least 48 hours (but sometimes as long as 2 weeks) in an attempt to equalize the developmental status of the duckling eggs. Nevertheless, hatching was still asynchronous; furthermore, according to a later report by Hailman and Klopfer (1962), such cold shock kills *chick* embryos at 24 hours of incubation, but has no effect on *duck* embryos of the same age. However, according to these authors, such treatment is lethal to duck embryos previously incubated for at least 32 hours. Nevertheless, it is highly apparent the cold treatment cannot reduce the developmental variability in duck eggs by any more than 24 hours.

Gottlieb (1963e) subsequently reported that a colder temperature, 29±1°F, for 3 days, is more effective in equalizing developmental status of a given hatch of ducks. In his original paper, Gottlieb (1961a) showed that it was possible to determine a specific 12-hour period, developmentally speaking, in which peking ducks showed greater tendency to follow the decoy than at other developmental ages. Of 22 naïve animals that were exposed to the silent model in the age period 26½ to 27 days from the beginning of incubation, 32 percent followed it, while 79 percent of those 24 subjects so treated during the developmental age period from 27 to 27½ days from the beginning of incubation, followed. The maximum following responsiveness was found in those presented with the silent decoy between 27½ to 28 days after commencement of incubation, for all 10 of these subjects followed. After this developmental age period, however, a sharp decline in following responsiveness was observed, for at the developmental age period 28 to 28½ days, only 44 percent of the 9 subjects followed. While Gottlieb claimed that his data showed that developmental age is a more sensitive indicator of following susceptibility than post-hatch age, several considerations prevent our agreeing with him. One is, of course, the fact that his chilling treatment, as shown later by Hailman and Klopfer (1962), did not necessarily synchronize the developmental stages of his experimental subjects very much. Another is the fact that he based his assertion upon a graphic presentation of the data that was disadvantageous to post-hatch age. It was a disadvantageous presentation because the proportion of followers for post-hatch age was depicted according to 4-hour post-hatch age intervals, while the proportions for developmental age intervals were calculated for 12-hour age intervals.

Other observations of Gottlieb (1961b) on the elicitation of following according to post-hatch age in pekin, wild mallard, and domestic mallard ducklings differed from those of Boyd and Fabricius (1965) with wild mallards, possibly because *silent* decoys were used. First, Gottlieb found that 40 percent of naïve pekin ducklings 3 to 12 hours old followed, while 57.5 percent of those 13 to 27 hours old did so. Of the naïve wild mallard ducklings, 40 percent followed at the younger age range, and 25 percent in the older age range followed. Among the domestic mallard subjects, 16 percent of the 3- to 12-hour-old hatchlings followed, while 14.5 percent of the 13- to 27-hour-old ones did. The poorer response of the wild and domestic mallards is congruent with Klopfer's (1962) observation that while mallards require auditory *and* visual stimulation to follow at their maximal level, pekins do not.

Data on the proportion of naïve pekin ducklings induced to follow a *vocal* decoy at different post-hatch and developmental ages were reported by Klopfer and Gottlieb (1962a). These data, because of their similarity to those obtained with silent decoys, further confirm the notion that pekins follow maximally to both visual only and visual plus auditory stimuli. Of 10 naïve pekin ducklings 10- to 13-hours-old, 50 percent followed the vocal decoy, and 67 percent of 30 ducklings 14- to 20-hours old followed it. With respect to developmental age, 57.1 percent of the 7 subjects in the first half of day 27 followed, 83.3 percent of the 18 ducklings in the latter half of day 27 did so, while 35.7 percent of 14 subjects in the first half of day 28 followed.

Several studies (Gottlieb and Klopfer, 1961, 1962; Klopfer and Gottlieb, 1962a, b; Gottlieb, 1963d) on differences in auditory responsiveness and visual responsiveness in the following behavior of naïve pekin ducklings have been executed. In any group of hatchling ducklings, these investigators observed that some individuals exhibit higher following response tendencies to visual than to auditory aspects of stimulation, and vice versa. They called this phenomenon "behavioral polymorphism," and subjected it to an analysis according to post-hatch and developmental age variables. Such "behavioral polymorphism," they suggested, might be highly adaptive in ensuring the elicitation of the following response to the mother in natural conditions, particularly since Collias and Collias (1956) and Klopfer (1959a) have shown that ducklings are susceptible to a "social facilitation effect" in the evocation of following behavior. Within certain age limits, if no more than three naïve ducklings are placed together with one age mate duckling that has already shown a high following tendency, the naïve ducklings will follow with about the same intensity as the "leader" (Klopfer, 1959a). Thus it appeared to Klopfer and Gottlieb that if different ducklings in the same clutch have different response tendencies, the social facilitation effect would promote the development of similar following behavior in the entire group, even when the individual members differ in developmental age.

However, the deduction of differences in auditory versus visual responsiveness as a function of developmental age was originally not made on the basis of following behavior *during the* initial exposure of naïve pekin duck hatchlings to stimuli but on the basis of their differential responses to auditory or visual components of the previously vocal decoy on a later test, generally given 10 to 14 hours later. Thus the postulation by these authors of differential auditory and visual responsiveness rested on the assumption that whatever aspect, auditory or visual, of the decoy principally responsible for the elicitation of following behavior on the part of the naïve pekin duckling would be evidenced by a greater amount of time spent in following that same specific aspect than toward the other aspect, presented successively, on the later test.

This assumption of a differential effect on the specific aspects of the initial following experience on later following behavior toward these aspects must be kept in mind in assessing Klopfer and Gottlieb's experimental data: it was not until Gottlieb's (1963d) last report of this present series that differential following responsiveness to auditory and visual stimulation as a function of post-hatch and developmental age in pekin ducklings was determined during the *initial* exposure itself, rather than on the basis of performance on later testing.

Thus, Klopfer and Gottlieb (1962a) found that auditory responsiveness appeared to be predominant in those pekins that had been exposed initially to the model during the first half of day 27 of development, while those exposed to the decoy during the second half of day 27 showed both visual and auditory response tendencies. This appeared to be correlated with the previous findings of higher response tendencies in terms of a higher number of followers among pekin ducklings exposed to a decoy during the second half of day 27 of development in comparison with the first half of day 27.

In another report, Gottlieb and Klopfer (1962) found a similar pattern of results with another group of naïve pekin ducklings. In this study, 40 percent of the hatchlings exposed to the vocal model during the last half of day 26 of development from the onset of incubation later showed greater following of auditory stimulation than of visual stimulation, while 20 percent in this developmental age exposure group later followed the visual stimulation more, and the remaining 40 percent made no response or showed equal following tendencies to both. Those that had been exposed to the vocal decoy during the first half of day 27 showed an even higher auditory following in the later test: 46.6 percent later showed greater auditory following than visual following, while 33.3 percent had greater visual following than auditory following on the later test, with 20 percent having either no response or equal following tendencies. After this developmental age period, however, a drastic change in the proportion of auditory and visual responders in the later test occurred as a function of the initial exposure: those that had been put with the vocal decoy at the latter half of day 27 produced

20 percent auditory responders, 46.6 percent visual responders, and 33.3 percent non-responders or equal responders: while, of those that had had this experience at the first half of day 28 of development, 26.6 percent later proved to be auditory responders, and 46.6 percent to be visual responders, with 26.6 percent showing either equal or no following of the visual and auditory components on the later test. All these results were obtained with animals that had been kept in individual isolation up to the time of the later test.

When the data were cast in terms of post-hatch age, there were no significant differences in auditory or visual responsiveness on the test as a function of post-hatch age, calculated in 3-hour intervals, at the initial exposure of these naïve pekins. However, when post-hatch age is cast in 11-hour intervals, more like the 12-hour developmental age intervals which these authors depicted, a similar trend may be seen in auditory and visual responsiveness on the later test session. The 6- to 17-hour age period exposure produced 42.1 percent auditory responders among the 19 subjects and 36.8 percent visual responders; while the 18- to 29-hour age period exposure produced 25.9 percent auditory responders and 33.3 percent visual responders. Unfortunately, animals older than 31 hours post-hatch were not tested; however, of the 14 subjects exposed at the age of 30 to 31 hours, 35.7 percent later showed auditory responsiveness, while 42.8 percent showed visual responsiveness, thus apparently supporting Gottlieb and Klopfer's suggestion that at the later post-hatch ages, visual components become somewhat more effective in eliciting following than auditory components do.

However, these results were from later testing, and may not truly reflect the actual relative auditory and visual sensitivities of ducklings at different post-hatch and developmental ages. This is shown in a later paper by Gottlieb (1963d), in which he studied the proportion of naïve pekin ducks that would follow a silent or a vocal decoy at different post-hatch and developmental ages and the amount of time they would spend in following the silent or the vocal decoy. At all ages, the vocal model induced a greater proportion of followers than did the silent model, and elicited a greater amount of following as well. Naïve pekins at less than day 27½ of development followed the silent model very little: 7.1 percent of 28 subjects followed it, while 38.7 percent followed the vocal model at this developmental age. Of those exposed during the second half of day 27 of development, 19.2 percent of the 26 exposed to the silent decoy followed it, and 44.8 percent of the 29 exposed to the vocal decoy followed. Responsiveness to the decoys was even higher among the naïve pekins presented with the models during the first half of day 28 of development: 42.2 percent of 26 subjects followed the silent model, while 70.0 percent of 30 subjects followed the vocal model.

When the data were recast according to post-hatch age, a fairly uniform responsiveness to the vocal decoys was found, and an initial rise and then a decrease in responsiveness to the silent decoys. At the post-hatch age of 8 to 21 hours, 17.7 percent of 34 pekin ducklings followed the silent model, while at the age of 22 to 33 hours, 31.2 percent of 32 subjects followed it, and at the age of 34 to 40 hours, 22.2 percent of 9 subjects followed. The corresponding percentages for the vocal model were 48.5 percent of 49 subjects, 54.3 percent of 35 subjects, and 50.0 percent of 6 subjects.

If these data which we have just cited are compared with those of Gottlieb and Klopfer (1962), it readily becomes apparent that they are not equivalent. First, visual responsiveness on the part of the ducks during the initial following experience in most of the developmental age categories is lower than the visual responsiveness on the later test as reported by Gottlieb and Klopfer (1962). Second, auditory response tendencies were much higher in the ducks during the first following experience during the developmental ages 27½ to 28 days and 28 to 28½ in Gottlieb's report than they were in the ducks that had been exposed during these very same developmental ages when they were tested for following behavior at the later session. It is therefore very apparent that there are changes in the relative responsiveness of pekin ducklings to visual and auditory stimulation with age. The responsiveness to stimulation which is present at one age cannot necessarily be determined by tests administered at another age.

Nevertheless, the main conclusion made by Gottlieb and Klopfer (1962)—that auditory responsiveness appears predominant before the developmental age of 27½ days from incubation—still holds. However, the initial postulation—that visual responsiveness equals or surpasses auditory responsiveness in chicks past that age—obviously does not. The observed increased visual responsiveness observed by Gottlieb and Klopfer (1962) therefore must be a function of the *later test age* which these authors utilized.

Comparison of the strength of following during the exposure to the models in terms of time in seconds spent in following as a function of developmental and post-hatch ages, according to Gottlieb (1963d), offered further interesting facts. When the pekins were placed with the silent decoy at less than day 27½ of development, the average following score was 41.8 seconds, but at later developmental ages, the average following scores were 67.2 seconds. On the other hand, pekins between 8 and 17 hours post-hatch had a mean following score of only 6 seconds, while those between 18 and 40 hours of age produced a mean following score of 84.9 seconds for the silent model. Much higher following scores, of course, were produced when the model was vocal: 252.8

seconds was the mean score of those exposed to this model when the subjects were at less than 27½ days of development, and 300.4 seconds was the score for those past day 27½ of development. The 8 to 17-hour-old (post-hatch) pekins had a following score of 102.4 seconds, and those 18 to 40 hours old had a mean following score of 346.4 seconds, to the vocal model.

These above results, however, were all obtained with pekin ducks, which respond at a maximum level to both silent and vocal moving decoys (Gottlieb, 1961b, Klopfer, 1962). A study by Klopfer and Gottlieb (1962b) which studied *wild mallard* ducklings did not find any predominance of auditory or visual following responsiveness as a function of initial exposure to the model at any developmental or post-hatch age. The auditory and visual responders on the later test were fairly evenly distributed among each of the developmental and post-hatch exposure ages.

The functional significance of the early sensitive period for the elicitation of following behavior has perhaps been suggested by Bjarväll (1967), who observed that the usual age of ducklings at the time of the nest exodus is past 16 hours. Thus, it would seem that, under normal conditions, all ducklings have already been imprinted before the exodus occurs. This imprinting may possibly occur by means of the small movements of the ducklings while they are with the mother during the several hours before the exodus.

Effects of Pre-Exposure Factors on Following. We have discussed several factors in connection with the elicitation of following behavior upon first exposure to a potential parent object. It has been found, in addition to the stimulus and age factors we have just now discussed, that there are several pre-exposure experiences which can influence the likelihood and intensity of following behavior during the initial exposure of hatchling ducklings to parental surrogates.

For example, Gottlieb and Klopfer (1962) reported that rearing pekin ducklings communally in groups of three altered the pattern of visual and auditory responsiveness in testing after initial exposure as a function of developmental or post-hatch age. The communally reared ducklings did not show the predominance of auditory responsiveness in the test session as a function of early initial exposure to the vocal model during the developmental ages of day 26½ to day 27½. However, the pattern of auditory and visual responsiveness as a function of exposure during the latter half of day 27 and the first half of day 28 was the same as it was for the individually isolated subjects. Similarly, auditory responsiveness as a function of post-hatch age of exposure to the vocal model was reduced in communally reared pekins that had been placed with the model at the age of 6 to 17 hours, since only 11.1 percent responded, in comparison with the 42.1 percent in the isolated group. Visual responsiveness was also reduced: 22.2 percent showed following responsiveness, while 36.8 percent of the isolated group did. However, there was no apparent influence of the communal rearing experience in those exposed during the age of 18 to 29 hours, and the proportion of auditory responders, visual responders, and non-responders in the later test session was essentially the same in the isolated and communally reared groups. As for those first exposed to the vocal decoy at the age of 30 to 31 hours (post-hatch), too few subjects were treated to make comparisons valid; but of 8 subjects, half failed to respond on testing, and the responders were equally divided among auditory and visual components. Smith and Nott (1970) have confirmed that social rearing before testing reduces mallard ducklings' responsiveness to a stationary but rotating auditory-visual stimulus, although this difference was not apparent on the first day of testing.

Moltz (1961) and Moltz and Stettner (1961) carried out an experiment with pekin ducklings, and found that the intensity of following upon exposure to an apparently silent green cardboard box as a function of age was influenced by the nature of the prior sensory experience received by the subjects. In this study, experimental subjects wore a latex hood which permitted them to see only diffuse light from the time of hatching, while the control subjects' hoods allowed them to see fully patterned light. Full patterned vision was permitted to all subjects upon exposure to the silent moving box. Those that had had diffuse light experience followed more than the corresponding controls at all ages, 12 hours, 48 hours, and 72 hours. The difference was very slight at the age of 72 hours, however.

The approximate following scores, in seconds, for the subjects at different ages were: 12 hours: diffuse, 610 seconds; patterned, 375 seconds; 24 hours: diffuse, 870 seconds; patterned, 330 seconds; 48 hours: diffuse, 670 seconds; patterned, 40 seconds; 72 hours: diffuse, 75 seconds; patterned, 50 seconds. Thus, the peak of following activity for the diffuse light-exposed subjects was at the age of 24 hours, while for the control subjects it was at the age of 12 hours. At the same time, while the control patterned light-exposed subjects showed a tremendous increase in avoidance of the model during the first five minutes of exposure as a function of increasing age during the exposure, after the age of 12 hours, the experimental diffuse light-exposed subjects showed only a slow rise in such avoidance behavior, a factor which suggested to the authors that the depression of fearfulness in the experimental subjects in comparison with the controls might be responsible for the greater elicitation of following behavior in the experimental subjects at the ages of 24 and 48 hours.

However, it does not appear that this adequately accounts for the whole of the decrease of following responsiveness in the animals 72 hours old, since the amount of fear shown by the experimental diffuse light-exposed subjects was less than that shown by patterned light-exposed control subjects at the age of 24 hours; yet the amount of following shown by the 72-hour old experimental subjects was less than that shown by the 24-hour old patterned light-exposed control subjects. Asdourian (1967), on the other hand, has suggested that prolonged darkness and isolation permit even 2-week old pekin ducks to follow or develop an attachment to a moving object.

An additional factor that may be of possible significance in evaluating Moltz and Stettner's data is that the experimental subjects were regularly handled in an attempt to encourage them to eat, while the control subjects apparently did not receive this extra stimulation. This handling could possibly activate a higher degree of following in the experimental subjects. This potential influence deserves investigation, particularly in different species, for there are, as we know, species-specific differences in the effects of the nature of sensory stimulation, of whatever modality, upon the elicitation of following in young birds. Certainly, it would appear that factors other than, or in addition to, increasing fearfulness or visual stimulation do play a role in the observed decline in the persistence of following as a function of increasing age in Moltz and Stettner's pekin ducklings.

In another paper, Moltz (1963) described an unpublished study in which he participated with one of his students, Mindel, on the effects of different types of retinal stimulation on the following behavior of pekin ducklings. At the age of 10 to 16 hours, the subjects were placed in stocks which restrained them and prevented locomotory movements. For 25 minutes the ducklings were subjected to one of the following visual stimulation conditions (no auditory stimulation being involved): seeing a green cardboard box move away; seeing it approach; seeing it alternately move away and approach; or seeing it stationary. Twenty-four hours later, this 25-minute period of exposure was repeated. Then the animals were removed from their restraining stocks and allowed to follow the moving green box. The median following scores of the four groups revealed that those that had seen the box move away continuously followed it the most, while those that had never before seen it move followed the least. The other two groups were essentially the same, and were intermediate in following performance.

Apparently, then, the experience of seeing the green box move away more effectively provided the stimulation which promoted the likelihood of later following behavior, whereas seeing the green box approach did not provide such stimulation to the same degree. The approaching green box, however, did promote more following on the test that did the stationary green box. So, as in many other studies, it appears in this one that the characteristic of motion in the object presented to the naïve hatchling is extremely important in promoting following behavior.

While Klopfer (1959a) found that pre-exposure to sound signals of different types apparently had no effect on the subsequent preference of individually isolated hatchling ducks of different surface-nesting duck species for following specific sounds, Weidmann (1955) raised the question of whether the call of ducklings, often heard prior to exposure to a parental surrogate, even when ducklings are socially isolated immediately upon hatching, might have any effects in promoting the preference of ducklings for following certain types of sounds. Weidmann noted this because both the sounds made by ducklings after hatching and the sounds most effective in eliciting following behavior consist of short, repeated notes.

To examine this question, Gottlieb (1963b, 1966) studied the contributory effect of auditory stimulation of pekin ducklings during the post-hatch period before placement at 10 to 21 hours of age or day 27 to 28½ of development with a vocalizing stuffed pekin duck which emitted pekin duckling calls or pekin maternal calls. These ducklings, although socially isolated, could hear the calls of neighboring age mates. Of 57 such experimentally naïve pekins presented with the stuffed pekin hen emitting a pekin duckling call, 33 percent followed, with a mean following score of 274.6 seconds; and of 60 similar pekin hatchlings presented with the same stuffed model emitting the pekin maternal call, 85 percent responded by following, with a mean following score of 589.6 seconds.

In another experiment, Gottlieb (1966) isolated the ducklings as before, but half of them were given additional auditory stimulation in the form of 4 to 12 hours of a loud recording of pekin duckling brooding calls prior to the simultaneous exposure to two stuffed pekin hens, each of which gave a different call, either duckling brooding calls or maternal calls. At least two hours of this sound stimulation had occurred just prior to the exposure to the stuffed hens. Of the 25 pekin ducklings that had had no extra auditory stimulation, 60 percent responded to the models by following, and all the followers preferred to follow the one that emitted the maternal call, with a mean duration of following of 260.2 seconds. Those ducklings that had had the extra auditory stimulation in the form of conspecific brooding calls, however, preferred even more strongly the stuffed model with the maternal call. Of these, 80 percent followed, with all preferring to follow the model with the maternal call, with a mean duration of following of 394.4 seconds. The degree of the preference shown by these pekin ducklings is emphasized by the fact that the mean duration of following of the stuffed model emitting the duckling call was only 1.9 seconds and .5 seconds for the two groups.

Since a further experiment showed that the exposure to pekin duckling brooding calls did not cause any manifestation of preference for maternal calls of the wood duck species in the same type of test situation involving a simultaneous choice between two models, each emitting a different call—either the wood duck maternal call or the pekin duckling call—Gottlieb concluded that the function of the duckling brooding call in the pekin duck species is to activate a higher degree of following responsiveness and a higher degree of preference for *conspecific* calls, whether maternal or duckling, rather than for maternal calls in general. Furthermore, the increased preference for conspecific maternal calls through stimulation with age mate calls is not through habituation to age mate calls or a waning of responsiveness to conspecific duckling calls through repeated experience with it, since no increase in preference for wood duck maternal calls could be induced by the experience with age mate brooding calls. Also of considerable importance is the fact that when the conspecific maternal call is available as an elicitor of following behavior, it shows much greater enhancement as a result of prior stimulation with the duckling call than does the duckling call itself.

In fact, a previous report by Gottlieb (1965a) offered results consistent with these conclusions. Prior to the placement in the following situation, he exposed passive pekin hatchlings to the exodus call of chickens and the wood duck, both foreign species. Subsequently, in the tests of following behavior he found that the innate preference of pekin ducklings for the maternal exodus call of their own species had not been depressed at all. Of great interest in this connection is Gottlieb's (1965c) further finding that conspecific maternal calls cause pekin duck embryos to increase their rate of bill clapping and calling. It would thus appear that such an increase in vocalization within the egg would serve to stimulate developmental processes in the entire clutch of eggs, as has been shown to be the case for the same species by Gottlieb (1965a), although it may or may not serve to synchronize hatching, as Vince (1964, 1966) has shown for species in which hatching is synchronous, as in the bobwhite quail. In Chapter 8 this particular question is discussed further.

Another report by Gottlieb (1965b) has suggested that exposure to the maternal call before the exodus from the nest possibly functions to raise the activity level of the hatchlings. Gottlieb has further suggested, on the basis of observations of mallard hens and young in the nest, that the increasing activity of the young in turn stimulates the mother to increase the rate at which she emits the exodus call. This reciprocal stimulation apparently continues until the mother leaves the nest and instigates the exodus, at which time the exodus call is at its highest rate. Gottlieb has reported that if young mallard ducklings are exposed to a recording of a high-rate exodus call, their responsiveness to it in a later test is less than that of controls which never heard it before, a finding indicating, according to Gottlieb, that the function of the increasing rate is to prevent habituation toward the call on the part of the ducklings. However, in several respects, our own observations (Hess and Petrovich, in press) of female mallard vocalizations during incubation, hatching, brooding, and nest exodus differ substantially from Gottlieb's. Several aspects of these differences will be discussed in Chapter 8.

Recently, Gottlieb (1971) has reported detailed investigations upon the role of auditory stimulation during the pre-hatching stage upon behavior before and after hatching, upon auditory preferences, and upon species identification.

Effect of Following on Later Behavioral Manifestations. Weidmann (1955) has pointed out that there is a distinct difference in the behavior of a duckling which has followed a releasing object and one that has never done so. "In such a situation the non-imprinted duckling will not alter its behaviour; even if it has meanwhile become tame it so to speak does not mind whether, e.g., a human is present or not. How differently does the imprinted duckling behave: it will stop all other activities and do what it can to find the lost parent again, i.e., it will search and give the distress call incessantly." Such behavior appeared to Weidmann to be "appetitive behavior," in the classical ethological sense. Non-socialized ducklings appeared to him to have lost (or never gained) appetitive behavior for the company of a parent or sibling. These observations of Weidmann for mallard ducklings were later confirmed by means of entirely different techniques by Hoffman, Searle, Toffey, and Kozma (1966). This latter investigation will be discussed when we consider the nature of the effects of early following experience on the later fear behavior of ducklings.

At any rate, one of the striking features of following behavior is that once it has been elicited, it is usually relatively easy to elicit it again at a later time, in comparison with ducklings that have never followed anything before, particularly when the same object that has induced the first incidence of following behavior is again presented. However, there are, as might be suspected, several factors that play a role in how well the first following behavior promotes the recurrence of following. One appears to be the age at which this first following took place. Another appears to be the stimulus characteristics, either visual or auditory, which elicited the first following. Another possibility is the amount of following during the initial instance of following. We shall examine each of these possibilities.

For example, Klopfer (1959a) found that while naïve hatchlings of different surface-nesting duck species had no *exclusive* preference for particular sound signals of different types, if they had been permitted to follow the experimenter while hearing one of these sound signals, they subsequently showed a significant preference for following that sound. Gottlieb (1965a) made a similar finding with hatchling pekin ducks: passive exposure to sound, as we mentioned earlier, did not affect the innate preference of these ducklings for calls of their own species. However, if they actively followed the source of a foreign sound, they would later follow it so long as the parental call was not heard. If actual preference for the foreign species' sound, instead of the conspecific parental call, were to be manifest in following behavior, a great deal of initial following of the former call would be necessary in order to produce this effect. It thus appears that there is a great deal of difference between no following (passive exposure) and some following in determining the elicitation of later following, at least with respect to sound stimulation.

However, Moltz, Rosenblum, and Stettner (1960), in another study with pekin ducklings, have suggested that such a difference between the effects of following and not following in the elicitation of following at a later time may possibly not be the case for visual stimuli, as Gottlieb (1965a) had found to be for sound stimuli. Two groups of 7- to 14-hour-old naïve pekins were formed: one was exposed to the object and permitted to follow or approach it; the other group was kept in a transparent restraining unit that prevented the subjects from either approaching or following the object during exposure, although they could see it without difficulty. For some, the object moved; for others, it was stationary; and for still others, it was absent. Some were exposed to a duck decoy; others, to a green box. The 25-minute exposure session was repeated daily, so that the animals had a total of three days exposure before all subjects were permitted free following of the moving object. In two such test exposures, there was no difference in the median following scores (in seconds) of those that had actively followed and those that had been restrained. The subjects that had never seen the object or had never seen it move did not follow.

However, a subsequent unpublished study mentioned in this report revealed that when the confined subjects were placed 7 inches away from the object, instead of 14 inches, as they were in the present study, their later following behavior was just like that of subjects which had never seen the object or had never seen it move. Thus, the evidence is equivocal with respect to the importance of following in subsequent elicitation of following by visual *silent* stimuli. Evidently being restrained 14 inches away from a moving object provides certain essential stimulation to the subjects or causes them to make essential responses that being restrained 7 inches away does not. Also, it must be kept in mind that the three daily exposures may have managed to provide the restrained ducklings with stimulation at a level close to an optimal amount whereas only one session of active following may have been sufficient to produce this same optimal amount of stimulation in the unrestrained group, thus making the other two sessions of active following relatively superfluous for these pekin hatchlings. The fact that those restrained 7 and 14 inches away were not equal in performance supports this notion, since the combined effect of the three exposure sessions was not optimal for those restrained 7 inches away.

Furthermore, a later study by Klopfer (1971), with the same breed —pekins—used by Moltz, Rosenblum, and Stettner (1960) showed that the ability of subjects to respond at the later testing session depended on whether they had had an opportunity to approach or follow the imprinting stimulus during the training session which took place between the developmental ages of 27 to 28¼ days after the start of incubation. Hence, Klopfer's (1971) findings must be regarded as not supporting Moltz, Rosenblum, and Stettner's (1960) contentions.

In many research reports on following behavior, it has been found that there is a substantial increase in the amount of following behavior on subsequent occasions. For example, an early report by Collias and Collias (1956) mentioned the fact that normally when a duckling is first taken out at the age of a few hours, it may follow only after a few minutes of exposure to the object. If tested again after a few hours, the duckling usually will follow immediately and consistently. This increase in following behavior did not seem to be closely associated with the age of the birds, so that maturation, in the sense of innately determined growth changes, did not appear to the authors to be solely responsible for this phenomenon, although it certainly appeared that it could play a role.

Weidmann (1955) also noted that once ducklings have already followed, such behavior can be maintained for 2 months. Furthermore, more stimuli can be left out of the releasing situation than was possible at first. For example, many ducklings subsequently will react to visual stimuli alone, whereas initially they would follow only if the object were vocal. Thus, we see that the initial experience of following will cause a duckling later to follow under conditions in which it would not have followed very readily had it been completely naïve and never followed before. Nevertheless, following behavior in ducklings normally declines with age, even with repeated elicitation of such following, as we have noted. Certainly, a duckling does not continue to follow its mother

indefinitely. Fabricius (1951a, b), for example, noted that following behavior was usually maintained by ducklings for about 8 weeks, and it
has generally been agreed that such is the case. Moltz and Rosenblum
(1958a) observed that persistence of following by pekin ducks of a green
cardboard box was very high on days 3 through 5, after which it fell off
to a minimal level on day 12. By day 15, the last day of testing, it was
rather low, but still could be seen to exist. This falling off after only
2 weeks, instead of 8 weeks, may be related to differences in the characteristics between a real female parent and a green cardboard box.

Another study on following behavior in pekin ducks, by Waller and
Waller (1963), exposed naïve ducklings to a green cube for two 15-
minute following sessions. For one group, this exposure first occurred
during the age of 10 to 18 hours; for the second, at 34 to 42 hours. For
another group, the exposures occurred at the ages of 80 and 104 hours.
There was no difference in the mean amount of following by the two
groups during the initial 15-minute session (scores were 181 and 133
seconds respectively), but during the second 15-minute session, the
younger group followed the green cube significantly more (357 seconds
versus 136 seconds). Thus, age during the initial exposure, as well as the
characteristics of the eliciting object, appears to influence the intensity
of following during the subsequent following session.

Even soon after the initial following experience at an early age, subsequent following by pekin ducks is not always higher than it was on
the initial session. Gottlieb (1961a) found, in every one of his groups,
a decrease in the proportion of pekin ducks that followed a silent decoy.
This decrease was with respect to the decoy to which they had been
exposed during the initial session.

However, Klopfer and Hailman (1964a) found a slight increase of following under such conditions. One group of naïve pekin ducklings was
initially exposed to a vocal white decoy: 38 percent of the 68 subjects
followed. Another group of naïve pekin ducklings was similarly exposed
to a vocal multicolored decoy: 37 percent of the 73 subjects followed.

In the second session, subjects of both groups were individually
exposed to both models, now silent. Of the first group, 44.7 percent
followed the model which they had first seen, while 48.0 percent of the
second group followed the model to which they had been first presented.
However, the white decoy did elicit less following from the first group
than the multicolored decoy elicited from the second group; the mean
following scores (in seconds) dropped somewhat for the plain decoy-
exposed group, while they rose somewhat for the multicolored decoy-
exposed group. In the initial session, the subjects exposed to the white
decoy spent less (but not significantly less) time in following its model
than did those exposed to the multicolored decoy.

A highly significant fact in Klopfer and Hailman's study is that the pekin ducklings that were initially exposed to the multicolored decoy showed a greater "faithfulness" to it than did those ducklings initially exposed to the white decoy during the subsequent test session when both decoys were placed together: 13 of the 67 white-exposed followed the multicolored model more than they did the white decoy on the test session, while only 4 of the 75 multicolored-exposed followed the white decoy more than they did the multicolored decoy. Conversely, 17 of the white-exposed stayed with the original decoy, while 32 of the multicolored-exposed remained faithful to the originally seen decoy.

Thus, there apparently is a very great difference in the efficacy of the specific characteristics of the object in ensuring later following under different conditions. Even though the ducklings initially showed little difference in the amount of following of these two different decoys, the multicolored model was obviously innately preferable, to the extent that several ducklings that had previously seen only a white decoy preferred to follow it instead. It may therefore be said that when the pekins followed the multicolored decoy, the experience has a much more complete effect on them than following the white decoy had on the other ducklings, since a much stronger preference was evident in the former than in the latter case. On the other hand, lack of preference for the imprinting model versus an unfamiliar one at a later test may not necessarily mean that the animal is perceptually unable to discriminate between the two models (Klopfer 1967, 1968).

This brings us to the question of the nature of the effects of initial following experience on the later behavior manifested by ducks. As we know, some researchers have equated social imprinting with following behavior, regardless of the age or conditions of occurrence. It does appear that the act of following often has the effect of establishing some sort of preference for the object that is eliciting the following. There are, of course, innately established preferences which so act as to make the subsequently manifested preferences either complete or incomplete, according to the nature of the stimulus characteristics which first release following behavior. There is no question that when the proffered object is innately acceptable, following it makes it even more highly preferable, to the extent that other stimulus characteristics, which earlier would have been equally efficacious, lose their relative potency.

However, there also appear to be other factors that play a role in the development of more or less firm following preferences by ducklings, particularly in the social sphere. This is one of the reasons why we do not feel that all cases of following behavior necessarily involve the development of social behavior or social preferences in the individual concerned. The age during which the following experience occurs appears to be another factor, in addition to that of the characteristics of the object, which influences the effectiveness of that experience. The very differences in the ease of elicitation of following behavior as a function of age, in terms of either hours since hatching or developmental stages, attest to this. In the next chapter, we will discuss our own research on the effects of age upon the completeness of the effects of the following experience in determining the preferences later shown by mallard ducklings.

A study by Waller and Waller (1963) illustrates some of the difficulties in equating all following behavior with social imprinting. As we mentioned earlier, hatchling pekin ducks were given the experience of following a moving green cube at the age of 10 to 18 hours and 34 to 42 hours or at the ages of 80 and 104 hours. A third group never saw the green cube until the preference test given to all subjects at the age of 14 days. The cube was placed at one end of a runway, and a duckling was placed at the other end; the amount of time spent in each section of the runway was recorded. It was found that the animals that followed the cube at the earlier age spent most of their time at the cube end of the alley, while those that followed it at the later age showed little preference for it over the duck portion. Those that had never seen the cube before, however, spent most of their time at the duck end of the alley.

However, Waller and Waller (1963) in another study, found that intervening experiences could influence the preferences shown in a simultanous choice test. One group of ducklings was exposed individually for 1 hour daily to the moving green cube, while another was similarly exposed for 1 hour daily to an age mate. All ducklings were housed individually in isolation between the exposure sessions. After 5 days of this procedure, the object to which the animals were exposed was switched to the other one for five succeeding days. A third group, which had been kept in individual isolation and had never been exposed to any object, was now exposed for 5 days in the same manner to the cube. At the age of 11 days, all animals were subjected to a preference test, in which they were exposed simultaneously to the moving cube and to a socialized age mate. All ducklings that had ever been exposed to age mates spent more time with the age mate than with the cube, so it appears that once pekin ducklings have had experience with an innately preferable object—an age mate in this instance—it tends to show greater following behavior to this object, in spite of earlier or intervening experience with a less preferable object. There is also the possibility that the age mate, being a living social object, fulfills more of the pekin duckling's social preferences than does an inanimate object. There may, in addition, be a greater stability of preference for the first-experienced social object if it is animate rather than otherwise.

There are indications that even inanimate objects, in the absence of competition from more adequate social objects, can acquire considerable incentive power for ducklings. This was shown by Peterson (1960), who had pekin and black ducks follow a yellow cylinder for six 45-minute periods distributed during the 1st and 2nd days of life. At the age of 3 days, the ducklings were individually presented with a learning situation in which they were required to peck at a response key in order to be able to see the yellow cylinder. It was found that the animals readily learned to do so, provided the cylinder was moving. When the cylinder did not move, the rate of response fell to zero. In other words, the moving cylinder, by virtue of the ducklings' having followed it at an early age, became a reinforcer for other behaviors. It functioned as a reinforcement, even when the pecking allowed the duckling to see it for only 1 second, a period of time too short to permit any following behavior.

However, Peterson's experiment did not prove that the behavior of the ducks was solely a product of the previous following experience. A replication of this experiment, with controls that had not followed the model, by Hoffman, Searle, Toffey, and Kozma (1966) has indicated that such is, indeed, the case. Pekin ducklings were first exposed to a silent moving object, a horizontally placed white plastic milk bottle, for 45 minutes at the age of 6 to 8 hours after hatching. Five more 45-minute presentations of the object were given within a 48-hour interval. During these six sessions, the duckling saw the milk bottle in a compartment separated from its isolation quarters by a screen; the duckling could follow, but not actually come into physical contact with, the milk bottle. Controls saw either nothing or only the empty compartment. Ducklings that had seen the moving milk bottle on the first days of life readily learned to peck a key which would result in their seeing the milk bottle for as little as 5 seconds, whether training was initiated at the 5th or 11th day of life, while the controls never could do this.

Another study, by Hoffman and Kozma (1967), showed that such key pecking behavior persists for a considerable period. It was still observable in 60-day old pekin ducks, which are almost full grown in size.

Following Behavior and Fear Behavior. Almost every investigator who has studied the following behavior of surface-nesting duck species has speculated on the reasons for the observed decline, with increasing age, of the ease with which the behavior can be elicited by an object. Since the disinclination to follow often appears concomitantly with the appearance of fear behavior toward the proffered social object, it has been suggested that perhaps an endogenous development of fear toward strange objects interferes positively with the elicitation of following behavior (Weidmann, 1958). It has also been sugested that there is a decrease in the internal motivation to follow an object (Fabricius, 1951a). At the present time, there is still no definitive proof of the reason for the decline of the readiness to follow with age and experience. The two mechanisms so far proposed are certainly not mutually exclusive: in fact, they may even both exist, so that in some cases the motivation to follow may decrease, thus permitting an endogenous increase in fearfulness to be more clearly manifest, since there are certainly instances in which ducklings show no fear of an object and no interest in following it. In other cases, the endogenous fear may hinder the tendency to follow an object, so that the two dispositions are in conflict.

Boyd and Fabricius (1965) have reported on: the incidence of following, with or without manifestations of avoidance; avoidance behavior without following; and complete indifference to silent models in naïve mallard ducklings. Following declined in incidence, from approximately 58.5 percent at the age of 10 to 20 hours to about 14.3 percent at the age of 240 hours. The sharpest decline was after the age of 35 hours. At the same time, the incidence of avoidance behavior rose, from 46.3 percent at the age of 10 to 20 hours, to 93.3 percent at the age of 65 to 80 hours, and 100 percent at the age of 240 hours. The percentages of unresponsive ducklings were: 19.5 percent at the age of 10 to 20 hours; 12.2 percent at 20 to 25 hours; 8.0 percent at 25 to 35 hours; 9.2 percent at 40 to 50 hours; 6.7 percent at 65–80 hours; and none at 240 hours. The authors obtained a similar trend of unresponsiveness with an acoustic stimulus: at the age of 10 to 20 hours, 6.0 percent; at 15 to 25 hours, 15.8 percent; at 25 to 35 hours, 3.7 percent; at 40 to 50 hours, 2.35 percent; at 65 to 80 hours, 5.6 percent; at 90 to 100 hours, 11.1 percent; and at 240 hours, 6.0 percent.

Such figures as these do not readily prove that there is an actual decline in the readiness to respond to a moving object or to an auditory signal, rather than an interference of following by an increase in fearfulness of the strange. Our own investigations with drugs which reduce fear are relevant to this point, and will be discussed in the next chapter.

It is clear, however, that once the disposition to follow a particular object has been established in a duckling, the placement of the individual into a fearful situation may cause it to show intensified following. This has been demonstrated by Moltz and his collaborators. In 1959, Moltz, Rosenblum, and Halikas reported an experiment in which pekin ducklings were initially made to follow a green cardboard box for twenty minutes in an alley during the age of 7 to 14 hours after hatching. This was repeated for 3 days. At the end of this time, the 32 animals that had shown the highest following scores during the 3 days were selected and given the following experience for 2 more days. On the 7th day, the animals were randomly divided into the following groups: one was placed in a glass compartment in the alley, without the object it had previously followed, and shocked every 15 seconds for 1 second, for a 15-minute period; the second group was similarly shocked, but not in the alley in which it had followed the object; the third group was similarly placed in the glass compartment in the alley, but not shocked; the fourth group was also put in the glass compartment, but outside the alley. This procedure was carried out for each group on the following 3 days, just before its members were given their regularly scheduled daily following sessions. The mean following score of each of these four groups during these four daily sessions was recorded. Those that had been shocked while inside the alley were found to have the highest median following score, 1025 seconds; those that were placed in the alley and not shocked showed the lowest median following score, 530 seconds. The other two groups, those placed in the compartment outside the alley, whether shocked or not, scored approximately the same, with median following scores of 758 and 751 seconds, respectively.

Thus it appeared to these authors that the introduction of conditioned "anxiety" in connection with the alley environment caused an increase in following behavior, while habituation to the alley without the object caused a decrease in following. It is, of course, analogous to the intensified clinging of the mother shown by a fearful toddler, in contrast to the willingness to play contentedly and the satisfaction with merely knowing where the mother is when the toddler feels secure in a familiar situation. The results of an earlier experiment by Moltz and Rosenblum (1958)—in which some ducklings were placed in the alley without the object which they had previously followed in the alley—further support this analogy. These ducklings later showed less following than did control ducks which had been placed in another environment for the same period of time. Thus, it is clear that when the environment is familiar, following of the object decreases.

Still other aspects of the effects of early following experience on the fear behavior of ducklings, as reflected in distress vocalizations, have been provided by an investigation by Hoffman, Searle, Toffey, and Kozma (1966) and Hoffman (1968). As mentioned earlier, individually isolated pekin ducklings were exposed to a horizontally positioned moving white milk bottle for six 45-minute sessions, beginning at the age of 6 to 8 hours, and within a 48-hour interval. On the 7th day from hatching, three ducklings were allowed to see the milk bottle for one full minute every other minute, and their distress calls during and between presentation periods were recorded. It was found that there was an extremely marked difference between distress call rates when the milk bottle was absent and those when it was present; one duckling, in fact, made almost no distress calls whenever the object could be seen, and made distress calls almost continuously whenever the object was out of view. When other ducklings, with a similar early exposure experience, were trained to peck at a key, an act which was rewarded by allowing the duckling to see the milk bottle for 5 seconds, it was found that distress vocalizations were at an extremely low rate, even when the model was not present. The ducks would peck the key regularly to see the milk bottle. Hoffman (1968) has made further studies on the effects of the absence of the imprinted model upon distress calling by ducklings.

In the 1966 Hoffman et al. study, when ducklings were subjected to extinction procedures, the rate of key pecking would increase tremendously, to be succeeded by a period of intense distress calling and diminishing key pecking. When pecking again was reinforced by the appearance of the milk bottle, the ducks again returned to their former minimal distress call rate and regular pecking rate. Still further experiments carried out along the same lines showed that the introduction of disturbances by noises, strange objects, or electric shocks had the effect of increasing both distress call rate and key pecking rate to produce the milk bottle. The authors pointed out the observed enhancing effect of aversive stimulation on behavior directed toward the milk bottle was the opposite from the suppressing effect that aversive stimulation normally has on food-directed behavior. This fact is all the more striking in view of the fact that food deprivation can be used to train animals to perform certain responses, including key pecking, for food reward.

An interesting sidelight to the reinforcing effect of the milk bottle on the behavior of the ducklings is found in another report, by Hoffman, Schiff, Adams, and Searle (1966). The pekin ducklings were exposed to the milk bottle, as in the above study. On the next 2 days, it was found, as in the earlier studies, that when the milk bottle was present for one minute during alternate minutes, the rate of distress vocalizations was much lower than otherwise: the mean number of distress calls during the presence of the milk bottle was 210 and 163 for the 2 days, and the mean distress calls during its absence was 632 and 485. On the following days, the subjects were paired so that each time one member of the pair emitted a distress call, it was permitted to see the stimulus. The other member of the pair also saw its own milk bottle each time the first member gave a distress call, but in its case the connection with its own distress calling was random. The first members of the pairs gave an average of 247 distress calls during the procedure, while the other members gave an average of only 87. The following day, members of the pairs were switched. Those that were now shown the object every time they gave a distress call did so for an average of 194 times, while the previously reinforced but now "yoked" ducklings gave an average of 183 calls. While the rate of distress calls for the latter ducklings was obviously reduced from that of the previous day, it was higher than that of the yoked members for the previous day, certainly because of the initial experience of having to emit a distress call in order to be able to see the milk bottle. The effects of presence and absence of the object upon distress vocalization were reported upon in Hoffman et al. (1970). It was found that the object exerts control over distress vocalization from the very beginning of the imprinting exposure, and that mere stimulus change per se was unable to have this kind of effect. Hence, the authors concluded, it would seem that ducklings have innate predispositions to emit filial-type responses in the presence of certain classes of environmental events.

These studies certainly show that experience with and following a moving object during the 1st or 2nd day of life, even when no physical contact is involved, can result in a duckling's acquiring a motivational system which is not apparent in ones which did not have this early experience.

Further congruent observations have been made by Stettner and Tilds (1966). Naïve hatchling pekin ducklings were made to follow a green styrofoam rectangle for the first time at the age of 7 to 14 hours, for 30 minutes. Subsequently, they were given daily following sessions through the age of 5 days. At the age of 14 days, the ducklings were placed in an unfamiliar open field. It was found that when the green styrofoam rectangle was present, the ducklings spent a considerable amount of time near it. When a fear object—a Raggedy Ann doll—was placed in the field, the ducklings stayed close to the green rectangle, even though this caused them to be closer to the doll than they would have tolerated were the rectangle not present.

Hole-Nesting and Other Ducks

The experimental data on the following behavior of young ducks of hole-nesting species, although brief, are mentioned herein separately because they indicate that there are considerable differences in the mechanisms eliciting and influencing following behavior in these species from those that operate in the case of the surface-nesting species we have been discussing. Klopfer (1959a, b, c) has provided the bulk of the available experimental observation on following behavior in the wood duck species. Unlike surface-nesting species, naïve wood duck hatchlings do not initially show a disposition to approach or follow a sound signal. However, also unlike the surface-nesting species, wood ducklings which have been exposed passively to a specific sound generally show a high preference for following it at a later age. In the case of surface-nesting species, as we have seen, active following of a sound signal is necessary in order to develop a preference for following that particular sound. But in the hole-nesting wood duck, passive exposure is sufficient to develop such a preference in following behavior. Klopfer also considered it highly possible that certain sounds are more readily learned as preferred evocators of following behavior by wood ducks than other sounds are, but was of the opinion that greater numbers of ducklings should be tested before coming to any conclusion on this aspect of following behavior in wood ducklings.

Several aspects of the natural situation are relevant to these observed differences between the hole-nesting wood ducks and ducks of the surface-nesting species. In the first place, Klopfer pointed out, surface-nesters usually can walk well before the age of 8 hours, but he had never observed any wood duckling walking before the age of 12 hours, with many too weak to even stand up until the age of 18 hours. Thus wood ducklings simply cannot approach the source of auditory stimulation at an early age, as surface nesters do, and it is possible that such approaches would actually be maladaptive. On the other hand, visual imprinting does not take place before the exodus from the nest, since the wood ducklings are in the dark. Therefore, hearing the call of the mother, even though no following takes place, apparently results in the immediate elicitation of following at the time when the exodus takes place. Furthermore, such learning of the mother's call may possibly compensate for any interference caused by fear responses to visual stimuli at the age of the exodus.

Gottlieb (1963a, c) has made naturalistic observations of the sequence of events preceding the exodus in the wood duck. When eggs pip, the female increases her vocalizations, and 20 to 36 hours later the intensity of these vocalizations reach a maximum. This is the time of the exodus, and the ducklings begin to follow when the female leaves the nest and calls outside it. Gottlieb suggested that the auditory stimulation from the mother may also serve to initiate following behavior in wood ducks in the same fashion as duckling calls in surface-nesting species appear to activate following behavior, as shown by Gottlieb (1966). Gottlieb (1965b) has further noted that the primary difference between wood duck and mallard hatchlings is that at the proper age, the time of the exodus, auditory stimulation alone is sufficient to induce wood ducklings to leave the nest and begin following, whereas with mallard ducklings, following is far more likely to occur with auditory stimulation if it is connected with some kind of visual stimulus.

The importance of species differences in the factors promoting following behavior and following preferences in ducks has been further demonstrated by Klopfer's observations (1959a) of the voiceless muscovy duck. Naïve hatchlings of this breed did not show any responsiveness to sounds, and could not be induced to acquire following behavior to sounds. Thus, Klopfer pointed out, even though the muscovy duck is a close relative of the highly vocal wood duck, its voiceless character would not tend to preserve the ability to respond to sound signals. This species has no specific nest site, unlike either wood ducks and surface-nesters.

Still another species observed by Klopfer (1959b), the shelduck, nests in burrows in normal conditions, but will also nest in thickets above the ground when burrows are not readily available. Like wood ducks, hatchlings of this species do not show any tendency to follow repetitive sound signals at the age of 18 to 26 hours. However, passive exposure to sound did not later cause them to show following behavior, as it did wood ducks. Instead, like surface-nesting species, the shelducklings had to follow the sound signals in order to develop specific preferences for following these sounds at a later time. Klopfer suggested that perhaps visual stimuli initiate following behavior upon emergence from the burrow in this species.

It is obvious, from our review of duck species, that species and breed differences play important roles in the elicitation, development, and maintenance of following behavior. Even further differences can be expected between duck and chicken species.

Wild and Domestic Chickens

Very little is known regarding following behavior in wild fowl—more specifically, the red jungle fowl—beyond the fact that it certainly does exist in response to a variety of potential parental objects (Hess, 1959a, b; Kruijt, 1962a, b, 1971). Snapp (1969) has shown that red jungle fowl chicks can respond differentially to different recorded maternal vocalizations. Therefore, the present review will deal only with aspects of following behavior in various breeds of domestic fowl, of which there are a very large number. Almost every experimenter, in fact, appears to have his own favorite chicken breed.

Eliciting Stimuli. As with ducks, the releasing stimuli of following behavior, both visual and acoustic, are relatively unspecific. A wide variety of shapes and spectral colors have been successfully used to elicit following behavior. People, guinea pigs, cylinders, cones, spheres, pyramids, duck decoys, hen models, toys, dusters, toilet floats, rotating discs, and flickering lights—all have been found to be effective visual stimuli. Here too, a summation of stimulation in more than one modality has greater effectiveness in eliciting following behavior: a vocal object is more likely to elicit approach and following behavior in naïve young chicks than is a silent one. Also, a moving object is superior to a motionless one.

Considerable differences between stimuli of one modality are evident, even though chicks certainly do not possess an extremely high degree of specificity in the stimuli which will release following behavior in them. Collias (1952) found that low frequency tones elicited approach behavior and contentment tones in young chicks, while high frequency tones induced withdrawal and distress tones. Fischer and Gilman (1969) exposed hatchling white rock × pilch broilers to a model emitting repetitive taps in one of seven different decibel levels. Moderate intensities (55 to 75 db signal added to 51 ±1 db ambient noise level) elicited much more following than did 85 and 95 db signals or no signal (i.e., the 51 ±1 ambient noise only). Signals of 85 and 95 db, in fact, were aversive to the human experimenters. Gottlieb (1965a) has reported differential following in response to different auditory signals in his white rock chicks at the developmental age of 20½ to 22½ days: 72 percent followed a rendition of the hen's call; 37 percent followed the mallard duck call; 26 percent followed the wood duck call; and the same number "followed" silence. The peak age for responsiveness to the chicken call was determined to be at the developmental age of 21½ to 22 days, since 90 percent of the chicks in this age group followed this auditory signal.

Gottlieb (1966) later reported that white rock chicks showed a far greater readiness to follow a model emitting a rendition of the maternal call of the species than one emitting the conspecific chick call: 72 percent of 79 chicks at the developmental age of 20½ to 22½ days followed the maternal call, while 60 percent followed the chick call. In addition, it took them, on the average, less time to begin following the maternal call than it did for the chick call: their latencies were 297.4 and 544.3 seconds, respectively. Finally, they followed the maternal call model longer than they did the chick call model, for the respective mean durations of following scores were 371.0 and 59.2 seconds. Earlier, Gottlieb (1965c) had found that in white rock chick embryos, as in pekin duck embryos, stimulation with the conspecific maternal call increases the rate of bill clapping and calling in the embryos at the developmental age of 20 to 20½ days after the beginning of incubation. While not tested, the possibility exists that in chicks the chick calls heard before and soon after hatching serve to activate responsiveness to conspecific maternal calls. There may be a reciprocal process involved, similar to the one suggested by Gottlieb (1965b) for the sequence of events leading to the exodus from the nest by ducks.

Auditory stimulation need not be emitted by the *model* to enhance following behavior in chicks: Sluckin and Salzen (1961) observed repeatedly that when Rhode Island reds and brown leghorns were evidencing decreased following of a model, intense following could be instantly reinstated by the experimenters' shouting, waving arms, clapping, or stomping.

Among visual stimuli, wide differences have been found in effectiveness of evoking following behavior in hatchling chicks. Jaynes (1956) exposed newly hatched 1 to 6-hour old New Hampshire red chicks to a green cube or to a red cylinder. The green cube elicited somewhat more following in the chicks than did the red cylinder, though not significantly so.

Guiton (1959) found that a light green box elicited greater amounts of following from brown leghorn chicks at the age of 20 to 54 hours than did a brick red box. The difference in following, although highly consistent, was not statistically significant.

Smith (1960) reported that 16 to 26-hour old light Sussex × brown leghorn chicks approached a flickering patch of light 6 inches in diameter just as much as they did a rotating black and white disk, while a plain white rotating disk did not attract them at all. Smith and Hoyes (1961), working with the same breed, reported that at the age of 18 to 30 hours, vertical and horizontal movements in a distant intermittent stimulus were both equally effective. Differences in the size of the distant intermittent stimulus were important in influencing the likelihood of approach behavior, while differences in the color of the distant flashing lights did not appear to play any differential role. Red, green, and white spheres also did not significantly differ in their effectiveness in eliciting approach behavior, but red and green were slightly better than the white for both the spheres and the flashing lights. The height of the stimulus above the chick was also found to be important; when the center of the 3 inch diameter flashing disk was 2 inches above the ground, most of the hatchlings approached it; but when the center of this disk was *20* inches above ground, most of them did not approach it.

Further and similar data were reported by Smith (1962a, b; Smith and Bird, 1963a). It appeared in these later reports that a rotating black 45° sector on a 12 inch white disk moving at a speed of one revolution per 1½ seconds was intrinsically more attractive to this breed of chicks than the flickering 6 inch diameter patch of light on a gray background, rather than equally attractive, as had been earlier reported by Smith (1960), although the data did not always show this to be the case.

James (1960c) found that barred rock × New Hampshire red chicks approached a .2/.2 sec flickering light more readily than they did a 5.0/.2 sec flickering light. Thus, it is apparent from these various studies that intermittent stimuli do vary in their ability to evoke approach responses from hatchling domestic chicks. It may be remembered that James (1959) found that domestic chicks did approach the flickering light he presented, but blue-winged teal and mallard ducklings did not. However, Bateson and Reese (1968) succeeded in demonstrating positive attractiveness of flicker to both wild mallard ducklings and "chunky" broiler chicks at the age of 1 day.

A more quantitative analysis of the effects of flicker as an attractant to young chicks has been conducted by Simner (1966) and Gottlieb and Simner (1969). Since chick embryos are exposed to their own cardiac rhythms, Simner (1966) suggested the possibility that this particular rhythm might prove to be highly attractive to hatchling chicks. Chicks of different ages (8, 26, 32, 48, 56, and 76 hours) were observed for amount of time spent near a source of flickering light. Different flicker rates which were above, within, and below the prenatal heart beat rate of chicks (3.8 to 4.4 cps) were presented to different chicks. The oldest chicks were found to spend more time near flicker than the youngest ones did. The strongest relative preference, however, was shown by the youngest subjects, and their preference was for the heartbeat flicker rate. Chicks tested longitudinally or cross-sectionally at different ages also tended to give more approach-stay behavior toward the heart beat stimuli range.

While a study by Kovach, Paden, and Wilson (1968), utilizing 3.5 cps flicker rate, obtained a steady and sharp increase in responsiveness in experimentally naïve chicks as a function of increasing age (12, 24, 72 hours), Simner (1968) found that naïve 8-hour old chicks were somewhat more responsive to 2.0 to 4.4 cps flicker than were the 26-hour old ones. Simner also found that the 50- and 72-hour old chicks were much more responsive than were these two younger age groups. Bateson and Reese (1968) have shown that flicker stimuli can also be used as a reinforcer to train naïve day-old chunky broiler chicks to press a pedal, with orange flicker superior to green flicker. Later studies (Bateson and Reese 1969) showed that previously socialized (to peers) subjects did not learn this task as quickly as did isolated ones. Dark-reared chicks 48 hours old were also able to learn the task faster than were light-reared peers.

Other kinds of stimulus variations have been studied for differential attractiveness. Schulman, Hale, and Graves (1970), for example, presented 14 to 22-hour old New Hampshire × barred Plymouth Rock chicks with red cardboard disks of 5, 10, 15, 20, 25, 36, and 71 cm diameters, with 20 birds randomly assigned to testing with each particular disk. Those that had disks 10–20 cm in diameter responded sooner and in greater proportion than those that had disks of other sizes.

Another type of stimulus variation is that of complexity. Bateson (1946b) reported that day old naïve Rhode Island red × light Sussex chicks approached a patterned model more than a plain gray one; furthermore, a highly conspicuous pattern, white with red stripes and red circles between the stripes, elicited significantly more approach than did red and gray stripes on the model. A conspicuous multicolored duck decoy model was also studied by Klopfer and Hailman (1964b) and compared with a plain white decoy. All chicks were at the developmental age of 21½ to 22¼ days at the time of the exposure, and both models were vocal. The chicks followed the white decoy for an average of 159.3 seconds, while the multicolored decoy was followed for an average of 202.8 seconds. Control chicks of the same age offered a simultaneous choice between both models silent followed the plain one for an average of 29.9 seconds and the multicolored one for 32.2 seconds, thus indicating the much greater attractiveness of vocal decoys over silent ones to domestic chicks.

The Kovach et al. (1968) study also undertook to compare the effectiveness of 3.5 cps. flicker, a yellow rotating pinwheel, and a blue ball in eliciting approach and following behavior in chicks of different ages. The flicker stimulus elicited much more approach and following behavior than did any other stimulus, especially at the age of 3 days, while it was not demonstrably more attractive to ½-day old chicks. Thus, flicker seems to have effects different from those of other stimuli.

Further flicker studies by Kovach (Kovach, 1971a, b; Kovach and Hickox, 1971), using 3 cps flicker (.166 on/.166 off rate), have shown that the color and intensity of the flicker light are important factors. The Rhode Island red chicks studied showed an inherent preference for blue stimuli. However, prior exposure to flicker or to continuous light, depending upon chromatism and intensity, had complex effects upon the approach preferences shown by chicks during testing. Such prior exposures during the first 3 days of life also influenced perceptual learning in these chicks begun on the 5th day of life and terminating no later than the 25th day of life, with prior exposure to blue resulting in superior perceptual learning rate. This has some similarity to Polt's (1969) finding that blue imprinting objects facilitate the learning of blue food-reinforced objects, but that yellow imprinting objects will not do the same for yellow food-reinforced objects.

The greater attractiveness of vocal objects over silent ones has been demonstrated also by Smith and Bird (1963b, 1964a, b). They found that the combined stimulation was more effective than auditory stimulation alone in eliciting approach behavior in their 24±6-hour old experimental subjects, brown leghorn × light Sussexs.

It appears that increasing length of exposure of chicks to an object may heighten the probability of a positive response to that object. Jaynes (1958a) reported that under certain conditions young chicks would begin following such an object in less than 10 minutes. However, 40 minutes of exposure was required in order to induce all experimental chicks to follow. Jaynes also claimed that it did not matter whether this 40 minutes occurred entirely on the 1st day of life or was distributed over the first 4 days of life: with accumulation of experience with the model, according to Jaynes, the chicks eventually would follow it.

Age Parameters in First Elicitation. Again, the notion of sensitive periods in the elicitation of following behavior has arisen with respect to chicks. Differences in the ease of inducing following or approach behavior in chicks as a function of age have been reported by some investigators. Klopfer and Hailman (1964b) have claimed that the developmental age of 21½ to 22¼ days from the beginning of incubation is the period when the following response is best elicited from vantress-cross chickens, but did not present specific experimental data in support of this contention. Gottlieb (1965a), an associate of theirs, however, has shown subsequently that this age period is one in which his chick subjects showed the strongest attraction to conspecific maternal calls.

Jaynes (1957) exposed communally reared hatchling New Hampshire red chicks to a green cardboard cube at different times after removal from a commercial hatchery. The criterion score for considering subjects followers was at least 60 seconds in the vicinity of the model during the last 5 minutes of the 30-minute exposure session: $5/6$ of those tested at 1 to 6 hours met this criterion, as did $5/7$ of those tested at 6 to 12 hours, $2/5$ of those at 24 to 30 hours, $3/5$ of those at 30 to 36 hours, only $1/5$ of those at 48 to 54 hours, and none at 54 to 60 hours. All chicks in each age group were experimentally naïve, of course. Thus, there was clearly a declining disposition to follow the model as a function of increasing age in these chicks upon initial exposure to the proffered model. However, those that did follow accumulated higher following scores with increasing age, perhaps because of increasing locomotor ability, which would permit them to follow for longer periods and farther distances. Greater following by older chicks therefore does not necessarily indicate greater attractive power of the stimulus at the later age, but may more accurately reflect differences in locomotor ability.

Smith and Nott (1970) have studied the approach responsiveness of brown leghorn × light Sussex chicks to a rotating (but stationary) white disk having a 45° red sector in relation to rearing experience and the age at which the initial test took place. This testing was done over a period of 14 to 18 subsequent days. At initial testing, which was at the age of 1, 2, 3, or 10 days, the 10-day old chicks were found to have less approach responsiveness than any other age group. However, in the subsequent days of testing, all chicks, except the 10-day old socially reared and naïve ones, were equally responsive to the stimuli, with the exceptional chicks (i.e., the 10 day-old ones) being less likely to approach the stimulus.

Guiton (1958) exposed brown leghorn chicks to a vocal stuffed brown cockerel at various ages from hatching. There was a steady decrease with age in the incidence of following behavior. All the 8 chicks 5 to 20 hours old followed the model, with a mean score of 8.6 for the group; 67 percent of the 6 chicks 30 to 36 hours old followed, with a mean score of 5.8 for the group; 57 percent of the 7 subjects 52 to 58 hours old followed, with a mean score of 5.3 for the group; and 22 percent of the 9 chicks 68 to 74 hours old followed, with a mean score of 2.0 for the group. Of those birds which followed, however, the mean score of following tended to remain fairly stable as a function of age, with respective scores of 8.6, 8.8, 9.3, and 9.0.

Other estimates of age-related differential sensitivity to the elicitation of approach behavior by chicks have been somewhat grosser. James (1960a) noted that if barred rock × New Hampshire red chicks were exposed to a flashing light a day after hatching, they would approach it more consistently than if they were exposed to it at the age of 7 days.

The question of the responsiveness of chicks, as a function of age to animals and inanimate objects, has been investigated in a series of papers by Gray and his associates. In these studies, the basic procedure was to rear chicks from the time of hatching in individual isolation compartments. These isolation compartments were abutted by two other compartments, which were visible from the chick's own compartment through two glass partitions. The platform in the floor of the chick's compartment was attached to a timer, which recorded, through the tilting of the platform, which side of it the chick was occupying—that is, which side compartment the chick was near. At the appropriate age, stimulus objects were placed in one or both compartments, and the location preferred by the chick noted. While following responses or approach (from a distance) tendencies were not specifically studied, the results of such research certainly are of some relevance to the problem of the responsiveness of chicks to objects. We shall now discuss these studies.

In the first experiment of this type, Gray (1961a) presented different age groups of isolated white rock chicks with a single object in one of the side compartments. The objects with which the chicks were presented were an age mate and 7 circles, each a different color—red, yellow, green, blue, white, black, and one that had a red upper half and a yellow lower half. Each chick at the appropriate age was successively shown all eight objects for 15 minutes. Thus each stimulus presented to a chick was an unfamiliar one; if a chick spent any time near an object, this was considered by Gray to indicate a certain degree of positive attraction of that stimulus for the chick. Chicks tested on the 1st day of life, at an age of about 6 hours, showed a clear preference only for age mates, and did not have any differential preference for any of the colored circles. Of interest was the fact that once a day-old chick had seen another chick or a black or yellow disc, its response to other objects was further depressed.

Chicks tested on the second day of life were positively attracted to all the stimuli, especially to the age mate and the red, yellow, black, and red-yellow circles. Chicks tested on the 3rd day of life showed the highest responsiveness to stimulus objects. However, the responsiveness to the black and yellow circles was significantly less than it had been with 2nd-day chicks. On the 4th and 5th days, the responsiveness of the tested chicks to all objects was generally low and there were no significant differences in preferences among the various objects.

Gray contended that his results showed that chicks are attracted to age mates or to color phenotypes of unfledged chicks (black and yellow) for the first 2 days of life, and that after that age—on the 3rd day—they are more attracted to objects resembling the mother. Gray suggested that it is not to the chick's advantage to follow its mother during its 1st day of life, since it appeared to him that the locomotor ability of chicks of that age is less well developed. Hence, Gray concluded that it might be more advantageous for chicks to stay with siblings in a flock. After the 1st day of life, Gray asserted, chicks will then show preferences for attributes of the natural mother.

These results do not give any information as to the effect of the exposure to the stimuli as a function of age upon later behavior since the chicks were tested at only one age. In another report, Gray (1961b) made the conclusion that the results of testing chicks that had been exposed to an object for 24 hours at different ages during the first 4 days of life provided further support for his proposition that there is, first, a process of sibling attachment and, then, a process of filial attachment in the life of chicks. The effects of the age of exposure were found to vary according to the color of the model and whether it was moving or stationary.

Since this report, a series of experiments (Gray, 1962, 1964; Gray, Weeks, Anderson, and McNeal, 1963; Gray, Sallee, and Yates, 1964) have attempted to show that there is a 24-hour cycle in the responsiveness of otherwise isolated young chicks to social stimuli. For example, Gray (1962) reported that white leghorn chicks exposed simultaneously to an adult hen and an age mate in the side compartments for 15 minutes at successive 3-hour intervals over a 24-hour period at different ages for different groups generally showed an increasing preference for the hen to a peak level at the fifth or sixth test session. Apparently Gray's chicks showed greater responsiveness to the age mate at the first tests than they did at any of the other succeeding tests. Although Gray had contended that his results mean that there is a "biological clock" in the preferential responses of young chicks to a hen or age mate, the fact must not be ignored that the repeated 15-minute exposures to the two objects may have been the factor promoting the rising preferences for the hen.

Much the same criticism may be directed at the results published for a similar experiment by Gray, Weeks, Anderson, and McNeal (1963). Again, otherwise isolated white leghorn chicks were simultaneously exposed to an age mate and an adult hen that had been placed in each glassed end compartment for 15-minute tests carried out every 3 hours over a 24-hour period. Different groups of chicks were thus tested at different ages—the 1st, 3rd, 6th, 10th, and 15th days of life. Again, as in Gray's (1962) report, the chicks showed the greatest responsiveness to the hen at the fifth or sixth test of the series. Responsiveness was primarily to the hen on the 1st day of life (a finding replicated in Gray, Sallee and Yates, 1970), while thereafter it was to the age mate, with increasing responsiveness to the hen on the fifth or sixth test still apparent. It is of interest that the absolute value of peak responsiveness to the hen dropped steadily as the age at which the chicks were tested was increased, to reach a relatively low plateau. Presumably the same trend had been earlier observed in Gray's (1962b) investigation. It is, however, very different from the conclusion Gray had drawn in his two 1961 reports to the effect that on the 1st day of life the chick prefers the age mate as a social companion and that the chick does not maximally prefer being near the hen until the 3rd day of life. The data reported in Gray, Sallee, and Yates (1970) also contradict this conclusion. We therefore must conclude that Gray's research reports manifestly lack internal consistency.

In still another experiment, Gray (1964) again exposed isolated white leghorn chicks to an age mate and an adult chicken for successive 15-minute tests, this time with 4-hour intertest intervals, over a 24-hour period, with different groups tested at different ages. Two different species, either male or female, were used as the adult chicken stimulus. Individual chicks were always tested for responses to the same adult: the leghorn hen or rooster, or the jungle fowl hen or rooster. In general, the hens elicited more responses from the chicks than the roosters did; at the first day of age, the leghorn hen elicited more responsiveness than did the jungle fowl hen. Since only six tests were given, instead of the eight in the earlier experiments, the peak of responsiveness to the leghorn hen was at the terminal tests, rather than just before. The changes in responsiveness to the leghorn rooster and the jungle fowl of both sexes as a function of testing had their own pattern for each of these three stimulus objects. While Gray maintained that these results supported the notion of a biological clock in the preferences shown by chicks, this, of course, is not the case, because of the successive testing procedure used.

Rather, it appears to us that these investigations of Gray show that the effect of the repeated testing with stimulus objects is in the direction of priming the preference for the leghorn hen, particularly on the 1st day of life, with the maximum level of preference for the leghorn female reached on about the fifth or sixth 15-minute trial and thereafter declining. We believe that this is in fact a phenomenon highly similar to the one described by Gottlieb (1963b, 1966), in which exposure to conspecific duckling calls enhances the innate preference of pekin duckling for conspecific maternal calls.

Our interpretation of Gray's research reports is further supported by another report (Gray, Sallee, and Yates, 1964), in which the successive testing method was abandoned, and a fresh group of white leghorn chicks was tested for 15 minutes at different times during the 1st day of life for responsiveness to an age mate and a conspecific hen. In this report all but two of the measured means for preferences were in the direction favoring the age mate, with the two in favor of the hen being rather small in magnitude. This is still further proof of our own deduction that leghorn chicks, on the first 15-minute test exposure, are likely to show a preference for an age mate, as was evident in all Gray's earlier reports. Our criticism of Gray's interpretation of his data does not mean that we are opposed to any notion of circadian rhythms in chick behavior. Rather, we feel that his experiments do not constitute adequate evidence of such biologically based rhythms. In this connection, it should be noted that Thorpe (1961) has discussed circadian and other biological rhythms in relation to imprinting.

Approach responses to stationary stimuli by young chicks over a period of 18 days after hatching have been observed by Abercrombie and James (1961). The stimulus offered was a turquoise plastic ball presented either alone or next to a group of five small holes through which a flickering light shone. Although the ball was stationary, the chick was introduced to it at some distance and permitted to approach it and stay near it if it wished. Barred rock × Rhode Island red chicks, commercially hatched, and at least 48 hours old when first placed in the experimental testing situation, were found to more readily approach the ball when the flicker was also present than when it was not. If the flicker was removed after 2 days of training, the chicks continued to show a high rate of approach responsiveness. While the group that never saw the ball with the flicker initially responded to it less than did the flicker-exposed group, the readiness to respond to it increased over several days, to the point that, by day 16 of age, their response to it was at the same level as that of the flicker-exposed group. On day 17, they were found to follow the ball just as much as did chicks from the flicker-exposed group. So, obviously, neither movement nor flicker needs to be present for chicks to develop an approach fixation to the ball.

Effects of Pre-exposure Factors on Following. It has uniformly been reported that prior exposure to age mates will cause chicks to show less following responsiveness to stimulation than otherwise. These findings are not at all incompatible with our interpretation of Gray's research data. As we noted, repeated exposure to both an age mate and an adult female initially served to increase responsiveness to the hen, but after the fifth or sixth 15-minute exposure, responsiveness to the hen dropped. This indicates that *continued* association with age mates, particularly in the absence of the hen, as in the group of research reports we are about to consider, has the effect of diminishing potential responsiveness to the conspecific hen or any other object that may be presented as a parental surrogate. When the proffered parental object is *not* the conspecific hen, the effect of socialization with age mates in damping potential responsiveness should be even more drastic.

One of the first reports on the effects of sibling socialization in chicks (Guiton, 1958) demonstrated that maintaining chicks together after hatching decreased both their disposition to follow and the intensity of following in those that did follow, at the age of 72 hours. During the first 6 minutes of exposure to the silent model, 43 percent of the 7 individually isolated chicks followed it, and none of the 6 socialized chicks did so; as soon as the model became vocal, all the isolated birds followed it, whereas only 17 percent of the socialized chicks did so. When the model was again silent, these proportions were maintained. The mean following scores of the subjects that followed was higher for the isolated subjects than for the socialized subjects: 7.3 was the average score for the isolated chicks when the model was silent, while the socialized ones, of course, did not follow at all; when the model was vocal, the mean following score of the isolated chicks was 19.9 and for the socialized ones, 3.0. The respective scores were 20.4 and 5.0 when the model was again silent.

In a subsequent study, Guiton (1959) investigated further aspects of the effects of prior socialization and individual isolation on the readiness of brown leghorn chicks to follow models. Seven chicks were kept in a group for 3½ hours beginning at the age of 20 to 54 hours, and then isolated to the age of 72 hours, when they were exposed to a red box. Nine chicks were isolated up to the age of 96 to 126 hours, and then exposed to the red box. The third group consisted of 6 chicks, which were kept together socially from the age of 20 to 54 hours until the test with the red box at the age of 96 to 126 hours. All chicks of the first group came to follow the model fully, with a mean total following score of 136 seconds. In the second group, 7 of the 9 subjects followed fully, with a mean total following score of only 41 seconds. In contrast, none of the subjects in the third group ever followed the model fully, and the mean total following score was 10 seconds. Of interest is the fact that a short period of isolation of birds with social experience increased the amount of following manifested, in comparison with subjects maintained in complete isolation, while ones that were maintained in social groups since the age of 20 to 54 hours were complete failures as followers.

In a later report by Guiton (1961), the deleterious effect of social experience on following was reconfirmed. More specifically, Guiton exposed 48-hour old brown leghorn cockerels, either individually or in a group, to a moving vocal model for 1 hour. More intense responses were found in the individually treated chicks than in the group treated ones. Furthermore, the individually exposed birds discriminated better between the model they had followed and a strange one than did the ones that had been exposed as a group.

Further indications of the effects of social experience with age mates on the elicitation of following behavior have been provided by James (1960b). Barred rock chicks 48 hours old were exposed to a blue plastic ball at the center of a set of five holes, through which a flickering light could be seen. Some of the subjects had been maintained in pairs, and others were left in individual isolation. The pair-raised chicks were found to show much less tendency to approach the flicker than did the completely isolated ones.

Sluckin and Salzen (1961) have confirmed that the effect of prior socialization with age mates usually serves to lower responsiveness to a silent moving model in 1-day old brown leghorn × light Sussex chicks. Furthermore, the older the chicks, the more drastic the inhibiting effects of the pretest social experience. Like Guiton (1959), they found that a short period of social experience—six hours—and then isolation caused 1-day old chicks to manifest enhanced responsiveness to the model. Even only a short period—six hours—of isolation after social life apparently can tremendously increase responsiveness of 1-day old chicks to a moving box. However, there were also indications that in 2-day old socialized chicks, short periods of isolation do not enhance responsiveness and longer periods—on the order of 24 hours—are necessary to produce a facilitating effect in chicks that have already lived with age mates for 48 hours.

An additional report on the effect of sibling socialization is one by Smith and Bird (1963c), who found that 26±6-hour old brown leghorn ×

light Sussex chicks that had been kept in separate compartments followed a 12-inch diameter rotating white disk having a 45° black sector significantly more than did those reared socially; in fact, the two-tailed statistical significance was between .0001 and .00006. Prior sibling socialization was found to reduce following responsiveness in other ways. For example, when chicks were exposed to the model in a group, following was more intense in those that had been housed separately. The same effect was observed in chicks which were exposed to the model in a group with a leader present.

A chronic sodium pentobarbital drug state apparently enhances the occurrence of following behavior in response to flicker stimulation by chicks at the age of 4 and 5 days (Macdonald, 1968). Bradford and Macdonald (1969) found, however, that hatchling chicks under the influence of this drug while being imprinted were not affected in their later following behavior as long as the drug dosage was not heavy.

Other pre-exposure factors that have been found to have an influence on the initial elicitation of following and approach behavior in chicks included: cold treatment (Salzen and Tomlin, 1963, Fischer, 1970), environmental complexity (Bateson, 1964a, b), testosterone propionate (James, 1960b, 1962), handling (Thompson and Dubanoski, 1964b), and embryonic visual stimulation on the 19th day of incubation (Adam and Dimond, 1971).

In Salzen and Tomlin's (1963) study, brown leghorn × light Sussex chicks, individually hatched, were tested for following behavior at the age of 12 to 24 hours with a white cylinder used as the eliciting object. Prior to this experience, some of the chicks were removed from the warm incubator and left for two to four hours in boxes in a 65°F environment. At the end of this exposure period, the animals were found to be cold to touch. During the first 5 minutes of exposure to the cylinder, few of the cold-treated chicks followed, but after 15 minutes, there were equal numbers of cold-treated and warm-treated chicks following. This finding was duplicated in a replication of the experiment. Thus, the effect of the cold treatment was to delay the appearance of following behavior, perhaps because of physiological effects on general motor activity. Also, all chicks were exposed to the model in a 75°F environment, thus permitting the cold-treated chicks to warm up to some degree. The total amount of following performed by the cold chicks, however, was less than that by the warm chicks: the longest distance traveled by a warm chick was 12½ feet, and by a cold chick, 2½ feet.

In 1961, we carried out an unpublished study in our laboratory in which vantress chicks were kept in individual lighted compartments since hatching and then regularly handled by stroking in the dark at 4-hour intervals before the imprinting exposure took place at the age of 24 hours. There was no difference in the amount of following between the handled and nonhandled groups. Since then, Graves and Siegel (1968) have studied the effects of handling in both light and dark conditions upon individually reared white rock chicks. At the exposure to a flickering light stimulus at the age of 24 hours, the non-handled control chicks proved to be no different in responsiveness from ones handled in the dark. However, the responsiveness was a great deal lower in those that had been handled in the light. On the other hand, when chicks had been allowed to see the experimenter's hand as it moved around, their responsiveness to the flickering light was slightly enhanced. The depressing of responsiveness to the flickering light by handling in the light was increasingly greater as the chicks were older at the time of the experience. When chicks were handled in the light at the age of 13 hours, the effect was the worst.

A study by Thompson and Dubanoski (1964b) indicated that, under certain circumstances, handling vantress chicks can enhance the intensity of following behavior shown upon exposure to a moving parental surrogate at the age of 30 and 54 hours. When the chicks were handled in the dark for 10 minutes at the age of 5 hours, and then exposed to the moving object at the age of 12 and 16 hours, they showed more following during 3-minute tests of following at 30 and 54 hours of age than did chicks that had been similarly handled at the age of 9 hours or not at all. The chicks of the latter two groups, of course, were also exposed to the moving parental surrogate at the age of 12 and 16 hours. It is unfortunate that the authors failed to report on the amount of following of the object during the initial exposure to it. It would be of great interest to know whether the handling of the 5-hour old subjects increased the amount of following on the initial exposures, or whether the handling had a true "sleeper effect" on following behavior.

Fischer (1970) has recently studied the effects of still another parameter—environmental temperature—upon the amount of following during the exposure to an object. Both the temperature during the pre-exposure brooding and that during the exposure itself were varied. Fischer's day-old leghorn chicks were found to follow the most when the exposure temperature was 16°F below the brooding temperature, provided that the exposure temperature was within the 68-84°F range.

The approach response of barred rock chicks to a flickering light was found to be depressed by 3 and 5 mg doses of testoterone cyclopentylpropionate at the age of 2 days, according to James (1960b, 1962), while hatchling barred rock × Rhode Island red chicks injected with this hormone at less than 24 hours of age showed no such depression of responsiveness to visual flicker. Similar results were obtained with white leghorn chicks, which were not affected by injections of testosterone propionate when given at less than 30 hours of age, but did show decreased approach tendencies to the flicker when injected at the age of 3 days, with a maximum age of 90 to 96 hours.

The effects of prior experience with environmental complexity on the tendency of chicks to follow or to approach objects has also been investigated to a limited extent. Bateson (1964a) kept Rhode Island red × light Sussex chicks in individual isolation for 3 days before their first exposure to a moving object. There were two different patterns that were used for the wall of the chicks' individual rearing compartments: black and white vertical stripes, and yellow and red horizontal stripes. At the age of 3 days, chicks were placed individually in a runway and faced with a moving model painted with one of these patterns. It was found that the chicks were significantly quicker to move toward the model and give other positive responses such as contentment tones or nestling movements when it was painted with the same pattern as the rearing compartment than when it was painted with the unfamiliar design. Those that had been reared in the presence of yellow and red horizontal stripes showed this facilitation to the greatest extent.

In another experiment, Bateson (1964b) reared the chicks in individual isolation with one of three different patterns: dark gray alone; dark gray and red horizontal stripes; and white with red stripes, and red circles between the stripes. After this rearing experience, the chicks were presented at the age of 3 days with a model painted with one of these three designs. A definite relationship was found between rearing conditions and model pattern with respect to latency of positive responsiveness. In general, those reared with gray walls were quickest to respond positively to a model, while those maintained with red and white walls were the slowest to do so. The red and gray model, on the other hand, elicited positive responsiveness the most quickly, and the white and red model, the most slowly. However, these differences were not significant.

In a further experiment, Bateson painted one wall of the runway in which the chicks' responses to the model were tested. The chicks in this experiment were reared in either white and red patterned compartments or in plain gray compartments. The testing models were likewise of either of these two patterns. The outer wall of the runway was painted with red and white vertical stripes. Again, the difference according to the earlier rearing condition in latency of positive responsiveness was significant. Those kept in plain gray compartments responded more quickly to a model—especially to the gray model—than did those that had been kept in white and red compartments. Bateson interpreted these results as indicating that chicks which had been maintained in the more complex environment had learned the characteristics of their environment more thoroughly than had those maintained in a relatively homogenous environment, and therefore showed a stronger discrimination between the familiar and unfamiliar.

Prenatal influences upon approach and response behaviors to the presented stimuli have recently begun to be studied. It may be that through such studies the structural—that is, organismic—bases of early social behavior may be found.

Strobel, Baker, and Macdonald (1967) and Strobel, Clark, and Macdonald (1968) have shown that irradiating day 7 (of incubation) or day 9 chick embryos (Cornish X white rock strain) with 400 r adversely affected their responsiveness to an auditory and flickering stimulus when tested at the age of 10 to 20 hours, whereas there was no discernible effect upon those irradiated at day 2, day 5, or day 12 of incubation. However, Oppenheim, Jones and Gottlieb (1970) were unable to find any adverse effects of prenatal irradiation in either white leghorn chicks or pekin ducklings upon responsiveness to a conspecific maternal attration call presented at the age of 15 to 30 hours after hatching. Perhaps the difference in results lies in the fact that Oppenheim et al. used a more nearly "natural" stimulus than did Strobel et al.

Not only prenatal but also genetic factors play a role in following behavior and imprinting in chicks. The studies bearing upon this area (Fischer, 1967; Graves and Siegel, 1968a, 1969; Gray, Yates, Davis and Mode, 1966; Hess, unpublished; Smith and Templeton, 1966) are discussed in Chapter 4.

Other Effects on Following Behavior.   A post-exposure factor influencing the degree to which initial following experiences affects later following behavior has been suggested by Gutekunst and Youniss (1963). All experimental subjects, newly hatched New Hampshire reds less than 24 hours old, were exposed to a silent moving green cube for 10 minutes. Some of the birds were anesthetized immediately after the following experience; others were not subjected to this procedure until 15 minutes later; and still others, not until 30 minutes later. A fourth group was never anesthetized. The following scores during the last 5 minutes of a 10-minute exposure period to the silent moving green cube 24 hours after the initial experience with it suggested that when the birds had been anesthetized immediately after the initial exposure, they were less inclined to follow on the test exposure. The respective scores of the four groups were: 135 (immediate anesthetization); 154 (15-minute interval); 163 (30 minutes later); and 161 (never anesthetized). It is quite apparent that anesthetization 30 minutes after the initial exposure does not at all influence the retention of the experience, and even a 15-minute interval shows only a small effect.

Still another post-exposure factor having possibly adverse effects upon the retention of the initial following experience has been indicated by Fischer, Campbell, and Davis (1965), who exposed 12-hour old vantress chicks to a red cube emitting chick peeps. All experimental chicks were immediately subjected to one ECS (electroconvulsive shock), and some were subjected to eight more, given at 4-hour intervals. Controls were given "placebo" shock treatment. At the age of 48 hours, all experimental and control subjects were tested for strength of following of the model. One ECS did not impair following responsiveness; in fact, it enhanced it in comparison with the placebo controls. However, nine ECSs did depress following behavior. Control subjects followed an average of 176.3 and 158.0 seconds during the test, while the single-ECS subjects followed an average of 316.5 seconds. The subjects that had nine ECSs followed an average of 57.7 seconds. It is not clear why the single-ECS subjects followed twice as much as the control subjects, but it is entirely clear that several convulsive shocks did serve to remove responsiveness to the model. These bidirectional effects of the ECS as a function of the number of ECS experiences certainly constitute a phenomenon worth further exploring, since if a single ECS immediately after initial following enhances later following, the administration of eight more ECSs at 4-hour intervals must not only eliminate this enhancement effect but also further depress responsiveness.

Haywood and Zimmerman (1964), using vantress broiler chicks, reared some in a complex visual and social environment, and others in a relatively restricted but not socially isolated environment. Each of these two groups was subdivided into six different age groups, according to the age of exposure to the mallard duck decoy emitting duck calls. These ages were 3, 6, 9, 12, 15, or 18 hours after hatching, and the exposure sessions lasted for 15 minutes. The complex environment constituted a concurrent experience in relation to following behavior in this experiment, since the effects of the complex environment were assessed by a later test session carried out 36 to 48 hours later.

The complex environment consisted of a black-walled enclosure with random stripes and blotches of white paint on the walls and with flashing overhead illumination. The chicks, kept four at a time in this enclosure, continuously heard two metronomes ticking and a loud radio program. Every half hour, each chick was stroked on its back for 15 seconds, heard a bicycle bell for 2 minutes, and received a mild puff of air. These chicks, of course, had ample experience with the experimenters during these procedures. The restricted chicks, on the other hand, were kept together in groups of four in wire mesh cages in a room relatively free from noise, and were able to see the experimenters going in and out in the course of obtaining the subjects for the tests.

The subjects that had been kept in the highly complex environment showed higher mean number of following responses during the later test session as a function of every initial exposure age, except the age of 12 hours, than did those kept in the less complex environment. The peak response for the complex environment subjects during the test session was given by those that first saw the moving decoy at the age of 6 hours, while for the other subjects the peak response at the test session was given by those that had initially seen the moving decoy at the age of 9 hours. Since these subjects were only comparatively restricted in relation to the experimental subjects, it is possible that the prolonged social experience they received (prolonged conspecific social experience, as we have already found, has a depressive effect on following responses) made the peak effect for them appear at an earlier age than it would have for completely isolated and environmentally restricted animals. In other words, had these authors also used animals that were kept in the dark in individual isolation, it is possible that the age peak, as measured by the later test session 36 to 48 hours later, would be about 12 hours after hatching for such animals. It is of interest in this connection that Haywood and Zimmerman's subjects with the less complex environmental experience had the same mean number of following responses as the complex environment subjects when the initial exposure to the vocal decoy had been at the age of 12 hours. When the initial exposure took place at the age of 18 hours, however, the complex environment subjects showed a relatively high level of responsiveness to the model during the test session, while the subjects that had the poorer environmental experience had no response at all on the test session.

These findings by Haywood and Zimmerman have been replicated and confirmed by a later study (Haywood, 1965). The 6-hour peak effect in terms of amount of following during exposure and strength of discrimination during test and the superiority of the complex-reared subjects were again observed.

A more truly concomitant experience which has been found to influence the degree of later following behavior by chicks has been reported by Pitz and Ross (1961). Hatchling vantress broiler chicks 12 to 15 hours old were exposed individually to a silent moving red cardboard box. Half of the experimental subjects heard a sudden, intense noise from a clapper whenever they were 6 inches within the object. The other half of the subjects heard the clapper whenever they were on the opposite side of the runway from the object. Control chicks were exposed to the moving object but never heard the clapper. This 15-minute exposure was repeated daily for 3 days. Then for 2 more days, all chicks were exposed to the model for 15 minutes without any auditory stimulation.

It was found that while there was no difference in the following behavior of the chicks on the first following session, there were differences
thereafter, thus indicating a "sleeper effect." The group that heard the
noise whenever in close proximity to the model followed it far more
than did those of the other two groups; the latter were indistinguishable from each other.

Effects of Following on Later Behavior.   As we have already seen with
ducks, the initial performance of following or approach behavior has an
influence on the later performance of that behavior. Collias (1962), for
example, pointed out that in domestic chicks there is usually an increase
in the amount of following performed as a function of mere experience
in following—a fact that had been observed to be the case with ducklings, as Collias and Collias (1956) had found. Gutekunst and Youniss
(1963) have reported data entirely in accord with this: 8 hatchling New
Hampshire red chicks exposed to a silent moving green cube when less
than 24 hours old for 5 minutes followed it for a mean of 75 and 93
seconds. Twenty-four hours later, upon re-exposure to the object, they followed it for a mean of 116 and 161 seconds in the two 5-minute sessions.
   Jaynes (1957) reported that there were unequal effects of a 30-minute
exposure to a moving silent green cube according to age in New
Hampshire red chicks. Some of those who had followed at earlier ages—
1 to 6 hours or 6 to 12 hours after removal from the commercial hatchery—no longer followed the model during the re-exposure to it 10
days later. On the other hand those groups that had been exposed to
the green cardboard cube at later ages—24 to 30 hours, 30 to 36 hours,
48 to 54 hours, and 54 to 60 hours—all showed an increase in the proportion of followers. In this instance, a "follower" was defined as a
subject which stayed with the model for 60 seconds or more during the
last 5 minutes of the half-hour exposure to the moving model. However,
the total amount of following by the followers *decreased* as a function
of the age of initial exposure to the model; in addition, such latent
effects of the initial exposure have not been replicated by any subsequent research. Jaynes did suggest, however, that the relative inability of
the younger chicks to follow the object may have been responsible for
their poorer performance at the later exposure. At any rate, this decrease does not agree with the increase reported by Collias (1962).
   When the effects of following are compared with those of no following we find that there is a great deal of evidence that following at an
early age does tend to have a considerable effect on later behavior in
different respects, especially in the intensity and likelihood of following and with respect to the preferred object for following.
   For example, a report by Salzen and Sluckin (1959) compared the per-

formance of Rhode Island red chicks that had never followed a silent red box (either because they had never seen it before or because they showed no disposition to follow it when they had been exposed to it for the first time) with the performance of other chicks that had followed the red box. The initial exposure to the red box took place at the mean age of 24 hours, and the 2-minute, 40-second test exposure was given from 1 to 6 days later. Since the test exposure could take place on any one of the 6 subsequent days (one fresh group of chicks tested on each day) the difference between the chicks that had followed and those that had not can be regarded as only suggestive. Nevertheless, It is of great interest that those chicks that had never seen the red box move showed a rather low level of responsiveness to the box. One group had spent 2 minutes and 40 seconds with the box while it made 10 "movements"; the other group had spent 9 minutes and 20 seconds with it while it made 50 movements. Of the former group, 22.5 percent responded by following the red box during the test session; of the latter group, 28.5 percent did so. The question of the effect of the extra experience with the moving box on the following tendencies of the second group, however, is a complex one.

On the test exposure, the performance of the initial followers was better for those that had seen the extra 40 movements; 29 percent of those in the 10-movement group followed the red box during the test session; and 39 percent of those in the 50-movement group followed. Thus it clearly appears that the extra following experience of the 50-movement group promoted the appearance of more following.

However, when the data with respect to the effects of greater exposure to the moving box on those that did not follow are examined, a curious fact emerges: of the 44 additional animals that were induced to follow through the extra 40 movements of the box, only 7 later showed any following disposition on the test exposure. This proportion is equivalent to that shown by chicks of the first group who did no following whatever during the initial exposure.

Since Salzen and Sluckin found that when the test exposure occurred later than 3 days after the initial exposure there was a rather precipitate drop in the proportion of birds responding positively, it may be that some of these 44 extra responders were simply tested too late. Another alternative exists in the fact that during the initial exposure to the red box, the age range of the subjects was from 18 to 30 hours. The slow responders thus may have been older animals, and therefore not as likely to retain responsiveness to the box as an effect of the experience. Nevertheless, the conclusion is inescapable that the extra experience in the 50-movement group acted primarily on those which had already been affected by the first 10 movements.

Further indications of the effects of the initial following experience for these particular chicks were later reported by Sluckin and Salzen (1961). Immediately after the initial exposure, which we have already described, the investigators tapped on the side of the runway enclosure that the chicks and the model had occupied. There were differences in the responsiveness of the chicks to this sound as a function of how many movements they had seen the box make: 25 percent, or 37, of the zero-movement group responded; 39 percent, or 58, of the 10 movement group responded; and 51 percent, or 76, of the 50-movement group did so. There were 150 experimental chicks in each treatment group.

Thus it appears very clearly that the likelihood of the chicks' responding to the sound was increased by a greater amount of experience in seeing the red box move. Furthermore, the likelihood of responding to the sound was also higher in those that had followed the red box than in those that had not followed the red box, with those that had seen 50 movements even better than those that had seen only 10 movements, since the respective proportions of sound responders was 61 percent and 52 percent among the followers, and 20 percent and 10 percent among the non-followers.

Another study (Collins, 1965) illustrates the complexities of assessing the meaning of the degree of following behavior manifested by a chick as a function of prior exposure. Here, unlike the above discussed studies, following was prevented by means of restraint for some chicks. This actual restraint appeared to have effects different from those of simple non-exposure or from those of the chicks' own disinclination to follow during the initial exposure.

White rock and leghorn chicks were exposed at the age of 48 hours to a silent moving dark red chicken model, half natural size, for 1 hour. Control chicks were similarly placed into the apparatus, but without the moving model present. For one group of chicks, active following of the model was permitted; for another, active following but no contact was permitted, since the model was behind a screen, which kept the chicks from being able to contact the model; the third group was restrained by a small screen enclosure, so that the moving model could be seen, but no following or any contact was possible. Five days later, at the age of 7 days, the chicks were all tested for their responsiveness to the model. Those chicks that had seen the moving model made more orienting responses to the model during the test than did those that had never seen it: the experimentals made from 10 to 14 such responses, while the controls made, at most, only one. Similarly, there was a tremendous difference between the experimentals and the controls in the median amount of time they spent in following the model during the test. The controls followed for medians of 4 to 7 seconds, while all the experimentals followed more than 100 seconds. As might be expected, those that could follow freely made the highest following score—218 seconds. However, among the restricted chicks, there was no superiority of the ones that could follow without making contact over those that could neither follow nor make contact, as their respective scores were 132 and 155 seconds. This difference from results obtained from other experimenters regarding the efficacy of following versus no following may be a function of the later age—48 hours—of the subjects used by Collins during the initial exposure session. Also, the model was silent.

It may be added parenthetically that an experiment indicates that contact-tactile factors apparently can operate to promote attachment behavior in domestic chicks (Taylor and Sluckin, 1964). Two groups of chicks were reared in individual pens which had folds of foam rubber hung on one of the walls. For one group, the inner folds of the foam rubber were rough and soft; for the other group, they were of smooth plastic. After 36 hours of such rearing from hatching, a cardboard was placed in front of the foam rubber, and contact with it was thus prevented. When it was raised again, the responses of the chicks to the foam rubber were noted. It was found that the chicks that had experienced the rough and soft inner folds were more attracted to those. Also, such chicks in a test of exploratory behavior in which a colored flag was placed in the compartment were found to orient to the foam rubber as a shelter and base from which to explore the flag. These results bear considerable similarity to those obtained in Harlow and Harlow's (1962) research with macaque monkeys reared with terry cloth mother surrogates.

Macdonald and Solandt (1966) have reported evidence relevant to the question of the effects of forcible immobilization of chicks during exposure to visual and auditory stimulation upon the degree to which they later prefer to be near the stimulus source. Macdonald and Solandt's procedure, essentially the same as that used by James (1959), consisted of exposing 12- to 20-hour-old white rock Cornish chicks to a flickering light and a metronome sound, both at a .5/.5 rate, for five 1-minute exposure sessions. This procedure was repeated for two more days. Some of these chicks were exposed while under the influence of Flaxedil, a drug which blocks overt motor responses; others were exposed without any drug influence; two control groups were neither drugged nor exposed to the stimulation. One of the control groups was placed in the runway apparatus without any flickering light or metronome sound present; the other control group remained in their home cage. On days 4 and 5, the exposure procedure was carried out for all experimental and control chicks, with no animal under drug influence. On both test sessions, the animals that had received stimulation and had been able to approach it actively showed the highest approach scores—152.3 and 151.9 seconds. The control chicks, on the other hand, made scores of only 25.3 and 58.4 or 30.3 and 50.1 during the test sessions. There was no difference, therefore, between the ones that had been in the exposure apparatus and those that had not. Those chicks that had been under the influence of the drug, on the other hand, showed little effect of the exposure to the flickering light and sound, although they did show somewhat higher scores on both test sessions than the controls had— 43.2 and 74.1 seconds. Thus, it appears that while the experience with the visual and auditory stimulation had some effect on the drug-immobilized group, actual approach behavior on the part of the undrugged experimental chicks was far more effective in promoting later positive approach behavior on the test sessions. Macdonald and Solandt's results also suggest that forcible confinement of chicks during exposure to a moving object may not adequately test the role of actual locomotion for the establishment of later approach behavior on the part of chicks, particularly when object choice is involved.

Effects of Following on Later Object Choice.   An investigation by Klopfer and Hailman (1964b) with vantress cross chicks has indicated that following behavior enhances later following of even a strange object if it is one that possesses attractive qualities. Here chicks were exposed at the developmental age of 21½ to 22¼ days to either a vocal white duck decoy or a vocal multicolored duck decoy for 20 minutes. Twenty-four hours later, the subjects were individually exposed simultaneously to both decoys, silent, and moving. Their following behavior was compared with that manifested by control chicks that had never seen either decoy. As had been the case in another study by these same authors (Klopfer and Hailman, 1964a) with pekin ducks carried out in the same fashion, chicks of both experimental groups preferred to follow the multicolored model, with those that had been originally exposed to this model showing the strongest preference. The control chicks, however, showed no preference for either of the two decoys. Furthermore, their following behavior toward the decoys was less than that shown by the two experimental groups toward either decoy.

A later paper by Klopfer (1965) extended further into this topic. Chicks were exposed to the white duck decoy or to the multicolored one, as in the earlier study. However, this time, some of the chicks were tested on motionless vocal models, and others were tested on moving vocal models. In the previous experiment, it will be recalled, the models were in motion and silent during the simultaneous choice test. It was found in Klopfer's experiment that when the models were in motion, the following scores of the subjects replicated those of the previous experiment by Klopfer and Hailman. However, when the models were stationary, the chicks preferred the model to which they had originally been exposed. Thus, it appears that the effect of the *model* that is followed during the initial following session is clearly evident only when reexposure with another model present occurs with the opposing models stationary. When models are in motion, it appears that other perceptual preferences act so as to interfere with the manifestation of any effect of the original exposure model. Again, as in the previous experiment, controls that had not previously seen either model followed the moving decoys very little and showed little attraction for them when they were stationary, in comparison with those that had previously followed.

However, it must be remembered that the effect of motion versus no motion in object choice may apply only to *inanimate* or small models, since Gray and Howard (1957) found that when Indian River chicks were made to follow a human for at least 10 minutes at the age of 31 and 37 hours, no definite choice was made between the person originally followed and a strange one during a 2-minute period, during which both persons stood still. When both persons began side stepping, 10 of the 12 chicks went to the one they had initially followed.

There has also arisen the question of the results of freely permitting chicks to follow a moving object on later preferential following behavior, in comparison with results obtained when the chicks see the object move but are physically restrained from engaging in locomotion to follow it, rather than when the chicks have never seen the moving object before or when they have shown no inclination to follow it during the initial exposure.

Investigations by Rice (1962a, b) have indicated that active following of a blue rubber ball by young vantress broiler chicks more effectively promotes a significant preference—82 percent—for being near the blue ball instead of an age mate than does dragging the chicks by a string attached to the ball for the same distance or length of time. The dragging experience, however, did have a positive effect on the chicks, for 59 percent showed a preference for the ball, and 33.33 percent made no choice. In contrast, totally isolated subjects without any social experience showed low responsiveness to either the ball or the age mate: 87 percent made no choice at all.

In a report by Thompson and Dubanoski (1964a) vantress chicks were exposed to a silent moving blue and yellow toy duck at the ages of 9, 12, and 16 hours. One group was permitted to follow the model freely as it moved; another group was carried in a small plastic box which moved with the box; and a third group was exposed to the model in a motionless condition, except that when the chick walked away from it, it was moved so as to remain within 1 foot of the chick. All chicks were tested, first, for amount of following of the model to which they had been exposed and, then, for amount of following of another model, a white stuffed replica of a hen, at the ages of 24 and 48 hours.

In all cases, the chicks followed the model to which they had been exposed during both test sessions, more than they did the unfamiliar model. Those that had followed it actively had by far the highest median following scores, while those that had been carried and those that had seen the model mostly stationary (and did not, in any event, actively follow the model) followed it only one-third as much as the first group did. The latter two groups were not significantly different from each other. It is of interest that during the first testing session, those animals that had actively followed the model showed more following of the white hen model than did those of the other two groups—a fact which indicates that initial following behavior activates the disposition to follow, as we have seen in other research investigations. In the second test, however, the white hen model was followed very little by these chicks, and it was no more attractive to them than to the chicks of the other two groups.

In a replication of this experiment, the model to which the chicks had not been exposed initially was changed to a blue and yellow toy doll, thus making the discrimination between the two objects more difficult (since they were both of the same combination of colors), and tests were at 38 and 62 hours of age. Despite the changes in procedure, very nearly the same pattern of results was obtained. The principal exception was that, in this case, the unfamiliar model elicited a higher level of responsiveness than had the white hen model in the first experiment, with the result that those chicks which had not actively followed the exposure model showed no consistent preference for either test model. During the first test session, the superiority of the group that had actively followed the model was such that they followed the model more than ten times as much as did those of the other two groups. In both test sessions, this group also followed the unfamiliar model more than did the other two groups, thus repeating the phenomenon noted in the first experiment.

However, these two experiments had a defect in that the original exposure object was presented first in the test session. Therefore, a third experiment was carried out, in which the original model was presented first for half of the subjects and the unfamiliar model was presented first for the others. In this instance, there was an even sharper difference than there had been in the other two experiments between the amount of following by those that had actively followed the model and that by those that had not done so. However, there was no preference at all for one model over the other among the subjects that had actively followed the model. The amounts of following by the other two groups, low as they were, actually indicated a preference for the unfamiliar model over the familiar one. The lack of preference for the exposure model led the authors to conclude that the original following experience generally has the effect of promoting following behavior rather than preference for the exposure object.

However, it must be pointed out that the two test objects were presented successively, rather than simultaneously, as in Klopfer (1965), wherein a preference for the original exposure model definitely was demonstrated. Clearly, then, the method of testing has a very decisive influence on the results obtained. The caution which is necessary in interpreting preferences shown in a successive testing procedure is shown by a recent experiment with commercial broiler chicks by Fischer (1966b), in which she compared the effects of following a red cube (emitting taps) for a continuous 12-minute session at the age of 18½ hours with the effects of following this model for two 6-minute sessions separated by 10, 20, or 30 minutes. At the age of 36 hours, the chicks were first retested on the red cube and then on an unfamiliar model, an orange double truncated cone. The familiar model—the red cube—was followed equally well by chicks of all groups, irrespective of whether the initial following experience had been massed into one session or two. However, the following of the strange model was considerably less in those chicks that had had more than one following session.

Nevertheless, acceptance of Fischer's assertion that the distribution of following experience acts to prevent following of strange objects must be tempered by consideration of Thompson and Dubanoski's (1964a) findings regarding the effects of presentation order on preferences shown in successive testing. Fischer may have thought that order effects in successive presentation did not interact with object preference, since in an earlier study in which she participated (Fischer, Campbell, and Davis, 1965), chicks showed a strong preference for following the original exposure model, *particularly* when the strange model was presented first in the successive series. However, the explanation for the results she obtained in this study can be readily found by reference to Gottlieb's (1966) report that pre-exposure to duckling calls enhances responsiveness to conspecific *maternal* calls. In Fischer, Campbell, and Davis' study, the original exposure model emitted hen broody calls and cackles, while the strange model emitted chick contentment calls. While we must be very careful in generalizing from ducks to chicks, or vice versa, Fischer, Campbell, and Davis' results are congruent with the notion that exactly the same phenomenon occurs with chicks: age mate vocalizations cause chicks to become increasingly responsive to conspecific maternal calls. We can suggest that this must be the case, because when the strange model, emitting chick calls, was presented first in testing, responsiveness to the familiar model, which emitted maternal calls, was *better* than when the latter was shown first in the testing.

Another point is that here again in chicks, we find an instance suggesting that initially the effects of age mate stimulation is to promote following responsiveness to maternal stimuli, as we found in the research of Gray and his associates, discussed earlier. This, of course, we consider to be the case only with small amounts of sibling stimulation, since beyond a certain point, stimulation from siblings acts to decrease responsiveness to maternal stimulation, as has been amply shown by several research investigations.

Other studies on the effects of following objects on the preferential object choice of chicks with respect to later behavioral manifestations have concentrated on the effect of the initial *model* followed on the choice later manifested between this model and others. For example, in one of the earlier laboratory investigations on following behavior in chicks (Jaynes, 1956), chicks were exposed either to a green cube or a red cylinder for daily half-hour sessions after the subjects had been obtained from a hatchery. The green cube subjects followed their model more than the red cylinder model followed theirs. However, during a 5-minute test after 4 days of experience in following, the green cube subjects showed a greater tendency to follow the previously unseen object—the red cylinder—than the red cylinder subjects showed to the green cube. Furthermore, the green cube subjects showed less of a behavioral differentiation between the two objects.

A later study by Jaynes (1958b) reported that chicks initially will equally follow a silent familiar object, a red cylinder, and a silent unfamiliar object (pink pyramid, yellow cube, green upright cylinder, or white trapezohedroid), successively presented, on the first day of life. However, on the second day, the chicks began to show less following of the strange object, and, as daily testing progressed, the chicks showed an increasing disinclination to follow a strange object as experience with the familiar one continued and a different strange object was presented daily. On the 5th day, both the familiar red cylinder and one of the four unfamiliar objects were simultaneously present for 45 minutes. Jaynes found that as exposure to the two objects continued, differential behavior toward them developed progressively and became fully established after 30 minutes. The development of differential behavior over a period of time Jaynes decided to call "emergent discrimination." However, it also shows that differential behavior toward an object that had been followed first may not be immediately apparent when it is presented successively with another object. This may be the reason that some studies have failed to show any differential preference of chicks for following the object which they had initially followed over an unfamiliar one.

For example, a study by Cofoid and Honig (1961) may possibly be subject to this factor. They exposed 16-hour old domestic white rock chicks to a violet-blue illuminated vocal moving porch light globe for 30 minutes. This procedure was repeated for 17 minutes on each of 3 subsequent days. On the two following days, the subjects were exposed to the violet-blue porch globe for five minutes, and then this color and five others, ranging from violet-blue to yellowish-green on the spectrum, were presented for 3 minutes, each in a different random order for each bird. The mean following scores for each of these spectral values tended to decrease slightly as the profferred stimulus became more and more dissimilar to the original exposure color. Thus, not only the problem of successive testing but also the problem of the shortness of the exposure places obstacles in the interpretation of the results. Furthermore, the range of stimuli presented was not particularly wide. Therefore, these results do not necessarily show a lack of discrimination, on the part of the chicks, between the familiar object and the unfamiliar ones.

Galassi and Walker (1968), on the other hand, found a rather sharp generalization gradient in the following by white leghorns of blue hexahedrons which varied in .75 inch increments or decrements from the training objects. It is possible, therefore, that color and shapes have different generalization gradients. Breed differences may also be rather important in this respect, since Galassi and Walker reported research by Perkins (1966), in which there had been a failure to find any generalization gradient in vantress broilers with respect to size variation. These broilers had been trained on a 4-inch diameter red ball, and were tested on one of a series of red spheres which ranged in size from 1 to 7 inches in diameter. Even the particular shape used for generalization studies may have an influential role. Goodwin and Hess (1969a, c) found, in studies of unrewarded pecking preferences of young vantress broiler chicks, that preference generalization gradients could be obtained for some series of stimuli but not for others.

The results of an experiment by Sluckin and Taylor (1964) provide still further indications that increased duration of exposure to simultaneously presented moving objects will tend to result in sharper differentiation between the familiar and unfamiliar as elicitors of following behavior than will shorter exposures. In Sluckin and Taylor's experiment, 36 to 54-hour old chicks, of an unspecified breed, were exposed to a moving object—either a red, black, or white cardboard box or a green foam pyramid. The chicks were tested for simultaneous discrimination between this object and a strange one, both in motion, either immediately or 5, 15, or 45 minutes later. It was found that greater discrimination between the familiar object and the strange one was obtained some minutes after the original exposure rather than immediately after it. In a second experiment, however, the simultaneous choice test was conducted with the models stationary, and it was observed that differential behavior toward them tended to decline rather than increase as a function of the length of the interval between initial exposure and testing. Hence, there is clearly a difference in results obtained on testing as a function of whether the models are stationary or moving, as Klopfer (1965) has found.

Since, in a third experiment, chicks showed greater following of the original model (without any strange object present) as a function of increased length of isolation from it, Sluckin and Taylor suggested that this may constitute a recovery from "drive satiation," and account in part for the increase in discrimination behavior seen in their first experiment. However, this postulation would not account for Jaynes' (1958b) findings of a similar increase in differential behavior with continued exposure to the strange and familiar objects, since his chicks were tested 24 hours after the last exposure to the familiar object, an interval certainly long enough to dissipate any possible habituation effects. Of course, it is possible that both increased length of isolation from the original exposure model and increased length of simultaneous exposure to the familiar and unfamiliar models during testing promote increasingly greater discrimination between the two models.

Still other experimental research (Kaye 1965a, b) is relevant to the question of the effects of the interval between initial exposure to the object eliciting following behavior and differential behavior toward that object and another. Kaye presented his hatchling barred rock × Rhode Island red chicks with either a moving silent green pyramid or a moving silent red cube until they had accumulated a following score of more than 30 seconds on each of two successive 5-minute trials. Then they were similarly exposed to the other object. The subjects were tested for their preference for the simultaneously presented objects either immediately or 24 hours later. All subjects were again tested 96 hours later. The subjects tested immediately after the successive exposures showed no preference for either of the objects; but those tested 24 hours later showed a significant preference for the object to which they had first been exposed, and maintained this preference on the retest at 96 hours as well. Curiously, those that had seen the two objects simultaneously during the test immediately after the successive exposure procedure also failed to show any preference for either object at the 96-hour retest. It therefore appears that when the chicks had been permitted to see the objects only *successively* during the early age, they later showed a preference for the one they had first seen; but when the chicks had had an early experience of seeing the two objects *simultaneously,* no differential preference ever became manifest.

Taylor and Sluckin (1964) have reported that rearing hatchling chicks, of an unspecified breed, for one day immediately after removal from the incubator with a moving box or with an age mate had significant and consistent differential effects on the social preferences of the chicks on the next day when both the box and an age mate were simultaneously present at opposite ends of the rectangular runway. Of the 10 socially reared chicks, 8 spent more than half of the 10-minute test period near the chick, with the other 2 preferring to remain in the "neutral" intermediate region. Of the 10 reared with the moving box, 9 stayed near it most of the time, and 1 stayed in the intermediate "neutral" region. In terms of mean time in seconds spent within 1 foot of an object, both groups of chicks manifested equally strong attachments toward the object with which they had been reared: the socially reared chicks spent an average of 442 seconds near the age mate chick, and the box-reared spent an average of 462 seconds near the box. The socially reared chicks spent an average of 11 seconds near the box, and the box-reared spent an average of 7 seconds near the other chick. Their scores for the intermediate neutral region were also similar, being 147 and 131 seconds, respectively. The strength of attachment to the object with which they had been reared during the first day was manifested in another behavior—that of struggling against the mesh barrier between themselves and the former companion. This behavior was shown by 9 of the socially reared chicks and 8 of the box-reared ones. It was never manifested toward the unfamiliar object.

Chicks that had had no social experience at all but which were maintained in individual isolation were found by Taylor and Sluckin to manifest a completely different pattern of response in the test situation. Of these 10 chicks, 4 stayed by the moving box, 4 stayed in the neutral region, and the other 2 stayed by the chick.

An experiment by Fischer (1966a) has indicated the role of the auditory component of the object initially followed upon later object preference. Commercial white giant × pilch broiler chicks were exposed to a red cube emitting bantam broody hen calls and cackles at the age of 24 hours. At the age of 36 hours, they were tested to the same model or to a different one, a double truncated orange cone, either silent or emitting the same sound or 1-day old chicks' peeps and pleasure calls. It was found that the effect of the familiar visual stimulus was much less than that of the familiar auditory stimulus. The original red cube emitting the original conspecific maternal call elicited a mean of 435.5 seconds of following. But when the cube emitted peeps, the average following score dropped to 159.5 seconds; when it was silent, the score was only 77.1 seconds. However, among all the auditory conditions, the red cube elicited more following than did the orange cone; when the orange cone emitted broody calls, it elicited a mean of 361.9 seconds of following; when it emitted peeps, 114.3 seconds of following; and when silent, it elicited only 46.1 seconds of following. Thus, we see clearly the activating role of the auditory component of the object eliciting following behavior as well as its role as an identifying agent. There are, of course, as we know, innate preferences for maternal calls over age mate calls in chicks. Also, hearing age mate calls enhances responsiveness to maternal calls, as we saw in the experiment of Fischer, Campbell, and Davis (1965). Within the *same* auditory conditions, however, let us repeat, visual factors indubitably play a differential role in the elicitation of following.

Other Effects of Following Experience on Aspects of Later Behavior. As we have already found with ducks, when chicks follow a specific object at an early age, that object can acquire the property of influencing the behavior of the animals in ostensibly nonsocial situations. For example, Campbell and Pickleman (1961) exposed white rock chicks to a silent moving blue cube for the first 4 days of life, with the first session carried out at an age within 20 hours after hatching. Controls were habituated to the exposure apparatus without the object for the same periods of time. The three strongest responders to the object were placed into a learning situation in which the object was placed in one arm of a T-maze. Over a period of ten days, they showed a significant increase in the number of responses to the arm of the T-maze which contained the object and in the speed of running to the end of that arm. The control chicks, on the other hand, had no such change in behavior, thus showing that the object which had elicited following in the chicks had acquired reinforcing properties of these chicks to the extent that a previously neutral environment was endowed with positive value that it never had for the chicks that had not followed the object.

Research by Polt (1969) (discussed in Chapter 4) has also indicated that the qualities of the imprinting object can influence behavior in other situations. Another instance of this appears to be in the "social facilitation of feeding" phenomenon. This phenomenon, which has been known for decades, refers to the fact that chickens eat more when with conspecifics than when alone. Recently, Strobel, Freedman, and Macdonald (1970) showed not only that communally fed chicks eat and gain more weight than do ones fed in isolation but that ones *reared* communally also eat more, even when fed in isolation. Further experiments by the authors revealed that rearing in isolation had its most harmful effects during the first 3 days after hatching, since chicks reared communally during that life period and then placed in isolation continued to eat well, while those kept in isolation during the first 3 days after hatching and then kept communally showed no social faciliation of feeding during two days of testing. These findings have important implications for understanding the interrelationships between socialization and feeding. For many years, psychologists seriously considered the notion that off-spring come to love their parents through having been fed by them. This kind of cause-effect sequence does not appear to hold in many cases. It might even be possible that socialization can reinforce eating behavior, but, of course, we do not have sufficient evidence to state whether this might be true, particularly since the nature of the early social experience of the hatchling birds is related to whether the social facilitation of eat-ing occurs. It may be, on the other hand, that social factors operate prin-cipally through arousal. It is obvious that explicit experimentation is needed in order to clarify the role of socialization in the development of eating behavior.

The question of how early social and following experiences leave their mark (in terms of neurophysiological events) on the young bird is ob-viously a difficult one that will someday result in a tremendous amount of research. A beginning in this direction was made by Eiduson, Geller, and Beckwith (1961). Of several chemical constituents of the brain, they found that RNA (ribonuclease acid) and true cholinesterase were signif-icantly and highly negatively correlated with the amount of following that young New Hampshire chicks had done in two 30-minute sessions car-ried out at the age of 16 and 40 hours after hatching. Such correlations, however, could not be found for chicks that had been exposed to the object only once, at the age of 16 or 40 hours.

More recently, Bateson, Horn, and Rose (1969) reported significantly greater incorporation of radioactively tagged lysine (an amino acid) into the forebrain of 14 to 19-hour old early-hatching chicks that had been exposed to a flashing light stimulus for one hour and then re-exposed for 45 minutes to the light than among control chicks kept isolated, either in darkness or in light. Similarly, Rose, Bateson, Horn, and Horn (1970) found that while 100 minutes of light stimulation or imprinting increased RNA synthesis (as indicated by incorporation of tritiated uracil) in the midbrain and forebrain roof and base, 76 minutes of exposure significantly increased RNA synthesis only in the group that were im-printed. All comparisons of RNA synthesis were made with chicks that had been maintained in complete darkness since hatching. Horn, Horn, Bateson, and Rose (1971) have extended this research by using "split-brain" chicks.

Following Behavior and Fear Behavior.   Fear behavior has been as much implicated in the development and maintenance of following behavior in chicks as it has in ducks. Although the notion of fear behavior as a factor in terminating the responsiveness (as measured by following be-havior) of young as a function of increasing age was developed with reference to ducks, it has been assumed by many that whatever explains the decline of following behavior in ducks will also explain the same phenomenon in chicks.

Certainly, it is evident that with increasing age, as with ducks, there is an increasing appearance of fear behavior toward strange objects, at least in those that have had no previous social experience. For example, Jaynes (1958b) reported that naïve chicks confronted with a specific object for the first time at the age of 7 days showed great terror of it, and certainly did not follow it as long as they were so fearful. Several authors have agreed that the greater difficulty of eliciting following behavior and other positive responses in chicks toward a parental surrogate may actually be ascribable to differences in mechanisms in totally isolated chicks and those in chicks that have been communally reared, as suggested by Guiton (1959) and Salzen (1962a, b; 1963). This difference in the causal mechanisms lies in the fact that chicks which have been maintained with their siblings and then placed individually into an apparatus for exposure to a moving object may not refuse to follow that object through fear of it, but may actually be searching for their companions from which they have been separated, giving "distress calls" for them. If chicks have been previously totally isolated, then, of course, such searching behavior is not performed, and there does appear to be a true fear of the strange environment and strange object. Thus, as Guiton (1959) has proposed, it seems that prior social experiences do not act so as to reduce the following tendency but to increase the selectivity with which the chicks perform such behavior, so that only familiar social objects will be able to elicit it. Guiton cited his earlier (1958) finding—that socially reared chicks cease following sooner than isolated ones—as a support for his hypothesis.

Guiton also suggested that this could be a possible explanation of the loss of the initial unselective response toward moving objects in chicks that have already been exposed to one moving object and then are confronted with another at a later time. Guiton proposed that, under natural conditions, socialization of chicks to siblings and the hen is the principal factor, rather than fear per se, which determines the age at which chicks no longer can be induced to approach or follow new objects. As long as chicks are kept in groups, Guiton observed, they show no sign of "emotionality" or fear of a moving object and little tendency to follow it. But if a chick is taken away from the group, it will make distress calls until it has rejoined the other chicks.

On the basis of his own experimental observations, Salzen (1962a, b, 1963; Sluckin and Salzen, 1961) initially agreed with Guiton's formulations, and suggested that during the initial socialization to age mates or during the initial following of a parental object by previously unsocialized chicks, selectivity with respect to the objects that can elicit following behavior develops, with the result that fear responses, in the form of avoidance of strange objects, arise as a consequence. It is to be noted that Sluckin and Salzen (1961) specifically suggested that the fear arises as a consequence of socialization or of the attachment of following responses to a specific object, not solely as a developmentally timed event which then acts to prevent the elicitation of approach and following behavior by strange objects. In other words, the process of attaching following and approach responses to a class of objects is one that brings its own end, according to these authors. When this process has not taken place—that is, when chicks have been socially isolated—Sluckin and Salzen proposed that removal of fear and avoidance tendencies by means of habituation or drugs then permits following to be elicited. This is not the case, they maintain, in socialized chicks, for it appears that the proffered model is ignored by such chicks.

Salzen (1962a, b; 1963) then went on to gather experimental data relevant to the question of fear behavior in response to a potential parent object. He reared brown leghorn × light Sussex chicks in individual isolation or in groups for periods varying from 0 to 7 days. At the end of the rearing experience, the chicks were placed alone with a silent moving or stationary object (a red cardboard box or a brown cardboard cylinder) or with one or more other chicks; the incidence of fear responses was then observed. It appeared to Salzen that the fear behavior might be independent of age but dependent upon the difference between the test situation and the rearing environment. All chicks, whether isolated or socially reared, showed fear of the test environment at all ages. The moving object was feared only by birds that had had a minimum of 24 hours of social experience with age mates, and therefore had a "familiar moving object percept." Thus, the fear of the new environment could also be alleviated in socially reared chicks if other chicks were also present; no such effect could be observed in isolated chicks.

Salzen (1963) further studied the ontogenetic development of fear behavior in brown leghorn × light Sussex chicks by investigating the relationship between the performance of the "immobility" response and length of social isolation. The immobility response of chicks is one that is usually elicited by turning it upside down and holding it down on its back for several seconds. It is considered a consequence of fear, particularly since in other animals it is readily elicited when the person that turns the animal on its back is one that has never handled the animal before and therefore is strange (Moore and Amstey, 1962). Isolated chicks tended not to show the immobility reaction at all, consonant with the results that have been obtained with mammals. In Salzen's study, socially maintained chicks did not show it until the age of 8 days, and showed it more strongly at the age of 14 to 16 days. However, they showed it less when they were tested in the presence of other chicks. Thus, it appeared that isolated chicks do not develop the type of fear responses conducive to the appearance of the immobility reaction, and that socially reared chicks' fear responses are attenuated by the presence of peers. While Salzen suggested that the socially reared chicks' fear reactions were largely due to separation from their companions, we feel that more research is needed before this type of conclusion is fully warranted.

Bateson (1963, 1964a, b, c) is another investigator who has studied the ontogentic development of fear behavior in relation to the responses of chicks to moving objects acting as potential parental surrogates. In his 1963 thesis, Bateson noted that when isolated Rhode Island red × light Sussex chicks were exposed at different ages for the first time to a moving object, the greatest avoidance of that object was apparent at the age of 3 days. Bateson's other papers (1964a, b, c) have studied the influence of the complexity of the rearing environment upon the chicks' avoidance responses upon presentation of a silent moving model.

Bateson (1964a) kept Rhode Island red × light Sussex chicks in individual compartments with black and white vertical stripes or yellow and red horizontal stripes from the time of hatching. At the age of 3 days, the age at which he had earlier found the most intense avoidance of moving objects, the chicks were individually exposed to either a model having the black and white stripes or one having yellow and red stripes. The chicks showed a much higher persistence of avoidance to the pattern they had not seen previously. Bateson (1964b) reared the chicks in individual compartments painted with one of the three following designs: dark gray alone; gray and red horizontal stripes; white and red stripes with red circles between the stripes. Retesting for avoidance behavior was done at the age of 3 days. In this case one of three designs (plain gray; red and gray; white and gray) was presented motionless for 20 minutes to individual chicks. It was found that the chicks that had been kept in the red and white compartments showed more avoidance behavior than did the chicks kept in compartments with either of the other two designs. The chicks kept in plain gray compartments, on the other hand, showed the least avoidance behavior, especially to the red and gray model. Those that had been kept in red and gray striped compartments showed the most avoidance to the white and red striped model and the same low degree of avoidance to the gray and the red and gray models.

Since it was possible that the gray-reared chicks showed the least avoidance because the walls of the testing apparatus were also gray, Bateson performed another experiment in which the chicks were reared as before and tested as before, except that the outer wall of the runway was painted with red and white vertical stripes. It was found that the chicks reared with gray walls still had the lowest avoidance scores, particularly to the gray model, and those reared with white and red walls had the highest avoidance scores, particularly to the white and red model. Clearly, the relationship between rearing conditions, model characteristics, and apparatus characteristics in the manifestation of avoidance behavior in chicks is complex indeed. It does appear that the effects of the environment upon the chicks' behavior toward an object are greatest in those that were maintained in individual compartments having the most complex design—the red and white stripes with red circles between the stripes—since chicks thus reared evidenced the most persistent avoidance behavior to potential social objects.

There have been several studies which indicate an increase in fear behavior and avoidance behavior in chicks with increasing age. Schaller and Emlen (1962) investigated several different chick species—white leghorn × New Hampshire red, white leghorn, mixed bantam, Plymouth rock, buttercup, minorca, and rose-comb bantam. While there were certainly differences among the various breeds, Schaller and Emlen found that avoidance behaviors in response to visual stimuli usually appeared in all these breeds before the age of 10 hours and then gradually increased in intensity to the age of 100 to 140 hours—that is, 4 to 6 days of age. Normally, the responsiveness was relatively low at the age of 10 hours or less, but achieved, in gradual steps, a near-plateau level by the age of 40 to 80 hours. Some birds were reared in complete darkness from the first few days of life up to varying periods. The avoidance behavior of deprived birds was equal to, or greater than, that shown by the control chicks maintained in normal visual conditions. Of interest is the fact that, on the first test, the birds visually isolated 1 or 2 days were equal to the controls in intensity of avoidance behavior, and then, on the next test, showed greater avoidance behavior than the controls did. On the third test, the avoidance response returned to the control level. This phenomenon did not, for some reason, occur in those isolated visually for 3 days. On the basis of the data obtained in their studies, Schaller and Emlen concluded: "Since birds raised in complete darkness during the first few days developed their avoidance tendencies to visual stimulus objects at a rate comparable to the controls, the ontogenetic process involved is, we feel, largely maturational, i.e., relatively independent of sensory experience."

Such an interpretation, however, has by no means been generally accepted. Salzen (1962a, b, 1963), for example, has concluded, on the basis of his experimental work, that fear behavior in chicks appears by virtue of experience rather than with age, since fear behavior was more prominent in chicks that were in surroundings having a higher degree of unfamiliarity to them during testing. Certainly, it has been found that environmental factors influence the manifestations of fear in young chicks. For example, Kaufman and Hinde (1961) observed that in both white leghorn and Rhode Island red chicks, environmental temperature, separation from age mates, and age were all factors in the rate of distress calls. At an environmental temperature of 110°F, socially reared chicks tested while separated from their companions showed a significant increase in distress calling after the age of 3 days; in isolated chicks, there was also an increase, but not a significant one. When chicks were tested in a cold 60°F environment, the rate of distress calls were maximal, with the result that no increase due to age could be observable. Kaufman and Hinde concluded that the question of the development of fear behavior is, indeed, a complex one, since different factors may operate in the various species and according to the experimental arrangements used, both pretest maintenance and test procedure itself.

A study by Candland, Nagy, and Conklyn (1963) and one by Phillips and Siegel (1966) illustrate further such complexities. Candland, Nagy, and Conklyn showed that the emotional behavior of white leghorn chicks, as reflected by the number of eliminations during an open field test, increased to a maximum during the first 2 weeks of life and then declined to a stable plateau. The number of chicks giving distress calls was highest during the first 8 days of life, and then decreased to a low level, where it remained thereafter. Candland, Nagy, and Conklyn then compared the incidence of freezing behavior and eliminations in an open field test with preferential object choice in chicks that had been reared from the age of 1 day to 25 days in individual isolation or in a group, with or without small manipulable objects present in the rearing environments. In the open field test, with a fear-provoking mechanical toy present, both communal rearing and the presence of the small objects in the rearing environment served to decrease the incidence of emotional behaviors in the subjects. In the social preference test, in which the manipulable objects were placed in one compartment and an age mate in another compartment, it was found that communal rearing caused chicks to spend more time with the age mate. Object rearing also caused chicks to spend more time with the objects than when the chicks had not been reared with them, in both isolated and communally reared groups.

The observations of Phillips and Siegel (1966) on two closely related lines of the same white rock chick breed have shown that the development of fear behavior is influenced by social experience and age in different ways in the two lines. These two lines of white Plymouth rock chicks had been developed on the basis of selection for high and low body weight at the age of 8 weeks, and the subjects were offspring from matings of F_6 generation animals of this breeding. Chicks were tested for responses to a sudden loud noise at one of the following ages: 6, 12, 18, 24, 36, 48, 72, 120, 144, and 168 hours. In spite of the complex differences between the two lines and social groups, it was still apparent that, generally speaking, the peak of fear behavior was at about the age of 2 to 3 days, an observation which agrees with that of Bateson (1963). It then declined to a plateau which remained well above the initial level.

Phillips' and Siegel's observation that newly hatched chicks 6 hours old show relatively little emotional responsiveness to the sound stimuli employed is congruent with reports of several other researchers that the level of emotionality appears at a low level in hatchlings soon after emergence from the shell and that novel stimuli are more readily tolerated at an early age. While, as Phillips and Siegel noted, distress calls can be heard before chicks hatch, they contend that the emission of such sounds are reflexive in nature and are later triggered by some of the same stimuli that elicit fear. They noted Fishman and Tallarico's (1961) report that no emotional response to a finger poke could be elicited from chicks at the age of 3 hours. Other reports by James and Binks (1963) and Fischer and Campbell (1964) have shown that apparently neither active nor passive avoidance responses can be learned by newly hatched chicks. Avoidance learning first appears at about the age of 3 days, and is shown by the majority of chicks at the age of 5 days. This indicates that maturational processes are, to a large degree, responsible for the appearance of such learning. Thus, fear responses may truly be said to appear as a function of maturation, with environmental factors serving to either hasten or retard the appearance of fear behavior. However, the function of fear in relation to following behavior is highly complex. At one point, when animals have not previously followed or become attached to an object, fear tendencies may serve to prevent the formation of any such attachment to any object. When such attachments have been already formed, fear may intensify the manifestation of such attachment and may be seen either in renewed following or in frantic search behavior when the object is absent.

The effects of early following experience on later responses in stress situations have been considered by Thompson and O'Kieffe (1962). These authors exposed vantress chicks to a silent moving object—a waddled bundle of linen wrapped in white cheesecloth—for 10 minutes at 9, 12, and 15 hours of age, and had them see it stationary in the meantime, from the age of 4 to 20 hours. At the age of 28 hours, these chicks and controls that had never seen the object were subjected to sound stress. One half of each group had the object present during the stress, and the others did not. Those that had lived with and followed the surrogate during the 1st day of life showed only a slight increase in the rate of distress calls, regardless of whether the object was present or absent. However, among those that had never seen the object before, seeing the object for the first time caused a doubling of the distress call rate, in comparison with those that did not have it present. The introduction of the sound stress caused the chicks of the latter group to double their distress call rate. The distress call rate was also doubled in the ones that did not have the strange object present. However, since their initial distress call rate was low, the introduction of sound stress had the effect of raising this call rate to the same level as that manifested by the experimental chicks that had lived with a parental surrogate.

Other Precocial Species

Ducks and chicks certainly have provided the bulk of experimental material for the study of following and early social behavior in precocial bird species, even though Lorenz's 1935 paper usually cited examples of the social imprinting process from the greylag goose.

Hinde (1955), and Hinde, Thorpe, and Vince (1956) reported on their studies of following behavior in young coots and moorhens. They confirmed that a large variety of moving objects, silent or vocal, could elicit following in hatchlings of these two species. A wooden moorhen model, a black box, and a large brown canvas hide were among the models used. They were able to get the young birds to address following to different models presented successively, just as chicks and ducklings can be so induced. The authors noted that such following behavior was independent of conventional reinforcement factors such as brooding or feeding.

Moorhens appeared to be more susceptible than coots were to fear tendencies—a factor which caused these birds to follow models less strongly than coots did. In fact, the increase of fear behavior in moorhens with advancing age was such that it was obviously much easier to elicit following in moorhens on the 1st day after hatching than if several days were allowed to pass. Hinde, Thorpe, and Vince suggested that fear behavior, as reflected in flight tendencies, being incompatible with following behavior, was an important factor in limiting the period of time in which young birds of these species could be positively conditioned to a model so that they would follow it.

Stevens (1955) reported that a young lesser white-fronted goose that separated from its flock at about the age of 5 days eventually came to follow him after 5 days in captivity. Stevens noted that this process was accompanied by a reduction of fear toward humans, which was initially extremely intense.

Melvin et al. (1967) have worked on imprinting bobwhite quail to a sparrow hawk, which, under natural conditions, is a predator of quail. One subject which had been attacked by the hawk, when the hawk inadvertently had not been fed prior to the experimental session, later showed an extremely strong attachment to the hawk, thus paralleling Hess' (1964) finding that toe stepping on ducklings enhances their attachment to the careless human being. Other studies of bobwhite quail have conducted by Porter and Stettner (1968a, b). As with domestic chicks, vocal models were found to elicit attachment behavior better than silent ones did. Hatchling quails were presented with a green rectangular box that emitted repetitive beeps. Then different groups were tested for attachment to some variation of the original stimulus object. It was found that the original auditory stimulus was more important in the formation of attachment than was the original visual stimulus. In another experiment, hatchlings were exposed during the 1st day of life to the beeping green rectangular box. On the next day, half of the young birds were exposed to a beeping red cylinder, while the other half saw it silent. On the 3rd day, those that had been exposed to the beeping red cylinder showed a stronger attachment to it than did the ones that saw it silent, even though all birds were shown the red cylinder as a silent object during the test. In other words, the birds were able to become attached to a new visual object when it was associated with the auditory characteristics of the original exposure object, and to show evidence of this attachment, even when these auditory characteristics were not present during a subsequent test.

Japanese quail (*Coturnix coturnix*) have been found to follow substitute parental objects readily (Ozmon, 1970; Martin Schein, personal communication). The proactive and retroactive effects of electroconvulsive shock (ECS) upon imprinting in this species have also been studied (Ozmon, 1969). Greylag geese were originally studied by Lorenz (1935), but little has been published regarding imprinting in this species. In recent years, Fabricius and Fält (1969) and Schutz (1969) have reported on studies of sexual imprinting and the possibility of innate reaction to nuptial male coloration in relation to the coloration of the imprinting object.

Turkeys can also be induced to follow substitute parent objects. Christopher and Hale (1968) found that presenting a turkey poult with a stimulus object for 20 minutes daily for 5 consecutive days results in sustained attachment to the substitute object. Schulman (1970) has found that, when tested in the presence of the substitute parent object after the 5-day imprinting procedure and 7-day isolation experience, 12-day old male turkey poults often may, even though not treated with any androgen injections, make their first response to the substitute object in the form of a sexual strut for a few seconds, after which, approach and following behavior ensue. Schleidt (1970) has similarly reported that immature turkey poults during the first 100 days of life commonly strut toward familiar social objects; siblings, a parent, or a human being —if imprinted to humans.

Approach and following behavior has been studied in a semi-precocial species—the ring-billed gull, *Larus delawarensis*—during its first days of life. Though these birds can move at an early age, they stay at or near the nest site, where they are fed by the adults. Evans (1970) has suggested that imprinting occurs in this species, and has discussed some of the possible bases and species survival advantages of imprinting for ring-billed gulls.

EARLY REARING AND SOCIALIZATION

A number of studies of the early socialization of birds have not centered their attention primarily upon the manifestation of following behavior. Such experiments usually have concerned themselves with the effects of early rearing experience and concomitant social experience during the early rearing period.

We will begin this topic by considering a group of experiments that have continuously reared young chicks individually, either with motionless stimuli that form part of their environment or to living stimuli with which they cannot make physical contact, for a period of time, usually several days; the chicks were than tested for preferences for being near the familiar stimulus rather than another, unfamiliar, one presented at the same time. While such a procedure may actually constitute a type of environment learning, we will discuss this group of experiments here because of the investigators' belief that they are relevant for understanding the nature of early socialization processes in birds.

In the first study utilizing such a procedure, Baer and Gray (1960) placed white rock chicks after hatching in individual isolation compartments. These compartments were constructed so that the chicks could see an adult guinea pig, either black or white, in another compartment next to their own and separated from it by a piece of transparent glass. Different groups of chicks saw the guinea pig for 24 hours at different ages from the 1st to the 4th day. On the 7th day of age, chicks were individually tested for half an hour for preferences for being near a guinea pig of the color they had seen or one of the other color. Both guinea pigs were simultaneously present, each being on one side of the chick's isolation compartment and visible through the glass partition. The amounts of time the chicks spent on the half of their own compartment next to each guinea pig were recorded automatically. It was reported that the chicks that had seen a guinea pig during the 2nd day of age showed the highest preference for the guinea pig that was the same color as the one they had seen, in comparison with other chicks which had seen a guinea pig on other days of life.

This type of procedure was repeated by Gray, but motionless geometric objects, instead of guinea pigs, were used as the exposure stimuli. These objects were: a circle with a diameter of 3½ inches, and an equilateral triangle with sides of 4 inches; both were black. Three groups of white rock chicks were exposed to one of these stimuli for 24 hours, at the 3rd, 4th, and 5th days of age, in their individual isolation compartments, as described above. At the end of the 24-hour exposure period (rather than at the 7th day of age, as in the earlier experiment), chicks were tested for their preference between the object they had just seen for 24 hours and the other one, both presented simultaneously for 15 minutes on each side of the chicks' individual isolation compartments. The day 3 group spent a mean of 3.65 minutes near the familiar model; the day 4 group, a mean of 5.77 minutes; and the day 5 group, a mean of 7.83 minutes. Since the chicks were not all tested at the same age, the results are not completely comparable with those of Baer and Gray (1960). In addition, the behavior of the chicks could be just as well ascribable to fear of the new object rather than to attachment to the old one, or perhaps to a combination of both factors. Thus, it is difficult to interpret these findings meaningfully.

In addition to the study by Candland, Nagy, and Conklyn (1963), which we have discussed earlier, two other studies have investigated the influence of static inanimate stimulus objects in the environment on the subsequent behavior of chicks toward these objects (Brown, 1964; and Taylor and Taylor, 1964). Candland, Nagy, and Conklyn, it will be remembered, found that the presence of small manipulable objects in the rearing environment caused the chicks that had seen them to show a greater preference for being near them than was evident in chicks that had never seen these objects before.

In Brown's (1964) study, the 5th post-hatch day appeared to be the most sensitive time for silver oklabar broiler chicks to develop a preference for a particular color for the large food box placed in their individual isolation compartments. Since the food box was of a size that permitted chicks to go *inside* of it, this may represent more fully a form of environment learning and not involve any type of social responses.

Social responses may or may not be more evident in the experiment by Taylor and Taylor (1964). Here, chicks of a commerical breed hatched in the laboratory were put in individual isolation upon hatching. Half of the chicks had a cardboard box suspended on one wall of the living compartment; the others had a foam rubber object similarly hung. After 48 hours of such rearing, the strength of social responses to the objects, simultaneously present in a larger pen, was tested. The box-reared subjects showed less of an attachment to the box than the foam-reared subjects showed to the foam object: 6 of the box-reared stayed in the area near the box, 9 stayed in a neutral area during the test period, and one approached both the box and the foam object; none of the foam-reared subjects ever went near the box, 4 stayed in the neutral area, with 12 remaining near the foam object. Attachment was also measured by the incidence of chicks that actually made physical contact with any of the objects. None of the 16 chicks that engaged in physical contact did this with the object that they had not been reared with. The greater attachment of the foam-reared subjects was also evident in the fact that 11 of the 12 approaching it touched it, and only 4 of the 6 box-reared approaching the box touched it. Taylor and Taylor suggested that the greater softness of the foam object and the opportunity to go *inside* it may have been responsible for the more intense attachments shown by the foam-reared subjects. An experiment by Taylor and Sluckin (1964a) has indicated that such tactile factors can achieve considerable influence in the development of approach behavior in domestic chicks.

However, all these rearing experiments that we have just discussed were of rather short range, and no follow-up was continued to relatively advanced ages. While long-range studies on the effects of early social experiences on the later behavior of birds are certainly fewer in number than those on the following response, they are sufficient in quantity to provide a large amount of evidence.

We will proceed to consider the effects of early rearing experience, first, in precocial bird species and, then, in altricial bird species. Precocial bird species, as we have mentioned earlier, are ones in which the young are feathered (or downy) at birth and can move about on their own soon after hatching. Because of their ability to leave the nest, even during the first day after hatching, they are sometimes called nidifugous birds. Altricial birds, on the other hand, are entirely helpless and relatively naked when hatched, and must stay in the nest for a few weeks and be cared for by the parents. Their physical and locomotor development is much less advanced, therefore, at hatching than is that of the precocial birds. They are sometimes termed nidicolous birds, since they do stay in the nest. In precocial birds, following activity and flocking behavior can form prominent components of the early primary socialization process, while in altricial birds, such obviously is not the case. It is often true, however, that altricial birds are reared in the nest in the company of siblings.

Precocial Bird Species

Long-range studies of the development of social behavior in domestic fowl are relatively recent. Various aspects of the effects of early social isolation on later social behavior of white rock chickens have been studied by Baron and Kish (1960) and by Baron, Kish, and Antonitis (1962). In the first study, 10 white rock chicks were maintained in complete social isolation from any living creature to the age of 4 weeks; 10 others were kept in pairs during this time; and 10 more were kept together in a group. At the end of the 4-week treatment period, animals were individually tested in an apparatus consisting of a compartment bilaterally flanked by two display compartments partitioned off by glass panes, similar to Gray's (1961a) apparatus. One of the compartments contained an age mate, and the other was empty. It was found that the isolated chicks spent significantly less time near the age mate than did the members of the other two groups, which did not at all differ from each other in this respect. All chicks were then placed in communal rearing groups, and then retested at the age of 10 weeks. None of the 3 groups were in any way distinguishable from the others in the amount of time spent in front of the compartment containing the age mate. Thus, it appears that socially isolated chicks can learn to prefer being near conspecifics rather than an empty space as a result of prolonged exposure to them.

The subsequent study (Baron, Kish, and Antonitis, 1962) on the effects of conspecific social isolation at different life periods had three groups of white rock chicks. The first group was kept in social contact for the first 10 weeks of life; another group, for only the first week of life, after which its members were individually isolated up to the age of 10 weeks; and the third was isolated during the first week of life and then kept socially during the subsequent 9 weeks. Several facets emerged from the results of social testing carried out on all subjects at the age of 5 and 10 weeks. As might be expected, the chicks that had been socially reared throughout showed the strongest social behavior toward age mates, and had the lowest activity scores at both test sessions. Activity scores were highest at all times for the isolated animals. However, while the isolated-social animals were indistinguishable from the social animals in activity and social scores at the age of 5 weeks, they were very much like the social-isolated animals in these two respects at the age of 10 weeks. While the authors concluded that contemporary isolation had the most effect on the degree of social behavior shown by chicks, their data show also that early social experiences have lasting effects, ones which may not be immediately apparent but which show up at a later time. This sleeper effect shows that, just because at one age an earlier experience does not appear to differentiate experimental animals from a control group, this is no reason to assume that at a later age the same will still be the case.

A somewhat different aspect of adult social behavior—fighting—has been studied as a function of early social experience in Japanese gray quails by Kuo (1960a, b). Half of these quails were kept in isolation from other species members from the time of hatching, with the remaining quails kept in group-living conditions during this time. Half of the subjects in each group were trained over a 2-month period to fight, beginning at the age of 8 months. At the end of training, at the age of 10 months, all quails were tested for fighting behavior. It was found that there was a higher proportion of intense fighters (25 percent) among untrained isolated birds than among untrained socially reared birds (10 percent). Among trained birds, there was still a higher proportion (60 percent) of intense fighters among the isolation-reared birds than among the socialized ones. When the birds were injected with testosterone propionate or with thiamine extract, the proportion of such fighters among all birds were increased, but there were still more fighters among the isolation-raised birds than among the socially-reared ones. In other words, both drugs and training had more effect, in terms of producing fighters, among isolated birds than among socialized ones. The effect of early isolation experience was, in fact, often greater than training experiences at maturity, though not significantly so. The effect of drugs in producing fighting behavior was minimal in comparison.

While the effects of such early isolation could be mitigated to some extent by later social rearing, Kuo found that such isolation-reared quails never lost their solitary habits and indifference to conspecifics.

Fisher and Hale (1957) reported the effects of isolation from members of the species from hatching to sexual maturity at an unspecified age on the sexual and aggressive behavior of 2 male New Hampshire and 4 male barred Plymouth rock chickens. When individually placed in a pen of females of both breeds, four waltzed, but none ever mounted a female or made any copulatory movements. This is in contrast to the behavior of 17 New Hampshire males which had been normally reared and then kept in all-male flocks since the age of 10 weeks: under similar conditions, 14 waltzed, 12 mounted, and 9 copulated with a female. After the isolated cocks had been penned together as a group for a few days, they were tested for a week for sexual behavior to nonreceptive females that had been reared in isolation but recently lived in a group for several weeks. One male showed the complete mating pattern, but directed it to the shoe of a person, after having waltzed to a female. After this testing, with all-male group living continued, 6 of the males were tested with sexually receptive normally reared hens.

These retests elicited these males' first complete sexual reactions to a species member: 5 waltzed, 2 mounted, and 1 attempted copulation. In a second retest, all 6 birds waltzed, 2 mounted and 1 gave a complete mating reaction, including copulation, to a hen. Continued tests with the females eventually resulted in 3 males carrying out complete mating patterns. However, Fisher, and Hale noted two highly unusual features of their sexual behavior: all males would waltz in front of the hens, but if a hen crouched, the sexually receptive female posture, the male would interrupt his waltz and walk away. Furthermore, no male was ever seen to mount, or attempt to mount, a squatting hen: all the mating behaviors were forced on a standing or fleeing hen, rather than performed on a behaviorally receptive hen. The one male that mounted people's shoes never mounted a hen. Thus we see that there were relativly persistent effects of the isolation experience upon the sexual behavior of these New Hampshire and barred Plymouth rock cocks.

Kruijt (1962a, b, 1964) has studied the effects of 9 to 16 months of social isolation from conspecifics on the adult social-sexual behavior of Burmese red jungle fowl cocks. The results of his investigations, although carried out with a different domestic fowl species, bear several similarities to those of Baron and Kish, particularly with respect to the specific behaviors exhibited by the isolated jungle fowl cocks during the tests with a receptive female. Specifically, Kruijt (1962b) noted that males that had lived at least 10 months in isolation from conspecifics would court the female by waltzing; but when the female responded by giving the sexually receptive crouch, they either paid no attention, or walked away, or persisted in waltzing, or attacked the female by kicking her, or failed to mount but pecked her head instead.

While, as Kruijt noted, such behaviors may sometimes be seen in normally reared males during initial encounters with females, they are persistent in isolation-reared males to the extent that there are no copulatory attempts such as normal males make. In contrast, all jungle fowl cocks that had had conspecific social experience, even though it was as members of an all-male group, during at least the first 11 months of life, even if there had been an intervening period of social isolation for as much as 14 months, established successful copulatory behavior with females after a few encounters with them. Two of the 11 isolated cocks did copulate with the female: 1 that had been isolated for only 9 months copulated in two tests, and the other, which had been isolated 14 months, took 14 such tests and 1 week of continuous living with a female before copulation with her occurred. Four of the unsuccessful cocks were retested at the age of 2 and/or 3 years; they were still unsuccessful in establishing copulatory behavior toward females. One of these that never tried to copulate with females would attempt to copulate with a feather held in his bill and perform the copulatory trampling on the floor of the pen.

Kruijt (1962b) also noted that the aggressive and escape behaviors of the isolated cocks were highly abnormal, even during the early isolation-rearing period. Mad dashing about the isolation cage, ducking in corners, and frequent screaming were especially apparent in a stage which they usually passed through. Such fits would sometimes last for hours, with the stimuli releasing such behavior not at all apparent. Sometimes it appeared as if they were attempting to escape from parts of their own body, particularly the legs and sometimes the tail. Kruijt remarked that such "hysterical fits" were unlike anything he had even observed in group-raised chicks. Sometime between 4 months and 1 year of age, such behavior changed to aggressive behavior in the isolated cocks. They would begin by directing aggression to their tail feathers, practically pulling them out. Later, humans might be attacked. Although escape behavior usually changed to aggressive behavior in isolated cocks, their behavior was still abnormal in comparison with group-reared cocks, with respect to both the objects chosen for the aggression and the greater temporal duration of such aggressive attacks.

In a more detailed exposition of his research findings, Kruijt (1964) confirmed the fact that all cocks raised in sight of humans but in isolation from conspecifics for at least 6 months and less than 10 months could show copulatory behavior with females, although their initial copulatory behavior was in many respects abnormal. Only 25 percent of other males kept in such isolation to later ages were able to show copulatory behavior. One of these males was 10 months old at test, and the other lived with a female for one week before showing copulatory behavior, as we earlier noted. Kruijt also found that similar periods of social isolation did not deleteriously affect the copulatory behavior of cocks that had been reared socially for as little as the first 2½ months of life for all such cocks could perform adequately. Kruijt concluded that early social deprivation of jungle fowl cocks did not remove the motor components of their social behavior, but affected the way in which the social behavior was released, oriented, and integrated. Unlike those of Fisher and Hale (1957), none of Kruijt's isolated cocks directed copulatory behavior toward humans.

In this report of Kruijt (1964), the behavior of partially isolated female birds of this species was noted. Some of these females were seen to go through a stage of excessive escape behavior, with a few later developing tail fighting. They did not attack humans, but most showed crouching in response to humans when adulthood was reached. When tested with courting males at ages between 9 and 12 months, they all avoided them strongly, and none was ever seen to crouch in response to the display of the male. All copulations which did occur were due to force on the part of the male.

Kruijt (1962b, 1964, 1971) suggested that his data indicated the existence of a sensitive period, during which cocks have the ability to organize copulatory activity. If isolated cocks are tested as late as the age of 9 months, copulatory behavior can be established. After this age, however, this becomes progressively more difficult, Kruijt also proposed that, as a result of deficiency in social experience, isolated cocks lack the normal ambivalence between aggression and escape behavior, a prerequisite for successful copulatory behavior.

Further research by Kruijt (1971) has shown that isolation from hatching until the age of 15 months or longer results in the permanent loss of copulatory ability in male jungle fowl. Such cocks, however, can still display to the hen. On the other hand, if isolation is not begun until the age of 10 weeks, lengthy isolation of 16 or more months does not prevent the establishment of copulatory behavior. Kruijt has suggested that the mechanisms underlying sexual behavior in male jungle fowls are set during the age period 6 to 10 weeks, probably through the performance of incomplete sexual behavior.

The findings of Wood-Gush (1958), that there were no clear-cut differences in the sexual behavior of socially isolated or homosexually reared 6½-month old brown leghorn cocks, are in accord with Kruijt's results with wild jungle fowl. Experimental results obtained by Siegel and Siegel (1964), although based on a different breed, are also remarkably congruent with those of Kruijt.

Siegel and Siegel reared cockerels of an unspecified breed in sex-mixed flocks until the age of 58, 70, or 84 days, when they were either isolated or put in all-male groups. At the age of 7 months, their mating behavior toward receptive females in a group was observed. Those cocks that had first been placed in isolation at the age of 84 days were no different in their sexual behavior toward tester female groups, in terms of incidence of waltzes, mounts, treads, and completed matings (copulations), from those put into all-male flocks at the same age. There were a few statistically significant differences at the .05 level between the isolated and grouped cocks when the removal had taken place at the age of 70 days. However, comparison between the isolated and grouped cocks of both 70- and 84-day groups makes them appear essentially identical. Both of these groups had had social experience almost equaling, or even exceeding, the 2½ months (75 days) that Kruijt had reported to be sufficient for the emergence of sexual behavior directed toward conspecific females. With the cocks isolated from the age of 58 days, however, a considerable decrement in sexual behavior was found. These cocks performed fewer mounts, fewer treads, and fewer complete matings. These differences were all significant at the .01 level. Presumably, such cocks would eventually bring their sexual behavior up to the normal level with increased social experience. However, it is of interest that these findings of a sufficiency of less than two months' social experience in allowing some immediate manifestation of sexual behavior to be apparent are completely in accord with those Kruijt obtained with the wild Burmese red jungle fowl.

A study by Bambridge (1962) has provided relatively clear evidence of a distinct preferential object choice as a function of early rearing and following experience in domestic chicks. Hatchling New Hampshire red × barred rock and pure barred rock chicks were reared with one of two silent moving objects (a blue or a yellow toilet float) for different periods. One group lived with its model from the 2nd to 9th days of life, and saw it move about for 10 hours daily. Another group had this experience from the 10th to 17th day and a third group saw and lived with the model during the entire period from the 2nd to the 17th day of life. In the meantime, all chicks were injected with testosterone propionate daily, beginning on the 5th day of life.

On the 19th and 20th days of life, the yellow and blue models were placed simultaneously in the chicks' individual living cages, and their sexual behavior to the models was observed for 10 minutes on both days. There was a clear-cut difference in the behavior of the birds that had been with the moving model (and therefore had followed it), beginning with the 2nd day of age and the behavior of those that had not seen a model until the 10th day of age. It made no difference whether the birds had been with the moving model for 8 or 15 days. Of 23 birds with this experience, 19 exhibited sexual behavior, with 18 treading only the model which they had been with. The remaining bird trod the familiar model 12 of 13 times. The late-exposed group, however, had only 1 bird that showed sexual behavior—it trod the model it had been with. Even during the early living experiences with the moving models, there was a difference in the mean amount of time that the subjects were observed to follow between those that were with a model beginning at the earlier age and those that did not begin until the 10th day of age. In fact, the amount of following was about six or seven times greater for the early-exposed chicks. Thus, we can clearly see that there is an effect of the age of exposure on the extent to which initial following experience will promote object choice at a later age. We may note, in concluding our consideration of Bambridge's report, that his findings are congruent with the fact that Noble and Zitrin (1942) had found that individually hand-reared isolated white leghorn chicks which had been given sex hormones reacted sexually to the human hand at the age of 24 days.

Further study (Guiton 1961, 1962a, b) has indicated that early social and following experiences can influence the object choice made in sexual situations by domestic chicks. Brown leghorn cockerels were either isolated or socially reared. Initial exposure to a vocal moving object (either a triangular green and brown box or a rectangular blue and orange box) took place for one hour on the second day after hatching. The model emitted a broody hen call. This exposure was repeated on each of the three subsequent days. Some of the birds were individually trained to follow the model, while others were trained in a group. Still others were habituated to the motionless model, and the remainder were placed in the exposure apparatus with no model in it. Tests of behavior toward the model were carried out at 1, 3, 6, 8, 12, and 24 weeks of age. Up to the age of 8 or 12 weeks, following behavior was predominant in those that had been trained to follow the model. At the age of 6 weeks, and especially at the age of 8 weeks, these birds tended to react aggressively to the model, in the same way that chicks normally react to their age mates. Such reactions were not seen in the birds that were habituated to the exposure apparatus, with or without the model being present. After 12 weeks of age, only 2 birds, both of which had been intensive followers, continued to respond to the model. These 2 birds continued to court the model by waltzing, even during the last test, carried out at the age of nearly 14 months, so that the effect of the early social experience with the model appeared permanent.

None of these subjects was given androgen treatment. This was done in the next study (Guiton 1962a, b). Young male brown leghorns were hand-reared and given androgen treatment during the first 3 weeks of life. Later testing revealed that even though the androgens induced sexual behavior, they did not intensify the effects of the early rearing experience on later sexual behavior. Guiton found that although such early hand rearing induced sexual attachments to humans, a preference for conspecific hens would be shown in a free choice situation at sexual maturity. Nevertheless, the effects of the early hand rearing were not lost. If a cock were given unrestricted sexual activity with conspecific females, it would then show an apparent and transient preference for humans through selective habituation of responsiveness to hens.

Another study (Ratner, 1965) has indicated that less than 2 months of social isolation—70 days from hatching—did not prevent white Cobb cocks from developing organized social behavior. This, again, is congruent with Kruijt's (1964) finding that wild Burmese red jungle fowl isolated from conspecifics up to 9 months from hatching still were able to develop mating behavior toward females, although with abnormalities in the initial expression of such behavior. Ratner tabulated the incidence of four patterns of social behaviors in normally reared and socially isolated cockerels. The isolated subjects showed these four patterns during isolation, but there was a consistent delay in their appearance.

The effects of early social experience or isolation on the social and sexual behavior of androgen-injected turkeys has been investigated by Schein and Hale (1959a, b). Male and female white Holland turkey poults were placed into isolation from species members or into small groups from the time of hatching. Some of the group-reared birds were subsequently placed into social isolation at the age of 10, 11, or 20 days. At the age of 32 days, all birds were put into a large community pen. Daily injections of testosterone propionate were begun on the 6th or 7th day of age to induce precocious male sexual behavior. Tests of sexual behavior as early as the age of 23 to 24 days and through 5 to 8 weeks of age showed that subjects of each group performed complete strutting patterns. Males in both group-reared and group-reared-isolated groups usually showed fully organized copulatory actions during the first test. Thus, the development of normal sexual behavior patterns in these turkeys did not appear to depend solely upon early social or sexual experience. In fact, Schulman (1970) has found that transitory struts are made by uninjected male turkey poults at the age of 12 days in response to a surrogate parent.

The treatment groups, however, did differ with respect to the stimuli which released sexual behavior. While birds that had had early group living experience reacted predominantly to a turkey head, those reared in isolation addressed their sexual behavior predominantly to the observer's hand. These results are similar to those of Noble and Zitrin (1942) with white leghorn chicks.

Later, Schein (1963a, b) reported on the sexual behavior of 6 survivors of the 1959 investigation that had reached the age of 5 years. Three of these birds had been reared in isolation from conspecifics; 2 of the others had been reared in groups of 5 birds—1 for 10 days, the other for 20 days, after which they were maintained in isolation until the age of 32 days, the sixth bird had been maintained in a group of other birds during the entire 32-day period. While the first 3 birds were those that showed sexual preference for humans at the age of 32 days, and the last 3 preferred other turkeys as sexual objects at the same age, all 6 were in adulthood and, at the time of the second investigation, tame to both turkeys and humans. They had all lived together in a standard turkey pen from the age of 32 days until the age of 5 years, at which time they were individually isolated for a period of ten days and then given a choice between the observer and a group of young females. All 3 of the group-reared turkeys showed a preference for conspecifics, while all 3 of the isolation-reared birds showed a preference for the human. Thus, the early preferences shown by these turkeys persisted in spite of 4 years of common group rearing experiences. Since 5-year old turkeys are at a relatively advanced stage, Schein asserted that it appeared extremely unlikely that any future changes in sexual preferences would develop in these turkeys.

A later study by Schein, Fitch, and Hart (1962) has indicated that the effects of early cross-species social experience on adult courtship behavior can be "sleepers." Newly hatched white leghorn chickens and newly hatched bronze turkeys were raised in pairs during the 1st week of life. Some control chickens were raised with chicks. During the 2nd and 3rd weeks of life, each bird was isolated and injected with testosterone daily. Thereafter they were all raised together. Although no selective sexual object preferences were manifest at the age of 21 days, in spite of the drug-induced precocial sexual behavior, tests at the age of 1 year showed definite sexual object preferences on the part of the experimental subjects. Of the 6 surviving chicken-paired turkeys, 2 courted only turkeys, 3 exhibited a preference for turkeys, and 1 preferred chickens. As for the chickens, out of the 9 survivors paired with turkeys during the first weeks of life, 7 courted only turkeys, and 2 preferred turkeys. The group of chickens that had been with other chickens during the first week of life produced 3 that survived to the age of 1 year. Of these 3, 2 courted chickens and turkeys equally, and 1 preferred turkeys. Although these sexual preferences deviate from normal, the fact that 1 of the chicken-reared chickens preferred turkeys indicates that the testing procedures may have been inadequate.

Sexual preferences as a consequence of early rearing experience have been studied for several years in various duck species by Schutz (1963, c, 1964, 1965). Schutz made a distinction between the process of attaching the following response to a specific object during the first few days of life and the process of attaching sexual behavior toward a class of objects, and contended that these two processes occur at different times in the life cycle. Also, he found that the latter process, although widespread among duck species, will occur only in males of sexually dimorphic species such as the mallard. In the females of these sexually dimorphic species, recognition of the mate has an innate basis. In the Chilean teal, on the other hand, a species in which males and females have the same coloration, sexual preferences are formed in both sexes on the basis of early rearing experience with the natural or foster species. Schutz also made a distinction between following and sexual preferences by pointing out that the duckling attaches the following reaction to his own mother, and therefore an individual-specific process is involved, while preferences for sexual-social behaviors are established on a species-specific level.

Pair formation does not involve the same individuals that had been reared together, a fact which Schutz cited in support of his assertions. Furthermore, he frequently observed that during the onset of the mating season individual birds would shift from their own species to the one they had been sexually attached to. Hence, extra-specific sexual preferences formed on the basis of early experience persist in the observed duck species in spite of considerable experience with conspecifics. Such observations also lend support to Lorenz's (1935) notion of *Kumpan*, which refers specifically to the fact that birds have different spheres of social and sexual activities which may be each directed to different species as a consequence of abnormal early experience. Schutz also found evidence that actual mating in the form of copulation is apparently not necessary in order for male mallards to maintain sexual objects preferences. For example, homosexual male mallards never do copulate, since neither member of the pair ever takes the female role. In spite of the absence of reinforcement from actual mating, these homosexual bonds are highly stable and do not dissolve in favor of ones which would lead to bona fide copulatory activity.

Schutz also found that there are often species-specific restraints on what objects an individual of a given species may attach sexual preferences to, with the severity of such restraints varying in different species. Domestic fowl, wild red jungle fowl, and coots are easily induced to attach sexual object preferences through early social rearing experience to different domestic ducks. But it was difficult to cause mallards to develop such sexual preferences for chicks and coots.

Altricial Bird Species

Klinghammer (1967) has extensively reviewed the effects of early rearing and social experiences on sexual and social object preferences in altricial birds. In the species so far studied there has been no determination of a precise sensitive period for the formation of social and sexual object preferences. This lack of sensitive period determination has been due to the nature of the extended parent-young relationship in these species. We will discuss Klinghammer's research in the next chapter, and now concern ourselves with other studies which have been involved with early social experience in altricial species.

We have already mentioned the initial studies on the effects of early socialization experiences in several species of altricial birds, including Craig (1914), Whitman (in Riddle and Carr, 1919), Portielje (1921, 1927, 1930), Heinroth and Heinroth (1924–1933), Cruikshank (1939), and Goodwin (1948). One of the directions in which differences between precocial and altricial bird species may take with respect to the effects of early social rearing experience was early expressed by Lorenz in a letter to Nice (cited in Nice, 1943):

> In jackdaws I have repeatedly found that when I got a brood of young, all at the same date, the eldest ones of that brood would show a normal sexual reaction (i.e., directed to own species) when reaching maturity, while the

young ones, who, when isolated from the parents were at the utmost 4 or 5 days younger, would become humanized and refused to give any sexual reaction to their kind. Anatidae [ducks], on the contrary, show normal behavior [to conspecifics], when hand-raised in company of their own kind.

In the first place, these findings indicate that the development of extra-specific sexual object preferences may develop at a later time in the jackdaw, an altricial species, than it does in precocial ducks. Nevertheless, in jackdaws, the younger the birds when hand raising is instituted, the more likely such preferences may be formed. There appears to be a sensitive period for such an effect, which ends very definitely at some stage in the development of these birds. Further research should elucidate the time of the ending of this sensitive period. Finally, the presence of siblings during hand rearing precludes the attachment of sexual feelings to humans in mallards but not in jackdaws. Other altricial species may vary with respect to the effect of conspecific sibling companionship on the formation of sexual object preferences.

Research by Nicolai (1956) with European bullfinches which he had hand-reared for varying periods of time indicates that even if isolated bullfinches accept the human keeper as a sibling partner substitute and address their first sexual activities toward him, as they normally do with one or two of their own sibling nest mates, this hand rearing does not necessarily result in the formation of sexual preferences for humans when adulthood is reached. This is because if an opposite-sex conspecific becomes available during adolescence, the relationship to the human gradually dissolved. If no such conspecific is available, the sexual ties to man become irreversible, and henceforth all social and sexual behavior will be directed to the keeper. This indicates the existence of a sensitive period for the attachment of sexual object preferences to a particular class of objects, a period which Nicolai has suggested may occur sometime before the end of the second year of life. Under normal conditions of conspecific rearing, Nicolai pointed out, the young bullfinches form pairs with siblings until the gonads begin to develop, at which time the sibling pairs break up rather suddenly, and actual mating and breeding pairs are formed. If bullfinches are not hand-reared in isolation from conspecifics, but in the company of nest mates, no sexual preferences for humans can be formed during the indicated sensitive period.

Three other finch species—zebra finches, hawfinches, and grass finches—have been observed. Immelmann (1959, 1965) placed zebra finch eggs in the nests of society finches, which reared them. The young zebra finches remained in the company of their foster parents between the ages of 33 and 66 days, and were placed in individual isolation until sexual maturity, at about 4 months of age. It was found that the effects of the cross-species rearing were different in the female and male zebra finch, just as it is different in male and female mallard ducks. The zebra finch, like the mallard duck, is a sexually dimorphic species, with the male colorful and possessing many morphological and behavioral sexual releasers, while the female does not. Thus, it was found that the cross-species rearing experience caused the male zebra finches to court and mate with society finch females in a free choice situation where a conspecific zebra finch female was also present. In fact, the conspecific female was, at times, actually attacked instead of merely ignored. No specific sensitive period has been delineated for the formation of sexual object preference in zebra finch males, although certainly it takes place before the age of 33 days.

Additional research by Immelmann (1969a) with male Australian zebra finches, Bengalese finches, and African silverbills—all estrildine finches— demonstrated that cross-species rearing with parents and siblings of a different estrildid species caused the subjects to preferentially or exclusively direct sexual behavior toward the foster species. There is also evidence that in grass finches the choice of objects for courtship and nest-building activities may be influenced by an imprinting process during early juvenile life (Immelmann, 1969b). In this species, courtship song, roosting behavior, and sociability were also found to be strongly influenced by infantile experience, according to Immelmann.

Relatively little is known regarding the hawfinch's development of sexual object preferences, but Kear (1960) has reported on one hand-reared female which had been taken from the nest at the age of 5 days and kept in the company of her brother and nestlings of other species. The hand-rearing period was for about six weeks. For 2 years, the female and her brother were kept together in an outdoors aviary; courtship took place, but no successful breeding. When the male died, the female then showed courtship behavior to Kear and treated him exactly as if he were her mate, showing nesting behavior and even "incubating" on a pile of seed, which actions indicate that the early 6-week hand-rearing experience did indeed influence sexual object choice, even though Kear was not the person that had hand-reared her.

The transfer of sexual activities to humans was noted in a hand-raised purple heron by von Frisch (1957) who had taken it at the age of 10 days. This heron, when it reached sexual maturity, courted von Frisch, attempted to copulate with him, and directed nest-building and nesting behavior toward him. Strangers which came near were not tolerated, and would be attacked. In all respects the heron treated von Frisch as if he were a female heron.

Mohr (1960) has indicated that the sparrow hawk can be induced to direct courtship and sexual activities to man if hand rearing is instituted no later than the 8th day of age. When hand rearing was begun at the age of 10 to 14 days, the birds would eventually be able to accept the human as a parent if they spent a great deal of time with him; however, they never would address sexual behavior to any human. At later ages, they would not even accept man as a substitute parent. Mohr described the behavior of a female sparrow hawk that had been hand-reared early enough to adopt him as a sexual partner when sexual maturity was reached. In all respects, the female treated Mohr like a male, soliciting him and performing female copulatory behavior with him.

Similar behavior has been noted on the part of a European white stork that had been hand-reared from the age of 8 days until sexual maturity (Löhrl, 1961). At that time, the bird showed the nest site to Löhrl, performed the greeting ceremony, and assumed the female copulatory posture.

Gwinner (1964) reported that male and female ravens, which he had hand-reared and given special attention during the pre- and post-weaning period, courted him at the time of sexual maturity. One female persistently courted him and performed nesting behavior with him, despite the availability of a male raven that courted her. However, as with other ravens which Gwinner had hand-reared, when he withdrew his company from her and left her with the male, she did eventually pair with the male raven, although she did not lay any eggs. Hence, it appears that in ravens the effects of early social experience with humans do not persist unless there is continued contact, because of competition with innate behavior patterns. It does appear, however, that early social rearing by humans is necessary in order for sexual behavior directed toward humans to be manifested.

An extremely interesting effect of early social experience has been reported for widow (whydah) birds by Nicolai (1964). Comprising the *Viduinae* species, these birds are parasitic upon *Estrildidae* species, each viduinid species laying eggs in the nest of only one particular host estrildid species. For example *Vidua macroura* parasitize *Estrilda astrild*. During the nestling period, during which the young widow birds are reared by the host species, the characteristics of the song of the host are learned by the parasites. The males learn to perform it, and the females learn to respond to it when it is later sung in conjunction with the species-specific song. During the breeding season, the male widow bird sings a song which interweaves components of the species-specific song patterns and those of the foster species. When a pair of the host species are seen building a nest, the male will begin to sing only the nest calls of the host species and direct the attention of the female of his own species to the host pair. Hearing the combination of species-specific and host songs thus directs the female to observe the activities of the host pair, and this observation stimulates her to copulate with the male of her own species and then to ovulate and lay eggs in the observed nest.

As we already know from Whitman's (in Riddle and Carr, 1919) and Craig's (1914) work, cross-species rearing will cause pigeons and doves to mate with members of the foster species in preference to their own species. However, such cross-species mating does not occur only as a result of early foster experience, for Lade (cited in Klinghammer, 1966) has reported that the effects of conspecific rearing can be overcome to some extent by means of isolation in close proximity with the foreign species for several months prior to the breeding season, with the result that the removal of fear through prolonged habituation and the drastic lowering of the thresholds for sexual behavior during the onset of the breeding season work together to permit the occurrence of interspecies mating when no access to conspecifics is permitted.

Since there are extremely wide color variations among adults of the same pigeon species, there has been a great deal of speculation and research on the effect of early rearing experience with conspecific parents of one or two colors upon the color chosen in mate selection at maturity. Goodwin (1958), for example, found a positive correlation between the color of the rearing parents and the adult sexual preferences for mates of a particular color in pigeons. Goodwin tabulated the colors of established feral pairs which he observed in the city of London. He noted a strong tendency for pied and red pigeons to be paired to mates of similar colors and no tendency for blue or bluish black pigeons to be paired to mates of similar colors. Goodwin suggested that either remaining in a particular habitat, where relatives having similar colors would be present, or the establishment of color preference during the nestling period could be responsible for this preferential mating which he observed.

Mainardi (1964) suggested that such a mechanism for the determination of color preferences in sexual behavior may be most evident in pigeons that live in towns, since in the wild, where many predators are present, mimicry in the form of the assumption of blue colors would have a greater selection pressure and be responsible for the greater incidence of blue pigeon forms in the wild. In town areas, on the other hand, there are fewer predators, and so there is a predominance of checkered or black pigeons as a result of preferences formed through early social experiences.

However, Warriner (1960) and Warriner, Lemmon, and Ray (1963) investigated the effects of early experience with parents of a particular color during the nestling period. Two species were used—white king pigeons and black king pigeons. Of 32 pairs of parent birds—half of them white kings and the other half black kings, half of the breed pairs of each hatched and reared the natural young, while the rest fostered a pair of young from eggs that had been laid within 2 days of their own eggs. Humans were not seen by the young during their first 2 weeks of life. The young of this experiment never saw pigeons of any color other than that of the rearing parent until the mating test at sexual maturity. At this time, the mating tests showed that the male birds consistently mated with females who were of the same color as the rearing parents, while females did not do so with a frequency greater than chance. Since the birds did not choose their own color to a significant extent, it was concluded that the sibling color, being the same, also did not have any significant effect on mate choice.

Of interest in this investigation was the fact that of the 6 males which did not choose mates of the same color as the rearing parents, 5 were of the same color as the parent birds that had reared the female with which they had paired. Nevertheless, the authors concluded that it may be possible that the observed difference of effect of the rearing experience on sexual selection in males and female might lie in the greater aggressiveness of the male and in the fact that the male may be more dominant to pair formation.

In another investigation, Kerfoot (1965) gathered evidence that females actually are influenced by early rearing experience in sexual object preference. Of 15 white females, half were raised by red parents, and half were raised by black parents; of 15 males, all were reared by white foster parents for the first 40 days of life, after which they were placed in visual isolation. The females did mate to a significant degree with males that were the color of the rearing parents. Thus, it does certainly appear that there may be an interaction between the sexual preferences of male and female pigeons in pair formation.

The effects of early social experience in altricial birds has also been studied with respect to the incidence of aggressive behavior by Kuo (1960b). Five species were studied: the masked jay thrush, normally a solitary and highly aggressive species which will attack and kill smaller birds; the Java gray sparrow and the house sparrow, both of which are highly aggressive birds; and the Peking robin sparrow and the South China white-eyed sparrow, two species which are normally highly sociable, tending to flock together and to be distressed when separated from companions.

In the first experiment, Kuo reared 48 young masked jay thrushes, which had been taken from their nests in the wild at the age of 5 to 10 days, in four different groups: one group of 8 lived with 10 adult Peking robin sparrows; another group of 8 lived with 10 adult South China white-eyed sparrows; a third group of 8 lived with 10 adult strawberry finches; and the fourth group of 24 lived with 20 parrots of various sizes ranging from parakeets to large cockatoos. For the first 6 months of such rearing, stranger birds lived for 1 day in the cage, with a new stranger bird introduced daily; for the second 6 months, the stranger bird stayed 1 week. During the 1-year rearing period, no experimental jay thrush was ever observed to attack the smaller birds or other birds of its own species, to show hostile attitudes, or to show dominating behavior. Although antisocial behavior never developed in these birds, neither did they ever build up positively social habits. None of them ever showed any discomfort on being removed from its companions or any "reunion" behavior when reunited, as Peking robin sparrows and South China white-eyed sparrows normally do. Neither did the thrushes ever show any caressing, fondling, or friendliness toward their own species of either sex or toward the smaller birds.

Java gray sparrows could not be reared from an early age, but experiments in which fully grown adults were severely beaten by a vicious masked jay thrush showed that the usual bullying of these sparrows could be reduced to a much lower level. Watching a member of their species being severely beaten by the thrush produced fear reactions which lasted for one week, but the normal level of aggressive behavior later returned. These results indicate that in this species, adult experiences, unless extremely traumatic, may have no lasting effect in mitigating aggressive behavior toward other species and conspecifics.

House sparrows reared from the age of 5 to 8 days in the company of baby white-eyed sparrows showed that aggressive behavior toward smaller birds could be reduced in house sparrows by such rearing. Only 1 of 20 house sparrows developed aggressiveness toward their own nest mates, and only 5 of 40 attacked smaller birds. The remainder were either friendly (53.33 per cent) or indifferent (46.67 percent) to strange birds of the same size as they. Like the masked jay thrushes, they never developed highly sociable behavior like that manifested by the white-eyed sparrows; they never showed restlessness upon temporary separation from companions; nor did they show any change in behavior upon reunion.

Kuo then proceeded to determine the effects of rearing in social isolation upon the social behavior of Peking robin sparrows and South China white-eyed sparrows, the two highly sociable species. Full-grown adults of both species and 5 to 7 day old white-eyed sparrows were equally divided into four groups, as follows, with 10 in each group: isolated for 1 month; isolated for 2 months; isolated for 4 months; and isolated for 6 months. At the end of the isolation period, the birds were placed in a multi-species group in an aviary. It was found that, despite the isolation, none of these birds ever developed antisocial habits. Some, however, did develop solitary habits as a result of the isolation, depending on the length of isolation and whether the isolation was during adulthood or early life. Of all the birds that did develop solitary habits, none became socialized during a subsequent 4-week social rearing experience. Among the adult robin sparrows, only 2 birds, both of which had been isolated for 6 months, developed solitary habits. Among the adult white-eyed sparrows, there was no loss of sociable habits until isolation had lasted for at least 4 months, when 1 of the 10 subjects in that group acquired solitary habits; also, 1 of the 10 isolated for 6 months developed solitary habits.

The development of solitary habits occurred with a greater incidence among the white-eyed sparrows that had been isolated beginning in the first week of life. Of the 10 isolated for 1 month, 2 did show solitary habits, as did 2 of the 10 isolated for 2 months. Of the 10 isolated for 4 months, 4 developed such behavior, as did 7 of the 10 isolated for 6 months. Thus, we see an increasing toll with increasing length of isolation beginning in the 1st week of life in these white-eyed sparrows.

It is apparent that, although there has been much research on early social behavior and the effects of early social experience in various bird species, there is still a great deal we do not know. At most, it appears that we have identified some of the factors capable of playing a role in the development of social and sexual behavior in birds. But how and when they play their roles are very large questions, indeed.

REFERENCES

ABERCROMBIE, BARBARA, and JAMES, H. The stability of the domestic chick's response to visual flicker. *Animal Behaviour,* 1961, **9,** 205–212.

ADAM, J., and DIMOND, S. J. The effect of visual stimulation at different stages of embryonic development on approach behavior. *Animal Behaviour,* 1971, **19,** 51–54.

ALLEY, R., and BOYD, H. Parent-young recognition in the coot *Fulica atra. Ibis,* 1950, **92,** 46–51.

ASDOURIAN, DAVID. Object attachment and the critical period. *Psychonomic Science,* 1967, **7,** 235–236.

BAER, DONALD M., and GRAY, PHILIP H. Imprinting to a different species without overt following. *Perceptual and Motor Skills,* 1960, **10,** 171–174.

BAMBRIDGE, R. Early experience and sexual behavior in the domestic chicken. *Science,* 1962, **136,** 259–260.

BARON, ALAN, and KISH, GEORGE B. Early social isolation as a determinant of aggregative behavior in the domestic chicken. *Journal of Comparative and Physiological Psychology,* 1960, **53,** 450–463.

BARON, ALAN, KISH, GEORGE B., and ANTONITIS, JOSEPH J. Effects of early and late social isolation on aggregative behavior in the domestic chicken. *Journal of Genetic Psychology,* 1962, **100,** 355–360.

BATESON, P. P. G. The development of filial and avoidance behaviour in the domestic chicken. Unpublished doctoral dissertation at Cambridge University, England, 1963.

BATESON, P. P. G. Effect of similarity between rearing and testing conditions on chicks' following and avoidance responses. *Journal of Comparative Physiological Psychology*, 1964, **57**, 100–103. (a).

BATESON, P. P. G. Relation between conspicuousness of stimuli and their effectiveness in the imprinting situation. *Journal of Comparative Physiological Psychology*, 1964, **58**, 407–411. (b).

BATESON, P. P. G. Changes in the activity of isolated chicks over the first week after hatching. *Animal Behaviour*, 1964, **12**, 490–492. (c).

BATESON, P. P. G., HORN, G., and ROSE, S. P. R. Effects of an imprinting procedure on regional incorporation of tritiated lysine into protein of chick brain. *Nature*, 1969, **223**, 534–535.

BATESON, P. P. G., and REESE, ELLEN P. Reinforcing properties of conspicuous objects before imprinting has occurred. *Psychonomic Science*, 1968, **10**, 379–380.

BATESON, P. P. G., and REESE, ELLEN P. The reinforcing properties of conspicuous stimuli in the imprinting situation. *Animal Behaviour*, 1969, **17**, 692–699.

BIERENS de HAAN, J. A. Die Balz des Argusfasans. *Biologisches Zentralblatt*, 1926, **46**, 428–435.

BJARVÄLL, ANDERS. The critical period and the interval between hatching and exodus in mallard ducklings. *Behaviour*, 1967, **28**, 141–148.

BOYD, HUGH, and FABRICIUS, ERIC. Observations on the incidence of following of visual and auditory stimuli in naive mallard ducklings *(Anas platyrhynchos)*. *Behaviour*, 1965, **25**, 1–15.

BRADFORD, JOHN P., and MACDONALD, GLENN E. Imprinting: pre- and posttrial administration of pentobarbital and the approach response. *Journal of Comparative and Physiological Psychology*, 1969, **68**, 50–55.

BROWN, LARRY. A critical period in the learning of motionless stimulus properties in chicks. *Animal Behaviour*, 1964, **12**, 353–361.

BRÜCKNER, G. H. Untersuchungen zur Tiersoziologie, insbesondere zur Auflösung der Familie. *Zeitschrift für Psychologie*, 1933, **128**, 1–110.

CAMPBELL, BYRON A., and PICKLEMAN, JACK R. The imprinting object as a reinforcing stimulus. *Journal of Comparative and Physiological Psychology*, 1961, **54**, 592–596.

CANDLAND, DOUGLAS K., NAGY, Z. MICHAEL, and CONKLYN, DANIEL H. Emotional behavior in the domestic chicken (white leghorn) as a function of age and developmental environment. *Journal of Comparative and Physiological Psychology*, 1963, **56**, 1069–1073.

CHRISTOPHER, S. B., and HALE, E. B. Specificity of visual imprinting in domestic turkeys. *American Zoologist*, 1968, **8**, 696. (Abstract).

COFOID, DIANNE A., and HONIG, W. K. Stimulus generalization of imprinting. *Science*, 1961, **134**, 1692–1693.

COLLIAS, NICHOLAS E. Some basic psychological and neural mechanisms of social behavior in chicks. *Anatomical Record*, 1950, **108**, 552. (Abstract). (a).

COLLIAS, NICHOLAS E. The socialization of chicks. *Anatomical Record*, 1950, **108**, 553. (Abstract). (b).

COLLIAS, NICHOLAS E. Social life and the individual among vertebrate animals. *Annals of the New York Academy of Sciences*, 1950, **51**, 1074–1092. (c).

COLLIAS, NICHOLAS E. The development of social behavior in birds. *Auk*, 1952, **69**, 127–159.

COLLIAS, NICHOLAS E. Social development in birds and mammals. In: Bliss, E. L., editor, *Roots of Behavior*. New York: Hoeber, 1962. 264–273.

COLLIAS, NICHOLAS E., and COLLIAS, ELSIE C. Some mechanisms of family integration in ducks. *Auk,* 1956, **73,** 378–400.

COLLINS, THOMAS B. The strength of the following response in the chick in relation to degree of "parent" contact. *Journal of Comparative and Physiological Psychology,* 1965, **60,** 192–195.

CRAIG, WALLACE. The voices of pigeons regarded as a means of social control. *American Journal of Sociology,* 1908, **14,** 86–100.

CRAIG, WALLACE. The stimulation and inhibition of ovulation in birds. *Journal of Animal Behavior,* 1913, **3,** 215–221.

CRAIG, WALLACE. Male doves reared in isolation. *Journal of Animal Behavior,* 1914, **4,** 121–133.

CRUIKSHANK, A. D. The behavior of some Corvidae. *Bird Lore,* 1939, **41,** 78–81.

CUSHING, JOHN E. Non-genetic mating preference as a factor in evolution. *Condor,* 1941, **43,** 233–236.

CUSHING, JOHN E., and RAMSAY, A. OGDEN. The non-heritable aspects of family unity in birds. *Condor,* 1949, **51,** 82–87.

DARLING, F. FRASER. *Island Years.* London: Bell & Sons, 1940.

EIDUSON, SAMUEL, GELLER, EDWARD, and BECKWITH, WILLIAM. Some biochemical correlates of imprinting. *Proceedings of the Federation of American Societies for Experimental Biology,* 1961, **20,** 345. (Abstract).

EVANS, ROGER M. Imprinting and mobility in young ring-billed gulls, *Larus delawarensis. Animal Behaviour Monographs,* 1970, **3,** part 3, 1–248.

FABRICIUS, ERIC. Some experiments on imprinting phenomena in ducks. *Proceedings of the Tenth International Ornithogical Congress,* (Uppsala, June 1950), 1951, 375–379 (a).

FABRICIUS, ERIC. Zur Ethologie junger Anatiden. *Acta Zoologica Fennica,* 1951, **68,** 1–175. (b).

FABRICIUS, ERIC. Experiments on the following-response of mallard ducklings. *British Journal of Animal Behaviour,* 1955, **3,** 122.

FABRICIUS, ERIC. Some aspects of imprinting. *Animal Behavior,* 1962, **10,** 181–182. (Abstract). (a).

FABRICIUS, ERIC. Some aspects of imprinting in birds. *Symposia of the Zoological Society of London,* 1962, **8,** 139–148. (b).

FABRICIUS, ERIC. Crucial periods in the development of the following responses in young nidifugous birds. *Zeitschrift für Tierpsychologie,* 1964, **21,** 326–337.

FABRICIUS, ERIC, and BOYD, H. Experiments on the following reactions of ducklings. *Wild Fowl Trust Fund Annual Report, Slimbridge, England,* 1954, **6,** 84–89.

FABRICIUS, ERIC, and FÄLT, LARS. Sexuell prägung has gräsandhonor. *Zoologiska Revy,* 1969, **31,** No. 4, 83–88.

FISCHER, GLORIA J. Auditory stimuli in imprinting. *Journal of Comparative and Physiological Psychology,* 1966, **61,** 271–273. (a).

FISCHER, GLORIA J. Distribution of practice effects on imprinting. *Psychonomic Science,* 1966, **5,** 197–198. (b).

FISCHER, GLORIA J. Hereditability in the following response of pedigreed white leghorns. *Psychonomic Bulletin,* 1967, **1,** 30.

FISCHER, GLORIA J. Arousal and impairment: Temperature effects on following during imprinting. *Journal of Comparative and Physiological Psychology,* 1970, **73,** 412–420.

FISCHER, GLORIA J., and CAMPBELL, GARY L. The development of passive avoidance conditioning in leghorn chicks. *Animal Behaviour,* 1964, **12,** 268–269.

FISCHER, GLORIA J., CAMPBELL, GARY L., and DAVIS, W. MARVIN. Effects of ECS on retention of imprinting. *Journal of Comparative and Physiological Psychology,* 1965, **59,** 455–457.

FISCHER, GLORIA J., and GILMAN, SARA. Following during imprinting as a function of auditory stimulus intensity. *Developmental Psychology,* 1969, **1,** 216–218.

FISHER, ALAN E., and HALE, E. B. Stimulus determinants of sexual and aggressive behavior in male domestic fowl. *Behaviour,* 1957, **10,** 309–323.

FISHMAN, R., and TALLARICO, R. B. Studies of visual depth perception. II. Avoidance reaction as an indicator response in chicks. *Perceptual and Motor Skills,* 1961, **12,** 251–257.

FRISCH, OTTO VON. Mit einem Purpurreiher verheiratet. *Zeitschrift für Tierpsychologie,* 1957, **14,** 233–237.

GALASSI, DONNA J., and WALKER, LAWRENCE C. Imprinting and shape generalization in white leghorn chicks. Midwestern Psychological Association meeting, Chicago, May 1968.

GOODWIN, DEREK. Some abnormal sexual fixations in birds. *Ibis,* 1948, **90,** 45–48.

GOODWIN, DEREK. The existence and causation of colour preference in the pairing of feral and domestic pigeons. *Bulletin of the British Ornithologists' Club, London,* 1958, **78,** 136–139.

GOODWIN, ELIZABETH BIRD, and HESS, ECKHARD H. Innate visual form preferences in the imprinting behavior of young chicks. *Behaviour,* 1969, **34,** 223–237. (a).

GOODWIN, ELIZABETH BIRD, and HESS, ECKHARD H. Stimulus generalization and responses to "supernormal" stimuli in the unrewarded pecking behavior of young chicks. *Behaviour,* 1969, **34,** 255–266. (b).

GOTTLIEB, GILBERT. Developmental age as a baseline for determination of the critical period in imprinting. *Journal of Comparative and Physiological Psychology,* 1961, **54,** 422–427. (a).

GOTTLIEB, GILBERT. The following-response and imprinting in wild and domestic ducklings of the same species *(Anas platyrhynchos). Behaviour,* 1961, **18,** 205–228. (b).

GOTTLIEB, GILBERT. A naturalistic study of imprinting in wood ducklings *(Aix sponsa). Journal of Comparative and Physiological Psychology,* 1963, **56,** 86–91. (a).

GOTTLIEB, GILBERT. The facilitatory effect of the parental exodus call on the following response of ducklings: One test of the self-stimulation hypothesis. *American Zoologist,* 1963, **3,** 518. (Abstract). (b).

GOTTLIEB, GILBERT. "Imprinting" in nature. *Science,* 1963, **139,** 497–498. (c)

GOTTLIEB, GILBERT. Following-response initiation in ducklings: Age and sensory stimulation. *Science,* 1963, **140,** 399–400. (d).

GOTTLIEB, GILBERT. Refrigerating eggs prior to incubation as a way of reducing error in calculating developmental age in imprinting experiments. *Animal Behaviour,* 1963, **11,** 290–292. (e).

GOTTLIEB, GILBERT. Imprinting in relation to parental and species identification by avian neonates. *Journal of Comparative and Physiological Psychology,* 1965, **59,** 345–356. (a).

GOTTLIEB, GILBERT. Components of recognition in ducklings. *Natural History,* February 1965, **74,** 12–19.(b).

GOTTLIEB, GILBERT. Prenatal auditory sensitivity in chickens and ducks. *Science,* 1965, **147,** 1596–1598. (c).

GOTTLIEB, GILBERT. Species identification by avian neonates: Contributory effect of perinatal auditory stimulation. *Animal Behaviour,* 1966, **14,** 282–290.

GOTTLIEB, GILBERT. *Development of Species Identification in Birds: An Inquiry into the Prenatal Determinants of Perception.* Chicago: University of Chicago Press, 1971.

GOTTLIEB, GILBERT, and KLOPFER, PETER H. Preliminary findings on the relation of developmental age to visual and auditory imprinting. *American Psychologist,* 1961, **16,** 350. (Abstract).

GOTTLIEB, GILBERT, and KLOPFER, PETER H. The relation of developmental age to auditory and visual imprinting. *Journal of Comparative and Physiological Psychology,* 1962, **55,** 821–826.

GOTTLIEB, GILBERT, and SIMNER, MARVIN L. Auditory versus visual flicker in directing the approach response of domestic chicks. *Journal of Comparative and Physiological Psychology,* 1969, **67,** 58–63.

GRAVES, HANNON B., and SIEGEL, P. B. Chick's response to an imprinting stimulus: heterosis and evolution. *Science,* 1968, **160,** 329–330. (a).

GRAVES, HANNON B., and SIEGEL, P. B. Prior experience and the approach response in domestic chicks. *Animal Behaviour,* 1968, **16,** 18–23. (b).

GRAVES, HANNON B., and SIEGEL, P. B. Bidirectional selection for responses of *Gallus domesticus* chicks to an imprinting situation. *Animal Behaviour,* 1969, **17,** 683–691.

GRAY, PHILIP H. Evidence that retinal flicker is not a necessary condition of imprinting. *Science,* 1960, **132,** 1834–1835.

GRAY, PHILIP H. The releasers of imprinting: Differential reactions to color as a function of maturation. *Journal of Comparative and Physiological Psychology,* 1961, **54,** 597–601 (a).

GRAY, PHILIP H. Developmental parameters of imprinting. *Dissertation Abstracts,* 1961, **21,** 2381–2382. (b).

GRAY, PHILIP H. Is the imprinting critical period an artifact of a biological clock? *Perceptual and Motor Skills,* 1962, **14,** 70.

GRAY, PHILIP H. Interaction of temporal and releasing factors in familial recognition of own and ancestral species. *Perceptual and Motor Skills,* 1964, **18,** 445–448.

GRAY, PHILIP H., and HOWARD, KENNETH I. Specific recognition of humans in imprinted chicks. *Perceptual and Motor Skills,* 1957, **7,** 301–304.

GRAY, PHILIP H., SALLEE, STELLA J., and YATES, ALLEN T. Developmental and chronological ages versus time of day as factors in released imprinting responses. *Perceptual and Motor Skills,* 1964, **19,** 763–768.

GRAY, PHILIP H., SALLEE, STELLA J., and YATES, ALLEN T. An innate period of familial preferences in chicks not imprinted. *Psychonomic Science,* 1970, **18,** 158–159.

GRAY, PHILIP H., WEEKS, SAM, ANDERSON, CHARLES D., and McNEAL, SHIRLEY. Further evidence of a "time of day at test" factor in the released social responses of isolated chicks. *Proceedings of the Montana Academy of Sciences,* 1963, **23,** 212–218.

GRAY, P. H., YATES, A. T., DAVIS, G. T., and MODE, C. J. Some aspects of the genetics of imprinting. *American Zoologist,* 1966, **6,** 568.

GUITON, PHILIP E. The effect of isolation on the following response of brown leghorn chicks. *Proceedings of the Royal Physical Society for the Promotion of Zoology and Other Branches of Natural History, Edinburgh,* 1958, **27,** 9–14.

GUITON, PHILIP E. Socialisation and imprinting in brown leghorn chicks. *Animal Behaviour,* 1959, **7,** 26–34.

GUITON, PHILIP E. The influence of imprinting on the agonistic and courtship responses of the brown leghorn cock. *Animal Behaviour,* 1961, **9,** 167–177.

GUITON, PHILIP E. The development of sexual response in domestic fowl in relation to the concept of imprinting. *Animal Behaviour,* 1962, **10,** 184. (Abstract). (a).

GUITON, PHILIP E. The development of sexual responses in the domestic fowl in relation to the concept of imprinting. *Symposia of the Zoological Society of London,* 1962, **8,** 227–234. (b).

GUTEKUNST, RALPH, and YOUNISS, JAMES. Interruption of imprinting following anesthesia. *Perceptual and Motor Skills,* 1963, **16,** 348.

GWINNER, E. Untersuchungen ueber das Ausdrucks and Sozialverhalten des Kolkraben *(Corvus corax corax L.) Zeitschrift für Tierpsychologie,* 1964, **21,** 657–748.

HAILMAN, JACK P., and KLOPFER, PETER H. On measuring "critical learning periods" in birds. *Animal Behaviour,* 1962, **10,** 233–234.

HARLOW, HARRY F., and HARLOW, MARGARET K. Social deprivation in monkeys. *Scientific American,* 1962, **207,** No. 5, 136–146.

HAYWOOD, H. CARL. Discrimination and following behavior in chicks as a function of early environmental complexity. *Perceptual and Motor Skills,* 1965, **21,** 299–304.

HAYWOOD, H. CARL, and ZIMMERMAN, DONALD W. Effects of early environmental complexity on the following response in chicks. *Perceptual and Motor Skills,* 1964, **18,** 653–658.

HEDIGER, HEINI. *Wild Animals in Captivity.* London: Butterworth, 1950. (translation of *Wildtiere in Gefangenschaft.* Basle, Switzerland: Benno Schwabe, 1942.

HEINROTH, OSKAR. Beitrage zur Biologie, namentlich Ethologie und Psychologie der Anatiden. *Verhandlungen des V. Internationalen Ornithologen-Kongresses,* 1910, **5,** 589–702.

HEINROTH, OSKAR, and HEINROTH, MAGDALENA. *Die Vögel Mitteleuropas.* Berlin: Litchterfelde, 1924–1933.

HESS, ECKHARD H. The relationship between imprinting and motivation. In: Jones, M. R., editor, *Nebraska Symposium on Motivation.* University of Nebraska Press, 1959. (a).

HESS, ECKHARD H. Imprinting. *Science,* 1959, **130,** 133–141. (b).

HESS, ECKHARD H. Imprinting in birds. *Science,* 1964, **146,** 1128–1139.

HESS, ECKHARD H., and HESS, DORLE B. Innate factors in imprinting. *Psychonomic Science,* 1969, **14,** 129–130.

HESS, ECKHARD H., and PETROVICH, SLOBODAN B. The early development of parent-young interaction in nature. In: *Life-Span Developmental Psychology: Methodological Issues.* H. W. Reese and J. R. Nesselroade, editors. In press.

HINDE, ROBERT A. The following response of moorhens and coots. *British Journal of Animal Behaviour,* 1955, **3,** 121–122.

HINDE, ROBERT A., THORPE, WILLIAM H., and VINCE, MARGARET A. The following response of young coots and moorhens. *Behaviour,* 1956, **9,** 214–241.

HOFFMAN, HOWARD S. The control of distress vocalization by an imprinted stimulus. *Behaviour*, 1968, **30**, 175–191.

HOFFMAN, HOWARD S., and KOZMA, FREDERICK, JR. Behavioral control by an imprinted stimulus: Long-term effects. *Journal of the Experimental Analysis of Behavior*, 1967, **10**, 495–501.

HOFFMAN, HOWARD S., SCHIFF, D., ADAMS, J., and SEARLE, JOHN L. Enhanced distress vocalization through selective reinforcement. *Science*, 1966, **151**, 352–354.

HOFFMAN, HOWARD S., SEARLE, JOHN L., TOFFEY, SHARON, and KOZMA, FREDERICK, JR. Behavioral control by an imprinted stimulus. *Journal of the Experimental Analysis of Behavior*, 1966, **9**, 177–189.

HOFFMAN, HOWARD S., STRATTON, JAMES W., NEWBY, VALERIE, and BARRETT, JAMES E. Development of behavioral control by an imprinting stimulus. *Journal of Comparative and Physiological Psychology*, 1970, **71**, 229–236.

HORN, G., HORN, ANN, L. D., BATESON, P. P. G., and ROSE, S. P. R. Effects of imprinting on uracil incorporation into brain RNA in the "split-brain" chick. *Nature*, 1971, **229**, 131–132.

HOWELLS, T. H., and VINE, D. O. The innate differential in social learning. *Journal of Abnormal Social Psychology*, 1940, **35**, 537–548.

HUDSON, WILLIAM H. *The Naturalist in La Plata*. London: Chapman and Hall, 1892.

HUNT, HATTIE E. Observations on newly hatched chicks. *American Journal of Psychology*, 1898, **9**, 125–127.

IMMELMANN, KLAUS. Experimentelle Untersuchungen über die biologische Bedeutung artspezifischer Merkmale beim Zebrafinken. *Zoologische Jahrbücher*, (Abt. Syst.) 1959, **86**, 437–592.

IMMELMANN, KLAUS. Objektfixierung geschlechtlicher Triebhandlung bei Prachtfinken. *Die Naturwissenschaften*, 1965, **52**, 169.

IMMELMANN, KLAUS. Über den Einfluss frühkindlicher Erfahrung auf die geschlechtliche Objektfixierung bei Estrilden. *Zeitschrift für Tierpsychologie*, 1969, **26**, 677–691. (a).

IMMELMANN, KLAUS. Ökologische und stammesgeschichtliche Betrachtungen zum Prägungsphänomen. *Zoologischer Anzeiger*, 1969, **183**, 1–12. (b).

IVOR, H. R. Bird's fear of man. *Auk*, 1944, **61**, 203–211.

JAMES, H. Flicker: an unconditioned stimulus for imprinting. *Canadian Journal of Psychology*, 1959, **13**, 59–67.

JAMES, H. Imprinting with visual flicker: Evidence for a critical period. *Canadian Journal of Psychology*, 1960, **14**, 13–20. (a).

JAMES, H. Social inhibition of the domestic chick's response to visual flicker. *Animal Behaviour*, 1960, **8**, 223–224. (b).

JAMES H. Imprinting with visual flicker: Effects of testosterone cyclopentylpropionate. *Animal Behaviour*, 1962, **10**, 341–346.

JAMES, H., and BINKS, CAROLYN. Escape and avoidance learning in newly hatched chicks. *Science*, 1963, **139**, 1293–1294.

JAMES, WILLIAM. What is an instinct? *Scribner's Magazine*, 1887, **1**, 255–365. Reprinted in: James, William, *The Principles of Psychology*. New York: Holt & Co., 1890.

JAYNES, JULIAN. Imprinting: The interaction of learned and innate behavior: I. Development and generalization. *Journal of Comparative and Physiological Psychology*, 1956, **49**, 201–206.

JAYNES, JULIAN. Imprinting: The interaction of learned and innate behavior. II.

The critical period. *Journal of Comparative and Physiological Psychology*, 1957, **50**, 6–10.

JAYNES, JULIAN. Imprinting: The interaction of learned and innate behavior. III. Practice effects on performance, retention, and fear. *Journal of Comparative and Physiological Psychology*, 1958, **51**, 234–237. (a).

JAYNES, JULIAN: Imprinting: The interaction of learned and innate behavior. IV. Generalization and emergent discrimination. *Journal of Comparative and Physiological Psychology*, 1958, **51**, 238–242. (b).

KATZ, D. *Animals and Men*. New York: Longmans, Green, 1937.

KAUFMAN, I. C., and HINDE, ROBERT A. Factors influencing distress calling in chicks, with special reference to temperature changes and social isolation. *Animal Behaviour*, 1961, **9**, 197–204.

KAYE, STUART M. Primacy and recency in the development of the following response in the domestic chick. *Bulletin of the Maritime Psychological Association*, 1965, **14**, No. 1, 13. (Abstract). (a).

KAYE, STUART M. Primacy and recency in imprinting. *Psychonomic Science*, 1965, **3**, 271–272. (b).

KEAR, I. Abnormal sexual behavior in the hawfinch *Coccothraustes coccothraustes*. *Ibis*, 1960, **102**, 614–616.

KERFOOT, EUGENE M. Some aspects of mate selection in domestic pigeons. *Dissertation Abstracts*, 1965, **25**, 4250.

KESSEN, WILLIAM. Comparative personality development. In E. F. Borgatta and W. W. Lambert, eds., *Handbook of Personality Theory and Research*. Chicago: Rand McNally, 1968.

KILHAM, PETER, and KLOPFER, PETER. The construct race and the innate differential. In: *Science and the Concept of Race*. Margaret Mead et al., editors. New York: Columbia University Press, 1968. 16–25.

KILHAM, PETER, KLOPFER, PETER, and OELKE, HANS. Species identification and colour preferences in chicks. *Animal Behaviour*, 1968, **16**, 238–244.

KLINE, LINUS W. Methods in animal psychology. *American Journal of Psychology*, 1899, **10**, 256–279.

KLINGHAMMER, ERICH. Imprinting in altricial birds: The ring dove *(Streptopelia roseogrisia)* and the mourning dove *(Zenaidura macruora carolensis)*. Unpublished doctoral dissertation, University of Chicago, 1962.

KLINGHAMMER, ERICH. Factors affecting choice of mate in altricial birds. In: Stevenson, H., W., Hess, E. H., and Rheingold, H. L., editors, *Early Behavior: Comparative and Developmental Approaches*. New York: Wiley, 1967. 5–42. (a).

KLINGHAMMER, ERICH. Imprinting in an altricial bird: The mourning dove *(Zenaidura macruora)*. Unpublished manuscript, 1967. (b).

KLINGHAMMER, ERICH, and HESS, ECKHARD H. Imprinting in an altricial bird: The blond ring rove. *(Streptopelia risoria)*. *Science*, 1964, **146**, 265–266.

KLOPFER, PETER H. An analysis of learning in young *Anatidae*. *Ecology*, 1959, **40**, 90–102. (a).

KLOPFER, PETER H. The development of sound preferences in ducks. *Wilson Bulletin*, 1959, **71**, 262–266. (b).

KLOPFER, PETER H. *Science*, 1959, **130**, 730. (Letter). (c).

KLOPFER, PETER H. *Behavioral Aspects of Ecology*. Englewood Cliffs, N.J. Prentice-Hall, 1962.

KLOPFER, PETER H. Imprinting: A reassessment. *Science*, 1965, **147**, 302–303.

KLOPFER, PETER H. Stimulus preferences and imprinting. *Science,* 1967, **156,** 1394–1396.

KLOPFER, PETER H. Stimulus preferences and discrimination in neonatal ducklings. *Behaviour,* 1968, **32,** 309–314.

KLOPFER, PETER H. Imprinting: Determining its perceptual basis in ducklings. *Journal of Comparative and Physiological Psychology,* 1971, **75,** 378–385.

KLOPFER, PETER H., and GOTTLIEB, GILBERT. Imprinting and behavioral polymorphism: Auditory and visual imprinting in domestic ducks *(Anas platyrhynchos)* and the involvement of the critical period. *Journal of Comparative and Physiological Psychology,* 1962, **55,** 126–130. (a).

KLOPFER, PETER H., and GOTTLIEB, GILBERT. Learning ability and behavioral polymorphism within individual clutches of wild ducklings. *Zeitschrift für Tierpsychologie,* 1962, **19,** 183–190. (b).

KLOPFER, PETER H., and HAILMAN, JACK P. Basic parameters of following and imprinting in precocial birds. *Zeitschrift für Tierpsychologie,* 1964, **21,** 755–761. (a).

KLOPFER, PETER H., and HAILMAN, JACK P. Perceptual preferences and imprinting in chicks. *Science,* 1964, **145,** 1333–1334. (b).

KOVACH, JOSEPH K. Effectiveness of different colors in the elicitation and development of approach behavior in chicks. *Behaviour,* 1971, **38,** 154–168. (a).

KOVACH, JOSEPH K. Interaction of innate and acquired: Color preferences and early exposure learning in chicks. *Journal of Comparative and Physiological Psychology,* 1971, **75,** 386–398. (b).

KOVACH, JOSEPH K., CALLIES, DUANE, and HARTZELL, REX. An automated procedure for the study of perceptual imprinting. *Perceptual and Motor Skills,* 1969, **29,** 123–128.

KOVACH, JOSEPH K., and HICKOX, JOHN E. Color preferences and early perceptual discrimination learning in domestic chicks. *Developmental Psychobiology,* 1971, **4,** 255–267.

KOVACH, JOSEPH K., PADEN, PHILIP, and WILSON, GREGORY. Stimulus variables in the elicitation and short-range reversibility of early approach and following responses. *Journal of Comparative and Physiological Psychology,* 1968, **66,** 175–178.

KRUIJT, J. P. Imprinting in relation to drive interactions in Burmese red junglefowl. *Animal Behavior,* 1962, **10,** 183. (Abstract). (a).

KRUIJT, J. P. Imprinting in relation to drive interactions in Burmese red junglefowl. *Symposia of the Zoological Society, London,* 1962, **8,** 219–226. (b).

KRUIJT, J. P. Ontogeny of social behavior in Burmese red junglefowl. *(Gallus gallus spadiceus* Bonnaterre). *Behaviour,* 1964, Suppl. **12,** 1–201.

KRUIJT, J. P. Early experience and the development of social behaviour in junglefowl. *Psychiatria, Neurologia, Neurochirugia,* 1971, **74,** 7–20. (Elsevier Publishing Company, Amsterdam).

KUO, ZING Y. Studies on the basic factors in animal fighting. IV. Developmental and environmental factors affecting fighting in quails. *Journal of Genetic Psychology,* 1960, **96,** 225–239. (a).

KUO, ZING Y. Studies on the basic factors in animal fighting. VI. Inter-species coexistence in birds. *Journal of Genetic Psychology,* 1960, **97,** 195–209. (b).

LACK, D. Some aspects of instinctive behaviour and display in birds. *Ibis,* 1941, **5,** (14th series), 407–441.

LÖHRL, H. Verhaltensweisen eines erfahrungslosen Weissen Storches. *Die Vogelwarte*, 1961, **21**, 137–142.

LORENZ, KONRAD Z. Der Kumpan in der Umwelt des Vogels. *Journal für Ornithologie*, 1935, **83**, 137–214, 289–413. Also in translation, as Companions as factors in the bird's environment. In: Lorenz, K., *Studies in Animal and Human Behaviour*. Translated by R. Martin. Cambridge, Mass.: Harvard University Press, 1970. Volume 1, 101–258.

LORENZ, KONRAD Z. The companion in the bird's world. *Auk*, 1937, **54**, 245–273.

LORENZ, KONRAD Z. Die Paarbilding beim Kolkraben. *Zeitschrift für Tierpsychologie*, 1939, **3**, 278–292.

LORENZ, KONRAD Z. *Studies in Animal and Human Behaviour*. Volume 1. Translated by R. Martin. Cambridge, Mass.: Harvard University Press, 1970.

MACDONALD, GLENN E. Imprinting: Drug-produced isolation and the sensitive period. *Nature*, 1968, **217**, 1158–1159.

MACDONALD, GLENN E., and SOLANDT, A. Imprinting: Effects of drug-induced immobilization. *Psychonomic Science*, 1966, **5**, 95–96.

MAINARDI, DANILO. Effetto evolutio della selezione sessuale basata su *imprinting* in Columba livia. *Rivista Italiana di Ornitologia*, 1964, **34**, 213–216.

MASCALL, LEONARD. *The Husbandlye ordring and Gouerment of Poultrie. Practiced by the learnedste and suche as haue bene knowne skilfullest in that Arte, and in our tyme*. London: T. Purfoote, 1581.

MELVIN, KENNETH B., CLOAR, F. THOMAS, and MASSINGILL, LUCINDA S. Imprinting of bobwhite quail to a hawk. *Psychological Record*, 1967, **17**, 235–238.

MILLS, THOMAS. W. *The Nature and Development of Animal Intelligence*. New York: Macmillan, 1898.

MOHR, H. Ueber die Entwicklung einiger Verhaltensweisen bei handaufgezogenen Sperbern (*Accipiter n. nisus* L.) und Baumfalken (*Falco s. subbuteo* L.). *Zeitschrift für Tierpsychologie*, 1960, **17**, 700–727.

MOLTZ, HOWARD. Imprinting: Empirical bases and theoretical significance. *Psychological Bulletin*, 1960, **57**, 291–314.

MOLTZ, HOWARD. An experimental analysis of the critical period for imprinting. *Transactions of the New York Academy of Sciences*, 1961, **23**, 452–463.

MOLTZ, HOWARD. Imprinting: An epigenetic approach. *Psychological Review*, 1963, **70**, 123–138.

MOLTZ, HOWARD, and ROSENBLUM, LEONARD A. Imprinting and associative learning: The stability of the following response in Peking ducks (*Anas platyrhynchos*). *Journal of Comparative and Physiological Psychology*, 1958, **51**, 580–583. (a).

MOLTZ, HOWARD, and ROSENBLUM, LEONARD A. The relation between habituation and the stability of the following response. *Journal of Comparative and Physiological Psychology*, 1958, **51**, 658–661. (b).

MOLTZ, HOWARD, ROSENBLUM, LEONARD A., and HALIKAS, NINA. Imprinting and level of anxiety. *Journal of Comparative and Physiological Psychology*, 1959, **52**, 240–244.

MOLTZ, HOWARD, ROSENBLUM, LEONARD, and STETTNER, L. JAY. Some paramasters of imprinting effectiveness. *Journal of Comparative and Psysiological Psychology*, 1960, **53**, 297–301.

MOLTZ, HOWARD, and STETTNER, L. JAY. The influence of patterned-light deprivation on the critical period for imprinting. *Journal of Comparative and Physiological Psychology*, 1961, **54**, 279–283.

MOORE, ULRIC, and AMSTEY, MARVIN S. Tonic immobility: Differences in susceptibility of experimental and normal sheep and goats. *Science*, 1962, **135**, 729–730.

MORE, SIR THOMAS. *Utopia*. Transl. by P. K. Marshall. New York: Washington Square Press, 1965.

MORGAN, C. LLOYD. *Habit and Instinct*. London: Edward Arnold, 1896.

MORGAN, C. LLOYD. *Animal Behaviour*. London: Edward Arnold, 1900.

NICE, MARGARET M. Studies in the life history of the song sparrow. II. The behavior of the song sparrow and other passerines. *Transactions of the Linnaean Society of New York*, 1943, **6**, 1–328.

NICE, MARGARET M. Development of a redwing (*Agelaius phoeniceus*). *Wilson Bulletin*, 1950, **62**, 87–93.

NICE, MARGARET M. Some experiences in imprinting ducklings. *Condor*, 1953, **55**, 33–37.

NICOLAI, J. Zur Biologie und Ethologie des Gimpels. *Zeitschrift für Tierpsychologie*, 1956, **13**, 93–132.

NICOLAI, J. Der Brutparasitismus der Viduinae als ethologisches Problem. *Zeitschrift für Tierpsychologie*, 1964, **21**, 129–204.

NOBLE, G. K., and ZITRIN, A. Induction of mating behaviour in male and female chicks following injections of sex hormones. *Endocrinology*, 1942, **30**, 327–334.

OPPENHEIM, RONALD W., JONES, JAMES R., and GOTTLIEB, GILBERT. Embryonic motility and posthatching perception in birds after prenatal gamma irradiation. *Journal of Comparative and Physiological Psychology*, 1970, **71**, 6–21.

OZMON, KENNETH L. Proactive and retroactive effects of electroconvulsive shock on imprinting in Japanese quail (*Coturnix coturnix japonica*). *Dissertation Abstracts*, 1969, **29**, 4874.

OZMON, KENNETH L. Imprinting and following in Japanese quail (*Coturnix coturnix japonica*). *Quail Quarterly*, 1970, **7**, 2–10.

PATTIE, F. A. The gregarious behavior of normal chicks and chicks hatched in isolation. *Journal of Comparative Psychology*, 1936, **21**, 161–178.

PERKINS, D. G. Effect of systematically varied stimuli on the following response during imprinting. Unpublished master's thesis at Bradley University, Peoria, Illinois, 1966.

PETERSON, NEIL. Control of behavior by presentation of an imprinted stimulus. *Science*, 1960, **132**, 1395–1396.

PHILLIPS, RICHARD E., and SIEGEL, P. B. Development of fear in chicks of two closely related genetic lines. *Animal Behaviour*, 1966, **14**, 84–88.

PITZ, G. F., and ROSS, R. B. Imprinting as a function of arousal. *Journal of Comparative and Physiological Psychology*, 1961, **54**, 602–604.

PLINY, C. P. S., the elder. *Naturalis Historia*, X, 27 A.D.

POLT, JAMES M. Effect of imprinting experience on discrimination learning in chicks. *Journal of Comparative and Physiological Psychology*, 1969, **69**, 514–518.

POLT, JAMES M., and HESS, ECKHARD H. Following and imprinting: Effects of light and social experience. *Science*, 1964, **143**, 1185–1187.

POLT, JAMES M., and HESS, ECKHARD H. Effects of social experience on the following response in chicks. *Journal of Comparative and Psyiological Psychology*, 1966, **61**, 268–270.

PORTER, RICHARD H., and STETTNER, L. JAY. Imprinting: Transfer of the following response after initial attachment. *Psychonomic Science*, 1968, **13**, 181–182. (a).

PORTER, RICHARD H., and STETTNER, L. JAY. Imprinting: Transfer of the following responses of bobwhite quail *(Colinus virginianus)*. *Journal of Comparative and Physiological Psychology*, 1968, **66**, 808–811. (b).

PORTIELJE, A. F. J. Zur Ethologie beziehungsweise. Psychologie von *Botaurus stellaris* (L.). *Ardea*, 1921, **15**, 1–15.

PORTIELJE, A. F. J. Zur Ethologie, beziehungsweise Psychologie von *Phalocrocorax carbo subcormoranus* (Brehm). *Ardea*, 1927, **21**.

PORTIELJE A. F. J. Versuch einer verhaltungspsychologischen Deutung des Balzgebarens der Kampfschnepf, *Philomachus pugnax* (L.) *Proceedings of the 8th International Ornithological Congress*, 1930.

RÄBER, H. Analyse des Balzverhaltens eines domestizierten Truthans *(Meleagris)*. *Behaviour*, 1948, **1**, 237–266.

RAMSAY, A. OGDEN. Familial recognition in domestic birds. *Auk*, 1951, **68**, 1–16.

RAMSAY, A. OGDEN, and HESS, ECKHARD H. A laboratory approach to the study of imprinting. *Wilson Bulletin*, 1954, **66**, 196–206.

RATNER, STANLEY C. Comparisons between behavior development of normal and isolated domestic fowl. *Animal Behaviour*, 1965, **13**, 497–503.

REGINALD of DURHAM (1165-1175). Libellus de admirandis beati Cuthberti virtutibus quae novellis patratae sunt temporibus. London: Nichols & Sons, 1835.

RICE, CHARLES E. Latent effects of imprinting on social behavior of the domestic fowl. *Dissertation Abstracts*, 1962, **23**, 1800. (a).

RICE, CHARLES E. Imprinting by force. *Science*, 1962, **138**, 680–681. (b)

RIDDLE, OSCAR, and CARR, HARVEY A., editors. *The Posthumous works of C. O. Whitman*. Volume III, *The Behavior of Pigeons*, Washington: The Carnegie Institution of Washington, 1919. Publication No. 257.

ROSE, S. P. R., BATESON, P. P. G., HORN, ANN L. D., and HORN, G. Effects of an imprinting procedure on regional incorporation of tritiated uracil into chick brain R.N.A. *Nature*, 1970, **225**, 650–651.

SALZEN, ERIC A. Imprinting and fear. *Animal Behaviour*, 1962, **10**, 183. (Abstract). (a).

SALZEN, ERIC A. Imprinting and fear. *Symposia of the Zoological Society, London*, 1962, **8**, 199–217. (b).

SALZEN, ERIC A. Imprinting and the immobility reactions of domestic fowl. *Animal Behaviour*, 1963, **11**, 66–71.

SALZEN, ERIC A., and SLUCKIN, WLADYSLAW. The incidence of the following response and the duration of responsiveness in domestic fowl. *Animal Behaviour*, 1959, **7**, 172–179.

SALZEN, ERIC A., and TOMLIN, F. J. The effect of cold on the following response of domestic fowl. *Animal Behaviour*, 1963, **11**, 62–65.

SCHAEFER, HALMUTH H., and HESS, ECKHARD H. Color preferences in imprinting objects. *Zeitschrift für Tierpsychologie*, 1959, **16**, 161–172.

SCHALLER, GEORGE B., and EMLEN, JOHN T. The ontogeny of avoidance behaviour in some precocial birds. *Animal Behaviour*, 1962, **10**, 370–381.

SCHEIN, MARTIN W. The permanent effect of imprinting in turkeys. *American Zoologist*, 1963, **3**, 518–519. (a).

SCHEIN, MARTIN W. On the irreversibility of imprinting. *Zeitschrift für Tierpsychologie*, 1963, **20**, 462–467. (b).
SCHEIN, MARTIN W., FITCH, ROBERT J., and HART, F. M. Sexual stimulus preferences of cross-species imprinted chickens and turkeys. *American Zoologist*, 1962, **2**. (Abstract).
SCHEIN, MARTIN W., and HALE, E. B. An hypothetical model clarifying the effect of early social experience on sexual behavior. *Anatomical Record*, 1959, **134**, 634. (Abstract). (a).
SCHEIN, MARTIN W., and HALE, E. B. The effect of early social experience on male sexual behaviour of androgen injected turkeys. *Animal Behaviour*, 1959, **7**, 189–200. (b).
SCHLEIDT, WOLFGANG. Precocial sexual behaviour in turkeys *(Meleagris gallopavo* L.) *Animal Behaviour*, 1970, **18**, 760–761.
SCHULMAN, ALLAN H. Precocial sexual behaviour in imprinted male turkeys *(Meleagris gallopavo)*. *Animal Behaviour*, 1970, **18**, 758–759.
SCHULMAN, ALLAN H., HALE, EDWARD B., and GRAVES, HANNON B. Visual stimulus characteristics for initial approach response in chicks *(Gallus domesticus)*. *Animal Behaviour*, 1970, **18**, 461–466.
SCHUTZ, FRIEDRICH. Objektfixierung geschlechtlicher Reaktionen bei Anatiden und Hühnern. *Die Naturwissenschaften*, 1963, **50**, 624–625.
SCHUTZ, FRIEDRICH. Die Bedeutung früher sozialer Eindrücke während der "Kinder- und Jugendzeit" bei Enten. *Zeitschrift für experimentelle and angewandte Psychologie*, 1964, **11**, 169–178. (a).
SCHUTZ, FRIEDRICH. Über geschlechtlich unterschiedliche Objektfixierung sexualler Reaktionen bei Enten im Zusammenhang mit dem Prachtkleid des Männchens. *Verhandlungen Deutsche Zoologischen Gesellschaft in München*, 1963, Leipzig: Akademische Verlagsgesellschafts Geest & Portig, K.-G., 1964. 282–287. (b).
SCHUTZ FRIEDRICH. Sexuelle Prägung bei Anatiden. *Zeitschrift für Tierpsychologie*, 1965, **22**, 50–103. (a).
SCHUTZ, FRIEDRICH. Homosexualität und Prägung: Eine experimentelle Untersuchung an Enten. *Psychologische Forschung*, 1965, **28**, 439–463. (b).
SCHUTZ, FRIEDRICH. Zur sexuellen Prägbarkeit und sensiblen Phase von Gänsen und der Bedeutung der Farbe des Prägungsobjekts. *Zoologischer Anzeiger Supplement*, 1969, **33**, 301–306.
SHAPIRO, L. JAMES. Experimental control and automation in a laboratory for imprinting research. *Journal of Comparative and Physiological Psychology*, 1970, **73**, 421–426.
SIEGEL, P. B., and SIEGEL, H. S. Rearing methods and subsequent sexual behaviour of male chickens. *Animal Behaviour*, 1964, **12**, 270–271.
SIMNER, MARVIN L. Cardiac self-stimulation hypothesis and the response to visual flicker in newly hatched chicks: Preliminary findings. *Proceedings of the 74th Annual Convention of the American Psychological Association*, 1966, **1**, 141–142.
SLUCKIN, WLADYSLAW. *Imprinting and Early Learning*. London: Methuen, 1964.
SLUCKIN, WLADYSLAW, and SALZEN, ERIC A. Imprinting and perceptual learning. *Quarterly Journal of Experimental Psychology*, 1961, **13**, 65–77.
SLUCKIN, WLADYSLAW, and TAYLOR, KEITH F. Imprinting and short-term retention. *British Journal of Psychology*, 1964, **55**, 181–188.
SMITH F. V. Towards definition of the stimulus situation for the approach response in the domestic chick. *Animal Behaviour*, 1960, **8**, 197–200.

SMITH, F. V. The experimental study of perceptual aspects of imprinting. *Animal Behaviour*, 1962, **10**, 182–183. (Abstract). (a).

SMITH, F. V. Perceptual aspects of imprinting. *Symposia of the Zoological Society, London*, 1962, **8**, 171–192. (b).

SMITH, F. V., and BIRD, M. W. Varying effectiveness of distant intermittent stimuli for the approach response in the domestic chick. *Animal Behaviour*, 1963, **11**, 57–61. (a).

SMITH, F. V., and BIRD, M. W. The relative attraction for the domestic chick of combinations of stimuli in different sensory modalities. *Animal Behaviour*, 1963, **11**, 300–305. (b).

SMITH, F. V., and BIRD, M. W. Group factors in the response of the domestic chick to a distant visual stimulus. *Animal Behaviour*, 1963, **11**, 397–399. (c).

SMITH, F. V., and BIRD, M. W. The approach response of chicks in groups in relation to the strength of the stimulus. *Animal Behaviour*, 1964, **12**, 252–258. (a).

SMITH, F. V., and BIRD, M. W. The correlation of responsiveness to visual and auditory stimuli in the domestic chick. *Animal Behaviour*, 1964, **12**, 259–263. (b).

SMITH F. V., and HOYES, P. A. Properties of the visual stimuli for the approach response in the domestic chick. *Animal Behaviour*, 1961, **9**, 159–166.

SMITH, F. V., and NOTT, K. H. The "critical period" in relation to the strength of the stimulus. *Zeitschrift für Tierpsychologie*, 1970, **27**, 108–115.

SMITH, F. V., NOTT, K. H., and YARWOOD, A. Brain protein synthesis and the approach response of chicks to a visual stimulus. *Brain Research*, 1970, **21**, 79–90.

SMITH, F. V., and TEMPLETON, W. B. Genetic aspects of the responses of the domestic chick to visual stimuli. *Animal Behaviour*, 1965, **2**, 121–122.

SNAPP, BARBARA D. Recognition of maternal calls by parentally naive *Gallus gallus* chicks. *Animal Behaviour*, 1969, **17**, 440–445.

SPALDING, D. A. Instinct, with original observations on young animals. *British Journal of Animal Behaviour*, 1954, **2**, 2–11. Originally appeared in *McMillan's Magazine*, 1873, **27**, 282–293.

STETTNER, L. J., and TILDS, BARRY N. Effect of presence of an imprinted object on response of ducklings in an open field and when exposed to a fear stimulus. *Psychonomic Science*, 1966, **4**, 107–108.

STEVENS, D. M. Transference of the "imprinting" in a wild gosling. *British Journal of Animal Behaviour*, 1955, **3**, 14–16.

STROBEL, MICHAEL G., BAKER, DONALD G., and MACDONALD, GLENN E. The effect of embryonic X-irradiation on the approach and following response in newly hatched chicks. *Canadian Journal of Psychology*, 1967, **21**, 322–328.

STROBEL, MICHAEL G., CLARK, GORDON M., and MACDONALD, GLENN E. Ontogeny of the approach response. A radiosensitive period during embryological development of domestic chicks. *Journal of Comparative and Physiological Psychology*, 1968, **65**, 314–319.

STROBEL, MICHAEL G., FREEDMAN, SIDNEY L., and MACDONALD, GLENN E. Social facilitation of feeding in newly hatched chickens as a function of imprinting. *Canadian Journal of Psychology*, 1970, **24**, 208–215.

TAYLOR, ANN, and TAYLOR, KEITH F. Imprinting to a static feature of the home environment. *Nature*, 1964, **204**, 1117–1118.

TAYLOR, KEITH F., and SLUCKIN, WLADYSLAW. An experiment in tactile imprinting. *Bulletin of the British Psychological Society*, 1964, **17**, No. 54, 10A. (Abstract). (a).

TAYLOR, KEITH F., and SLUCKIN, WLADYSLAW. Flocking of domestic chicks. *Nature*, 1964, **201,** 108–109. (b).

THOMPSON, WILLIAM R., and DUBANOSKI, RICHARD A. Imprinting and the "law of effort." *Animal Behaviour*, 1964, **12,** 213–218. (a).

THOMPSON, WILLIAM R., and DUBANOSKI, RICHARD A. Early arousal and imprinting in chicks. *Science*, 1964, **143,** 1187–1188. (b).

THOMPSON, WILLIAM R., and O'KIEFFE, M. W. Imprinting: Its effects on the response to stress in chicks. *Science*, 1962, **135,** 918–919.

THORNDIKE, EDWARD L. Instinct. *Biological Lectures, Marine Biological Laboratory, Woods Hole, Mass., 1898*, 1899, **7,** 57–68.

THORPE, WILLIAM H. Some problems of animal learning. *Proceedings of the Linnaean Society, London*, 1944, **156,** 70–83.

THORPE, WILLIAM H. The learning abilities of birds. Part II. *Ibis*, 1951, **93,** 252–296.

THORPE, WILLIAM H. Sensitive periods in the learning of animals and men: A study of imprinting with special reference to the induction of cyclic behaviour. In: Thorpe, W. H., and Zangwill, O. L., editors. *Current Problems in Animal Behaviour*. Cambridge, England: Cambridge University Press, 1961. 194–224.

VINCE, MARGARET A. Some experiments on "imprinting" in moorhens and coots. *Bulletin of the British Psychological Society*, 1955, **26,** 17.

VINCE, MARGARET A. Social facilitation of hatching in the bobwhite quail. *Animal Behaviour*, 1964, **12,** 531–534.

VINCE, MARGARET A. Potential stimulation produced by avian embryos. *Animal Behaviour*, 1966, **14,** 34–40.

WALLER, PATRICIA F., and WALLER, MARCUS B. Some relationships between early experience and later social behavior in ducklings. *Behaviour*, 1963, **20,** 343–363.

WARRINER, CLELL C. Early experience as a variable in mate selection among pigeons. *Dissertation Abstracts*, 1960, **21,** 672.

WARRINER, CLELL C., LEMMON, WILLIAM B., and RAY, THOMAS S. Early experience as a variable in mate selection. *Animal Behaviour*, 1963, **11,** 221–224.

WATSON, JOHN B. The behavior of noddy and sooty terns. *Papers of the Marine Biological Laboratory, Tortugas, Carnegie Institution of Washington*, 1908, **2,** 187–255.

WEIDMANN, ULI. Some experiments on the following and flocking reactions of mallard ducklings. Paper presented at meeting of A.S.A.B., October 19, 1955.

WEIDMANN, ULI. Some experiments on the following and the flocking reaction of mallard ducklings. *British Journal of Animal Behaviour*, 1956, **4,** 78–79.

WEIDMANN, ULI. Verhaltensstudien an der Stockente. II. Versuche zur Auslösung und Prägung der Nachfolge- und Anschlussreaktion. *Zeitschrift für Tierpsychologie*, 1958, **15,** 277–300.

WOOD-GUSH, D. G. M. The effect of experience on the mating behaviour of the domestic cock. *Animal Behaviour*, 1958, **6,** 68–71.

4

The Laboratory Analysis of Social Imprinting and Socialization in Birds

The first time I heard of imprinting was during my student days at Johns Hopkins University when I came into possession of a mimeographed English translation of Lorenz's 1935 paper on the topic. Since my major interests included perception and comparative psychology, I was very much interested in learning about this phenomenon. Later, when I had already begun teaching at the University of Chicago, I read the work of Ramsay (1951) at McDonogh School, not far from my residence in Maryland. Ramsay's work studied imprinting by utilizing foster parents as imprinting objects for hatchling birds. Because I was interested in doing experimental work in the area of imprinting, I contacted Ramsay in the spring of 1952. We soon began to collaborate on a laboratory investigation of imprinting in Maryland, resulting in our joint 1954 paper.

Since then, Ramsay and I and our associates have continued to study imprinting in various duck and chicken species and other birds in Maryland and at the University of Chicago. Table 4–1 shows the different precocial bird species with which we have worked during the past and the comparative degree to which each retains the effects of the early social experience with a vocal moving parental surrogate. Some species appear to be more strongly influenced by such early social experience; however, the ratings which we have assigned are dependent on the conditions under which the animals were tested for degree of imprint-

TABLE 4–1   NUMBER AND IMPRINTABILITY OF DIFFERENT BIRD SPECIES
USED AS SUBJECTS IN HESS LABORATORY RESEARCH
TOTAL EXPERIMENTAL SUBJECTS = 10,150
E = excellent; G = good; F = fair; P = poor

Species		Estimated number	Laboratory imprintability
Ducks			
Wild mallards		5,000	E+
Domesticated mallards		150	E
Pekins		200	G
Rouens		100	F
Wood ducks		50	P
Black ducks		200	G
	Total	5,700	
Geese			
Canada geese		60	E+
Pilgrim geese		50	G
	Total	110	
Chickens			
Jungle fowl		100	G
Cochin bantams		300	G
New Hampshire reds		100	G
Rhode Island reds		100	G
Barred rocks		200	G
Vantress broilers*		3,000	G+
White rocks		100	F
Leghorns		200	P
	Total	4,100	
Other Fowl			
Pheasants		100	P
Eastern bobwhite quail		50	G
California valley quail		20	F
Turkeys		70	F
	Total	240	

*Most animals were imprinted in runway and mallard decoy situations; however, some of the vantress broilers were imprinted on colored spheres.

ing. Some species are more readily influenced by experience with a foreign object than are others. Also, our laboratory procedures, except in the recent ones on the effects of prior sibling socialization (Hess, 1964; Polt and Hess, 1964, 1966), normally involves hatchlings being isolated from siblings and any other social object until the imprinting experience. These animals are also completely isolated between the imprinting experience and the testing procedure, which involves a simultaneous choice situation between the proffered imprinting object and a strange one.

MALLARD DUCKS

Experimental Procedure

In the initial experimental work, we hatched, in our own incubators, wild mallard duckling eggs which we had collected from our duck pond area. Near the time of hatching, the incubators were checked approximately every hour and the chicks were removed as soon as they had hatched. They were individually isolated in small 5- by 4- by 4-inch light-proof cardboard boxes. The time of hatching was recorded, both on the box itself and in the permanent records for each duckling. The ducklings remained in the cardboard boxes in an incubator used as a brooder until imprinting and testing had been completed; only after testing had been carried out were they placed in full daylight and given food and water. Thus every precaution was observed in order to prevent the animals from having any visual or social experience prior to imprinting exposure and the test.

During the imprinting exposure itself, the ducklings were exposed to commercially made papier-mâché mallard duck decoys which had been fitted with off-center wheels that caused them to move with a waddling motion. They also contained small loudspeakers inside which emitted a continuous taped recording of a human rendition of "Gock, gock, gock." In some cases, the model we used contained a thermostatically controlled internal heating element and wore a felt skirt that permitted the duckling to go underneath the decoy for warmth.

The original apparatus used for exposing the ducklings was a 12-foot long rectangular runway 1½ feet wide and 1½ feet high, illuminated with three 15-watt bulbs, one at each end of the runway and one in the middle. The room containing the imprinting apparatus was kept dark during imprinting and during the later testing. In addition, the runway had a hinged wire screen cover to make it difficult for the ducklings to see out although they could easily be seen.

Two main methods of imprinting exposure were used. In the first, the duckling was kept with the model for 10 minutes. Although the movement of the model was accommodated to that of the duckling being exposed, the model was kept in motion as much as was possible for the entire exposure period. Usually the duckling traveled between 150 and 250 feet during the allotted 10-minute period. In the second method, the duckling was with the imprinting object for 30 minutes and the model was moved for a short distance every 5 minutes, with the distance being 12 feet for each 5-minute period, or a total of 72 feet during the 30-minute imprinting exposure.

Later (Hess, 1957) we constructed a more convenient imprinting apparatus (shown in Figure 4-1) consisting of a circular runway 12 inches wide and 12½ feet long. It was enclosed by walls of Plexiglas 12 inches high. The mallard duck decoy was suspended 2 inches above the floor of the runway by means of an elevated arm radiating from the center of the apparatus. The arm caused the decoy to rotate about the runway at speeds and intervals controlled by a panel located about 5 feet from the apparatus and shielded from view from the apparatus by a curtain. As before, the decoy contained a loudspeaker which continuously emitted the gock call from a tape.

During the imprinting exposure procedure itself, the birds were individually released into the runway by means of a cord, pulley, and clip arrangement. Treadles on the floor of the runway activated counters which indicated the amount of following by the young animal. At the termination of the exposure, usually 10 to 20 minutes long, a trap door

Figure 4–1 Apparatus used in the study of laboratory imprinting consists primarily of a circular runway around which a decoy duck can be moved. In this drawing, a duckling follows the decoy. The controls of the apparatus are in the foreground. (Reprinted by permission from Hess, E. H. *Science*, 1959, **130**, 134. © Science, 1959.)

in the floor of the runway returned the duckling to its box, thus making it unnecessary for experimental subjects to be handled by us at any time.

The testing procedure, identical for all our research investigations with mallard ducklings, sometimes carried out as early as 5 hours after imprinting exposure and sometimes as late as 70 hours in our initial research (Ramsay and Hess, 1954) and always 24 hours later in subsequent research, was begun by mechanically releasing the individual ducklings from their box halfway between two duck models placed 4 feet apart. One of these models was the one to which the duckling had been exposed during the imprinting session—a drake—while the other was a strange one—a female mallard. The only difference between these models was their coloration. The duckling was given four successive 1-minute tests in the imprinting apparatus itself, whether rectangular or circular. For the first minute, the models were both silent. At the end of this minute, whatever choice the duckling had made, sound was turned on in both models, with the drake emitting the gock call and the female model emitting quacks such as are normally given when the young are called. For the third 1-minute test, the female model was placed in motion and the drake remained motionless; both models emitted their respective calls. During the last minute of testing, the female mallard model both moved and called while the drake model was silent and motionless. We deemed these four 1-minute tests to be in order of increasing difficulty for the duckling to remain with the original model it had been exposed to, as the female mallard model was made to be more and more attractive to the duckling.

If the duckling went over to the imprinting exposure object, the drake model, during a test period, it was given 15 percentage points. If, in addition, the duckling emitted contentment calls while in the presence of that model, it was given an additional 10 percentage points. Thus, if, in every one of the four tests, the duckling went to the imprinting model, it gained a score of 60 percentage points. It could achieve the remaining 40 percentage points required to obtain a perfect imprinting score of 100 percent only if it also gave the pleasure (contentment) notes to the imprinting model during each of these four tests. These criteria for imprinting are very stringent, indeed; a score such as 60 percent actually denotes significant attachment on the part of the duckling, since if a duckling prefers to be with the imprinting model four times out of four occasions, this certainly is not chance behavior.

Effects of Age of Exposure

In Ramsay and Hess (1954), we reported on the results of experimentation with 92 ducklings, 54 of which had been run according to the 10-

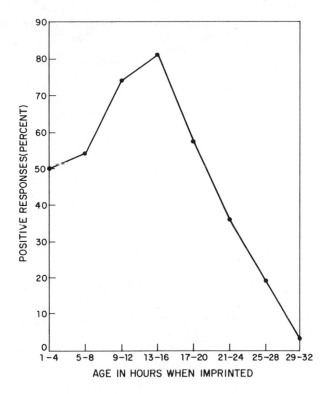

Figure 4–2 Percentages of positive responses made by ducklings in test series.

minute procedure and the remaining 38 run by the 30-minute method. In these ducklings, while we saw no gross effect of the length of the interval between laboratory imprinting exposure and testing, we found extremely clear indications of an age-related period of sensitivity to the imprinting exposure situation, both in terms of the average scores obtained during the later testing procedure and in terms of the number of ducklings that achieved perfect imprinting scores. Figure 4–2 shows the mean percentage scores made by the animals of each exposure age group, with the highest mean score of more than 80 percent made by animals 13 to 16 hours old at the time of the imprinting exposure. The mean scores are essentially zero after the age of 28 hours. Table 4–2 gives the number of ducklings tested at each age group, the number in each group giving a positive response during each of the four tests, and the mean total percentage score for all four tests. The .5 scores indicate ducklings which went in the direction of the imprinting object before it was moved and which remained with the model.

Only 9 animals out of the total of 92 ducklings gave a positive re-

TABLE 4–2 RESPONSES OF DUCKLINGS IMPRINTED AT DIFFERENT AGES TO LABORATORY IMPRINTING OBJECT ON LATER FOUR-PART TEST

Number	Age in hours	Number giving positive response*				Average (percent)	Number making perfect score
		Test 1	Test 2	Test 3	Test 4		
13	1 to 4	12	11	3	1	51.9	0
20	5 to 8	18.5	18.5	6	0	53.6	0
15	9 to 12	15	15	8	6.5	74.1	2
15	13 to 16	15	15	11.5	7	80.8	6
10	17 to 20	9	9	3	2	57.5	1
11	21 to 24	7	5	3	1	36.4	0
4	25 to 28	1	1	0	1	18.7	0
4	29 to 32	0	0.5	0	0	31.3	0

*.5 scores are ducklings that went in the direction of the imprinting object before it was moved and that remained with the model.

sponse in all four of the tests for imprinting strength. Two of them were 9 to 12 hours old during the initial exposure, 6 were 13 to 16 hours old, and the last 1 was 17 to 20 hours old. If these data are presented graphically in terms of the proportion of ducklings in each age group that made perfect scores, as is done in Figure 4–3, the influence of the age at the time of the imprinting experience upon the extent to which duckling will approach and prefer to stay with the object which they had seen becomes extremely clear. The sharpness with which the age of

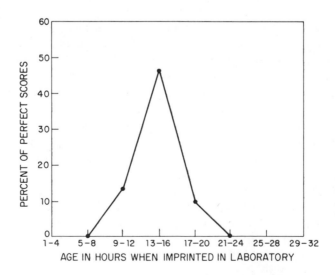

Figure 4–3 Percentages of perfect scores of mallards imprinted in various age groups.

the animal influences the retention of the laboratory imprinting experience is shown by the fact that both of the animals in the 9 to 12 hour age group that made perfect retention scores were 12 hours old at the time of the exposure, and the one animal in the 17 to 20-hour age group which showed perfect imprinting was 18 hours old. Thus, the range of perfect scores was actually only from 12 to 18 hours, since no animal younger than 12 hours or older than 18 hours made perfect scores in this experiment.

Our findings do not accord completely with those of Fabricius (1957), since he had reported that the period from hatching up to the age of 12 hours was the most sensitive in his mallard ducklings. It is possible that our testing procedure was more sensitive than that used by Fabricius. Another possible source of the difference in the reported data may lie in the fact that Fabricius reported that normal walking and running were not established in his ducklings until they reached the age period of 16 to 28 hours after hatching. All our ducklings were able to walk and run many hours before this age period. While 4 of the 8 ducklings that were placed in the imprinting situation before reaching the age of 2 hours could not even crawl in a straight line but crawled in a clockwise direction, 6 ducklings which were exposed to the parental surrogate between the age of 3 and 4 hours for a 10-minute period traveled an average distance of 75 feet within this time period. The maximum distance traveled in this experiment was 250 feet, and the minimum following score was 16 feet.

The effect of the laboratory imprinting experience is particularly evident in the results obtained when we exposed 24 naïve ducklings of various ages to the testing situation (Ramsay and Hess, 1954). These ducklings, never having been exposed to the imprinting siuation, showed no inherent preference for either of the two models. They were first tested with the models silent and then with the drake calling gock and the female model calling quack. The calls were then reversed in the models two or more times. At no tlme were the models moved, and each duckling was allowed as much as 5 minutes to make a response. None of the 24 ducklings moved toward either model as long as they were both silent. Fifteen ducklings showed no preference between the call notes. Of the 15, 10 made no move toward either sound, and 5 responded to each call once. Of the remaining 9 ducklings, 8 chose the gock call consistently and one chose the quack repeatedly. In another experiment, 15 ducklings were similarly tested for preference between the recorded duck quack and a human rendition of a duck quack. Two of the ducklings definitely chose the human quack, and 1 the recorded quack. Those ducklings therefore showed no real auditory preferences.

While the effect of increasing age beyond the age of 16 hours is in

the direction of decreasing the susceptibility to the laboratory imprinting experience in mallard ducklings, it is possible to produce some
retentiveness of the experience in ducklings which are well past this
optimum imprinting age. Two ducklings, 28 hours old, and 2 ducklings,
38 hours old, were each placed with the imprinting object in the company of 2 other ducklings that had already been well imprinted to the
model. Upon later testing, all 4 animals made better scores than would
otherwise have been expected. Each of the 2 imprinted at the age of 28
hours made a score of 75 percent, and each of the 2 imprinted at the
age of 38 hours made a score of 50 percent during the test period.

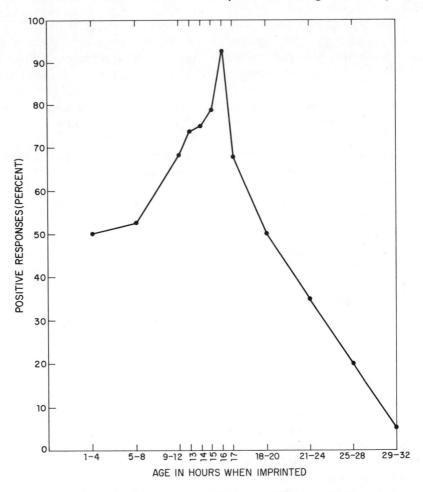

Figure 4–4 Critical age for laboratory imprinting in mallards expressed as the percent
of positive responses.

Thus we have fully confirmed the "social faciliation" effect noted by Collias and Collias (1956) and reported by Klopfer (1959).

Further experiments (Hess, 1957) carried out with additional subjects substantiated our initial findings with respect to the effects of age upon the behavior of the ducklings toward the two objects during the testing situation. These additional subjects, incubated and brooded as before in individual isolation, were exposed to the parental surrogate in the circular runway apparatus and tested at a later hour, as had been done in Ramsay and Hess (1954). The 10-minute procedure in which the animals followed the drake decoy for about 150 to 200 feet was utilized. The additional data, when added to those which we had previously obtained, produced an even clearer curve showing the relation between the age at laboratory imprinting and the strength of preference for the imprinting object at the later test. Figure 4–4 (compare with Figure 4–1) shows the mean imprinting test scores obtained by the ducklings as a function of age at the initial exposure. It also shows that during the age period from 13 to 17 hours the effect of the laboratory imprinting experience rises gradually to a maximum level at the age of 16 hours, after which it falls off rather sharply. Similarly, Figure 4–5 offers constructive comparison with Figure 4–2. Again, the ability of the ducklings to form

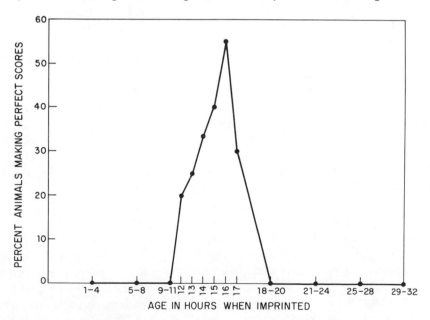

Figure 4–5 Critical age for laboratory imprinting in mallards expressed as the percent of animals making perfect scores.

irreversible preferences for the imprinting object rose after the age of 12 hours to a maximum at the age of 16 hours, thereafter falling off rapidly.

Releasers of Imprinting

Ramsay and Hess (1954) also made an exploratory study of the effects of various stimuli acting as releasers in evoking the following reaction in ducklings during the exposure to a potential parent object. We have already mentioned the fact that naïve ducklings of various ages did not have any inherent preferences for the drake model or the female mallard model. It was also found that of 7 ducklings of various ages exposed only to the recorded natural quack of the hen duck calling her young, only 4 responded to this sound during the later test period. These 4 made an average score of 50 percent in the test period; the other 3 did not make any response to either model, thus making the mean score of the group 28.6 percent. In contrast, however, of thirty-eight mallard ducklings exposed to the male model calling gock, only 1 failed to respond at all during the later test. The group's mean score in this test was 57.5 percent.

Thus, while visual stimuli appeared important in conjunction with auditory ones, Ramsay and Hess (1954) also found that motion was not at all necessary for the ducklings to show a strong preference for the imprinting model on the later test. Four ducklings were kept with a motionless drake model for half an hour while it emitted the standard gock call continuously. Three of the 4 ducklings had a score of 75 percent on the test, and the fourth had a perfect score of 100 percent. This fourth duckling was the only one that was exposed at the sensitive age period of 13 to 16 hours. These ducklings responded at a higher level than did Fabricius' (1951) ducklings that were exposed to a stuffed female mallard.

Furthermore, while Ramsay and Hess' ducklings had no obviously universal auditory preferences, it was found that they did have form preferences. Three ducklings were individually imprinted to a motionless calling drake decoy for 30 minutes, and 3 others were similarly exposed to a small box which also emitted the gock call. This half-hour exposure took place during the 1st day of life. When the ducklings were approximately 2 days old, they were given the following preference tests: drake model and box, both giving the standard gock call; drake model silent, box calling; and drake model calling, box silent. The drake-imprinted ducklings made a mean score of 61.1 percent, and the box-imprinted ducklings made a mean score of 27.8 percent to their respective models on the test. Thus, it is very apparent that, even with the limited number of subjects tested, ducklings do have inherent preferences for the form of the parental object, since the drake-imprinted ducklings showed a far greater effect—more than twice as much—than did the box-imprinted ones. (Similar effects in the case of color and form preferences were seen later on the part of chicks by Schaefer and Hess, 1959.) It is also significant that 2 of the drake-imprinted ducklings responded to it even when it was silent and the box was calling, but none of the box-imprinted ducklings responded to it when it was silent and the drake was calling.

Other research investigations which we have conducted have clearly indicated the superiority of vocal models over silent ones In the laboratory imprinting situation. When the model is vocal, twice as many ducklings of the sensitive age period will follow it; in addition, they will follow twice as much.

Later research (Hess, 1962b) showed that when the same shape—a 6½ inch diameter sphere—was used in different colors, the colors elicited differential amounts of following in 12 to 16 hour old naïve socially isolated mallard ducklings. The most effective color was blue (evoking 50.0 feet of mean following), followed, in descending order, by green (32.5 feet), red (30.0 feet), orange (14.2 feet), and yellow (5.7 feet). The scores for achromatic spheres were: black, 31.2; gray, 9.6; and white, 13.7 feet of mean following.

Field Observations

Naturalistic field studies reported by Ramsay and Hess confirmed that the attachments formed by ducklings kept with a drake decoy during the entire period of imprintability on the 1st day of life were strong enough to cause such ducklings to avoid real live females calling their young actively, whereas untreated naïve ducklings of the same age would ignore the calling drake model and go to join the female mallard. Even small amounts of imprinting experience had evident effects on the social behavior of ducklings released into the field: a group of day-old ducklings that had had less than 10 minutes of experience in following a silent drake decoy in the runway the previous day went to a silent floating drake decoy and persisted in staying with it in spite of the female mallard's persevering attempts to lure them away. Another group of drake-imprinted ducklings that had had no experience in following a silent model followed the floating drake decoy briefly, and then left it to join the more familiar model with wheels resting on nearby land.

Another event occurring during the field studies showed the strength of the laboratory imprinting experience in influencing the behavior of ducklings. Three young mallards previously imprinted on a male model were at the edge of a duck pond with the decoy as it was emitting the gock call. A female mallard with 2 of her own ducklings came up to these 3 ducklings. All the ducklings became intermingled; but when the female left, only her own ducklings followed her, and the 3 imprinted on the drake decoy stayed with it. Thus, we can see how this type of field study can supplement laboratory experimentation on this behavior process, a point which is discussed in Chapter 8.

The Law of Effort: $I_e = \log E$.

One of the questions which we attempted to explore in our 1954 report was that of how long birds must be exposed to the imprinting object if laboratory imprinting is to be complete and irreversible to the extent that perfect 100 percent scores are made in the test with the imprinting object and a strange object simultaneously present. Both the imprinting methods we used—the 10-minute procedure and the 30-minute procedure—produced a few ducklings that achieved the perfect imprinting score in the test situation. Both methods, in fact, were just as effective in terms of proportions of ducklings that made 100 percent scores. Thus, amount of time, qua time, spent with the imprinting model did not appear to be a very strong factor in promoting the effectiveness of the exposure to the model in promoting an attachment to it.

Incidental observations made during the course of the experimentation reported by Ramsay and Hess (1954) appeared to suggest that ducklings which walked more during the exposure to the laboratory imprinting object were better scorers on the later test. This led to specific experimentation on the effects of the amount of walking during the imprinting experience in comparison with the effects of the amount of time spent with the model in terms of the degree of attachment evident in the test session. The results of this experimentation were reported in Hess (1957).

First, we studied laboratory imprinting strength as a function of the distance traveled by ducklings during a 10-minute exposure period. We used the circumference of the runway—12½ feet—as a unit, and had animals follow the drake decoy for 0, 1, 2, 4, and 8 turns. This resulted in 10-minute laboratory imprinting experiences in which the ducklings walked 1, 12½, 25, 50, and 100 feet, respectively. All ducklings were between 12 and 17 hours old, so as to equalize the degree of age-related sensitivity.

Figure 4–6 depicts the scores obtained during the testing procedure, the same as used in Ramsay and Hess (1954) and administered 24 hours later, as a function of the number of feet that the model had been followed. There is a rapid rise in the test scores between 1 and 25 feet. After the distance of 50 feet, there appears to be a relative leveling off

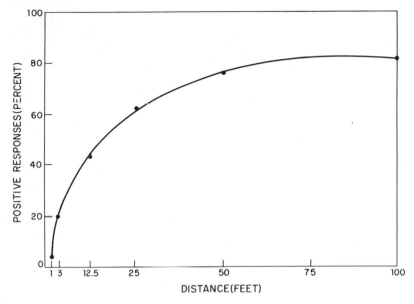

Figure 4–6 Strength of laboratory imprinting as a function of distance traveled by ducklings, with exposure time held constant.

of the effectiveness as a function of increasing distance. The curve produced by the scores, in fact, appears to be essentially logarithmic.

While we had not yet observed any evidence indicating amount of time during exposure to be an important factor in promoting the attachment of ducklings to the parental surrogate, we decided to test for this factor explicitly by having ducklings follow the drake model for the same distance in different amounts of time. The results are shown in Figure 4–7. As often as not, in fact, the effect of giving animals more time in which to follow the model for a specific distance was to depress the test score very slightly, thus showing that the small differences in test scores for equal distances of following as a function of exposure time merely reflect random fluctuations from a basic value which is dependent on the actual amount of following that had been performed during the laboratory imprinting experience.

These experimental results led us to conclude that it is the total amount of effort expended by the duckling during the exposure to the parental surrogate that is a primary factor in promoting the degree to which the duckling forms an attachment to the object. The more the duckling follows—that is, the more energy the duckling expends in order to be with the object—the more likely it is to achieve the perfect imprinting criteria score in our testing procedure. We carried out a few

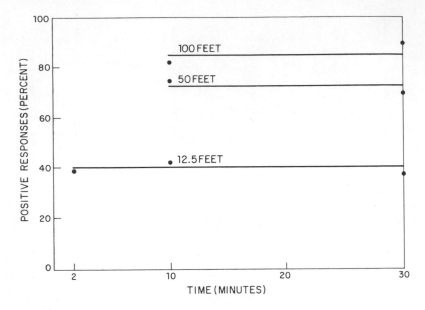

Figure 4–7 Strength of laboratory imprinting as a function of duration and exposure in minutes. Time had little effect on the test scores of the ducklings when the distance traveled was held constant.

other supplementary experiments that also served to indicate the importance of effort on the part of the duckling in promoting the occurrence of laboratory imprinting (Hess, 1955).

First of all, we exposed naïve individually isolated ducklings at the optimum age to 2 identical drake decoys placed 3 feet apart. A light over each decoy could be turned on and off so that only one model at a time was illuminated in the otherwise dark experimental apparatus as it gave the gock call. When a duckling reached an illuminated and calling model, the light and sound were switched off in that model and turned on the other one. In this fashion, the ducklings were shuttled back and forth between the two models, so that they expended effort to be with a parental surrogate without the surrogate itself moving in space. Ducklings that were shuttled 4 or 16 times between the models achieved test scores similar to those obtained by ducklings that had followed a moving drake decoy for 12 and 50 feet. Thus, the complex perception of following a moving object is not required in order for laboratory imprinting to be effective.

We carried out the shuttle experiment again, but this time made it much harder for the ducklings to traverse the distance between the 2 drake decoys. This was accomplished by placing two hurdles 4 inches in height between the 2 models. The ducklings learned in a few trials to get over the hurdles and otherwise behaved as in the first shuttle experiment. The ducklings, 12 to 17 hours old, were shuttled between the models 4 times. The scores that these ducklings obtained in the imprinting test procedure showed that the additional effort required on their part to traverse the four shuttles involving a total distance of 12 feet when the obstacles were present served to enhance the attachment they had for the drake decoy, in comparison with the scores obtained by ducklings that followed for a distance of 12 feet in the earlier shuttle experiment without obstacles, or for a distance of 12½ feet in the circular runway, also without obstacles. The difference in the test scores obtained as a function of the presence or absence of obstacles during the laboratory imprinting exposure was a significant one, since the scores obtained by subjects that climbed over hurdles while traversing 12 feet were the same as those obtained by animals that followed a vocal moving drake decoy for more than 25 feet in the circular runway without obstacles. In still another experiment (Hess, 1958), we had the young ducklings follow the drake decoy in the circular runway in a tilted position, thus forcing them to follow the model uphill, or had the ducklings climb over hurdles placed in the level runway; we obtained similar results.

We also carried out an experiment in which we attempted to imprint 10 ducklings at the critical age upon the drake decoy without their following it but at the same time with their seeing the decoy move. We did this by restraining them in a holder attached to the rear of the vocal moving drake model. During the 15-minute exposure period, the decoy moved 8 times around the 12½ foot runway, thus traveling a total of 100 feet. When we later tested these ducklings in the standard four-part testing procedure 24 hours later, we found that ducklings which had been observed to attempt to get from the holder to the model's tail, and visibly struggled to do so in vain, showed evidence of laboratory imprinting having taken place; whereas those that were not seen to struggle at all in this fashion were not, according to their test scores, imprinted to the drake decoy. As may be seen from Table 4–3, all those that struggled

TABLE 4–3   IMPRINTING TEST SCORES OF TEN INDIVIDUAL DUCKLINGS AT CRITICAL AGE PERIOD CARRIED BEHIND MOVING DECOY

Non-strugglers	Strugglers
1. 0	1. 75
2. 25	2. 100
3. 0	3. 100
4. 25	
5. 25	
6. 0	
7. 25	

obtained test scores no lower than 75 percent, while none of these never seen to struggle obtained scores higher than 25 percent on the test.

These results are at variance with those reported by Moltz, Rosenblum, and Stettner (1960) (see Chapter 3 for details) in an experiment in which pekin ducklings were exposed to a silent moving pekin duck decoy or to a green box for 25 minutes daily for 3 days, beginning on the very 1st day of life at an age of approximately 7 to 14 hours. Some of the ducklings, it will be recalled, were permitted to follow the moving object actively, while others were restrained in a transparent enclosure. The restraint was such that while chicks could stand, turning was accomplished with difficulty. The authors reported that the chicks that were restrained during experimental exposure for 3 days but were able to observe the moving decoy later followed it just as intensively as did those that had been permitted to follow it actively. Moltz, Rosenblum, and Stettner discount the possibility of struggling by the confined ducklings as causing the high level of following activity of the exposure model during test: "Some birds sit quitely during confinement and then follow vigorously when the opportunity is afforded." However these authors used a completely different criterion from that used by us—that is, amount of following rather than choice in a simultaneous presentation situation. In fact, their ducks were given a 5-minute choice test 1 hour before the following session on day 4 and another 1 hour afterward. "The results obtained did not furnish an estimate of imprinting effectiveness that was either internally consistent or in accord with the following scores obtained in the alley," according to Moltz, Rosenblum, and Stettner. The behavior during the choice test was measured in terms of the number of seconds spent with the familiar object rather than of which object was approached. Hence, the reported data are not at all comparable with ours and, in view of the difficulties of using amount of following as a criterion of the effectiveness of exposure to a parental object in producing a manifest attachment, we do not feel that these reported data of Moltz and his associates obtained with pekin ducklings constitute negative evidence for our conclusion that energy expenditure during the laboratory imprinting experience enhances the occurrence of laboratory imprinting in mallard ducks. More direct evidence is necessary in order for our position to be contravened. We will have much more to say on the topic of energy expenditure and imprinting when we discuss our research with chickens.

As a result of all these findings, we came to the conclusion (Hess, 1958) that there is a lawfulness in the way in which effort expended by critical period age ducklings during the imprinting exposure to a parental surrogate positively enhances the formation of an attachment to that surrogate. We expressed this lawfulness in accord with the type of experimental results we had obtained, shown in Figure 4–6, as a formula: the strength of imprinting equals the logarithm of the effort expended by the animal during the laboratory imprinting experience occurring during the period of optimum susceptibility to imprinting, 12 to 17 hours of age.

Still other experimental facts we have obtained support the hypothesis of the importance of effort in the laboratory imprinting process in mallard ducklings. It may be recalled that in Ramsay and Hess (1954) it was found that of 7 ducklings exposed passively to the recorded natural quack of the female mallard calling her young, only 4 showed responsiveness to this sound when later tested. The inefficacy of auditory stimulation without concomitant visual stimulation or energy expenditure was shown by another experiment in which we exposed 30 mallard eggs during the last 48 hours of incubation to a constantly played tape recording of a mallard hen calling her young (Hess, 1959c). We did this because some investigators of the laboratory imprinting phenomenon have suggested that the vocalizations of the incubating parent might result in an imprinted attachment to that vocalization even before the time of hatching. However, when the laboratory-hatched mallard ducklings were tested, they chose this sound no more frequently than they did the strange gock call. Gottlieb (1965) has reported that the rates of bill clapping and vocalizations are increased in white rock chick embryos and pekin duck embryos as a consequence of stimulation with the conspecific maternal call. Hence, our failure to get mallard embryos to show an active preference for the quacking of a female mallard as a consequence of the passive exposure to it suggests that the effect of such prenatal stimulation from the female duck's vocalization is not in the direction of promoting an immediate attachment for that vocalization in the case of laboratory-hatched mallard ducklings, but may serve as an activating agent for becoming immediately imprinted to it and to the female mallard after hatching. More recent research upon this question is discussed in Chapter 8.

Drugs

We began experimentation on the effects of tranquilizers on the formation of imprinted social attachments in mallard ducklings because we were interested in assessing the role played by fear responses on the part of ducklings in ending the period of susceptibility to the laboratory experience. We had noted in our initial research (Ramsay and Hess, 1954) that fear in response to strange moving objects first appeared in our mallard ducklings near the age of 20 hours. Later research (Hess, 1957) determined that almost 80 percent of ducklings 24 hours old show fear or avoidance behavior and that the proportion of ducklings showing such behavior increases rapidly to 100 percent at the age of 32 hours or older.

Thus, it occurred to us that we could reduce the fearfulness of older ducklings by means of giving them tranquilizing drugs such as meprobamate and perhaps increase their imprintability. Preliminary tests showed that meprobamate did, indeed, reduce the emotional responsiveness of ducklings without markedly influencing their motility or coordination. Such ducklings, even at an age when marked fear is normally a certainty, evidenced no fear of strange objects or persons. The action of meprobamate, administered orally, was clearly evident at 20 minutes after administration and disappeared in about 5 hours.

Then we carried out an experiment in which we administered meprobamate, chlorpromazine (both tranquilizers), or nembutal (a barbiturate) to experimental animals. Control animals were given .33 cc distilled water. Ducklings were imprinted and tested under one of the following four conditions: 1) drug at the age of 12 hours, imprinting at the age of 24 hours, test 24 hours later when the drug effect had worn off; 2) drug at the age of 12 hours, imprinting at the age of 14 to 16 hours, test 24 hours later when the drug effect had worn off; 3) imprinting at the age of 16 hours, testing 24 hours later while under the influence of a drug; and 4) drug at the age of 24 hours, imprinting at the age of 26 hours, test 24 hours later when the drug effect had worn off. Naturally, all animals were subjected to the same hatching, individual isolation, imprinting, and testing procedures that we had used before.

The percentage scores made in the imprinting test situation by the animals of the different experimental groups are shown in Table 4–4.

TABLE 4–4 MEAN PERCENTAGE SCORES OF DUCKLINGS UNDER DIFFERENT CONDITIONS OF LABORATORY IMPRINTING, TESTING, AND DRUG ADMINISTRATION

Group	Control H_2O	Meprobamate 25mg/kg	Nembutal 5mg/kg	Chlorpromazine 15mg/kg
1. Drug at 12 hours, imprint at 24 hours, test without drug	14	54	31	57
2. Drug at 12 hours, imprint at 14 to 16 hours, test without drug	62	8	28	63
3. Imprint without drug at 16 hours, test under drug	61	65	61	58
4. Drug at 24 hours, imprint at 26 hours, test without drug	19	17	16	59

The results obtained with these drugs surprised us a great deal. For example, 26-hour old ducklings normally imprint rather weakly, but those put into the imprinting exposure situation while under the influence of either meprobamate or nembutal imprinted even less well in spite of the removal of fear.

In all cases in which the animals had been put into the laboratory imprinting situation during the optimum age of 16 hours without being under the influence of any drug but were tested for the effects of imprinting while drugged, absolutely no interference with the effects of the imprinting experience is evident. But if 14- to 16-hour-old ducklings were exposed to the drake model while under the influence of meprobamate or nembutal and then were tested when the drug had worn off, interference with the retention of the imprinting experience was very evident, especially in the case of the animals drugged with meprobamate where evidence of imprinting in the test was practically nil, while nembutal apparently halved the degree of imprinting. Chlorpromazine, on the other hand, had no such interfering effect. However, when one of these three tranquilizers had been administered at the age of 12 hours and the ducklings then exposed to the imprinting situation at the age of 24 hours, the later test scores of these animals were higher than were those of the control animals, with the enhancing effect much less marked in the case of nembutal.

Out of this complex of results it is possible to hypothesize that meprobamate and chlorpromazine act by reducing neural metabolism, since it is known they do not affect general metabolism. In such a case, we could expect the high scores resulting from imprinting at the age of 24 hours (group 1) because neural metabolism had been slowed and thus the sensitive period for imprinting extended to permit imprintability at a later age than normal (Hess, 1960). No slowing of neural metabolism could occur in the animals given distilled water. Second, while the control and nembutal groups treated at the age of 24 hours showed marked emotionality at the age of 26 hours, no such responses were observable in the meprobamate or chlorpromazine groups. In spite of this, only the chlorpromazine group showed evidence that imprinting had occurred.

To explain the effect of meprobamate upon the 24-hour ducks, we considered the law of effort, which postulates that the strength of imprinting is a function of effort expended or distance traveled during imprinting in animals that are at the optimal age for imprinting. It may be that since meprobamate is a muscle relaxant drug, these effects of meprobamate cut into muscular tension or proprioceptive impulses from the muscles, and thus nullified the effectiveness of the imprinting experience in spite of the fact that the animals under its influence were able to walk. This notion appeared even more tenable in the light of the fact that we had been able to obtain adequate imprinting with the use of chlorpromazine.

In 1958, carisoprodol was made available to us, and we proceeded to test the hypothesis that meprobamate interferes with imprinting via its muscle-relaxant properties. This we could do with carisoprodol because it is a congener of (chemically related to) meprobamate and is almost purely a muscle relaxant, with little or no tranquilizing action (Hess, Polt, and Goodwin, 1959). Using the same hatching, individual isolation, imprinting, and testing procedures, we had the following three experimental groups of animals: 1) 10 ducklings given 125 mg/kg carisoprodol at the age of 12 hours after hatching, then imprinted at the age of 24 hours, and tested 24 hours after imprinting when the drug had worn off; 2) 42 mallard ducklings given 125 mg/kg carisoprodol at the age of 12 hours after hatching, then imprinted between 14 and 16 hours of age, and tested 24 hours after imprinting when the drug had worn off; 3) 9 subjects imprinted at the age of 14 to 16 hours, without any drug influence, but tested for imprinting strength while under the influence of 125 mg/kg carisoprodol administered 2 hours before the test which was performed 24 hours after the imprinting exposure. Twenty ducklings, serving as controls, were given water just before the imprinting session at the age of 16 hours after hatching.

Table 4–5 shows the scores obtained in the testing session by the three experimental groups of ducklings, in comparison with the appropriate control groups from Hess (1957). When Table 4–5 is compared with the data with respect to the effects of meprobamate as shown in Table 4–4, it becomes evident that our hypothesis was confirmed. Just as meprobamate does, carisoprodol completely prevents ducklings from forming an attachment to the drake model which has been offered as a parental surrogate, when the exposure to it during the critical age period takes

TABLE 4–5 MEAN PERCENTAGE SCORES OF DUCKLINGS UNDER DIFFERENT CONDITIONS OF TESTING AND DRUG ADMINISTRATION

	Scores at test	
Group	Control*	Carisoprodol
1. Drug at 12 hours, imprint at 24 hours, test without drug	14	34
2. Drug at 12 hours, imprint at 14 to 16 hours, test without drug	62 to 65[†]	11
3. Imprint without drug at 16 hours, test under drug	61	67

*Figures for control animals, except the 65 percent recorded in this column, are from Hess (1957).
[†]Score of 20 controls that had never been given any drug.

place with the animal under its influence. Furthermore, testing under the influence of carisoprodol does not at all interfere with the manifestation of imprinting. However, the extension of the period of imprintability, possibly through retardation of neural metabolism, which had been observed with meprobamate, did not materialize to the same extent with carisoprodol, for animals which had been drugged with carisoprodol at the age of 12 hours and then exposed to the imprinting object at the age of 24 hours later achieved scores resembling those obtained by ducklings that had been similarly treated with nembutal and placed in the imprinting situation at the age of 24 hours.

These results concerning the effects of drugs on the duration of the sensitive period for imprintability and the retention of the effects of the imprinting experience are of great interest in the light of the fact that in informal experimentation in which we have had week-old mallard ducklings learn a color discrimination problem involving food reward while under the influence of meprobamate, there was no evidence at all that there was any depressing influence on their ability to learn the color discrimination or in their ability to retain the effects of the learning when later tested after the drug had worn off. This is, indeed, in stark contrast to the fact that meprobamate causes ducklings under its influence while being exposed to an imprinting object to later act as if the experience had never occurred at all. There will be further discussion of the effect of drugs upon laboratory imprinting when the relevant research conducted with vantress broiler chicks is discussed later in this chapter.

Primacy versus Recency

We have attempted (Hess, 1959a) to determine the effects of exposure to more than one moving vocal model during the sensitive period for laboratory imprinting. Two groups of 11 mallard ducklings each, hatched in our laboratory and visually and socially isolated as usual, were successively exposed to two different models—a drake decoy and a female mallard decoy—at the age of 14 to 16 hours. The drake decoy emitted the standard gock call, and the female mallard decoy gave the quack. One group was first imprinted on the drake model and then on the female model, while the reverse order was used for the other group. The imprinting procedure carried out with each of the two models was identical, involving 8 turns of the models about the circular runway, so that each model could be followed for a maximum of 100 feet.

Twenty-four hours later, ducklings were individually placed in the four-part test situation with both models present. Fourteen of the 22 ducklings showed a preference for the model which they had followed first in the imprinting exposure situation, and 5 showed a preference for the one they had followed most recently. Only 3 showed no preference at all. Thus, it is highly apparent that the first-experienced social object is, generally speaking, the one which retains the prepotent effect on the later social preferences shown by the mallard duckling in a free choice test with both objects simultaneously present. This conclusion will be further supported by the data presented in the next section.

Effect of Sibling Socialization.

Heretofore, all our laboratory imprinting research involved the use of naïve ducklings that were completely isolated in small cardboard boxes in a dark brooder-incubator as soon as possible after hatching. These animals, at the time of the laboratory imprinting experience, were bereft of both social and visual experience. After the imprinting experience, they were further kept in social and visual isolation until the time of the testing for imprinting several hours later. In two recent experiments (Hess, 1964; Ramsay and Hess, 1967) we are about to discuss, however, this procedure was departed from to the extent that ducklings were given 2 hours of social experience with age mates at some time prior to the imprinting experience.

In the first experiment, 144 ducklings were given 2 hours of social experience during the critical age period of 12 to 17 hours after hatching. This was done by removing the ducklings from their individual isolation boxes and placing them with a group of 10 age mates in a lighted area. The ducklings were marked with a felt pen for identification purposes. After socialization experience, they were returned to their numbered individual boxes and kept inside them in a brooder-incubator until the imprinting experience, after which they were again returned to the numbered individual boxes and placed in the brooder-incubator until the time of the testing session. The laboratory imprinting exposure occurred at different times for different groups of ducklings.

The model to which the chicks were exposed was the standard drake decoy emitting the usual gock call. During the first 2 minutes of the exposure, the decoy was made to move slowly back and forth, "coaxing" the duckling to approach it. This was usually effective in getting subjects to follow. The model was moved about the circular runway apparatus 8 times in a period of 10 minutes, making it possible for the duckling to follow it for a maximum of 100 feet during the imprinting exposure session. Relatively few ducklings had to be exposed to the model for several turns before they would begin to follow it.

The procedure for testing for imprinting strength, carried out 24 hours after the imprinting exposure session, utilized the same 4 1-minute

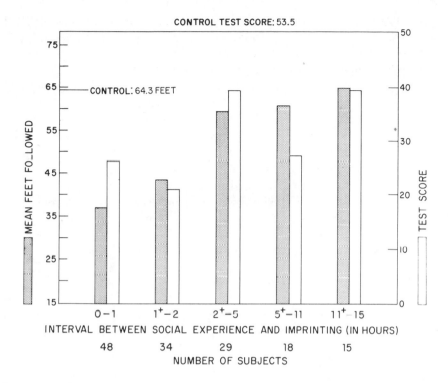

Figure 4–8 The effects of the interval between social experience during the critical period and exposure to the laboratory imprinting model in ducklings. Control N was 33 subjects.

series of simultaneous exposure to the imprinting object and a strange object as used in our earlier research.

Figure 4–8 shows the mean amounts that the different groups of ducklings followed the drake decoy during the laboratory imprinting experience itself and the scores which they obtained when later tested for evidence of imprinting. It is very obvious that all but one of the groups followed the model less than did normal naïve controls 14 to 16 hours old, and that all socialized groups obtained imprinting test scores lower than those obtained by the controls on the test. However, an extremely striking feature of these data is the fact that the shorter the interval between the socialization and the laboratory imprinting experiences, the greater the depressing effect of the socialization experience upon the amount of following of the drake decoy by the experimental subjects during the exposure experience. The compensatory effect of the increasing length of isolation upon the interference caused by the 2-hour socialization experience was such that those isolated 11¼ to 15 hours followed the model just as much as had the naïve unsocialized 14- to 16-hour-old controls. Nevertheless, even though these animals followed just as much as did the younger controls, they did not obtain test scores as high as those obtained by the controls.

These data appear to indicate that mallard ducklings are essentially incapable of being attracted to or of forming attachments to a parental surrogate soon after having had 2 hours of social experience with other ducklings during the critical age period of 14 to 16 hours after hatching. However, long after the critical period has passed and at an age—25 to 31 hours—during which socially and visually isolated ducklings show virtually no following or any formation of attachment for a potential parent object, socialized ducklings appear to have been "primed" by the social experience so that they follow at a near-optimal level.

However, the test scores obtained by animals of this socialized group shows that despite this facilitation of following through the 11¼ to 15 hours of isolation, they were still unable to form an attachment to the drake decoy to the same degree as did individually isolated naïve ducklings exposed to the decoy at the critical age period. Thus, it is apparent that the lesser imprinting sensitivity of such animals, caused both by the prior socialization experience and by their increased age, did not permit the ducklings to form as firm an attachment to the decoy, even though they followed as much as would be optimal for animals at a critical age period.

Figure 4–9 is a rearrangment of the data obtained with these animals in such a way that the effect of the critical period on the process of imprinting becomes more apparent. In this figure, the age of the animals at the time of the laboratory imprinting procedure is related to the mean number of feet that the drake decoy was followed and the mean scores which were made on the test session 24 hours later. As before, no socialized group had imprinting test scores as high as those of the controls. It is again obvious that when both the social experience and the exposure to the imprinting model (with no intervals between socialization and imprinting greater than 2 hours for the 14- to 15-hour age group) occur at the critical age period itself, there is almost a complete depression of following and later test scores. With increasing age concomitant with increasing temporal duration of the interval between sibling socialization and exposure to the proffered imprinting object, there is an increase in both the amount of following of the model during the exposure and the test scores obtained in the simultaneous choice test. These increases are exactly the reverse of the decreases in following and test scores as a function of increasing age of imprinting exposure obtained when completely naïve and unsocialized ducklings are used.

In the second experiment on the effect of sibling socialization upon

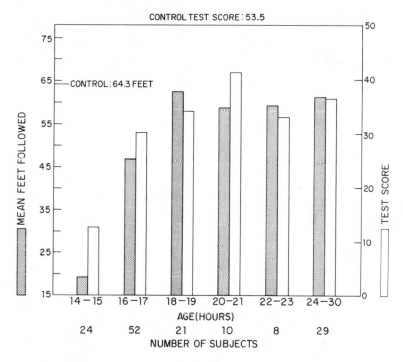

Figure 4–9 Mean number of feet followed and test scores of groups that had social experience during the critical period and that were imprinted in the laboratory at different ages. Control N was 33.

the imprintability of mallard ducklings on a parental surrogate, we used 84 ducklings, which were given 2 hours of social experience with age mates at a time earlier than the critical period and were then given the laboratory imprinting experience during the critical age period, 13 to 16 hours after hatching. As before, there were varying intervals of visual and social isolation in the individual numbered cardboard boxes between the socialization with siblings and the exposure to the imprinting experience. The lengths of these intervals ranged from zero to eleven hours.

Figure 4–10 shows the mean number of feet that the animals of the different groups, divided according to the length of isolation, followed the drake decoy and the mean test scores which they obtained on the later testing session. As before, socialization deleteriously affected the imprintability of the experimental ducklings. In this figure, however, it is apparent that the effect of the length of the isolation after the socialization experience was precisely the inverse of that observed in the first experiment. Evidently, then, when imprinting is carried out during the

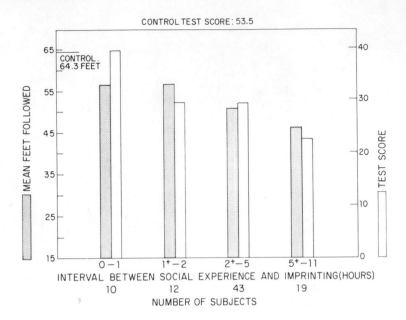

CONTROL TEST SCORE: 53.5

MEAN FEET FOLLOWED

TEST SCORE

CONTROL.
64.3 FEET

INTERVAL BETWEEN SOCIAL EXPERIENCE AND IMPRINTING(HOURS)

| 0−1 | 1⁺−2 | 2⁺−5 | 5⁺−11 |
| 10 | 12 | 43 | 19 |

NUMBER OF SUBJECTS

Figure 4–10 The effect of the interval between social experience and laboratory imprinting in ducklings imprinted during the critical period only. Control N was 33.

critical age period itself, the earlier the ducklings have already been socialized to their age mates, the less they are influenced by the exposure to a potential imprinting object, in terms of both the amount of following and the mean test scores in the simultaneous choice test. The reduction in following behavior due to sibling socialization is to an even greater degree than that found by Gottlieb and Klopfer (1962) with pekin ducklings, a more domesticated breed than mallards.

The imprinting test scores were lower for every one of the socialized groups than for the naïve isolated controls, even though they were all exposed to the imprinting situation at the age of 14 to 16 hours after hatching. The increasingly depressive effect of socialization as a function of earlier age indicates that strong emotional attachments can be formed in mallard ducklings long before the time of the critical period that we have demonstrated in our previous research. This is a situation which is beneficial to the survivability of mallard ducklings in natural conditions, since it further ensures that the ducklings quickly form attachments to the parental object even before walking ability is fully established. Our findings are therefore consonant with Lorenz's (1935) report that, in the natural situation, imprinting in mallard ducklings occurs earlier than the 13- to 16-hour age peak which Ramsay and Hess (1954) reported for socially and visually deprived laboratory ducklings.

The reality of sibling socialization as a factor influencing the later social behavior of ducks is shown by an incidental observation made of a different duck species, a hybrid cross of black duck × Florida duck that was reared after hatching with wood ducks. The result of the rearing with wood ducks of the same age was that at sexual maturity and throughout his adult life the hybrid directed his sexual attentions exclusively to wood ducks. This observation is of particular interest since other hybrid ducks which we have produced have failed to show sexual behavior directed toward the species of the females which reared them.

Thus, again, the importance of the first social experience in the formation of social behavior as a consequence of processes occurring during the sensitive age period for imprinting is confirmed by our research investigations. This research has several theoretical implications for regarding the nature of the imprinting process, which we shall discuss in Chapter 7.

We may point out, however, that our results are contrary to Fabricius' (1951) conclusion that duck siblings do not imprint on each other. He had come to this conclusion because he had observed that while hatchlings have a strong flocking impulse, they will follow the parent object when flocking and following are in conflict. As our experiment shows, this is not the case in ducklings socialized to age mates before the first encounter with a parental object. It certainly should be the case for ducklings already imprinted to the parent object.

Another experiment of ours (Hess and Hess, 1969) emphasizes even more strongly the importance of naturally occurring conditions in imprinting. Certainly many researchers have deliberately avoided imprinting several ducklings at the same time to the same surrogate so as to prevent the ducklings from possibly imprinting onto each other. Yet ducklings do, in the wild, normally first experience the mother in the company of siblings. Thus, it may be that ducklings are genetically programmed to imprint primarily to the parent when siblings are present, but primarily to siblings when the parent is absent.

Thus we exposed hatchling mallard ducklings in two groups of 5 animals each to a duck decoy and 6 ducklings individually to the same decoy. There was no difference in the degree of imprinting by group-imprinted and individually imprinted ducklings when tested at the age of 3 weeks, and all subjects had a daily half-hour experience with the surrogate after imprinting until the test.

In the same experiment (Hess and Hess, 1969), we also individually imprinted some ducklings at the age of 15 to 16 hours to a human being so as to compare the effects of imprinting to a duck decoy with those of imprinting to a human being. Daily half-hour exposure sessions were given, as with the group-imprinted ducklings, until the test at the age of

3 weeks. This test consisted of giving each duckling a simultaneous choice between the duck decoy and a human being. All ducklings—both the decoy-imprinted and the human-imprinted—chose whatever they had been imprinted to, but it was an extremely striking fact that those imprinted to the duck decoy immediately dashed over to it, whereas human-imprinted ones required at least 5 seconds, some as many as 70 or 120 seconds, to go over to the human. This seems to suggest rather strongly that mallard ducklings have an innate disposition to imprint to members of their own species. It is interesting that Hoffman et al. (1970), on the basis of research using completely different methods, concluded that "imprinting begins with predispositions to emit a filial-type response to specific classes of stimulation."

Genetic Studies and Further Naturalistic Observations

Table 4–6 shows four duck species with which we have worked and their relative ability to imprint in terms of scores obtained in the four-part test situation carried out 24 hours after the standard 10-minute imprinting exposure period. Since the decreasing scores down the list from wild mallards to rouens appear to be concomitant with increasing domestication, it would seem that imprintability has a genetic basis in these species.

We have carried out an experiment which attempted to demonstrate the genetic bases of the laboratory imprinting phenomenon in mallard ducklings. We formed two groups of ducklings from ones which we had used in our research investigations: one was composed of those which obtained perfect test scores of 100 percent in the test situation as a consequence of a laboratory imprinting experience when exposed during the critical period age; the other was composed of those which, at the same age, refused to have anything to do with the model during the exposure to it and also gave no evidence of having formed any attachment to it when tested at a later age. All these latter ducklings had zero test scores. The 6 members of the first group (forming 3 breeding pairs)

TABLE 4–6   ESTIMATED PERCENTAGES OF SUBJECTS OF EACH SPECIES THAT SHOW IMPRINTING AS RESULT OF TEN MINUTES OF LABORATORY EXPOSURE DURING CRITICAL AGE PERIOD

	Percent
Wild mallard	82
Domestic mallard	78
Pekin	65
Rouen	35

—the "imprinters"—were allowed to breed only with each other; the 6 members of the second group (also forming 3 breeding pairs)—the "non-imprinters"—were likewise given only each other as breeding partners. We thus obtained two groups of offspring, which we proceeded to expose to the laboratory imprinting situation when they reached the critical age period. The imprinter offspring were easy to imprint, while the non-imprinter offspring proved to be relatively intractable. The imprinter offspring, furthermore, obtained a mean score of 85 percent on the later test for imprinting, more than three times as high as the mean score, 16 percent, obtained by the non-imprinter ducklings' offspring on the same test. These differences were statistically highly significant.

Genetic programming of this kind also appears to exist in the two domestic chicken strains studied by Kilham, Klopfer, and Oelke (1968) and by Kilham and Klopfer (1968). These were yellow vantress-cross and black sex-linked. Chicks that had no previous social experience showed no preference for being with peers of their own or the other breed. Neither did rearing for 24 to 30 hours with the breed not their own produce any consistent preference. But rearing with their own breed for the same period of time did result in chicks showing a definite preference for their own breed. That it was not just simply the color differences that were responsible was shown by the fact that even when yellow vantress cage mates were dyed a dark blue the own-breed preference was not prevented from developing.

We have continued to make field observations on the effects of laboratory imprinting on the long-range behavior of mallard ducklings. We have, for example, repeatedly observed an increased amount of homosexual courtship behavior in our subjects, both male and female, that had been imprinted on the drake model. While these observations may not be statistically valuable, they perhaps point to some long-range, irreversible effects of the laboratory imprinting process. The most intriguing aspect of this homosexual behavior that has been observed lies in the fact that under natural feral conditions the male mallard duck acquires a sexual preference for the female of his species through the early imprinting experience with the mother. But female ducklings are also imprinted on the mother. This is a situation analogous to the Freudian theory of psychosexual development, which shows how the male of the human species develops his sexual role but fails to account adequately for the psychosexual development of females. Seriously, however, the observations of Schutz (1965) are relevant: in sexually dimorphic species, such as mallards, males show an imprinting to the sexual object as a consequence of early rearing experience, while the females seem to react on the basis of genetically present "releasers" which are presented by the colorfully plumed male during courtship behavior.

It may be pointed out that Schutz's female mallard ducklings had experience with females, while our experimental females, which *did* show an effect of the early experience upon mate selection, experienced a male mallard model.

Also of importance in our naturalistic studies was the repeated observation that if we accidentally stepped on the toes of a duckling while we were in the process of imprinting it to ourselves, the duckling made no attempt to run away from us. In fact, the duckling strove to stay even closer to us as a direct result of our having subjected it to the painful experience of being stepped on. This was analogous to Spalding's (1875) observation that a chick being imprinted on a human being would not run away from this person even when it was repeatedly hit with a small branch in an effort to drive it away. The positively enhancing effect we saw, however, was even beyond the mere failure to alienate the duckling as a result of our unintentional maltreatment of it. It struck us that this phenomenon showed that imprinting differed very much from usual learning processes, since in the latter, the administration of aversive stimulation normally leads to the avoidance of the associated object when there is an option to do so. In contrast, in our situation the duckling could have run away from us, but did the opposite instead. This led us to perform an experiment in our laboratory directly testing the hypothesis of the enhancing effect of aversive stimulation on imprinting by electrically shocking naïve hatchling chicks of the appropriate age while in the imprinting exposure situation. The details and results of this experiment will be discussed later in the next section when we turn our attention to our experimental research on the imprinting phenomenon in chickens.

DOMESTIC CHICKENS

As Table 4–1 shows, we have worked with a variety of chicken breeds. However, most of our work was initially with chickens of white rock stock, and our most recent research has utilized primarily the vantress broiler breed, which is closely related to white rock.

Effects of Age of Exposure

In our original research report (Ramsay and Hess, 1954), we published data we had obtained with 26 hatchling Cochin bantam chicks which we had treated just the same as we had the mallard ducklings. In other words, they were removed as soon as possible after hatching, placed into individual cardboard boxes, put into the laboratory imprinting situation with the drake decoy at the designated time, and then further socially and visually isolated until the time of the test procedure involving a simultaneous choice between the drake and hen duck decoys. The 10-minute procedure in the rectangular runway was used for the imprinting experience itself, and the same four-part test procedure for testing of imprinting strength was also used. The only difference in the testing procedure was that we used the clucking of a real mother hen for the female model during the testing session instead of the quacking of a female duck.

As Table 4–7 indicates, the bantam chicks showed much less evidence of imprinting in the test situation than did the mallards. None of the chicks, furthermore, ever made perfect imprinting scores in the test, and none of them responded positively to the laboratory imprinting model in test 4. The highest score that any individual chick was able to make in the test was 75 percent, and this was made by one chick in the 13- to 16-hour exposure group. We then performed an additional test in which we had the female model quiet and immobile and the male motionless and calling. The results of test 5, as shown in Table 4–7, confirm that even though only a few animals were tested, the period of maximum sensitivity to the imprinting exposure is at the age of 13 to 16 hours, the same as in ducks, despite the differences in length of incubation, which is 21 days for chickens and 27 days for ducklings.

Releasers of Imprinting

In Ramsay and Hess (1954), we also reported an experiment which we carried out on 13 Cochin bantam chicks in an attempt to determine whether inherent preferences existed. We exposed the naïve chicks to

TABLE 4–7   RESPONSES OF COCHIN BANTAM CHICKS IMPRINTED AT DIFFERENT AGES TO LABORATORY IMPRINTING OBJECT ON LATER FIVE-PART TEST

Number	Age in hours	Number giving positive response*				Average all 4 parts (percent)	Number giving positive response on Test 5*
		Test 1	Test 2	Test 3	Test 4		
5	1 to 4	1	0	0	0	5	1 (20.0%)
5	5 to 8	1	0	0	0	5	2 (40.0%)
3	9 to 12	0.5	0	0	0	4.2	2.5 (83.3%)
4	13 to 16	3	2	1	0	37.5	4 (100%)
3	17 to 20	0.5	0	1.5	0	16.7	2 (66.7%)
3	21 to 24	2.5	0.5	0	0	25.0	1 (33.3%)
3	25 to 28	1	1	0	0	16.7	2 (66.7%)

*.5 scores are chicks that went in the direction of the imprinting object before it was moved and that remained with the model.

both sounds which we had used in the laboratory imprinting test situation—the standard gock call, and the recorded clucking of a hen. All but 2 of the 13 chicks chose the clucking over the gock. This is certainly in contrast to the fact that the majority of the naïve mallard ducklings that we had tested for preferences between the standard gock and the recorded quacking of a female duck showed no preference for either call. Only 9 of them showed any preference, and for 8 this preference was for the gock. Later we will discuss further research on the question of the efficacy of the stimulus elements of an imprinting object (Schaefer, 1958; Schaefer and Hess, 1959).

The Law of Effort

While we have not carried out an experiment identical to the one we carried out with mallard ducklings in which we varied time and distance followed, we have several reasons for believing that the law of effort is just as valid with chicks.

In the first place, we replicated the experiment in which naïve ducklings were carried in a small transparent container on the back of a moving drake decoy by using 10 hatchling chicken subjects (Hess and Ramsay, unpublished research, 1955). These chicks were, of course, individually isolated immediately after hatching and maintained in social and visual isolation except for the laboratory imprinting exposure and test situation. As had been done with ducks, the decoy moved 8 times around the 12½-foot circular runway in a period of 15 minutes.

During the exposure to the drake decoy, chicks were observed for struggling behavior in the form of trying to get to the model or the model's tail. Those that were seen to do this were placed in one category, and those that remained absolutely still during the entire procedure were placed in another category. The upper part of Table 4–8 shows the individual imprinting test scores obtained by the chicks 24 hours later as a function of whether or not any effort had been expended to be with the model despite the restraint. Atlhough the mean imprinting test score for the entire group at 37.5 percent, the nonstrugglers had a mean score of 0 percent, and the strugglers had a mean test score of 53.6 percent.

Another experiment was carried out with 25 other chicks treated exactly as in the above experiment. The only difference was that the model was stationary instead of moving. It remained in the runway for the same period of time—15 minutes. The lower part of Table 4–8 shows the imprinting test scores obtained by these chicks 24 hours later. Just as in the first experiment, all of the non-strugglers obtained zero scores

TABLE 4–8 IMPRINTING TEST SCORES OF 33 INDIVIDUAL
CHICKS CARRIED BEHIND MOVING OR STATIONARY
DECOY AT CRITICAL AGE PERIOD

MOVING MODEL	
Non-strugglers (percent)	Strugglers (percent)
1. 0	1. 2.5
2. 0	2. 25
3. 0	3. 100
Mean 0%	4. 40
	5. 90
	6. 50
	7. 45
	Mean 53.6%

STATIONARY MODEL	
Non-strugglers (percent)	Strugglers (percent)
1. 0	1. 90
2. 0	2. 30
3. 0	3. 15
4. 0	4. 65
5. 0	5. 30
6. 0	6. 65
7. 0	7. 45
8. 0	8. 25
Mean 0%	9. 100
	10. 65
	11 25
	12. 100
	13. 65
	14. 45
	15. 100
	Mean 57.7%

on the test. The mean score of the strugglers was 57.7 percent, very similar to the score of the strugglers in the first experiment.

Although we used only 35 subjects, the congruence between the two groups—the ones that were "carried," and the ones that were "still"—is extremely good, thus very strongly supporting the validity of our data on this question. The wider range of test scores obtained in this experiment, in comparison with the ones obtained by mallard ducklings, as seen in Table 4–3, is, of course, a function of the fact that, on the whole, domestic chicken species do not have the capacity to form as much of an imprinted attachment to a parental surrogate as mallard ducklings do. Since wild red jungle fowls are known to be extremely capable of imprinting, the relatively lower imprintability of other chickens appears to be related to domestication.

More information indicating the influence of energy expenditure on imprinting in chickens has been provided by experimentation on the effects of drugs similar to that which we have reported with ducks.

Drugs

In the series of experiments (Hess, Polt, and Goodwin, 1959) we are about to describe, the imprinting and testing apparatus used, as shown in Figure 4–11, was a 12 inch wide circular runway having a 12-foot length (almost 3 meters) in its center line. Lighting for the runway was from the rear of the white matte plastic sheeting which formed the

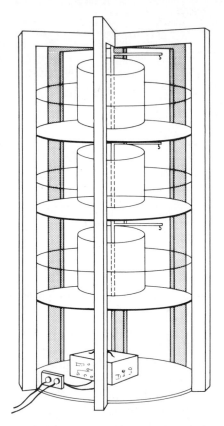

Figure 4–11 Three-tiered laboratory imprinting apparatus used for chick imprinting studies at the University of Chicago laboratories.

inner wall of the runway, and was provided by six 15-watt light bulbs. The model to which the DeKalb leghorn chicks were exposed at the age of 14 to 16 hours was a green sphere 6½ inches in diameter and fitted with a loudspeaker which emitted the standard gock call.

Chicks were hatched in our laboratory and individually isolated in individual cardboard boxes as soon as possible after leaving the shell. The time of hatching was recorded on the numbered box as well as in the permanent records. This social and visual isolation was maintained up to the laboratory imprinting procedure and continued thereafter until the time of the test for imprinting strength.

The imprinting procedure itself involved placing the chick individually 18 inches away from the silent motionless green sphere. After 2 minutes, the gock sound was turned on in the motionless model. After the sound had been on for 2 minutes, the green sphere was moved near the chick. After 1 more minute, the model began to move around the runway, completing 4 turns, with regular pauses of 14 seconds after every 6 seconds of movement, in approximately 13 minutes. The test for imprinting retention was prepared by hanging the green sphere and one or two spheres of the same size but different colors from gallows placed 72° apart in an arc on the edge of a round table 2½ feet in diameter. Translucent plastic panels formed walls at the boundary of the table. The chick was placed in the center of the table and therefore equidistant from the models. If a chick went within 12 inches of a sphere, and stayed there for at least 1 minute, it was considered as having chosen that sphere. It was given 10 minutes to make such a choice. The testing was terminated upon the choice, or at the expiration of 10 minutes.

Four groups of vantress broiler chicks were utilized in this experiment. All treatments were carried out at the age of 12 hours, and laboratory imprinting was at the age of 14 to 16 hours. The first group was given water before the imprinting experience, the second was similarly given 400 mg/kg meprobamate, and the third was given 400 mg/kg carisoprodol. The fourth group was never given any drugs or water. Table 4–9 shows the imprinting test scores obtained by chicks of each of the three series of the four groups. According to these scores, both meprobamate and carisoprodol depress imprintability of chicks under their influence. The fact that in each of the three series we tested the rank order of the test scores obtained by chicks of the three experimental groups was the same despite the small number of each group in any single series is further substantiation of the validity of the data for drawing inferences regarding the action of meprobamate and carisoprodol on imprintability. An interesting facet of these results is that even though chicks normally imprint less well than mallard ducklings, as shown by the normal control

TABLE 4–9 MEAN POSITIVE RESPONSIVENESS TO IMPRINTING MODEL ON LATER TEST BY THREE SERIES OF VANTRESS BROILER CHICKS AS A FUNCTION OF THREE DIFFERENT LABORATORY IMPRINTING CONDITIONS

Series	Control H_2O	Meprobamate 400mg/kg	Carisoprodol 400mg/kg	Control— no drugs or H_2O
1.	30.8	10.5	7.5	
2.	53.0	21.0	9.3	
3.	41.6	20.0	10.0	
Mean	41.2	16.3	8.7	40.8
Number Subjects	17	24	23	25

test scores of 41.2 percent in contrast to the 62 percent or 65 percent achieved by ducklings, the administration of carisoprodol or meprobamate reduced the imprintability of both species to the very same level, on the order of 16 percent and 9 percent for chicks and 8 percent and 11 percent for ducklings.

Recently a possible explanation for the effects of meprobamate upon laboratory imprinting has become evident, in the light of current biochemical investigations demonstrating a relationship between learning and protein synthesis in the brain. Thus, it appeared that the interfering effects of meprobamate upon the imprinting process might be based upon impairment of RNA synthesis. Studies reported in Chapter 3 have involved the investigation of brain protein synthesis in response to an imprinting situation.

Hence, an experimental procedure was conducted to investigate the effects of meprobamate upon the absolute RNA levels in the chick brain before, during, and after the demonstrated critical period under conditions of minimal environmental stimulation—that is, in the absence of a specific imprinting exposure experience (Kubos, Petrovich, and Hess, in preparation).

Thirty-six vantress broiler chicks were hatched in our laboratory incubators and individually isolated, according to the usual procedures, with the time of hatching determined within 15 minutes since eggs were checked every half hour. Three main groups, according to the age at sacrifice, were formed: 6-hour-old chicks, 15-hour-old chicks, and 24-hour-old chicks. Each main group was further broken down into two subgroups of 6 animals each, with one subgroup given a dose of 25 mg/kg meprobamate administered intraperitoneally two hours ($\pm$5 minutes) before sacrifice, and the other given a dose of control vehicle at the same time. The subjects were systematically distributed among groups according to their hatching order, so as to avoid confounding the results with the length of time spent in the incubator.

The animals were removed from their boxes, quickly injected, and returned to their boxes under quiet and dim illumination conditions, so as to minimize sensory stimulation. Sacrifice was conducted under similar conditions. The sacrifice consisted of decapitation, removal of the brains, placement of the brains into individually numbered vials, and

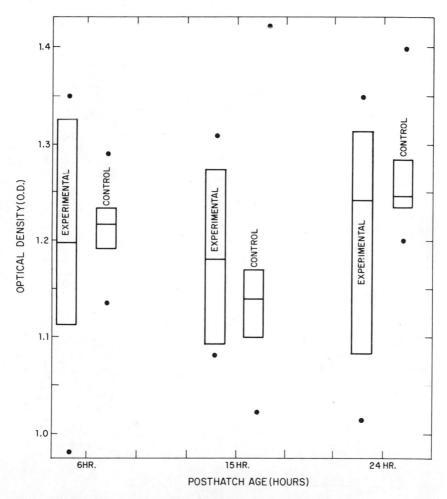

Figure 4–12 The left members of each pair of bars represent the groups given meprobamate and the right members of each pair represent the vehicle control groups. The drug or vehicle was administered 2 hours prior to decapitation. Dots represent the extreme values while the bars represent 50% of the data, according to the method of J. Tukey (*Exploratory Data Analysis: Limited Preliminary Edition.* New York: Addison-Wesley 1970, pp. 5–1 to 5–2.) 1.0 Optical Density (O.D.) is equivalent to 50 μg of RNA.

immediate freezing in dry ice (−78°F) until biochemical analysis for RNA content.

The results of the biochemical determination of RNA content of the six groups are depicted in Figure 4–12, where the data are plotted according to the Tukey method (Tukey, 1970). From this figure, it can be seen that the effect of meprobamate is to increase, by twofold to fourfold, the variability in the absolute RNA level in chick brains. In all groups receiving meprobamate, the RNA variability was at least twice that of the corresponding groups of the same ages that received control

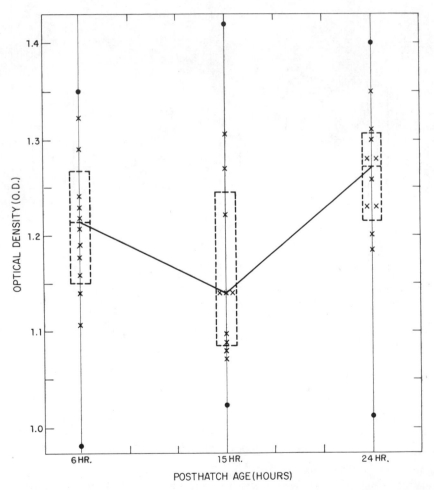

Figure 4–13 Drug and vehicle control groups in each age group pooled so as to depict the effect of age. Dots represent the extreme values while the bars represent 50% of the data, according to the method of J. Tukey (1970). 1.0 Optical Density (O.D.) is equivalent to 50 μg of RNA.

vehicle. The 15-hour experimental group, furthermore, evidenced effects of meprobamate upon absolute RNA that were different from those of the 6-hour and 24-hour experimental groups. The 15-hour experimental group had the lowest mean absolute RNA level, and it was the only experimental group having a higher trimean RNA level than its corresponding control group. Furthermore, as shown in Figure 4–13, in which age groups are pooled, 15-hour-old animals had a much lower absolute RNA level than the 6-hour- or the 24-hour-old animals. Figure 4–13, in fact, is the inverse of the normal critical period sensitivity curve, which shows that absolute RNA level in chick brains during these ages is highly negatively correlated with imprintability. This negative relationship certainly appears to be due to genetically programmed biochemical events, and deserves further experimental investigation, so that the time course of absolute RNA level as a function of age may be known more fully. The effects of meprobamate in increasing the range of variability in absolute RNA level, however, constitute a phenomenon that is presently difficult to assess. Nevertheless, the study does show that meprobamate affects the absolute RNA level, a level which reflects within a system the net result of opposing effects of synthesis and metabolism.

Effect of Light Stimulation and Sibling Socialization

We have amassed considerable evidence supporting other reports in the literature that certain conditions of sibling socialization has the effect of markedly reducing following behavior and imprintability to a parental surrogate in domestic chicks.

First, we carried out two studies (Polt, 1966; Polt and Hess, 1964) in which we assessed the role of light experience without concomitant social experience and the role of 2 hours of age mate experience immediately prior to the imprinting exposure at the age of 16 or 48 hours.

In the first study, 56 vantress broiler chicks, hatched in our laboratory, were divided into four treatment groups according to the age of the imprinting exposure and the reception or deprivation of patterned light experience.

We did this because an earlier unpublished pilot experiment by Hess and Goodwin (1961) produced socially naïve 24-hour old chicks that followed the imprinting model better than usual. In this case, it appeared possible that the patterned light experience they had received since hatching was responsible for this. In addition, Moltz and Rosenblum (1958) had found stronger following in pekin ducklings that received diffuse light stimulation rather than patterned light stimulation since hatching.

All subjects were maintained in darkness in individual isolation compartments up to the time of the laboratory imprinting experience, except that the experimentals were placed individually in a wooden isolation box 4 by 4½ by 5½ inches for 2 hours just prior to the imprinting procedure. The isolation box received light from a 100-watt bulb suspended over it.

The imprinting apparatus was the same one described in the previous experiment. The potential parent object offered was a blue ball about 6½ inches in diameter. A speaker inside the ball emitted a recorded and continuous human rendition of "Come, chick, chick, chick."

After the 2 hours of light experience, the experimental animals were returned to their individual isolation boxes for transportation to the imprinting room. With the room in darkness, the chick was eased onto the runway next to the model. The experimenter took his post at the control panel, which was located behind a one-way screen for the purpose of observing the chicks. The lights and sound were turned on in the apparatus. The model remained stationary for 10 minutes, and then made 4 turns with regular pauses around the runway, for a total distance of 40 feet. The 40 feet were traversed in about 13 minutes. The control animals were subjected to the same procedure, except that they had never been in the isolation compartments for light experience and so were simply transported to the imprinting room in their individual cardboard boxes.

Table 4–10 shows the mean amount, in feet, that each of the experimental and control groups followed the blue ball in the laboratory imprinting situation. The chicks imprinted at the age of 48 hours showed a marked, and statistically significant, increase in the amount they followed the blue ball after they had had just 2 hours of light experience. The amount they followed, however, was the same as that shown by the 16-hour-old animals, since, with the control 48-hour-old animals that had had no patterned light experience, the amount of following manifested was significantly less than that shown by 16-hour-old visually

TABLE 4–10 MEAN AMOUNT OF FOLLOWING BY CHICKS OF DIFFERENT AGES AND PRIOR VISUAL EXPERIENCE DURING FIRST EXPOSURE TO LABORATORY IMPRINTING MODEL

Number	Age at exposure	Prior light experience	Mean distance in feet model followed
12	16 hours	patterned light	25.0
14	16 hours	dark (deprived)	21.0
16	48 hours	patterned light	22.3
14	48 hours	dark (deprived)	13.3
56			

naïve chicks. These results suggest a reason why some other investigators, such as Moltz and Rosenblum (1958), found good following in animals past the critical age period which Ramsay and Hess (1954) have delineated.

However, the fact that the light experience caused the chicks exposed to the laboratory imprinting situation at the age of 48 hours to follow the vocal moving ball more does not necessarily indicate that they imprinted better as a result of this extra following. This is confirmed by the results of the second study.

In this second study, we used four groups of laboratory hatched vantress broiler chicks consisting of 10 subjects each. Two groups of chicks were both visually deprived and socially isolated until the time of imprinting and afterward until the time of testing: one group was given the laboratory imprinting experience to the vocal blue ball at the age of 16 hours, and the other received this experience at the age of 36 hours. The other two groups of chicks were maintained in the same way as the controls, except that they received 2 hours of social experience with age mates in a brooder containing 10 other chicks and illuminated by a fluorescent bulb. These 2 hours of age mate experience occurred just before the laboratory imprinting exposure.

The imprinting apparatus and procedure were exactly as in the first study described above. After imprinting, all animals were placed in their individual isolation boxes and they remained there in social and visual deprivation until the time of testing, which occurred 20 to 28 hours (with a mean of 24 hours) after the imprinting exposure itself.

The testing took place in the imprinting apparatus. Approximately 5 feet away from the blue ball was placed a group of 4 decoy chicks in a transparent plastic "corral" which restrained them from moving about in the darkness. With the imprinting room in darkness, the experimental chicks were eased onto the runway at a point equidistant between the imprinting object and the group of siblings. Then the experimenter went to the control panel and turned the lights on. Like Ramsay and Hess (1954), we gave the individual chicks 4 immediately succeeding 2-minute test periods. In the first 2-minute period, the imprinting model was silent and stationary. In the second 2-minute period, it was stationary and calling. In the third 2-minute period, it was moved, silent, to the center position where the chick had been placed. In the final 2-minute test period, the model, in the same center position, called. If, at the end of a 2-minute period, the chick was with the model, it was given a score of 25 percentage points. Thus, if the chick went to *and* stayed with the model during all 4 of the test periods, it earned a total imprinting test score of 100 percent.

The results of this experiment are listed in Table 4–11. Here we see

TABLE 4–11 MEAN AMOUNT OF FOLLOWING BY CHICKS OF DIFFERENT AGES AND PRIOR SOCIAL EXPERIENCES DURING FIRST EXPOSURE TO PARENTAL MODEL AND MEAN SCORES ON LATER TEST OF LABORATORY IMPRINTING STRENGTH, TOGETHER WITH RANK CORRELATIONS BETWEEN FOLLOWING SCORES AND TEST SCORES OF INDIVIDUAL CHICKS

Number	Social experience and age at laboratory imprinting	Mean distance in feet model followed	Mean test scores (percent)	Spearman rank correlation between following scores and test scores of individuals
10	Isolation, 16 hours	18.3	57.5	+.76
10	Social, 16 hours	30.8	10.0	−.78
10	Isolation, 36 hours	5.0	20.0	+.02
10	Social, 36 hours	33.3	15.0	+.08

the effects of age and social experience upon the mean distance, in feet, that the blue ball was followed, and the mean scores obtained by each group during the testing situation. It also shows the rank correlation between the following scores and test scores of individuals in each group.

These rank correlations and the mean test scores show that the only group that can truly be regarded as showing evidence of laboratory imprinting was the one consisting of animals maintained in complete social and visual deprivation up to the time of the imprinting experience, which occurred at the critical age period. The animals that had been socialized just prior to the laboratory imprinting exposure at the very same age period, however, were evidently imprinted on their siblings and not at all on the blue ball. The essentially nil test scores and the high negative correlations between following and test scores in the case of this group demonstrate that such is the case. The fact that the socialization experience at the critical age period was effective enough to completely prevent the formation of any demonstrable attachment to the blue ball in the testing situation is a proof that the first object, or class thereof, experienced during the sensitive period for laboratory imprinting is the one that is learned by hatchling chicks, just as we have demonstrated in mallard ducklings (Hess, 1959a). In other words, primacy, and not recency, of experience is the prepotent factor in the laboratory imprinting process.

The data also demonstrate the difficulty of establishing imprinting in chicks that are past the critical age period. While both the isolated and socialized 36-hour-old chicks achieved somewhat higher test scores than did the socialized 16-hour-old imprinted chicks, neither group, of course, could achieve as high a degree of imprinted social attachment to the ball as did the 16-hour-old chicks. Furthermore, it also appears that the 36-hour-old socialized chicks did not form as strong an attachment to their siblings through exposure to them at the age of 34 to 36 hours as the 16-hour-old chicks had formed to their siblings through exposure to them at the age of 14 to 16 hours. While further research is needed to definitely establish this point, two facts are suggestive: there was a slightly higher test score by the 36-hour socialized chicks, in comparison with that of the 16-hour socialized chicks; and there was no correlation at all between individual following and test scores in the 36-hour socialized chicks. The effects of increasing age in preventing the formation of attachment to the ball during the exposure to it are dramatized further by the fact that although the 36-hour-old isolated chicks followed a mean of only 5 feet during the laboratory imprinting session, their imprinting test scores were actually slightly higher than those obtained by the 36-hour-old socialized chicks which had followed almost seven times as much during the exposure session.

At any event, it becomes clear that there is a positive correlation between following and imprinting strength only when the laboratory imprinting exposure to completely naive chicks is made during the critical age period. In other words, the law of effort applies only to such animals. Contrary to what many researchers have assumed, following, by itself, does not necessarily indicate the formation of social imprinting bonds between the young and the parental object. Chicks which are not susceptible to imprinting to a parental surrogate, either because of age or because of prior socialization, simply cannot be induced to form the same degree of imprinting to such an object, even if they manifest an increased readiness to perform following behavior. This is completely congruent with the results obtained by Salzen and Sluckin (1959), wherein day-old Rhode Island red chicks showed greater attachment to a stationary box as a result of increased experience with it only if they were already susceptible to imprinting as evidenced by their behavior during the initial exposure. That is, there was not demonstrable increase in the amount of attachment shown by chicks that had not responded to the box during the first 10 movements of the object as a result of seeing it make 40 more movements. But there was an increase in the attachment shown by chicks that had already responded to the box during the first 10 movements as a result of the 40 more movements, in comparison with chicks that were permitted to see only 10 movements and that responded to it. Other details regarding this experiment have already been given in Chapter 3.

A further point of importance is the fact that the socialization experience affected the amount of following in chicks in a fashion different from that in mallard ducklings. In mallard ducklings, as will be recalled from earlier in this chapter, prior socialization caused the reduction of following of the drake decoy during the critical age period. This comparison becomes even more interesting in view of the fact that Gottlieb and Klopfer (1962) reported that social experience caused pekin ducklings to follow less than ones reared in social isolation; however, the reduction found by them was less than that which we found in our mallards. This difference in the degree of reduction suggests that increasing domestication of an animal species may be concomitant with a correspondingly lesser reduction of following of a parental surrogate in socialized hatchlings to the point where there is actually a facilitation in the amount of following in the laboratory imprinting situation, as in the vantress broiler chick subjects we used in these two pilot experiments. And, of course, chicken species imprint less well than do duck species: the maximum imprinting test score obtained by chickens at the critical age period, as we have seen (Ramsay and Hess, 1954), is often lower than that obtained by wild mallard ducklings, thus showing that social imprinting is present in a less strong form. Even among chickens, furthermore, there is a wide variability in the ability to imprint. Certainly it is obvious that species characteristics strongly determine the effects of certain operations upon the manifested imprinting phenomenon.

Still another point which we may briefly mention here is that in both chicks and ducklings we find evidence that there are completely different processes involved in the exposure of naïve animals at the critical age period to a potential parent object and in the exposure of socialized animals, or older animals, to this object. This accords entirely with our theoretical position that the phenomenon of imprinting is different from other processes in the development of behavior. This, of course, is an issue which we will later discuss, in Chapter 7, both with respect to the experimental data which we have reported above and with respect to several other experimental findings.

These studies led us to expand our investigation of the effects of age and sibling socialization experience on following behavior in vantress broiler chicks (Polt, 1966; Polt and Hess, 1966). This investigation involved a total of 370 chicks from a series of successive hatches.

In the experiment, the chicks were hatched in the laboratory, as in the previous experiments. They were placed, within 2 hours of hatching, in individual small cardboard boxes, so that they remained in social and visual deprivation until the time of the laboratory imprinting exposure at the appropriate age, except, in the case of the experimental animals only, for 2 hours of social experience with 10 age mates in a lighted brooder section. As before, chicks were marked with a felt pen for identification upon placement with siblings. During the isolation, chicks were kept without food or water, neither of which was received until the chicks had been used experimentally.

Immediately after socialization, the chicks were returned to their individual isolation boxes and transported to the imprinting room for exposure to the imprinting object. Unsocialized control chicks were simply taken from the darkroom to the imprinting apparatus. The darkroom was maintained at brooder temperature.

The identical apparatus and imprinting exposure procedure were used as in the pilot studies. The same imprinting object—a blue ball approximately 6½ inches in diameter, and emitting the recorded "come, chick, chick, chick" call was offered as a parental surrogate. After the chick had been eased onto the dark runway next to the model, the experimenter went to the control panel out of view and turned on the lights and sound. The model was stationary for 10 minutes, and then moved about the runway for 4 times, for a total of 40 feet, in about 13 minutes, with regularly scheduled pauses during each turn.

Table 4–12 shows the following performed by chicks of each experimental and control group as a function of age. The decreasing sensitivity of the naïve isolated chicks as a function of increasing age is shown by the steadily decreasing group mean following score and the declining proportion of chicks in each group that followed the blue ball for 1 foot or more during the laboratory imprinting exposure. Furthermore, of those that did follow at least this much, the mean amount of following

TABLE 4–12 MEAN AMOUNT OF FOLLOWING AND PERCENTAGE OF SUBJECTS FOLLOWING ONE FOOT OR MORE BY CHICKS OF DIFFERENT PRIOR SOCIAL EXPERIENCE

Number	Age at laboratory Imprinting (hours)	Mean feet of following	Percent following one foot or more	Mean feet of following by those that followed at least one foot
		ISOLATED CHICKS		
70	16	16.3	73.5	22.4
50	24	10.5	61.0	16.9
50	36	7.8	54.5	14.4
50	48	6.4	49.0	13.3
		SOCIALIZED CHICKS		
50	16	23.5	79.5	30.1
30	24	22.9	77.5	29.9
30	36	28.7	81.0	35.8
40	48	24.6	74.5	33.9

also steadily decreased as a function of increased age. A rather different picture emerges from the results obtained from the socialized experimental chicks, however. Among these chicks, the group mean scores of following during the laboratory imprinting exposure varied only from 22.9 to 28.7 feet. Also, the proportion of followers tended to remain at the same level, 77.5 to 81.0 percent, until the age of 48 hours, where a small drop to 74.5 percent is evident. The mean amount of following performed also tended to be relatively stable, ranging from 29.9 to 35.8 feet.

Comparing the isolated control chicks with the socialized ones in following performances, we see that the socialization experience had the effect of increasing the amount of following performed by each age group. At the age of 16 hours, the amount of following by the socialized chicks was significantly more—at the 1 percent level—than that performed by the controls. The increased amount of following by each of the other socialized groups was significantly more than that of the corresponding isolated control groups at the 1 percent level.

The question, then, is: What factors promote increased following in socialized chicks? Results obtained by other experimenters (Guiton, 1958, 1959, 1961; Sluckin and Salzen, 1961; Smith and Bird, 1963) with domestic chicks have all shown that prior socialization of chicks with their age mates decreases following behavior in response to the parental surrogate upon imprinting exposure. These experiments, however, involved chicks either much older or having had many more hours of social experience than was received by chicks in our experimental investigations. Thus, the results obtained by these experimenters do not contradict those obtained by us, but, rather, complement them. Obviously, then, the effects of age, presence or absence of social experience, amount of social experience, and length of isolation since social experience—all are factors that lend considerable complexity to the phenomenon of following behavior.

The reminder that not all cases of following behavior constitute imprinting, as demonstrated by our initial experiment (Polt and Hess, 1964), further emphasizes that these data show that the processes occuring in older or socialized chicks are not the same as those seen in completely naïve socially isolated chicks during the critical age period. The present data with respect to socialized chicks suggest that there is a habituation to strange objects, a habituation which has the effect of facilitating following of a strange object by chicks which are past the critical age period and which have had 2 hours of sibling experience just prior to the laboratory imprinting exposure. The existence of such association learning processes in these chicks thus indicates why some experimenters, particularly those maintaining their animals communally, might look upon imprinting as a type of association learning.

Still other experiments we have conducted have lent considerable support to the notion of age-related changes in the behavior of chicks which may be correlated with the development and decline of imprintability in naïve isolated chicks. Particularly of interest in this connection were the developmental courses of locomotor and fear behaviors.

Normal Developmental Changes

Since our earlier research had shown that for laboratory imprinting to be effective ducklings must follow or expend effort to reach the imprinting object, we hypothesized that the observed initial rise in imprintability as a function of age might be related to the development of locomotor activity. Ducklings and chicks which have just emerged from the shell normally evidence considerable incoordination in walking and normally cannot cover great distances. Also, if an imprinting object moves faster than the young bird is able to walk, it will not be able to spend as much time in following the object, since it falls behind the model. Thus, only part of the very young bird's walking effort can be directed toward the imprinting object. If a circular runway is used, the model will catch up with the young animal again after completing a full turn. What often happens under these circumstances, as we have observed, is that the young bird will emit the so-called distress notes until the model reappears in view from behind. At this point, the animal will turn around and move toward the approaching model, emitting the contentment or conversational notes. Some following will occur and often what may be considered positive responses, such as pecking at the model and trying to slip under it. Soon the model outpaces the hatchling, and the same process is repeated. Thus the animal, while not actually covering any appreciable distance, can expend considerable effort in attempting to reach and keep up with the model. We thus decided to assess the development of locomotor ability during the first hours of life in chicks by means of the following experiment.

Sixty vantress broiler chicks of white rock stock, hatched in our laboratory and visually and socially isolated in individual numbered boxes, were divided into age groups, from 1 to 24 hours, according to the time of testing (Hess, 1959b). The testing was conducted by placing chicks individually 3 feet away from a group of 2 or 3 siblings which were located under a lamp which provided warmth and light. Since chicks orient positively to light and warmth, it was not necessary to confine the stimulus chicks in any way, as they did not wander from the light source. The innately present flocking tendency on the part of the chicks tested was therefore used to promote approach behavior toward the group of age mates. The time in which it took a chick to join its age mates was recorded as soon as the chick rose from a squatting position. The test period lasted for 10 minutes. Two more tests were given each chicks, so that it received 3 tests in a period of 1 hour.

Figure 4–14 shows the total average speed of the different age groups as well as the average speed for each of the 3 trials for each age group. It can be seen that there is an increase in performance over the 3 trials for the age groups older than 4 hours and less than 17 hours. At 17 hours and older, the animals apparently reach a relative plateau of lomomotor speed, which, under these circumstances, they do not exceed, as shown by fluctuations of performance between trials after that time and by the leveling of average speed. It is obvious that there is an improvement of lomocotor ability as a consequence of increasing age.

Then we set out to assess in a similar fashion the development of fear behavior in chicks as a function of age in an effort to determine its relation to the observed decline in the imprintability of chicks with decreased age. We did this because several investigators have noted the emergence of fear behaviors as related to the decline of imprintability. Certainly, if a chick runs away from an object it will not imprint to it.

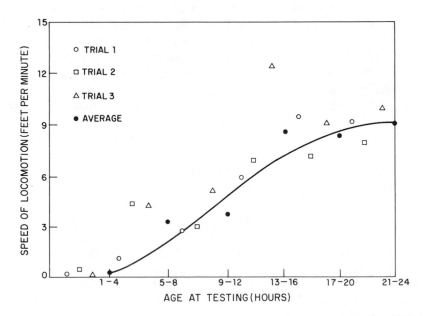

Figure 4–14 Speed of locomotion of 60 vantress chicks of different ages during three trials.

One hundred thirty-seven white rock chicks, visually and socially isolated since hatching, were divided into nine age groups from 1 to 36 hours (Hess, 1959b). At the appropriate age, each chick was individually placed into a 10-minute imprinting exposure situation, where it was confronted with a stationary vocal drake decoy 1 foot away from it and emitting the gock call in the 10-foot circular runway. For 2 minutes the model was stationary, and then for 8 minutes it moved about the circular runway with regular pauses. A total distance of 20 feet was traversed. If the chick emitted distress notes in the presence of the decoy, it was considered to have shown a fear response. The occurence of fear was thus considered as an all-or-none phenomenon; the intensity of fear behavior in terms of duration was not recorded.

Figure 4–15 shows the rapid increase in the incidence of fear beginning at the age of 13 to 16 hours after hatching. By the age of 29 to 32 hours and thereafter, the proportion of chicks that showed any fear in the 10-minute laboratory imprinting observation period was at the level of 100 percent. This development of fear behavior with age is strikingly similar to Harlow's finding (personal communication, 1959) that initially there is no emotional response to strange situations on the part of infant rhesus monkeys until the age of 30 to 90 days. At this age they begin to appear.

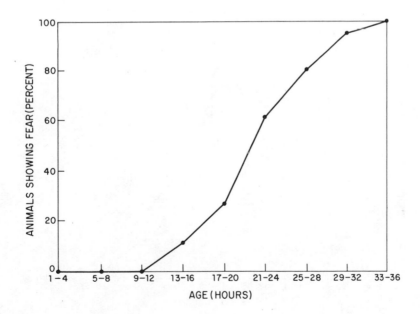

Figure 4–15   Percentages of 137 white rock chicks showing fear responses at different ages.

The combined effect of locomotor ability and the development of fear responses is shown in Figure 4–16. Here one curve shows the hypothetical ability of chicks to move at an optimum rate of 3 feet per minute. This is the speed necessary to follow the proffered imprinting object in many of our experimental investigations. All chicks 17 hours and older are able to move at least this fast when properly motivated unless they are in poor physical condition. The development of loco-motor ability is thus shown as a facilitatory influence on imprintability in Figure 4–16. The other curve shown in this figure is the fear response curve of Figure 4–15 which has been turned upside down in order to emphasize its depressive influence on imprintability. The third curve shows the laboratory imprinting test scores of white rock chicks as a function of the age of exposure to a laboratory imprinting situation, using the 10-minute exposure method and straight alley runway and drake decoy reported by Ramsay and Hess (1954) as well as the same four-part imprinting test procedure. This curve, in essence, is a con-firmation of the curve reported in our 1954 paper, which used a differ-ent chicken breed. While the earlier reported curve for Cochin bantams differs in the exact imprinting test scores at the different age groups, the peak of the laboratory imprinting test scores remains at exactly the same age for white rock chicks.

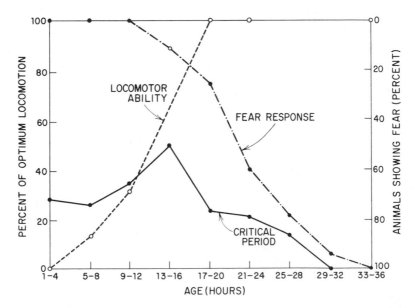

Figure 4–16 Hypothetical and empirical curves of the critical period of chicks (white rock stock).

The empirical curve of imprintability of white rock chicks beyond the age of 12 hours is consistently lower than the hypothetical curve of the critical period which is formed by the intersection of the locomotor and fear curves. This is certainly partly due to the measurements used for the locomotor and fear indices. If, for example, a 1-minute period observation for fear behavior had been used, the incidence of fear behavior might have been slightly lower for each age group. Similarly, the use of more stringent locomotor ability criteria would also lower the lomotion curve. Furthermore, the level of imprintability in the species and breed determines the height of the imprintability curve. Therefore, it is not the exact identity of curves which assume importance but, rather, the resemblence of curves that does: both resemble normal distribution curves, with a peak at a certain time and generally lower points before and afterward.

Of particular interest is the fact that actual laboratory imprintability of chicks less than 9 hours old is greater than the theoretical curve predicts—that is, the shape of the actual curve at these points is not the same as that of the theoretical curve. This difference is the result of the fact that newly hatched chicks only a few hours old will expend considerable effort approaching and following an imprinting model, even when they cannot keep pace with it. Thus, although the speed of the chicks of that age is relatively low, they can and do expend considerable effort to be with siblings or an imprinting object. This finding, therefore, is consonant with our law of effort, since it shows that effort, and not actual locomotion itself, in terms of moving from one place to another, is the effective factor in the laboratory imprinting phenomenon.

Not only the ability to locomote but also other factors temper the ability of the hatchling chick to imprint during its earliest hours of life. Chicks that have just emerged from the shell not only move poorly but also tire easily, so that their attention span is very short. They fall asleep at frequent intervals, even in the presence of a laboratory imprinting object which they have struggled to reach.

Further experimentation (Hess and Schaefer, 1959) has shown that other behavior patterns emerge with a certain lawfulness in the development of chicks. In this experimentation, 124 naïve and socially isolated leghorn chicks were observed for 2 minutes in the runway of the circular imprinting apparatus with a motionless mallard decoy present 6 inches away. During the first 20 seconds of the observation, the decoy was silent; during the remainder of the observation, it was vocal. The following behaviors were recorded: orienting toward the model, approaching the model, latency of approach, dominance of emission of distress notes, contentment (conversational) notes, or quietness.

These criteria were judged according to objective methods. For example, "orientation" was defined as consisting of stretching of the neck, jerky movements, opened eyes, and "looking" at the decoy. If these responses were not displayed during the first few seconds of the observation by the subject, it was considered to have not made this immediate orientation. This judgment was made without respect to whether the orientation appeared to be primarily visual or primarily auditory. In the judgment of the dominance of contentment tones or distress notes, aside from the fact that these two behaviors are clearly recognizable as different, it was true that during the 2-minute observation period one type of vocalization always occurred more frequently than the other. Usually if one behavior replaced another, it would be a sharp change at the moment at which the animal settled under or near the model.

The results of the observation are shown in Figures 4–17, 4–18, and 4–19. These graphs offer strong evidence of the regularity with which the behaviors concerned emerge during the early development of young leghorn chicks.

As may be seen in Figure 4–17, the proportion of socially and visually naïve animals fixating or orienting to the drake decoy and the proportion moving toward or approaching the model both decrease rather sharply from universal occurrence at the ages of 1 to 8 hours to nonexistence by the age of 29 hours. Figure 4–18, on the other hand, depicts the change in the dominant character of the vocalizations emitted by the naïve chicks as a function of age of first exposure to the decoy. Like the fixation and approach curves on Figure 4–17, the contentment vocalization curve on Figure 4–18 starts at a high level at the age of 1 to 8 hours and falls to zero at the age of 29 hours. The distress vocalization curve is almost the inverse of the contentment vocalization curve: up to the age of 16 hours, distress notes occur at a minimal level, after which their incidence rises sharply, to reach a maximum level at the age of 29 hours.

Thus, according to these data, there seem to be the following age phases in the organization of behavior in leghorn chicks: from hatching to 8 hours of age, the chicks appear to respond essentially wholly positively to a surrogate parental object. After this time to the age of 16 or 17 hours, ambivalence sets in and increases to the point where at the age of 29 hours the chicks all respond negatively to the surrogate parental object.

The data presented in Figure 4–19 support this division of phases in the development of the behavior of these chicks. Here we see that the proportion of animals remaining quiet in the experimental situation showed no appreciable change as a function of age. This indicates that the changes in contentment and distress vocalization, as shown in Figure 4–18, really are interrelated. The decreasing responsiveness of the

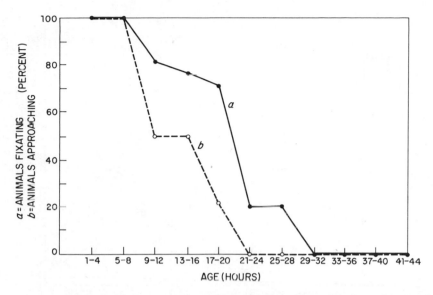

Figure 4–17   Percentages of 124 leghorn chicks (a) fixating, (b) approaching the stimulus object at different ages.

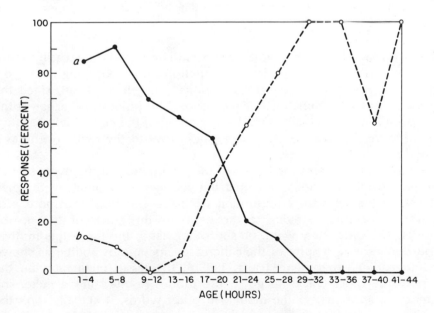

Figure 4–18   Percentages of animals emitting (a) contentment tones, (b) distress tones in experimental situation at different ages.

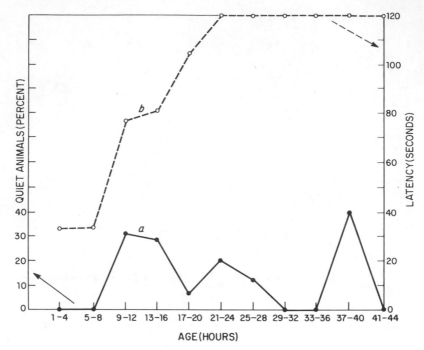

Figure 4–19 (a) Percentages of animals remaining quiet in experimental situation at different ages. (b) Latency of approach to the stimulus object. The mean for each age group is shown.

chicks toward the decoy is further substantiated by the increasing mean amount of time in the experimental situation for approaching the decoy, up to the point where often no response was made at all, since the observation was terminated at 120 seconds. This point was reached at the age of 24 hours, foreshadowing the beginning of the completely negative phase in the behavior of the naïve chicks toward the drake decoy as a function of increased age.

A particularly interesting aspect of the locomotion of the experimental animals toward the decoy was that the younger the animals were when placed in the laboratory imprinting exposure situation, the more pronounced was their striving to move under the cover of the nearby model. The older they were, on the other hand, the more this motivation diminished. In spite of their increased locomotor ability, as shown in our earlier experiments (Hess, 1959b), the lesser inclination on the part of the older chicks to go to the model resulted in an increasing latency of approach to the model. In other words, it actually took the younger chicks less time to reach the model despite their poor locomotor ability. Some of the youngest chicks, in fact, could hardly walk at all but tumbled their way to the model, using both feet and wings as supports, an effort which left them exhausted when the 6-inch-long journey was completed.

The observed plateau from the age of 21 hours in approach latency, furthermore, agrees with the report of Andrew (1966) that there were no latency differences observable in 28- and 48-hour old chicks. Since Andrew found the same to be the case for older chicks, up to the maximum age of 8 days, that were tested, it is obvious that this trend of low responsiveness in naïve chicks, beginning at the age of 21 hours, persists for a rather long time, indeed.

These data are remarkably congruent with the observations on the effects of age upon the imprintability of chicks, as measured by scores in the later test situation. In other words, the known effect on the laboratory imprinting experience on visually and socially naïve chicks of different ages, as determined by behavior at a later age, is completely consonant with the observed behavioral changes in the naïve chicks observed in this experiment. That is, there are changes in the responsiveness of chicks to potential parental surrogates as a function of constitutional changes within the chicks. These changes in responsiveness are correlated with changes in the degree of the effect that the exposure to the potential imprinting object has on the chicks' later behavior.

The data, therefore, support our contention that the behavioral processes which may be observed during the critical age period are different from those current after the critical age period has passed. The principal factor appears to be maturationally scheduled appearance of fear behavior. Therefore, after the critical period has passed, it is necessary to deal with this fear behavior by means of habituation through either repeated or prolonged exposure to the potential parent object. In such cases, then, conventional learning processes are obviously present. During the critical period, habituation plays a relatively small role, one reason being the relative absence of fear. We shall return to a consideration of this point in the next chapter.

Effects of Painful Stimulation

The lack of fear in chicks during the earliest hours of life seemed to us to suggest a possible explanation for a phenomenon that we had repeatedly observed in mallard ducklings which we had imprinted individually to ourselves. This was the fact that whenever we stepped on a duckling's toes, it would not show any fear toward us, as would certainly be the case with older animals (Hess, 1959a). Instead, such a duckling would stay even closer to us. It appeared that it was impossible to elicit fear in these ducklings so that laboratory imprinting would be interfered with. On the contrary, the reaction from the painful stimulation to the toes was directed to an increased intensity of contact with us.

The importance of emotionality in the laboratory imprinting process in chicks has been strongly indicated in a preliminary study (Hess, 1962b), in which the behavior of 200 vantress broiler chicks, all 14 to 16 hours old—the peak of imprinting susceptibility—in a 10-minute laboratory imprinting exposure session, was observed. It was found that all chicks that defecated during the imprinting situation were those that followed the model. In a very large number of the cases, defecation would occur just before following began. Not all the animals that followed the model defecated, but none of the non-followers in this group ever defecated. In an expansion of this observation (Goodwin, 1967), 331 additional animals were studied; only 4 of the defecators failed to follow. Defecation, of course, is widely known as an indicator of emotionality. This relationship between the occurrence of defecation and of following again confirms the notion that the arousal of emotionality in the young chick is an important component of the behavior in the laboratory imprinting exposure situation.

Thus, we postulated, on the basis of our observations, that the deliberate administration of painful stimulation such as electric shock should serve to enhance laboratory imprinting in critical age period animals that possessed few fear processes and had positive responsiveness to parental objects dominant in their motivational system. If fear processes were present, then the effect of painful stimulation should be in the direction of enhancing these fear processes and thus reduce imprintability.

Therefore, we undertook a systematic analysis on the effect of electric shocks of different intensities and frequencies upon the following behavior of naïve socially isolated chicks of different ages in the laboratory imprinting situation.

In the first experiment (Kovach, 1963; Kovach and Hess, 1963), the subjects were 60 vantress broiler chicks which we hatched in our laboratory and kept in visual and social isolation in individual numbered cardboard boxes from the time of hatching. We used the same 10-foot circular runway imprinting apparatus and a blue ball, approximately 6½ inches in diameter, as the imprinting object. The ball emitted a recorded human rendition of "Come, chick, chick, chick," as in our socialization studies.

The 60 subjects were divided into two different treatment and three different age groups, thus making each subgroup consist of 10 members each. The experimental chicks received 11 electric shocks, each of approximately 3 ma intensity and half-second duration during the standard laboratory imprinting procedure, while the controls received none. The shocks were delivered through electrodes attached to the wings of the chick. The controls also wore these electrodes, but they did not, of course, receive shocks during the imprinting exposure. The three different ages of exposure to the imprinting model were 18, 32, and 48 hours.

The laboratory imprinting procedure was essentially identical to that used in our investigations on the effects of socialization on imprinting in chicks (Polt, 1966; Polt and Hess, 1964, 1966). That is, the chicks were eased next to the model from its box in darkness, after which the experimenter retired behind the control panel and turned on the light and sound. For 10 minutes the model was stationary, and then it made 4 turns around the runway, with regular pauses, in about 13 minutes. Successive turns, however, were in reversed direction, rather than in the same direction as before, so as to avoid dragging the chick by the 12-foot long wires leading from the wing electrodes in the event it did not follow. The electric shocks were administered to the chick according to the following schedule: once during the first turn, twice during the second turn, three times during the third turn, and four times during the fourth turn.

Figure 4–20 shows the total amount of following of the model for each of the three age groups as a function of shocking or no shocking. It may be seen that the administration of shock doubled the amount of following performed by the chicks 18 hours old, but halved it in older

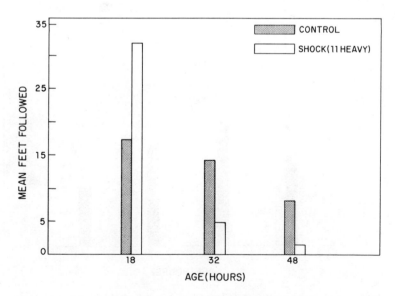

Figure 4–20 Mean number of feet followed by groups of chicks given 11 heavy shocks at three different ages and compared with the following of the non-shocked controls.

chicks past the critical age period, at the age of 32 and 48 hours. At the age of 48 hours, the amount of following in control animals is so low that there is little statistical difference between the experimental and control animals.

Another experiment was carried out by us (Kovach and Hess, 1963) to further elucidate the effects of electric shock upon the elicitation of following behavior by a model at different ages in naïve chicks. We also utilized two different intensities and two different frequencies of shocks during the laboratory imprinting exposure situation. Three age groups—14, 18, and 32 hours—at the time of imprinting exposure were obtained from 120 chicks. Within these three age groups were four different treatment groups. The first was a control group; the second consisted of animals which received 11 shocks of 3 ma intensity, administered according to the same schedule utilized in the previous experiment. The third group received 27 shocks of a lighter intensity, 1 ma; and the fourth group received 27 shocks of the heavier intensity, 3 ma. The 27 shocks for the third and fourth groups were scheduled as follows: 3 shocks during the initial 10-minute exposure to the stationary ball; 6 shocks during each of the 4 turns of the ball around the runway. In all other respects, the laboratory imprinting procedure for animals in each of the groups was the same as for animals in the previous experiment just discussed.

Figures 4–21, 4–22, and 4–23 show the total amount of following of

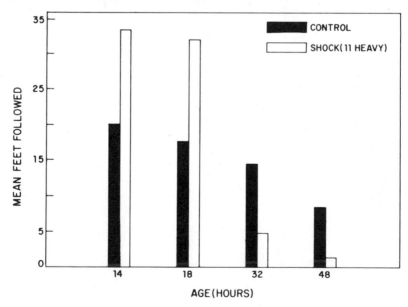

Figure 4–21   Mean number of feet followed by groups of chicks given 11 heavy shocks at four different ages and compared with the following of non-shocked controls.

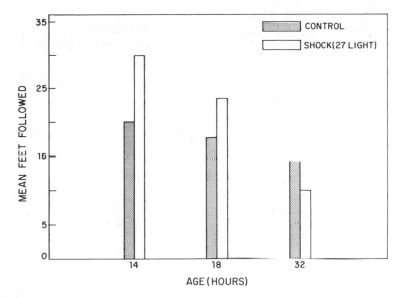

Figure 4–22 Mean number of feet followed by groups of chicks given 27 light shocks at three different ages and compared with the following of non-shocked controls.

the model for each of the various intensities and frequencies of shock administration for the three age groups. In animals that received 11 shocks of the 3 ma intensity (Figure 4–21), the 14-hour-old chicks followed approximately one-third more than did the control animals; as before, the shocked 18-hour animals followed almost twice as much as the controls of the same age did. However, in the 32-hour group, the amount of following by the shocked animals was only one-fourth of that performed by the control subjects.

When the chicks were given 27 shocks of 1 ma intensity, as shown in Figure 4–22, the amount of following was one-third higher for shocked 14-hour-old chicks than for non-shocked control chicks of the same age. In the 18-hour group, the amount of following was one-third higher for the shocked chicks than for the controls. In the 32-hour group, the amount of following for the shocked chicks was about half as much as that of the controls.

Figure 4–23 delineates the effect of 27 shocks of 3 ma intensity upon the following behavior of the different age groups. It is apparent that the amount of following was about one-fifth less in 14-hour-old shocked animals than in the controls. In the 18-hour-old chicks, shock definitely decreased the amount of following: the shocked chicks followed only one-fourth as much as did the controls. The effect was just as drastic in the 32-hour-old chicks.

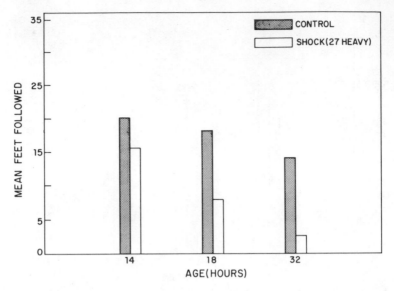

Figure 4–23 Mean number of feet followed by groups of chicks given 27 heavy shocks at three different ages and compared with the following of the non-shocked controls.

These data conclusively demonstrate that the effects of electric shock on the following behavior of naïve socially isolated chicks, when confronted with a laboratory imprinting object, is highly dependent on the animal. They constitute further evidence of the importance of the critical period in the behavioral processes involved in laboratory imprinting, and support the postulation that the imprinting process is fundamentally different from the usual association learning processes with respect to the effect of aversive or painful stimulation. Administration of rather strong *and* frequent electric shock (27 heavy) in the course of the laboratory imprinting exposure during the critical period interferes only slightly with the animal's tendency to follow, probably through incapacitation rather than primarily through the operation of any fear tendencies which would be minimally, if at all, present at this age.

Animals shocked at lesser intensities or with lesser frequencies, on the other hand, follow more than unshocked controls if—and only if—they were at the critical age period. The administration of any intensity of shock at any frequency when the experimental chicks are past the critical age period, however, always serves to decrease the tendency to respond to a laboratory imprinting model, and the effects are exactly the same as in association learning processes, because of the presence of fear behavior at those later ages, since the shocks thus serve to activate the fear response system of these older animals.

Further research, of course, is necessary to demonstrate the effect of the electric shocks on laboratory imprinting itself—that is, the attachment of the young chick for the model to which it was exposed, in preference to a strange one. This is because, as our sibling socialization studies have shown, differential amounts of following in different treatment and age groups are not necessarily correlated with the test scores obtained at a later time. It does appear to us that, since there was no prior socialization of chicks, the increased amount of following by the shocked chicks that were in the critical age period would provide an increased degree of attachment for the imprinting object. The effects, of course, should increase and reach a plateau level, as we saw in our law of effort studies. The greater the sensitivity of the individual chick, as determined by its maturational stage and its genetic constitution, to the effects of laboratory imprinting experience, the greater should be the enhancing effect of stimulation upon the formation of a preference for the associated object. With chicks past the critical age period, however, we predict with absolute confidence that the effects of the electric shock stimulation would invariably further reduce the already lowered sensitivity of the experimental chicks.

These results led us to consider the role of autonomic activity as a function of the age of naïve socially isolated chicks in the elicitation of following behavior (Kovach, 1963, 1964). We did this because of the fact that if fear behavior does not exist to any considerable extent in chicks 16 hours or younger, then the facilitation of following behavior by means of electric shock may act through autonomic arousal.

Effects of Autonomic Drugs

Eight different autonomic drugs—amphetamine sulfate, ephedrine sulfate, adrenaline chloride, ergotamine tartrate, hexamethonium chloride, neostigmine methylsulfate, and atropine sulfate—have been studied for their influence upon following behavior in naïve socially and visually isolated chicks of different ages when placed in the imprinting exposure situation. Ergonovine maleate—which, unlike the ergobasic ergonovines, has no known autonomic action, but confines its action to powerfully contracting uterine smooth muscles—was another compound used for additional information.

Ten chicks were used in each age and drug group studied in this investigation. For each drug there were five different age groups—8, 14, 18, 24, and 32 hours—of chicks exposed to the laboratory imprinting object, a blue ball approximately 6½ inches in diameter. Individual isolation from hatching up to the time of the laboratory imprinting exposure and afterward to later testing was observed. The imprinting procedure was carried out in the identical fashion as in the electric shock studies, except that no electrodes or electric shocks were necessary. Also, the initial exposure to the stationary model was 5 minutes instead of 10. Drugs were injected subcutaneously between 10 and 70 minutes —usually 1 hour—before the imprinting exposure. Controls were injected with distilled water containing .9 percent benzyl alcohol.

The first group of drugs studied were racemic amphetamine sulfate, ephedrine sulfate, and adrenaline chloride (epinephrine). These are all sympathetic amines having central and peripheral stimulation effects. Amphetamine and ephedrine promote the accumulation of epinephrine and norepinephrine in the organism, since they are competitive inhibitors of amino oxidase, and thus the destruction of epinephrine and norepinephrine is prevented.

The doses given to the chicks prior to the laboratory imprinting experience were 8 mg/kg for racemic amphetamine sulfate, 20 mg/kg for ephedrine sulfate, and .04 mg/kg for adrenaline chloride. Figure 4–24

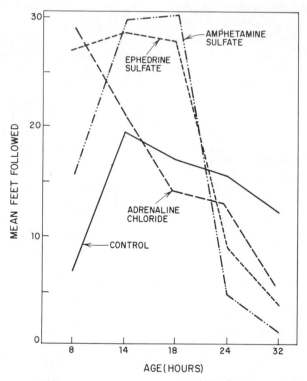

Figure 4–24 Mean number of feet followed during laboratory imprinting while under the influence of ephedrine, epinephrine, or amphetamine as compared with the following of non-drugged controls.

shows the amount of following performed by each age and drug group in comparison with the undrugged controls. In this figure, it is clear that, like electric shocks, ephedrine sulfate and amphetamine sulfate facilitate the amount of following over that of the control animals injected with water when the drugged animals were 8, 14, and 18 hours old. However, in chicks 24 and 32 hours old, the amount of following was substantially depressed.

By themselves, the results obtained with ephedrine sulfate and amphetamine sulfate would seem to indicate that the accumulation of epinephrine and norepinephrine—that is, excitation of the sympathetic nervous system—promotes the following tendency during the critical age period but diminishes it after the critical period has passed. The effects of epinephrine itself, in the form of adrenaline chloride, however, are not the same, for there is an observable facilitating effect only at the age of 8 hours, with little difference from the control level at the ages of 14, 18, and 24 hours, and a considerable interference at the age of 32 hours. At the age of 18 and 24 hours, there was a slight interference. Rajecki and Saegert (1971) have shown facilitatory effects of methamphetamine hydrochloride upon the following behavior of DeKalb leghorn chicks 12 to 24 hours old.

The problem of the effects of epinephrine in the elicitation of following behavior was further studied by using ergotamine tartrate, a water soluble ergot alkaloid which abolishes some effects of epinephrine and sympathetic stimulation. This drug has a direct action on the smooth muscles of blood vessels and the uterus, and thus acts as a peripheral sympathetic blocking agent through its vasoconstrictor effect. It was given in the dose of .4 mg/kg. As shown in Figure 4–25, ergotamine tartrate increased following at the age of 8 hours, but had absolutely no effect on following behavior one way or the other in comparison with the controls at any of the later ages.

Ergonovine meleate, an ergot alkaloid which has the special distinction of having no adrenergic blocking action, unlike the other ergot alkaloids, was given in the dose of .1 mg/kg. Its principal effect on the organism is as an oxytocic, causing powerful contraction of uterine muscles, being highly selective in this regard. As shown by Figure 4–25, it had the effect of enhancing following behavior in 8-hour old chicks to almost the same degree as ergotamine tartrate. It did not change the amount of following behavior performed by 14-hour old chicks, but considerably enhanced following behavior in 18- and 24-hour old subjects. There was only a rather slight enhancement of following in the 32-hour old subjects.

All the above drugs are ones involved in the sympathetic division of the autonomic nervous system. Thus, it also seemed advisable to study

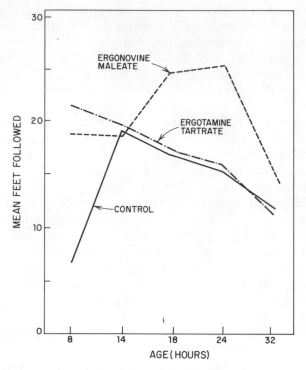

Figure 4–25 Mean number of feet followed during laboratory imprinting while under the influence of ergonovine maleate or ergotamine tartrate.

the effects of drugs belonging to the parasympathetic division. Parasympathetic post-ganglionic nerve fibers are cholinergic, and excitation for pre-ganglionic to post-ganglionic nerves is transmitted by acetylcholine. Acetylcholine is also liberated at the endings of the motor nerves to voluntary muscles. Acetylcholine has two types of actions: muscarinic, and nicotinic. The muscarinic actions of acetylcholine on the whole correspond to those of parasympathetic stimulation; the nicotinic effects of acetylocholine include stimulation of all autonomic ganglia, of voluntary muscle fibers, and of secretion of adrenaline by the adrenal medulla. The muscarinic actions correspond to those of acetylcholine released at the postganglionic nerve endings of the parasympathetic and cholinergic sympathetic fibers.

The three drugs studied in connection with the acetylcholinic actions of the parasympathetic division were hexamethonium chloride, neostigmine methylsulfate, and atropine sulfate. Hexamethonium chloride was given in the dose of 15 mg/kg. It antagonizes the nicotinic actions of acetylcholine on the ganglia—that is, the depolarization of the ganglia by acetylcholine is prevented by hexamethonium, although hexamethonium does not itself stimulate or depolarize the ganglia. The net effect is to block the transmission of impulses by the sympathetic ganglia. Since the vasoconstrictor effect of nicotine is abolished through hexamethonium's antagonism of acetylcholine, it essentially promotes vasodilation and a fall in blood pressure.

Atrophine sulfate is also an antagonist of acetylcholine, but at the peripheral level. A poisonous alkaloid extracted from belladonna, it is a competitive antagonist of the muscarine actions of acetylcholine. Thus, it antagonizes most of the effects of stimulation of parasympathetic and cholinergic sympathetic nerves. It does not prevent the release of acetylcholine, but antagonizes the effects of acetylcholine on the effector cells after it has been released from post-ganglionic nerve endings. Atropine also produces both stimulant and depressant actions on the central nervous system. It has the effect of accelerating the heart rate since the action of acetylcholine on the pacemaker of the heart is antagonized. It is used to relieve spasms, and, when applied topically, it enlarges the pupil of the eye. In this experiment, it was given in the dose of .2 mg/kg to the experimental subjects.

Neostigmine methylsulfate, however, promotes acetylcholine by inhibiting cholinesterase, a substance which itself inhibits acetylcholine. Thus neostigmine promotes formation of acetylcholine indirectly and enhances the muscarinic effects of acetylcholine. It is used to relieve postoperative atony of intestines and the urinary bladder. This cholinergic drug was given in the dose of .1 mg/kg to the subjects.

The effects of these three parasympathetic drugs on the following behavior of naïve socially isolated chicks of different ages in the imprinting exposure situation are depicted in Figure 4–26. It is apparent that when acetylcholine is enhanced by the use of neostigmine methylsulfate, the following tendency of the subjects is not at all facilitated. There are, in fact, slight interfering effects at the ages of 14 and 24 hours, and strong interfering effects at the age of 32 hours (not statistically significant, however). The curve of following behavior as a function of age in chicks under the influence of neostigmine sulfate is highly similar to that of the control subjects, except at the age of 32 hours.

The results obtained with atropine sulfate and hexamethonium chloride are extremely interesting, since they have nearly opposite effects on the following behavior of the chicks, except at the age of 8 hours. It seems as though the antagonism of the peripheral muscarinic effects of acetylcholine by atropine sulfate considerably depressed following behavior at all ages except 8 hours, where some facilitation occurred. But when the nicotinic effects of acetylcholine are removed and the trans-

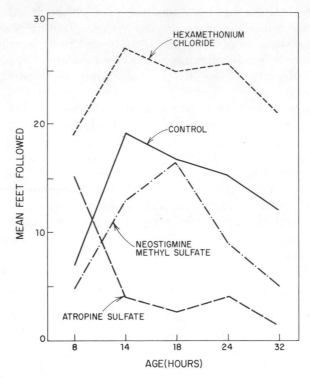

Figure 4–26 Mean number of feet followed during laboratory imprinting while under the influence of hexamethonium, neostigmine, or atropine as compared with the following of non-drugged controls.

mission of excitation of post-ganglionic fibers is prevented by the use of hexamethonium, there is a considerable enhancement of following behavior at all ages. The enhancement was statistically significant at the ages of 8 and 24 hours.

The effects of these various autonomic drugs indicates that the mechanisms involved in the facilitation and depression of following behavior at different ages by different drugs are highly complex. It is not possible, for example, to conclude that fear mechanisms, or even adrenergic stimulation, facilitate following during early ages and interfere with it at later ages, in the light of the results obtained from the use of blocking agents and ergonovine maleate. Since all the drugs, except neostigmine methylsulfate, facilitated following behavior at the age of 8 hours, it appears that any agent which will produce general activation of the nervous system will increase following tendencies at the earliest ages. The facilitation at the age of 8 hours suggests that the lack of following found in normal chicks of this age is not due to incomplete muscular development. Also, it raises the possibility that chicks may be able to form imprinted attachments to the potential parental surrogate at that age, a possibility which has been supported by our sibling socialization studies (Polt, 1966; Hess and Polt, 1964, 1966).

All subjects in the drug study were tested for following behavior at the age of 52 to 60 hours without the influence of any drug. The test procedure consisted of exposing the animals individually to the stationary ball for a period of 1 minute, then moving the ball at the rate of 10 feet per minute, for 4 turns around the 10-foot runway.

Table 4–13 shows the mean number of feet followed by the different age and drug groups during the initial laboratory imprinting exposure period and during the re-exposure at the age of 52 to 60 hours when the drug influences had completely worn off. The correlation between following during the initial exposure and the re-exposure was +.83. In fact, there was only one instance in which the amount of following in the two cases was significantly different—at the 5 percent level— and this was for the ephedrine sulfate group exposed to the ball at the age of 8 hours. This result can be expected when 45 comparisons are made.

Since the testing did not involve requiring the animal to make a discrimination between the model to which it had been initially exposed and a strange one simultaneously present, we cannot offer any conclusions regarding the effects of the drugs upon the imprinted attachments formed by the drugged chicks in comparison with the undrugged controls. Obviously, this is a question which requires experimental investigation, particularly in the light of the fact, as shown by our sibling socialization studies (Polt, 1966; Polt and Hess, 1964, 1966), that increases in following behavior by means of the introduction of external variables, such as patterned light experience or prior socialization, do not necessarily mean that greater social attachments are formed. In such cases, in fact, the following behavior that is exhibited may be completely independent of imprinting.

Autonomic Drugs and Shock

We thought that perhaps the facilitating effects of electric shock and drugs which were observed in the earliest ages might summate when simultaneously present in the imprinting exposure situation (Kovach, 1963). To this end, we selected six of the autonomic drugs we had studied. Three of them—amphetamine sulfate, ephedrine sulfate, and hexamethonium chloride—increased following behavior in chicks 8, 14, and 18 hours old. A fourth—ergotamine tartrate—had facilitating effects

TABLE 4–13 MEAN NUMBER OF FEET FOLLOWED BY DIFFERENT AGE GROUPS UNDER THE INFLUENCE OF DRUGS DURING INITIAL LABORATORY IMPRINTING (II) SESSION AND DURING RETENTION TEST (RT) AT 52 TO 60 HOURS OF AGE

Condition	8-hr. groups		14-hr. groups		18-hr. groups		24-hr. groups		32-hr. groups	
	II	RT	II	RT	II	RT	II	RT	II	RT
Controls	6.8	6.0	19.1	19.5	16.9	15.9	15.3	15.5	11.6	13.0
Amphetamine	15.1	21.6	29.8	26.6	30.3	26.6	4.6	4.8	1.0	5.8
Ephedrine	26.9	17.0*	28.5	27.8	27.7	25.3	8.9	15.1	3.6	7.0
Epinephrine	29.6	22.6	21.6	21.5	14.0	16.2	12.8	10.6	5.4	3.9
Hexamethonium	19.0	14.0	27.0	30.2	25.0	19.0	25.6	23.1	21.0	14.8
Ergonovine	18.3	12.6	18.2	16.6	24.2	21.8	25.0	27.3	14.0	18.0
Ergotamine	21.9	17.8	19.8	19.5	17.6	16.6	15.7	14.7	12.0	16.6
Neostigmine	4.8	11.2	13.0	17.3	16.6	22.8	9.0	14.0	5.0	11.0
Atropine	14.2	7.4	4.0	3.4	2.6	2.1	4.0	5.0	1.2	1.9

*Different from initial performance at .05 level.

only at the age of 8 hours. A fifth—neostigmine methylsulfate—never had facilitating effects, and actually caused a slight depression of following at the age of 14 hours. The sixth—atropine sulfate—had been found to facilitate at the age of 8 hours and to depress following at the ages of 14 and 18 hours.

The ages of 8, 14, and 18 hours were chosen for the laboratory imprinting exposure session because the facilitating effects upon following behavior that have been observed with electric shock or drugs have been most evident at these earliest ages. As in the other studies, the 180 vantress broiler chicks were hatched in our own laboratory, individually isolated in small cardboard boxes upon hatching, maintained there in visual and social deprivation until the time of the imprinting exposure, and returned to the boxes after the exposure until the time of the re-exposure test.

The drugged subjects received the same doses as in the previous study, usually 1 hour before the laboratory imprinting exposure. During the imprinting procedure itself, carried out as in the electric shock studies, the electrodes attached to the wings of the chicks delivered one 3 ma shock during the initial 5 minutes of the observation when the blue ball was stationary, and delivered 10 more shocks of the same intensity at the end of each successive 2 minutes thereafter, during which period the model moved about the 10-foot runway, with regularly scheduled pauses. It moved approximately 57 feet during this 20-minute period.

Re-exposure to the moving model was carried out at the age of 52 to 60 hours without any drug influences or shock. This was done in the same way as in the previous drug study, with the chick exposed to the stationary model for 1 minute and then to the moving model as it traversed the 10-foot runway for 4 turns in 4 minutes.

Table 4–14 shows the mean number of feet that the model was followed by the different drug and age groups during the initial imprinting exposure and the later test. As in the earlier drug study, there was a high correlation between the amount of following during the initial exposure and during the re-exposure.

Even though the subjects in this study had the opportunity to follow the model for a greater distance—17 feet more—than in the earlier drug study, comparison of the corresponding drug groups under conditions of shock and no shock reveals that in 16 out of the 18 comparisons possible among drugged animals, the mean amount of following during the initial laboratory imprinting exposure was lower for the shocked animals than for the non-shocked ones. Naturally, not all these differences are statistically significant. Nevertheless, while the

TABLE 4–14 MEAN NUMBER OF FEET MODEL FOLLOWED DURING INITIAL
EXPOSURE BY SHOCKED CHICKS UNDER THE INFLUENCE
OF DIFFERENT DRUGS AND MEAN NUMBER OF FEET
MODEL FOLLOWED DURING SUBSEQUENT RE-EXPOSURE
WITHOUT SHOCK OF ANY DRUG INFLUENCE

| | Age at initial laboratory exposure to model | | | | | |
| | 8 hours | | 14 hours | | 18 hours | |
Drug	Impr.	Test	Impr.	Test	Impr.	Test
Amphetamine sulfate	16.9	9.6	21.1	14.1	7.8	9.5
Ephedrine sulfate	16.6	9.9	16.1	9.7	11.0	9.2
Hexamethonium chloride	17.5	10.4	4.9	2.8	9.6	0.0
Ergotamine tartrate	3.2	1.5	1.5	0.0	3.1	1.5
Neostigmine methylsulfate	2.0	0.0	1.9	1.8	5.0	5.0
Atropine sulfate	9.2	11.3	7.7	11.1	2.4	0.0

drugged animals that had not been shocked during the imprinting procedure had tended to follow the most at the ages of 14 and 18 hours,
the additional effect of shock had the strongest interfering effects on
the following behavior of drugged animals of those same ages. The
effects of the added shock, in fact, tended to be at least double at those
ages in comparison with the earlier age of 8 hours, so that the highest
following in drugged and shocked subjects tended to occur at the age
of 8 hours, with progressively less following with greater age of exposure. In all probability, it appears that had even older animals been
used, at the ages of 24 or 32 hours, we would have obtained still
further depression of following behavior in shocked animals under a
drug influence.

The results obtained with the individual drugs in the shock and non-
shock conditions are extremely interesting. For example, hexamethonium, which had facilitated following in non-shocked animals of all ages
failed to do so in shocked animals 14 and 18 hours old. The amount of
following in subjects given ergotamine tartrate, neostigmine methylsulfate, or atropine sulfate was essentially nil for both the initial exposure and the re-exposure situations.

These results led Kovach (1963) to conclude that they could not be
accounted for in terms of the notions of sympathetic arousal and excitation of fear mechanisms, which had appeared reasonable with respect
to the observed facilitatory and interfering effects in following behavior
when drugs or shock were used separately. Instead, Kovach turned to
the notion of an optimal level of excitation responsible for facilitation of
following behavior. Beyond such an optimal level, he suggested, further
increasing the intensities of excitation results in the depression of following behavior.

Effects of the Object on Following and Imprinting

We have repeatedly observed that vocal models are twice as effective as silent ones in eliciting following behavior during the imprinting exposure, both in terms of the doubling of the number of chicks that follow and in doubling the total amount of following performed. Subsequent research has also demonstrated that visual aspects of the laboratory imprinting object themselves influence not only the amount of following behavior and approach tendencies in naïve socially isolated chicks but also their demonstrated preference for the specific object to which they had been exposed initially when later required to make a discrimination between a simultaneously presented strange object and the familiar one (Schaefer, 1958; Schaefer and Hess, 1959; Hess, 1959a). In other words, chicks have a preference for following certain types of objects as parental surrogates over other types of objects, just as it has been demonstrated that chicks peck more at objects of certain colors than at those of others (Hess, 1956) and more at certain shapes than at others (Fantz, 1957). Thus, the potential parental object can truly be called a "releaser" of following behavior and attachment formation.

Our investigation concerned itself with the importance of form and color aspects of a laboratory imprinting object in determining not only the elicitation of following behavior but also the formation of an imprinted attachment to that object on the basis of preferences shown in a later free choice test.

In the first experiment of this investigation, 160 vantress broiler chicks from our own laboratory were used. They were placed immediately after hatching in small cardboard boxes in pairs, and kept in these little boxes until the time of the laboratory imprinting exposure. They were placed in pairs so as to facilitate drying of the down. Just before the imprinting exposure, the chicks were placed individually into cardboard boxes and transported to the imprinting room. The chicks were 13 to 16 hours old, at the height of sensitivity to imprinting, as determined by our previous work.

The laboratory imprinting procedure itself was similar to that in our other studies. The chick was eased onto the runway from the box at a distance 24 inches from the model in darkness. The experimenter then went to the control panel behind a one-way screen and turned on the lights in the apparatus. For a period of 1 minute, the model (one of eight to be later described) was silent and stationary. Then for 2 minutes, the stationary model began to emit a continuous rendition of the gock call. After this time, the model, still vocal, was moved to within 6 inches of the chick, if the chick had not already moved to within this distance of the model. It remained in this position for 2 further minutes, after which it began to make 4 circuits about the run-way, moving at the speed of 2 inches per second, and making regular pauses so that each 120 inch turn was traversed in a period of 200 seconds. After the exposure had been completed, the lights were turned off in the apparatus and the chick returned to the cardboard box, where it remained by itself until the testing procedure 24 hours later, at the age of approximately 38 hours.

Eight different models were used. All were spheres approximately 6½ inches in diameter and equipped with a loudspeaker. There was one each of the following colors: red, orange, yellow, green, blue, white, gray, and black (Ostwald denominations for the respective colors were 6 pa, 4 pa, 1 pa, 22 pa, 14 pa, a, g, p). Thirteen subjects were used for each of the chromatic balls, and 10 were used for each of the archomatic ones.

The later test procedure utilized a 3.5 foot diameter round enclosed platform bordered by five gallows placed at 72° intervals. For the chicks that had been exposed to one of the chromatic stimuli, all five chromatic spheres were hung from the gallows; for the chicks exposed to one of the archromatic stimuli, all three chromatic spheres were hung in the test apparatus.

The test session consisted of placing the chick, in the dark, on a little circle in the center of the platform so that it was equidistant from all stimuli. If a chick went within 12 inches of a sphere, it was considered

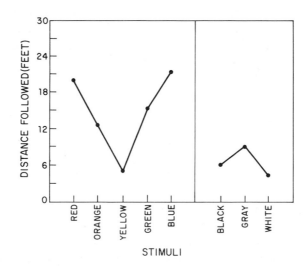

Figure 4–27 Mean distances followed in feet by eight groups of animals to eight different stimuli differing in color or reflectance.

as having chosen that sphere and observed for another minute to confirm the choice. If the chick had not made any such choice within a period of 10 minutes, it was considered to have made no choice, and the experiment was terminated.

Figure 4–27 depicts the mean amount of following of the laboratory imprinting object during the exposure session. As can be seen, the red and blue balls elicited the greatest amounts of following, and the achromatic and yellow balls the least.

The effect of the specific model experienced during the imprinting exposure upon the choices made in the later test session is shown in Figures 4–28 and 4–29. As can be seen from these figures, there were clear differences in the preferences shown by the chicks as a function of what model they had been exposed to. A particularly interesting aspect of the test data obtained with the chromatic stimuli is that there is a high correlation between the amount of following during the laboratory imprinting session and the percentage of animals in that group that chose the same model during the test session. This fact, graphically presented in Figure 4–30, is all the more impressive in view of the fact that the chicks had five stimuli from which to choose during the test session.

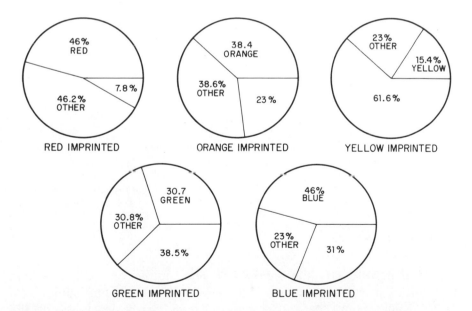

Figure 4–28 Influence of laboratory imprinting: percentages of animals preferring to approach one out of five differently colored stimuli 24 hours after having been imprinted to the one indicated. The gray sectors indicate the percentages of no choice. (N = 65, or 13 for each color.)

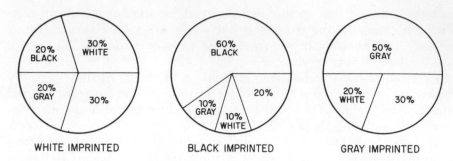

Figure 4–29 Influence of laboratory imprinting: percentages of animals preferring to approach one of three stimuli of different reflectances 24 hours after having been imprinted to the one indicated. (N = 30, or 10 for each shade.)

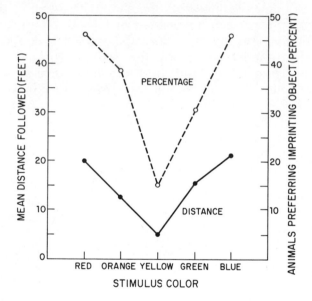

Figure 4–30 The law of effort applied. A comparison of the performances of five groups of animals during laboratory imprinting (in terms of feet followed) and during later testing (in terms of percentages of animals choosing the imprinted stimulus) shows that the more effort a group expended during laboratory imprinting, the better its score became during testing.

This demonstrated relationship between amount of following and strength of preference in the chicks exposed to chromatic stimuli is a further confirmation that our law of effort, which we developed on the basis of experimentation with mallard ducks, is valid in the case of chicks.

These results gain further depth when compared with those obtained with naïve chicks of two different ages that were tested in exactly the same way for preferences among either the five chromatic stimuli or the three archromatic stimuli. One group of 25 naïve visually deprived and unimprinted vantress broiler chicks was tested in the preference situation on the five chromatic stimuli at the age of 13 to 16 hours after hatching; the other group of 58 similarly naïve chicks was tested in the same fashion on the five chromatic stimuli or on the three achromatic stimuli at the age of 30 to 36 hours after hatching. The preferences shown by these naïve controls are illustrated in Figure 4–31. These preferences, based upon simultaneous free choice between the stimuli, reflect the potency of these stimuli in eliciting approach behavior at different ages in naïve chicks. Consonant with what was found with the imprinted chicks, yellow proved to be the least attractive of the chromatic stimuli for the naïve chicks. In fact, none of the older naïve chicks chose it.

The influence of the exposure in promoting an attachment to the exposure model in preference to strange ones as a function of the characteristics of the model is very evident in these data when the proportion of failure to make any choice at all in each group is considered. Among the naïve animals, of those that had not previously formed any attachment to any of the models, from 40 to 72 percent failed to approach any of the proffered stimuli. This shows that the chicks that had been exposed to the yellow sphere essentially did not form an attachment to it at all. However, the chicks which had been exposed to an achromatic stimulus, while following at the same level as those exposed to the yellow ball, showed a higher degree of attachment for the object to which they had been exposed than did the yellow-exposed subjects to the yellow ball. This higher degree is largely only apparent, because in the test situation they were confronted with three stimuli

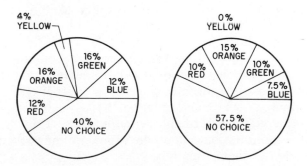

Figure 4–31 Percentages of naïve animals preferring to approach one of five differently colored stimuli presented simultaneously (a) 13 to 16 hours after hatching (25 young controls), (b) 30 to 36 hours after hatching (40 old controls).

instead of five, a factor which would permit a greater likelihood of approaching the familiar stimulus. Also, the greater percentage choice for black-exposed subjects for that stimulus than the gray-exposed had for their stimulus is a reflection of the variability that is to be expected as a consequence of the low amount of following performed by all members of this group. Thus, no true differentiation for these achromatic stimuli on later testing may be expected under such conditions.

The changes in preferences shown by the naïve controls in the test situation as a function of age are of interest. In the first place, it appears as if the innate preferences present in 13- to 16-hour-old chicks result in the more effective formation of attachment to some stimuli than to others. Without any laboratory imprinting experience, however, the preferences of naïve animals tend to change slightly. Furthermore, there is a decreasing tendency to make any choice at all as a function of increasing age, as shown by the higher percentage of older controls that did not approach any of the chromatic spheres, thus confirming our observations that the older the chicks are, the less of a response they have to a laboratory imprinting situation. These data also show that the shift in the approach preferences of the experimental chicks was due to the laboratory imprinting and not to maturational processes.

The demonstrated color preferences for imprinting objects gains further substantiation through the fact that although the subjects exposed to the colored balls were run from three hatches, there was a consistent relationship among the stimuli in terms of the preferences shown: yellow always was the least preferred color, orange and green were always followed more, and red and blue were followed the most. Such consistency is statistically highly significant.

We have concluded that hue qualities, rather than brightness qualities, were the effective factors in influencing the behavior of the chicks. We came to this conclusion because, first, of the marked differences in the overall behavior of the animals with respect to the chromatic and achromatic stimuli. The chromatic stimuli, it will be recalled from Figure 4–27, elicited more than twice as much following as did the achromatic ones. Second, there were no marked differential preferences for any of the stimuli in the achromatic series during following. Neither was there any consistent preference for following or for approaching in the simultaneous discrimination test among either naïve or imprinted chicks in terms of a white-gray-black brightness continuum. Thus, it is apparent that brightness could not have been the primary dimension to which the chicks responded in these situations.

The imprinting color preferences of these chicks is very similar to the imprinting color preferences of naïve socially deprived mallard ducklings at the critical age period. The ducklings' preferences, as indicated by the

TABLE 4–15 MEAN NUMBER OF FEET MODELS OF DIFFERENT COLORS
FOLLOWED DURING LABORATORY IMPRINTING
SESSION AT CRITICAL AGE PERIOD BY SOCIALLY
AND VISUALLY NAÏVE CHICKS AND DUCKS

	Mean number of feet followed	
Color	Ducks	Chicks
Yellow	5.7	5.0
Blue	50.0	21.0
Red	30.0	20.0
Green	32.5	16.0
Orange	14.2	12.0
Black	31.2	6.0
White	13.7	4.5
Gray	9.6	9.0

amount of following in a standard laboratory imprinting exposure session was, from high to low, as follows: blue, green, red, orange, and yellow. Table 4–15 shows the mean following scores elicited from chicks and ducks by each of the five colored and three achromatic spheres. The ducklings' color preferences correlate $+.90$ with those shown by chicks (Schaefer and Hess, 1959). Species differences certainly are to be expected, particularly since it has been found that different breeds of chicks have different color preferences in their pecking behavior (Hess, unpublished research).

Further investigations have revealed that the form aspects of a laboratory imprinting object also influence following behavior in naïve socially isolated vantress broiler chicks (Schaefer, 1958; Schaefer and Hess, 1959; Hess 1959a). One hundred eighty chicks, hatched in our laboratory and placed in pairs in small cardboard boxes to prevent visual experience were individually exposed to one of nine different models at the maximally sensitive age of 13 to 16 hours. The imprinting experience in the circular runway was exactly the same as that described in the previous experiment with the spheres of different colors.

The nine different models were of three different colors—yellow, red, and blue—and of three different shapes—plain sphere of the same size as in the previous experiment, sphere with added "tail" and "wings," and sphere with added "tail," "wings," and "head." Figure 4–32 depicts the mean amount of following elicited during the imprinting laboratory exposure session by each of the nine models. It is readily apparent that the simple sphere tended to elicit greater following, and that the more additions put on it, the less the following that was elicited. Just as we

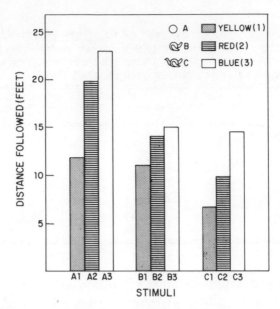

Figure 4–32 Effectiveness of models in eliciting the following reaction, expressed as a function of stimulus complexity and color.

had found earlier, blue proved to evoke more following than red, and red in turn was superior to yellow in this respect. If all subjects that were exposed to a specific shape without regard to color are considered, the mean following scores were: sphere, 18.25 feet; with wings and tail, 13.5 feet; with head, wings, and tail, 10.32 feet. If all subjects that were exposed to a particular color regardless of shape are considered, the mean following scores were: blue, 17.50 feet; red, 14.57 feet; and yellow, 9.85 feet. This type of regularity is completely supportive of the notion of the laboratory imprinting object as a releaser of following behavior in the chicks, since there is clearly an additive effect of stimulus elements that are simultaneously present.

Further regularity of this sort is obtained in terms of the number of chicks exposed to each type of imprinting model that followed it during the exposure to it and the number that did not. With shape held constant, 40 followed the plain sphere, while 20 did not; 32 followed the sphere with wings and tail, while 28 did not; 33 followed the sphere with head, wings, and tail, while 27 did not. With color held constant, 41 followed the blue models, while 19 did not; 37 followed the red models, while 23 did not; and only 27 followed the yellow models, while 33 did not.

Twenty additional vantress broiler chicks, treated in the same way as in the above experiment, were exposed to a stuffed adult male brown leghorn. Only 2 of these chicks followed the model at all, and these 2 followers followed for an average of 9.5 feet, certainly minimal, and certainly less than the average following score racked by the animals that were exposed to the yellow sphere with all superstructures added to it.

This surprising result with the stuffed rooster as a model led us to consider the possibility that the size differences in the different shape models might have also been responsible for the observed decrements in following behavior as further structures were added to the plain spheres. This is because as wings, tail, and head were added, the laboratory imprinting model became larger. The stuffed brown rooster was larger than any of these. Thus, the possibility that increasing size decreases the amount of following is one that certainly should be experimentally investigated.

Subsequent research (Goodwin and Hess, 1969a) has attempted to determine the laboratory imprinting preferences of naïve hatchling vantress broiler chicks for different two-dimensional shapes. These shapes were constructed out of light-weight bristol board, and had an area of approximately 38 square inches.

In the first experiment, five colored circles—red, orange, yellow, green, and blue, in the same Ostwald designations as used in Schaefer and Hess (1959)—were employed as laboratory imprinting stimuli. No sound was used during the exposure to the stimuli. The naïve socially isolated chicks, 14 to 18 hours old, were exposed individually to one of the colored circles in the circular runway apparatus for a period of 2 minutes, during which the stimulus moved toward the chick from a point 18 inches from the chick to a point 6 inches from the chick and stayed there for a period of 50 seconds, after which it was again moved 18 inches from the chick. Ten seconds later, this movement toward the chick was repeated with return to the original starting point scheduled as before, after which the observation was terminated.

During the observation (with the experimenter behind the one-way vision screen) the chicks were scored for behaviors toward the stimulus. Positive scores were earned for making intention movements toward the stimulus, for making approach responses of one or two steps toward the model, for making contentment notes to the model when it was nearby, for looking at the model. Negative scores were given for making distress notes in the presence of the model or for avoiding the model by moving away from it when it was nearby.

Eight or 9 animals were exposed individually to each stimulus, with a total of 44 experimental subjects. The average scores elicited for each color was: red, 4.50; orange, 1.44; yellow, 1.55; green, .56; and blue,

2.28. Thus, as was found with three-dimensional spheres by Schaefer and Hess (1959), red and blue were the most effective colors; and orange, yellow, and green, the least effective. The higher ranking of red over blue in this instance is not surprising, since Schaefer (1958) on occasion obtained this in his study. Furthermore, color preference studies conducted by Kovach (1971a, b) and Kovach and Hickox (1971) with a different breed—Rhode Island red—obtained relative preferences similar to these. Also, the animals studied by Goodwin and Hess (1969a) were tested at the end of April and at the beginning of May, while Schaefer tested his subjects in June and July; seasonal influences may thus be present. Hence, these results indicated some degree of good comparability with the ones obtained with three-dimensional stimuli, even though there did not seem to be as high a degree of differentiation among the two-dimensional circles of different colors as Schaefer (1958) and Schaefer and Hess (1959) had obtained with solid spheres of different colors.

Additional research (Goodwin and Hess, 1969a) has assessed the relative attractive value of different two-dimensional forms, all of the same color. A total of 84 chicks, 13 to 16 hours old, with an average age of 14 hours, socially and visually naïve, were exposed for 2 minutes to a silent stimulus which moved as in the above experiment. Six different forms were used, with 13 to 15 subjects exposed to individual forms. The behavior of the chicks was scored in the same fashion as with the colored circles. The mean scores obtained for the stimulus forms were: triangle, 2.250; square, 1.700; pentagon, 1.346; star, 1.1785; hexagon, .9615; circle, .3571.

Since the relative differentiation between stimuli was not great, stimuli were made vocal after the initial 2-minute period of silent presentation, for 8 minutes, in the hope of eliciting actual following behavior, in another experiment. Chicks were, as before, 13 to 16 hours old (with the majority 14 hours old) and socially and visually naïve at the beginning of the exposure to a single stimulus. The movement of the model while it was vocal depended on whether or not the chick began to follow it. If the chick began to follow, the model was kept moving ahead of the chick, but never more than $3\frac{1}{3}$ feet away, until the total experimental time of 10 minutes had elapsed. The model was kept ahead of the chicks as much as possible, in an effort to keep chicks from running ahead of the model and seeing the loudspeaker mounted on the other side of the stimulus and thus receiving visual stimulation not equivalent to that desired.

If, however, the chick did not follow, the model, after 2 minutes of vocal presentation during which the motion of the model was as during the previous 2 minutes of silent presentation, was immediately rendered silent and moved away from the chick on the opposite side of the apparatus so that it was out of sight. The model was silent for 1 minute. Then it was again vocal and began movement toward the model, with regularly scheduled pauses of 12 seconds after every 6 seconds of movement. When the model was within 6 inches of the chick, it reversed its direction of intermittent movement. By the time the 10-minute experimental session ended, if the chick had not followed at all, the model was again out of sight of the chick, and still vocal.

During the exposure, the number of feet that the model was followed was recorded. Then different stimulus forms were used: serrated circle, oval, circle, hexagon, pentagon, square, rectangle, diamond, triangle, and star. In spite of the large number of subjects—from 42 to 45—exposed to each form, there was still not a great differentiation in the mean scores, in terms of number of feet of following, of individual stimuli. Table 4–16 shows the mean feet of following to each of the ten forms used, ranked in order of decreasing effectiveness. For the purpose of comparison with previous research utilizing other stimuli, the scores of individual subjects were limited to 40 feet in the computation of the averages shown in Table 4–16.

The rankings between the six stimuli—triangle, square, pentagon, star, hexagon, and circle—in Table 4–16 and the rankings for the same stimuli when presented silent correlate +.77. The differences in mean following are rather small between adjacently ranking stimuli, with seven pairs of adjacently listed forms on Table 4–16 differing in mean following scores by less than 1 foot. Thus, the preference ranking cannot be considered an absolute one; this is amply confirmed by the fact that sequential testing of different hatches to these ten stimuli produced preference

TABLE 4–16 MEAN NUMBER OF FEET VOCAL TWO-DIMENSIONAL MODELS OF DIFFERENT FORMS FOLLOWED BY SOCIALLY AND VISUALLY NAÏVE CHICKS AT CRITICAL AGE OF 13 TO 16 HOURS

Form	Mean feet followed
Square	20.52
Pentagon	19.77
Horizontal oval	19.52
Horizontal diamond	18.32
Triangle	17.55
Serrated circle	17.27
Star	16.19
Horizontal rectangle	15.40
Circle	13.62
Hexagon	12.98

rankings which differed in exact preference order from that of the composite total for all 438 experimental subjects.

These very small differences in the efficacy of the stimuli, which differ only in form and not in color, deserve attention. They are congruent with the finding of Smith and Meyer (1965) that there were much smaller differences in the approach responses of socially naïve 12- to 14-hour-old leghorn chicks to a hen outline versus a rectangle than between the responses to red versus white stimuli or between silent and vocal stimuli. It also appears that there is a cross-species generality regarding these small differences in attractive qualities of potential imprinting objects as a function of two-dimensional form, since Klopfer (1971) presented data upon which he drew the conclusion that pekin ducklings in an imprinting situation discriminate imprinting objects primarily on the basis of solidity of objects, with different two-dimensional representations being treated as equivalent.

At any rate, both the rankings for the six silent stimuli and that for the ten vocal stimuli disagree with Schneirla's contention that disks are more attractive to neonate chicks than are angular ones when presented as distant stimuli for filial attachment behavior (Schneirla, 1965, p. 37).

Genetic and Neurological Studies

Initial genetic studies with bantam chicks showed that with them, as we had found with ducks (Hess, 1957), the ability to imprint on a parental object is genetically based, and apparently can be bred for or against. Further studies, in which two strains of Cochin bantams—one buff, and the other black—were crossed, suggested that imprintability may be sex-linked. This is because a cross between a male black good imprinter and a female buff non-imprinter produced black imprinters, while a cross between a female black good imprinter and a male buff non-imprinter produced black non-imprinters.

Genetic work in the area of imprinting in other laboratories has had mixed results, depending upon the investigators' frames of reference. Gray, Yates, Davis, and Mode (1966) report finding that differences in chicks' responses toward different objects were based on inherited tendencies. Fischer (1969), using the white leghorn breed (which was probably the breed utilized in the Gray et al. study), discovered practically no heritability component in the laboratory imprintability of this breed. This breed is one which we have found (Hess, 1959a) to imprint very poorly in our experimental situations. In line with our own unpublished findings, Fischer (1969) predicted that "selection for following in white leghorns would probably be difficult." Smith and Templeton (1966) have, furthermore, reported that no statistically significant genetic contribution to responsiveness in a laboratory imprinting situation could be found in F_3 brown leghorn × light Sussex chicks. The genetic contribution was estimated to be approximately 18 percent for this breed.

Graves and Siegel (1968), on the other hand, have supported the notion that imprintability has a genetic basis. A total of 669 domestic chicks from five 2 × 2 mating sets that formed 10 F_1 crossbred types and 9 F_1 purebred types were exposed to flicker as day-old hatchlings. Their response and approach to this flicker were recorded. Crossbreds were found to have higher response and approach tendencies than did purebreds. While variances for these trials were large, these tendencies appeared to be heterotically inherited, in the view of the authors, particularly in relation to the known genetic composition of the breeds. Additive inheritance also appeared to have a low, but significant, effect on these response tendencies (Graves and Siegel, 1966). Graves and Siegel considered that the response and approach traits were probably adaptive during the phylogenetic development of domestic fowl, and are probably best understood in relation to imprinting. Further recent studies (Graves and Siegel, 1969) showed that related chicken lines are indeed very different in response and approach tendencies. They reported much greater success in breeding for fast response and approach tendencies than for slow response and approach tendencies. The heritabilities of the response-approach and staying-near behaviors were estimated to range from .22 to .42, with median values at .28 and .32.

As for the neurophysiological bases of imprinting, we have made pilot studies on the effects of cerebral lesions on the following behavior of naïve vantress broiler chicks in an imprinting exposure situation and attachment formation as a result of such exposure. This was done partly because we noted that some chicks which had been operated upon lacked the fear response even though they were old enough to have it fully developed. Also, Collias (1950) had reported that decerebrate chicks will not follow a clucking or retreating object, but that if basal portions (paleonstria) of cerebral hemispheres are left intact, the social responses will be normal.

The types of lesions that were made are shown in Figure 4–33. Chicks that had a type 1 (amygdaloid) lesion were able to achieve good imprinting test scores as a result of exposure to the laboratory imprinting object (in accordance with our usual procedures) at the age of 3 days. This is considerably superior to control chicks which follow and imprint only occasionally so late in their first few days. Even so, chicks with this lesion were unable to form any imprinted attachments as a result of laboratory imprinting exposure carried out for the first time at the age of 5 days or at the age of 7 days. Newly hatched chicks with these amygdaloid lesions, on the other hand, would readily follow, even

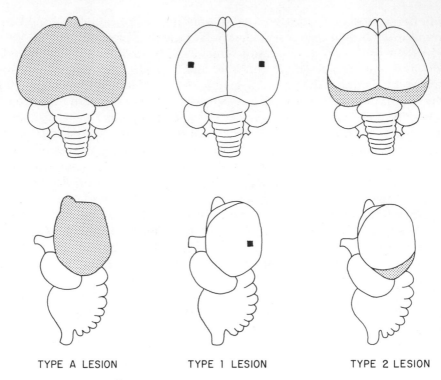

TYPE A LESION   TYPE 1 LESION   TYPE 2 LESION

Figure 4–33 Three types of lesions in the chick brain used to study the effects of extirpation on imprintability.

when the stuffed brown leghorn rooster that had dismally failed to elicit following in normal critical age period chicks was shown to them.

Type 2 lesions did not promote the formation of imprinted attachments to parental surrogates, in spite of the fact that such lesions completely removed fear responsiveness to strange objects. Chicks that were completely decerebrate—type A lesion—were exposed to the laboratory imprinting object only at the age of 2 days. They followed the object well, but when imprinting strength was considered, the results of the later discrimination test were inconclusive. Control animals given sham operations behaved essentially like normal chicks of the same age.

Although the number of animals used in this study is small, this seems to be a fruitful avenue of approach, one which we hope will be tapped more fully for its potential.

Informal Observations

Many years ago I imprinted a hatchling jungle fowl chick to myself during his first day of life. I permitted him to follow me regularly from that time on. Up until the time of sexual maturity this jungle fowl showed an extreme attachment to me. He emitted distress calls whenever I had to leave the laboratory. If he was out loose from the cage, he would follow me up and down stairs, through the laboratory and my house.

However, when he matured, his behavior suddenly changed. He no longer would display affectionate behavior to me, and sometimes attacked. As a result, he was placed in a cage by himself. Every time after that when he was taken out of the cage, he would court and perform mating behavior to the legs of anyone who was nearby. If he was given a choice between trousered and bare legs, he preferred the trousered legs. His attacks toward me may be related to Kruijt's (1971) observations of aggressive "tail-fighting" in isolation-reared male jungle fowl chicks several weeks old. Such aggressive behaviors could also be directed to colorful stationary objects in the cage with the isolated cockerel.

When my jungle fowl cock was three years old, various white leghorn and vantress hens were placed in his cage with him. He disregarded them completely. Even after many months of companionship with an adult hen in his small cage, the cock never showed any diminishing of his responsiveness to human legs. He lived to be more than 11 years old, and during that time never courted females of his own species, but continued to waltz to people. This is similar to Räber's (1948) and Schein's (1963) turkeys. Since Guiton (1966) failed to find this type of effect in brown leghorn cocks, it may be that the breed that he used has lost, through the process of domestication, this ability for irreversible sexual object fixation.

This breed difference in the ability to form imprinted social attachments during the 1st day of life is also indicated by the fact that pilot work with the colored spheres either with or without the additional head, wings, or tail superstructures showed that when white leghorn chicks were used as subjects, more following was elicited in them by models that had the superstructures, while the reverse, as we know, was the case with vantress broiler chicks. This is still another reason that we are so careful to specify the breed used for laboratory subjects when arriving at our conclusions regarding following behavior and the formation of imprinted social attachments in the filial-maternal sphere.

Other Experiments with Chicks

It appeared to us that it was possible that the laboratory imprinting experience could have an influence upon the behavior of animals in situations that did not seem to be related to social imprinting. More specifically, would the laboratory imprinting experience provide a degree of perceptual sensitization that could influence learning in other situations?

To approach this question, we conducted the following experiment reported by Polt (1969). Twenty vantress broiler chicks were imprinted to a 7 inch diameter blue ball, and 20 others were imprinted to a 7 inch diameter yellow ball, beginning at the age of 16 hours. The exposures were repeated at the ages of 36, 60, and 84 hours. Each exposure lasted 1 hour. At the age of 3 days, chicks were given ten training trials to discriminate between yellow and blue food boxes in a discrimination apparatus. Half of the yellow-imprinted and half of the blue-imprinted had the blue as the positive stimulus (rewarded with food), and all the others had yellow as the positive stimulus.

It was found that the chicks that had the same color for the laboratory imprinting object as they had had for the positive food box were able to show evidence of learning during the ten trials, with the blue-imprinted, blue-rewarded chicks showing a very highly significant responsiveness to the blue food box. The greater effect shown by the blue-imprinted in comparison with the yellow-imprinted is congruent with earlier findings (Schaefer and Hess, 1959) that chicks imprint more strongly to blue balls than to yellow ones. In spite of this, however, control chicks which had never had any laboratory imprinting experience showed neither any preference for either of the two colors nor any evidence of greater responsiveness to the positive food box during the ten training trials.

We have also carried out some experimentation on the effects of social isolation during the earliest part of life on the development of behavior in chicks (Hess, Polt, and Goodwin, 1959). We had observed that if chicks, of whatever breed, are isolated from their own kind or from other living creatures from the moment of hatching by placement in small individual compartments in which food, water, heat, and light are provided, a variety of aberrant behaviors can be observed in individual chicks by the fourth day of age. Some chicks exhibit "catatonic" behavior; they remain completely immobile in a corner, not responding to external stimulation. Others become extremely flighty, running to and fro at the approach of a human hand. Still others may become very aggressive and hostile, giving strong attack responses. Other varieties of such "pathological" behavior can be seen in these socially isolated chicks.

We took 15 De Kalb leghorn chicks that had just hatched, transferring them directly from the incubator into their individual compartments. This transfer was done in dim light, so that the chicks had a minimum of visual experience of the experimenter. Five chicks served as controls, 5 others were given carisoprodol, and the other 5 were given meprobamate. The drugs were administered by adding them to the drinking water, so that no contact between the chick and the experimenter was necessary. In addition, this constituted a continuous, self-drugging procedure. At the age of 4 days, all chicks were tested in two different situations. One was a field test, which consisted of observing the chick for a short period and then reaching for the chick with and noting its specific reaction to the approaching hand. The other situation consisted of exposure to a group of age mates that had been socially reared in laboratory brooders.

No abnormal behaviors were observable in the experimental animals that had received meprobamate or carisoprodol, but they were clearly evident in the control group. Of course, since small numbers were used, we cannot make any sweeping generalizations.

OTHER PRECOCIAL SPECIES

Most of the observations made with other precocial bird species have been limited to the apparent ability to form filial attachments to a mallard duck decoy, as Table 4–1 shows.

However, we made other observations of a long-range nature. For example, a blue goose which was reared by turkeys from hatching was found to spend its time with turkeys. In another case, a female turkey that had been reared in isolation became sexually imprinted on humans. Similarly, two male turkeys, though subsequently reared with other turkeys after initial hand rearing, recognized men as competitors and pursued them around the enclosure in which they were kept.

LABORATORY IMPRINTING AND SOCIALIZATION IN TWO DOVE SPECIES

While the observations of Whitman (in Riddle and Carr, 1919) and of the Heinroths (1924–1933) have shown that social imprinting occurs in certain altricial bird species, little experimental research has been done subsequently. In addition, the life histories of altricial birds which have been reported to show abnormal sexual fixations are usually relatively unknown. As may be recalled, altricial bird species are ones in which the hatchling young cannot follow the parent, and the helplessness of the young requires that rather intensive care (in laboratory, hand feeding as well) be provided if they are not reared by their own parent.

It may be recalled that our socialization studies (Polt, 1966; Polt and Hess, 1964, 1966) demonstrated that following behavior per se does not necessarily mean that laboratory imprinting of filial behavior to a parental object is taking place. Only when naïve socially isolated precocial birds are exposed at a particular age is following behavior truly correlated with the formation of laboratory imprinting. The existence of social imprinting in altricial bird species is further evidence that imprinting and following behavior are not identical entities.

In certain altricial birds, there is now evidence that laboratory imprinting to a sexual object and taming to a foreign species are separate and sometimes independent processes (Klinghammer, 1967a, b). The experiments we shall now discuss are further indications of this fact.

We used two different species of dove—the blond ring dove (Streptopelia risoria, a species sometimes called S. roseogrisia), and the North American mourning dove (Zenaidura macruora carolensis)—that differed in the degree of domestication and in social living habits (Klinghammer, 1962, 1967a, b; Klinghammer and Hess, 1964). The blond ring dove has been a domesticated species for almost a thousand years, whereas the mourning dove is wild. The question of domestication with respect to the effects of early social experience in dove species was brought into consideration because of our earlier findings that domesticated mallard ducklings do not show imprinting as strongly as do wild mallard ducks.

Blond Ring Dove

We raised four groups of blond ring doves (Klinghammer, 1962, 1967 a, b; Klinghammer and Hess, 1964). The first group consisted of 25 birds which were isolated in individual cages until they were tested for sexual imprinting when they had become adults. The nestling squabs were removed from their nest and hand-reared at different ages between days 4 and 14. On each of these days, except days 3, 12, 13, and 14, 3 birds were so removed. On the other days, only 1 bird was taken from its nest for hand rearing. The second group consisted of 11 birds, also hand-reared in isolation, but only to the time of weaning, after which they lived in a community cage with other ring doves. One bird was removed from the nest on each day of the period from day 4 to day 14. Their exposure to human beings was limited to that necessary for feeding and cleaning.

The third group consisted of 6 birds which were raised by their own parents until the time of weaning and then were isolated in individual cages until the time of testing at adulthood. The last group contained 6 more birds which were raised by their parents and then kept in a community cage with other doves until the testing at sexual maturity. The exposure of this group to human beings was the same as that received by the second group which had been hand-raised to weaning and then kept in community cages.

Auditory isolation for socially deprived birds was not considered necessary, since Lehrman (1958) showed that as long as doves are visually isolated (but not auditorily isolated), pair formation and the brooding cycle do not begin. Also, it is known that vocal cues do not influence mate choice in doves. Vocal cues merely serve as a means of recognition among birds already mated to each other.

At the age of 8 or 9 months, and a little older for a few of the birds, testing for mate selection was commenced for all birds. The testing was carried out in a room 1.8 by 1.5 by 2.1 meters high, illuminated from the ceiling by a 40-watt fluorescent bulb. A wooden perch ran the length of the cage at a distance of 1.5 m from the ground and about 60 cm from the only open side (which was covered with wire netting). On one end of the perch was placed a small nest box, and on the other end a small wire cage (60 by 45 by 40 cm) containing a perch and a nest box as well as a choice bird of the opposite sex. The human participant in the test, acting as an alternative potential object for mate choice, sat in a chair placed in the corner opposite the wire cage. An observer who recorded the behavior of the bird during the test situation was about 60 cm away from the wire-covered open side, behind a door with a glass window. An intercom system permitted communication between the observer and the human participant.

After the person and the choice bird were in their places, the experimental bird was placed on the center of the perch. After a few minutes, the experimental bird usually approached either the person or the choice bird. At that time, the choice bird was released from its cage so that it could make advances to the experimental bird at the same time as did the human participant. During the entire test, the observer in the other room, using a check list based on an inventory of behaviors performed by dove species, noted the actions of the experimental bird, and a protocol was taken.

Four response categories were possible. The bird could: court the person; court the other bird; alternate between courting the person and the bird; or ignore both. In terms of these responses, it was found that the members of the first group, which had been hand-reared during the nestling stage and isolated thereafter, showed a strong preference for the human being as a mate, with the strongest preferences shown by those that had been removed from the nest between 7 and 9 days of age. Figure 4–34 shows the percentage of birds in each age group (according to the time of removal from the nest for hand rearing) that chose the human being or the conspecific ring dove.

All the birds that lived in community cages after weaning, irrespective of the mode of earlier rearing, chose the conspecific doves as a mate. They were all so inhibited by the presence of the person in the test cage, however, that no courtship behavior would occur unless the person left

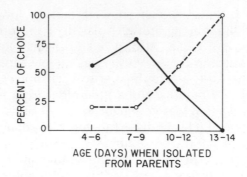

Figure 4–34 Percent of choice by 25 ring doves in a free choice situation between a human being (solid line) and a ring dove (dashed line) of the opposite sex. All birds were kept in visual isolation from other doves from the day they were removed from their parents until they were tested as adults.

the cage. This was not the case with birds that were kept in isolation after weaning and cared for by humans. Birds of these two groups were able to respond by either assuming the male role in copulation with the choice objects (in the case of the human, with the hand), showing a decided preference for one of the two objects, or by exhibiting all courtship behavior except actual copulation. At other times, these birds would assume the appropriate female role with the female copulatory behavior patterns. When the objects were either ignored or passively avoided, the birds were considered to have made no preference.

Of the birds raised by parents until weaning and then individually isolated, 2 chose the human being, 2 chose the dove, 1 chose both, and the sixth ignored both.

These results indicate that social imprinting does occur in the blond ring dove and that the optimum time for it to occur with the human being as an object is at the age of 7 to 9 days. Squabs that were removed from their parents after the 12th day of age chose a dove in a free choice situation. On the other hand, only half of the birds that were taken from the nest at days 4 to 6 chose the human being. While one might expect all birds removed before a certain age to choose human beings in a mate selection situation, this obviously is not the case.

The explanation for this may possibly lie in the onset of fear behavior. As may be seen from Figure 4–35, the onset of fear of humans in nestling squabs occurs between the 7th and the 10th days of life. This is precisely the same period as that of the maximum sensitivity to the formation of a social bond to human beings. It may be that, in the case of the blond ring dove, when there is interaction with a new object, such as occurs when a human being removes the bird and raises it by hand,

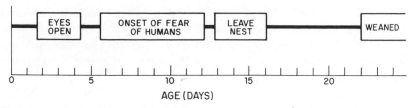

Figure 4–35 Normal development of blond ring doves from the time they hatch until they are weaned.

that a social bond may be formed more effectively when this experience is accompanied by a certain level of fearfulness. Birds removed earlier, when fear responsiveness is either zero or extremely low, never do show fear of the human, while after 12 days from hatching, the fear is sufficiently strong to prevent the establishment of any social bond to the human being. A social-fear response test conducted after weaning in the case of the hand-reared birds confirmed the effect of age at the onset of hand rearing in the development of fearfulness. The test consisted of slowly moving the hand to the bird. Those removed before the age of 9 days showed no fear, while those removed at the age of 9 days and later did, as shown by Figure 4–36.

However, pre-weaning rearing experience is not the sole factor which determines the sexual object choice of sexually mature blond ring doves. This is shown by the fact that all birds which lived in a group with other conspecifics after weaning chose them. Those that had been reared by hand for 2 or 3 weeks and then left with other doves for 7 to 8 months showed no detectable lasting effect in comparison with those that remained with conspecifics for the entire time. Similarly, of 6

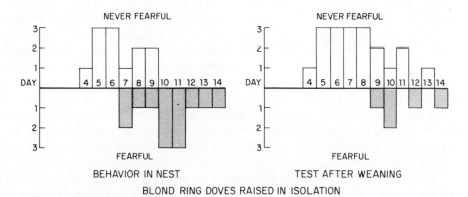

Figure 4–36 The fear responses of blond ring doves when tested during the nest stage and after weaning.

parent-raised birds kept in individual isolation after weaning, 3 showed responsiveness to a human being as a sexual object, with 2 of these 3 showing a definite preference for the human being. These complementary findings indicate the influence of post-weaning social experience upon sexual object choice in blond ring doves.

In this species, the evidence supports the notion that not only the early experience during an optimum period but also continued experience throughout the bird's life have an effect on adult behavior. Certainly, experience during an optimum period between 7 and 9 days of age does have lasting effects, as shown by the hand-reared isolated birds. Thus, it appears that in this species two mechanisms have evolved which result in pair formation at sexual maturity. Thus, we may conclude that in this respect we may consider this imprinting to be reversible in the sense that preferences for sexual objects can be altered in the blond ring dove. The effects of the early experience, however, are never completely lost in some birds, according to the conditions of their subsequent experience, as the results show.

These experimental data show that taming and social imprinting are separate behavioral processes in the blond ring dove. In other words, these birds certainly could be tamed through extended experience with the human being, even after weaning had taken place. But such taming did not automatically insure that the human being would be chosen as a sexual object. Further light on the phenomenon of imprinting in altricial bird species is shed by the results of our experiment with the North American mourning dove.

North American Mourning Dove

As we have already mentioned, there are several behavioral differences between blond doves and mourning doves. Still another point of difference is that while ring doves usually will begin to court and mate with a conspecific or with a member of another species (if sexually attracted to that species) within one hour, mourning doves normally require days to exhibit all the behavior patterns concommitant with courtship. Thus, arbitrarily setting a 1-hour time limit for testing sexual object choice for both species of dove would actually be a flaw in experimental design. Further data on mourning dove behavior illuminate the importance of assessing relevant behavior patterns as a function of the particular species being investigated.

An initial experiment (Klinghammer, 1962) assessed some of the factors which appear to influence the development of mate selection in mourning doves. One mourning dove was raised with a ring dove nest mate, and remained with ring doves until sexual maturity. Six doves were raised by ring dove foster parents with their own mourning dove siblings, and remained with both species until sexual maturity. Two other mourning dove groups were hand-reared from the time of separation from the parents until weaning or sexual maturity. Five subjects were hand-reared until maturity and isolated during that time from all other mourning doves. Their exposure to human beings was maximal. Four other birds were hand-raised with conspecific siblings, and then kept in a community cage with other mourning doves. These birds never saw ring doves, and had maximal exposure to humans as did the other group. An additional 3 birds were removed from their wild parents on approximately the 9th and 13th days of life and then were hand-raised until weaning. Since the recently wild-caught adult mourning doves did not rear young in captivity, no mourning doves could be raised by their own species. Therefore, the young doves or eggs were placed with incubating or brooding ring doves when the phases of the breeding cycle of eggs and young coincided with those of the foster ring dove parents.

The test for sexual object choice was carried out at the time of sexual maturity. It was the same test as was used for the blond ring dove, but allowed additional time for the development of sexual behavior in the light of the observed species differences. While it had rarely been necessary to test ring doves for more than 2 hours, the mourning doves required a few weeks to several months to be tested. The ring-dove-reared mourning doves took the longest to be tested because of their relative wildness.

All 3 surviving mourning doves that were hand-raised and kept in isolation until the time of the test ignored other mourning doves and ring doves completely, even after several months of experience with them in the same room, while humans were treated as sexual partners and rivals. However, unlike ring doves, human-imprinted mourning doves would never allow themselves to be touched by humans, particularly outside the breeding season. They would peck or preen the experimenter's head, ears, or hair, sit on his hands or shoulder, but avoided being held. This is correlated with the fact that in the natural situation mourning doves also avoid bodily contact with other doves except during the breeding season.

Those that had had sibling experience, however, never chose man as a sexual object, despite their very apparent tameness to the experimenter. In contrast, however, all the mourning doves that were raised by ring dove parents were extremely fearful of man; they could not be handled at all. Since all the subjects were males, no suitable mourning dove female was available as a test object; they were all tested on a female ring dove that would accept mourning doves as a mate. One male mated and raised a hybrid offspring with the female ring dove. Five others showed no choice, and the remaining one died before it could be tested at sexual maturity.

The 3 birds removed at the 9th and 13th days of life and hand-raised until weaning feared humans, and the 2 survivors preferred mourning doves as mates.

These preliminary results with mourning doves indicated that when imprinting occurs to humans in these birds, it occurs with greater strength than in the case of ring doves.

The existence of stronger imprinting in these mourning doves than in the ring doves appears to be correlated with their greater wildness. There is evidence that when mourning doves are bred in captivity for several generations, as has been done in Germany, imprinting exists in an attenuated form, so that there is some reversibility.

Because of the small number of subjects, we were unable to determine with statistical significance any period of sensitivity for the hand-rearing experience to result in sexual imprinting; however, a fear response test conducted after weaning by slowly moving the hand toward the bird in its cage gave results similar to that obtained with the blond ring doves. As figure 4–37 indicates, there is a sharp break at the age of 8 days in the occurrence of fear behavior. Mourning doves removed at less than the age of 9 days showed no fear on the test, while fearfulness did occur in those removed afterward. Furthermore, no bird hand-raised individually after the age of 8 or 9 days showed imprinting to humans.

This initial experiment indicated that it would be worthwhile to investigate the critical period of sensitivity to imprinting in mourning doves. Wth this goal in mind, we conducted another study with additional subjects.

In this subsequent study, 18 mourning doves were removed from the nest at various ages and given one of the following social experiences:

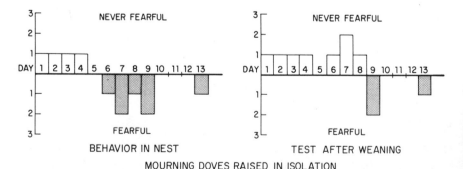

Figure 4–37   The fear responses of North American mourning doves when tested during the nest stage and after weaning.

complete isolation from conspecifics until sexual maturity (7 subjects); isolation and hand rearing until the age of 22 to 52 days (5 subjects); or maintenance with siblings until weaning, at which time they were placed into community cages with conspecifics (6 subjects) (Klinghammer, 1967a, b).

At sexual maturity, the free choice test situation was again utilized to determine the preference of the subjects for a human being or a conspecific mourning dove. Testing in this instance consisted of placing an experimental bird into a large room containing unpaired mourning doves of both sexes. Under such conditions, the bird would begin to respond to or advance toward either a mourning dove or the human, and from then on react primarily to the selected partner. If a bird selected the human, and the human left the room, the bird might eventually respond to a mourning dove; but upon the reappearance of the human being, an event which usually occurred several times each day, any beginning relationship with another dove would be at once interrupted, and the bird would react once again to the human being. Thus, it was easy to assess mate selection, since such an experimental bird would never pair with a mourning dove. Testing was carried out during the latter part of April or during May, since it is during this time that there is the maximum physiological readiness for reproductive behaviors.

As in the research with ring doves, it was found that the 8th day of life is the approximate point of the critical period for the development of an imprinted social bond to the human being, thus confirming the suggestion of the fearfulness test conducted after weaning in the pilot study of Klinghammer (1962). Birds that were removed from the nest before that age would, if individually isolated, select a human being as a mate. If hand-raised with a sibling, they chose conspecifics as a mate, but were nevertheless tame to human beings and did not show fear of human beings. Birds taken from the nest after the 8th day of age, however, all showed fear of human beings at the time of sexual maturity.

Raising with a sibling, regardless of the age of removal from the nest, always resulted in the formation of a sexual preference for conspecifics in these mourning doves. But hand raising, with or without sibling social experience, always resulted in permanent taming to human beings. In other words, the early experience had a permanent effect in this respect, even though it did not permanently influence sexual object choice.

When the mourning doves were hand-raised in isolation until sexual maturity and then placed with conspecifics, they showed a gradual shift in sexual preferences from breeding season to breeding season, until, by the fourth breeding season, the biologically appropriate object—the mourning dove—was predominantly the chosen object in sexual selection. Although these birds did come to direct sexual behavior toward conspecifics, they never behaved normally in the sense that they never formed a pair with another mourning dove of the opposite sex that went through a normal breeding cycle. If mate selection were to be determined solely on the basis of the occurence of sexual behavior, then it would be said that there was a reversal from the first year of life. However, if all aspects of sexual behavior and mating are to be considered, then it can be said that the effects of the early experience were lasting.

The changing preference in mating behavior may be related to the lowering of thresholds to releasers for sexual behavior at the peak of the breeding season through physiological processes, and habituation of aversive responses to other doves through prolonged acquaintance.

While sexual choice of the human being by the mourning dove will occur only if experience with the human being has begun prior to the 8th day of life, such is not the case with the determination of another mourning dove as a sexual object. Differences in biological adequacy and the possible presence of innately determined responses to conspecific stimuli appear to play a role in this. The influence of later conspecific social experiences in reversing the effects of the bond to the human being that had hand-reared the birds in question is further shown by the fact that the group of birds which had been hand-reared beginning on or before the 8th day of life and kept in isolation until 52 days of age, after which they were placed in a community cage with other mourning doves until sexual maturity, chose mourning doves as sexual partners. Thus it appeared, on the basis of these results, that early experience on the nest before the 8th day of life may be a prerequisite for keeping mourning doves together, until, some time after 52 days of age, learning experiences can take place that result in species members mating with each other.

Some initial observations on *Zenaida graysoni,* a dove from the island of Socorro in the Pacific Ocean off the coast of Mexico, indicate that in both the absence and the presence of species' members, other species— in this particular case, ring doves—are courted (Klinghammer, 1967a). One parent-raised female that had copulated successfully with a male conspecific solicited ring doves in the characteristic female solication posture when she was isolated from her own kind. In addition, she occupied a nest jointly with a ring dove pair and laid her own eggs in the nest.

Another observation by Klinghammer, of a male *Z. graysoni* which had raised several broods of young with a female of his species, revealed that he courted ring doves persistently after living in an aviary with them for about one year. This finding is the more remarkable in view of the fact that, although his former mate had died, there were several additional members of his own species of both sexes available and in breeding condition in the loft. In addition, his own female offspring, raised by him and his former mate, and living under the same conditions, solicited ring doves repeatedly.

REFERENCES

ANDREW, R. J. The relation between the following response and precocious adult behaviour in the chick. *Animal Behaviour,* 1966, **14,** 501 505.

COLLIAS, NICHOLAS E. Some basic psychological and neural mechanisms of social behavior in chicks. *Anatomical Record,* 1950, **108,** 552. (Abstract)

COLLIAS, NICHOLAS E., and COLLIAS, ELSIE C. Some mechanisms of family integration in ducks. *Auk,* 1956, **73,** 378–400.

FABRICIUS, E. Zur Ethologie junger Anatiden. *Acta. Zoologica Fennica,* 1951, **68,** 1–175.

FANTZ, ROBERT L. Form preferences in newly hatched chicks. *Journal of Comparative and Physiological Psychology,* 1957, **50,** 422–430.

FISCHER, GLORIA J. Heritability in the following response of white leghorns. *Journal of Genetic Psychology,* 1969, **114,** 215–217.

GOODWIN, ELIZABETH BIRD. Innate visual form preferences in young chicks. Unpublished doctoral dissertation, University of Chicago, 1967.

GOODWIN, ELIZABETH BIRD, and HESS, ECKHARD H. Innate visual form preferences in the pecking behavior of young chicks. *Behaviour,* 1969, **34,** 223–237. (a).

GOODWIN, ELIZABETH BIRD, and HESS, ECKHARD H. Innate visual form preferences in the imprinting behavior of hatchling chicks. *Behaviour,* 1969, **34,** 238–254. (b).

GOODWIN, ELIZABETH BIRD, and HESS, ECKHARD H. Stimulus generalization and responses to "supernormal stimuli" in the unrewarded pecking behavior of young chicks. *Behaviour,* 1969, **34,** 255–266. (c).

GOTTLIEB, GILBERT. Prenatal auditory sensitivity in chickens and ducks. *Science,* 1965, **147,** 1596–1598.

GOTTLIEB, GILBERT, and KLOPFER, PETER H. The relation of developmental age to auditory and visual imprinting. *Journal of Comparative and Physiological Psychology,* 1962, **55,** 021–026.

GRAVES, H. B., and SIEGEL, P. B. *Bulletin of the Ecological Society of America,* 1966, **47,** 200. (Abstract)

GRAVES, H. B., and SIEGEL, P. B. Chick's response to an imprinting stimulus: Heterosis and evolution. *Science,* 1968, **160,** 329–330.

GRAVES, H. B., and SIEGEL, P. B. Bidirectional selection for responses of *Gallus domesticus* chicks to an imprinting situation. *Animal Behaviour,* 1969, **17,** 683–691.

GRAY, PHILIP H., YATES, ALLEN T., DAVIS, G. T., and MODE, C. J. Some aspects of the genetics of imprinting. *American Zoologist,* 1966, **6,** 568.

GUITON, PHILIP E. The effect of isolation on the following response of brown leghorn chicks. *Proceedings of the Royal Physical Society Edinburgh,* 1958, **27,** 9–14.

GUITON, PHILIP E. Socialisation and imprinting in brown leghorn chicks. *Animal Behaviour,* 1959, **7,** 26–34.

GUITON, PHILIP E. The influence of imprinting on the agonistic and courtship responses of the brown leghorn cock. *Animal Behaviour,* 1961, **9,** 167–177.

GUITON, PHILIP E. Early experience and sexual object-choice in the brown leghorn. *Animal Behaviour,* 1966, **14,** 534–538.

HEINROTH, OSKAR, and HEINROTH, MAGDALENA. *Die Vögel Mitteleuropas.* Berlin: Lichterfelde, 1924–1933.

HESS, ECKHARD H. An experimental analysis of imprinting: A form of learning. Unpublished Progress Report submitted June 1, 1955, to United States Public Health Service (Grant No. 776).

HESS, ECKHARD H. Natural preferences of chicks and ducklings for objects of different colors. *Psychological Reports,* 1956, **2,** 477–483.

HESS, ECKHARD H. Effects of meprobamate on imprinting in waterfowl. *Annals of the New York Academy of Sciences,* 1957, **67,** 724–732.

HESS, ECKHARD H. "Imprinting" in animals. *Scientific American,* 1958, **198,** No. 3, 81–90.

HESS, ECKHARD H. The relationship between imprinting and motivation. In: M. R. Jones, editor, *Nebraska Symposium on Motivation, 1959.* Lincoln: University of Nebraska Press, 1959. (a).

HESS, ECKHARD H. Two conditions limiting critical age for imprinting. *Journal of Comparative and Physiological Psychology,* 1959, **52,** 515–518. (b).

HESS, ECKHARD H. Imprinting. *Science,* 1959, **130,** 133–141. (c).

HESS, ECKHARD H. Effects of drugs on imprinting behavior. In: L. Uhr and J. G. Miller, editors, *Drugs and Behavior.* New York: Wiley & Sons, 1960. 268–271.

HESS, ECKHARD H. Imprinting and the critical period concept. In: E. L. Bliss, editor, *Roots of Behavior.* New York: Hoeber, 1962. 254–263. (a).

HESS, ECKHARD H. Experimental Analysis of Imprinting. Unpublished Progress Report for Grant MY-776 for activities from June 1958 to June 1962. (b).

HESS, ECKHARD H. Imprinting in birds. *Science,* 1964, **146,** 1128–1139.

HESS, ECKHARD H., and HESS, DORLÉ B. Innate factors in imprinting. *Psychonomic Science,* 1969, **14,** 129–130.

HESS, ECKHARD H., POLT, JAMES M., and GOODWIN, ELIZABETH. Effects of carisoprodol on early experience and learning. In: J. G. Miller, editor, *The Pharmacology and Clinical Usefulness of Carisoprodol.* Detroit: Wayne State University Press, 1959. 51–65.

HESS, ECKHARD H., and SCHAEFER, HALMUTH H. Innate behavior patterns as indicators of the "critical period." *Zeitschrift für Tierpsychologie,* 1959, **16,** 155–160.

HOFFMAN, HOWARD S. The control of distress vocalization by an imprinted stimulus. *Behaviour,* 1968, **30,** 175–191.

HOFFMAN, HOWARD S., STRATTON, JAMES W., NEWBY, VALERIE, and BARRET, JAMES E. Development of behavioral control by an imprinting stimulus. *Journal of Comparative and Physiological Psychology,* 1970, **71,** 229–236.

KILHAM, PETER, and KLOPFER, PETER H. The construct race and the innate differential. In: M. Mead, et al, editors, *Science and the Concept of Race.* New York: Columbia University Press, 1968. 16–25.

KILHAM, PETER, KLOPFER, PETER H., and OELKE, HANS. Species identification and color preferences in chicks. *Animal Behaviour,* 1968, **16,** 238–244.

KLINGHAMMER, ERICH. Imprinting in altricial birds: The ring dove (*Streptopelia roseogrisia*) and the mourning dove (*Zenaidura macroura carolinensis*). Unpublished doctoral dissertation, University of Chicago, 1962.

KLINGHAMMER, ERICH. Factors influencing choice of mate in altricial birds. In: H. W. Stevenson, E. H. Hess, and H. L. Rheingold, editors, *Early Behavior: Comparative and Developmental Approaches*. New York: Wiley, 1967. 5–42. (a).

KLINGHAMMER, ERICH. Imprinting in an altricial bird: The mourning dove (*Zenaidura macroura*) Unpublished manuscript, 1967. (b).

KLINGHAMMER, ERICH, and HESS, ECKHARD H. Imprinting in an altricial bird: The blond ring dove (*Streptopelia risoria*). *Science*, 1964, **146**, 265–266.

KLOPFER, PETER H. An analysis of learning in young Anatidae. *Ecology*, 1959, **40**, 90–102.

KLOPFER, PETER H. Imprinting: Determining its perceptual basis in ducklings. *Journal of Comparative and Physiological Psychology*, 1971, **75**, 378–385.

KOVACH, JOSEPH K. Some physiological and behavioral correlates of the imprinting phenomenon: arousal and the following behavior. Unpublished doctoral dissertation, University of Chicago, 1963.

KOVACH, JOSEPH K. Effects of autonomic drugs on imprinting. *Journal of Comparative and Physiological Psychology*, 1964, **57**, 183–187.

KOVACH, JOSEPH K., Effectiveness of different colors in the elicitation and development of approach behavior in chicks. *Behaviour*, 1971, **38**, 154–168. (a).

KOVACH, JOSEPH K. Interaction of innate and acquired: Color preferences and early exposure learning in chicks. *Journal of Comparative and Physiological Psychology*, 1971, **75**, 386–398. (b).

KOVACH, JOSEPH K., and HESS, ECKHARD H. Imprinting: Effects of painful stimulation on the following behavior. *Journal of Comparative and Physiological Psychology*, 1963, **56**, 461–464.

KOVACH, JOSEPH K., and HICKOX, JOHN E. Color preferences and early perceptual discrimination learning in domestic chicks. *Developmental Psychobiology*, 1971, **4**, 255–267.

KRUIJT, J. P. Early experience and the development of social behaviour in jungle fowl. *Psychiatria, Neurologica, Neurochirugia*, 1971, **74**, 7–20. (Elsevier Publishing Company, Amsterdam).

LEHRMAN, DANIEL S. Induction of broodiness by participation in courtship and nest-building in the ring dove (*Streptopelia risoria*). *Journal of Comparative and Physiological Psychology*, 1958, **51**, 32–36.

LORENZ, KONRAD Z. Der Kumpan in der Umwelt des Vogels; die Artgenosse als auslösende Moment sozialer Verhaltungswiesen. *Journal für Ornithologie*, 1935, **83**, 137–213, 324–413.

MOLTZ, HOWARD, and ROSENBLUM, LEONARD A. The relation between habituation and the stability of the following response. *Journal of Comparative and Physiological Psychology*, 1958, **51**, 658–661.

MOLTZ, HOWARD, ROSENBLUM, LEONARD A., and STETTNER, L. JAY. Some parameters of imprinting effectiveness. *Journal of Comparative and Physiological Psychology*, 1960, **53**, 297–301.

POLT, JAMES M. The effects of social experience on imprinting. Unpublished doctoral disseration, University of Chicago, 1966.

POLT, JAMES M. Effect of imprinting experience on discrimination learning in chicks. *Journal of Comparative and Physiological Psychology*, 1969, **69**, 514–518.

POLT, JAMES M., and HESS, ECKHARD H. Following and imprinting: Effects of light and social experience. *Science*, 1964, **143**, 1185–1187.

POLT, JAMES M., and HESS, ECKHARD H. Effects of social experience on the following response in chicks. *Journal of Comparative and Physiological Psychology*, 1966, **61**, 268–270.

RÄBER, H. Analyse des Balzverhaltens eines domestizierten Truthans (*Meleagris*). *Behaviour*, 1948, **1**, 237–266.

RAJECKI, D. W., and SAEGERT, SUSAN. Effects of methamphetamine hydrochloride on imprinting in white leghorn chicks. *Psychonomic Science*, 1971, **23**, 7–8.

RAMSAY, A. OGDEN. Familial recognition in domestic birds. *Auk*, 1951, **68**, 1–16.

RAMSAY, A. OGDEN, and HESS, ECKHARD H. A laboratory approach to the study of imprinting. *Wilson Bulletin*, 1954, **66**, 196–206.

RAMSAY, A. OGDEN, and HESS, ECKHARD H. The influence of sibling experience on imprinting in wild mallards. Unpublished manuscript, 1967.

RIDDLE, OSCAR, and CARR, HARVEY A., editors. *The Posthumous Works of C. O. Whitman*, Vol. III. *The Behavior of Pigeons*, edited by H. A. Carr. Washington: The Carnegie Institution of Washington, 1919. Publication No. 247.

SALZEN, ERIC A., and SLUCKIN, WLADYSLAW. The incidence of the following response and the duration of responsiveness in domestic fowl. *Animal Behaviour*, 1959, **7**, 172–179.

SCHAEFER, HALMUTH H. Imprintability of chicks as a function of varied stimulus elements in the imprinting object. Unpublished doctoral dissertation, University of Chicago, 1958.

SCHAEFER, HALMUTH H., and HESS, ECKHARD H. Color preferences in imprinting objects. *Zeitschrift für Tierpsychologie*, 1959, **16**, 161–172.

SCHEIN, MARTIN W. On the irreversibility of imprinting. *Zeitschrift für Tierpsychologie*, 1963, **20**, 462–467.

SCHNEIRLA, T. C. Aspects of stimulation and organization in approach/withdrawal processes underlying vertebrate behavioral development. In: D. S. Lehrman, R. A. Hinde, and E. Shaw, editors. *Advances in The Study of Behavior*. New York: Academic Press, 1965. Volume 1.

SCHUTZ, FRIEDRICH. Sexuelle Prägung bei Anatiden. *Zeitschrift für Tierpsychologie*, 1965, **22**, 50–103.

SLUCKIN, WLADYSLAW, and SALZEN, ERIC A. Imprinting and perceptual learning. *Quarterly Journal of Experimental Psychology*, 1961, **13**, 65–77.

SMITH, F. V., and BIRD, M. W. Varying effectiveness of distant intermittent stimuli for the approach response in the domestic chick. *Animal Behaviour*, 1963, **11**, 57–61.

SMITH, F. V., and TEMPLETON, W. B. Genetic aspects of the response of the domestic chick to visual stimuli. *Animal Behaviour*, 1966, **14**, 291–295.

SMITH, T. L., and MEYER, M. E. Preference of chicks in the original stimulus situation of imprinting. *Psychonomic Science*, 1965, **2**, 121–122.

SPALDING, D. A. Instinct and acquisition. *Nature*, 1875, **12**, 507–508.

TUKEY, JOHN W. *Exploratory Data: Limited Preliminary Edition*. New York: Addison-Wesley, 1971. Chapter 5.

5

Food, Olfactory, Auditory, and Environmental Imprinting

Several decades ago, there was a lively controversy in the psychology literature over the pecking behavior of chickens during their first few days of life. It had been noted that chicks' ability to peck accurately at grain improved during the earliest days of life. Then an argument arose, as part of the then-current instinct-versus-learning discussion, as to whether this improvement was due to maturation or to learning.

Experiments by Bird (1933) and others supported the notion that maturation processes are primarily responsible for the initial increase in pecking accuracy during the first few days of life. Bird stressed, however, that beyond this point, delayed pecking acts to depress pecking accuracy. In 1935, Padilla picked up this point and reported on his experiments on the effects of extremely prolonged delayed pecking practice. He compared hand-fed chicks permitted only 75 pecks per day after the enforced delay period had ceased with similarly reared chicks that were allowed unlimited pecking. He found that while delayed chicks needed more practice to reach the level of normal accuracy, within certain limits the amount of practice did not greatly affect the development of pecking accuracy. He therefore concluded that maturation simply sets the physiological level of accuracy of pecking response, given a certain amount of practice. Up to the age of 8 days, delay in pecking practice from the time of hatching had no deleterious effects on the eventual attainment of normal pecking accuracy in the chicks, but such delays longer than 8 days did. Chicks delayed for 14 days were found to be perfectly healthy, and autopsies could not reveal any visual defects. But even though they obviously could see the grain, they were unable to peck at it and literally starved to death in the midst of plenty. Only 2 weeks of intensive training could get the chickens to peck at food. This dramatic effect was most evident in chicks that had been prevented from pecking practice since hatching, for chicks that had already pecked for 8 days and then kept in the dark for 14 days regained most—but not all—of their pecking accuracy in 3 or 4 days. This phenomenon of failure to peck at food after more than 8 days of enforced delay in practice since hatching is, then, definitely an effect of early experience as such. Tucker (1957) has reported experiments which confirm fully that lack of early visual experience makes normal pecking accuracy almost impossible to achieve.

While Padilla said that his 14-day-delay chicks had either lost the pecking instinct or, at the very least, had it extremely disorganized, Poulsen (1951) points out that some of these chicks did peck aimlessly into the air, as Padilla had noted, and proposes that these chicks had not lost the pecking drive at all, but had, instead, failed to learn, as a result of the delay experience, what to peck at. This phantom pecking reported by Padilla was also noted by Tucker (1957). Since it is a real phenomenon, it does appear possible, as Poulsen suggested, that it was the object-response relationship that had suffered a rupture, not the response itself.

Experiments by Hess (1953, 1965a, b, 1962, 1964) have confirmed that the normal increase in pecking accuracy during the first 3 days of life is due to maturation, and that at the age of 3 days, when pecking accuracy normally reaches its usual level, chicks learn what objects are food objects to be pecked at, thus giving substantial support to Poulsen's suggestion. First, we will confine our attention to Hess' work on the development of pecking accuracy, and will later devote our attention to the question of the learning of food objects.

Hess (1953, 1956b) fitted newly hatched and visually naïve chicks with hoods containing prisms that displaced their field of vision 7 degrees to the right or the left. Half of these hooded chicks were given ample opportunity to practice pecking while feeding at scattered grains on the floor, while the other half were fed from bowls of mash, where accuracy did not matter in obtaining food. All chicks were tested daily for pecking accuracy by presenting them with small brass brads embedded in modeling clay which would show a mark from each peck. Control chicks, whose vision was not displaced, showed the usual increasing accuracy of pecking by producing less and less dispersion of their pecks around the brass brads. When the chicks were about 3 days old, they were extremely accurate in pecking. The displaced-vision chicks also showed the same amount of tightening of the dispersion of pecks, but to the right or left of the brad, in accordance with the type of prism they wore. Thus, experience with the displacing prisms could not cause them to alter their innate visual-pecking coordination.

Learning, then, has no role in the increase of pecking accuracy during the first 3 days of life, for otherwise the prism-wearing chicks would have learned to adjust their pecking to the displaced image, which they did not. As a matter of fact, prism-wearing chicks found it increasingly difficult to survive, and could have even starved to death if obtaining food had depended upon true pecking accuracy. Nevertheless, the experiments of Shepard and Breed (1913), Bird (1925, 1926, 1933) and of Cruze (1935) show that visual experience is necessary in attaining pecking accuracy, if not learning. These experiments showed that 3 days of patterned visual experience are necessary for the appearance of normal pecking accuracy. During this time, there is a gradual rise of accuracy if at least a minimal of pecking activity is permitted—about 75 pecks per day, certainly more than 25 (Bird, 1925, 1926, 1933). The effect of the visual experience appears to be to trigger the maturation of the visual-pecking coordination system.

LEARNING OF FOOD OBJECTS

In the past century, many observations have been made that the young chicks usually will peck at a rather large variety of objects, both edible and inedible. It has also been generally agreed that the chick early learns quickly what objects are most profitably pecked at for feeding purposes, and also to ingest grit for grinding the food in the crops. Almost a century ago, Preyer (1881) noted that his newly hatched chick first pecked equally at egg white, egg yolk, and millet seed. On the second exposure, the chick pecked more at egg yolk. While Preyer interpreted this as indicating an inherited preference for egg yolk, Romanes (1883) differed, preferring to see it as an instance of extremely rapid discrimination learning.

Eimer (1890), on the other hand, suggested that the young chick has an innate preference for millet, since his chicks pecked more at this seed than at other objects presented to it. Then Mills (1896) stated that "a chick will peck at any light spot, or object, if small, be it food or not."

Morgan (1896) remarked that chicks

Strike first with perfect impartiality at *anything* of suitable size: grain, small stones, bread-crumbs, chopped up wax matches, currants, bits of paper, buttons, beads, cigarette-ash ends, their own toes and those of companions, maggots, bits of thread, specks on the floor, their neighbours' eyes—anything and everything, not too large, that can or cannot be seized is pecked at, and if possible, tested in the bill. . . . There does not seem to be any congenital distinction between nutritious and innutritious objects, or between those which are nice and those which are nasty. This is a matter of individual acquisition. They soon learn, however, what is good for eating, and what is unpleasant, and rapidly associate the appearance with the taste.

Thorndike (1899a) took a position similar to Morgan's in stating that "the chick instinctively pecks at all sorts of objects of suitable size, e.g., tacks, match ends, printed letters, the eyes and toes of his mates, his own excrement, etc. The pecks at bits of food and small stones bring satisfaction, and the chick that, when first confronted by the situation 'grains of wheat, match ends, & excrement,' was as likely to peck at one as at another, becomes a chick who inevitably pecks at the wheat." Thorndike (1899b) presented chicks with small colored squares and counted the number of pecks made to each square. He found that all the squares were reacted to, but not equally. "These differences are due probably to accidental position or movements. . . . I should attach no importance whatever to the quantitative estimate given." The notion of trial-and-error learning of food objects by chicks is still postulated today, as one may see in Baeumer (1955).

However, the idea has only recently begun to be appreciated that even though chicks do peck at very many different objects, they do have innate preferences for pecking objects. Englemann (1941) showed that even though chicks were reared on paste in a brooder, they evidenced innate preferences for grain of certain shapes from the very first time that they saw them. The preferred shapes were those that most nearly approximated natural grains. The notion that chicks do show innate partiality toward certain objects for pecking has been substantially supported by several workers, including Curtius (1954), Fantz (1954), Hess and Gogel (1954), Hess (1956a), and Goodwin and Hess (1969a, c). Experiments by Hess (1962, 1964), utilizing natural pecking preferences, have agreed with early naturalistic observations that chicks do learn what objects are to be eaten, and at a critical period early in life, with the ultimate result that *both* the early proponents of innate pecking preferences and the proponents of rapid learning in altering pecking preferences turned out to be right.

When Robert Fantz (1954) studied the innate pecking preferences of young chicks for small objects of different shapes, he did so by counting the number of pecks newly hatched chicks made to the different shapes that were presented to them. During the course of this study,

Figure 5–1 A schematic diagram of a portion of the interior of the octagonal Hess Pecking Apparatus. As may be seen, two stimuli are visible through the circular holes in the panel of a single side wall of the apparatus. Enlarged representations of the stimuli are shown at the upper right of the figure. The small circles and triangles seen in these stimuli consist of white tissue paper, which may be pecked through to obtain grains of feed from the open feed holder in back of the stimulus. One of the triangles shown has been pecked through. The stimuli that do not provide food reward are placed upon blind feed holders, so that the tissue cannot be pecked through. Each peck upon a stimulus activates the lever upon which the blind or open feed holder is mounted; the lever movement is recorded upon a mercury counter. The readings from the 16 counters thus indicate how many times each of the 16 stimuli have been pecked during a given experimental session. The position of the stimuli are regularly changed so as to prevent bias due to position preferences.

Fantz attempted to determine the effects of rewarding chicks for pecking at shapes which they normally did not prefer. To do this, he used the Hess Pecking Preference Apparatus, shown in Figure 5–1. The chicks could obtain food by pecking a small hole in the stimulus which had a hollow holder in back which was filled with fine grain. It was found that if chicks are rewarded in this manner for about 2 hours for pecking at shapes which they do not usually peck much at, and are *not* rewarded for pecking at a stimulus which they do normally prefer to peck at, they eventually will peck more at the innately less preferred stimulus, not only during the period of food reward but also during extinction, when there is no more food reward. The effect of such a short period of food reward upon pecking preferences is rather stable, and can last as long as 10 days of daily testing without any further food reward.

It is obvious that in such a situation the chicks have learned what objects are to be pecked at in order to obtain food, and this accords with the naturalistic observations made by so many workers. This learning would appear to be very much like ordinary discrimination learning situations such as having to learn which of two differently colored food boxes contains feed. Research by Hess (1962, 1964), however, has shown that, on the contrary, this food learning differs a great deal from ordinary discrimination learning situations and gives support to Poulsen's (1951) contentions. The first indication of this difference was found in an experiment in which Hess varied the age at which food reward experience was given.

In this experiment, Hess used two stimuli: one was a white triangle on a green background, and the other was a white circle on a blue background. Approximately 280 leghorn chicks, divided into six groups, were given 2 hours of food reward experience for pecking at the innately less preferred stimulus, triangle-green, at the appropriate age, and were subsequently tested without the presence of any food reward for daily two-hour periods. At no time was any food reward given for pecking at the innately preferred stimulus, circle-blue.

The chicks of the first group were 1 day old when they were given the food reward experience. During the food reward period, they were presented with triangle-green only, so as to increase the number of opportunities for pecking at this stimulus and obtaining food, for the pecking level of chicks at this age is normally low, in comparison with that of older chicks. However, on subsequent testing days, both circle-blue and triangle-green were present. These chicks made 16,000 rewarded pecking responses to the triangle-green; yet, for 6 days following the food reward experience, it had no apparent effect on the innate pecking behavior. The chicks made more than 16,000 pecks over the 6 testing days, with an average of 27 percent to triangle-green, which is within the normal range for triangle-green preference when circle-blue is also present. The results for this group are shown in Figure 5–2.

The second group of chicks was rewarded at the age of 2 days for pecking at triangle-green but not for pecking at circle-blue. In the food reward situation, over 27,000 pecks were made, with 98 percent of them to the triangle-green. In subsequent testing, there was a short-term effect of the reward upon pecking behavior: on the first day without reward, 83.5 percent of the pecks were to triangle-green. However, the preference for triangle-green rapidly dropped from this level during the 5 days of testing, and on the last 2 days the pecks to triangle-green were 16 and 24 percent of the total. Since these preferences were at the

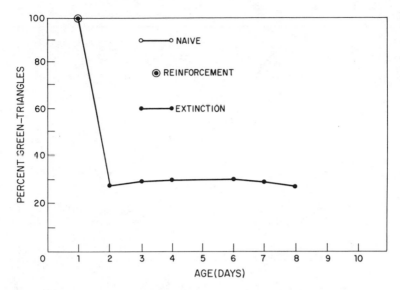

Figure 5–2 This graph, and the succeeding six (Figures 5–3 through 5–8) depict the proportion of total pecks that were directed to the triangle-green stimulus during pre-reinforcement control periods, reinforcement sessions, and extinction periods by each of the six experimental groups in the study. Pre-reinforcement control periods in which no reinforcement was given for pecking at any stimulus are indicated by open circles; reinforcement sessions are indicated by circled solid circles; and post-reinforcement extinction sessions are indicated by solid circles. This graph shows the percentage of pecks made to the triangle-green during reinforcement and post-reinforcement periods by the group of chicks reinforced at the age of 1 day.

normal level, any effect of food reward had completely vanished by that time. The results obtained from this group are shown in Figure 5–3.

The group rewarded at the age of 3 days, on the other hand, behaved quite differently from the first two groups. There were 45,000 rewarded pecking responses, or 99 percent of all pecks, made to triangle-green during the food reward period. During the 7 days of testing without any food reward, the response to triangle-green remained at a very high level, never dropping below 93 percent of the cumulative total of nearly 83,000 pecks. Even on the very last day of testing, pecking responses to triangle-green were 94 percent of the total. As shown by Figure 5–4, the effect of food reward was both permanent and potent.

The fourth group had its preference tested for 2 days at the ages of 3 and 4 days prior to the food reward experience. During this time, the animals performed within the normal preference range, giving 23 percent of the pecks to the triangle-green. At the age of 5 days, they were given food reward for pecking at triangle-green. During this time, 98 percent of their responses, or 40,000 pecks, were to this stimulus. During the 5

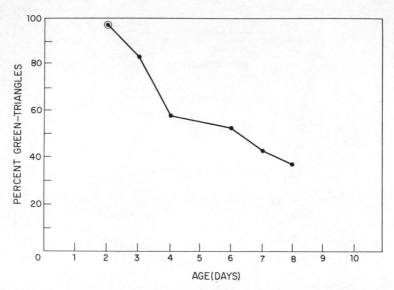

Figure 5–3 The responses of chicks given food reward for pecking at the triangle-green stimulus at the age of 2 days, during the reinforcement session and during the post-reinforcement extinction sessions.

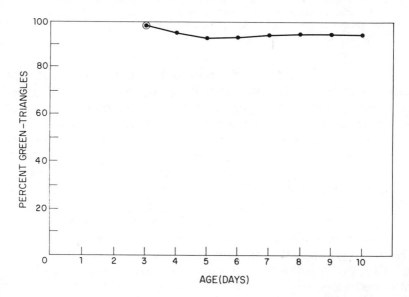

Figure 5–4 The responses of chicks given food reward for pecking at the triangle-green stimulus at the age of 3 days, during the reinforcement session and during the post-reinforcement extinction sessions.

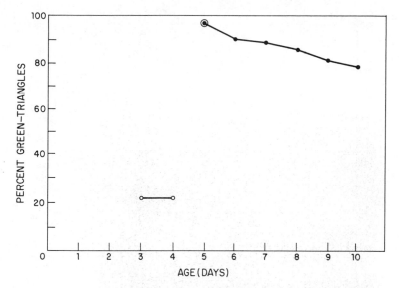

Figure 5–5 The responses of chicks given food reward for pecking at the triangle-green stimulus at the age of 5 days, during the pre-reinforcement control sessions, during the reinforcement session, and during the post-reinforcement extinction sessions.

subsequent days of testing with no food reward, a definite effect of the reward experience upon pecking behavior could be seen. However, as shown in Figure 5–5, the effect was not as strong as it had been for the group rewarded at the age of 3 days. The preference for triangle-green gradually diminished over the period of testing to a total of 79 percent of cumulative pecking responses. On the last day, 69 percent of the pecks were to the triangle-green.

The fifth group, rewarded for pecking at triangle-green at the age of 7 days, showed no effect of the food reward experience upon their pecking preference. Their preference was tested at the ages of 4, 5, and 6 days: during these days, 35 percent of their pecks were made to triangle-green. During the following 3 days, when no reward was given, only 14 percent of the total cumulative pecking responses were to triangle-green, even lower than it had been before the food reward experience. This is shown in Figure 5–6. On the last day, 3 percent of the pecks were to triangle-green.

The last group, reinforced at the age of 9 days, similarly showed no effect of the food reward experience upon innate pecking preferences. Their preference for triangle-green during the 4 days prior to food reward experience was 10 percent of all pecks. After withdrawal of reward, as shown in Figure 5–7, they pecked 20.5 percent at triangle-green.

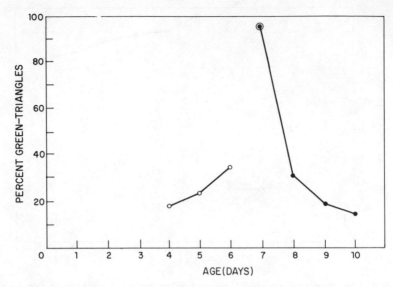

Figure 5–6 The responses of chicks given food reward for pecking at the triangle-green stimulus at the age of 7 days, during the pre-reinforcement control sessions, during the reinforcement sessions, and during the post-reinforcement extinction sessions.

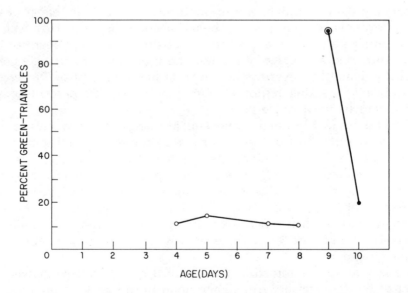

Figure 5–7 The responses of chicks given food reward for pecking at the triangle-green stimulus at the age of 9 days, during the pre-reinforcement control sessions, during the reinforcement session, and during the post-reinforcement extinction session.

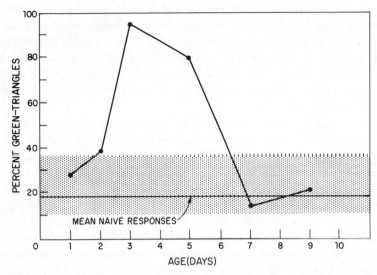

Figure 5–8 The mean rate of response to the triangle-green stimulus during the post-reinforcement extinction sessions, for each of the six experimental groups rewarded at different ages, as compared with the range of response to the triangle-green stimulus normally obtained from unrewarded control chicks. Thus, the reinforcement session had an evident effect only upon the chicks reinforced at the ages of 3 or 4 days.

The results of all six groups are summarized in Figure 5–8, in which the cumulative total percent of pecking responses to triangle-green during the no-reward testing period is plotted by the age at which the food reward experience had taken place. The resulting curve suggests very strongly that there is a period of maximum effectiveness for food reward to modify innate pecking preferences, and that the peak of this period is on the 4th day of life, or at the age of 3 days. It may be that the peak is, in fact, at the age of 4 days, and, in addition, that there would be an even smoother curve if there were data for the effect of food reward experience at the ages of 4, 6, and 8 days.

Nevertheless, the general conclusion is inescapable: there is a definite critical period during which food reward is most effective in modifying innate preferences of chicks for pecking at certain objects. The farther the chick is from the age of 3 days, the less effective is food reward experience.

The presence of a critical period for the chick's learning of food objects distinguishes it from ordinary learning problems in which food is used as a reward and in which discrimination between two different visual stimuli is required. That there should be a critical period for learning food objects seems reasonable, since at the age of 3 days a chick can no longer depend on the yolk sac for nutritional resources, but must acquire food by pecking at appropriate objects or it will die. It is of great interest that at this very age the chick has just acquired its highest level of pecking accuracy, which is complete at the end of the 3rd day of its existence. And then in the next few hours, on the 4th day of its life, qualities of food objects are learned so strongly that extinction is not readily achieved.

Further research upon the modification of innate pecking preferences by means of direct food reward has indicated that the existence of a critical period is not the only difference between it and ordinary discrimination learning. As we have seen in Chapter 4, while the drugs meprobamate and carisoprodol have no effect on the retention of ordinary association learning after their influence has worn off, they prevent animals from retaining the effects of a social imprinting experience (Hess, 1957; Hess, Polt, and Goodwin, 1959). In view of this, Hess (1962, 1964) carried out another experiment to determine whether the use of these two drugs would permit this early learning of food objects to be retained.

A total of 170 Leghorn chicks, 3 days old at the start of experimentation, were divided into four different treatment groups. One group consisted of animals which were given 16 mg carisoprodol 1½ hours before being given the food reward experience; in another group, the animals were given 16 mg meprobamate 1½ hours prior to the food reward experience; in the third group, the subjects were given .2 cc of water 1½ hours earlier; and the final group served as controls, having been given neither food reward nor any drug. The three experimental groups were rewarded with food for a period of 2 hours when they pecked at triangle-green but not when they pecked at circle-blue.

On each of 6 days following the food reward experience, all experimental groups were given 2 hours of testing without any food reward. The control animals were similarly placed in the Hess Pecking Preference Apparatus for 2 hours on each of these days, but food reward was never given to them.

Figure 5–9 shows the results obtained, in terms of percentage of pecks to triangle-green during the 6 days of testing without food reward or the administration of drugs. All three experimental groups had been pecking at triangle-green during the food reward period at a level of precisely 99 percent. The control group pecked at the triangle-green between 7 and 21 percent during the 6-day testing period, while the group given water showed the effect of food reward by pecking between 55 and 58 percent at triangle-green. The other two experimental groups, those given carisoprodol or meprobamate, however, showed a preference that is much closer to the normal preference range of the control group than

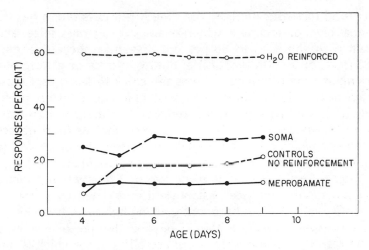

Figure 5–9   The mean rate of response to the triangle-green stimulus during 6 days of post-reinforcement extinction testing in animals that had been reinforced at the age of 3 days under the influence of carisoprodol, meprobamate, or given distilled water, as compared with the mean rate of response of controls which had received no food rewards.

that of the group reinforced with food and given water: the animals that had been reinforced under the influence of carisoprodol performed at a level between 21 and 29 percent for triangle-green, while those that had been given meprobamate pecked at a level of 10 to 12 percent at triangle-green. It can be easily seen that the animals that were trained under the influence of either drug, even though they were 3 days old at the time of food reward experience, behaved during the no-reward testing period as if they had never received any food reward.

The adverse effects of carisoprodol and meprobamate on the retention of the effect of food reward experience on pecking preferences provide still another difference between the processes involved in the modification of innate pecking preferences—that is to say, the learning of food objects and ordinary discrimination or association learning involving food as a reward.

Thus, it may be seen how the chick's behavior toward food objects is organized during the first days of life. The normal chick living in natural circumstances will peck at an extremely large variety of objects, but has natural preferences for objects according to their size, shape, color, and shininess. It appears that most of the preferences are for objects which are most like natural grains on which chicks usually feed when maintained in a natural environment (Fantz, 1954). However, the chick does exist largely on the food from its yolk sac during the first 2 or 3 days of life. During this period, its ability to peck accurately at pieces of grain or other food increases until, by the time it is 3 days old, it has acquired the normal level of accuracy, which enables it to strike, seize, and swallow grain with about 75 to 80 percent first-strike success. Then, at the age of 3 days, or the 4th day of life, the experience of getting nutriment by pecking at certain objects enables the chick to learn very rapidly the characteristics of food objects. Normally, innate pecking preferences coincide fairly well with the characteristics of actual food objects. However, if the environment happens to be such that its food objects have characteristics which are not optimally preferred, the chick will learn to peck primarily at these objects and thus alter its innate pecking preferences. Food reward experience at the age of 3 days when optimal pecking accuracy has already been established thus determines, more or less permanently, the chick's subsequent pecking behavior. If pecking opportunities are experimentally withheld beyond the age of 8 days, so that an object-response relationship is not established, the chick is unable to peck in order to obtain food unless given very intensive training, as in Padilla's (1935) study. If dark-reared chicks are required to feed themselves by pecking in the dark, as in Tucker (1957), pecking at food objects is still possible by training at the age of several months. However, such trained pecking is by no means normal, since there is no visual-motor guidance, grain recognition is absent and pecking accuracy is zero. In other words, the pecking behavior does not materially change in character, and remains much at the same level it had been during the period of dark rearing. Furthermore, Tucker reported that chicks that were only monocularly blinded for 10 weeks showed off-target pecking and never were normal in pecking accuracy. Thus, it is very evident that early experiences are of importance in the food behavior of the domestic chicken.

We therefore propose that there is a phenomenon of food imprinting in domestic chicks. We do not claim originality in this proposal since Poulsen (1951) has already suggested this on the basis of the finding that chickens that have been dark-reared and force-fed for at least 14 days are unable to use pecking behavior to obtain food. While it may appear initially strange to think of the social imprinting process as providing a model for the learning of food objects, we feel that there is evidence to support such a notion. First, our experimental research described above has shown that there is a critical period for the modification of innate pecking preferences, just as there is in social imprinting. In both cases there is a process of preferential attachment of specific behavior to specific objects. Second, the administration of carisoprodol or meprobamate results in the ineffectiveness of the exposure experience in both innate pecking preference modification and social imprinting. Third, the modification of innate pecking preferences during the critical period is apparently permanent.

In short, we propose that food imprinting is a food learning that is achieved through an imprinting process. The theoretical aspects of food imprinting and the ways in which it is similar to and different from other kinds of imprinting is discussed in Chapter 7.

The notion of food imprinting, furthermore, has received support from a later experiment by Burghardt and Hess (1966) on a very different species, the snapping turtle (*Chelydra serpentina*). Newly hatched turtles were given their first feedings at the age of approximately 10 days. Some were given ground horsemeat; others were given killed guppies; and still others received a small piece of redworm daily for 12 days. When given a choice between all three foods, 16 of the 20 turtles chose the item which they had already been fed. After this test, the turtles were fed for 12 days on a food other than that which they had originally eaten. On retest, there was again a strong preference for the food item which they had first eaten, in spite of the intervening experience with another food: 16 of the 20 chose the original diet item.

A subsequent experiment by Burghardt (1967) showed that a single meal given to naïve hatchling snapping turtles was sufficient to cause a preference for the particular food given at that meal when the subjects were given a choice test occurring 2 weeks after the first meal and 1 week after the only intervening meal, which had been of a different food. The primacy effect was much stronger with those subjects that first ate meat than in those that first ate redworms (*Eisenia foetida*), a result which indicates that experience interacts with innate preferences in this learning experience.

In this experiment, however, the subjects were 1 week older than the ones in Burghardt and Hess (1966). Hence, it may be that there is no temporally limited critical period for food learning in snapping turtles, as there is in chicks, in which case the food learning could not be regarded as a true imprinting process but as an instance of one-trial learning. Furthermore, it is apparent that long experience with other foods is able to alter the food preferences of snapping turtles.

Returning to the subject of food imprinting in chicks, it must be noted that there do appear to be circumstances under which the phenomenon does not occur. Hess (unpublished) has had his students in his experimental laboratory courses perform the pecking preference experiment for several years without ever encountering any problems in demonstrating the preference modification phenomenon. However, Hess' procedure always involved placing a group of about 50 chicks simultaneously in the pecking apparatus. Careful and extensive unpublished research by Robert

T. Brown (personal communication, 1968) and studies by Meyer and Frank (1970) and Frank and Meyer (1970) indicate that the modification phenomenon does not occur when groups of 2 to 10 chicks are used, but can occur when at least 16 chicks are given the experience together in the apparatus. Apparently, then, chicks trained individually or in very small groups in a pecking apparatus do not imprint to the stimuli which signal food. This may well be due, at least in part, to the fact that chicks generally engage in lower per capita pecking levels when kept individually or in small groups than when kept in larger groups.

In addition, the situation may be very different when actual food objects are utilized as the sole source of solid nourishment for an entire day. Burghardt (1969) used groups of 8 chicks each, which were fed with either rapeseed or canary seed exclusively on the 3rd day of life. The other seed was fed on the 4th day of life. Subsequent preferences between both seeds, simultaneously and freely available, were found to be in favor of the seed type first eaten.

Chicks that ate canary seed first showed a strong preference for canary seed during the 8-day test period, while those that ate rapeseed first showed no clear preference. However, previous pilot experiments showed that chicks innately prefer canary seed, with the preference for canary seed ranging from 54 to 66 percent, and that for rapeseed 34 to 46 percent (percentages based on weight eaten), so that it is easier to increase the preference for a preferred food than for a nonpreferred one.

In spite of the demonstrated preference for canary seed, all chick groups showed an increasing preference for rapeseed during the 8 test days. This appears to indicate that perhaps metabolic feedback from the two different seeds can summate with the early experience variable.

The notion that the involvement of actual food objects more reliably produces the modification phenomenon has received support from work by Capretta (1969), in which chicks were fed red or plain tan mash from the age of ½ to 1½ days. From the age of 1½ to 2½ days, chicks ate either green or plain tan mash. Subsequent tests showed a higher preference for red mash by those that ate it during the first exposure period. That this shift—and primacy effect—could be obtained as a result of experience before the age of 3 days, in contrast to the finding of most effectiveness at the age of 3 days in our own pecking apparatus, appears to indicate the very great difference that there can be between actual food objects and signals for food objects.

However, the observed social facilitation effect observed in the pecking preference modification in the pecking apparatus, where artificially constructed stimuli were reinforced by mash grains, must be interpreted with caution. This is because our unpublished experiments have also shown that social facilitation has no obvious influence on *what* chicks peck at, although, to be sure, the *total amount* of pecking is, indeed, raised, probably through arousal effects. For example, we took several white vantress broiler chicks which we knew to prefer pecking at red-orange colors, and placed them into the pecking preference apparatus at the same time as a group of white leghorn chicks which we knew to prefer pecking at blue. They were all allowed access to a range of non-reinforced colors, including red, orange, yellow, green, and blue. We obtained a bimodal curve of pecking preferences to these colors—one peak to red-orange, and the other to blue. Then we found that we could manipulate the heights of the two humps in the preference curve by making appropriate changes in the number of chicks of each breed that were in the pecking apparatus at the same time. This experiment thus confirmed the observation reported by Dove (1935); the leaders of the flock stimulate others to peck and eat, but they do not influence just what items in the trough are actually pecked at.

Some aspects of the nature of the process occurring in the phenomenon of social facilitation of eating in chicks have been indicated recently by Strobel, Freedman, and Macdonald (1970). These researchers found, of course, that chickens eat more when together than when alone. However, it was also found that social rearing during the first 3 days after hatching was necessary for 3- and 4-day-old chicks to exhibit social facilitation of eating. Chicks reared in individual isolation since hatching and then kept with other chicks showed no social facilitation effect. Whether they would eventually demonstrate social facilitation of feeding through prolonged communal rearing with conspecifics is, of course, a question requiring further experimentation. Nevertheless, it is an important finding, in contrast to the fact that chicks reared communally for 3 days since hatching and then placed into isolation continued to eat just as much as did those that were permitted to remain with their peers. In addition, brief exposures to a flickering light stimulus enabled chicks that were otherwise kept in isolation to exhibit the social facilitation effect when tested at the age of 3 and 4 days.

Hence, it seems that social stimulation can enhance eating behavior in chicks. The question of whether it acts as a direct reinforcer of eating behavior requires experimental clarification, particularly since the necessary social experience apparently must occur at a time when chicks can live primarily from the yolk sac reserves, and do not have to eat to survive until the age of 3 days.

The food imprinting process in chicks, like the social imprinting process, uses particular visual preference systems as a tool for learning the characteristics of the environment. Just as Fantz (1965) has pointed out in the case of the visual preferences evidenced by human infants, the visual preferences in social imprinting (Schaefer and Hess, 1959) and in food imprinting (Fantz, 1957; Hess, 1964; Goodwin and Hess, 1969a, c) prevent both random exploration of the environment and rigid fixation on parts of the environment, and permit systematic exploration of the milieu in which the chick finds itself. Schaefer and Hess (1959) have reported that the chromatic color preferences of vantress broiler chicks for imprinting objects was precisely the reverse of the chromatic color preference of the same breed for pecking objects. More recently, Goodwin and Hess (1969b) has shown that such a reversal is also true in the case of radially symmetric regular polygon forms from circles down to triangles when imprinting behavior is considered with respect to its "attention" and "approach" components. Following behavior, an activity less similar to pecking behavior than is attention behavior toward the imprinting object, also showed a negative correlation, but less strong, with pecking preferences.

In other words, the visual form and color preferences of vantress broiler chicks for food and for pecking behaviors are in opposition, so that there is no confusion between food and social objects. The similarities and differences in food and social imprinting processes and their theoretical implications will be considered further in Chapter 7.

Experiments by Brown (1964) appear to suggest that after chicks have learned what food is through imprinting, they then learn the characteristics of the part of the environment where food is likely to be. Brown observed this by offering large food boxes of different colors on different days after hatching, and found that the age of exposure to the food box had an important influence in the preferences subsequently exhibited. Since the food boxes also afforded some degree of shelter, however, the response systems of the chicks in this situation were not related solely to the acquisition of food, but perhaps also to environmental imprinting. We will consider the possibility of environment imprinting after discussing the question of olfactory imprinting.

OLFACTORY EXPERIENCES

The olfactory sense plays an important role in the life of animals in many situations, particularly among those that, unlike man, have a high olfactory acuity. With such animals, the olfactory sense plays an important role in regulating relationships between members of the same species, as in sexual behavior, in promoting predator or prey recognition, and in identification of food or territory when visual aspects are not predominant. The imprinting of the maternal bond in goats, described by Klopfer, Adams, and Klopfer (1964) appears to be mediated by the olfactory sense. This maternal imprinting will be discussed more fully in Chapter 6.

Social Regulation

The idea that early olfactory experience could determine later responses to specific olfactory stimuli was apparently first expressed by Fielde (1903, 1904) with respect to social behavior. Fielde carried out numerous experiments with ants, investigating the experiential factors influencing the acceptance or rejection of individuals on the basis of their odors. Ant fights are caused by differences in odor; ants from different colonies, even if of the same species and variety, will fight each other. However, Fielde found that if ants of different species, even of different genera, were reared together from hatching on, they would live harmoniously together. But, surprisingly enough, the bonds thus formed were strictly between individuals, for this early learning did not cause the ants to accept unknown odors. Fielde stressed two particular facts as important in understanding this phenomenon. First, ants inherit an odor from the queen from whose eggs they have developed. Second, worker ants change in odor as they grow older. Hence, if ants that had known each other were separated for more than 40 days, they would no longer know each other, because of the degree of change in their odor qualities. However, Fielde found that these ants would accept the exact same odor that they had experienced in their earliest days, for they accepted eggs and newly hatched young laid by the same queen that had laid the ones with which they had been acquainted in early life, even after as much as months or years of separation from these highly specific odors.

These findings definitely show an effect of early experience as such, for it is only during the rearing period that ants are willing to accept completely new odors. Afterward, new odors are rejected unless they have resulted from a gradual change of a familiar odor. This gradual change must be experienced by the ant, for if there is a separation of individual ants for more than 40 days, the new odor which has been acquired during the interim will not be accepted. Any odors met during the rearing stage are permanently accepted—that is, for the remainder of the ant's life.

This learning, while obviously occurring during a definite sensitive period, probably cannot be regarded as an imprinting process, and 40 days is much too long a period for it to be regarded as a *critical* period, since ant species are involved, and 40 days would constitute a rather large portion of the usual life cycle.

Olfactory Cues in Environment or Locality

A dramatic example of long-term retention of an early odor experience is shown in the amazing ability of some species of salmon and trout to return to the specific stream in which they had hatched and lived as small fry, after 2 to 6 years hundreds of miles away in the ocean. An explanation of this phenomenon has been offered by Hasler (1960) in that this ability is derived from irreversible early olfactory learning or imprinting of the parent stream odors by young salmon. The parent stream odor involved remains the same year after year and season after season. Hasler and Wisby (1951) had earlier shown that fish are able to discriminate between highly diluted water samples from two different streams. A learned discrimination of such stream water was found to be retained by the fish for several months following initial training.

Studies of homing in salmon show that when these fish have plugged nasal sacs they cannot return accurately to the home stream after displacement. Hasler (1960) has proposed that the odor guiding salmon to their original tributary from the mouth of the river is highly specific, and does not serve merely as an attractant. Of course, it is also possible that the fish learn the sequence of olfactory stimuli to which they had been exposed during their first trip to the sea as young salmon. Displacement experiments should explore this question. It is to be noted, however, that the parent stream odor can guide the salmon only upon arrival at the mouth of the main stream. It is possible that the main stream is located from the open sea by means of a sun compass mechanism, since laboratory experiments have demonstrated that young salmon do, indeed, have such a mechanism. In conclusion, the possibility that the parent stream has an odor which is learned by imprinting is an extremely exciting one; it will take further experiments to discover this odor which remains so invariantly specific for a particular stream.

AUDITORY EXPERIENCES

Some authors have suggested that there may be auditory imprinting, especially in song learning in birds. As is well known, in many species, the song is entirely innate; in others, it is learned; and in still others, there is a mixture of learned and innate components. In some species where there are learned components, there appears to be a sensitive or receptive period during which songs are normally learned permanently and irreversibly (Lanyon, 1957; Thorpe, 1961; Nicolai, 1964; Marler and Tamura, 1964; Immelmann, 1966).

Nicolai (1964), for example, has suggested that widow birds, which parasitize the broods of estrildine birds, learn the host species' song during the nestling period by means of an imprinting process. This song, together with the innate species-specific song, is sung by a male widow bird when it sees an estrildid pair (of the particular species that is parasitized by the species to which the widow bird belongs) building its nest. Since the hatchling widows resemble the host hatchlings in plumage and color, and since there are several different estrildine species, it is of importance for survival that the widow pair parasitize the correct species. The use of the host's song apparently serves to synchronize the widow pair's physiological state with that of the host pair, so that the parasitic eggs will hatch at the same time as the host eggs.

Thorpe (1961) has suggested that in the chaffinch there is imprinted song learning. Poulsen (1954) has also suggested an imprinting-like mechanism in the song learning of the linnet. Thorpe noted the following similarities between song learning in the chaffinch and classical social imprinting: maturational bases of the sensitive period involved; impossibility of learning new material once the sensitive period has passed— that is, there are relatively critical consequences of the experiences during the sensitive period; preference for specific classes of things; sufficiency of reasonably short exposure to relevant stimuli; delayed manifestation of the effect of the experience during the sensitive period; absence of *conventional* rewards as as requisite for learning.

Since that time, more has been discovered regarding the ontogeny of courtship song in several bird species. Nottebohm (1970) has recently reviewed the literature in this area. One of these studies, by Marler (1970), which involved white-crowned sparrows, has shown that the most sensitive period for learning the species-specific song is at the age period 10 to 50 days. Before the age of 10 days and after the age of 100 days, auditory exposure cannot affect the song. Furthermore, the song learning is selective in that only dialects of the *conspecific* song can have any effect on song development during the age of 10 to 50 days. The local "culture" of white-crowned sparrows is thus passed on from generation to generation. Immelmann (1969a) has shown that infant experience determines the development of courtship song in zebra finches. There are probably several other bird species in which there are sensitive period processes in song learning.

For any bird species manifesting sensitive periods in song learning, it should be determined whether or not a *critical* period, in our sense, is involved. For example, Thielcke-Poltz and Thielcke (1960) found that a single minute of exposure during the sensitive period was sufficient to cause song learning in blackbirds. But even here, a sharply limited critical period appropriate to the life span of the species involved has not been demonstrated so far. If there is no critical period, we cannot regard the learning as an imprinting process but, rather, at the most a *susceptible* period learning process.

Gottlieb (1966) and others have suggested that auditory imprinting may occur in chicks and ducklings in the period immediately before hatching since the females of both species have been observed to vocalize to the eggs during the final stages of incubation. However, as we mentioned in Chapter 4, laboratory-hatched ducklings to which we played female mallard sounds before hatching failed to show a preference for these sounds. Nevertheless, the possibility of auditory imprinting has been suggested by ongoing preliminary research being conducted by Slobodan Petrovich and me. We found that some ducklings that had been incubated by their own female parent and thus had heard and responded to her maternal calls imprinted better to decoys that emitted mallard clucks than to ones that emitted other sounds. It may be that the female's responses to the ducklings' vocalization promoted the higher imprintability to the conspecific call. Furthermore, we have found in this research that immediate posthatching experience with the female mallard on the nest can highly determine the degree of filial attachment to her and make imprinting to a human sound virtually impossible.

ENVIRONMENTAL PREFERENCES

That animals of different species have distinct preferences for specific types of environments is of no surprise to anyone who has ever considered the habits of animals. For the most part, the relationship between what an animal needs, in the way of shelter or food, and where it is to be found is so obvious as to hardly require mentioning. Most animals have rather specialized activities which are correlated with specific sectors of the environment, or what ecologists call the "niche."

In the majority of cases, it appears that the environmental preferences of animals are determined by constitutional factors which have developed in the complex interplay of forces during the evolutionary process. And, of course, there is probably also learning of the environment by the individual in the sense that the animal may learn where it is likely to be able to obtain food or where its home site is located in relation to other aspects of the territory in which it lives. However, there have been some suggestions made that specific territories or specific aspects of the environment may be very readily and very permanently learned during an early period in the animal's life by means of a mechanism similar to the imprinting process found in the development of social behavior in some animals, particularly birds. The existence of imprinting processes in the learning of food characteristics by chickens (Hess, 1962, 1964) also makes it reasonable to look for habitat learning processes which occur during highly specific sensitive life periods.

Thorpe (1944, 1945) apparently was the first to suggest the possibility of "locality imprinting." In other words, the immediate locality first perceived by a newly hatched or newly born organism may be learned by an imprinting process in some species so that it is chosen as the breeding grounds of that individual upon adulthood. As evidence suggesting such a possibility, Thorpe cited Rau's (1934) observation that bembecine wasps tend to maintain their nesting colonies in the exact same spot year after year—more than 20 years in one instance—even though several sites of greater suitability are easily available. Several other cases of locality restriction by hymenopterous insects were mentioned as possibilities by Thorpe. However, he cautioned that considerable examination of individual cases was needed to determine the relevant factors promoting locality restriction.

The problem of habitat selection in relation to early environmental experience has thus become an important but yet relatively little-studied problem for students of animal behavior. While the notion of habitat selection has received some impetus from the findings regarding host specificity through chemical conditioning during the larval stage, we will confine ourselves at present to the learning of the presumably visual and spatial aspects of the environment. As Hinde (1959) has pointed out, changes in habitat preference in a species through non-genetic factors (such as imprinting) could ultimately have effects in the genetic factors that are involved in habitat preferences. Tinbergen (1951) has noted that in Eskimo dogs there apparently is a highly sensitive period, around the time of the assumption of sexual maturity, for the learning of territorial boundaries.

There has been much speculation and suggestive evidence regarding environmental selection as well as suggestions concerning the possibility of a sensitive period for such learning. For example, in a study by Loehrl (1959), hand-bred flycatchers returned after the winter to the locale where they had been reared if they were released at least 2 weeks prior to the completion of the juvenile molt and were free to fly about within this territory during this time. If they were not released until or after the completion of the molt, they failed to return, either because, as Klopfer (1962) suggested, food supplies had diminished within that area and therefore reduced its reinforcing aspects, or because it was hormonally time to fly directly south for the annual migration and there was no available opportunity to learn the characteristics of the environment beforehand because physiological conditions impelled the birds to migrate rather than to explore and learn the immediate territory.

Klopfer (1963) obtained evidence that there is an innate preference for pine leaves over oak leaves in chipping sparrows, as shown by wild-trapped adults and by 2- to 4-month-old isolated birds reared without sight of any foliage. Isolates reared in the presence of oak leaves, however, showed a decreased preference for pine. These results are similar in character to those obtained with some insect species with respect to

host specificity which we have already discussed. The selection of nesting materials and habitats by zebra finches nesting for the first time was
found to be influenced by rearing experiences, while subsequent nest-
ings were found to depend more on previous nesting experience, according to Sargent (1963). Thus, the fledgling period, found to be more
influential than the nestling period for the acquisition by young birds of
information regarding the nest, could have effects reaching through a
considerable period of time, since the first nesting experience influences
subsequent choice of materials and habitats. Immelmann (1969b) has
concluded from his research that in several species of grass finches the
choice of objects for nest building is determined by an imprinting-like
process in early juvenile life. Roosting behavior in these grass finches was
also found to be strongly influenced by infant experiences.

Just as Klopfer (1963) had found with respect to the foliage preference
of chipping sparrows, Wecker (1963) observed that there is an innate
preference for field type environments in the prairie deer mouse. The
offspring of wild-caught deer mice also showed a distinct preference
for field environments over wooded environments, irrespective of where
they were reared, while deer mice that had been bred and reared in the
laboratory for several generations and their offspring reared in woods
showed no such preference for either type of environment. But laboratory rats reared in the field environment showed a significant preference
for it. Apparently then, twelve to twenty generations of laboratory rearing is sufficient for this species to lose its hereditary control over the
habitat selection response, although there still appears to be some innate bias for the field environment and against the woods environment,
since early rearing promoted a preference for the field environment but
could not promote a preference for the woods.

As for chickens, Hess (1959) showed that day-old hatchlings which
saw a large stationary cutout form 1½ feet away from their isolation
compartments from the age of 22 to 46 hours subsequently preferred to
be near that form rather than another form of similar size but of different shape. This age period of exposure appeared to be the most
sensitive in promoting such an attachment to a form (Hess, 1964). In
another experiment (Hess, 1959), day-old chicks were reared for 1 day
in boxes which were patterned with either small triangles or small
circles on the walls. These chicks were subsequently found to show
less of a preference for *pecking* at the specific shapes to which they had
been exposed during this rearing period than did either chicks that had
been reared in boxes with a different pattern on the walls or those that
had never seen any triangles or circles at all, showing either that the
environmental exposure to these forms at this age did not cause them
to regard these shapes in the same way as they would have otherwise

or that they were responding to the novelty provided by the unfamiliar stimulus. This could have been determined to some extent by testing for the relative environmental preference of these chicks for being near walls of the different patterns in the same way, as had been done in the first experiment. It is notable, though, that these chicks were *not* in the sensitive period for *food* imprinting Hess (1962). The pecking drive of hatchling and day-old chicks has been found to be rather low, in comparison with later ages, as shown by our own laboratory investigations (Goodwin and Hess 1969a). Also, in the imprinting exposure situation, it has been found (Goodwin and Hess 1969b) that chicks will peck much more at the floor or at walls than at the imprinting object. Therefore, if these day-old chicks reported in Hess' (1959a) experiment were susceptible to social imprinting, the exposure to the forms on the walls of the small enclosure in which they were housed might possibly result in some sort of social imprinting to these forms.

Gray (1960) has subsequently confirmed Hess' original findings that chicks can show attachment to a motionless cutout geometric form which they had seen during rearing by preferring to be near it rather than an unfamiliar one, although Gray appeared to find a rather different age of sensitivity from that determined by Hess. Chicks were exposed to the sight of one form from their isolation compartment during either the 3rd, 4th, or 5th day of life. Those that were exposed on the 5th post-hatch day, or at the age of 4 days, were thought to show the greatest attachment to the motionless objects, in contrast to Hess' earlier findings that the 2nd day of life—the age of 1 day—was the most efficacious in promoting this type of attachment. Only further experimentation with regard to species differences, procedural differences, and the use of a larger number of subjects can determine the source of this discrepancy in results. Here, as in rat experiments involving environmental enrichment (Walk, Gibson, Pick, and Tighe, 1959), the importance of the attention-getting value of the cutout form was stressed by Gray as a factor in the determination of the attachment shown by the chicks.

Further experiments on environmental preferences in relation to early rearing experiences in chicks have been carried out by Brown (1964). While Gray (1960) did not specifically associate food with the environmental conditions except indirectly, Brown exposed his chicks to large food boxes, the interior of which were painted in different colors. While the food boxes formed only a part of the living compartment, they were big enough for the chicks to go inside them, where, in fact, they were often found. Even though only part of the environment was therefore involved, it certainly was a part of considerable importance to the chicks, being related to food-getting behavior and perhaps also to shelter seeking. The interior of the food boxes was painted either a medium gray or one of the following Ostwald (Jacobson, Granville, and Foss, 1948) colors: vermilion (6 pa), bright orange (4 pa), bright lemon yellow (1 pa), peacock blue (16 pa), or royal blue (13 pa).

In the first experiment, Brown exposed his chicks to a differently colored food box on each of the first 5 days of life. When tested for a choice between the five colors by placement in front of a large quarter-circle arc formed by the boxes, it was apparently found that the 35 subjects tested under 24-hour food deprivation and the 35 subjects tested while satiated were not significantly different in their preference behavior toward the food boxes. While a larger number of subjects is needed to clarify this, it did appear that the fact that the boxes held food was of relatively minor importance to the chicks, and that perhaps the shelter or visual aspects of the food boxes played a larger role in the preferences shown by these chicks. They showed a greater preference for the colors most recently seen, with the preferences stronger the more recently the colors had been seen, with the exposure ages of 3 and 4 days (4th and 5th day of life, respectively) showing the most effect.

In the second experiment carried out by Brown, chicks were exposed to a particular color on only one of the first 5 days of life. It was found that learning of the food box color, as determined by subsequent choice behavior, could be seen only in the chicks that had been exposed during the 5th day of life, or at the age of 4 days. Since this was the last exposure day used in this experiment, this result might reflect an effect of recency. Therefore, Brown carried out a third experiment in which the individual exposure days were from the 4th day of life up to and including the 8th day (that is, 7 days old). Only the chicks exposed during the 4th or 5th day showed a significant preference for the color to which they had been exposed. Thus, the three experiments taken together showed that the ages of 3 and 4 days appear to be the most sensitive for environmental learning of this type. These ages are somewhat different from the ones found by Hess (1959) and Gray (1960) to be most effective for their experimental conditions. While Brown stated that his animals treated on the 3rd post-hatch day were the same age as Hess' (1962) 3-day-old chicks in the pecking preference modification situation, this was obviously an error. (Actually, Brown's chicks exposed on the 4th day of life were the same as Hess'.) Since Gray's (1960) chicks showed a maximum effect resulting from exposure to a large cutout at the age of 4 days, or the 5th day post-hatch, and Hess (1964) found the 4th and 6th days of life to be sensitive to food imprinting, with the 4th day much more effective than the 6th day for this learning, it may be that Brown's experiments have combined aspects of both environmental and food learning. Environmental learning in this case would involve the learning of stationary stimuli, with stimuli signaling the availability of food forming an important category. However, such an interpretation of Brown's results would have to be tempered by the fact that the same pattern of results were obtained by Brown regardless of whether subjects were hungry or satiated at the time of testing.

Furthermore, Gray's (1960) data also cannot be explained through reference to food imprinting. In this connection, it might be noted that Gray did not analyze the effects of the 2nd day of age in this experiment, whereas Brown did include chicks of this age. Certainly, the discrepancy between Gray and Hess, in the stated ages regarded as most effective for the type of environmental learning studied by them, requires clarification. However, Hess' own findings, that the 2nd day of life can affect environmental preferences, has been supported by the report of Taylor and Taylor (1964) that chicks exposed for the first 48 hours with a soft foam object subsequently show a marked approach response to this object, whereas those reared with a cardboard box did not show such an effect.

As a final point, it should be mentioned that Hess (1962, 1964) has left open the possibility that the 5th day of life might also show strong effects of food reward in modifying innate pecking preferences in the chick, as pointed out earlier in this chapter. Thus, the possibility of interaction of several factors in these phenomena must be seriously considered. Such factors as localization of food supply, decreasing yolk sac supply, and locomotor ability in relation to the need for shelter are among these.

The possibility of habitat imprinting in mallard ducks was suggested by Hess (1964) on the basis of informal observations that when there were both nesting sites on the ground and elevated nest boxes over a pond available for use in a natural and free-living environment, only mallard ducks which had been hatched in an incubator chose the elevated nesting boxes, while those that had been hatched in open ground nests chose to nest on the ground. Furthermore, it was noted that elevated nests were far less subject to predation than were open ground nests.

While Gottlieb (1965) has reported that the mallards investigated did not use elevated nest boxes, Burger (1964) and Bjärvall (1970) also have reported that mallards will use elevated nest boxes. The effects of early environmental experiences in influencing female mallards to use elevated nest boxes instead of ground nests were suggested by the fact that during the initial four years of research by Hess (1972) at Lake Cove from 1958 through 1961 there were 5 elevated nest boxes available for use but none of the resident wild mallard females used them. However, in the spring of 1962, after 35 incubator hatched mallard ducklings had been introduced the year before, all 5 nest boxes were occupied by females. During the eight succeeding years, more and more mallards used the nest boxes, and additional ones had to be constructed to keep ahead of demand. Each year the ducks were always provided with a few more nest boxes than were actually used, so that all those that chose to use elevated nests would have one available. By the spring of 1969, there were a total of 32 nest boxes available, and, since then, there have always been a few vacant nest boxes

Since nest box usage began so precipitiously, an experiment (Hess, 1972) was set up to investigate whether something analogous to environmental imprinting might actually have taken place in the incubator-hatched ducks that chose to use elevated nest boxes. Fifteen young mallards were *hatched* in a simulated open ground nest in the laboratory and kept there for 1 or 2 days by means of a light wire mesh over them. Similarly, another 15 young were hatched in a simulated nest box in the laboratory and kept there for 1 or 2 days. The laboratory in which all animals were kept was well illuminated by natural light and maintained at a temperature of 29 to 25°C.

After such rearing for 1 or 2 days, the simulated nest-box ducklings were banded on the right leg, and the simulated ground-nest ducklings were banded on the left leg. Blue bands were employed to indicate that the rearing had taken place for a period of 1 day, and yellow bands were utilized to indicate that the rearing had taken place for a 2-day period. Since some of the ducks lost their leg bands during the succeeding summer, autumn, and winter months, it was not possible to follow up *all* 30 ducks during the following spring. Nevertheless, of the 7 banded ducks that were found using elevated nest boxes, *all* were found to have been reared in the simulated nest boxes for 2 days. All of the 10 banded ducks found in natural ground nests, on the other hand, had been reared either on the simulated ground nest for 1 or 2 days or in the simulated elevated nest box for only 1 day. Table 5–1 shows the number of banded ducks in each rearing category that were found using nests of either type.

TABLE 5–1   NUMBERS OF BANDED DUCKS FOUND IN GROUND AND ELEVATED NESTS ACCORDING TO TYPE OF EARLY REARING

	Using elevated nests		Using ground nests	
	"Box"—reared	"Ground"—reared	"Box"—reared	"Ground"—reared
1 Day	0	0	3	2
2 Days	7	0	0	5

More data, obtained in the spring 1971, give further support to the notion that environmental experience during the *2nd* day of life influences nest site choice. In the first place, 5 female mallards that had been hatched the year before by their mother in a *nest box* and allowed to remain there only *1* day were all found using *ground nests* These 5 females had been removed from their mother after their 1st day and kept in the laboratory. Despite constant handling by human beings and intensive efforts to tame them, they always remained wild. In the second place, of the 29 ducks using elevated nest boxes in the spring of 1971, 7 were identified as ones that had been hatched in the laboratory incubator in 1970.

In the third place, the previous findings that elevated nest users have greater success in hatching and rearing young have continued to be substantiated. In 1971, 3 out of 12 gound-nesting females hatched young and left the nest with them, with the clutches of the remaining 9 destroyed by ground predators and crows. On the other hand, 27 of the 29 elevated box users were successful in hatching young and leading them from the nest.

All these facts appear to suggest an environmental imprinting occurring on the 2nd day of life in mallard ducklings, since the effects of the experience are apparent a year later and the experience in question is limited to an extremely brief period at a very particular priod in the life cycle. That is, preferential attachment to specific environmental features may be achieved through an imprinting process. The permanance of the effects of a brief experience suggests this. In Chapter 7 the theoretical aspects of environmental imprinting are discussed. More research is required to determine if environmental imprinting actually exists in mallard ducks, as has been suggested by our findings. Bjärvall's (1970) own observations, however, have led him to conclude that increased population pressure may be an important factor in promoting the use of elevated nests by mallards. Further experiments are needed to assess the relative roles of early experience and population pressure.

Nevertheless, it is an incontestable fact that female mallards will choose to use elevated nest boxes under specific circumstances. In recent years, conservationists (e.g., Burger, 1964; Bjärvall, 1970) have become interested in promoting the use of elevated nest boxes by wild mallards and wild black ducks because of the decreased destruction of eggs and offspring by ground predators. In addition, Gottlieb's (1965) observation of no elevated nest usage must necessarily be interpreted in the light of the evidence obtained at other places.

The possible occurrence of environmental learning during the 2nd day of life, after social imprinting has already firmly taken place, would certainly appear to be related to the fact that the nest exodus normally takes place early on the 2nd day of life for mallard ducks (Hess, 1972). As may be recalled, Bjärvall (1967) has also documented the fact that the nest exodus normally does not take place until well after the period of maximum social imprintability that has been demonstrated in laboratory imprinting experiments.

Laboratory imprinting experiments, furthermore, have shown that imprinting can occur much earlier than the critical period peak of 13 to 16 hours (e.g., Polt and Hess, 1966). Certainly, it would appear that the function of the 13 to 16-hour peak imprintability found in laboratory imprinting occurs because at that time it becomes highly important for the hatchling to become imprinted to its mother if it has not already done so. The imprinting process must be completed before the nest exodus takes place; otherwise the duckling may be in danger of losing its mother.

Once securely attached to its mother, however, the young bird can then be free to move about in the environment, since its attachment to the mother will keep it from putting itself into dangerous situations. Indeed, Bateson (1969) has also emphasized the fact that imprinting to the mother is a temporal precursor of environmental exploration.

Experiments by Ramsay and Hess (1971) on the ability of previously imprinted (to a duck decoy) ducklings to learn a conditioned hiding response to a danger signal have shown that this ability appears most evident in the ducklings that were trained between the ages of 36 and 60 hours. It is possible that even though this conditioned learning certainly was not accomplished through an imprinting process (because it extinguished rapidly), it may be correlated with environmental imprinting in this species, since an awareness of the characteristics of the environment would appear to be necessary for such learning to occur.

Also, it was noted informally that for several months after the experiments had taken place, ducklings that had learned the conditioned hiding response thereafter avoided man, regardless of whether they were permitted their freedom or penned so that fear responses to man might be habituated out. This observation is highly interesting because it was the sight of the experimenter's face that had served as the unconditional reinforcer of the fear response at the time that the danger signal was emitted during the experiments. In other words, it might be that the innate fear response was imprinted to the sight of man, since these ducklings were already socially imprinted to the decoy when exposed to the experimenter's face during the conditioned learning procedure. The possibility of fear imprinting should be investigated further.

Bateson (1964a, b, c) has also studied the effects of early environmental experience on the behavior of chicks, particularly with respect to behavior in the social imprinting situation. Since the focal concern was upon the effects of homogenous versus patterned stimulation in the rearing cages on the responses of chicks to homogenous versus patterned stimuli which were in motion and therefore potential social objects, these experiments have been discussed more fully in Chapter 3.

However, we do wish to recall that these experiments have shown that there is a very definite influence of the type of environmental stimulation during the 3 days of life on the responses made by the chick to specific types of potential social stimuli. This appears to be related to the suggestion of Sluckin and Salzen (1961) and Sluckin (1962) that social imprinting is a type of perceptual learning. Sluckin and Salzen noted, as other investigators have observed informally, that the relationship of environment conditions to the social imprinting phenomenon is a very important one. For example, even if a chick has ceased following a social imprinting model intensely, this does not mean that the model has lost its attractiveness to the chick, for if there is a sudden disturbance, such as movement or noise, the chick will resume strong following during the disturbance. In his 1962 paper, Sluckin stated his contention that imprinting is perceptual learning, since prior perceptual experiences appear to have a considerable influence on behavior in the social imprinting situation. We will discuss his viewpoint in Chapter 7.

REFERENCES

ALLEN, J. R., and LITTLEFORD, R. A. Observations of the feeding habits and growth of immature diamondback terrapins. *Herpetologica*, 1955, **11**, 77–80.

BAER, DONALD M., and GRAY, PHILIP H. Imprinting to a different species without overt following. *Perceptual and Motor Skills*, 1960, **10**, 171–174.

BAEUMER, ERICH. Lebensart des Haushuhns. *Zeitschrift für Tierpsychologie*, 1955, **12**, 387–401.

BATESON, P. P. G. Effect of similarity between rearing and testing conditions on chicks' following and avoidance responses. *Journal of Comparative and Physiological Psychology*, 1964, **57**, 100–103. (a).

BATESON, P. P. G. Relation between conspicuousness of stimuli and their effectiveness in the imprinting situation. *Journal of Comparative and Physiological Psychology*, 1964, **58**, 407–411. (b).

BATESON, P. P. G. An effect of imprinting on the perceptual development of domestic chicks. *Nature*, 1964, **202**, 421–422. (c).

BATESON, P. P. G. The development of social attachments in birds and man. *Advancements of Science*, London, 1969, **25**, 279–288.

BIRD, CHARLES. The relative importance of maturation and habit in the development of an instinct. *The Pedagogical Seminary and Journal of Genetic Psychology*, 1925, **32**, 68–91.

BIRD, CHARLES. The effect of maturation upon the pecking instinct of chicks. *The Pedagogical Seminary and Journal of Genetic Psychology*, 1926, **33**, 212–234.

BIRD, CHARLES. Maturation and practice: Their effects upon the feeding reactions of chicks. *Journal of Comparative Psychology*, 1933, **16**, 343–366.

BJÄRVALL, ANDERS. The critical period and the interval between hatching and exodus in mallard ducklings. *Behaviour*, 1967, **28**, 141–148.

BJÄRVALL, ANDERS. Nest-site selection by the mallard *(Anas platyrhynchos)*: A questionnaire with special reference to the significance of artificial nests. *Viltrevy Swedish Wildlife*, 1970, **7**, 151–182.

BROWN, LARRY T. A critical period in the learning of motionless stimulus properties in chicks.*Animal Behaviour*, 1964, **12**, 353–361.

BROWN, ROBERT T. Failure to obtain modification of pecking preferences. Unpublished manuscript, 1968.

BURGER, GEORGE V. Experiments with nest boxes for mallard ducks at Remington Farms. *Transactions of the Northeast Fish and Wildlife Conference*, Hartford, Connecticut, 1964. Mimeographed.

BURGHARDT, GORDON M. The primacy effect of the first feeding experience in the snapping turtle, *Psychonomic Science*, 1967, **7**, 383–384.

BURGHARDT, GORDON M. Effects of early experience on food preference in chicks. *Psychonomic Science*, 1969, **14**, 7–8.

BURGHARDT, GORDON M., and HESS, ECKHARD H. Food imprinting in the snapping turtle, *Chelydra serpentina*. *Science*, 1966, **151**, 108–109.

CAPRETTA, PATRICK J. The establishment of food preferences in chicks *Gallus gallus*. *Animal Behaviour*, 1969, **17**, 229–231.

CRUZE, WENDELL W. Maturation and learning in chicks. *Journal of Comparative Psychology*, 1935, **19**, 371–409.

CURTIUS, ANNETTE R. Über angeborene Verhaltensweisen bei Vögeln, insbesondere bei Hühnerkücken. *Zeitschrift für Tierpsychologie*, 1954, **11**, 94–109.

DOVE, W. F. A study of the individuality in the nutritive instincts and of the causes and effects of variations in the selection of food. *American Naturalist*, 1935, **69**, 469–544.

EIMER, GUSTAV HEINRICH THEODOR. *Organic Evolution*. Translated by J. T. Cunningham. London and New York: Macmillan, 1890.

ENGLEMANN, C. Über den Geschmacksinn des Huhns. VI. Über Formvorliebe bei Hühnern. *Zeitschrift für Tierpsychologie*, 1941–42, **5**, 42–59.

FANTZ, ROBERT L. Object preferences and pattern vision in newly hatched chicks. Unpublished doctoral dissertation, University of Chicago, 1954.

FANTZ, ROBERT L. Form preferences in newly hatched chicks. *Journal of Comparative and Physiological Psychology*, 1957, **50**, 422–430.

FANTZ, ROBERT L. Ontogeny of perception. In: Schrier, A. M., Harlow, H. F., and Stollnitz, F., editors, *Behavior of Non-Human Primates*. New York: Academic Press, 1965. Volume 1, 365–403.

FIELDE, ADELE M. Artificial mixed nests of ants. *Biological Bulletin*, 1903, **5**, 320–325.

FIELDE, ADELE M. Power of recognition among ants. *Biological Bulletin*, 1904, **7**, 227–250.

FRANK, LAWRENCE H., and MEYER, MERLE E. Food imprinting in domestic chicks as a function of social contact and number of companions. *Psychonomic Science*, 1970, **19**, 293–294.

GOODWIN, ELIZABETH BIRD, and HESS, ECKHARD H. Innate visual form preferences in the pecking behavior of young chicks. *Behaviour*, 1969, **34**, 233–237 (a).

GOODWIN, ELIZABETH BIRD, and HESS, ECKHARD H. Innate visual form preferences in the imprinting behavior of hatchling chicks. *Behaviour,* 1969, **34,** 238–254. (b).

GOODWIN, ELIZABETH BIRD, and HESS, ECKHARD H. Stimulus generalization and responses to "supernormal stimuli" in the unrewarded pecking behavior of young chicks. *Behaviour,* 1969, **34,** 255–266. (c).

GOTTLIEB, GILBERT. Components of recognition in ducks. *Natural History,* February, 1965, **25,** 12–19.

GOTTLIEB, GILBERT. Species identification by avian neonates: Contributory effect of perinatal auditory stimulation. *Animal Behaviour,* 1966, **14,** 282–290.

GRAY, PHILIP H. Evidence that retinal flicker is not a necessary condition of imprinting. *Science,* 1960, **132,** 1834–1835.

HASLER, ARTHUR D. Guideposts of migrating fishes. *Science,* 1960, **132,** 785–792.

HASLER, ARTHUR D., and WISBY, WARREN J. Discrimination of stream odors by fishes and its relation to parent-stream behavior. *American Naturalist,* 1951, **85,** 223–238.

HESS, ECKHARD H. Maturation and learning in the development of pecking accuracy in chicks. *American Psychologist,* 1953, **8,** 367. (Abstract).

HESS, ECKHARD H. Natural preferences of chicks and ducklings for objects of different colors. *Psychological Reports,* 1956, **2,** 477–483 (a).

HESS, ECKHARD H. Space perception in the chick. *Scientific American,* 1956, **195,** No. 1, 71–80. (b).

HESS, ECKHARD H. Effects of meprobamate on imprinting in waterfowl. *Annals of the New York Academy of Science,* 1957, **67,** 724–732.

HESS, ECKHARD H. The relationship between imprinting and motivation. In: M. R. Jones, editor, *Nebraska Symposium on Motivation,* 1959. Lincoln: University of Nebraska Press, 1959.

HESS, ECKHARD H. Imprinting and the critical period concept. In: E. L. Bliss, editor, *Roots of Behavior.* New York: Hoeber, 1962. 254–263.

HESS, ECKHARD H. Imprinting in birds. *Science,* 1964, **146,** 1128–1139.

HESS, ECKHARD H. The natural history of imprinting. *Annals of the New York Academy of Sciences,* 1972, **193,** 124–136.

HESS, ECKHARD H., and GOGEL, WALTER C. Natural preferences of the chick for objects of different colors. *Journal of Psychology,* 1954, **38,** 483–493.

HESS, ECKHARD H., POLT, JAMES M., and GOODWIN, ELIZABETH. Effects of carisoprodol on early experience and learning. In: J. G. Miller, editor, *The Pharmacology and Clinical Usefulness of Carisoprodol.* Detroit: Wayne State University Press, 1959. 51–85.

HINDE, ROBERT A. Behaviour and speciation in birds and lower vertebrates. *Biological Review,* 1959, **34,** 85–129.

IMMELMANN, KLAUS. Zur ontogenetischen Gesangsentwicklung bei Prachtfinken. *Verhandlungen der Deutschen Zoologischer Gesellschaft (Göttingen),* 1966, Suppl. 30, 320–332.

IMMELMANN, KLAUS. Song development in the zebra finch and other estrildid finches. In: R. A. Hinde, editor, *Bird Vocalizations.* Cambridge, England: Cambridge University Press, 1969. (a).

IMMELMANN, KLAUS. Ökologische und stammesgechichtliche Betrachtungen zum Prägungsphänomen. *Zoologischer Anzeiger,* 1969, **183,** 1–12. (b).

JACOBSON, E. N., GRANVILLE, N. C., and FOSS, C. E. *Color Harmony Manual.* 3rd edition. Chicago: Container Corporation of America, 1948.

KLOPFER, PETER H. *Behavioral Aspects of Ecology.* Englewood Cliffs, N.J.: Prentice-Hall, 1962.

KLOPFER, PETER H. Behavioral aspects of habitat selection: The role of early experience. *Wilson Bulletin,* 1963, **75,** 15–22.

KLOPFER, PETER H., ADAMS, DONALD K., and KLOPFER, MARTHA S. Maternal imprinting in goats. *Proceedings of the National Academy of Sciences,* 1964, **52,** 911–914.

LANYON, WESLEY E. The comparative biology of the meadowlarks *(Sturnella)* in Wisconsin. *Publication of the Nutall Ornithological Club,* 1957, **1,** 1–67.

LANYON, WESLEY E. The ontogeny of vocalization in birds. In: W. E. Lanyon, and W. N. Tavolga, editors, *Animal Sounds and Communication.* Washington, D. C.: American Institute of Biological Sciences, 1960. 321–347.

LOEHRL, H. Zur Frage des Zeitpunktes einer Prägung auf die Heimatregion beim Halsbandschnäpper *(Ficedulla albiocollis). Journal für Ornithologie,* 1959, **100,** 132–140.

MARLER, PETER. A comparative approach to vocal learning: Song development in white-crowned sparrows. *Journal of Comparative and Physiological Psychology Monograph,* 1970, **71,** No. 2, part 2, 1–25.

MARLER, PETER, and TAMURA, M. Culturally transmitted patterns of vocal behavior in sparrows. *Science,* 1964, **146,** 1483–1486.

MEYER, MERLE E., and FRANK, LAWRENCE H. Food imprinting in the domestic chick: A reconsideration. *Psychonomic Science,* 1970, **19,** 43–44.

MILLS, THOMAS WESLEY. *The Nature and Development of Animal Intelligence.* New York: Macmillan, 1896.

MORGAN, CONWAY LLOYD. *Habit and Instinct.* London: Edward Arnold, 1896.

NICOLAI, J. Der Brutparasitismus der Viduinae als ethologisches Problem. *Zeitschrift für Tierpsychologie,* 1964, **21,** 129–204.

NOTTEBOHM, FERNANDO. Ontogeny of bird song. *Science,* 1970, **167,** 950–956.

PADILLA, SINFOROSO G. Further studies on the delayed pecking of chicks. *Journal of Comparative Psychology,* 1935, **20,** 413–443.

POLT, JAMES M., and HESS, ECKHARD H. Following and imprinting: Effects of light and social experience. *Science,* 1964, **143,** 1185–1187.

POLT, JAMES M., and HESS, ECKHARD H. Effects of social experience on the following response in chicks. *Journal of Comparative and Physiological Psychology,* 1966, **61,** 268–270.

POULSEN, HOLGER. Maturation and learning in the improvement of some instinctive activities. *Videnskabelige Meddelser fra Dansk naturhistorisk Forening,* Copenhagen, 1951, **113,** 155–170.

POULSEN, HOLGAR. On the song of the linnet *(Carduelis cannabina* L.). *Dansk Ornithologisk Forenings Tidsskrift,* 1954, **48,** 32–37.

PREYER, THIERRY WILLIAM. *Die Seele des Kindes. Beobachtungen über die Geistige Entwicklung des Menschen in den Ersten Lebensjahren.* Jena: 1881. Translated by H. W. Brown, as *The Mind of the Child.* New York: Appleton, 1888.

RAMSAY, A. OGDEN, and HESS, ECKHARD H. Sensitive age parameters and other factors in conditioning to a danger call in mallard ducklings. *Zeitschrift für Tierpsychologie,* 1971, **28,** 164–174.

RAU, PHIL. A note on the attachment of the wasp, *Bembix nubilpennis,* to their nesting sites. *Psyche,* 1934, **41,** 243–244.

ROMANES, GEORGE JOHN. *Mental Evolution in Animals.* London: Kegan Paul, Trench, & Co., 1883.

SARGENT, THEODORE D. The role of experience in the nest building of the zebra finch. *American Zoologist,* 1963, **3,** 519. (Abstract).

SCHAEFER, HALMUTH, and HESS, ECKHARD H. Color preferences in imprinting objects. *Zeitschrift für Tierpsychologie,* 1959, **16,** 161–172.

SHEPARD, J. J., and BREED, FREDERICK S. Maturation and use in the development of an instinct. *Journal of Animal Behavior,* 1913, **3,** 274–285.

SLUCKIN, WLADYSLAW S. Perceptual and associative learning. *Symposia of the Zoological Society of London,* 1962, **8,** 193–198.

SLUCKIN, WLADYSLAW S., and SALZEN, ERIC A. Imprinting and perceptual learning. *Quaterly Journal of Experimental Psychology,* 1961, **13,** 65–77.

STROBEL, M. G., FREEDMAN, S. L., and MACDONALD, G. E. Social facilitation of feeding in newly hatched chickens as a function of imprinting. *Canadian Journal of Psychology,* 1970, **24,** 207–215.

TAYLOR, ANN, and TAYLOR, KEITH F. Imprinting to a static feature of the home environment. *Nature,* 1964, **204,** 1117–1118.

THIELCKE-POLTZ, H., and THIELCKE, G. Akustisches Lernen vershieden alter schallisolierten Amseln *Turdus merula* L., und die Entwicklung erlernter motive ohne und mit künstlichem Einfluss von Testosteron. *Zeitschrift für Tierpsychologie,* 1960, **17,** 211–244.

THORNDIKE, EDWARD L. Instinct. *Biological Lectures, Marine Biological Laboratory, Wood's Hole, Massachusetts, 1898.* 1899, **7,** 57–68. (a).

THORNDIKE, EDWARD L. The instinctive reaction of young chicks. *Psychological Review,* 1899, **6,** 282–291. (b).

THORPE, WILLIAM H. Type of learning in insects and other arthopods. Part III. *British Journal of Psychology,* 1944, **34,** 66–76.

THORPE, WILLIAM H. The evolutionary significance of habitat selection. *Journal of Animal Ecology,* 1945, **14,** 67–70.

THORPE, WILLIAM H. *Bird Song: The Biology of Vocal Communication and Expression in Birds.* Cambridge, England: Cambridge University Press, 1961.

TINBERGEN, NIKO. *The Study of Instinct.* Oxford: Oxford University Press, 1951.

TUCKER, ARLENE. The effect of early light and form deprivation on the visual behaviors of the chicken. Unpublished doctoral dissertation. University of Chicago, 1957.

WALK, RICHARD D., GIBSON, ELEANOR J., PICK, HERBERT L., JR., and TIGHE THOMAS J. The effectiveness of prolonged exposure to cutouts vs. painted patterns for facilitation of discrimination. *Journal of Comparative and Physiological Psychology,* 1959, **52,** 519–521.

WECKER, STANLEY C. The role of early experience in habitat selection by the prairie deer mouse, *Peromyscus maniculatus* bairdii. *Ecological Monographs,* 1963, **33,** 307–325.

6

Sensitive Periods
and Imprinting in Humans
and Other Mammals

Up to now, we have discussed sensitive periods and imprinting processes in non-mammalian species, particularly birds. We have suggested that imprinting processes may exist in situations other than in primary socialization experiences in certain bird species, and have discussed some of these, including food, olfactory, environmental, and song imprinting.

A very natural response to these studies of sensitive periods and imprinting is to ask whether such phenomena exist in human beings. In this chapter, we will attempt to explore some aspects of this question. It is, of course, important always to be cautious of superficial similarities.

IMPRINTING OF THE MATERNAL BOND

If care of the young is to be carried out, such an activity must provide incentives for the parent. The complex of activities performed in caring for the offspring is, indeed, amazing, and yet often deceptively simple. Naturally, endocrinological and physiological factors play important roles in sensitizing the mother or, as in some species, both parents to certain types of stimuli, particularly releasing stimuli emanating from their offspring.

Some species, such as mice, rats, cats, dogs, monkeys, or birds, will readily adopt foster young, even of a different species. Sometimes they will do this even when they are not in the particular physiological state brought about by the normal sequences of events following parturition or hatching. However, this does not necessarily mean that such animals cannot discriminate between their own young and those of others (see Jensen, 1965). Notable examples of fostering are found in the birds parasitized by the European cuckoo, who lays its eggs in other birds' nests. When the foreign egg hatches, the fledgling usually pushes the foster parents' own young out of the nest and is fed by the foster parents, simply because he so potently presents the necessary characteristics of baby birds which release parental activities, even when he is larger than the foster parents themselves.

In some other cases, however, the mother discriminates her own young from those of others, and will refuse to care for foster young, even of the same species. This phenomenon is found in some herd animals, such as sheep and goats, and in the Alaska fur seal. In these animals, the formation of the social bond between young and parent is limited by the mother herself in accepting only her own young and rejecting all others.

Collias (1956) observed that mother sheep and goats (as well as other herd animals) become strongly and quickly attached to their offspring very shortly after birth, and butt away any other young who try to approach them. Sheep- and goat-owners have always known, of course, that ewes and dams will not readily adopt foster young, with the result that orphan lambs and kids must be hand-reared by humans if they are to survive, for even though they approach females, they are refused and butted away. The difficulty of securing adoption is emphasized by the fact that if a mother's own young is temporarily removed for a short period of time immediately after birth for warming during cold weather, she may reject it upon return. Rather specialized techniques have been developed to bring about adoption. For example, a mother who has just given birth to her own young and lost it may be induced to adopt a young orphan (not more than 2 days old) which has been rubbed with her own offspring's afterbirth or placenta or if the orphan is covered with the skin of her dead one (Gibson, 1951). Washing with strong detergent (Gibson, 1951) and spraying the baby orphan with kerosene or with mother's milk can also be helpful in bringing about acceptance. However, such acceptance usually can be effected only during the first 2 hours after the foster mother has herself given birth, and is more likely to occur if the orphan itself is only a few minutes old.

Of particular interest to us is the fact that there is actually a highly limited sensitive, probably critical, period for the formation of the attachment of the ewe or dam to her young. Collias (1953) noted that if the young is removed from the mother immediately or shortly after birth and kept away for 2 hours or more, the mother will refuse it and actively butt it away as if it were a strange kid. If the separation is 45 minutes or less, the infant may be accepted forthwith. On the other hand, young removed at the age of 1 hour after parturition for a period of 2 or 3 hours will then be accepted without hesitation. Blauvelt (1955) also observed that there is a 2-hour period after birth during which a goat mother shows responsiveness to any newborn; afterward she will ignore and reject any newborns. Hersher, Moore, and Richmond (1958) made the observation that goat mothers allowed to be with their young for 5 to 10 minutes after birth would accept them after a ½- to 1-hour separation. At a later age, 2 to 3 months, the kids could be separated from their mothers for as long as 6 to 10 hours and still be accepted by the mother.

While Hersher, Richmond, and Moore (1963b) did not regard this as evidence of a critical period, but only of a sensible or susceptible period, the work of Klopfer, Adams, and Klopfer (1964) has suggested very definitely that the first few minutes after parturition is actually the peak of a 2-hour critical period for acceptance of the kid by mother goats. They found that rejection was prevented by 5 minutes of contact following birth, even when the separation was as long as 3 hours. It is quite possible that sheep mothers undergo a similar highly limited sensitive period during which contact with the young should occur to ensure acceptance (Smith, 1965).

This maternal imprinting in goats, while highly similar in several important characteristics to the filial imprinting we have found in precocial birds, contrasts sharply with it, since it is the mother who comes to recognize and prefer her own offspring rather than vice versa. Newly born fallow deer and domestic goats, as Klopfer (1964) has observed, will readily follow a human parent-substitute (just as mother hens and ducks will readily call to strange young the same age as their own), but do not usually form a lasting preferential attachment to their foster parent, as geese and ducks do when they have this type of early experience; and they readily return to adults of their own kind during the first few days of life. Of course, as Hess (1962) has found with lambs, prolonged contact with humans in the same fashion as with the natural mother does promote preferential social attachment.

What factors mediate this maternal imprinting phenomenon? Since sheep and goat mothers spend the first few minutes after birth in nuzzling and licking the young, it may be that olfactory characteristics of the young are learned during this first licking and nuzzling, and that preference and discrimination are based upon olfactory differences between kids. While Klopfer (1964) mentions other possible factors promoting maternal attachment in goats, Smith (1965) has singled this out as the most likely sensory modality mediating the ewe-lamb attachment and suggests that the lamb may have a distinctive odor discernible in the amniotic fluid. A report by Klopfer and Gamble (1966) has shown that olfactory contact is the normal means by which goat mothers learn to recognize their own young. Naturally, the olfactory essences promoting maternal attachment cannot be identified without extensive chemical assays, but it does appear obvious that experimentation can and should be carried out to define the role of the olfactory sense in maternal imprinting in sheep and goats.

The notion that this maternal attachment process is a true imprinting phenomenon, as we have defined it, is supported by several facts. One is that it has a critical period approximately 2 hours long and having an extremely short duration peak. This peak occurs 10 minutes after birth, and is apparently timed by physiological events. Furthermore, it is a process which does not influence the nature of the behavior itself, but which has the function of influencing the *object* to which the behavior will be directed so that others tend to be excluded. Again, there is an irreversibility of effect, for once an attachment has been formed to the specific neonate offspring, no other can be made as easily. In fact, if no attachment has been formed by the time the critical period has passed, none can be formed in the same manner. This also explains why in twin births the second twin may sometimes be rejected by the mother if it is not noticed soon enough by the mother because she is busy caring for the first twin.

Furthermore, there seems to be a prior disposition to react to own young with maternal behavior, since Klopfer (1971) has reported that while alien kids can be accepted *only* if initially presented at parturition, the female's own kids still can be accepted when initial presentation is a few hours later. The acceptance of own kids, however, appears to be lowered the longer the duration of the initial contact with the alien kid immediately after parturition.

The entire critical period of 2 hours after parturition may be important, since Blauvelt (1955) and Hersher, Moore, and Richmond (1958) have found that if brief separations of the mother and young of sheep and goats occur shortly after birth, even after the peak of sensitivity has passed, some disturbances in the maternal-infant bond are created. Such disturbances are apparent in that the maternal specificity is less than normal at a later time. Even so, the first 10 minutes after birth are the most crucial in the formation of an exclusive attachment of the mother to her young.

A second point of difference between maternal imprinting in sheep and goats and filial imprinting in precocial avian species is that the process is repeated at the birth of subsequent offspring, by virtue of the fact that mother sheep and goats experience more than one birth of off-spring, whereas the offspring themselves experience their own birth or hatching only once. This difference does not, of course, alter the validity of our point regarding the irreversibility of maternal attachment in ewes and dams as a characteristic tending to make it appear to occur through a true imprinting process.

Another important fact supporting the contention that the maternal attachment process in the goat is actually a classical imprinting phenom-enon is that it has an association learning counterpart. Other imprinting processes all have association learning counterparts. These are described and discussed in Chapter 7. Hersher, Richmond, and Moore (1963a, b) reported that sheep and goat mothers could be forced to adopt foster young by placing them in stanchions continuously so that they could not butt the young animals away as they tried to nurse from them. While the normal maternal imprinting process takes only 5 or 10 minutes to accomplish, it takes an average of 10 days, or approximately 14,400 minutes, before the foster mother will not butt away the young when she is released from the stanchion. While these researchers contend that this shows that the critical period for maternal imprinting can be con-siderably prolonged beyond its normal time, we do not agree. We feel that this proves even more strongly that the processes of true imprinting, which occur very rapidly during a naturally established critical period, are fundamentally different from the processes of association learning, which can be used at a later time to produce a superficially similar re-sult after compartively extensive training. That the bond formed by such forced fostering is different from that formed naturally is shown by the interesting fact that kids and lambs which have been forcibly fostered are not susceptible to "animal hypnosis" (tonic immobility), as normally reared kids and lambs are (Moore and Amstey, 1962). This appears to be related to the fact that the forcibly fostered young experience a great deal of ambivalent behavior from their foster mother, whereas normally reared ones do not.

Yet another point of similarity between maternal imprinting in goats and filial imprinting in precocial birds is that decreased social input apparently can result in the peak of the critical period occurring some-what later than it normally does. Just as chicks and ducks are imprinted to the mother or siblings when only a few hours old when kept in social groups and yet show maximum imprintability at the age of 16 hours when kept in total social isolation, goats separated from their newborn kids for as long as 8 hours after parturition will accept them upon reunion, provided that they have been completely isolated during this time and not in contact with other animals (Moore and Moore, 1960). This does not mean, of course, that the peak of the critical period has been shifted 8 hours, for the degree of the shift was not at all determined by this experimental procedure. What it does mean is that, within limits, total social isolation promotes the likelihood of natural acceptance at a somewhat later time than usual in spite of separation, just as it promotes the likelihood of natural social imprinting in precocial birds under similar circumstances.

Apparently there is at least one other mammalian species—the Alaskan fur seal (Bartholomew, 1959)—in which maternal imprinting takes place, and certainly also through olfactory cues. Just as kids and lambs initially do, the seal pup will attempt to nurse from any female it sees (though in normal conditions the kid or lamb does not see other members of the flock for a time after birth, since as Hersher, Richmond, and Moore [1963b] and Smith [1965] point out, the ewe or dam segregates herself from the flock shortly before birth), with the result that only the young animal's own mother will permit nursing. However, kids and lambs come to approach solely their own mother as a result of the rebuffs from other females, but seal pups never seem to form a definite discrimination between their own mother and other females, as they approach every returning female when they are hungry. This is correlated with the fact that while sheep and goat mothers remain with their young in the herd, the Alaskan fur seal mother spends only the first 2 days with her pup, and then goes to sea and returns to nurse the young at weekly intervals. When she returns, she calls, and all the hungry pups within earshot approach and attempt to nurse while she smells each one in turn. If she finds her own pup, it is the only one permitted to nurse; otherwise, no pup will be fed.

Whether the mother seal's acceptance of the young is contingent upon contact with her pup during the first few minutes after birth or sometime afterward is not now known. Mother seals do not lick or groom their young during the immediate period after parturition, but do smell it some. However, the discrimination must be formed fairly quickly, for the mother leaves her young in 2 days; before then she defends it vigorously.

Whatever other species have this phenomenon of maternal imprinting await discovery and enumeration. While several references in the literature (Baerends and Baerends-van Roon, 1950; Tinbergen, 1951; Thorpe, 1956) have given the impression that Noble and Curtis (1939) showed that parental imprinting occurs in cichlid fish through experience with the first batch of young, Greenberg (1963) points out that Noble and Curtis actually did not, and presents experimental results which fail to give any support to such a notion. Among jewel fish (*Hemichromis bimaculatus* Gill) and ports (*Aequidens portalegrensis*), exchange of young, whether of the same species or of the other species, is successful only if the foster young are wrigglers or matching in age and behavior the parents' own brooding phase. Otherwise they are often eaten.

GUINEA PIG SOCIALIZATION

We have observed in our laboratories several times that young guinea pigs can readily be induced to follow substitute maternal objects. More recently, Shipley (1963), Sluckin (1968), Gaston, Stout, and Tom (1969), and Harper (1970), have described following behavior in young guinea pigs toward moving objects. Sluckin's work showed that naïve guinea pigs as old as 7 days could be motivated to follow a small moving object and then show preference for it over a strange object as a consequence of four successive daily 1-hour exposures after the initial session. These data show that it is questionable whether true imprinting (according to our criteria of extremely short sensitive period and irreversibility) actually exists in the guinea pig.

Our own research work during the past few years (Beauchamp and Hess, 1971) has demonstrated that, especially for male guinea pigs, the effects of extra-species social experience are relatively temporary. All male guinea pigs have an innate preference for conspecific females as sexual partners when they reach sexual maturity, regardless of whether they were raised with their own species or with another species. However, the effect of extra-species rearing experience is to permit male guinea pigs to make sexual responses to the foster species. This is noteworthy, since colony-reared male guinea pigs normally never show any sexual behavior toward anything that is not a female of their own species. What is more, there is no sensitive period for the development of non-species directed sexual behavior, as we have found there is, for example, no difference in the acquisition of such behavior if the rearing experience is during the first or second 3 weeks of life.

HUMAN BEINGS

The currently increasing prevalence of notions of the existence of sensitive periods or phases and of structures within the human child, which cause him to be selectively responsive toward specific aspects of the environment through the possession of certain innate drives for love and stimulation and which, furthermore, impel him to perform certain specific actions in response to these environmental stimuli, is worth noting as a strong indication of a growing, though still not unified, trend in conceptualizing the nature of the human child and his developmental processes.

We find such concepts very clearly in Bowlby (1953) with respect to the development of social behavior in man. Bowlby noted that while it is a platitude that man's social responses are profoundly affected by his social experiences, the notion that the precise age at which he has these social experiences might be vitally important had not received serious attention, even though the idea of critical or sensitive phases in morphological, neurological, and physiological development had long been a biological truism. Just as in embryology the organization of a group of cells which governs their subsequent growth is determined by their environment at a particular critical phase, Bowlby suggested that "it looks very much as though something of the same kind underlies the development of psychopathic personality." For example, psychopathic character apparently does not follow maternal deprivation in older children or adolescents, but may do so when the deprivation occurs before about 5 years of age, according to Bowlby's own experiences. He noted the widespread existence of the notion of the importance of experience during the early life years in other areas of development, notably abilities in the auditory and visual sensory modalities.

> If these perceptual organisations are consolidated by experience in the third or fourth years they are maintained throughout life even if deafness or blindness intervenes. But if deafness or blindness supervene earlier, say before the second birthday, the organisation fails to consolidate, and if hearing and vision are restored all has to be learned afresh—and learned with infinitely greater difficulty because the plastic phase of development is over and different organisations for communication and perception of form have become organised and consolidated. . . . There is good reason to think something similar occurs in regard to social perceptions and social responses. Children of between six months and three years of age who are separated from their mothers often undergo intense emotional experiences of rage and despair and then they proceed to organise their social relations on a new pattern; often one in which no particular human being is being sought after and loved. It would appear that if this new psychopathic organisation is permitted to consolidate around the age of three or four years, it tends to become permanent.

Furthermore, according to Bowlby, these changes in perceptual sensitivities and development of social response systems, eventuating in final "setting" of perceptual and behavioral patterns, originate in *structural* changes in the child. These structural changes occur principally in the physiology and anatomy of the brain as maturation proceeds. However, the precise structural alterations accompanying these changes in sensitivities and behavior patterns await experimental discovery. Bowlby (1953, 1958, 1960), also pointed out that there are several congruent features between the ethological findings regarding the development of social behavior in some animal species and the psychoanalytic principles regarding the same development in humans: the innate drive to make a love relation with a parent-figure, the strong influence of the individual's early love object on the selection of a love object in adult life (a process which in humans may, in abnormal cases, be carried to the point of pathological fixation), and the critical or sensitive phases of development of instinctual responses with reference both to the nature of the object selected and the organization of the motor patterns adopted. Bowlby's recent book *Loss and Attachment* (1969) also compares social imprinting in animals with socialization processes in human infants.

Another psychoanalyst who has posited critical consequences resulting from interpersonal experiences during highly specific life periods is Bender (1954), who wrote:

> A serious deformity in personality may occur in a child when there is a critical change in parent relationships before the latter part of the first half year of life, because this is a period when children first identify with their parents and show a definite and individual relationship to people around them.... Our experiences have led us to believe that unless the child has had the continuous affectionate care of one mothering adult up to the age of nine months he can not develop a clearly differentiated relationship with the mother.

However, this was not, in Bender's opinion, the sole period of vulnerability: "It appears that a very critical break in total family identification during the second, third, and fourth years may produce a similar personality distortion." Bender postulated that the effects of maternal deprivation lay in the *retardation* of personality development; true affectional ties, as a consequence, cannot be established by the deprived child, leading to the relatively ineradicable inability to be controlled by social forces, to defects in language development and in temporal conceptualization. Thus, in Bender's view, the family plays a highly positive and formative role in the development of personality: "The family is uniquely suited to develop the capacity for love."

Other writers have espoused the notion that there are sensitive periods in human maturation which play a positive role in the formation of character, not merely periods of vulnerability to damage. An example of the latter position is Allport (1955), who was frankly skeptical that the first 5 years of life are those in which the individual's personality is irrevocably formed. However, he was willing to concede that "a disordered affiliative relationship may leave an ineradicable scar by age 3-5." But in normal circumstances, Allport contended, the child who has not had adverse experiences is "free to become. He is not retarded, but well launched on a course of unimpeded growth." On the other hand, Nash (1954), like Bowlby and Bender, has proposed that there are formative periods in human maturation similar to the critical periods in the development of animal behavior, particularly where behavior patterns become attached to relatively simple "innate releaser mechanisms." In such sensitive maturationally determined periods, Nash suggested, the child is especially receptive to certain types of stimuli, and quickly attaches certain behavior patterns to them.

Spitz (1959, 1965) has continued this trend of thought by conceptualizing a series of specific maturationally timed stages in the psychical development of the child, during which he is particularly sensitive to specific types of experiences. The function of each stage, according to Spitz, is the development of a so-called psychological organizer, somewhat similar in the nature of its action to the embryological "organizer" postulated by Spemann (1938). Such psychic organizers are established during specific critical periods, according to Spitz. The specific organizers he hypothesized were: structuring of perception and establishing of the beginning of the ego, or establishment of the first rudiments of the reality principle, beginning at the age of 3 months; integrating object relationships with drives and establishing the ego as an organized psychic structure, ending between the ages of 6 and 10 months, when the so-called 8-months' anxiety can be seen; and developing of object relationships on the human pattern and the organizing of semantic communication during the age period from 6 or 10 months to 18 months, when global speech patterns, in which single words function as sentences, are predominant. After this third organizer has been established around the age of 18 months, the adult sense of speech is subsequently acquired. Spitz did not say just when he considered the adult sense of speech to be fully acquired.

At each of these critical periods, emphasized Spitz, there must be maturational and developmental (psychological) compliance for optimal development. Synchronicity between maturational and psychological factors was regarded as absolutely essential for normal development; otherwise, Spitz postulated, if the appropriate psychological conditions are not present at the time of maturational readiness, then other psychological items which are available are seized upon and distorted. Such asynchronicity thus results in disturbances and fixation of ego energies upon inappropriate objects, according to Spitz. As an example of such adverse consequences, Spitz cited exactly the same behavior pattern as Halliday (1948) earlier had: the normal 6- to 8-month old child's tendency to hit everything within reach, put everything in his mouth, and chew them. In normal development, this destructive-appearing activity, according to Spitz, "would be progressively modified into filling in, into manipulating, into constructive building, into the role-playing activity of the 3 to 4 year old. But if this development is arrested at the earlier level and the destructive activity, which is normal at this level, persists in the 3- to 4-year old then we get the picture of the senselessly destructive toddler, who smashes everything in sight, bites everybody in his way and ends up pulling a kettle of boiling water onto himself." Naturally, Spitz did not rigidly postulate the same pathological consequences from the same cause, for he pointed out that many kinds of deviation can result from the same antecedent event, and that the same abnormal fixations can occur for different reasons.

The notion that there is an early period in human development which plays the role of establishing primary social relationships, and therefore an enduring pattern of social behavior, has been expressed by several writers other than Bowlby and Spitz. The exact periods proposed by these writers vary: Gray (1958) proposed the period of 6 weeks to 6 months; Hess (1959), the first $5\frac{1}{2}$ months of life; Rollman-Branch (1960), the first 6 months of life, and Ambrose (1963), the age period from 5 to 12 months. Scott (1958) was not initially certain as to the possible location of the sensitive period for primary socialization in humans, but contended that since primary socialization periods were so universal in the animal kingdom, there was "every reason for suspecting that a similar period exists in human development." Later Scott (1963) stated that it was likely that this period was between 6 weeks and 6 months of age. Nevertheless, he considered later ages as also sensitive to psychological damage resulting from pathological social experiences.

Ambrose (1963), in considering Gray's (1958) paper attempting to prove the existence of an imprinting-like primary socialization process in human beings during the age period 6 weeks to 6 months, stated that Gray's proof was inadequate with respect to relevant details. However, Ambrose did feel that there are, in fact, very good grounds for supposing that there is an early and very sensitive period in the development of the human infant's basic social response system. Furthermore, Ambrose contended that this sensitive period depends upon the nature of the type of caretaking to which the child has been exposed.

On the basis of his own earlier research with the smiling response (Ambrose, 1961), Ambrose suggested that the sensitive period for supra-individual learning of the human face—the human analogue of supra-individual learning of the species in precocial birds—starts at approximately the 5th week of life and ends at approximately 12 weeks of age for family-reared infants and at approximately 18 weeks age for institutionalized infants. Thus, it appears, just as it does in the cases of social imprinting that we already have discussed that the end of the sensitive period is delayed when the social-sensory input to the organism is below normal. Even if this proposed period should, indeed, be vital for the development of the child's capacity to form and maintain human relationships, Ambrose emphasized that, in his opinion, this does not mean that later vicissitudes, such as separation from the mother or change to other caretakers, do not also have far-reaching effects on the quality of the subsequent affectional relationships that the child forms. On the contrary, the nature of the response to such vicissitudes would be profoundly affected by the social behavior patterns set up during this early period in question.

Ambrose did not posit any further sensitive periods in human behavioral development other than to state that 3 or 4 months after the formation of the attachment to the mother, through supra-individual learning, the infant begins to learn that there are other human beings in the world and to transfer his perception of, and responsiveness to, his mother to these new people. Depending on the infant's relationship with his mother, he will either approach or avoid other people. Hence, it seems that the quality of the child's relationship with his mother influences his capacity to establish and maintain adaptive human relationships in general.

Somewhat similar notions regarding the development of attachment behavior have been espoused by Ainsworth (1964), a close colleague of Bowlby. These notions do, however, differ from those of Ambrose in the number and exact timing of the stages proposed. Four stages were defined: 1) From birth to the age of 8 to 12 weeks, there is an undiscriminating responsiveness to people. 2) From then to the age of 6 to 7 months, there is differential crying in response to the mother and to others; however, there continues to be attachments to people other than the mother. 3) Then there is a sharply defined attachment to the mother and a precipitate drop in undiscriminating friendliness; this phase begins without abrupt transition from stage 2 and overlaps to some extent with the next phase. 4) Apparent at about 9 months of age, the fourth phase is reflected when the baby follows other people, such as father, siblings, and extra-family friends and relatives, about. From phase to phase, there are changes in the expression of the capacity for attachment to other people.

Ainsworth strongly emphasized that the baby plays a very active part in the development of attachment behavior, since all his behavior patterns, down to the seeking responses in feeding, show initiative on his part. Ainsworth postulated that it is probably primarily through his own activity that the child becomes attached to people, rather than through stimulation or through the passive satisfaction of mere creature-comfort needs. There is, in other words, a reciprocal interaction between the child and the people who are responsible for his care or those who are otherwise in continuous or frequent contact with him, and it is this reciprocal interaction which forms the basis of social behavior patterns.

While Ainsworth did not go into detail regarding the possibilities of deleterious sequelae of abnormal events during these periods in attachment behavior, it is clear, from her other publications, such as two papers in 1962, that maternal deprivation, defined as insufficient interaction between the infant and a mother-figure, rather than mere lack of sensory stimulation, has deleterious effects.

Of importance is the fact that both Ambrose (1963) and Ainsworth (1964) have postulated that attachment to the mother takes place long before the child shows fear of strangers, so that fear of strangers is *not* a criterion of attachment to the mother, as has often been assumed (e.g., Gray, 1958). Freedman (1961) has likened the baby's fear reaction to strangers to the flight response to a potentially dangerous situation, since the infant buries his face in the mother's shoulder and screams when he sees a stranger. Therefore, since the mother is already there, the reaction is not one made in response to a perceived threat of losing the mother. Further support for the notion of the separability of infant-mother attachment and fear of strangers has been made by Schaffer (1963), who observed that these two behavior items do not arise simultaneously in the child, that there are children who show a high degree of attachment to specific individuals in their environment and yet very little fear of strangers, and that there are still other children who are very afraid of strangers but are not attached to familiar persons. Hence, these two behaviors are not merely opposite sides of the same coin, concluded Schaffer, even though they may come to interact with each other.

Ainsworth (1963) further observed that after the attachment to the mother takes place, the baby becomes attached to several other people, including ones who do not feed him. Thus, as also suggested by Wilson (1963), feeding a baby will not necessarily insure that he will love you; the same has been found to be true in birds and other animals. While observing the development of attachment behavior in Uganda infants where several caretakers may be involved with the child, Ainsworth (1963) found that the figures selected for attachment by the baby were sometimes persons who took no part in his routine care but who merely played and interacted with him, leading Ainsworth to conclude that "something other than mere satisfaction of bodily needs determined attachment to specific figures." Furthermore, just as appeared to be the case with Harlow and Harlow's (1965) mother- and surrogate-reared monkeys, a secure attachment to the mother appeared to Ainsworth to be essential for the child's being able to form attachments to other people and to form a base from which to explore the world, developing skills and knowledge.

Schaffer (1963) also has pointed out that the mother is not *always* the person to whom attachment behavior is shown most frequently and intensely, although she is most often at the top of the child's hierarchy. However, there were cases observed by Schaffer in which persons other than the mother were selected for the top of the hierarchy for the child, even though the total amount of time they spent with him was very much less. Normally, Schaffer contended, it is the rule that several individuals are attached to by the infant, and protest at being left is evoked by any of a number of persons, not just one.

In the same paper, Schaffer theorized that there are three principal stages in the development of attachment behavior. The first consists of appetitive "stimulus-seeking" behavior by the baby, the second of "indiscriminate attachment" behavior and the third of "specific attachments." In complete agreement with the thesis of Rheingold (1961), Schaffer felt that searching of the environment for stimulation is one of the most prominent characteristics of the young infant, and forms the origin of attachment behavior. Human beings in themselves appear to form the most stimulating part of the infant's environment, and the child's supply of non-social stimulation is usually dependent on the adult, since the young infant's motor equipment initially does not permit him to move around and produce for himself the interesting sights and sounds which he needs to relieve his boredom, according to Schaffer. Therefore, when the adult disappears and the baby is left to his own devices, the baby has only very limited means at his disposal to entertain himself, and eventually the natural reaction is to cry. "Right from the beginning the infant is no mere passive being to whom nothing matters but food and warmth," Schaffer noted. "Whatever label will eventually be found most appropriate for the tendency we are now discussing— stimulus hunger, curiosity, arousal seeking, exploratory drive—it seems likely that this function is one of the most important attributes with which a child comes into the world," Schaffer continued. This notion is congruent with Casler's (1961) suggestion that the pathological sequelae of early institutionalization have their origin in stimulation deprivation. But a most striking feature of this function, Schaffer stressed, is that the tendency to seek environmental stimulation "may be found to different degrees in different individuals. . . . There are babies who seem satisfied with very little stimulation and are usually described as 'easy' and 'content,' while others appear simply ravenous for stimulation, who cry most readily at its lack and where mothering entails an almost continuous supply of one form or another of excitation."

Therefore, it was clearly postulated by Schaffer that both certain internal structural characteristics of the child, to which the adults in his environment must adjust, and the nature of his social environment, stimulating and fostering his attachment behavior, determine the intensity of the attachment behavior which he does show. In mother-infant interaction, active mutual adaptation, and therefore reciprocal stimulation, the basis of socialization and intellectual capacities, must occur from the very beginning. The eventual intensity of the attachments formed depend, in Schaffer's words, "both on the strength of the particular child's need and the extent to which the people around him are prepared to satisfy it."

The studies on the effects of bereavement, maternal deprivation, and institutionalization also have furnished some evidence of sensitive periods in human behavioral development. In reviewing these studies on the effects of disturbances in the infant-mother relationship, Yarrow (1961, 1964, 1965) has suggested, in direct analogy with the social imprinting phenomenon in animals, that there is a specific developmental period during which vulnerability to separation from the mother or parents is the greatest. "The most sensitive time may be the period during which the infant is in the process of establishing stable affectional relationships, approximately 6 months and two years" (1964). Yarrow further hypothesized that the effect of separation depends on whether or not focused relationships have already been established by the child, and emphasized that definitive studies were needed to establish the validity of this postulation. According to Yarrow (1964):

> In a broader sense, each developmental stage may be viewed as critical in terms of the child's capacities, in terms of the central developmental tasks or the focal psychological conflicts of specific developmental periods. One might hypothesize that each developmental period has its own sensitivities and vulnerabilities. . . . For example, the young infant may be less disturbed by a permanent separation than the child past two years of age who is able to understand more clearly the implications of permanent separation. Thus although vulnerability and loss of a mother-figure may be greatest at one particular period, separation may continue to be a potentially disturbing experience, but to a lesser degree, at other developmental periods. This concept of changing vulnerabilities also suggests that one needs to be aware of the particular developmental sensitivities and focal conflicts at different ages. For example, the height of the Oedipus period can be particularly traumatic. Similarly hospitalization for surgery may be most traumatic at the developmental period in which there is particular concern about body integrity.

Still another expression of the concept of sensitivities during early personality development has been given by Saul (Saul and Wenar, 1965), who has postulated:

> The child who during his first six years has had favorable relations with those responsible for his rearing, has a stable core of good relations toward others and can withstand a good deal of injurious influence thereafter. Conversely, a child treated badly during his first six years will never become adequately mature. Babies are easily driven into psychotic, prepsychotic, and other

seriously disordered states. Most persons fall between the two extremes: they have sufficiently good relationships before the age of six to continue maturing despite other warping influences, but they retain throughout life some problems in their feelings toward others and toward themselves.

ARE THERE *CRITICAL* PERIODS IN HUMAN DEVELOPMENT?

Thus, we see a definite and growing trend, particularly among Europeans, to conceptualize the behavioral development of the human individual as containing periods of sensitivity or susceptibility to environmental events, especially in the spheres of social-emotional behaviors and intellectual activities. Some of these writers, indeed, have espoused the view that certain of these periods are critical ones. About the evidence regarding human development with reference to the classification of sensitive periods, which we have set up in Chapter 2, the question may be asked whether there are, in fact, any truly critical periods in human behavioral development. A critical period, according to our proposed classification, is very short in duration, and the effects of specific events during this period are extremely long-lasting, probably lifelong, and relatively immune to erasure by subsequent events. Such critical period processes have been seen in the social imprinting phenomena in precocial birds.

Thus, we must first ask whether any of the sensitive periods that have been found or postulated in humans fits any of the criteria for critical periods, as we have defined them, found in other animals. Critical periods have been found lasting 2 hours in sheep (Klopfer, Adams, and Klopfer, 1964), 36 hours in ducks and chickens (Hess, 1957), 1 week in dogs (Tinbergen, 1951), and 3 days in rats (Bell, Reisner, and Linn, 1961; Denenberg, 1962; Levine and Lewis, 1959). We cannot arbitrarily set a specific time limit on the length of a sensitive period for it to be regarded as a true critical period—a time period of 1 week certainly could not be regarded as a critical period for a creature such as a fruit fly. Therefore, some proportionality with respect to the normal expected life span of the species in question is indicated. On this basis, it appears reasonable in the case of the human child to consider a sensitive period lasting at the most 2 or 3 months as a critical period. Longer periods than that certainly would be more accurately regarded as susceptible periods rather than as critical periods. As Murphy (1964) has pointed out, for example, one cannot speak of imprinting in the ethological sense when the process in question has to go on for 200 days and nights or more. Also, while Money, Hampson, and Hampson (1957) have proposed that the age period 0 to 2½ years is a *critical* one, we feel that this is really a *susceptible* period. Wolff (1970), using a *strict* definition of critical periods, has concluded that there are none in human beings.

Very few of the sensitive periods proposed by the theorists we have just considered fall within this 3-month time limit. The first period proposed by Spitz (1959)—the one resulting in the emergence of the first psychic organizer—usually by the age of 3 months, is one of these. Ambrose's (1963) proposed critical period from the age of 5 to 12 or 18 weeks is the only other one which meets the critical period time limit criterion we have proposed. Neither of these two periods has been conclusively demonstrated to exist.

However, the degree of the postulated effect of events occurring during these periods is, in both proposed cases, of the type that we have seen in critical periods in other animals. Certainly, the process of primary ego formation is vital to the remainder of personality and intellectual development; failure in its development can be seen in the autistic children described by Rimland (1964). Ambrose has emphasized the widespread effect of the first affectional relationship with the mother or caretaker on the quality of subsequent affectional relationships. Nevertheless, we must, in view of the limited present evidence, be conservative as to whether there are actually any critical periods in human development. But we certainly can be completely affirmative that there are a number of highly susceptible periods and many optimal periods in human development. These periods, of course, do not occur in rigid sequence, but overlap considerably, and some are concurrent. Some of these susceptible periods do have what may be called "critical" consequences; but criticality of consequences alone is not sufficient to make a sensitive period a critical one. In fact, there can be critical consequences without there being any sensitive period at all: for example, once a person is killed, an event that is possible at any time, he will remain dead.

Granted that sensitive periods of different types and with different degrees of crucialness in the determination of later behavior and abilities do exist in humans as well as in other animals, what are their bases? As Schaffer (1963) has pointed out, determining the sensitive age ranges is but a beginning of the inquiry and not the end. "The function of the age variable is merely to direct our attention to a certain phase of development; it cannot by itself provide us with any clue as to *why* this function emerges just at this time, i.e., what processes are responsible for its occurrence. To this challenging problem we have as yet no definite answer."

SOCIAL IMPRINTING IN HUMAN BEINGS?

Related to the question of whether any critical periods exist in human development is the perennial question of whether social imprinting occurs in man. Ever since the discovery of the social imprinting phenomenon in precocial birds, there has been much speculation as to whether at least a similar phenomenon exists in human babies. As Ambrose (1963) has pointed out, this issue is very important, very complex, and very difficult. Taketomo (1968) has examined several of the attempts that have been made to suggest imprinting processes in humans, and found them all rather inadequate. From our own point of view, since no *critical* periods have yet been conclusively demonstrated to exist in behavioral development in humans, we do not feel that any imprinting processes have been demonstrated to exist in the human species. Nevertheless, it is still valuable to explore this question as a means of possibly seeing new and better ways of understanding the course of human behavior development. As Bateson (1969) has warned, it is, of course, necessary to observe closely the actual processes of behavior development and social attachment processes in babies in order to gain any notion of the kinds of processes that actually occur.

Many aspects of the classic social imprinting phenomenon have attracted the attention of psychoanalysts. In particular, the notion of imprinting as a rapidly formed and ineradicable attachment to a specific type of object, particularly when abnormal objects have been attached to, used by some theorists, has been linkened to that of pathological "fixations" (Rapaport, 1961, cited in Saul and Wenar, 1965; Sutherland, 1963). Such pathological fixations, according to Sutherland, are derived from traumatic frustration experiences in early development which appear to set up subsystems in the person, subsystems that continue to actively seek expression. They are relatively little influenced by subsequent experiences. But, as Sutherland pointed out, it is not really known whether or not maturationally determined sensitive periods are associated with the formation of pathological fixations. Nevertheless, many theorists do seem to concur that there are certain properties of specific states of the person involved in the genesis of these fixations, just as in the case of imprinting.

As has been seen in the social imprinting phenomenon, young animals of certain species have a highly specific drive to attach themselves to the company of a parent figure. The same drive has been increasingly postulated by a number of psychoanalytically oriented theorists in the field of child development, and has been suggested as a possible indicator of an imprinting-like social attachment process in human beings. While the flood of literature on the effects of maternal deprivation or inadequate maternal care certainly has shown that the infant has *need* of the mother, it is quite a different thing to actually postulate that the infant has a *drive* for the mother. Such a viewpoint as the latter implies that the infant can and does play an active role in the formation of early social relationships, rather than that he passively receives whatever social stimulation the mother chooses to give him, or that the mother acts solely as a means of provision of creature-comfort needs, and the infant becomes attached to her for that reason.

Early psychoanalytic views, while implying the infant's active role in infant-mother relationships, did not seem to place sufficient emphasis on it. Freud emphasized the passive satisfaction of the infant's bodily needs through maternal care and the need for erogenous (skin) stimulation, especially in the oral zone. Social drives on the part of the child did not play any great role in the Freudian system until the time of the development of the Oedipus complex.

With Halliday (1948), we find clearly stated the notion that the infant has an innate drive to receive love from the mother. Bowlby (1953) also expressed a similar notion in pointing out the similarity between imprinting and the formation of social relationship in human babies. And, of course, writers dealing with the subject of the possibility of imprinting in human beings, such as Gray (1958), Caldwell (1961, 1962), Ambrose (1963), Rollman-Branch (1960), generally imply that such drives exist. Rollman-Branch (1960), for example, suggested that the similarity between the marasmus and death of infants deprived of motherly contact around the age of 6 months and the flight and fear reaction of animals who have not been imprinted implies that object relationships are a primary need of both animals and men, rather than merely a subsidiary to the satisfaction of physical needs.

In spite of having stated that nothing is known of imprinting in man, Bowlby (1953) still felt that there were several similarities between the social imprinting process in precocial birds and the development of social attachment in humans. He likened the child's intense need for attachment from the age of 3 or 7 months to more than 3 years to the following responses of other mammals. Furthermore, he suggested, on the basis of his clinical experiences, that the phase during which differentiation between the mother and other people takes place, and during which the following response is at a maximum, is critical for the development of the child's reaction to his parents and also for his adult social responses such as the sexual and the parental. All those proposed points are analogous with the classical social imprinting phenomenon, as Bowlby pointed out.

However, actual following behavior cannot take place until the baby can crawl around to some extent. Other writers have expressed the opinion that the primary socialization of the human child occurs before he can crawl. Gray (1958), for example, suggested the period between the age of 6 weeks and 6 months as the period of primary socialization, and that the smiling response is homologous to the following response of young precocial birds, particularly since it ends with a fear response to strangers, inasmuch as young birds show distress behavior when confronted with novel objects after the critical period for imprinting has passed. The fear response of young infants to strangers has also been likened by Freedman (1961) to that shown by young birds. He stated that the child's fear response is a flight response, because the infant buries his face in the mother's shoulder; such behavior is not the same as that shown when loss of the mother is threatened. Certainly, it has been observed that the infant commonly shows distress at the mother's departure at a much earlier age than it does fear of the stranger; according to Ainsworth, the respective average times for the appearance of these behaviors is 15 weeks and 8 months. Such fear of strangers beginning at the latter age has been pointed out by many other writers, particularly Spitz (1950), as well as Hess (1959), Rollman-Branch (1960), Ambrose (1963), Ainsworth (1964), and Morgan (1965).

However, Ambrose (1963) contended, just because there is a period of positive responsiveness and positive attachment, followed by the fear response, this is not sufficient to establish the existence of a social imprinting phenomenon in human beings. This is because the distress behavior evident in young chicks or ducklings already imprinted to siblings or to another parent object may possibly reflect a searching for the lost companionship rather than fear of the new situation per se. Thus, while fear may cause incompatible responses in birds which have been completely isolated socially since hatching, this may not be the case in socially maintained ones.

Even though Ambrose criticized the grounds on which Gray (1958) attempted to demonstrate the existence of social imprinting in human beings, he felt that there were, indeed, other very good bases for supposing that there is an analogy between early social learning in human babies and social imprinting in precocial birds. We have already mentioned Ambrose's postulation of a critical period in supra-individual social learning in children. In the first place, according to Ambrose, there is a broad similarity in the nature of the innate releasing situations for smiling in babies and following in chicks and ducks, and these releasing situations are mother objects in both cases. Not only are there close similarities in causation, but there is also a close similarity in function; and this function is that of keeping the young organism close to the mother object. Whereas the young chick or duck can follow, the human infant is utterly incapable of doing so for several months. However, the human baby's crying normally does serve to bring his mother to him from a distance, and his smiling serves to keep her there when she is already nearby. Ambrose also pointed out that another similarity between smiling in human babies and following in chicks and ducks is that both develop in response strength in the period of supra-individual learning of the species without any conventional reward such as food.

Finally, Ambrose postulated that a better criterion for the beginning of social imprinting and the beginning of supra-individual species learning in babies is when fixation upon an object is possible, rather than when learning is first evident, as Gray (1958) had proposed. A bird, Ambrose pointed out, cannot learn its parent unless it can follow, and it cannot follow its parent unless it can keep the parent fixated. Thus, the commencement of visual learning is conditional upon the achievement of the ability to fixate an object. In line with this, Ambrose suggested that the mother's eyes are the first objects to consistently elicit visual fixation by the infant, particularly since the studies of Ahrens (1954) and others have indicated that the smiling response is initially elicited by the eyes alone, later requiring more and more completeness in the representation of the human face to release smiles. Caldwell (1962) has also suggested that *visual pursuit* is the "following" of the parent-figure in the infant.

Also a point of similarity between the smiling response and the filial responses in social imprinting in birds, on the basis of Ambrose's (1961) data, is that lowered sensory input apparently causes the susceptible or critical period in question to terminate at a later time than usual. Institution-reared infants continue to smile indiscriminately longer than do family-reared babies, and also commonly begin smiling later. This similarity appears to indicate that there is, indeed, a strong resemblance between primary social learning in human infants and the same process in precocial birds.

In this connection, we would like to note that only recently has there been experimental evidence that the human infant is born with a preference for the normal human face (Jirari, 1970), just as ducklings have an innate preference for the characteristics of their species-specific mother (Hess and Hess, 1969). Jirari found this preference in newborns that had no opportunity to associate creature comforts with other human beings, so that associative learning processes could not possibly be responsible for the observed preference. Jirari showed schematic faces and "scrambled" faces (having the same schematic elements but placed randomly on the stimulus board) to 36 babies no older than 24 hours. The schematic normal faces elicited markedly more visual following than did the scrambled faces, even in infants only a few hours old.

Thirty-one newborns of the same age were also shown a real face and a mannequin face. The real face elicited more visual following by the babies than did that of the mannequin. If babies less than a day old can differentiate such face stimuli, differing principally in degree of realism, then it is evident that the human infant is programmed, prior to birth, to respond to actual human faces.

These findings are, therefore, in direct opposition to the commonly held belief that human neonates cannot discriminate between normal faces and abnormal ones. This belief, of course, was based on the fact that hitherto there were no adequate techniques available to find out whether they could. At any rate, it becomes clear that, among human beings, social attachment behavior is built upon a definitely organized basis that is present at the time of birth, just as it is in other social species having interaction between parent and offspring.

Hence, we have yet another way in which social imprinting processes in birds and primary socialization processes in human beings are similar: there is, in both cases, a built-in preference for the characteristics of the actual conspecific parent.

Further similarities between the two process have been noted by Hinde (1961), who has theorized that the human infant's crying is functionally equivalent to the distress calls of a nidifugous bird. Hinde also suggested that each of the various behavior patterns which contribute to the infant-mother relationship, and ultimately to the development of typical responsiveness to other people, has its own sensitive period, which may be limited in the manner postulated by James' (1887) Law of Transitoriness of Instincts. The lack of the importance of food or other conventional rewards in promoting the tie of the infant to his mother (as shown by Wilson, 1963) is certainly congruent with the fact that precocial birds form the attachment to the mother-figure before they have any real need for food, being able to draw upon nourishment from the yolk sac until the 3rd day of age, according to Hinde.

However, the existence of all these similarities does not necessarily force the conclusion that there is actually a phylogenetic connection between the imprinting phenomenon in birds and filial attachment to parents in human infants. Hinde pointed out that the synapsid and diapsid reptiles, from which mammals and birds arose, have been distinct since at least the Permian period of the Paleozoic era. Thus parental care and, therefore, infant-to-mother attachment behavior have evolved independently in the two groups. Therefore, the similarities would indicate more accurately that these behaviors constitute analogies rather than homologies, and that they arose from similar forces in the evolutionary process.

This view of Hinde's would undoubtedly be completely correct if the development of social attachment were the only instance in which the imprinting process operated. But we must also point out that if imprinting is a type of learning process which can be applied to a variety of situations in which specific behavior patterns are attached to a class of stimulus objects—such as food imprinting in chicks and turtles, maternal imprinting in sheep and goats, or environmental imprinting in a variety of species—then the imprinting mechanism must be one which is phylogenetically very old, since it apparently exists even in the turtle. Thus, it seems possible that the imprinting process could have been independently seized upon by both mammals and birds for use in the development of social behavior systems as well as of other object-response relationships. Thus, the homology, if it exists at all, would be only through the phylogenetic transmission of the imprinting process, and not through the phylogenetic transmission of parental care and filial attachment system. For the time being, we must still regard the existing similarities as somewhat analogous and certainly not as true homologies.

Other kinds of possible imprinting processes in humans and other mammals have been suggested by some writers. For example, Salk (1962) has suggested that the fetus is imprinted to the maternal heartbeat. However, because of the great length of the probable exposure, imprinting certainly is not probable as the learning process occurring, but most probably simple habituation is. The possible imprinting of sex orientation and sex role in the young child, as suggested by Money, Hampson, and Hampson (1957), also cannot be seriously considered as a true imprinting process, because of the long life period involved. Spiegel's (1965) application of imprinting to hypnosis is certainly highly questionable.

Nevertheless, the attempts of several researchers and theorists to find if there are, indeed, imprinting processes have brought to light cases of rather permanent or rather rapid learning which have strong effects upon behavior. These lend further support to our suggestion that there are different kinds of learning, particularly whenever any kind of sensitive period may be involved. The far-reaching effects of different kinds of early experience for the human child and for the adult he becomes are cases in point. Hence, searching for sensitive period phenomena probably will aid us more fully to understand the normal and abnormal development of behavior in humans, even if actual imprinting never is found. The importance of consistent and stable maternal attachments during the first years of life, as demonstrated by Bowlby (1969), certainly has gone far to help us in determining improved methods of managing orphaned children as well as those living in normal families.

REFERENCES

AHRENS, ROLF. Beitrag zur Entwicklung des Physiognomie- und Mimikerkennens. *Zeitschrift für experimentelle und angewandte Psychologie*, 1954, **2,** 412–454.

AINSWORTH, MARY D. The development of infant-mother interaction among the Ganda. In: B. M. Foss, editor, *Determinants of Infant Behaviour II.* Second

Tavistock seminar on mother-infant interaction, London, 1961. New York: Wiley, 1963. 67–112.

AINSWORTH, MARY D. Patterns of attachment behavior shown by the infant in interaction with his mother. *Merrill-Palmer Quarterly*, 1964, **10**, 51–58.

ALLPORT, G. W. *Becoming. Basic Considerations for a Psychology of Personality.* New Haven and London: Yale University Press, 1955.

AMBROSE, JOHN A. The development of the smiling response in early infancy. In: B. M. Foss, editor, *Determinants of Infant Behaviour*. First Tavistock Seminar, London, 1959. New York: Wiley, 1961. 179–201.

AMBROSE, JOHN A. The concept of a critical period for the development of social responsiveness in early human infancy. In: B. M. Foss, editor, *Determinants of Infant Behaviour II*. Second Tavistock Seminar on mother-infant interaction, London, 1961. New York: Wiley, 1963. 201–225.

BAERENDS, G. P., and BAERENDS-van ROON, J. M. An introduction to the ethology of Cichlid fishes. *Behaviour Supplement*, 1950, **1**, 1–243.

BARTHOLOMEW, GEORGE A. Mother-young relations and the maturation of pup behaviour in the Alaskan fur seal. *Animal Behaviour*, 1959, **7**, 163–172.

BATESON, P. P. G. The development of social attachments in birds and man. *Advancement of Science*, London, 1969, **25**, 279–288.

BEAUCHAMP, GARY K., and HESS, ECKHARD H. The effects of cross-species rearing on the social and sexual preferences of guinea pigs *(Cavia porcellus)*. *Zeitschrift für Tierpsychologie*, 1971, **28**, 69–76.

BELL, ROBERT W., REISNER, GERALD, and LINN, THEODORE. Recovery from electroconvulsive shock as a function of infantile stimulation. *Science*, 1961, **133**, 1428.

BENDER, LAURETTA. *Aggression, Hostility, and Anxiety in Children.* Springfield, Illinois: Thomas, 1954.

BLAUVELT, H. Dynamics of the mother-newborn relationship in goats. In: B. Schaffner, editor, *Group Processes*. Transactions of the first conference, 1954. New York: Josiah Macy, Jr. Foundation, 1955. 221–258.

BOWLBY, JOHN A. Remarks. In: J. M. Tanner, editor, *Prospects in Psychiatric Research*. Proceedings of Oxford Conference of Mental Health Research Fund, 1952. Oxford: Blackwell Scientific Publications, 1953. 80–86. (similar material in: John A. Bowlby. Critical phases in the development of social responses in man and other animals. *New Biology* (Penquin Books), 1953, **14**, 25–37.

BOWLBY, JOHN A. The nature of the child's tie to his mother. *International Journal of Psychoanalysis*, 1958, **39**, 350–373.

BOWLBY, JOHN A. Grief and mourning in infancy and early childhood. *Psychoanalytical Study of the Child*, 1960, **15**, 9–52.

BOWLBY, JOHN A. *Attachment and Loss*. New York: Basic Books, 1969. Volume I.

CALDWELL, BETTYE M. The development of social behavior. *American Psychologist*, 1961, **16**, 377. (Abstract).

CALDWELL, BETTYE M. The usefulness of the critical period hypothesis in the study of filiative behavior. *Merrill-Palmer Quarterly*, 1962, **8**, 229–242.

CASLER, LAWRENCE. Maternal deprivation: A critical review of the literature. *Monographs of the Society for Research in Child Development*, 1961, **26**, No. 2, Serial No. 80, 1–64.

COLLIAS, NICHOLAS E. Some factors in maternal rejection by sheep and goats. *Bulletin of the Ecological Society of America*, 1953, **34**, 78.

COLLIAS, NICHOLAS E. The analysis of socialization in sheep and goats. *Ecology,* 1956, **37,** 228–239.

DENENBERG, VICTOR H. An attempt to isolate critical periods of development in the rat. *Journal of Comparative and Physiological Psychology,* 1962, **55,** 813–815.

FREEDMAN, DANIEL G. The infant's fear of strangers and the flight response. *Journal of Child Psychology and Psychiatry,* 1961, **1,** 242–248.

GASTON, MICHAEL G., STOUT, ROBERT, and TOM, ROLAND. Imprinting in guinea pigs. *Psychonomic Science,* 1969, **16,** 53–54.

GIBSON, ELEANOR J. Maternal behavior in the domestic goat. *Anatomical Record,* 1951, **111,** 483. (Abstract).

GRAY, PHILIP H. Theory and evidence of imprinting in human infants. *Journal of Psychology,* 1958, **46,** 155–166.

GREENBERG, BERNARD. Parental behavior and imprinting in cichlid fishes. *Behaviour,* 1963, **21,** 127–144.

HALLIDAY, JAMES LORIMER. *Psychosocial Medicine.* New York: Norton, 1948.

HARLOW, HARRY F., and HARLOW, MARGARET K. The affectional systems. In: A. M. Schrier, H. F. Harlow, and F. Stollnitz, editors, *Behavior of Non-Human Primates.* New York: Academic Press, 1965. Vol. II, 287–334.

HARPER, LAWRENCE V. Role of contact and sound in eliciting filial responses and development of social attachment in domestic guinea pigs. *Journal of Comparative and Physiological Psychology,* 1970, **73,** 427–435.

HERSHER, LEONARD, MOORE, A. ULRIC, and RICHMOND, JULIUS B. Effect of post partum separation of mother and kid on maternal care in the domestic goat. *Science,* 1958, **128,** 1342–1343.

HERSHER, LEONARD, RICHMOND, JULIUS B., and MOORE, A ULRIC. Modificability of the critical period for the development of material behavior in sheep and goats. *Behaviour,* 1963, **20,** 311–320. (a).

HERSHER, LEONARD, RICHMOND, JULIUS B., and MOORE, A. ULRIC. Maternal behavior in sheep and goats. In: H. Rheingold, editor, *Maternal Behavior in Mammals.* New York: Wiley, 1963. 203–232. (b).

HESS, ECKHARD H. Effects of meprobamate on imprinting in waterfowl. *Annals of the New York Academy of Science,* 1957, **67,** 724–733.

HESS, ECKHARD H. The relationship between imprinting and motivation. In: M. R. Jones, editor, *Nebraska Symposium on Motivation, 1959.* Lincoln: University of Nebraska Press, 1959. 44–77.

HESS, ECKHARD H. Experimental analysis of imprinting. Progress report for Grant MY-776 from June 1958 to June 1962. Unpublished manuscript, 1962.

HESS, ECKHARD H., and HESS, DORLÉ B. Innate factors in imprinting. *Psychonomic Science,* 1969, **14,** 129–130.

HINDE, R. A. The establishment of the parent-offspring relation in birds with some mammalian analogies. In: W. H. Thorpe and O. L. Zangwill, editors, *Current Problems in Animal Behaviour.* London: Cambridge University Press, 1961. 175–193.

JAMES, WILLIAM. What is an instinct? *Scribner's Magazine,* 1887, **1,** 355–365.

JIRARI, CAROLYN GOREN. Form perception, innate form preference, and visually mediated head-turning in the human neonate. Unpublished doctoral dissertation, University of Chicago, 1970.

JENSEN, GORDON D. Mother-infant relationships in the monkey *Macaca nemestrina:* Development of specificity of maternal response to own infant. *Journal of Comparative and Physiological Psychology,* 1965, **59,** 303–308.

KLOPFER, PETER H. Maternal "imprinting" in goats: The role of chemical senses. *Zeitschrift für Tierpsychologie,* 1966, **23,** 588–592.

KLOPFER, PETER H. Parameters of imprinting. *American Naturalist,* 1964, **98,** 173–182.

KLOPFER, PETER H. Mother love: What turns it on? *American Scientist,* 1971, **59,** 404–407.

KLOPFER, PETER H., ADAMS, DONALD K., and KLOPFER, MARTHA S. Maternal "imprinting" in goats. *Proceedings of the National Academy of Sciences,* 1964, **52,** 911–914.

KLOPFER, PETER H., and GAMBLE, JOHN. Maternal "imprinting" in goats: The role of chemical senses. *Zeitschrift für Tierpsychologie,* 1966, **23,** 588–592.

IRVINE, SEYMOUR, and LEWIS, GEORGE W. Critical period for effects of infantile experience on maturation of stress response. *Science,* 1959, **129,** 42–43.

MONEY, JOHN, HAMPSON, JOAN G., and HAMPSON, JOHN L. Imprinting and the establishment of gender role. *Archives of Neurology and Psychiatry,* 1957, **77,** 333–336.

MOORE, A. ULRIC, and AMSTEY, MARVIN S. Tonic immobility: Differences in susceptibility of experimental and normal sheep and goats. *Science,* 1962, **135,** 729–730.

MOORE, A. ULRIC, and MOORE, FRANCES. Studies in the formation of the mother-neonate bond in sheep and goats. Symposium on Mechanisms of Primary Socialization. Paper presented at 1960 American Psychological Association Meeting.

MORGAN, GEORGE ARTHUR, JR. Some determinants of infants' responses to strangers during the first year of life. *Dissertation Abstracts,* 1965, **25,** 7371.

MURPHY, LOUIS B. Some aspects of the first relationship. *International Journal of Psychoanalysis,* 1964, **45,** 31–48.

NASH, JOHN. Critical periods in human development. *Bulletin of the Maritime Psychological Association* (Canada), 1954 (Dec.), 18–22.

NOBLE, G. K., and CURTIS, B. The social behavior of the jewel-fish *Hemichromis bimaculatus* Gill. *Bulletin of the American Museum of Natural History,* 1939, **76,** 1–46.

RHEINGOLD, HARRIET L. The effect of environmental stimulation upon social and exploratory behaviour in the human infant. In: B. M. Foss, editor, *Determinants of Infant Behaviour.* New York: Wiley, 1961. 143–177.

RIMLAND, BERNARD. *Infantile Autism: The Syndrome and Its Implications for a Neural Theory of Behavior.* New York: Appleton-Century-Crofts, 1964.

ROLLMAN-BRANCH, HILDA S. On the question of primary need. *Journal of the American Psychoanalysis Association,* 1960, **8,** 686–702.

SALK, LEE. Mother's heartbeat as an imprinting stimulus. *Transactions of the New York Academy of Sciences,* Series II, 1962, **24,** 753–763.

SALZEN, ERIC A. Discussion. *Science and Psychoanalysis,* 1968, **12,** 184–189.

SAUL, LEON J., and WENAR, SOLVEIG. Early influences on development and disorders of personality. *Psychoanalytic Quarterly,* 1965, **3,** 327–389.

SCHAFFER, H. RUDOLPH. Some issues for research in the study of attachment behaviour. In: B. M. Foss, editor, *Determinants of Infant Behaviour II.* Second Tavistock seminar on mother-infant interaction, London, 1961. New York: Wiley, 1963. 179–199.

SCOTT, JOHN P. Critical periods in the development of social behavior in puppies. *Psychosomatic Medicine,* 1958, **20,** 42–54.

SCOTT, JOHN P. The process of primary socialization in canine and human infants. *Monographs of the Society for Research in Child Development*, 1963, **28**, No. 1, 1–47.

SHIPLEY, W. U. The demonstration in the domestic guinea pig of a process resembling classical imprinting. *Animal Behaviour*, 1963, **11**, 470–474.

SLUCKIN, WLADYSLAW. Imprinting in guinea pigs. *Nature*, 1968, **220**, 1148.

SMITH, F. V. Instinct and learning in the attachment of lamb and ewe. *Animal Behaviour*, 1965, **13**, 84–86.

SPEMANN, HANS. *Embryonic Development and Induction*. New Haven: Yale University Press, 1938.

SPIEGEL, H. Imprinting, hypnotizability, and learning in the psychotherapeutic process. *American Journal of Clinical Hypnosis*, 1965, **7**, 221–225.

SPITZ, RENÉ A. Anxiety in infancy: A study of its manifestations in the first year of life. *International Journal of Psychoanalysis*, 1950, **21**, 138–143.

SPITZ, RENÉ A. *A Genetic Field Theory of Ego Formation: Its Implications for Pathology*. New York: International Universities Press, 1959.

SPITZ, RENÉ A. *The First Year of Life. A Psychoanalytic Study of Normal and Deviant Development of Object Relations*. In collaboration with W. Geoffrey Cobliner. New York: International Universities Press, 1965.

SUTHERLAND, J. D. The concepts of imprinting and critical period from a psycho-analytic viewpoint. In: B. M. Foss, editor, *Determinants of Infant Behaviour II*. Second Tavistock seminar on mother-infant interaction, London, 1961. New York: Wiley, 1963.

TAKETOMO, YASUHIKO. The application of imprinting to psychodynamics. *Science and Psychoanalysis*, 1968, **12**, 166–183.

THORPE, WILLIAM H. *Learning and Instinct in Animals*. London: Methuen, 1956.

TINBERGEN, NIKO. *The Study of Instinct*. Oxford: Clarendon Press, 1951.

WILSON, JERE P. Nursing experience and the social smile. Unpublished doctoral dissertation, The University of Chicago, 1963.

WOLFF, PETER H. Critical periods in cognitive development. *Hospital Practice*, 1970, **5**, No. 11, 77–87.

YARROW, LEON J. Maternal deprivation: Toward an empirical and conceptual re-evaluation. *Psychological Bulletin*, 1961, **58**, 459–490.

YARROW, LEON J. Separation from parents during early childhood. *Review of Child Development Research*, 1964, **1**, 89–136.

YARROW, LEON J. Conceptual perspectives on the early environment. *Journal of the American Academy of Child Psychiatry*, 1965, **4**, 168–187.

7

Theoretical
Interpretations
of Imprinting

We began our own explorations in imprinting in the context of the primary formation of social attachments in precocial birds. Not long ago (Hess, 1962a) we defined imprinting as "the primary formation of social bonds in infant animals." Now, however, we no longer regard imprinting as simply primary socialization. Rather, we see imprinting as a particular type of learning process—that is, a tool (in the same sense as eating or breathing are tools), which may be used by a species for the formation of a filial-maternal bond, pair formation, environment attachment, food preferences, and perhaps other cases involving some sort of object-response relationship. It is, furthermore, a genetically programmed learning, with some species-specific constraints upon the kind of object that may be learned and upon the time of learning. In other words imprinting is a genotype-dependent ontogenetic process.

In line with our position, then, we believe in viewing imprinting in its evolutionary context and in terms of the survival function which it serves for a given species. This, of course, is the basis of the ethological approach to the study of behavior.

By focusing on the *process* of imprinting in this larger view, it becomes essential to determine the basic features of the process in distinction to the secondary features entailed by the specific situation to which imprinting has been applied by the observed species. While Thorpe (1961a, b) and others such as Poulsen (1951) have spoken of imprinting in cases other than primary socialization, theorizing on the nature of imprinting as a behavioral process apart from a specific context has not yet really emerged. In fact, it may be said that except for Thorpe (1961a, b), Hess (1964) has come the closest to this, through considering the common features of social and food imprinting in chicks. Thorpe (1961a, b), on the other hand, suggested a kinship between the imprinting process and those underlying circadian and other biological clocks. Poulsen (1951) was the first to suggest that chicks become imprinted to food objects—that is, in order for chicks to eat food, they must attach the characteristics of food objects as permanent releasers of pecking and eating behavior.

Most theorizing on imprinting has been based upon primary socialization or laboratory imprinting experiences in certain precocial bird species, and therefore are really theories upon this socialization rather than upon imprinting as a specific type of learning process. Such theorizing can be hampered by a confusion between the process of imprinting and the specific tools used in the service of the process. Following behavior, for example, indubitably is independent of imprinting, yet there are those who regard its every occurrence as a gospel indicator of imprinting. Such researchers, therefore, have theories of following behavior rather than of imprinting. One writer—Salzen (1970)—has echoed our feelings in declaring that "imprinting is commonly misconceived as the eliciting of the following response or as the acquisition of a response. . . . [Rather], imprinting is a process of goal or object acquisition and *not* response acquisition."

A theoretical interpretation of imprinting is handicapped at the outset by the fact that not only do people have very different concepts as to what imprinting is but also, as a consequence, they differ as to what facts they consider to be relevant to the consideration of any imprinting phenomenon. Under such circumstances, attempting to theorize on the nature of imprinting can automatically put one in a double bind. While all processes of animal behavior should be studied without prior preconceptions which will have the Procrustean effect of determining what is observed, investigators often are unable to do this. The study of imprinting is no exception. It is certainly true that the desire to find an all-encompassing unity in natural phenomena tends to preclude the observation of incongruent factors. The weltanschauung of the observer tends to make him see more of the same; any deviations from the known order can easily be suppressed, intentionally or unintentionally. Analogously, we do not really 'see" the retinal images that are produced by stimulation from the external world. For example, although we usually receive elliptical retinal images of a given disk, we have the apparent experience of seeing a perfectly circular shape the entire time.

Certainly, we all agree that behavioral scientists are devoted to the discovery of the truth. But at the same time, most of us begin our search with very strong opinions as to what the truth is or how it should be obtained. We are immersed in our own scientific "cultures," which have their own sets of beliefs and sanctions.

We have mentioned earlier (Chapter 1) the confrontation between the European proponents of ethological methods in the study of animal behavior and the United States adherents to behavioristic methods. The opposition between these two methods has been particularly apparent in the social imprinting phenomenon. It is not that we are claiming that there is any degree of unanimity between all behaviorists and between all ethologists with respect to theoretical conceptualizations on imprinting. Rather, our main point is to stress that there is a considerable polarity between the two approaches, which has resulted in the gathering of very different experimental data on the social imprinting phenomenon. This immensely wide range of data is certainly apparent from our review of imprinting and socialization in birds (Chapters 3 and 4). In a large number of cases, differences in species and differences in experimental techniques serve to make the body of data very heterogenous indeed, and also highly fragmentary. If we were to take any two studies of social imprinting at random, there would be a good chance of their data not being comparable because of these factors which we have cited.

Experimental design, as we all know, is very much influenced by the experimenter's "culture." Early social behavior is sufficiently multifaceted so as to be capable of supporting a wide variety of conflicting theories on the basis of a judicial selection of facts and specific experimental design. It is quite easy, for example, for an experimenter who does not believe in the existence of a sensitive period for imprinting to design an investigation in which animals are exposed or tested at a large number of different ages except the specific sensitive age. This can be done, may we add, without *any* conscious bias on the part of the investigator. Since under such conditions the experimenter obtains no age-related differences, he then will conclude that there are no sensitive periods for imprinting. There are, we know, other behavioral processes for which sensitive periods may easily be overlooked. An example is infantile handling of rats.

Similarly, the belief that imprinting constitutes conventional association learning of the parent by the young animal can cause an experimenter not only to use animals which are past the critical age period but also to do such things as exposing them for several daily sessions before making any tests of the effects of the exposure. In our own view, imprinting may not be at all involved under such circumstances but, rather, habituation of fear behavior through incremental conditioning. In our opinion, true social imprinting normally takes place only during the critical age period between hatchlings and their own parent in natural conditions, and ordinary association learning processes are much more likely to be operant in the socialization experiences of a young animal past the critical period.

In this chapter, then, we will, first, consider theoretical interpretations of social imprinting, and then, turn to the theoretical implications of regarding imprinting as a genetically programmed learning process applicable to several different kinds of situations, existing in a wide range of animal species, and thus possibly phylogenetically very old.

SOCIAL IMPRINTING

Lorenz's (1935) notion that there is a limited period of greater sensitivity to an imprinting experience in the formation of social bonds has held up rather well over the years. However, the specific limits of the sensitive or critical period for social imprinting for a given species have not always been agreed upon, primarily because of methodological or ideological differences between researchers. The very concept that an investigator holds with respect to what social imprinting is consequently controls both whether he will find the critical or sensitive period as well as its temporal limits, if it is at all apparent to him.

Related to the question of the placement of a critical period for social imprinting is that of what the processes may be that contribute to the ending of the ability to imprint to a social object. While several suggestions have been made along this line, it still is not known what are the precise *causative* factors resulting in the termination of the sensitive period for social imprinting. One correlative factor is that once social imprinting has taken place, exposure to a new object becomes less likely to result in the development of an imprinted attachment to that object. Another is that as the animals become older, there is an increasing incidence of fear behavior upon exposure to strange objects, whether the animals have been previously imprinted or not. These two factors have been considered by various authors as possible inhibitors of social imprinting.

However, it is also possible that a positive motivation leading to social imprinting susceptibility wanes, either as a result of actual imprinting having taken place or with increased age. With such waning motivation, fear behavior may then arise and replace the earlier tendencies. Ultimately, the questions regarding the onset and termination of the sensitive period may require neurophysiological and biochemical studies before any definitive answers may be obtained.

Lorenz's (1935) postulate, that the object to which filial behavior comes to be directed through social imprinting never is forgotten, has led to considerable disagreement through divergent interpretations of the term "irreversibility." Normally, for example, young birds will follow the parent object less and less as they achieve increasing autonomy. This fact, thought some, mediated against the idea of the irreversibility of imprinting. However, in Lorenz's terms, it does not, particularly since he did not consider social imprinting solely with respect to actual following of the maternal object or solely with respect to maternal attachment.

Another observable fact leading to doubt, in the minds of some, of the irreversibility of social imprinting as well as of the sensitive period was that young birds very often can be trained to follow other objects after having already been imprinted to a particular non-conspecific social object or at a relatively advanced age in socially naïve subjects. Such training, however, usually involves considerably more experience than is sufficient during the sensitive period itself. Furthermore, the following of new objects does not necessarily mean that the old object will no longer be followed. It has, for example, been observed in many cases that thoroughly imprinted young can be transferred away from the company of the imprinted social object and kept in the exclusive company of other objects without ever developing mature social responses to the new objects. Hess (1959a), for example, owned a red jungle fowl cock who persisted courting humans despite long—considerably longer than that originally with humans—experience with conspecific hens, which he utterly ignored.

While it is true that the newly hatched chick or duckling does not perform adult sexual behavior, the postulated relationship between filial imprinting and adult sexual object choice cannot be considered an impossibility, since it has been demonstrated in several species that some motoric components of adult sexual behavior are performed by the very young. For example, Andrew (1966) has observed contact behavior and climbing (mounting) in chicks less than 1 day old. He also found that pelvic thrusts can be elicited in the chick of this age when it is highly excited. These juvenile copulatory movements, however, occur independently of imprinting, since they are still found in 1-week-old socially isolated chicks. Andrew also observed "titbitting," an element of adult courtship behavior, in newly hatched chicks, in the form of ground pecking performed when near a stationary imprinting object. Bambridge's (1962) study also shows that precociously induced sexual behavior is directed toward the imprinting object. Furthermore, in at least one species—the turkey—pharmacological induction of precocial sexual behavior is unnecessary. Schulman (1970) has reported initial sexual struts performed by laboratory-imprinted 12-day old male poults toward the laboratory imprinting objects. These initial struts were performed just before the poults began following the imprinting object. In addition, Schleidt (1970) has confirmed that these strut postures are normally performed by group-reared male and female turkey poults toward siblings and the hen or substitute guardian. Male poults perform them much more frequently than the females, and after the age of 100 days, there is a very large increase in the frequency of the struts among the males.

Although social imprinting so clearly occurs, particularly in natural conditions between hatchlings and their own parent, there has been relatively little unanimity of thought regarding the nature of the underlying mechanism of this imprinting. At least three clearly identifiable viewpoints (with, of course, some overlap between them as well as distinct schools within each) can be described: 1) social imprinting as a process differing in some fundamental respects from other learning processes, particularly when occurring in actual natural conditions, as we ourselves believe; 2) social imprinting as a process having features derived from the sensory inexperience of the animal and constituting a perceptual-exposure learning phenomenon; and 3) social imprinting as a process fundamentally similar to other learning processes. These latter two theoretical positions have been built upon evidence obtained by studies of the laboratory imprinting process.

The Type 3 Imprinting Theory

The type 3 theory is at nearly opposite poles from the type 1 theory, particularly because of its insistence upon disavowing the concept of a genetically programmed learning process differing from other learning processes which are not as obviously genetically programmed. While the type 3 theory may agree to the existence of a genetically programmed sensitivity or arousability to environmental influences, it denies that there are any special classes of sensory events related exclusively to the elicitation of affiliative behavior or that there are any specific neurosensory mechanisms related to social imprinting.

The principal proponent of the type 3 theory is Howard Moltz (1960, 1963), who has treated the imprinting process from an epigenetic viewpoint (see Chapter 1 for a description of the epigenetic philosophy). It is, however, part of a larger mainstream which has conceived of the imprinting process as primarily identical with the association learning process commonly seen in laboratory experiments involving primary reinforcement factors and discrimination learning. Verplanck (1955), for example, provided a rather clear example of this type of thinking. He regarded imprinting as "simple S-R learning occurring under somewhat special circumstances." The phrase "special circumstances" foreshadows the type 2 theory, as we shall see. According to Verplanck's formulation, the young animal has an initial weak tendency (the source of which, however, is unidentified) to follow moving objects; this tendency is strengthened by repetition of the behavior. The exclusion of other objects as elicitors of such behavior is sequentially accomplished through the appearance of a "species-specific tendency to fear and to escape" from new objects even though of the same class of those initially potentially capable of eliciting following behavior. The original object followed continues to be followed through a "transfer phenomenon called proactive inhibition in other contexts."

Steven (1955) provided still another example of the association learning interpretation of imprinting. He found that through taming a wild gosling which was habituated to humans to the extent that it would follow them around. He regarded this as showing a "relation between imprinting and the process of habituation," since he thought that the gosling's imprinting had been transferred to the human being and away from the wild parents.

We can see that the notion of association learning in the sense of discrimination which emerges through repeated experience with the relevant object influenced the way in which many social imprinting experiments were designed. Some early investigators, for example, used commercially hatched subjects instead of laboratory-hatched ones, so that the exact ages of the experimental subjects were not known. Exposures to the social object commonly were repeated over a period of days, in congruence with the usual discrimination learning paradigm.

A series of experiments by Jaynes (1956, 1957, 1958a, b) illustrates such an approach to the study of social imprinting. While Jaynes held the opinion that innate behaviors were involved in the affiliative actions of neonatal chicks toward parental surrogates, that there were innate preferences for object qualities, and that there is a critical period for acquiring filial responsiveness, his method of studying imprinting involved giving exposure sessions each day over the first 4 days of life and then giving "retention sessions" to test for the imprinting. He concluded that imprinting is a positive function of practice, and that its retention is a function of neonatal practice. The discrimination of the imprinting object was thought to "emerge" through extended experience with the familiar and strange social objects. This, however, occurred even in the absence of any apparent differential reward, according to Jaynes.

Moltz, the main supporter of the type 3 theory of social imprinting has not been so much concerned with the *process* or mechanism of imprinting as with the *following response* and thus his theory is essentially a theory of following behavior. He used the term "imprinting" to denote "the procedure of visually presenting to an animal a large moving object during the first several hours of its life under conditions that insure that the object is not associated with such conventional reinforcing agents as food or water" (Moltz, 1960, p. 294). Moltz's measurement of the effects of this procedure has been in terms of amount of following behavior.

Thus, by focusing on the following response itself, rather than on the *process of filial attachment*, Moltz moved his inquiry to a different area even though he maintained the use of the term "imprinting." It is important to remember, then, that the differences between Moltz's position and those of other researchers can be largely semantic.

This semantic difference is not purely arbitrary on Moltz's part; it derives from his epigenetic viewpoint regarding behavioral processes. In the epigenetic viewpoint, all species-typic response patterns are thought to arise from the "integrative influence on the development of both intraorganic processes and extrinsic stimulative conditions" (Moltz, 1963, p. 125). In other words, the behavior patterns involved in social imprinting are regarded as "organized during ontogeny through the progressive interaction between the developing organism and its sensory environment" (Moltz, 1963, p. 125). Moltz has opposed such notions to ones regarding imprinting as having instinctive elements which are directly and specifically provided for through genetic factors expressed during the growth process itself.

Since following behavior, a tool which can be used for the social imprinting process in some species, can be exhibited independently of imprinting, and may be elicited through conventional training procedures or habituation, the question of genetically programmed learning of the parent and filial attachment, as reflected or as expressed in, for example, following behavior, is essentially avoided by Moltz.

The avoidance of the problem of genetically programmed elements in the behavior observable in precocial birds during the initial social imprinting exposure on the 1st day of life is evident in still other ways in Moltz's scheme. While Lorenz (1935) and other ethologically oriented researchers on social imprinting have agreed that the initial following behavior during the process of filiative attachment is released by the characteristics of the social object through an endogenous, genetically based, and selective mechanism, Moltz disavowed this entirely. Instead, he preferred to relate the development and organization of the following response to processes and events in ontogeny. Since the motor acts of following are morphologically complete upon hatching in precocial chicks and ducklings, Moltz's position would require an investigation of embryonic behavior, as he himself admits.

Therefore, to explain why following occurs toward a parent object as a result of a laboratory imprinting exposure, Moltz (1960) pointed to the fact that for a time after hatching young precocial birds do not show as high a degree of emotionality as they do at a later time. Moltz suggested that as a result of seeing a potential parent surrogate, an attention-provoking object, at the same time that there is a low anxiety drive, "the object acquires the capacity to elicit certain autonomically controlled components of the drive state" (Moltz, 1960, p. 304). As a result of this conditioning, Moltz deducted, the object acquires the capacity to function as a reinforcer, and therefore becomes capable of mediating new learning. At later ages, the young bird has achieved greater locomotor skills and is more capable of exploring and attending to features of the environment. Earlier, only the imprinting object appears to elicit consistent attention on the part of the young bird, according to Moltz, but at the later time, a larger number of environmental components can do so, with the result that anxiety is aroused. Then the bird follows the object as a means of reducing this anxiety. In line with this notion, Moltz (1960) predicted that irrespective of age, the simultaneous occurrence of a low anxiety drive (tranquilizer-induced) and a visually dominant (but unfamiliar) object will result in a vigorous following of that object if anxiety (induced through shock or novel stimuli) is subsequently aroused in its presence. A study by Hoffman et al. (1968), while concluding that ducklings *do* innately have a disposition to emit filial responses, has supported the notion that the imprinting object *does* function to reduce arousal in hatchlings. A study by Bateson (1969) has voiced similar ideas: wild mallard ducklings kept individually in black and white striped boxes exhibited less moving around than did ones kept individually in dull gray boxes, and that birds being exposed to a "conspicuous" training object decreased their distress calling when they were permitted to be in the company of the object. If they were not allowed to be with the object, then they went about the enclosure in a random fashion.

However, Moltz's theory regarding imprinting as "essentially a classical-instrumental conditioning sequence centering on the arousal and reduction of emotionality" (Moltz, 1963, p. 125) has severe limitations, as he himself (Moltz, 1963) acknowledged in the later paper. Principally, young chicks or ducks may be found to *approach* an object at a stage when its characteristics have not yet been learned and little or no signs of anxiety are manifest. Thus, Moltz modified his proposal in some respects. Impressed by Schneirla's (1959) scheme of approach and withdrawal behavior from an epigenetic viewpoint, Moltz elaborated his conceptualization of imprinting upon it.

As an initial point of departure in the modified scheme, Moltz noted that in a large number of cases experimental subjects will start to follow the imprinting object when it begins to move away. In addition, Moltz reported that he never had an instance in which the young bird began following an object as it *approached*. Such an observation has not been substantiated in chicks, since Schulman, Hale, and Graves (1970) found that chicks are more likely to move toward approaching imprinting objects than to follow retreating ones. (Of course, "following" is not even possible when an imprinting object approaches the young bird; the young bird can only "approach" if it moves toward the approaching model.) Therefore, Moltz suggested that the reduction of retinal innervation as a result of the decreasing stimulation from the receding object induces a particular constellation of visceral and cardiac events and incipient approach movements.

In connection with this, Moltz noted that Schneirla (1959) has proposed that early in development low intensity stimuli arouse approach processes in the animal. Schneirla assumed that the activation of A-processes through approach response is reinforcing; on the basis of this, the birds can rapidly learn to approach and follow low intensity visual stimuli. In this way, they learn the characteristics of the particular object to which they were oxposed, and come to search for it when it is absent.

Moltz seized upon Schneirla's concepts of stimulus intensity as a means of explaining differential effectiveness of different imprinting objects. (Interestingly, Schneirla (1965) later disagreed with some aspects of Moltz's theory.) Since Moltz preferred not to believe in the existence of any genetically patterned neural mechanisms corresponding more closely to certain stimulus configurations than to others with respect to the elicitation of differential following behavior, he then suggested that preferences in the characteristics of imprinting objects might be more closely related to the excitation of sensory elements in the bird's eye than to the excitation of some specific preformed neural pattern. As a consequence, Moltz (1963, p. 129) considered it "gratuitous to conceive of imprinting stimuli as comprising a special class of sensory events, uniquely related to the expression of filial behavior. . . . The stimuli eliciting this [filial] attachment seem neither to derive from any specific avian characteristics nor to activate any specific neurosensory mechanism related to imprinting as such."

This proposal has some similarity with one that has been made by Sackett (1963). The latter author suggested that the releaser functions involved in the evocation of fixed action patterns (such as locomotor coordinations in the laboratory imprinting situation) are organized and integrated by peripheral visual neural units, the retinal ganglion cells, which are sensitive to certain specific aspects of environmental stimulation. Thus, he considered it possible that fixed action patterns in response to visual releasers result from the evocation of activity in one or a combination of various stimulus-specific cell groups in the retina. The types of differentially responsive cells which he listed were with respect to: sustained edges; convex edges; changing contrasts; dimming; and darkness.

While Sackett's proposals may serve as a start in elucidating the nature of the neurological processes that determine visual preferences and visual releasers in animal behavior, including laboratory imprinting behavior in chicks or ducks, some of his specific suggestions as to what sorts of visual stimulation should be more effective actually do not fit some of the extant data on preferences (e.g., Klopfer, 1967b). Furthermore, Sackett also proposed differential maturation of the different types of retinal ganglion cells as an explanation of the sensitive period for imprinting. Specifically in the case of imprinting, Sackett thought that the maturation of cells sensitive to movement could be primarily responsible for the onset of the sensitive period. Movement, he thought, would be perceived for the first time at some hours after hatching, and stand out in great temporal distinctiveness to visual stimulation perceived prior to maturation of these cells.

However, it has never seemed to us that the young chick or duckling does not perceive movement during its first hours. It can make considerable and rather obvious efforts to approach a parent object, even though its locomotor capacity is not fully functional (despite the morphological completeness of the movement pattern). Also, it may be noted in passing that Sackett's theory does not account for the sensitive period in the learning of *food* objects by young chicks, a process which can involve visual preferences just as much as social imprinting does, because the *same* innate preferences are shown before and after the sensitive period for food imprinting when the imprinted food object is absent (Goodwin and Hess, 1969a).

As for Moltz (1960), his specific suggestion was that the degree of flicker from a laboratory imprinting object might be related to the extent to which an animal orients to it and also to the probability of the object's dominating the environment. Later, Moltz (1963) suggested that there might be an inverted U function of effectiveness of relevant parameters of each stimulus class applicable to the characteristics of the imprinting object.

In considering the question of the critical period for initiating attachment to the imprinting stimulus, Moltz (1963, p. 130) suggested that

> For each vertebrate form there is a period of development during which behavioral arousal is largely or exclusively determined by stimulus intensity and, moreover, that this period is non-recurrent, terminating early in ontogeny as the animal's perceptual environment expands to permit greater

specificity of afferent control, as associative learning enters to modify previous behavioral adjustments, and, most likely, as maturation of the nervous system selectively changes neural excitatory thresholds to facilitiate more precise sensory-motor integration.

In this statement we see an area of some overlap with the type 2 theory of imprinting, since specific sensory sensitivity is postulated as accounting for the period of sensitivity to a laboratory imprinting exposure. However, while this statement concedes the existence of a sensitive period for social imprinting, it does not provide an explanation of the temporally distinct critical periods for food imprinting shown in the laboratory.

Moltz (1963) has proposed that the processes maintaining the performance of following, and therefore attachment, to the imprinting object are different from those that were responsible for the original elicitation. These processes, he suggested, might well be those of selective learning, with fear reduction functioning as the reinforcing agent. This, it must be noted, is a somewhat different proposition from the type 1 postulation that following or attachment behavior elicited after the critical period for imprinting is really due to conventional association learning processes, whereas the imprinting processes during the critical period itself are not. Rather, the type 1 theory maintains that when an animal has been imprinted to an object, that object continues to act as a releaser of affiliative behavior, while other objects have lost this function for that animal and can elicit such behaviors only through habitutation and regular learning processes.

Schneirla's (1965) critique of Moltz's theory expressed the view that anxiety reduction had not been shown to be a *necessary* factor in imprinting. He preferred to view *approach* systems as being the necessary factor and to view withdrawal systems as secondary. He noted that while withdrawal processes do not occur as early as approach processes in ontogeny, such withdrawal processes to strange objects could also act to facilitate approach processes with respect to familiar objects.

The Type 2 Imprinting Theory

Now we shall turn to a consideration of type 2 theories, which essentially seek an understanding of imprinting as a function of the context in which it occurs—that is, in terms of the young animal's sensory inexperience. As early as 1955, Thorpe stated that imprinting was "very rapid unrewarded perceptual learning." Smith (1962a) explicitly assumed that "imprinting involves a process of selection or discrimination." But he did not make an analysis of this notion.

Hinde (1961, 1962a, b, 1963) was apparently the first to develop in any detail the idea of perceptual learning as comprising the nature of social imprinting, although Ewer (1956) and Dilger and Johnsgard (1959) made earlier suggestions in this direction. Hinde's position was that the young bird at the time of hatching does not have size or pattern constancy, because of its visual inexperience. "The parent may appear in many shapes, sizes and even colours according to its posture, distance, background and the light conditions." Thus, it would be adaptive for the young bird to be able to respond to a wide range of stimuli.

This is similar to Ewer's (1956) suggestion that imprinting might "be a sort of evolutionary concession to the imperfectly developed sensory capacities of the newly born or hatched young." Dilger and Johnsgard (1959), on the other hand, pointed out:

> If the critical features of the normal environment which make up the Umwelt for each species, are rather rigid and "predictable" then the animal can "afford" to have its responses "built-in," so to speak, in a rigid manner exemplified by the common releaser-sign stimulus-RM type of response. If, on the other hand, the animal's Umwelt is a rather plastic one in any regard, then the responses to this type of situation are likely to be learned in some fashion.

Later, in discussing our own theory with regard to the phylogenetic status of imprinting, we will have a few comments regarding our appraisal of Hinde's (1962a, b) and Ewer's (1956) suggestion that imprinting is based upon sensory imperfection on the part of the animal undergoing imprinting.

Hinde contended that the establishment of the mother-offspring relation in birds as manifest in the social imprinting process does not involve a special form of learning, and that the observed characteristics are different only in degree from those of other forms of instinctive behavior. Thus, while, like type 3 theorists, Hinde specifically disavows the notion of the uniqueness of imprinting, he has not done this on the grounds of rejection of the notion of a genetically programmed provision for the occurrence of this type of learning, as Moltz has done. In fact, Hinde stated that "the degree of specificity in responsiveness thus seems to have been selected for in evolution, the optimum varying with the behavior in question." In other words, Hinde admits the notion that there are innately determined stimulus preferences in imprinting, rather than merely that there is a nonrecurrent period early in ontogeny during which behavioral arousal is principally influenced by stimulus intensity, as Moltz has.

Hinde's main point, therefore, was that "thus most authors (including Lorenz, personal communication) now agree that imprinting is peculiar only by virtue of its context and consequences and cannot be regarded as a distinct form of learning." He did not consider that Hess (1959a, c) had proven that imprinting is a special form of learning, and claimed either lack of evidence or an obscurity of the relevance of Hess' specific points with regard to this question.

The context which Hinde (1962a, b, 1963) considered was with respect to the concomitant features occurring in the natural situation as well as in the laboratory itself. Such features included the correlation between perceptual and motor abilities (relevant for the fixation and following of the object) with the beginning of the sensitive period for imprinting, the role of fear, decreased following tendency, or possible incompatible responses such as searching for lost companions (applicable only in the case of chicks previously socialized to siblings or to some other social object) with the ending of the sensitive period, and the positive consequence of the imprinting experience.

The perceptual aspect of the social imprinting phenomenon was a factor that particularly engaged Hinde's (1961, 1962a, b) attention. He pointed to certain similarities between studies of the effects of early perceptual experience upon later behavior, specifically the enhancing value of the "attention-getting" properties of the stimuli to which the young animals are exposed. In his opinion, the relationship between perception and motivation deserved very careful consideration as the basis for an interacting system in the behavioral development of the young bird. Furthermore, it intrigued him that while adult birds can

> respond appropriately even to particular postures of their own species on the first occasion that they see them, young nidifugous birds often have only a very generalised responsiveness to the characteristics of their own species. . . . Is it possible that the recognition of a complex pattern, such as that displayed even by specific releasing structures on the parent bird, would require too complex a mechanism until powers of size and distance constancy have been acquired?

Hinde (1963), furthermore, stated his belief that there are particular sensitive periods for specific responses—that is, each response has its own distinct sensitive period in which it is learned. Also, Hinde distinguished between sensitive periods for learning response X which are critical for the subsequent performance of response X and sensitive periods for learning response X which are critical for the subsequent performance of response Y.

Unlike the proponents of the type 1 theory, Hinde (1962a, b, 1963) did not believe that imprinting could be regarded as a type of learning process available for application to different situations. He thought that even if one can legitimately ask whether learning occurring in these other contexts shares characteristics with classical imprinting, it is not useful to ask whether or not such learning is imprinting. He felt this because natural selection forces can result in convergent behavior mechanisms. Therefore, Hinde (1963) concluded that "superficial comparisons" made between these specific cases occurring in different species are nothing more than pointers for analysis—they should not lead us to believe that they rely on similar mechanisms.

Certainly, we ourselves are in perfect agreement with the necessity for exercising every caution in making comparisons between different species: In fact, this notion has served as one of our own cardinal guiding principles. We have, however, come to the conclusion that imprinting is a type of learning process which can serve as a behavioral tool in different contexts and in different species. We differ from Hinde in that we believe that selection may possibly call forth the same learning tool for specific situations in different species, even though the necessities for dealing with these specific situations probably have arisen convergently.

Bateson (1966) has presented an elaboration of the theoretical relationship between perception and social imprinting. In contrast to the type 1 notion that imprinting represents a specific type of learning process, Bateson offers the view that the observed characteristics of social imprinting are determined by the situation in which this learning occurs. This viewpoint, Bateson believes, is more parsimonious and more capable of analysis than is the type 1 theory of uniqueness of imprinting and also has stronger experimental foundation.

The unique situation in which social imprinting occurs, according to Bateson, lies in the fact that the young birds have had rather limited experience and have been subjected to few changes in sensory input. The selective responsiveness exhibited toward aspects of the environment derive from relatively simple preferences. These initially broad preferences, generally for "conspicuous" objects, are restricted by experience (in a sense similar to Jaynes' 1958b notion of "emergent discrimination"): the structuring and refining of preferences through the learning occurring during imprinting markedly affect the responses of the animal to novel stimuli. This is because, even though the processes of information acquisition may not change, the kind of information that is acquired by means of such processes is influenced by the animal's past experience. For example, there is less interference from previously established preferences and habits when learning occurs early in the life cycle, making the preferences then established likely to develop more rapidly and be more stable than those formed at a later time. In other words, Bateson has a more or less "foundational" viewpoint regarding the early development of behavior and perceptual capacities.

While Schneirla (1959) took the position that low intensity stimulation elicits approach and high intensity stimulation provokes withdrawal, Bateson (1966) has argued that the behavioral organization of the young precocial bird at the time of hatching is much greater than such a notion presupposes. Bateson proposed that "rather than passively filtering and classifying their input young birds actively search for a certain class of stimuli." This type of "searching" is thought of as in the cybernetic sense, and is typical of the "appetitive behaviors" described by ethologists. When a member of this class of stimuli is encountered by a young bird, the responses are directed toward it and the bird begins to learn its specific characteristics.

This learning process, furthermore, was considered by Bateson to be based primarily upon *length* of visual contact with the object in question. Rather than expenditure of effort as a crucial factor in influencing the effectiveness of the imprinting experience, as Hess (1957, 1959c) has postulated (type 1), Bateson believed that the amount of visual experience represents a simpler explanation of Hess' results on the relationships between distance of following or struggling to be near the imprinting object and degree of imprinting as evidenced in a later free choice test. However, Bateson did not entirely discard the notion that effort per se could have a positive influence on the imprinting process, since Lewis (1964) has reported that the more an animal works for a reward in the course of habit acquisition, the less readily is that habit removed through extinction procedures.

The limits of the sensitive or critical period for social imprinting should not be thought of as solely the results of invariant maturational processes, according to Bateson, (1969), but also as influenced by the conditions under which the birds are reared. The role of developmental processes in setting the *beginning* of the sensitive period, as indicated by Gottlieb's (1961a, 1963d, e) experimental results, was considered by Bateson to be the largely responsible factor. Since there appear to be several behavioral changes correlated with the sensitive period for imprinting, Bateson (1966) has favored the investigation of the possibility that developmental changes in the organization of retinal process, as proposed by Sackett (1963), could possibly account for the beginning of the critical period for imprinting. We have already discussed the limitations of Sackett's theory earlier in this chapter.

With respect to the *ending* of the critical period for imprinting, Bateson (1966, 1969) has argued that, also in this case, the notion of purely endogenous changes in motivation is inadequate, because the length of the sensitive periods appears to be affected by rearing experience. Among factors affecting the ending of the sensitive period were thought to be prior social experience with siblings, diffuse versus patterned light experience, and complexity, or "conspicuousness," of the patterned environment. The relationship between unfamiliarity and fear, as pointed out by Hebb (1946), Bindra (1959), and Guiton (1959), appeared to Bateson as a highly relevant factor in the ending of imprintability. In fact, he concluded that one of the causes of the end of the sensitive period "is undoubtedly that the birds learn the characteristics of the environment in which they are reared and avoid dissimilar objects" (1966). Fear, therefore, comes about because of prior learning, and it is this prior learning which can prevent later learning, in Bateson's scheme, rather than that fear tendencies as such hinder the learning. In a similar sense, also, the process of imprinting itself serves to bring about its own end, since the imprinted object becomes a familiar object, and results in new objects being experienced as unfamiliar and hence feared. Bateson cited as a factor casting doubt on the validity of Schneirla's claim that the young bird possesses innate withdrawal tendencies to high intensity stimulation the frequent observation that the hatchling may not withdraw from new stimuli until after learning the characteristics of something else. Schneirla (1965), however, has pointed out that withdrawal responses do not appear as early as do approach responses in hatchling chickens and ducks.

Bateson (1969, 1970) has also emphasized the very active role that is taken by the young chick or duckling in the social imprinting process. Young birds that have not yet been imprinted can be found to be appetitively "searching" for an appropriate object. In support of this, Bateson (1969) cited the fact that birds reared in boxes with conspicuous walls are quieter than those reared in boxes with plain walls, just as imprinted birds walk about disorientedly when the imprinting object is missing, and becomes quiet and contented when the imprinting object is present. The imprinting object thus functions as a constellation of consummatory stimuli for the appetitive searching behavior, and this consummatory function is further indicated by experiments that demonstrate that the imprinting object can easily be used as a reinforcer of relatively arbitrarily chosen instrumental behavior such as stepping on a pedal (Bateson and Reese, 1968), just as Hoffman et al. (1970) have reinforced key pecking with the appearance of the imprinting object. This reinforcing property of the imprinting object or of the actual parent has been proposed by Bateson (1969) as being responsible for keeping the brood together.

In general, Bateson's theoretical position has been that the underlying bases of the critical period for imprinting are determined by at least two factors: developmental stage, and the opportunity for developing (that is, acquiring) a preference or attachment to some thing or to some aspect of the environment. He has proposed that the sensitive period in imprinting comes to an end when the birds have become

familiar with the sensory aspects of their surroundings and can discriminate between their surroundings and a laboratory imprinting
object. The end of the sensitive period does not, in his view, end the
process of imprinting, because the subjects normally proceed to learn
further sensory details of the object which they prefer (Bateson, 1970).
The characteristics of imprinting are not attributable to imprinting being
a special kind of learning, but derive from the situation in which imprinting occurs, according to Bateson (1969, 1970).

Another proponent of the type 2 theory of social imprinting is Sluckin
(1964, with Salzen, 1961), whose position was rather similar to that of
Bateson, differing principally in lesser theoretical points. Like Bateson,
Sluckin emphasized the relative lack of sensory experience in the young
bird at the normal time of the social imprinting experience and therefore the effect of the perceptual experiences during this period of high
sensitivity to the imprinting experience. The imprinting experience was
seen as consisting of a sharpening of discrimination between the object
presented and others. Thus, as did Bateson, Sluckin saw the young bird's
preferences as refined and structured through the social imprinting
experience. Furthermore, Sluckin (with Salzen, 1961) argued that fear
is not in itself the cause of the end of the sensitive or critical period for
imprinting, but that imprinting ends as a result of its own action through
increasing the selectivity of the animal's responses, particularly since
following tendencies can wane even though no fear is at all evident.
In fact, fear responses, thought Sluckin, themselves could be the result
of imprinting having occurred.

However, while Bateson attributed the characteristics of social imprinting primarily to the context in which it occurs, Sluckin did not go to
this extreme in denying inherent characteristics of social imprinting,
even though he did believe that there are many points in common between imprinting and other cases of learning. Such was indicated by
the fact that Sluckin (1964) stated, "While in some ways imprinting is
seen to be much more like other forms of learning, in other ways the
difference between imprinting-like learning and other learning is now
clearer and sharper." In fact, Sluckin suggested in a much later section
of his book: "Imprinting, as distinct from initial filial responses, cannot
be readily fitted into the framework of existing learning theory. Perhaps
the time is ripe for new theoretical formulations concerning both basic
motives and learning."

With this goal in mind, Sluckin introduced the notion of "exposure
learning" as relevant to the process of social imprinting. This exposure
learning, however, operates in social imprinting because of the particular
condition of the young bird that is only a few hours old. Exposure
learning, according to Sluckin, consists of perceptual registering of the

characteristics of the environment by the organism, a kind of absorption, so to speak, which results in the organism becoming familiar with its environment. Since the organism does lack a considerable background of prior sensory experience, its perceptual organs could have a particularly strong need or drive to function per se—that is, a "Funktionslust"—resulting in both a high degree of impressionability and consequently the development of the capacity to deal competently with the environment.

Together with this Sluckin considered the approach and following tendencies evident in the social imprinting of nidifugous birds as innate and primary drives, just as much as exploratory and manipulatory behaviors are based on primary drives rather than being acquired. These approach and following behaviors are considered as *released* by stimuli, in opposition to the type 3 theory. Through imprinting, then, some percepts come to acquire relatively permanent releaser value, according to Sluckin's theoretical system.

Social imprinting as a process has characteristics which differ to some extent from those possessed by other conditioning processes, according to Sluckin. For example, the imprinting object itself functions as both the unconditional stimulus and the conditional stimulus, since it is in itself a reinforcer of the behavior involved. What is more, the removal of the imprinting object does not necessarily result in extinction through removal of reinforcement, as is normally the case in instances of conditioning.

Nevertheless, Sluckin also emphasized that some characteristics of social imprinting can also be found in other learning situations. For example, there are sensitive periods for forms of learning other than social imprinting; social imprinting functions to alter the probability of the occurrence of specific behaviors, and this imprinting can vary in degree of thoroughness.

Some of the characteristics which have been proposed for social imprinting were disavowed by Sluckin. Social imprinting is not an instantaneous process, he felt, but rapidly incremental. He disagreed with Hess (1959a, c, 1964) about the question of primacy in imprinting and regarded punishment as an *extraneous* factor in imprinting rather than as an important aspect of it, as Hess has proposed.

While Sluckin conceded that there is no conclusive evidence that the capacity for imprinting can occur beyond the juvenile stage, he did not like ever to exclude any possibility of imprinting occurring in social learning at later ages, in opposition to the type 1 theory that imprinting as such cannot occur at all once the sensitive or critical period has passed. While Sluckin did agree that imprinting has a critical period which can be expressed in terms of developmental age, he pointed out that the length of the sensitive period appears to vary as a consequence of social rearing with siblings or visual experience such as reduction of sensory input.

Salzen (1962a, b, 1966, 1967, 1970), who has two published joint papers with Sluckin, concluded that, on the basis of the available evidence, "the recognition of imprinting as a distinct and peculiar phenomenon then becomes of doubtful value" (1966). In this sense, Salzen (1966) is closer to Bateson in denying uniqueness in imprinting than he is to Sluckin's position. In addition, Salzen (1968) has specifically aligned himself with the epigenetic viewpoint, thus making himself a type 2 theorist leaning toward type 3. Furthermore, he has deemphasized the critical period and the permanence of laboratory imprinting procedures (Salzen and Meyer, 1968).

While Salzen (1966) agreed that the stimulus object in social imprinting situations has innate releasing properties (with some objects better releasers than others), he also has enumerated three other factors which may operate in addition to the phenomenon of social imprinting and its effects on later social and sexual behavior. The first of these factors is the avoidance of strange objects via the disruption of established, persistent patterns of sensory input (the "neuronal models") by strange or unfamiliar patterns of sensation. This disruption releases previously inhibited neural processes of emotional behavior in the form of fear and avoidance responses. Such a suggestion is not very far removed from the cybernetic "search image" models mentioned by Bateson (1966), and is strongly similar to some of Schneirla's (1965) notions. At any rate, it is clear that in Salzen's (1966) view, social imprinting itself causes fear of strange objects, rather than fear arising independently of social imprinting and then preventing it.

The second factor which Salzen (1966) considered pertinent was that of stimulus satiation effects. In other words, strange stimuli which are repeatedly presented eventually fail to elicit fear responses, thus permitting positive behavior tendencies to appear. Finally, Salzen (1966) considered "social inertia" as the third factor in social imprinting. Because of such inertia, the animal may choose members of its own species as objects to which to direct adult sexual behavior simply because they were present at the time of the relevant learning, the earlier filial attachment processes having taken place.

In Salzen's (1966) scheme, the proposed neuronal hypothesis led him to suggest that familiarity of objects, whether acquired early or later in life, is an essential factor. Strange objects do not become familiar because the animal withdraws from them, and therein lies the basis of the irreversibility attributed to imprinting, Salzen (1966) proposed. Together with the social inertia factor, Salzen (1966) suggested, it would appear that deviant social and sexual behavior of an animal was due to early experience, whereas there is actually an interaction of different behavior phenomena. Salzen continued to emphasize the reversibility of laboratory imprinting procedures in further papers (e.g., Salzen and Meyer, 1968). However, Salzen's position does not yet adequately account for cases of early imprinting experience which have proved to have extremely persistent effects, such as was the case with the jungle fowl cock which was human-imprinted, then kept for many years in close contact with hens, and yet never in all these years courted hens, but directed sexual behavior exclusively to humans (Hess, 1964). In this case, the hens, even though familiar to the cock, still failed to elicit sexual behavior in him.

Furthermore, young chicks and ducklings normally begin to explore the environment and cease staying strictly with the mother object. In other words, the young animal does not spend its time thereafter constantly avoiding objects that are not familiar and thus withdrawing from them. Bateson (1969), for example, has pointed out that the phenomenon of avoiding strange objects that occurs as a consequence of the imprinting process does not continue indefinitely. "It looks very much as though exploration of the environment begins when imprinting has done its job and the young bird has established a firm bond with its mother," Bateson (1969, p. 285) has suggested. This is much the same conclusion we drew from Bjärvall's (1967) research, which demonstrated that the nest exodus normally takes place after the experimentally demonstrated critical period peak for social imprinting in mallard ducklings.

King (1966) has expressed ideas that are similar to Salzen's. He proposed two basic hypotheses: novel stimuli elicit fear response in both young and adult organisms, and certain stimuli which are always found in the person of the natural mother elicit pleasant feelings in the offspring. King further proposed that association of the mother with novel or fear-provoking stimuli can lead to the permanent reduction of fear toward such objects. Conversely, the mother normally takes the young away from dangerous objects so quickly that they never get a chance to become familiar with them, thought King. Thus, King appeared to rely more upon concepts of association learning and habituation of fear responses as an explanation of various aspects of the mother-infant relationship than upon concepts of innately based releasers of filial and fear responses.

Fabricius, one of the earliest researchers on imprinting, has evolved toward a type 2 position regarding the nature of imprinting. Although most of his earlier work was largely descriptive, he did state (1951a, b) at the outset that he did not believe that there were any essential differences between social imprinting and other learning processes in the sense that no hard-and-fast line could be drawn between them. In recent papers (Fabricius, 1962a, b, 1964; Kovach, Fabricius, and Fält, 1966), he has considered imprinting in relation to other types of learning processes and its perceptual learning component, as well as the interrelationships of factors in the natural situation.

Like other type 2 theorists, Fabricius nevertheless has not regarded the processes of social imprinting as identical with those of conventional learning. For example, Fabricius (1962b) did not consider the reinforcement in social imprinting as limited solely to conventional reward, but as possibly including "some specific brain activity elicited by the stimulus situation of keeping near the object that elicits the following response." In this connection, Fabricius also applied the classical ethological principle that the very performance of an instinctive action, rather than the result to which such an action leads, is in itself rewarding. Fabricius' 1966 paper with Kovach and Fält similarly calls attention to the fact that the imprinting process involves the formation of an association between a stimulus and a response. He specifies, however, that the attachment of a new response such as shock avoidance to the imprinted stimulus "does not follow the familiar additive and subtractive properties of S-R bond transfer."

Fabricius agreed that the following reaction during the imprinting experience, whether to siblings or to the parental object, is released by the imprinting stimulus acting as an innate sign stimulus. The innate sign stimuli for imprinting, however, are rather few and simple, with the function of imprinting being to supplement them with acquired, conditioned elements, so that the response becomes more selective. In addition, Fabricius regarded the appearance of fear or escape behavior as an important factor in the waning of the tendency of the young birds to respond to a potential imprinting object. However, he did not regard it as the only factor involved, since he felt that "there could be other factors as well, perhaps internally determined, which independently cause a decrease of the readiness for the following response. . . ." Examples of such factors were thought to include social experience, drug administration, in addition to the biological ones of growth and of maturation of certain responses.

Fabricius (1964) distinguished between following behavior and the imprinting process, between its sensitive period and its peak, the period of maximum imprintability.

In the Kovach, Fabricius, and Fält (1966) paper, the suggestion was made that the long-range effects of imprinting are based upon an acquisition process comparable to perceptual learning rather than upon a unique formation of "social bond," thus placing Fabricius and his associates squarely among the type 2 theorists. The perceptual acquisition, it was further suggested by these authors, may facilitate subsequent learning in which the original imprinting stimulus is involved, and may lead to social attachment under favorable conditions. In this connection, they proposed that the critical period in imprinting and, more specifically, the peak of sensitivity to the imprinting experience may play its role primarily through limiting the available range of the kind of responses upon which the acquisition process is based. Furthermore, these authors also pointed out that the imprinting experience in nature is provided by the very first sensory impression. This primacy of the received sensory impressions occurs when the organism's system is "experientially uncluttered," they noted. Again, this is a characteristic type 2 notion.

Nevertheless, Kovach, Fabricius, and Fält noted that their own data suggested that there are lasting effects from these first sensory impressions only if they are associated with a specific *response* on the part of the organism, as Klopfer and Hailman (1964a, b) have postulated. While Kovach et. al. did not comment on whether there appeared to be any relation between amount of effort, intensity of response, and the effectiveness of the experience, it would seem that in their view visual experience alone is not sufficient to promote the occurrence of imprinting, as Bateson's (1966) position would predict.

Another theorist that we will consider among the type 2 category is Klopfer, although several facets of his theory are of the type 1 category. However, since Klopfer has never taken the position that imprinting is a unique process, he is essentially a type 2 theorist. The closest Klopfer ever came to differentiating definitely between imprinting and other types of learning was when he stated (Klopfer, 1967a) that experiments involving prolonged exposure were unrelated to imprinting: "The kinds of preferences developing from longer term exposure are presumably capable of developing at any time in the animal's life and may be likened to the process of habituation or facilitation, that is, to conditioning. The consequence of the latter processes may indeed be indistinguishable from the consequences of imprinting, but this does not reflect a similarity in the mechanism itself." Similar thoughts were earlier (1964) expressed by Klopfer.

Since one or another of many of imprinting's features can be found in some other learning process, Klopfer (1961) asserted that the only factor possessed uniquely by the imprinting phenomenon was its temporal fixity as to when in the life of the animal it could occur.

One type 2 feature of Klopfer's theoretical position was that, as Klopfer and Hailman (1964a) postulated, imprinting, as a process, was considered to constitute the establishment of a stimulus preference rather than simply an intensification of following behavior, although these authors also were of the opinion that imprinting involves endowing an object with the capacity to elicit following behavior when it is present, so that the young animal will have greater occasion to perform directed following behavior. Klopfer (1967a), furthermore, has emphasized that the motor act of following is experimentally independent of the innately determined perceptual preferences for characteristics of parental surrogates. Like Hinde (1962b), Klopfer agreed that the existence of the imprinting process in phylogenetically disparate animals "might result from the similarity in the selective pressures which in certain situations favor rapid, stable, one-trial learning."

Choice between objects, and not merely following behavior, constituted the criterion which Klopfer chose to indicate imprinting to the object followed. Klopfer's own definition of imprinting, one which he constructed so as to "avoid a semantic quarrel," was as follows: "the development of a stable preference for an object or pattern as a consequence of a relatively brief exposure to that pattern" (Klopfer, 1964, p. 173). A further and "most important restriction is that the exposure must be effective only during a limited and specific developmental stage" (ibid).

As early as 1959, Klopfer stated his belief that although social imprinting is not absolutely different from other forms of learning, since it does not necessarily possess the extremely high level of stability that Lorenz (1935) had originally proposed, it nevertheless is restricted to a particular sensitive period, and is not effective unless the animal exerted itself to make a response to the object involved. Klopfer and Hailman (1964), while concluding that followers do show an effect of the imprinting experience and non-followers do not, also pointed out that they were not able to discern any direct function of the amount of initial following on subsequent choice or following. It may be pointed out also that Klopfer (1964, 1967a) has stated that following behavior and imprinting should not be confused with each other, because following does not necessarily result in social imprinting (a point which has been stressed by Polt and Hess, 1964, 1966), nor does imprinting depend absolutely on the elicitation of the following response.

Klopfer's zoological viewpoint is evident in his observations (1959b) regarding the so-called social facilitation of imprinting in naïve unimprinted ducklings that are led by a previously imprinted duckling, and the variability in individual members of a brood with respect to both the strength of response and the particular aspect of the proffered imprinting object which is responded to. The different responses learned by the individual ducklings, Klopfer suggested, could be advantageous together with the leadership principle. Klopfer also believed that while physical factors insure an association between parents and young in the case of altricial species, thus permitting a gradual learning of the characteristics of the parents, in precocial species factors which keep the young from separating or dispersing from the parents must be present either at birth or very soon thereafter. Of course, there are exceptions to each of these categories, with rapid learning or imprinting occurring among precocials and with innately established preferences for the parental object in some altricial species, according to Klopfer. It should, however, be kept in mind that there is an extremely limited period—the age of 8 days—which has been found to be decisive for the occurrence of imprinting in an altricial dove species, as found by Klinghammer (1962).

Klopfer (1959a) has further suggested that the process of behavioral evolution has involved shifting the establishment of responses to the parental object from a point before hatching to one after hatching, and entailing a rapid learning process. During further evolution and radiation, the time of the learning process could be shifted further in ontogeny or back to a point before emergence from the egg, Klopfer suggested. Klopfer thus introduced the concept that there may be several processes which are intermediate between imprinting and conventional learning, just as in a taxonomic group there may be forms intermediate to two morphologically disparate species and are spread between the two species as a morphological progression from one to the other. This is one of the ways in which Lorenz's 1955 remarks regarding the relationship between imprinting and other learning processes may be interpreted.

Consonant with such biological viewpoints, Klopfer (1962) has promoted the notion of species and breed differences in social imprinting, an emphasis which can be found also in Hess' (1959a, c) type 1 theory of social imprinting. As an example, Klopfer cited Gottlieb's (1961a, b) work comparing wild mallards with domestic pekins. This study had come to the conclusion that wild mallards respond to a relatively narrower range of stimuli than do domestic pekins; while more domestic pekins will follow a given object, the mallards that do respond to it follow more intensively. Congruently, Klopfer's (1962) own unpublished research indicated to him that pekins follow at their maximum level to both adequate and inadequate stimuli, whereas when wild mallards are presented with adequate stimuli, they follow more intensively than to the inadequate stimuli, and certainly at a much higher level than do the pekins. This finding tended to disprove Haldane and Spurway's (1956) notion that imprinting capacities are not impaired by domestication.

Other concepts tending toward the type 1 schema have been endorsed by Klopfer and Hailman (1964a). For example, they maintained that the visual qualities of the imprinting object are important in promoting the formation of an imprinted attachment; even though different objects may not evoke differential following behavior in pekins, they may later show differential strength of preference. Further results by Klopfer (1967b) on stimulus preferences for imprinting in pekins strengthened this viewpoint. Klopfer thus concluded that these species-specific constraints on the qualities of the imprinting object showed that the "tabula rasa" notion of imprinting is inadequate: the young duckling is not as structureless as such a notion implies, since imprinting cannot be elicited with just any set of stimuli. Such selectivity, furthermore, is not simply on the basis of "conspicuousness" in Bateson's (1966) sense or "strikingness" in Hailman's (1959) sense, since the specific preferences shown by ducklings in the laboratory situation were not systematically related to dimensions such as color or flicker.

Similarly, Klopfer (1967a) considered the factors determining the temporal limits of the critical period for social imprinting to lie, at least in part, in the functional readiness of the sensory systems implicated in the process, with the time during which the stimuli relevant for social imprinting happen to be available in the environment possibly also playing a role in the initiation of the critical period. Finally, with respect to the factors responsible for the termination of the critical period, Klopfer suggested that this occurs through the development of conflicting responses, and not necessarily those of fear, since reduction of sensory (perceptual) input, as shown by various experiments, often appears to have the effect of extending the length of the critical period of responsiveness. Therefore, Klopfer suggested that the "terminus of the critical period is reached when the [sensory] input has attained a particular level."

Gottlieb, originally Klopfer's student, and a colleague of Kuo, has a zoological type 2 viewpoint containing some type 3 epigenetic elements. His zoological viewpoint is evident in his emphasis upon observation of imprinting in natural conditions (e.g., Gottlieb, 1965b). The type 2 feature of his viewpoint can be seen in his study of the role of prenatal sensory experiences upon the responses of hatchling ducks to the auditory and visual characteristics of the parent (Gottlieb, 1971). In other words, he has sought an understanding of the imprinting phenomenon through investigation of the sensory experiences of the young bird. His use of the term "epigenesis," it must be noted, however, is different in important ways from our use of this term, as seen in Chapter 1. "Epigenesis" in Gottlieb's (1971) work refers to embryological and postnatal behavior development, with innate behavior being due to "predetermined epigenesis" and acquired behavior being due to "probablistic epigenesis." Regarding critical periods in embryogenesis of behavior, Gottlieb has said: "The existence of critical periods is ascribable to organic factors: whether a critical or sensitive period is shorter or longer, or occurs earlier or later, is ascribable to stimulative factors. It is by virtue of the uncertain interplay between organic and stimulative factors that sensitive periods in behavioral development become probabilistic occurrences rather than absolutely predictable events" (Gottlieb, 1968, p. 163).

The Type 1 Imprinting Theory

Now we shall consider the Type 1 theory, principally our own. Historically, the first of the type 1 theories—that is, theories which advocate fundamental differences between social imprinting and other types of learning processes in general—is that of Konrad Lorenz in 1935 and 1937. We have already outlined the basic features of this theory when we discussed the historical bases of the study of imprinting in chapter 3. Lorenz, of course, does not hold precisely the same views today. As a result, our theory is now the only type 1 theory still around, even though several type 2 theorists and others have come to add some aspects of our type 1 theory to their own schemes of imprinting. In 1955, Lorenz stated that he believed there was a continuum between imprinting and other learning processes, a notion earlier put forth by Fabricius in 1951. Also, as mentioned above, Hinde (1962) reported that Lorenz placed less emphasis upon the uniqueness of imprinting and more upon the characteristics forced upon social imprinting by the context in which it occurs. At a recent ethology conference meeting (1963), Lorenz and Schutz (subsequently published by Schutz in 1964, 1965) took the view that true imprinting lies only in the context of sexual imprinting—that is, only in cases in which the young become fixated on their parent object and learn the supra-individual recognition marks which characterize the species. Subsequently, according to Schutz, there is a period of time during which the animal cannot absorb further relevant stimuli. When the animal does become sexually mature, it directs its sexual behavior to the species members which represent those to which it has been imprinted. Cases which involve exposure of a young animal to the parent so that it learns to follow the parent are not within the context of the imprinting phenomenon, in Lorenz's view.

Schutz (1964, 1965) has presented evidence in favor of Lorenz's earlier (1935) postulation that social imprinting involves species learning, through the observation that when sexual maturity is achieved, the individuals do not pair with the same ones with which they had been reared, but with others of the same class. By implication, then, following behavior is individual-specific, since ducklings follow their own mother. In our own view, social imprinting does involve general species characteristics: the following behavior is elicited at first by species characteristics, but later association learning of the individual parent's characteristics can take place to promote the individual parent-young bond.

Schutz (1965) also postulated that sexual preference and the following response differ physiologically in their processes during the specific critical periods. He also postulated that this sexual learning occurs at a time later than that of imprinting of the following reaction, because approximately one-third of individuals that were kept with their own species from hatching to the age of 1 to 3 weeks and then kept for a period of 5 to 6 weeks (the usual interval) with an imprinting object later showed evidence of sexual preference for the latter object. If it really does require 5 to 6 weeks to obtain this sexual preference, then we cannot consider it to be a sexual *imprinting* phenomenon but, rather, a learning process of some other kind.

Lannoy (1967) has distinguished between sexual imprinting and following a social object. Following behavior is not dependent upon a critical period for its formation, whereas with sexual imprinting there is a "primacy of experience" effect in our own sense (Hess 1959a, c), thus indicating the importance of a sensitive, perhaps critical, period for this imprinting, according to Lannoy. In fact, he believes that the primacy feature is the *only* aspect that truly distinguishes imprinting from other learning.

While Lannoy is in essential agreement with us that following behavior does not necessarily indicate imprinting, his rejection of any other distinction between imprinting and other learning is not at all in accordance with our own position. Like Schutz (1965), Lannoy agreed that sexual imprinting typifies what Lorenz originally meant in his 1935 exposition on imprinting. While following behavior is directed toward a specific mother, sexual imprinting is generalized to other individuals, according to this position.

Lannoy has made some interesting suggestions of his own regarding the phenomenon of sexual imprinting. Like Lorenz, he emphasized that the fixed action patterns involved in sexual imprinting were identical, regardless of whether the object to which they were directed was species-specific or not. Imprinting, he suggested, therefore determines the taxis component of sexual behavior rather than the fixed action component, since it is the nature of the object eliciting sexual behavior which is determined through imprinting. To us, however, this proposal stretches the meaning of the term "taxis" too far beyond its usual limits. Taxes continuously steer a behavior, and it certainly does appear that an object eliciting sexual behavior has aspects that serve this function if sexual behavior is to result in successful mating and impregnation. However such an object also seems to have aspects that serve to trigger sexual behavior. For example, courtship activity in many species is preparatory to actual physical contact. If sexual imprinting actually does occur, then specific experimentation would have to be conducted to determine whether the imprinted object acts as a pro-pulsory instigator or as an error-correcting feedback mechanism.

Such schemes of social imprinting as being limited primarily to the learning of sexual objects bear several similarities to the phenomenon known as latent learning. We do not, however, believe that the concept of imprinting should be drastically limited and specialized to sexual imprinting in only a few kinds of animals, mostly waterfowl. It appears to us that the examples that we have been able to find, including those of food imprinting, indicate that there is a phenomenon of imprinting as a distinct type of learning process. That is, in this learning process there is necessarily a critical period before and after which such learn-ing is rather impossible. When the learning does occur during the critical period, it is extremely permanent. In these ways, the imprinting process, as we conceive it, is different from latent learning. We shall now attempt to describe in detail our concept of imprinting as a genetically programmed learning of a specific type, one that can be used as a tool by a species as an adaptive mechanism for use in different situations related to the survival of the species. Not all species, naturally, can be expected to use an imprinting process for learning something. Never-theless, the range of species that do so probably is much wider than is now known.

IMPRINTING AS A GENETICALLY PROGRAMMED LEARNING PROCESS

Semantics is certainly an extremely important part of the theoretical contention among researchers on the question of the nature of imprint-ing. Obviously, imprinting involves the establishment of a connection between a specific object or a class of objects and a particular class of behaviors. But this fact must not be thought to automatically make imprinting exactly the same as other association learning processes. The laws which have been found to apply in the association learning processes which have been experimentally studied in psychological laboratories do not necessarily apply to imprinting (in *our* sense). This is one of the fundamental points of our theoretical position on imprinting.

In recent years, the innate features of social imprinting have been thought to be circumscribed, principally because of the fact that in species which manifest this phenomenon in primary socialization, there is an inborn disposition to become very rapidly attached to a parental object. It has been thought by many researchers that imprinting involves the absence of an innate recognition of the natural parent, since ani-mals can be induced, through relatively brief exposure, to direct filial behavior to an object that is not the natural parent. Even so, there have been recurrent observations that there are apparently species-specific constraints of some kind upon the kinds of objects to which animals will readily imprint, and that among the stimuli to which animals will respond, some more readily elicit a display of filial behavior than do others.

An experiment, by Hess and Hess (1969) has shown that when imprinting is extended to ten half-hour experiences, over a three-week period after the initial imprinting session on the first day of life, mallard ducklings will show a 100 percent choice for the object to which they were imprinted. However, there was a considerable difference in the speed with which the subjects joined the imprinting object when given a free choice between this object and a strange one with respect to the particular object used as a parent surrogate. The ducklings would immediately dash over to the mallard decoy when that was their imprinted object, but when a human being was their imprinted object, most of the ducklings took more than half a minute and none took less than five seconds to go to the human being. Since the visual characteristics provided by a duck decoy produce far more evident social imprinting than do those of a completely unrelated species—human beings—we must consider that young ducks innately possess a schema of the natural imprinting object, so that the more a social object fits this schema, the stronger the imprinting that occurs to this object. This innate disposition with regard to the type of object learned indicates that social imprinting is not just simply an extremely powerful effect of the environment upon the behavior of an animal. Rather, there has been an evolutionary pressure for the young birds to learn the right thing —the natural parent—at the right time—the 1st day of life—the time of the sensitive period that has been genetically provided for.

Later, we will have more to say on the role of evolutionary processes in the development of social imprinting and other imprinting processes as well as in the development of other learning mechanisms. For the present, we wish to emphasize strongly that whenever a behavior mechanism is being investigated, it is essential to consider it in the context of the natural function which it serves.

Differences Between Imprinting and Other Learning.

Imprinting involves to a very high degree a behavior which is indispensable for the survival of the animal under natural conditions. In the case of both social and food imprinting, this is clear. Not only must the animals *want* to follow the parent or *want* to eat food: they *must* learn what object(s) is(are) to be the target(s) of such behavior. The drive to learn these objects is so strong that the associated processes accomplishing this learning are contrary to those involved in usual association or rote learning situations.

In earlier publications (e.g., Hess, 1964), we have stated a total of five principal distinctions between social imprinting and association learning processes. In the first place, we have found in our research that the "critical period" is a basic characteristic of imprinting, for we have never failed to find its existence and importance. Extremely limited critical periods—during which the animal is highly susceptible to the effects of certain kinds of experience, with chicks and ducklings being maximally so at the age of 13 to 16 hours (peak critical period), and outside of which the animal is not sensitive—have never been found in cases of association learning. Outside the critical period, true imprinting is not possible, but only association learning. This has not yet been fully recognized by experimenters who are of the opinion that the same physiological and neurological processes are to be found in social imprinting and association learning.

Second, the drugs meprobamate and carisprodol differentially affect the process of learning in social and food imprinting and in learning a color discrimination problem involving food reward. Third, the distance which chicks or ducks follow an object during the exposure to it at the critical age—or, roughly, the amount of energy expended in attempting to be with the model—is related in a logarithmic fashion with the later demonstrated strength of imprinting in a free choice situation involving the imprinting object and a strange one. In contrast, spacing, rather than massing, of effort of practice trials is more effective in regular association learning. Fourth, painful or aversive stimulation will enhance the drive of the animal being imprinted to be with the model; in aversive conditioning, the animal acts so as to avoid whatever is associated with the painful stimulation. Fifth and finally, primacy of experience, rather than of recency, has the greater influence in the formation of an imprinted attachment, whereas recency is often seen to be prepotent in many laboratory learning situations such as bar pressing and maze running.

These five differences have received considerable support from our research. As time has gone on and more experiments have been conducted, these five differences have been confirmed and amplified.

Another possible difference between imprinting and other learning processes has been suggested by results reported by Fischer, Campbell, and Davis (1965). A single electroconvulsive shock immediately after a 12-minute imprinting experience enhanced the amount of following performed by chicks on a later test. The mean scores were 316.5 and 176.3 seconds for ECS and control chicks, respectively. While these authors also demonstrated that *nine* ECS after imprinting depressed test following, with mean scores of 57.7 and 158.6 seconds for ECS and control chicks, respectively, as is the case with other kinds of learning, this does not mean, of course, that imprinting, as a process, is like those involved in other instances of learning, since administration of *nine* ECS amounts to what may be called "brain frying," and constitutes rather severe treatment which, to say the least, should be expected to have pervasive effects.

The above enumeration of differences between imprinting and other types of learning, particularly ordinary association learning, serves as a quick summary of our position. We shall now discuss these differences in more detail.

The Imprinting Object as an Unconditional Stimulus

There are certainly points of both similarity and dissimilarity between the imprinting process, as we conceive it, and other types of learning. To be sure, as we have said, there is an attachment between certain behaviors and the stimulus object in question during the exposure session. However, it is extremely important to note that in classical conditioning situations, the object in question does not initially elicit the desired behavior. This is accomplished through its temporal association with another object which does elicit it. In contrast, the imprinting object by itself elicits the behavior under consideration: it is *not* initially a neutral stimulus as far as the animal is concerned.

We may note that the disposition of young chicks to approach a flickering light, for example, has been shown by Strobel, Baker, and Macdonald (1967) and Strobel, Clark, and Macdonald (1968) to have neurophysiological correlates which are in the process of formation in the central nervous system during the 7th and 9th—especially the 7th—days of incubation. This appears to indicate that radiosensitive periods for the formation of the ability of hatchling chicks and ducklings to imprint to a parent object could be found, since the approach to flickering light in chicks bears marked similarity to the filial behavior on the part of chicks and ducklings to parent objects during the 1st day of life.

The naïve animal in the critical age period has the potentiality of responding to a very large variety of objects and situations in the appropriate fashion. Some of these objects, to be sure, are much more potent in this respect than others. But among a group of equally effective but also completely distinctive stimuli, the imprinting exposure will result in the object to which the animal has been presented remaining effective as an elicitor of the behaviors and the others, which had been initially equally potent in this respect, losing their efficacy. It may be noted that this change in the effectiveness is with respect to *dissimilar* (and equally effective) stimuli: objects possessing a degree of similarity to the object used in the imprinting exposure may also be able to elicit the behavior in question in accordance with a generalization gradient. The point being made here is that while in classical conditioning situations, the unconditional stimuli remain as such before and after the conditioning session, and also serve to direct the conditioned response to the conditioned stimuli, in the true imprinting situation, there are *many* unconditional stimuli for the animal when it has not yet been exposed to the imprinting object during the critical age period. After imprinting has taken place during this time, the stimuli to which the animal had been exposed retain their status as unconditional stimuli, while the others lose this capacity, so that there are *fewer* unconditional stimuli as a result of the experience. When imprinting fails to occur at all, then there are *no* unconditional stimuli for the behaviors in question—at least in the case of the precocial species we have studied. In the case of the failure of association learning to occur, there are, of course, no changes in the number of unconditional stimuli. It may seem that we are belaboring the point, but we do so because it is one that is not obvious to many people.

There are important consequences of the fact that the imprinting object is from the outset an unconditional stimulus rather than a neutral one which acquires a certain meaning for the animal. In classical conditioning, as a rule the conditioned stimulus will gradually lose this meaning when it is no longer associated with the unconditional stimulus. This process is called extinction. Extinction may take longer to accomplish in the case of avoidance conditioning where aversive stimulation serves as the unconditional stimulus, but it does take place; if a rat is not shocked regularly, it may discontinue the performance of the required avoidance behavior.

In social and food imprinting, however, the object itself is an unconditional stimulus, which means that the question of extinction does not enter in the same degree or in the same fashion. In fact, in normal conditions it may not enter at all. In studies of learning in very young organisms, it has often been found that occasional repetition of the learning is necessary to prevent forgetting. However, this does not occur in cases where social imprinting has been involved: the imprinting object is not forgotten when there is a prolonged absence. In addition, the imprinted object is its own reinforcer. Furthermore, as shown by other studies (Campbell and Pickleman, 1961; Peterson, 1960; Hoffman, Schiff, Adams, and Searle, 1966; Hoffman, Searle, Toffey, and Kozma, 1966; Bateson and Reese, 1968; Hoffman et al., 1970), it can act as a reinforcer for other behaviors. Furthermore, an object can act as an unconditional reinforcer for animals past the critical age period only if they already have been imprinted on it. Otherwise, animals past the critical period which have not been exposed to any appropriate object during the critical period will then not be able to respond with the appropriate behavior toward it, even though they would have been responsive to it had it been presented to them at the proper time. In such cases, the object, of course, cannot thenceforth be an unconditional reinforcer either for the behavior in question or for others.

It has been suggested at various times by other researchers that reinforcing events, such as eating, warmth, and contact from the parent, can play a role in the formation of social imprinting. While it does appear that physical contact can play an important role in social imprinting (particularly through intensification of sensory input), food and warmth from the parent cannot. In the first place, social imprinting in chicks and ducklings occurs on the 1st day of life, when yolk sac reserves render eating superfluous until the 3rd day of life, at which time eating becomes necessary. Experimental evidence of Klopfer and Hailman (1964a) on the effects of heat reinforcement failed to indicate any positive or negative effect upon imprinting. Our own unpublished research has not indicated any greater attractive effect of a decoy with a heating element placed inside it, in comparison with one without it. The benefits which an *individual* gains as a result of having imprinted to a parental object do not directly influence the behavior of that individual. The reinforcing effects, however, are probably on the *phylogenetic* level, because it is survival rate, and therefore the heritable behavior pool, which is influenced.

While the imprinting object is the same as the unconditional stimulus or reinforcer in learning theory jargon, it is also the releaser in ethological terms. Many aspects of the imprinting exposure situation are conveniently described from the ethological viewpoint. Releasers, of course, vary in the potency with which they elicit a specific behavior. Not only may potential imprinting objects be regarded as releasers of a certain system of behaviors, but it may also be said that the animals, by virtue of their specific sensitivity at a particular age period, show appetitive behavior toward an imprinting object. This appetitive behavior is in the Craig-Lorenz sense (Hess, 1962b). In the case of social imprinting, the animals search (in the ethological and cybernetic sense) for a situation in which all behaviors normally performed in the presence of the parental object may be released. Three principal behavior processes are then released: the approach response; the following response; and the attachment formation. In our opinion, the last-mentioned occurs most effectively during the critical age period.

The Critical Age Period

The critical age period is vitally important in the imprinting phenomenon. Without the critical age limitation, there is no true imprinting process. There is, shall we say, a genetically programmed place in the ontogeny of the animal to learn to direct certain classes of behavior— mostly fixed action patterns—which are already possessed and are morphologically complete even before the necessary time, toward the objects experienced during this period through an imprinting process. The acquisition of the objects as releasers for these fixed action patterns, which function as consummatory acts ending the appetitive sequence, is the goal of the imprinting process. As Bateson (1966) has pointed out, the ethological notion of "searching"—that is, appetitive behavior— has been regarded with suspicion in the past, but, now that computers have been found to be able to do the same thing, it has now become more acceptable to behavioral scientists in disciplines other than ethology. These scientists are now conceding that animals have behavioral strategies which will eventually result in the matching of sensory input with a specific innate or learned "model" which has been established.

The limits of the critical period for imprinting are genetically programmed, rather than maturationally determined, as we earlier proposed (Hess, 1959a). We have made this change in our thinking for several reasons. Firstly, the occurrence of *early* imprinting apparently cuts off or diminishes sensitivity to any further imprinting from then on (Polt and Hess, 1964, 1966; Hess, 1964). For example, chicks or ducklings socially imprinted to their siblings at the age of 6 hours will not show optimal social imprinting toward a parent surrogate at later ages, even though isolated subjects show very strong social imprinting as a result of specific experience at the age of 13 to 16 hours. Not only early social imprinting, but also primacy effects, shuts off imprintability to further social objects. There are additional factors which serve to influence the precise temporal boundaries of the sensitive period for social imprinting: sensory input (Moltz and Stettner, 1961; Klopfer, 1964); drugs (Hess, 1957, Hess, Polt, and Goodwin, 1959); and social facilitation (Klopfer, 1959a, Hess, 1959a, c) and Collias and Collias, 1956).

The course of maturation, as has been shown by numerous studies on early experience, can be set in motion or speeded up simply through sensory input and not because there has been any opportunity for extra learning. Studies on infantile handling of rats (e.g., Levine, 1960) have provided rather clear instances of this; Lemmon and Patterson (1964) reported on the effect of maternal stimulation in accelerating the onset of the ability of baby goats to avoid a visual cliff; Klopfer, Adams and Klopfer (1964) showed the effect of social stimulation in hastening the end of the disposition of a mother goat to accept her own offspring which has been separated from her since birth.

Moltz and Stettner (1961) and Klopfer (1964) observed that reduction of visual experience (translucent light or dark rearing) permits greater responsiveness in ducklings or in chicks in an imprinting situation than is shown by others of the same age that have had full patterned vision experience. While it certainly is incontestable that greater sensory input has the effect of accelerating developmental schedules, as we earlier mentioned, we have, however, been puzzled by the fact that Moltz and Stettner's full-light reared ducklings showed the same curve of imprintability as a function of age as do our own *dark*-reared ducklings, with the peak at 12 hours of age, while their diffuse-light subjects showed a peak imprintability at 24 hours of age. It would seem that diffuse-light reared subjects should have an imprintability curve resembling more closely the dark-reared subjects' curve than the full-light reared subjects would have. Breed differences between pekins and mallards may be in part responsible for this puzzling finding.

At any event, the effect of sensory experience upon the temporal boundaries of the sensitive period for social imprinting experiences certainly exists. It seems to exist also in food imprinting in chicks, since Padilla's (1935) dark-reared chicks apparently were able to learn to use pecking behavior as a means of obtaining food, but with intensive training necessary in order to bring this about. Chicks kept in the dark for the first 8 days of life, however, were able to learn this behavior spontaneously. Since we had found that full-light-reared chicks were completely unable to imprint to food objects by the time they were 7 days old, it appears that in Padilla's dark-reared chicks an extension of the sensitive period had taken place.

In the light of all this, it becomes clear that the genetic program's role is in providing a topography or order of events in the maturational sequence, rather than a "railroad timetable" based on highly specific ages. The topography of social imprinting has been indicated in several ways. The correlations between the rise and fall of imprintability and definite changes in other behaviors are an important source of data for elucidating this topography. Hess (1959b) has demonstrated that isolated socially naïve chicks show a definite progression in speed of locomotion and in incidence of fear behavior during the hours after hatching. The increasing speed in locomotion is correlated with increasing sensitivity to an imprinting experience, while the increase in fear tendencies is correlated with decreasing likelihood of imprinting as a result of exposure to an imprinting object. We do not, it must be remembered, claim that there are any direct causal relationships implied by these two correlations.

A report by Tolman (1963) on the relationship between age and wakefulness of chicks precisely illustrates this last statement, and provides still further support of our theoretical position on the nature of social imprinting. Tolman observed 12 individually isolated chicks (4 leghorns, 8 New Hampshires) every hour for 24 hours, counting the total number that were observed to be maximally wakeful—that is, active, standing, moving around the cage, for each 4-hour block. The graph which he presented to portray the obtained data, in terms of percent of birds that were thus awake, was almost indistinguishable from the one which we use (Ramsay and Hess, 1954), based on 92 ducklings depicting the percentage of subjects in each 4-hour age group that achieve a perfect imprinting score on the imprinting test 24 hours after the initial exposure. From his data, Tolman drew the conclusion that the critical period for social imprinting could be interpreted in terms of internal changes in arousal level, although "it is not an intended implication of this note that all determinations of the critical period may be artifacts of natural arousal changes." One other factor which he mentioned as playing a role in specific experimental results was communal rearing, acting to reduce the uniformity of such arousal changes.

There is at present no justification for regarding this arousal level as *causing* the observed developmental course of imprinting sensitivity. We could just as well say that the arousal curve obtained by Tolman is simply a consequence of the isolated chicks' increasing readiness and then decreasing sensitivity to imprint, as would be predicted by the appetitive behavior concept. More important, however, the arousal curve does not touch at all on the problem of the rapidly increasing incidence of fear behavior in chicks exposed to a social object after the age of 16 hours; an increasing tendency to react with fear cannot be predicted given the fact that wakefulness or activity *declines* after that time.

Experimental results by Fischer (1967) showed that 12-hour-old chicks that followed an imprinting object more had higher mean activity scores during the fifth minute of adaptation (just before the model actually began to move) to an imprinting situation than did chicks that did not follow the object much, with no differences during the first and third minute of adaptation between those that followed more and those that followed less. This higher level of activity, of course, indicates *reactivity* to the situation rather than merely activity alone on the part of the chicks that were strong followers. This, however, as Fischer pointed out, does not answer the question of whether the chicks that followed strongly did so because they were more responsive or because they were less fearful (less freezing behavior, in other words), or perhaps both.

Here again, at any rate, we can discern evidence of the role of internal processes in the effects of a social imprinting experience.

The importance of the critical period in the social imprinting phenomenon has been underscored by the finding of Hoffman, Searle and Kozma (1966) that only ducklings that had been exposed to an imprinting model six times (45 minutes each, beginning at the age of 6 to 8 hours) during the first 48 hours of life were able to learn a key peck response that was rewarded by the presentation of the imprinting object. Neither those exposed at the age of 198 to 246 hours nor unexposed controls could do so. Imprinted ducklings also showed behaviors very clearly related to the presence or absence of the imprinting object.

In this connection, it is also worth noting that since late-exposure subjects were familiar with the object and yet failed to learn the key peck response, this indicates that familiarity alone on the part of the subjects exposed during the critical period is not the factor enabling them to learn the key peck response. Rather, the early-exposed subjects, because they experienced the imprinting object during the sensitive period, had developed a positive attachment to it and therefore had an incentive to learn the key press response.

Thus, the appetitive behavior of the animal results in the acquisition of releasing objects for the specific motor patterns for a specific behavior system, and a previously existing void in the innate schema is completed, just as Lorenz (1935) postulated. There is a genetically determined space for the animal to learn a specific thing by means of imprinting during its ontogeny. If the animal does not meet any object which fits the requirements of the schema, or meets one that does not fill the void completely, then the acquisition of this releasing object is absent or incomplete, respectively.

It is important to recognize the existence of absent or incomplete imprinting. There are degrees of imprinting, just as there are degrees of completeness in other kinds of learning. Of course, this factor does not mean that imprinting is the same as other kinds of learning. We know that in social imprinting, for example, the young bird has an innate preference for the natural living parent as a releasing object for social behaviors. The results of Hess and Hess (1969) show that objects resembling the natural parent result in demonstrably stronger social imprinting in mallard ducklings than does an object belonging to a very different species—the human being. When the natural parent is available for social imprinting, all the necessary elements are present, and there is perfect imprinting. Perfect imprinting is much less likely to occur when artificial models or foreign species are used as imprinting objects. Waller and Waller (1963) have observed that pekin ducks prefer a sibling duck over a green cube, even if they had been exposed first to a green cube and then to siblings. At any event, incomplete imprinting will result in abnormal social behaviors, not only toward conspecifics but toward the inadequate parental model as well.

Even though artificial models *are* inadequate, it is surprising to observe the degree of positive behavior that a young bird being imprinted to them may display. In a laboratory imprinting situation, such models do not respond to the young animal's distress cries by coming to it, except by chance; they push against the young birds if they are in its way; usually do not adjust their speed to that of the young; do not stay with them when they settle down; and so on. Yet, in spite of this highly unmaternal behavior, young chicks and ducklings which have been exposed to such models when socially naïve and during the critical age period can go to this entirely inadequate surrogate instead of avoiding it and searching further for a suitable parental object which will actually provide protection and succorance.

Permanence

Laboratory imprinting procedures during the critical age period can have strong and often permanent effects upon the preferences of the animal. However, since laboratory imprinting procedures often result in less than complete imprinting because of the use of biologically inappropriate objects, the effects of such procedures are *not* absolutely irreversible. Animals may, for example, be trained to follow new objects immediately after intensive laboratory exposure to a parental surrogate. But if young ducklings are imprinted to their own parent in feral conditions the imprinting is complete and *irreversible*. This appears to be because the most optimal and biologically appropriate social imprinting object is involved in such cases. Furthermore, young ducklings appear to be genetically programmed to respond to characteristics of the natural parent during the critical age period, as suggested by findings of Hess and Hess (1969).

In our opinion, permanence is a necessary criterion of imprinting. Unless the effects of an experience are permanent, imprinting cannot be involved. Nor can imprinting be involved if there is no critical period limitation for the occurrence of the learning in question.

Effects of Aversive Stimulation

The strength of the drive of a young chick or duckling for a parental object has been even further proved by our electric shock experiments (Hess, 1964; Kovach and Hess 1963). If we step on a chick or duckling or shock it while it is being imprinted, we cannot succeed in driving it away. Instead, as long as incapacitation does not occur through excessively high shock levels or stepping too hard, the following behavior of chicks at the critical age period is actually enhanced by the shock, and they stay even more closely by the punitive imprinting object. This "masochism" does not occur in usual association learning situations, for in such cases, the administration of painful stimulation normally produces escape or avoidance behavior with respect to the associated object.

But if the chick has already passed the critical age period at the time of the imprinting exposure, the administration of electric shock acts in the expected way: the following behavior is reduced, the more so the older the chick. This constitutes still further proof that after the critical age period has passed, true imprinting does not, in fact, occur; rather, more conventional, trial-by-trial association learning processes take place. In such cases, the inducement of following in chicks involves the habituation of fear responses through conditioning. Once again, the role of the genetic program, as reflected by the change in the prevalent learning process, is evident. During the critical age period itself, as we have seen, aversive stimulation energizes positive behavior toward a parental object; but after the critical age period, such stimulation energizes fear behaviors instead.

There is actually a positive effect of aversive stimulation upon filial behavior in imprinting and not merely a failure of the young animal to be able to learn to passively avoid, escape, or react to aversive pain or electric shock stimulation, as might be suggested by reports of James and Binks (1963) and Fischer and Campbell (1964). James and Binks found that none of their seven New Hampshire barred rock chicks less than 15 hours old could learn active avoidance or escape; of those 25 to 43 hours old, all but one learned to escape, but none learned to avoid; all those at least 49 hours old learned both. However, these findings may be situation-specific, as we have observed socially naïve chicks and ducklings actively avoid a laboratory imprinting model as early as 18 hours after hatching. Fischer and Campbell's results, showing the failure of passive avoidance learning in 3-day old leghorn chicks and its ready acquisition at the age of 6 days (with 75 percent of subjects learning this at the age of 4 days), must be tempered by the consideration that the required response was in conflict with social approach behavior toward an age mate, and that the chicks were communally reared. The flocking tendency of chicks is less strong at the age of 1 week than at the age of 3 days, or at least shorter distances are necessary at the earlier age in order to satisfy the flocking drive in younger chicks. If some goal other than a social object were used, passive avoidance learning might become evident; alternatively, it might be possible to offer a choice between two social objects—one associated with shock, and the other not.

This enhancing effect of aversive stimulation directly associated with the object to be learned upon the learning itself may not exist in processes other than social imprinting. It certainly is evident in the social imprinting of chicks and ducklings. Melvin, Cloar and Massingill (1967) have cited an accidental observation of intensified affiliative behavior in a bobwhite quail that had been attacked by a sparrow hawk while being imprinted to this hawk. While Sluckin (1964) has objected that "punishment is, in fact, an entirely extraneous factor in imprinting, whereas it is an integral factor of escape and avoidance conditioning," we believe that punishment is not as extraneous in social imprinting as he believes. Rather, we believe that in the development of the parent-offspring relationship in the evolution of many species, including that of man, aversive stimulation has come to promote rather than weaken the tie during its formation. For example, should a mother duck accidentally step on a duckling during the exodus from the nest, it clearly would not be adaptive for that duckling to then run away from her. Furthermore, if there were any actually dangerous events, such as attacks upon the young, it would be highly advantageous for them to strive harder than ever to reach and be with the mother so that she could provide protection.

The observation of mother animals with their very young offspring often reveals that the mothers are by no means gentle in their handling of the infants. They can be amazingly rough, pushing—shoving, stepping, and energetically licking their babies. It is a common sight to see a mother cat pick up her tiny kitten by the neck with her teeth. None of this ever drives the young away from the mother. Even when a mother happens to be abnormally cruel in her treatment of her young, the infant can be strenuously persistent in staying with her. Harlow and Harlow (1962) had female monkeys that had been reared in total social isolation for 6 months from birth. These females, when they became mothers, were inordinately abusive to their first-born infants, one of which actually died as a result, and another had to be rescued. But in spite of all this abuse, the infants strove all the more to nurse from their mothers and to stay with them. Another experiment, by Rosenblum and Harlow (1963), in which surrogate mothers emitted aversive blasts of air on the baby monkey, resulted in the finding that the babies clung all the more tenaciously. Here again, the enhancing effect of aversive stimulation upon the infant-mother bond is demonstrated.

Also among humans, we find evidence that physical punishment of the child by the parent does not result in the child's associating the punishment with the parent. If a child is punished for a misdemeanor, the child associates the punishment with the act, not with the parent Polt (1966). Menaker (1956), in fact, has suggested than an overly punitive parent may cause the formation of extremely strong masochistic attachment—that is, intensified affiliative behavior directed to the parent. It seems as if the child who is in a punishing relationship reacts by idealizing the parent and picturing that parent as all-powerful and loving.

Law of Effort

Our postulated logarithmic and positive relationship between expenditure of directed energy in the imprinting exposure situation and the strength of manifest imprinting bond as evidenced in a free choice test situation has generated one of the literature's enduring controversial topics. Nearly every serious writer on imprinting has made some comment on it.

In this connection, we will first mention Fischer's (1966) report, since we have stated (Hess 1959c, 1964) that the law of effort indicates that it is not temporal spacing of effort or practice trials that promotes effective learning in imprinting, as it does in association learning, but that the converse is true. Our ducklings do not learn the imprinting object more quickly or more stably when they are given a greater amount of temporal association with the model, if the amount of following— that is, expended effort—remains constant. Instead, the strength of the resultant learning remains the same.

Fischer (1966) reported that while an interexposure interval between two successive 6-minute imprinting experiences at the age of 18½ hours had no positive or negative effect on following responsiveness to the familiar model, on the later test, at the age of 36 hours, it did have the effect of markedly decreasing following responsiveness to a subsequently presented strange model when the interval had been 10, 20, or 30 minutes' duration. A 1-minute interruption in the middle of a 12-minute imprinting session (consisting of turning off the lights, transporting the chick to the isolation room, and back, replacing apparatus, turning on lights) had no effect on these two measures.

These findings support our own, in that the chicks followed the familiar model just as well as a result of one continuous exposure session as they did when the experience is distributed over two sessions. However, Fischer concluded that, nevertheless, there was a facilitating effect of distribution, in that the strange model was followed less as a result. Since she used the successive presentation test method, with the familiar model shown first, we do not know whether imprinting scores derived from a simultaneous choice method as used by us would reflect a distribution effect.

Our findings—based on socially naïve mallard ducklings exposed at the age of 13 to 16 hours (see Chapter 4) and tested with a simultaneous choice between the familiar and a strange model in a four-part pro-cedure—are certainly clear enough. The same appears to be true, with-out exception, for the chicks we have studied under the same conditions.

But, as we shall soon see in the following discussion, some researchers have not obtained this kind of relationship. Indeed, there are many who have doubted that any kind of response other than merely seeing the object is necessary for social imprinting to occur. For the large part, differences in interpretation of data and experimental procedures have been responsible for this confusion. This is because the law of effort ap-plies only to the situation in which it was found: where previously isolated socially naïve chicks and ducklings (precocial species) are placed in the imprinting situation during the *critical period*. Animals previously socialized or past the critical period will not demonstrate the relationship we postulated. And, of course, different species are probably differ-entially affected by a given amount of energy expenditure. Animals of species A may follow less than animals of species B and yet imprint as well, presumably because they are more sensitive to the effects of such experience.

Sensitivity to the imprinting experience—that is, a strong readiness to imprint—appears to be related to whether the law of effort is operative or not. We might mention a study by Salzen and Sluckin (1959) in this connection, even though they used chicks that had a mean age of 24 hours, and therefore most were beyond the peak critical age of 13 to 16 hours. Nevertheless some of them may have been at that peak age. Our interest in this lies in the fact that they had two experimental groups, the first of which was exposed to 10 movements of a red box, and the second to fifty movements of this same box. In the second group, a certain number of animals followed the box during the first 10 move-ments, and the extra 40 movements induced 44 additional animals to follow. But when the later test was carried out, these additional 44 ani-mals showed *no higher incidence of following* than did animals of the first group which did not follow during the 10 movements that were presented to them. In contrast, however, the animals of the second group that had already started to follow during the first 10 movements demon-strated a marked effect from being exposed to the extra 40 movements: *39 percent* of them followed on the test session. This is higher than the proportion of followers that were permitted to see only 10 movements during the exposure session that followed when tested in the second session—*29 percent*. Thus, the relative improvement attributable to the extra experience given to susceptible subjects was 10 percent. The rather low percentages of followers during the test session for members of both groups is probably a consequence of their relatively advanced age at the time of the initial exposure experience.

There have been several studies comparing the effects of restraint or confinement preventing actual following behavior with those of following itself. Moltz, Rosenblum, and Stettner's (1960) is an example of such a study. Pekin ducklings, 7 to 14 hours old, were either confined to a transparent restraining unit or permitted to follow the imprinting object freely. Some of the ducklings were restrained 14 inches away from the object, and others were restrained 7 inches away. Those that were restrained at the farther distance were able to show as much evidence of imprinting as were the unrestrained ones, while those that were restrained only 7 inches away were no different from the unrestrained ones that did not follow. The conclusion is inescapable that those that were far from the model made responses to it that resulted in becoming imprinted to it, while those that were near to it did not. That is, the near ones appear to have paid less attention to the model than the far ones did.

Struggling to get to the model is one such response made by restrained animals that we have noted in our own chicks and ducklings. However, Moltz et al. claimed that some ducklings did not appear to make such responses, but sat quietly and yet were able to show vigorous following when permitted to do so on the test session.

A report by Macdonald and Solandt (1966) may possibly be relevant to this. We say "possibly" because they used a flickering light as the relevant stimulus rather than a social object, and it is not certain to us whether a social imprinting process is involved when a spatially fixed flickering light is proffered. At any rate, these researchers found that if 12 to 20-hour old chicks were pharmacologically immobilized with Flaxedil, a drug which "leaves the sensorium intact," the chicks showed almost no effects of the imprinting exposure when later tested. They concluded that the form of response required for imprinting to occur must be relatively fine if restrained birds that show little or no overt behavior actually can become imprinted. It is this last which we consider in need of explicit and careful study.

Until such study is carried out, it is clear that the many studies (e.g., Baer and Gray, 1960; Smith, 1962b; Moltz, 1963; Thompson and Dubanoski, 1964; Collins, 1965) using restraint to prevent following do not test for the role of the response to the model in determining the strength of imprinting. Just because no overt following of a moving decoy occurs, it does not necessarily mean that there is no expenditure of effort involved. One study, by Thompson and Dubanoski (1964a), apparently lends some support to the law of effort. However, methodological considerations with respect to the testing procedure they used make it necessary to be cautious in this regard.

Bateson (1966) has questioned the law of effort on rather different grounds. He suggested that the relevant factor may be amount of directed *visual* experience rather than simply amount of energy expended by the animal's motor apparatus. It certainly is true that directed visual experience is necessary in order for the locomotor effects of the imprinting experience to have any effect on the strength of the imprinted bond formed. However, it has also become apparent that mere exposure to an imprinting object without following efforts will not be effective in producing evident imprinting. For example, Klopfer and Hailman (1964a), while failing to find any positively correlated functions between amount of following and subsequent choice in pekin ducklings, did discover that those that did not follow at all failed to show any evidence of imprinting on test. Klopfer (1971) reported evidence that pekin ducklings must move during the imprinting exposure in order to show later effects of the experience. Similarly, Kovach, Fabricius, and Fält (1966) reported that only chicks that followed the imprinting object were able to solve an avoidance or discrimination problem involving the imprinted stimulus as a discriminanda better than the controls; the non-followers—even they too had seen the imprinting object—did not. Work by Gottlieb (1965a) has indicated that passive exposure of pekin ducklings to a foreign sound did not result in their responding to it, but if they were permitted to actively follow the source of this sound, they later would follow it. This foreign sound could become preferred as an elicitor of following if it were followed a great deal. Otherwise, if the pekin maternal call were also present, the ducklings would prefer to follow it.

Hence, if visual experience of the imprinting object is actually the relevant variable rather than directed muscular responses, this visual experience must be more than passive reception, just as the locomotory responses required must be directed with reference to the imprinting object. It may be well in this connection to mention that in our laboratories chicks and ducklings apparently can be imprinted to a sound alone, and hence visual stimulation is not the only modality in which imprinting operates. Thus, it would appear that both directed sensory input and directed approach, following, or, at the very least, orientation of some sort must be involved in the formation of the imprinting bond to the parent object.

Certainly, in a precocial species we would find the effort-visual experience in the orientation actions of the young toward the parent to be implicated as the process by which the imprinting may take place. In sum, passive sensory exposure has not been shown to be sufficient to result in an imprinted attachment; the animal itself must be *involved* in responding to the sensory input. The rise in activity of isolated birds correlated with potential imprintability found by Tolman (1963) is one indication of this fact. Also, our observations of chicks being imprinted have shown that those that defecate during the exposure session almost invariably show filial behavior to the imprinting model (unpublished data). In conclusion, then, it still appears justifiable to us to stand by our law of effort, as applied to the situation from which it was derived.

The law of effort, furthermore, has been useful in explaining various facets of social imprinting. For example, as we noted (Hess, 1959c), mallard ducklings exposed to an auditory stimulus before hatching did not show an imprinted response to it. We conjectured that the inability of these ducklings to follow when still in the egg might be the reason. Bateson (1966), of course, would attribute this failure of auditory imprinting to lack of visual stimulation. However, as mentioned earlier, we do know that auditory imprinting can be obtained in this species after hatching has occurred, so that visual stimulation emanating from a specific object is not necessary in order for social imprinting to occur.

In other imprinting situations, such as environmental imprinting, the relevant responses may not be overt. Even in such a case, it is quite possible that more than mere passive reception of relevant stimulation forms the basis of the learning that takes place.

Primary versus Recency

The final difference between imprinting and most association learning which we will discuss in this section in the efficacy of primacy rather than recency in influencing behavior tendencies when equally effective imprinting stimuli are involved. It is, indeed, most unfortunate that we cannot adequately assess Kaye's (1965) experimental results on this question, since he did not report the age at which his experimental subjects were exposed to the two successive imprinting objects. However, the findings of Polt and Hess (1964, 1966) on the deleterious effects of prior sibling exposure upon imprinting to a parental surrogate is clear substantiation of the primacy principle in chick imprinting, a principle initially established with mallard ducklings as subjects. The latter experiments (Hess, 1959a, c) were conducted with the animals socially naïve and at the peak of the critical period, 13 to 16 hours after hatching.

As food imprinting also has the primacy phenomenon (Burghardt, 1967; Burghardt and Hess, 1966, involving the snapping turtle; Burghardt, 1969; Hess, unpublished research), this shows that imprinting is foundational in nature, as Sluckin (1964) suggests. Certainly there is no "backward learning," as there is in serial rote or maze learning in infrahuman animals. Nor is there retroactive inhibition of old learning by the new experience.

Similarities between Imprinting and Other Learning

As we have previously pointed out, in nature we usually find multiple mechanisms to accomplish the same purposes. The existence of these multiple mechanisms can result in their being confused with each other, even when they are characterized by different processes. The imprinting process is one that has been subject to a great deal of confusion with trial-by-trial conditioning or discrimination learning. Not only have theoretical biases of researchers served to confuse these two processes, but also the fact that both imprinting and a more commonly known association learning process can result in the performance of very similar-appearing behavior by the organism.

The existence of alternative methods for the development of a given behavior does not necessarily mean that the long-range effect on the performance of that behavior will be the same for all the possible methods of developing it. But we can say with certainty that the existence of alternative learning mechanisms for the acquisition of a particular thing is certainly beneficial to the survival of the species.

The principal alternative learning mechanisms which we will consider here are the imprinting mechanism and association learning. In each of the imprinting situations—not only social imprinting but also environmental imprinting and food imprinting—we have observed that the imprinting has an association learning counterpart. As we have repeatedly pointed out, after the critical period has passed, conventional association learning methods are required if some form of the behavior desired is to be developed. Thus, chicks and ducklings which are no longer in the critical age period or which have already been completely imprinted to a parental object will show fear responses to a new object. Such fear responses must be habituated and the animal gradually trained to follow the new object. Such training requires an inordinately longer period of time to accomplish than an original social imprinting process does.

In the case of food imprinting in chicks, we similarly find that older chickens can be placed in a Skinner box and trained to peck at colored lights in order to obtain food. The pecking response to the colored light, acquired by means of the association learning process, can soon be extinguished by withdrawal of the food reward, whereas, in our food imprinting experiments, the 3-day-old chicks which had been rewarded for pecking at a stimulus which they innately preferred less were never observed to lose their new pecking preference, even after long periods without reinforcement (see Chapter 5).

Lastly, the environmental imprinting, which appears to exist as a result of experience during the 2nd day of life in ducks (see Chapter 5), also has an association learning counterpart which may be deduced from the fact that a wild-caught animal may be easily trained to sleep or otherwise spend long periods in a particular place quite different from the habitat in which it was reared.

These association learning counterparts of specific imprinting processes can utilize stimuli to which the animal has not been imprinted. As was earlier mentioned, there is, for every imprinting situation, be it food, social, maternal, or environmental, a wide range of stimuli which initially have the potentiality of releasing the behavior in question. Through the imprinting process, a specific number of these stimuli are experienced by the animal and thus retain their unconditional reinforcing effect. The remaining stimuli lose their unconditional reinforcing property and therefore become neutral stimuli. Responses later conditioned to these stimuli will follow all the classical laws of conditioning and trial-and-error learning. In other words, after such training, the animal can easily generalize to other objects and thus increase the range of objects to which it can make conditioned responses of this type.

Furthermore, it is important to note that the occurrence of imprinting to a object or class of objects does not at all preclude the additional occurrence of association learning with respect to these same objects. In other words, both imprinting and association learning may be, and possibly often are, successively existent in the same animal, and both produce behaviors in that animal which appear superficially the same. However, in our view, the conditioned responses and the imprinted responses of the animal are completely different in terms of the conditions of their origins and also in terms of their long-range effects on the character of the animal's behavior.

Phylogenetic Status of Imprinting

The existence of imprinting as a mechanism providing for the very rapid learning of a highly specific thing during a genetically programmed developmental period in the life of the animal points to the great importance of this particular learning for the survival of the species to which that animal belongs. In our view, imprinting is a behavior-determining mechanism which is evolutionarily available to a species for rapidly learning a vitally important thing. In the case of food imprinting, for example, it is obvious that around the 3rd day of age the chick, in order to survive and ultimately reach reproductive capacity, must have a sensitivity to food objects. Under natural conditions, these food objects are often called to the attention of the chick by its mother. The refusal to learn food objects or to eat at this time would surely result in the death of the chick, since its food reserves from the yolk sac are no longer sufficient to maintain its life. The basic vital function of the social imprinting experience is perhaps not as immediately obvious, but it does provide for the continuation of a social species through cohesiveness of the individual members of the species.

In both chicks and ducklings, the existence of a rather sharp peak of high sensitiveness at the age of 13 to 16 hours points to the urgency of the social learning at this time if it has not yet been accomplished. In the natural situation, there is opportunity to associate with the parent and siblings from the moment of hatching. Experiments by Polt and Hess (1964, 1966) have indicated that in chicks imprinting can be completed to the extent of preventing any further imprinting to a new object during the first hours after hatching. Similar findings for ducks have been made by Hess (1964). Therefore, this probably is normally the case in natural conditions. The peak sensitivity to imprinting at 13 to 16 hours of age would seen to operate as a fail-safe mechanism, for if social imprinting has not yet occurred by that age, it becomes extremely imperative that it do so. In this way, the high level of sensitivity should guarantee that social imprinting will occur toward practically whatever social object, even if inadequate, is available in the environment.

In line with this, Bjärvall (1967) has observed that the majority of mallard duckling are more than 16 hours old at the time of the exodus from the nest. We ourselves have observed that the exodus usually takes place 24 to 26 hours after hatching. Before the exodus, the young normally make several short excusions of a few inches or so from and back to the nest. In this fashion, the imprinting to the parent takes place, and serves to make the duckling completely ready to follow the mother reliably by the time the exodus occurs. The peak sensitivity at the age of 13 to 16 hours, the same age as with chicks, ensures that imprinting actually has occurred by the time of the exodus. Work by Hoffman (1968) has shown that neither individual exposure nor extensive following is necessary for pekin ducklings to become attached to a surrogate object so that it acquires control over the ducklings' distress vocalization. Klopfer (1971) has shown that some movement must occur for pekin ducklings to imprint in the laboratory. Hence, it does seem that the early movements of the ducklings in the presence of the mother normally result in complete imprinting before the exodus occurs.

Bjärvall's observations on the time of exodus also lend some support to the notion of environmental imprinting occurring on the 2nd day of life. The possibility of the existence of environmental imprinting occurred to us because we have observed that mature wild mallards that have grown up around our lake choose nest sites in accordance with their early nest experience. Nests are available either in the surrounding marshes or in elevated nest boxes. The laboratory subjects that had been hatched in our incubators were the only ones that chose to nest in the elevated boxes, while the nest-hatched birds nested on the ground.

Preliminary experimentation with ducklings has indicated that the 2nd day of life is a sensitive period for the formation of such nest preferences in mallard ducks (Hess, 1972), just as chicks exposed to a large cutout (Hess, 1959a) show a strong preference for staying near the familiar cutout rather than a strange one when the exposure has taken place during the age of 22 to 46 hours. Thus, the period of sensitivity may exhibit temporal distinctiveness from those involved in food and social imprinting.

Assuming that environmental imprinting does exist, its comparison with food and social imprinting presents some problems that are in need of experimental clarification. While with both social and food imprinting, the existence of releasers and the elicitation of specific motor actions by these releasers are very clear, this is not yet quite the case with environmental imprinting. As our observations have shown, wild ducks will nest in a specific type of place in accordance with their environmental experience, presumably during the 2nd day of life. Obviously, the nest site itself elicits nesting behavior in these adult ducks. But what is it that happens during the 2nd day of life?

At that age, ducklings and chicks orient themselves to specific aspects of the environment. Movements in accordance with temperature gradients, for example, are very obvious at that time, and particularly more so than during the 1st day of life. In chicks, for example, it has been noted (unpublished data) that on the 1st day of life they will expend considerable energy in keeping up with an imprinting model which is exposed to them in an 80°F room heated by a single radiator. Non-followers, furthermore, do not show any significant degree of positive orientation toward this radiator. But on the 2nd and 3rd days of life, non-imprinted chicks will generally go near the radiator and stay there, paying no attention to a moving or stationary imprinting model. Imprinted chicks of the same age, on the other hand, will persist in following the model and ignore the relatively warmer area near the radiator.

While similar behavior probably would be seen in ducklings, it is among *nesting* ducklings and chicks that the situation becomes less clear, since the temperature conditions presumably are largely controlled by the mother. A nest, being stationary, does not elicit following behavior. It can, of course, elicit approach behavior from a chick or duck that has made a short excursion from it.

Investigation of imprinting at different phylogenetic levels should lead to a clarification of the primary and secondary features of the imprinting process as applied to different situations. For example, in comparing food imprinting and social imprinting in chicks, we can see that the features that are common to both situations include: a) the existence of the critical period; b) the existence of differentially effective releasers for the behaviors involved; c) abnormal and maladaptive behaviors when the requisite imprinting does not occur at all, with failure to eat in the case of chicks that have not imprinted to any food objects, failure to make social contacts in the case of those that have not imprinted to any social objects, and perhaps failure to nest adequately in the case of those ducks that have failed to imprint to an environment (although, by definition, ducklings *must* be in an environment of some sort at the sensitive period, so that perhaps it is difficult to observe cases of failure of environmental imprinting to occur); and d) having an association learning counterpart. We would also like to mention as a particular point e) that the great resistance of food imprinting to extinction is apparently on a par with the life-long affects that have been observed for social and environmental imprinting.

A still further similarity is that: f) in both food and social imprinting, a response on the part of the young animal toward the imprinting object is necessary in order for the imprinting exposure to have any demonstrable effect. Whether or not there is also some sort of law of effort in food or environmental imprinting during the critical period, as there is in the case of social imprinting, is yet to be determined experimentally.

In comparing social and food imprinting in chicks, we find the following additional similarities which have not yet been tested for with respect to environmental imprinting in ducks: in both cases, meprobamate and carisoprodol have an inhibiting effect on the learning, and our unpublished research and that of Burghardt (1969) have strongly suggested that primacy also is more effective than recency in the establishment of food imprinting in chicks, as is the case in social imprinting. In the case of a completely different species—the snapping turtle—Burghardt and Hess (1966) and Burghardt (1967) have reported that primacy is effective in food learning. Burghardt's (1967) report indicated that even only one meal can produce a food preference in favor of the first-fed food, even though there is an interaction between the learned and the natural food preferences. It is possible that primacy is prepotent in environmental imprinting as well.

Some of the secondary characteristics of the specific imprinting process can be seen in the differences between social and food imprinting in chicks and environmental imprinting in ducklings: a) the temporal location of the critical period involved is at the 1st day of life in the case of social imprinting for both chicks and ducklings, at the age of 3 days for food imprinting in chicks, and at the 2nd day of life for environmental imprinting in ducks; and b) the object and reinforcer for the learning involved are social, food, and nest, respectively, with the reinforcement relevant for one imprinting process being not directly relevant as a reinforcer for the other imprinting processes.

It is probable, nevertheless, with regard to point (b), that when one imprinting process has occurred, then it can function to limit the range of things that can be involved in other imprinting processes. For example, if the mother duck is the object to which the duckling has been imprinted, then she naturally can cause the duckling to be in certain environments which she prefers and to which the duckling subsequently becomes imprinted. And then, being with the imprinted mother (who prefers to be at certain places) and being attracted to certain environments result in certain food stuffs being exposed to the duckling, and thus limiting the possible variety of food objects to which it has the opportunity to become imprinted.

It is also possible that when one imprinting process has occurred, the young animal possesses a greater readiness for a subsequent imprinting process involving a different sphere of behavior. Preciselywhat mechanisms would be involved in this is not certain, but maturational ones could not be excluded from consideration. As a concrete example of this phenomenon, Strobel, Freedman, and Macdonald (1970) have shown that social rearing during the first 3 days after hatching, or even just brief exposure to a flickering light stimulus during this time, permits chicks to show the phenomenon of eating more food when in the company of other chicks than when alone ("social facilitation"). It would seem at first as if social stimuli actually reinforces eating behavior, which is quite a reversal from the commonly held notion that social behavior is reinforced by eating. This notion has often been applied to the development of social behavior in human infants. However, this reversal does not touch upon the whole truth, because our observations have led us to conclude that social facilitation serves to increase the *amount* of pecking or eating behavior in chicks, rather than to channel this behavior in terms of *what* specific objects are pecked at or eaten. Thus, it seems that we have to understand the cause-effect sequence by examining the developmental processes set in motion by the imprinting experience. It seems to us that the imprinting process, particularly the normal imprinting to the real mother, serves to unlock a series of behaviors that otherwise do not appear until much later if the animals are maintained in total isolation. Thus, social imprinting may activate a maturational process which then places the young bird into readiness for other kinds of imprinting or learning experiences, involving environment, food, or other things.

In returning to the subject of secondary characteristics of specific imprinting processes, we note: c) that even though both social and food objects have visual qualities, the effective visual qualities for each situation are different. Schaefer and Hess (1959) have shown that color preferences are completely reversed in relative order in the case of food and social imprinting. Goodwin and Hess (1969b) demonstrated that shape preferences among two-dimensional regular polygons, from triangle up to hexagon and circle, are also preferred in a precisely reversed order between food and social imprinting. Size also sharply differentiates between social and food imprinting objects: small objects can elicit intensive pecking, whereas large ones do not, with social behavior occurring toward large objects. Even among objects small enough to release regular pecking behavior, it is clearly apparent that forms ¼ inch in diameter elicit much less pecking than do ones of the same shape that are ⅛ inch in diameter (Goodwin and Hess, 1969a). In fact, an attempt to determine pecking preferences with forms ½ inch in diameter proved to be abortive, since the level of pecking behavior to these forms was extremely low. The effective *visual* qualities involved in environmental imprinting are as yet unclear.

Since the reinforcing objects differ in social and food imprinting, we can also expect to find that: d) different factors correlate with the beginning and ending of the relevant critical periods. In the case of social imprinting, increase in sensitivity appears to be correlated with increasing locomotor ability, decrease with increasing fear behavior, whereas in food imprinting, the increase in sensitivity appears to be correlated with a decrease in yolk sac supplies, with the decrease in sensitivity correlated with an observed temporary distintegration of innate pecking preferences (Goodwin, and Hess, 1969a). The correlation of these factors, however, does not in any sense indicate *causative* factors.

A still further secondary characteristic may possibly be found in that: e) the effects of aversive stimulation in enhancing social imprinting during the critical period may be a phenomenon peculiar to social imprinting, since it does not appear that noxious-tasting food objects would be more readily learned as *food* objects. Of course, there is the possibility that noxious food objects are more rapidly learned as non-food objects than real food objects are learned as food objects. On the other hand, the *aversive* stimulation from *hunger* may enhance food imprinting. This is possible since food imprinting occurs when chicks are first capable of experiencing hunger. This might perhaps be tested by exposing hungry and satiated chicks to the food imprinting situation. It would be necessary, of course, to control for the number of pecks performed by the hungry and satiated chicks.

Imprinting is a behavior process which is phylogentically very old. In fact, we are willing to entertain the notion that imprinting is the oldest, most primitive type of learning process. This idea is rather different from that expressed by Ewer (1956) more than a decade ago. She suggested, "Imprinting may be a stage in which a motor response has been perfected and the learning period which occurs first has become vestigal but has not yet disappeared." This seems to imply that a species has its members first learn a given response, then imprint it, and then finally inherit this response. While this might be so for some specific behaviors, we might add that some theorists would argue for the opposite order or progression in behavior development—that is, from innate to imprinted and then learned. We would, of course, hesitate to apply such a progression to the development of any given behavior in the evolutionary history of a specific species. However, it might very well be that in behavioral evolution—that is, the emergence of specific kinds of acquisition of behavior—fully innate behaviors were first, then imprinted ones, and finally incrementally learned ones. The incrementally learned behaviors, imprinted ones, and innate ones have all radiated into different subtypes and categories. These three major categories, furthermore, are not intended to be completely inclusive; they merely serve as illustrations of possible categories.

It is not necessarily the application of imprinting to the learning of specific things which has evolved, but the process itself. Any homologies that may be found in imprinting processes in different animal species are more probable in the imprinting as a process rather than in the nature of the thing learned. For example, the filial-parental relationship probably has evolved independently in several animal groups, as Hinde (1961) pointed out, so that the existence of an imprinting mechanism in the formation of the filial-parental bond in different species does not necessarily indicate a homology in the *social* learning processes in these species if they are not closely related species. Even in closely related species, the postulation of a homology in the social learning process must be applied with considerable caution.

We should further state that we do not believe that imprinting is a mechanism that has evolved for a given situation because of sensory imperfection on the part of the animal that is learning, as Ewer (1956) and Hinde (1962a, b) have suggested. This position of ours might be deduced from our earlier discussion of Sackett's (1963) suggestions in connection with Moltz's type 3 imprinting theory. As Goodwin and Hess (1969c) have shown, chicks have the same innate pecking preferences for two-dimensional forms before and after the sensitive period for food imprinting. Also, in the case of maternal imprinting (Klopfer, Adams, and Klopfer, 1964), olfactory imperfection on the part of the mother goat seems highly improbable. On the contrary, heightened olfactory sensitivity appears implicated.

Our reservations, of course, also apply to the notion that imprinting is "exposure learning" (Sluckin, 1964) or "perceptual learning" (Bateson, 1966). Such views of imprinting do not seem entirely adequate to us, particularly since they were based upon imprinting research in the laboratory, often involving sensorially deprived young. Our work (Hess and Hess, 1969) has shown that ducklings have an innate preference for the conspecific as a parental object, whereas Bateson (1966) has emphasized only the "conspicuousness" of the proffered imprinting object as influencing the young's stimulus preferences and Sluckin (1964) has spoken of the imprinting process as involving a sharpening of discrimination between the imprinting object and others. In other words, we do not feel that the perceptual learning view of imprinting does adequate justice to the degree to which the hatchling is genetically programmed to react in specific ways to specific stimulus constellations. Not only is the young bird's behavior highly organized at the time of hatching, as Bateson (1966) has emphasized, but also its *perceptual* organization, in our view. Our recent observations of actual imprinting between ducklings and their own biological mother have impressed us with the rapidity with which the young show absolute attachment to the mother and fear any new objects. This is in contrast to the usual laboratory imprinting situation, which must last for hours before the subjects show similar fear of any new objects. This is, indeed, evidence of a rather strong perceptual organization on the part of the animal if the preference for a specific imprinting object is manifested so markedly.

On the other hand, we do not yet know enough about environmental imprinting to be able to assess the degree of perceptual organization with respect to the environment. It might be that environmental imprinting involves some form of exposure learning but finding whether this is so requires, of course, specific experimentation when adequate techniques become available.

Recently, Lorenz (1961, 1965) has presented a scheme of the nature of adaptive modification of behavior in animals. While we have already described Lorenz's conceptualization in our earlier writings (Hess, 1962b, 1970), it bears repeating here with respect to the phylogentic status of imprinting as a behavior mechanism effecting adaptation of the species. Lorenz's theory, we believe, can serve to bring into perspective the various mechanisms determining behavioral adaptation of a species.

In his presentation, Lorenz advanced the theory that organisms have evolved so as to make learning an adaptive process in the modification of behavior, just as they have evolved fixed action patterns in the service of their survival. Lorenz posited that whenever an organism manifests adaptive behavior, this indicates that the organism has been so formed as to fit the environment in a fashion that will promote its survival. Fitting the organism to environmental requirements implies the acquisition of information regarding the nature of this environment. Lorenz pointed out that there are only two ways in which such information may be acquired: the process of phylogeny, which evolves behavior in the same fashion as any other morphological structure or physiological function; and the process of ontogeny, which involves modification of behavior, or learning, during the individual's life.

Lorenz has pointed out several general analogies between these two processes. For example, a species may be said to experiment by means of mutation, while an individual experiments by means of trial and error in instrumental learning. In evolution, part of the progeny is risked through mutation: a single mutation does not have a high probability of achieving better adaptiveness to the environment, but when one does, selection preserves it and it is disseminated quickly among the species. Similarly, one trial in normal trial-and-error learning has a small chance of being adaptive, but when it is, it is repeated and its place in the behavior repertoire solidified. The incremental process of behavior change is also evident in classical conditioning processes. Both evolution and learning processes, therefore, create and adaptively change the structure of the neural apparatus which determines behavior.

With this framework, it follows, according to Lorenz, that since learning processes are evolved during phylogenesis, they are not the function of an unorganized aggregate of neural elements. The organism is structured to learn, and to learn specific things in specific ways. This theoretical position is, indeed, a far cry from earlier views held by neurologists a few decades ago, when they were hindered by the lack of adequate analytical tools and by ignorance of the functioning of the brain, and thus were unable to perceive the highly complex functional structure of this organ. Chauvin (1959), a neurophysiologist of that not-too-distant time, humorously declared that if the skull were stuffed with cotton instead of containing the brain, the functioning of the higher nervous centers would not have been understood any better or any worse.

Learning thus gains the status of a *specific* survival-achieving function of the organism in the Lorenzian system. Lorenz (1961, 1965) postulated that learning occurs only at evolutionarily preformed places where genetically determined learning mechanisms are waiting to perform just that function. These learning mechanisms, Lorenz asserted, are very often unable to modify any but one very circumscribed system of behavior. As an example, he cited the fact that honeybees can use ir-regular forms such as trees and rocks as landmarks to find their way to the hive. But they are unable to use these forms as signals indicating the presence or absence of food. Forms that bees will learn to use as food signals must be geometrically regular, preferably radially symmetric, according to Lorenz. No one, Lorenz claimed, has been able to demon-strate *diffuse* modifiability of any arbitrarily chosen innately determined element of behavior.

While Lorenz (1961, 1965) postulated the existence of two major sources—evolution and learning—for behavior modification, it must also be pointed out that neither Lorenz nor any other ethologist conceives of two parallel and independent mechanisms determining behavior, least of all among neurophysiological processes. While Lorenz suggested that learning processes might have similar physiological process, (with this to be determined by future research), he denied that there is only one neurophysiological process in the determination of behavior into which learning does not enter. Rather, there are many physiological processes that innately determine behavior and are as different from each other as they are from learning, for the same reason that a tooth differs from a nose or foot. Such mechanisms as the innate releaser mechanism, fixed action pattern, orientation, and optomotoric reactions not only have different neurophysiological origins but also are completely different from each other in their functions. Placing all of them together into a single neurophysiological group would certainly result in their being defined solely by exclusion of learning processes, and such a group would not be conceptually useful.

It is with these different physiological processes in mind that etholog-ists have spoken of the intercalation of learned and innate behaviors. Just as learned and innate behaviors interweave with each other, differ-ent innate behavior mechanisms intercalate with each other, an example being the classic discovery of fixed action pattern and taxic orientation components in the egg-rolling behavior of the herring gull (Lorenz and Tinbergen, 1938).

For our theoretical position on the nature of the imprinting process, we would like to extend Lorenz's schema of the evolution of adaptive behavior by suggesting the evolution of different learning processes which are possessed as behavioral tools by the species. Just as there are different innately determined behavior mechanisms which inter-weave with each other and with learning, so also, in our opinion, are there different learning processes which interweave with each other and with innately given mechanisms in the behavior of the individual or-ganism. We have already shown how imprinting processes and associa-tion learning processes interweave with each other during ontogeny.

There probably are other learning processes which do the same. All these separate learning processes, like the separate innate processes, can exist and coexist in the same species and in the same individual.

The genetic program, evolved by the species, is of importance in the development of behavior in the individual during ontogeny. It is our view that imprinting processes occur only during a specific critical period—a period which is genetically determined. Association and classical conditioning processes, on the other hand, are not as strictly limited to specific periods, although in some individual cases there are indubitably sensitive period limitations on the use of these processes for the learning of specific things. As will be remembered from our presentation in Chapter 2, we have postulated three major types of sensitive periods: the critical period, the susceptible period, and the optimal period. Each of these sensitive periods involve less and less rapid learning, with learning during the optimal period and in cases where there is no sensitive period at all conforming the most closely to the classical learning paradigms, although, to be sure, the association learning of the particular things, such as language, during the relevant optimal period is demonstrably easier and more quickly accomplished than at a later time.

It will also be remembered that we have postulated these three principal types of sensitive periods primarily for purposes of simplification, since since there are very likely intergrades between these three categories. We do suggest, however, that the specific constellation of laws governing the learning processes associated with the sensitive periods are probably different for each type. Of course, some particular features of one process may also be present to some degree in one or more other processes. We feel that this kind of reasoning is as justifiable as considering a giraffe to be a different animal from a mouse even though both are vertebrate mammals and have the same number of neck bones.

In recent decades, there has been considerable controversy over the question of whether there is more than one learning process. None of these bitter theoretical controversies ever touched upon the question of the involvement of sensitive periods in learning processes as a differentiating factor. They have usually focused on the question of whether classical conditioning and instrumental trial-and-error learning could be explained by the same principles or whether they should be regarded as two distinct learning processes.

The goal of parsimony in explanation and conceptualization is certainly a commendable one. But the postulation of unitary principles for all learning processes is merely illusory simplicity. The contortions necessary in order to use the same principles of explanation for both classical conditioning and instrumental learning (cf. Osgood, 1953; Hilgard, 1956) are highly complex and anything but simple to a neophyte that attempts to understand them. Fortunately, most contemporary American learning theorists are willing to accept the notion of two major types of learning processes among those they have studied in the laboratory.

However, the desire to "simplify" and create unifying principles to explain many behavioral phenomena is still highly evident in the resistance of many theorists to the notion of imprinting as a unique learning process governed by laws which are not the same as those found for the association learning situations which have been studied in psychological laboratories. Behavioristically oriented animal psychologists frequently evidence a distinct dislike for the unique, the incongruent, in behavioral data. This is in strong contrast to the attitude of ethologists, who have proclaimed a constant readiness to observe the existence of new behavior-determining mechanisms. While ethologists do believe in unifying principles as much as do behaviorists, they have constructed and used their unifying principles in very different ways.

The desire to find simple explanatory principles for every phenomenon can be self-defeating. Many times in the past history of psychology and other sciences there have been vain hopes of finding single principles that would be all-explanatory. For example, when the reflex arc was discovered, it was thought that ultimately the functioning of the entire nervous system could be explained on the basis of the reflex arc principle. Naturally, it was eventually found that the higher neural levels required other explanatory principles. It should be evident to scientists that we must never assert categorically than a phenomenon or mechanism which has not yet been revealed does not exist; it can only be said that it has not yet been observed.

It is not even remotely possible at this point to set up a complete scheme of the possible different learning mechanisms which exist along the phylogenetic scale. However, there has been a beginning made in this direction through the work of Bitterman (1965). Bitterman compared learning processes in five different species—monkey, rat, bird, turtle, and fish. On the basis of his research, Bitterman has come to the conclusion that there are discontinuities in behavioral evolution along the phylogenetic scale concomitant with the emergence of new neural structures. The phylogenetic differences in learning behavior among animals are not, Bitterman asserted, one of degree, as has been so long and popularly assumed. Higher animals are not more adaptive in their behavior just because they have a greater number of neural elements in their sensory and motor systems. In place of such a notion, Bitterman suggested that the evolution of intelligence is not merely the improvement of earlier-existing processes and the increase of originally present neural elements but the actual appearance of completely new modes of intelligence and distinct neural mechanisms parallel with the appearance of new brain structures such as the cortex and therefore new modes of neurological organization.

Consideration of these many phylogenetic factors brings us to another extremely important point. This is that while laboratory work can be helpful in the study of imprinting, the natural situation in which imprinting occurs must always be the basic reference point. Furthermore, natural imprinting must be studied in itself. "Granting the indispensableness of the laboratory, it is well, after finishing with our animal, to observe him yet again in the field," Watson (1914) said—a dictum which some of his followers were not sufficiently aware of. Thus, we must specifically examine what factors follow each other or occur together, what the basic survival function of the adaptation in question is, and so on. An experiment by Hess and Hess (1969) provides an illustration of this point. Ducklings were initially imprinted individually or in a group of 5 members to a mallard decoy at the critical age. Ten more half-hour sessions were given over a 3-week period, with the ducklings run individually or in a group as in the initial session. Comparison of the test scores of the group-imprinted and the individually-imprinted ducklings revealed absolutely no differences in the latencies to reach the imprinted object. All ducklings in the free choice situation between the familiar decoy and a human being chose to go to the decoy on which they had been imprinted.

Because it is more difficult to observe a number of birds simultaneously than only one, it has been customary to expose birds individually to a social imprinting object, despite the fact that in the natural situation ducklings and chicks are together in a group during the period that imprinting to the parent takes place. An additional reason for this procedure has been to prevent the possibility of the young imprinting to each other rather than to the model. While it is true beyond doubt, as Polt and Hess (1964, 1966) and Ramsay and Hess (unpublished research; Hess, 1964), have shown, that chicks and ducklings imprint to their siblings when a parent object is absent, and then can fail to imprint to a parent, even when isolated from their siblings for a time, the identity of the scores of the group-imprinted and individually imprinted ducklings in Hess and Hess's (1969) report suggests strongly that simultaneous exposure to siblings at the time imprinting to a parent object is taking place does not have any deleterious effect upon that imprinting, since both the parental surrogate and the siblings are experienced together when the first exposure to them took place, just as in the natural situation. Fabricius (1951a, b), it may be remembered, noted that while the flocking tendency of naturally reared ducklings is very strong, when being with the parent-object conflicts with being with siblings, the former will be chosen. He was, however, erroneously led by this observation to conclude that sibling imprinting does not take place.

Why does the simultaneous exposure to siblings not interfere with the formation of the attachment to the parent? Some indication that such exposure may actually serve, during its initial stage, to activate and enhance the parental attachment may be seen in research by Gray (1962, 1964; Gray, Weeks, Anderson, and McNeal, 1963; Gray, Sallee, and Yates, 1964), in which it was found that upon initial *simultaneous* exposure to an age mate and to an adult hen during the 1st day of life, the chicks would stay near the age mate during the first 15-minute test period but gradually switch over to the adult hen and show a peak preference for the hen by the fifth or sixth 15-minute test period. Gottlieb (1963b, 1966) has shown that early prior exposure to conspecific duckling calls enhances the innate preference of pekin ducklings for conspecific maternal calls. Although different species are involved in these two studies, it would seem that successive exposure to sibling and maternal auditory signals is a positive factor in the attachment of the young to the parent, whereas in the case of visual exposure, the stimuli from siblings and the parent must be *simultaneous* in order for this to be the case.

However, we certainly cannot afford to make any absolutely definite conclusions on the basis of this evidence. It may be, for example, that in the natural situation, where the simultaneous exposure persists for several days, any initial difference in the efficacy of group versus individual exposure to the imprinting object would be effaced, particularly since *all* animals would then indubitably have gained no less than the optimal amount of relevant stimulation and made the required responses for the stimulation to have its effect. But in the laboratory situation, animals may be exposed to the relevant object for a very short period of time, say half an hour, so that only the primary imprinting takes place. Would there then be a difference in individual versus group exposure with respect to the effect of the imprinting exposure?

Smith and Bird (1963), while using chicks 18 to 30 hours old at the initial exposure, have made some observations that give some faint indication of what the possible effects may be when chicks or ducklings 13 to 16 hours old (the critical period peak) are exposed simultaneously to siblings and to the parent. While the chicks in question had been reared in individual isolation before the imprinting exposure, some were exposed individually, while others were exposed in a group of 3, and still others in a group of 3 with a well-imprinted leader present. The first test was at the age of 18 to 30 hours, and consisted of 2 trials of 5 minutes each; then 3 trials each of 3 minutes duration on the following 2 days were given. The total scores for all 5 tests showed that the group-run individuals were slightly more responsive to the imprinting model than were those run individually. Unfortunately, data are not given regarding the scores on the very first exposure, and also we do not know to what extent these subjects would have preferred the imprinting model they had been exposed to over a strange one, if given a simultaneous free choice.

It appears relevant to mention the studies that have dealt with the "social facilitation effect" in the initial imprinting exposure. In our own research, it was indicated that social facilitation—that is, having subjects exposed to an imprinting object while with an age mate that has already been thoroughly imprinted to that object—will result in evident imprinting even in subjects that were as old as 24 hours when exposed. Other observations on the enhancing effect of such social facilitation have been made by Collias and Collias (1956) and by Klopfer (1959a).

In a series of papers, Klopfer and Gottlieb (1962a, b; Gottlieb and Klopfer, 1961, 1962; Gottlieb, 1963d) have considered social facilitation, particularly with respect to the observation that individual ducklings in a brood will show maximum responsiveness to different stimulus aspects of the imprinting object and that there are age-related changes in responsiveness to specific aspects, primarily auditory and visual, of the imprinting model. These authors called these individual and age-related differences *behavioral polymorphism*. They regarded this behavioral polymorphism as especially adaptive in conjunction with the social facilitation effect and as acting so as to guarantee that all members of a brood will be able to respond to the parental object during the primary imprinting experience. Once again, then, it appears strongly possible that the response to the presence of siblings in the natural situation has evolved in such a way as to positively promote also the response to the presence of the parent as the primary social object.

Behavioral polymorphism promises to be a fruitful concept with respect to the study of imprinting and other behaviors in chicks and ducks. Over the years, we have been impressed by the individual differences among members of the same hatch. Research by Goodwin and Hess (1969a) has shown that although there are reliable pecking preference trends for two-dimensional forms in vantress broiler chicks, specific batches of chicks may not show precisely the same general preference gradient. Individual chicks, of course, are highly idiosyncratic in the specific pecking preferences they show, as has been indicated by many informal experiments with single chicks. It is, rather, in group data that the typical preference gradient is obtained. It is as if there is a pool of behavior tendencies upon which individual members of a species may draw and reflect in their own behavior. Such variability, of course, has considerable adaptive value in permitting the animals to survive changes in the environment.

Both social and food imprinting experiences serve to structure and refine initially broad preferences which are genetically based. The persistently observed individual and group variation in social and food imprinting preferences appears to maximally promote the survival of hatches of chicks (and perhaps other precocial species) in the natural and domesticated situations. It is, indeed, testimony to their phylogenetically evolved nature that such preferences and their variation should be maintained in the face of domestication, which has, in recent times, made it less and less necessary for young chicks to depend on their own behavioral resourcefulness for survival, since they are often kept in warm brooders and provided with ample food and water supplies.

While we have a rather broad concept of imprinting, we also feel very strongly that this concept must not be used promiscuously. We are not at all ready to regard any specific case of very rapid or very permanent learning as an instance of imprinting in our sense. Imprinting, in our minds, is both rapid, permanent, and with a limited genetically programmed time during the life cycle in which it occurs.

Thus, before we can seriously entertain the notion that young salmon, as Hasler (1960) suggests, might imprint to the olfactory qualities of the home waters in which they are reared, experimentation would have to be conducted to determine if it takes place rapidly and within a very limited sensitive period. The permanence of this olfactory learning is not, by itself, a sufficient indicator of an imprinting phenomenon, but must be accompanied by the other two factors of rapidity and critical period in order to be considered as such. After all, young salmon do spend a long period of time in their home waters before going out to the ocean. Similarly, Nicolai's (1964) suggestion that parasitic young widow birds *(Viduinae)* imprint the song of their specific *Estrildidae* host during the nest period must be regarded with caution, since he has not shown when this learning occurs or how long it takes. Some of the other instances of song learning which have been discussed in the literature may possibly be attributable to imprinting as such if the sensitive period is short enough and if limited experience is sufficient for the learning to take place.

The sudden appearance of inextinguishable day-night rhythms in 7-month old continuously light-reared mayflies *(Ecdyonurus torrentis)* after a single exposure to light-dark alternation in a 24-hour period (Harker, 1953) also cannot be considered imprinting, even though this learning is very rapid and permanent, for it is not limited to a specific life period for its occurrence. For the very same reason, Leyhausen's (1965) suggestion that cat species learn the upper limits of prey size through a process akin to imprinting is tempered by the apparent absence of a critical period for this learning. It is very much like the may-fly day-night rhythm learning, and these two may represent a category of rapid and persistent learning different from both imprinting and truly incremental trial-and-error learning processes. Both of these are quite obviously cases of genetically determined learning, and may represent an important category.

Thorpe (1961a, b) has suggested that the setting of circadian and other biological rhythms and the imprinting process have some features in common. This proposition, however, is one that requires careful exploration through the appropriate physiological techniques. While sensitive periods in learning—whether critical, susceptible, or optimal—undoubtedly have physiological correlates, just as much do biological rhythms, the similarities that do exist must not divert attention from the differences that also exist.

We might say that one of the reasons why social imprinting has captured the interest of scientists is its obvious potential effect upon the evolution of a species, since sexual behavior is affected by this imprinting. This, in turn, would influence the biological bases of the imprinting phenomenon. Cushing (1941) early expressed the notion of imprinted mating preferences as influencing the course of evolution, particularly the establishment of isolated breeding populations through the acquisition of different factors conditioning sexual preferences, a concept later favored by Spurway (1955). Kalmus and Smith (1966) have regarded imprinting's effects on sexual selection as similar to phenotypical assortative mating.

A recent example of this kind of concept is illustrated by Immelmann (1969), who has suggested that imprinted ecological preferences may be a first step to sympatric speciation. He also suggested the possibility of imprinted mating preferences increasing the influence of any ecological imprinting processes and, in turn, favoring the development of homogamy, thus leading to the development of groups which do not interbreed with each other.

In all cases of imprinting that we have observed, there is a very important survival need which is involved in the consequences of the imprinted learning: attachment of parent and young in social species; ingestion of edible food objects, shelter, and mating. Every single one of these is essential for the survival of the particular species, and it is selection pressure which has formed the characteristics of the imprinting which takes place in these situations. It is learning without which the species in question would not survive.

REFERENCES

ANDREW, R. J. Precocious adult behaviour in the young chick. *Animal Behaviour,* 1966, **14,** 485–500.

BAER, DONALD M., and GRAY, PHILIP H. Imprinting to a different species without overt following. *Perceptual and Motor Skills,* 1960, **10,** 171–174.

BAMBRIDGE, R. Early experience and sexual behavior in the domestic chicken. *Science,* 1962, **136,** 259–260.

BATESON, P. P. G. The characteristics and context of imprinting. *Biological Review,* 1966, **41,** 177–220.

BATESON, P. P. G. The development of social attachments in birds and man. *Advancements in Science,* London, 1969, **25,** 279–288.

BATESON, P. P. G. Imprinting and the development of preferences. In: J. H. Crook, editor, *Social Behaviour of Birds and Mammals.* New York: Academic Press, Inc. 1970. 109–132.

BATESON, P. P. G., and REESE, ELLEN P. Reinforcing properties of conspicuous objects before imprinting has occurred. *Psychonomic Science,* 1968, **10,** 379–380.

BATESON, P. P. G., and REESE, ELLEN P. The reinforcing properties of conspicuous stimuli in the imprinting situation. *Animal Behaviour,* 1969, **17,** 692–699.

BINDRA, DALBIR. *Motivation: A Systematic Reinterpretation.* New York: McGraw-Hill, 1959.

BITTERMAN, MORTON E. The evolution of intelligence. *Scientific American,* 1965, **212,** No. 1, 92–100.

BJÄRVALL, ANDERS. The critical period and the interval between hatching and exodus in mallard ducklings. *Behaviour,* 1967, **28,** 141–148.

BURGHARDT, GORDON M. The primacy effect of the first feeding experience in the snapping turtle. *Psychonomic Science,* 1967, **7,** 383–384.

BURGHARDT, GORDON M. Effects of early experience on food preference in chicks. *Psychonomic Science,* 1969, **14,** 7–8.

BURGHARDT, GORDON M., and HESS. ECKHARD H. Food imprinting in the snapping turtle, *Chelydra serpentina. Science,* 1966, **151,** 108–109.

CAMPBELL, BYRON A., and PICKLEMAN, JACK R. The imprinting object as a reinforcing stimulus. *Journal of Comparative and Physiological Psychology,* 1961, **54,** 592–596.

CHAUVIN, REMY. Notions modernes sur l'ethologie. *Psychologie Francaise,* 1959, **4,** 1–11.

COLLIAS, NICHOLAS E., and COLLIAS, ELSIE C. Some mechanisms of family integration in ducks. *Auk,* 1956, **73,** 378–400.

COLLINS, THOMAS B., JR. Strength of the following response in the chick in relation to the degree of "parent" contact. *Journal of Comparative and Physiological Psychology,* 1965, **60,** 192–195.

CUSHING, JOHN E. Non-genetic mating preference as a factor in evolution. *Condor,* 1941, **43,** 233–236.

DILGER, WILLIAM C., and JOHNSGARD, PAUL A. Comments on "species recognition" with special reference to the wood duck and the mandarin duck. *Wilson Bulletin,* 1959, **71,** 46–53.

DREVER, JAMES. The concept of early learning. *Transactions of the New York Academy of Sciences,* 1955, **17,** 463–469.

EWER, R. F. Imprinting in animal behaviour. *Nature,* 1956, **177,** 227–228.

FABRICIUS, ERIC. Some experiments on imprinting phenomena in ducks. *Proceedings of the Tenth International Ornithological Congress (Uppsala, June 1950),* 1951, **10,** 375–379. (a).

FABRICIUS, ERIC. Zur Ethologie junger Anatiden. *Acta Zoologica Fennica,* 1951, **68,** 1–175. (b).

FABRICIUS, ERIC. Some aspects of imprinting. *Animal Behaviour,* 1962, **10,** 181–182. (Abstract). (a).

FABRICIUS, ERIC. Some aspects of imprinting in birds. *Symposia of the Zoological Society of London,* 1962, **8,** 139–148. (b).

FABRICIUS, ERIC. Crucial periods in the development of the following response in young nidifugous birds. *Zeitschrift für Tierpsychologie, 1964,* **21,** 326–337.

FISCHER, GLORIA J. Distribution of practice effects on imprinting. *Psychonomic Science,* 1966, **5,** 197–198.

FISCHER, GLORIA J. Comparisons between chicks that fail to imprint and ones that imprint strongly. *Behaviour,* 1967, **29,** 262–267.

FISCHER, GLORIA J., and CAMPBELL, GARY L. The development of passive avoidance conditioning in leghorn chicks. *Animal Behaviour,* 1964, **12,** 268–269.

FISCHER, GLORIA J., CAMPBELL, GARY L., and DAVIS, W. MARVIN. Effects of ECS on retention of imprinting. *Journal of Comparative and Physiological Psychology,* 1965, **59,** 455–457.

GOODWIN, ELIZABETH BIRD, and HESS, ECKHARD H. Innate visual form preferences in the pecking behavior of young chicks. *Behaviour,* 1969, **34,** 223–237 (a).

GOODWIN, ELIZABETH BIRD, and HESS, ECKHARD H. Innate visual form preferences in the imprinting behavior of hatchling chicks. *Behaviour,* 1969, **34,** 238–254. (b).

GOODWIN, ELIZABETH BIRD, and HESS, ECKHARD H. Stimulus generalization and responses to "supernormal stimuli" in the unrewarded pecking behavior of young chicks. *Behaviour,* 1969, **34,** 255–266. (c).

GOTTLIEB, GILBERT. Developmental age as a baseline for determination of the critical period in imprinting. *Journal of Comparative and Physiological Psychology,* 1961, **54,** 422–427. (a).

GOTTLIEB, GILBERT. The following-response and imprinting in wild and domestic ducklings of the same species *(Anas platyrhynchos). Behaviour,* 1961, **18,** 205–228. (b).

GOTTLIEB, GILBERT. A naturalistic study of imprinting in wood ducklings *(Aix sponsa). Journal of Comparative and Physiological Psychology,* 1963, **56,** 86–91. (a).

GOTTLIEB, GILBERT. The facilitatory effect of the parental exodus call on the following-response of ducklings: One test of the self-stimulation hypothesis. *American Zoologist,* 1963, **3,** 518. (Abstract). (b).

GOTTLIEB, GILBERT. "Imprinting" in nature. *Science,* 1963, **139,** 497–498. (c).

GOTTLIEB, GILBERT. Following-response initiation in ducklings: Age and sensory stimulation. *Science,* 1963, **140,** 399–400. (d).

GOTTLIEB, GILBERT. Refrigerating eggs prior to incubation as a way of reducing error in calculating developmental age in imprinting experiments. *Animal Behaviour,* 1963, **11,** 290–292. (e).

GOTTLIEB, GILBERT. Imprinting in relation to parental and species identification by avian neonates. *Journal of Comparative and Physiological Psychology,* 1965, **59,** 345–356. (a).

GOTTLIEB, GILBERT. Components of recognition in ducklings. *Natural History,* February 1965, **74,** 12–19. (b).

GOTTLIEB, GILBERT. Species identification by avian neonates: Contributory effect of perinatal auditory stimulation. *Animal Behaviour,* 1966, **14,** 282–290.

GOTTLIEB, GILBERT. Prenatal behavior of birds. *Quarterly Review of Biology,* 1968, **43,** 148–174.

GOTTLIEB, GILBERT. *Development of Species Identification in Birds.* Chicago: University of Chicago Press, 1971.

GOTTLIEB, GILBERT, and KLOPFER, PETER H. Preliminary findings on the relation of developmental age to visual and auditory imprinting. *American Psychologist,* 1961, **16,** 350. (Abstract).

GOTTLIEB, GILBERT, and KLOPFER, PETER H. The relation of developmental age to auditory and visual imprinting. *Journal of Comparative and Physiological Psychology,* 1962, **55,** 821–826.

GRAY, PHILIP H. Is the imprinting critical period an artifact of a biological clock? *Perceptual and Motor Skills,* 1962, **14,** 70.

GRAY, PHILIP H. Interaction of temporal and releasing factors in familial recognition of own and ancestral species. *Perceptual and Motor Skills,* 1964, **18,** 445–448.

GRAY, PHILIP H., SALLEE, STELLA J., and YATES, ALLEN T. Developmental and chronological ages versus time of day as factors in released imprinting responses. *Perceptual and Motor Skills,* 1964, **19,** 763–768.

GRAY, PHILIP H., WEEKS, SAM, ANDERSON, CHARLES D., and McNEAL, SHIRLEY. Further evidence of a "time of day at test" factor in the released social responses of isolated chicks. *Proceedings of the Montana Academy of Science,* 1963, **23,** 212–218.

GUITON, PHILIP E. Socialisation and imprinting in brown leghorn chicks. *Animal Behaviour,* 1959, **7,** 26–34.

HAILMAN, JACK P. Why is the male wood duck strikingly colorful? *American Naturalist,* 1959, **93,** 383–384. (letter).

HALDANE, J. B. S., and SPURWAY, H. Imprinting and the evolution of instincts. *Nature,* 1956, **178,** 85–86.

HARKER, JANET E. The diurnal rhythm of activity of mayfly nymphs. *Journal of Experimental Biology,* 1953, **30,** 525–533.

HARLOW, HARRY F., and HARLOW, MARGARET K. Social deprivation in monkeys. *Scientific American,* 1962, **207,** No. 5, 136–146.

HASLER, ARTHUR D. Guideposts of migrating fishes. *Science,* 1960. **132,** 785–792.

HEBB, DONALD O. On the nature of fear. *Psychological Review,* 1946, **53,** 250–275.

HESS, ECKHARD H. Effects of meprobamate on imprinting in waterfowl. *Annals of the New York Academy of Sciences,* 1957, **67,** 724–732.

HESS, ECKHARD H. The relationship between imprinting and motivation. In: Jones, M. R., editor, *Nebraska Symposium on Motivation, 1959.* Lincoln: University of Nebraska Press, 1959. 44–77. (a).

HESS, ECKHARD H. Two conditions limiting critical age for imprinting. *Journal of Comparative and Physiological Psychology,* 1959, **52,** 515–518. (b).

HESS, ECKHARD H. Imprinting. *Science,* 1959, **130,** 133–141. (c).

HESS, ECKHARD H. Imprinting and the critical period concept. In: E. L. Bliss, editor, *Roots of Behavior.* New York: Hoeber-Harper, 1962. 254–263. (a).

HESS, ECKHARD H. Ethology. In: R. Brown, E. Galanter, E. H. Hess, and G. Mandler, *New Directions in Psychology,* New York: Holt, Rinehart, & Winston, 1962. (b).

HESS, ECKHARD H. Imprinting in birds. *Science,* 1964, **146,** 1128–1139.

HESS, ECKHARD H. Ethology and developmental psychology. In: P. Mussen, editor, *Carmichael's Manual of Child Psychology.* Third edition. New York: Wiley & Sons, 1970. Volume 1, Chapter 1.

HESS, ECKHARD H. The natural history of imprinting. *Annals of the New York Academy of Sciences,* 1972, **193,** 124–136.

HESS, ECKHARD H., and HESS, DORLE B. Innate factors in imprinting. *Psychonomic Science,* 1969, **14,** 129–130.

HESS, ECKHARD H., and PETROVICH, SLOBODAN B. The early development of parent-young interaction in nature. In: H. W. Reese & J. R. Nesselroade, editors, *Life-Span Developmental Psychology: Methodological Issues.* In press.

HESS, ECKHARD H., POLT, JAMES M., and GOODWIN, ELIZABETH. Effects of carisoprodol on early experience and learning. In J. G. Miller, editor, *The Pharmacology and Clinical Usefulness of Carisoprodol.* Detroit: Wayne State University Press, 1959. 51–65.

HILGARD, ERNEST R. *Theories of Learning.* Second edition. New York: Appleton-Century-Crofts, 1956.

HINDE, ROBERT A. The establishment of the parent-offspring relation in birds, with some mammalian analogies. In: W. H. Thorpe, and O. L. Zangwill, editors, *Current Problems in Animal Behaviour.* London: Cambridge University Press, 1961.

HINDE, ROBERT A. Some comments on the nature of the imprinting problem. *Animal Behaviour,* 1962, **10,** 181. (Abstract). (a).

HINDE, ROBERT A. Some aspects of the imprinting problem. *Symposia of the Zoological Society of London,* 1962, **8,** 129–138. (b).

HINDE, ROBERT A. The nature of imprinting. In: B. M. Foss, editor, *Determinants of Infant Behaviour II.* Second Tavistock seminar on mother-infant interaction, London, 1961. New York: Wiley, 1963. 227–233.

HOFFMAN, HOWARD S. The control of distress vocalization by an imprinted stimulus. *Behaviour,* 1968, **30,** 175–191.

HOFFMAN, HOWARD S., SCHIFF, D., ADAMS, J., and SEARLE, JOHN L. Enhanced distress vocalization through selective reinforcement. *Science,* 1966, **151,** 352–354.

HOFFMAN, HOWARD S., SEARLE, JOHN L., TOFFEY, SHARON, and KOZMA, FREDERICK, JR. Behavioral control by an imprinted stimulus. *Journal of the Experimental Analysis of Behavior,* 1966, **9,** 177–189.

HOFFMAN, HOWARD S., STRATTON, JAMES W., NEWBY, VALERIE and BARRETT, JAMES E. Development of behavioral control by an imprinting stimulus. *Journal of Comparative and Physiological Psychology,* 1970, **71,** 229–236.

IMMELMANN, KLAUS. Ökologische und stammesgeschichtliche Betrachtungen zum Prägungsphänomen. *Zoologischer Anzeiger,* 1969, **183,** 1–12.

JAMES, H., and BINKS, CAROLYN. Escape and avoidance learning in newly hatched chicks. *Science,* 1963, **139,** 1293–1294.

JAYNES, JULIAN. Imprinting: The interaction of learned and innate behavior. I. Development and generalization. *Journal of Comparative and Physiological Psychology,* 1956, **49,** 201–206.

JAYNES, JULIAN. Imprinting: The interaction of learned and innate behavior. II. The critical period. *Journal of Comparative and Physiological Psychology,* 1957, **50,** 6–10.

JAYNES, JULIAN. Imprinting: The interaction of learned and innate behavior. III. Practice effects on performance, retention, and fear. *Journal of Comparative and Physiological Psychology,* 1958, **51,** 234–237. (a).

JAYNES, JULIAN. Imprinting: The interaction of learned and innate behavior. IV. Generalization and emergent discrimination. *Journal of Comparative and Psysiological Psychology,* 1958, **51,** 238–242. (b).

KALMUS, H., and SMITH, SHEILA MAYNARD. Some evolutionary consequences of pegmatypic mating systems (imprinting). *American Naturalist,* 1966, **100,** 619–635.

KAYE, STUART M. Primacy and recency in imprinting. *Psychonomic Science,* 1965, **3,** 271–272.

KING, DONALD LEE. A review and interpretation of some aspects of the infant-mother relationship in mammals and birds. *Psychological Bulletin,* 1966, **65,** 143–155.

KLOPFER, PETER H. An analysis of learning in young Anatidae. *Ecology,* 1959, **40,** 90–102. (a).

KLOPFER, PETER H. The development of sound preferences in ducks. *Wilson Bulletin,* 1959, **71,** 262–266. (b).

KLOPFER, PETER H. *Science,* 1961, **133,** 923–924. (letter).

KLOPFER, PETER H. *Behavioral Aspects of Ecology.* Englewood Cliffs, N.J.: Prentice-Hall, 1962.

KLOPFER, PETER H. Parameters of imprinting. *American Naturalist,* 1964, **98,** 173–182.

KLOPFER, PETER H. Is imprinting a cheshire cat? *Behavioral Science,* 1967, **12,** 122–129. (a).

KLOPFER, PETER H. Stimulus preferences and imprinting. *Science,* 1967, **156,** 1394–1396. (b).

KLOPFER, PETER H. Imprinting: determining its perceptual basis in ducklings. *Journal of Comparative and Physiological Psychology,* 1971, **75,** 378–385.

KLOPFER, PETER H., ADAMS, DONALD K., and KLOPFER, MARTHA S. Maternal "imprinting" in goats. *Proceedings of the National Academy of Science,* 1964, **52,** 911–914.

KLOPFER, PETER H., and GOTTLIEB, GILBERT. Imprinting and behavioral polymorphism: Auditory and visual imprinting in domestic ducks (*Anas platyrhynchos*) and the involvement of the critical period. *Journal of Comparative and Physiological Psychology,* 1962, **55,** 126–130. (a).

KLOPFER, PETER H., and GOTTLIEB, GILBERT. Learning ability and behavioral polymorphism within individual clutches of wild ducklings. *Zeitschrift für Tierpsychologie,* 1962, **19,** 183–190. (b).

KLOPFER, PETER H., and HAILMAN, JACK P. Basic parameters of following and imprinting in precocial birds. *Zeitschrift für Tierpsychologie,* 1964, **21,** 755–761. (a).

KLOPFER, PETER H., and HAILMAN, JACK P. Perceptual preferences and imprinting in chicks. *Science,* 1964, **145,** 1333–1334. (b).

KOVACH, JOSEPH K., FABRICIUS, ERIC, and FÄLT, LARS. Relationships between imprinting and perceptual learning. *Journal of Comparative and Physiological Psychology,* 1966, **61,** 449–454.

KOVACH, JOSEPH K., and HESS, ECKHARD H. Imprinting: Effects of painful stimulation on the following behavior. *Journal of Comparative and Physiological Psychology,* 1963, **56,** 461–464.

LANNOY, JACQUES de. Zur Prägung von Instinkthandlungen (Untersuchungen an Stockenten *Anas platyrhynchos* L. und Kolbenenten *Netta rufina* Pallas). *Zeitschrift für Tierpsychologie,* 1967, **24,** 162–200.

LEMMON, WILLIAM B., and PATTERSON, GEORGE H. Depth perception in sheep: Effects of interrupting the mother-neonate bond. *Science,* 1964, **145,** 835–836.

LEVINE, SEYMOUR. Stimulation in infancy. *Scientific American,* 1960, **205,** No. 5, 81–86.

LEWIS, M. Some nondecremental effects of effort. *Journal of Comparative and Physiological Psychology,* 1964, **57,** 367–373.

LEYHAUSEN, PAUL. Über die Funktion der Relativen Stimmungshierarchie (Dargestellt am Beispiel der phylogenetischen und ontogenetischen Entwicklung des Beutefangs von Raubtieren). *Zeitschrift für Tierpsychologie,* 1965, **22,** 412–494.

LORENZ, KONRAD Z. Der Kumpan in der Umwelt des Vogels; die Artgenosse als auslösende Moment sozialer Verhaltungsweisen. *Journal für Ornithologie,* 1935, **83,** 137–213, 289–413. Also in translation, as Companions as factors in the bird's environment. In: Konrad Lorenz, *Studies in Animal and Human Behaviour.* Translated by R. Martin. Cambridge, Mass.: Harvard University Press, 1970. Volume 1. 101–258.

LORENZ, KONRAD Z. The companion in the bird's world. *Auk,* 1937, **54,** 245–273.

LORENZ, KONRAD Z. Morphology and behavior patterns in closely allied species. In: B. Schaffner, ed., *Group Processes.* New York: Josiah Macy Jr. Foundation, 1955. 168–220.

LORENZ, KONRAD Z. Phylogenetische Anpassung und adaptive Modifikation des Verhaltens. *Zeitschrift für Tierpsychologie,* 1961, **18,** 139–187.

LORENZ, KONRAD Z. *Evolution and Modification of Behavior.* Chicago: University of Chicago Press, 1965.

LORENZ, KONRAD Z., and TINBERGEN, NIKO. Taxis und Instinkthandlung in der Eirollbewegung der Graugans. I. *Zeitschrift für Tierpsychologie,* 1938, **2,** 1–29.

MACDONALD, GLENN E., and SOLANDT, A. Imprinting: Effects of drug-induced immobilization. *Psychonomic Science,* 1966, **5,** 95–96.

MELVIN, KENNETH B., CLOAR, F. THOMAS, and MASSINGILL, LUCINDA S. Imprinting of bobwhite quail to a hawk. *Psychological Record,* 1967, **17,** 235–238.

MENAKER, ESTHER. A note on some biologic parallels between certain innate animal behavior and moral masochism. *Psychoanalytic Review,* 1956, **43,** 31–41.

MOLTZ, HOWARD. Imprinting: Empirical bases and theoretical significance. *Psychological Bulletin,* 1960, **57,** 291–314.

MOLTZ, HOWARD. Imprinting: An epigenetic approach. *Psychological Review,* 1963, **70,** 123–138.

MOLTZ, HOWARD, ROSENBLUM, LEONARD A., and STETTNER, L. JAY. Some parameters of imprinting effectiveness. *Journal of Comparative and Physiological Psychology*, 1960, **53**, 297–301.

MOLTZ, HOWARD, and STETTNER, L. JAY. The influence of patterned-light deprivation on the critical period for imprinting. *Journal of Comparative and Physiological Psychology*, 1961, **54**, 279–283.

NICOLAI, J. Der Brutparasitimus der Viduinae als ethologisches Problem. *Zeitschrift für Tierpsychologie*, 1964, **21**, 129–204.

OSGOOD, CHARLES E. *Method and Theory in Experimental Psychology*. New York: Oxford University Press, 1953.

PADILLA, SINFOROSO G. Further studies on the delayed pecking of chicks. *Journal of Comparative Psychology*, 1935, **20**, 413–443

PETERSON, NEIL. Control of behavior by presentation of an imprinted stimulus. *Science*, 1960, **132**, 1395–1396.

POLT, JAMES M. The effects of social experience on imprinting. Unpublished doctoral dissertation, University of Chicago, 1966.

POLT, JAMES M., and HESS, ECKHARD H. Following and imprinting: Effects of light and social experience. *Science*, 1964, **143**, 1185–1187.

POLT, JAMES M., and HESS, ECKHARD H. Effects of social experience on the following response in chicks. *Journal of Comparative and Physiological Psychology*, 1966, **61**, 268–270.

POULSEN, HOLGAR. Maturation and learning in the improvement of some instinctive activities. *Videnskabelige Meddelser fra Dansk naturhistorisk Forening, Copenhagen*, 1951, **113**, 155–170.

RAMSAY, A. OGDEN, and HESS, ECKHARD H. A laboratory approach to the study of imprinting. *Wilson Bulletin*, 1954, **66**, 196–206.

RAMSAY, A. OGDEN, and HESS, ECKHARD H. The influence of sibling experience on imprinting in wild mallards. Unpublished research.

ROSENBLUM, LEONARD A., HARLOW, HARRY F. Approach-avoidance conflict in the mother-surrogate situation. *Psychological Reports*, 1963, **12**, 83–85.

SACKETT, GENE P. A neural mechanism underlying unlearned, critical period, and developmental aspects of visually controlled behavior. *Psychological Review*, 1963, **70**, 40–50.

SALZEN, ERIC A. Imprinting and fear. *Animal Behaviour*, 1962, **10**, 183. (Abstract). (a).

SALZEN, ERIC A. Imprinting and fear. *Symposia of the Zoological Society of London*, 1962, **8**, 199–217. (b).

SALZEN, ERIC A. The interaction of experience, stimulus characteristics, and exogenous androgen in the behaviour of domestic chicks. *Behaviour*, 1966, **26**, 286–322.

SALZEN, ERIC A. Imprinting in birds and primates. *Behaviour*, 1967, **28**, 232–254.

SALZEN, ERIC A. Imprinting and environmental learning. In: L. R. Aronson, E. Tobach, D. S. Lehrman, and J. S. Rosenblatt, editors, *Development and Evolution of Behavior*. San Francisco: Freeman & Co., 1970.

SALZEN, ERIC A., and MEYER, CORNELIUS C. Reversibility of imprinting. *Journal of Comparative and Physiological Psychology*, 1968, **66**, 269–275.

SALZEN, ERIC A., and SLUCKIN, WLADYSLAW. The incidence of the following response and the duration of responsiveness in domestic fowl. *Animal Behaviour*, 1959, **7**, 172–179.

SCHAEFER, HALMUTH H., and HESS, ECKHARD H. Color preferences in imprinting objects. *Zeitschrift für Tierpsychologie*, 1959, **16**, 161–172.

SCHNEIRLA, T. C. An evolutionary and developmental theory of biphasic processes underlying approach and withdrawal. In: M. R. Jones, editor, *Nebraska Symposium on Motivation*, 1959. Lincoln: University of Nebraska Press, 1959. 1–43.

SCHNEIRLA, T. C. Aspects of stimulation and organization in approach/withdrawal processes underlying behavioral development. In: D. S. Lehrman, R. A. Hinde, and E. Shaw, editors, *Advances in the Study of Behavior*. New York: Academic Press, 1965. Volume 1.

SCHLEIDT, WOLFGANG. Precocial sexual behaviour in turkeys *(Meleagris gallopavo L.)*. *Animal Behaviour*, 1970, **18**, 760–761.

SCHULMAN, ALLAN H. Precocial sexual behaviour in imprinted male turkeys *(Meleagris gallopavo)*. *Animal Behaviour*, 1970, **18**, 758–759.

SCHULMAN, ALLAN H., HALE, E. B., and GRAVES, H. B. Visual stimulus characteristics for initial approach response in chicks *(Gallus domesticus)*. *Animal Behaviour*, 1970, **18**, 461–466.

SCHUTZ FRIEDRICH. Die Bedeutung früher sozialer Eindrücke während der "Kinder- und Jugendzeit" bei Enten. *Zeitschrift für Experimentelle und Angewandte Psychologie*, 1964, **11**, 169–178.

SCHUTZ, FRIEDRICH. Sexuelle Prägung bei Anatiden. *Zeitschrift für Tierpsychologie*, 1965, **22**, 50–103.

SLUCKIN, WLADYSLAW. *Imprinting and Early Learning*. London: Methuen, 1964.

SLUCKIN, WLADYSLAW, and SALZEN, ERIC A. Imprinting and perceptual learning. *Quarterly Journal of Experimental Psychology*, 1961, **13**, 65–77.

SMITH, FREDERICK V. The experimental study of perceptual aspects of imprinting. *Animal Behaviour*, 1962, **10**, 182–183. (Abstract). (a).

SMITH, FREDERICK V. Perceptual aspects of imprinting. *Symposia of the Zoological Society of London*, 1962, **8**, 171–192. (b).

SMITH, FREDERICK V., and BIRD, M. W. Group factors in the response of the domestic chick to a distant visual stimulus. *Animal Behaviour*, 1963, **11**, 397–399.

SMITH, FREDERICK V., *Attachment of the Young: Imprinting and Other Developments*. Edinburgh: Oliver & Boyd, Ltd., 1969.

SPURWAY, H. The double relevance of imprinting to taxonomy. *British Journal of Animal Behaviour*, 1955, **3**, 123–124.

STEVEN, D. M. Transference of the "imprinting" in a wild gosling. *British Journal of Animal Behaviour*, 1955, **3**, 14–16.

STROBEL, MICHAEL G., BAKER, D. G., and MACDONALD, GLENN E. The effect of embryonic X-irradiation on the approach and following response in newly hatched chicks. *Canadian Journal of Psychology*, 1967, **21**, 322–328.

STROBEL, MICHAEL G., CLARK, GORDON M., and MACDONALD, GLENN E. Ontogeny of the approach response: A radiosensitive period during embryonic development of domestic chicks. *Journal of Comparative and Physiological Psychology*, 1968, **65**, 314–319.

STROBEL, MICHAEL G., FREEDMAN, S. L., and MACDONALD, GLENN E. Social facilitation of feeding in newly hatched chickens as a function of imprinting. *Canadian Journal of Psychology*, 1970, **24**, 207–215.

THOMPSON, WILLIAM R., and DUBANOSKI, RICHARD A. Imprinting and the "Law of Effort." *Animal Behaviour*, 1964, **12**, 213–218. (a).

THOMPSON, WILLIAM R., and DUBANOSKI, RICHARD A. Early arousal and imprinting in chicks. *Science*, 1964, **143**, 1187–1188. (b).

THORPE, W. H. The nature and significance of imprinting. *British Journal of Animal Behaviour,* 1955, **3,** 121.

THORPE, W. H. Studies of problems common to the psychology of animals and men. In: W. H. Thorpe, and O. L. Zangwill, editors, *Current Problems in Animal Behaviour.* Cambridge, England: Cambridge University Press, 1961. 167–174. (a).

THORPE, W. H. Sensitive periods in the learning of animals and men: A study of imprinting with special reference to the induction of cyclic behaviour. In: W. H. Thorpe, and O. L. Zangwill, editors, *Current Problems in Animal Behaviour.* Cambridge, England: Cambridge University Press, 1961. 194–224. (b).

TOLMAN, CHARLES W. A possible relationship between the imprinting critical period and arousal. *Psychological Record,* 1963, **13,** 181–185.

VERPLANCK, W. S. An hypothesis on imprinting. *British Journal of Animal Behaviour,* 1955, **3,** 123.

WALLER, PATRICIA F., and WALLER, MARCUS B. Some relationships between early experience and later social behavior in ducklings. *Behaviour,* 1963, **20,** 343–363.

WATSON, JOHN B. *Behavior: An Introduction to Comparative Psychology.* New York: Holt, 1914.

8

A Look to the Future: The Natural History of Imprinting

Up to now, we have been dealing primarily with laboratory imprinting situations. We have constantly attempted to relate the findings of our own research in laboratory imprinting to the function of imprinting in natural conditions. But now, after almost twenty years of this work, we have just begun to realize that this was not enough. We have suddenly concluded that if we want to find out what imprinting really is, we must look very carefully at the real imprinting experiences that occur between hatchlings and their biologically appropriate parent.

We have already made some beginnings in this direction, particularly since much of our recent work has, indeed, indicated that we need to know what actually happens in a real imprinting experience. We have known for a long time that while hatchling ducks and chicks can respond to a lot of different substitute mother-objects, there is very definitely a variation in the ability of different kinds of objects to elicit filial attachment behavior from hatchlings. It just simply is not true that any object will do as a substitute parent. The literature is replete with findings that support this idea.

It may seem ironic, after having spent so much time and thought on laboratory imprinting, for us now to wonder whether it has been really relevant to the study of natural imprinting. We may even ask why, in all these years since Lorenz's classic 1935 paper, laboratory imprinting seemed to be relevant. This may be because laboratory imprinting procedures so bombard the hatchling with inappropriate stimuli that the response system for which it is programmed to perform at that age finally is squeezed out of it. In short, laboratory imprinting is a sort of brainwashing that forces a hatchling that is searching (in the appetitive sense) for a mother to accept a substitute. The best analogy we can think for this at the moment is the well-known law of specific nerve energies. Eyes respond to visual stimuli, not to auditory stimuli, and ears respond to auditory stimuli, not to visual ones. Yet an eye which is bumped, or electrically stimulated, will cause us to see "light," because that is the response that is programmed into the brain as a reaction to messages from visual nerves. We do not mean by this that there are specific nerve energies involved in social imprinting, but it has struck us that laboratory imprinting really does inundate a hatchling with a tremendous dose of biologically inappropriate stimuli, and thus elicits the behavior which the duckling is programmed to give immediately— almost instantaneously—to the biologically appropriate mother. Laboratory imprinting requires more time and more effort, among other things, to have an effect, and the more so, the more the object differs from the real mother.

We have, indeed, learned a great deal about laboratory imprinting— primacy versus recency, the law of effort, the sensitive period, the effects of drugs, the efficacy of different kinds of stimuli, the effects of different kinds of autonomic drugs, and so forth—all of which still appear to be valid. Laboratory imprinting, as we have found, is viewed by many researchers as being a straightforward learning phenomenon, measured in terms of number of feet of following, number of seconds close to the object, distress calls, and so on. Mother surrogates usually have been offered to hatchlings at specified lengths of time. The prior experiences of the hatchlings, from the time of hatching up to the imprinting exposure, have been limited, often through maintaining hatchlings in visual and social isolation so as to prevent contamination of the young bird's responses to the imprinting object. Hence, most imprinting experiments have been conducted as *deprivation experiments,* with the result that the animals involved are behaviorally abnormal. This is because the hatching, handling, and maintenance of the young birds in man-constructed artificial laboratory settings, bearing little resemblance to the natural outdoors setting, prevent the birds from obtaining normal environmental experience. They are placed in a precisely constructed apparatus with numerous controls and other experimental equipment. They are imprinted on *biologically inappropriate* objects, such as flickering lights, inanimate decoys, milk bottles, pyramids, and cubes. Furthermore, the hatchlings may be required to push levers or do other things which they would never perform in natural conditions. These artificial conditions have resulted in the tremendous variation in the results, conclusions, and theoretical speculations regarding imprinting on the basis of experimental data, because much information bearing upon the actual imprinting phenomenon has been missed. In fact, the artificiality has become so extreme that the only criterion for any research work being in the area of imprinting may be the researcher's use of the word "imprinting" in reporting his work. Klopfer's (1967) question, "Is imprinting a Cheshire cat?" is highly apropos in this respect.

So we have begun looking at the behavior of naïve ducklings in relation to real duck mothers. The first thing that became apparent to us is that after a few minutes of experience with a real mother—that is, almost immediately—the duckling in question will display fear and a whole host of other behaviors. In laboratory imprinting situations, on the other hand, such behaviors usually do not make their appearance until hours later. In some instances, when a duckling has spent as little as 10 minutes with a real mother, it is impossible to get that duckling to show filial behavior toward a male mallard duck decoy or a human being: it shows fear and avoidance of such objects. While such ducklings will, of course, join siblings when the mother is absent, they will not immediately follow a maternal surrogate. In contrast, it has been reported repeatedly in the literature, and, indeed, we have observed this ourselves, that even after *extensive* laboratory imprinting experience, a duckling can readily be induced to follow something else. Our own primacy-versus-recency experiment (Hess, 1959), involving the use of two different duck decoys, illustrates this perfectly, and so does a recent report by Kovach, Paden, and Wilson (1968). This transfer of following behavior after extensive laboratory imprinting is, indeed, in great contrast to the zero reversibility found in natural imprinting to the real mother.

Obviously, to get at the real heart of the matter, we must intensively analyze natural imprinting experiences. As a result of these initial observations, we have begun making minute and thorough examination of motion picture records of several natural imprinting experiences. We are currently making very careful and detailed film and binocular observations of female mallards and their offspring in natural settings, beginning with the onset of incubation, and going through incubation, hatching, exodus from the nest, and the subsequent weeks of life—that is, we are making an *ethogram* of imprinting. We are monitoring as many as possible of the many behavioral, physiological, and environmental events occurring during the development of the parent-young relationship in nature. In doing this, we must first study the natural process through methods which do not alter the animals' environment or interact with their behavior—that is, they must not introduce contaminating variables into the experimental situation. Other aspects of the research can involve manipulation only to the extent that the natural situation is still left as intact as possible, with the experimental variation being measured in relation to the natural situation. *Hence, the control is always the actual natural parent-offspring relation in a feral setting.* It is never a state in which animals are deprived as completely as possible and are permitted to experience only the few variables which are introduced experimentally.

Our data resulting from the observation of imprinting in the natural setting, based upon the wild and semi-wild mallard duck population resident at the Lake Cove research station, are, of course, far from being complete. This is because knowledge of the genetic and ecological factors that affect early and contemporary experiences and behavior of animals is necessary for understanding the complex interactions in observed events. Our data do, however, indicate some of the factors which strongly influence natural imprinting events.

For example, observation of actual egg laying, incubation, and hatching events in the natural setting immediately reveals several differences from laboratory events. Detailed records which have been made over a period of 6 years at Lake Cove show that among unrestricted female mallards living out-of-doors, egg laying normally begins in the latter part of February. Eggs are laid at daily intervals with an occasional skip, and total number laid may vary. Normally, incubation begins after 10 to 12 eggs have been laid. The pipping of the eggs normally takes place sometime between 24 and 27 days after the onset of incubation, with the exact time of occurrence being determined by the total incubation duration, which may be between 25 and 28 days from onset to hatching. Pipping generally occurs during the morning hours, between dawn and noon. The following day, usually during the morning hours, the eggs hatch, with an interval of 6 hours or so between the hatching of the first and the last ducklings in the clutch. Then, during the next day, or, infrequently, two days later, the female leaves the nest with the young for the nest exodus if weather conditions are reasonably favorable. Exodus often occurs during the morning, but usually not until the middle or late morning. Therefore, the average age of the ducklings at the time of the nest exodus is normally 24 to 26 hours after hatching, although on occasion they may be as old as 48 hours. Bjärvall (1967) has reported similar observations. It should be noted that the exodus from the nest thus normally occurs well past the critical period peak for imprintability that has been observed in laboratory imprinting (Hess, 1957).

In a laboratory incubator, however, the length of incubation from onset to hatching is approximately 22 to 26 days. There are also extreme variations, so that laboratory incubation can be as short as 21 days or as long as 28 days for individual eggs. Whatever the variations, hatching in a typical laboratory incubator normally occurs over a period of 2 or 3 days. This is the case even when all eggs are placed into the incubator after deep chilling to terminate any partially developed embryos, as was done by Gottlieb (1963d) in order to try to synchronize all ducklings to the same developmental age.

Not only are there practical problems in assessing the post-hatch age of ducklings for laboratory imprinting experiments when there is this time spread, and an inconvenience to experimenters when ducklings must be removed during night hours, but the question has also been raised as to whether the ducklings that hatch sooner are developmentally different from those that hatch later. Closely related to this question is whether the act of hatching is strictly developmentally timed or not. Gottlieb (1961, 1963d) has addressed himself to the first question through the deep chilling technique described above.

In the natural setting, however, the situation is *quite different,* since the hatching of wild mallard eggs is synchronous. Bjärvall (1967), for example, has reported that naturally incubated eggs hatch within 3 to 8 hours of each other. At Lake Cove, where wild mallard breed freely, records have been made over several breeding seasons with respect to hatching synchronism. These records show that, at Lake Cove, wild-incubated eggs of the same clutch normally hatch within 6 hours of each other.

Hatching synchronism of this sort should be of value in ensuring that all young of a single clutch were at reasonably similar stages of locomotor ability and experience at the time that the female mallard leads them for the nest exodus. This would be of greater adaptive value than if 2-day old ducklings were in a nest when others were still hatching, as would be the case if natural hatching followed the same pattern as incubator hatching.

To investigate this problem, records were kept for one season with respect to the number of days each wild female's clutch was incubated. Records were also kept of the noon-time temperature for each day of incubation. A total of 40 clutches were thus studied during the successive months of March, April, May, and June.

These records showed that the incubation duration of the naturally incubated eggs varied between 25 and 28 days. However, the females which had clutches *early* in the spring had the *longest* incubation duration, while those which had clutches very *late* in the spring had the *shortest* incubation durations. This progressive shortening of incubation duration from onset to hatching was found to be inversely correlated with the steady rise in the mean noon-time temperature during the season.

This relationship is depicted in Figure 8–1, which shows the mean

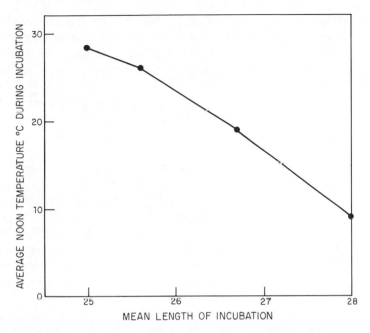

Figure 8–1 The correlation between mean noon temperature during the incubation of clutches of eggs by female mallards in natural conditions and the mean length of incubation duration in days from onset to hatching. Each point represents data collected for a one-month period during which incubation took place. The first point is for the month of June; the second, for May; the third, for April; and the fourth, for March.

number of days of incubation and the mean noon-time temperature for the clutches in each of the successive months of March, April, May, and June.

Other possible influential factors in hatching synchronism may include diurnal photoperiod variations, humidity, or other environmental changes, as well as endogenous factors. Nevertheless, the results of a laboratory experiment that has been performed at Lake Cove support the notion that environmental temperature does play a role in incubation duration and hatching synchronism. This experiment was based on the fact that in the natural situation the female mallard goes off the nest for feeding and bathing. Whenever she leaves the nest, the eggs that she is incubating may cool off. The degree to which they cool is, of course, related to the environmental temperature. Hence, in March or April the eggs may chill to about 7 to 10°C when the female leaves the nest, whereas in June or July the eggs may cool very little.

In this laboratory experiment, there were two groups of 60 laboratory incubated wild mallard eggs each. These two groups were treated identically, except in the degree to which they were cooled daily. Each day, for a 2-hour period, the eggs were removed from the laboratory incubator. One group was placed in a $7 \pm 1°C$ room, and the other was placed in a $27 \pm 1°C$ room. All eggs were turned three times daily until day 24 of incubation, at which time the daily cooling procedure was also terminated.

The eggs that had cooled daily in a $7 \pm 1°C$ room hatched during the second half of day 27 and during day 28 of incubation—that is, over a 36-hour period. On the other hand, the eggs that had cooled daily in a $27 \pm 1°C$ room hatched during day 25, 26, and the first half of day 27 of incubation—that is, over a 60-hour period, which is within the usual 2 to 3-day hatching asynchronism for laboratory incubated eggs.

While the cooling process did not achieve the 3 to 8-hour synchronism found in the natural situation, the results do indicate the importance of environmental factors in this phenomenon, since the strong cooling did reduce asynchronism appreciably. In this group, furthermore, the incubation duration was longer than in the other group, thus confirming the relationship between incubation duration and environmental temperature found in natural conditions.

These data on the effects of environmental temperature upon incubation duration and upon hatching synchronism indicate the necessity for reassessing the question of the developmental age of mallard ducklings at the time of hatching. It is obvious that one would not be justified in regarding a duckling hatched in June after 25 days of incubation as developmentally younger than one that hatched in March after 28 days of incubation. Gottlieb (1961, 1963d) has defined developmental age solely in terms of *number of days* since onset of incubation; our experimental findings strongly suggest that such a definition is untenable. Since the time of hatching can be speeded up or slowed down, it appears that the act of hatching may very well be either a developmental stage indicator or a developmental stage initiator.

We have also used Gottlieb's own techniques of chilling and identical incubation commencement upon duck eggs. We have tested several such ducklings for imprintability at the post-hatch age of 16 hours. Those that had left their shells at different times after incubation onset, even as much as 24 hours apart, were found to be *no different* in imprintability, presumably because they had the same post-hatch age—16 hours.

For these reasons, we have concluded that age in terms of time since hatching is a much more adequate measure of developmentally timed sensitivity to environmental events than is a measure based upon number of days since the onset of incubation. Certainly, it would be of far greater adaptive usefulness for species survival if the learning of the parent by the young or the attachment of the young to the parent were genetically programmed so as to take place within a certain time after hatching, rather than within a certain number of days after the onset of incubation. Hatching synchronism would also be of great survival value for the species for the same reason.

In the light of these considerations, it is astonishing that for so many years Gottlieb's claim that developmental age in terms of number of days since incubation onset—a claim which was actually unsubstantiated by data, as discussed in Chapter 3—was taken at face value and uncritically cited. We have, finally, felt compelled to point out the improper basis of his data presentation upon which he based his conclusions regarding developmental age (Iless, 1972; Iless and Petrovich, in press). Williams (1972) has also presented a critique regarding Gottlieb's methodology.

An additional factor that may possibly play a role in the natural hatching synchronism is the occurrence of vocalizations between parent and young before hatching. This vocalization may possibly be strongly involved in hatching synchronism. Its role in the auditory imprinting process suggested by Gottlieb (1966) and others needs further investigation. We will discuss this particular point after we have dealt with the characteristics of these parent-young vocalizations. We began investigating these vocalizations with the observation that a few days before ducklings hatch, the female mallard will make certain cluck-like sounds. To investigate this phenomenon, the experimental method depicted in Figure 8–2 was employed. Figure 8–2 shows one of the several experimental methods that we have set up for studying the imprinting process in the natural setting. Any sounds that are made within the nest box in which the female is incubating eggs are picked up by means of a concealed microphone. A speaker placed underneath the eggs allows taped sounds to be presented to the female. A thermistor probe permits the continuous recording of nest box temperature at the level of the eggs. Each nest box being monitored is between 300 and 700 feet from the laboratory building housing the tape recorders and the tele-thermometer.

The recordings of the female mallard's vocalizations toward the end of incubation showed that sometimes they consist of single clucks, sometimes of bursts of three, four, or five clucks. They reach a high output rate when a duckling hatches. This vocalization was found to be initiated before the eggs are pipped and to continue periodically until, and during the time of, the nest exodus. Since it was not observed that females which had just begun incubating or which had been incubating for 2 weeks ever made these vocalizations, the question arose as to whether there were stimuli emitted from the eggs that elicited the observed vocalizations from the incubating female.

We investigated this question by using 3½ inch Quam loudspeakers installed just underneath the eggs in the nest, as shown in Figure 8–2.

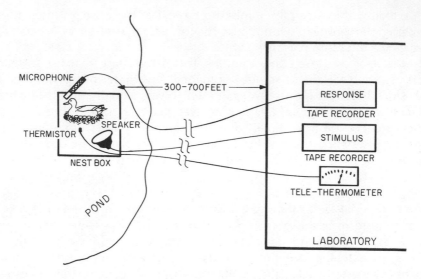

Figure 8–2 Schematic representation of one of the experimental methods of studying imprinting in the natural setting. The nest box in which the female mallard is incubating eggs is a structure elevated above the water of a large pond. The different nest boxes in the pond are all located between 300 and 700 feet from the laboratory building housing the recording equipment. This permits the observation of the natural incubation process without the experimenter disturbing or being seen by the female mallard.

Each loudspeaker was wrapped in an extremely thin and pliable plastic material to insulate them from water. They were placed cone upward at a depth of approximately half an inch in the nest. The loudspeakers were used to play sounds from a remotely located Uher 4000-L tape recorder. The tape was a recording that had been obtained from a hatching mallard egg in the laboratory. The taped sounds of the duckling in the hatching egg consisted of bill clapping and vocalization. These sounds had been recorded at the speed of 7½ inches per second on a Nagra IV-D tape recorder via a microphone placed close to the egg. A 1-minute sample of these sounds was then used as a master tape sound to make the stimulus tape, which consisted of an initial 1-minute silent period followed by the 1-minute duckling sound period, another 1-minute silent period, and so on, ending with the seventh minute, which was silent. The sound pressures made when a hatching duckling vocalizes had previously been determined by a Scott Type 450 sound pressure meter to be approximately 50 to 60 decibels at a distance of about 6 to 8 inches from the eggs. The Scott meter was used after a loudspeaker had been installed at the nest to insure that the volume setting on the Uher tape recorder resulted in the same sound pressure as that emitted by an actual hatching egg. By this means, the sounds of the hatching egg were emitted as the females sat upon their eggs. Every female except one was tested for only one session during her reproductive cycle. Some were tested during their first week of incubation (days 1, 2, and 3), some during their second week (day 10), some during their third week (days 14 to 22), and some in their final week, either close to having or actually having, pipped eggs. One female was tested twice, on day 2 and 3 of incubation.

Recordings of the females' responses when the 7-minute stimulus tape was played at different points during the incubaton period revealed that the specific stage of the reproductive cycle of the individual female had a definite influence upon the nature of her responses to the hatching sounds. As shown in Figure 8–3, in the first few days of incubation, the 11 females gave no vocalization response to the sounds of the hatching duckling. One of these females, tested at the second day of incubation, immediately flew off the nest when the sound was presented. This female

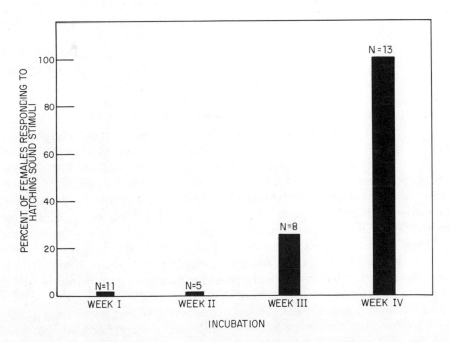

Figure 8–3 The responsiveness of incubating female mallards to a tape recording of sound stimuli emitted by a duckling that had pipped but had not yet emerged from its shell, in relation to the incubation stage of the female mallards' own eggs. The bars represent the percentage of females in the particular weeks of incubation that responded by vocalizing when presented with the hatching sound stimuli.

was subsequently retested. Two others gave a panting sound while fluffing up their feathers, a behavior regarded by students of mallard behavior as being a threat response. This response is illustrated by Figure 8–4a and *b,* which depict the same female, one of those tested in the first few days of incubation, before the sound stimulus was played, and while the sound stimulus was played. Comparison of *a* and *b* shows that the stimuli elicited feather fluffing.

On the other hand, all 13 females tested during the last days of incubation gave the vocalization response to the duckling sounds. In fact, the degree of vocalization was strongly correlated with how soon the incubating eggs were going to pip. While it would appear plausible to hypothesize that sounds from the female's own eggs enhance the probability of her making vocalizations to the stimulus tape, two observations demonstrated that this is not necessarily the case. In these two observations, the tested females turned out to have been sitting upon infertile eggs. *These two females still made the vocalizations to the sounds of a hatching duckling at a time when their own eggs would have been hatching if they had not been infertile.* Therefore, the length of time that they had been on the nest apparently played a role in their responsiveness to these sounds.

None of the 5 females tested during the second week of incubation responded to the hatching duckling sounds, and only 2 of the 8 female mallards tested in the third week of incubation gave vocalizations upon the playing of the hatching sounds. Figure 8–3 shows the results obtained for the females in each week of incubation. The data in Figure 8–3 seem to indicate that among female mallards incubating their clutches in natural conditions, there is a rapid development of vocal responsiveness to the sounds of a hatching duckling toward the end of the normal incubation period. These data, of course, are still preliminary, since some of the female mallards were incubating for the first time and thus probably had had no prior experience with hatching eggs. According to the identification bands worn by the females, some of them were in their second breeding season, some in their third, some in their fourth, and 2 were in their seventh. Ongoing and future research will permit us to examine the effect of previous experience upon the female's vocalization responses to hatching duckling sounds.

In this initial experiment, only 1 female was tested more than once, and in this case the retesting was conducted simply because she flew off the nest during the first test. Hence, another experiment was conducted. It involved daily testing of individual females throughout the entire incubation periods. Twenty females were studied, 5 of which had been imprinted to human beings during the first days of life after laboratory incubation, and the remaining 15 were females found in the

(a)

(b)

Figure 8–4 (a) and (b) are before-and-after photos of a female mallard that has just begun incubating a clutch of eggs. (a) shows the female just before the playing of the stimulus tape of sounds made by a hatching duckling. (b) shows her immediate response, panting and feather fluffing, to the hatching sound stimuli. This is a response given only during the first few days of incubation, when female mallards are not ready to respond positively to hatching duckling sounds.

field.* Testing with the tape-recorded duckling sounds was carried out daily with each female, beginning on day 1 of incubation and continuing through the day that the eggs hatched. The data obtained from this testing parallel those of the initial experiment, even though there are differences between the human-imprinted and field mallards, as shown in Figures 8–5 and 8–6. As shown by these figures, the differences consisted of the human-imprinted females responding to the hatching duckling sounds earlier in the reproductive cycle and in making more vocalizations in response to these sounds. The differences between the human-imprinted and the field mallards in the vocalization responses may well be due solely to sampling error rather than to any early experience effects, since there were only 5 females in the human-imprinted group. Further research is being conducted to determine whether this is the case.

In any event, it is clear in Figures 8–5 and 8–6 that none of the females gave the vocalization responses to the hatching duckling sounds from the 1st through the 18th day of incubation. On the 19th day of incubation, 2 of the 5 human-imprinted mallards gave a few vocalization responses, while none of the field mallards did. Upon the actual day of hatching, which was on day 27 for all subjects, all females gave vocalization responses to the stimulus tape sounds.

This experiment, together with the initial one, demonstates that the female's vocalization response to the sounds of a hatching duckling is not made at every incubation stage, but is made primarily during the last week of incubation, particularly just before pipping, through pipping, and during hatching. The fact that 2 of the tested females had been sitting for approximately 24 days upon infertile eggs and nevertheless gave very strong vocalizations to these sounds indicates strongly that the females are themselves "primed" to make these responses. Whether this phenomenon is strictly under neuroendocrine control or whether other factors such as experience also play a role and to what extent, will be investigated in forthcoming research. Nevertheless, it does appear at present that there may be neuroendocrine factors which prime the female mallard's vocalization responses, which are then elicited by the sounds made by the young in the eggs.

The question of whether the vocalizations proceed stricly from young to parent was then investigated by playing a recording of a female mallard's vocalizations to ducklings which were still in the egg but which had pipped and were scheduled to hatch about 24 hours later.

*Since there is a possibility that some females that have been released to the field after laboratory experimentation lose their identifying leg bands, it must be kept in mind that some human-imprinted female mallards might have been among the field mallards.

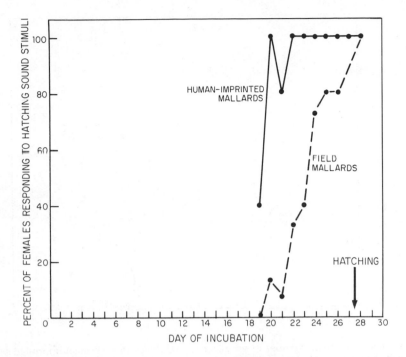

Figure 8–5 The responsiveness of incubating female mallards to a tape recording of sound stimuli emitted by a hatching duckling. Each of 5 females known to have been imprinted to human beings when they were ducklings during the previous spring and each of 15 females found incubating in the field and not known to have been laboratory imprinted were tested daily with the recorded hatching sound stimuli. The points represent the percentage of females on each day of incubation that responded by vocalizing when presented with the hatching sound stimuli. Since none of the females responded during the first portions of incubation, none of the zero scores for these days are plotted on this graph.

The recording consisted of a 1-minute sample of female vocalizations which had been made in response to a hatching duckling.

Two groups of 3 pipped eggs each were used. The test procedure was as follows: The speaker was placed 1 foot from the eggs, and the volume setting on the Uher 3000-L tape recorder adjusted so that the sound pressure at the level just above the pipped eggs was 55 decibels, as determined by the Scott sound pressure meter. This level is similar to the usual 50 to 55 decibels sound pressure which occurs in an actual nest; preliminary experimentation showed that female vocalizations played at the level of 50-55 decibels sound pressure to pipped eggs resulted in good responses from the hatching ducklings. In this experiment, the eggs were given 10-minute trials at 6 different times: 24 hours before

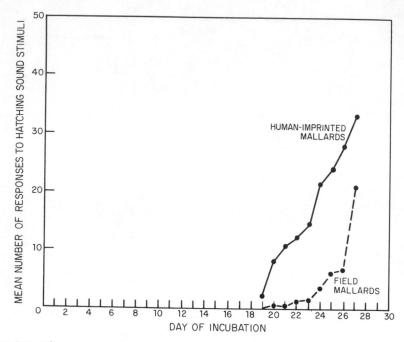

Figure 8–6 The mean number of vocalizations made by the 5 human-imprinted female mallards and by the 15 field mallards during the test session on each day of incubation. Again, zero scores obtained during the first portions of incubation are not plotted on this graph.

scheduled hatching, 3 hours before scheduled hatching, 2 hours before scheduled hatching, 1 hour before scheduled hatching, during actual hatching, and 1 hour after actual hatching. Each 10-minute trial consisted of 5 repetitions of the 1-minute female vocalization sample interspersed with 1-minute silent periods.

The data obtained for the two groups of subjects were highly similar. They show that the degree to which pipped ducklings initiate vocalization when the female mallard is silent changes as the time of hatching approaches and again after actual hatching. This is evident in Table 8–1, which gives both the number of duckling vocalizations during the silent and female vocalization periods at each test session for both groups and the percentage of all duckling vocalizations that were emitted during the silent periods in each test session. In the first place, there was a steady decrease in the relative proportion of duckling calls that were made during silent intervals of the successive tests approaching the actual hatching time. For example, 24 hours before hatching, 34 percent of all duckling vocalizations were made during the silent intervals, while at 3 hours before scheduled hatching, 24 percent of them were. From

TABLE 8–1 NUMBER OF VOCALIZATIONS EMITTED BY PIPPED, HATCHING, AND HATCHED DUCKLINGS DURING FEMALE VOCALIZATION AND SILENT INTERVALS OF TEN-MINUTE TEST SESSIONS

Pre- and post-hatch time in hours	Number of duckling vocalizations during 5 one-minute female vocalization intervals in test session		Number of duckling vocalizations during 5 one-minute-silent intervals in test session		Total vocalizations	Percent of total vocalizations that were made during silent intervals
	Group 1 (N = 3)	Group 2 (N = 3)	Group 1	Group 2		
H − 24	64	36	37	14		
total	100		51		151	34
H − 3	90	77	28	24		
total	167		52		219	24
H − 2	122	127	22	42		
total	249		64		313	20
H − 1	137	132	12	37		
total	269		49		318	15
H − 0 (hatching)	116	139	12	12		
total	255		24		279	9
H + 1	209	210	122	124		
total	419		246		665	37
total	738	721	233	253	1,945	—
total	1,459		486		1,945	—

that time on, there was a steady rapid fall in the percentage of total calls that were emitted during the silent intervals, and during the actual hour of hatching, only 9 percent of the total calls were ones that were made during the silent intervals of the test session. One hour after hatching, however, the proportion of vocalizations made during silent periods went back up to 37 percent. There was also a progressive increase in the total number of vocalizations made by the ducklings during the female vocalization periods, starting with 100 emitted at the test session 24 hours before scheduled hatching, rising to a level of about 250 during the test session 2 hours before scheduled hatching and through the actual hatching hour, with a level of 419 emitted during the test session 1 hour after actual hatching.

Taken together, these data indicate the possibility that the female's vocalization is initiated by sound stimuli from the young at some point when the female is ready for making such responses to the young. Once the female's vocalizations have begun, they apparently serve as a stimulus promoting hatching synchronism. That is, if ducklings respond to her vocalizations, the activities of the individual members of the same clutch become similar and facilitate their hatching within 3 to 8 hours of each other. Impekoven (personal communication, 1971) has conducted research indicating that the female pekin's vocalizations have the effect of increasing the frequency of hatching or pipping movements by pekin ducklings in the egg. Impekoven's work further indicated that the ducklings perform more hatching or pipping movements when the female's calls are made contingent upon their own activity than when they are not. There may, of course, be still other possible factors promoting the observed hatching synchronism in natural conditions. For example, the young may possibly interact with each other in hearing each other's calls. Vince (1964, 1966a, b, 1968 a, b; with Cheng, 1970) has shown conclusively that hatching synchrony in quail is caused by such interaction between the young themselves while in the eggs. Such a phenomenon, of course, has not been demonstrated in the mallard species. Nevertheless, it certainly should not be excluded as a possibility when investigating the causal factors underlying the fact that incubator hatched ducklings hatch over a period of days, while ducklings of the same genetic stock hatched by the female mallard accomplish hatching in a matter of only hours.

The next step in investigating parent-young communication in relation to hatching synchronism is to provide eggs in the laboratory incubator with the same sort of auditory stimulation and communication as are given by a real female to her own eggs, and to compare the effects of this auditory stimulation in comparison with, and in conjunction with, the regular cooling periods during incubation. This step, which is currently being conducted at Lake Cove, is illustrated by Figure 8–7. Microphones and speakers were installed in the laboratory incubator and in an actual nest where a female was incubating her eggs, which had begun at the same time as those in the laboratory incubator. This two-way arrangement permits the incubator eggs to have the same auditory feedback as the female's own eggs: whenever the incubator eggs emit sounds, the female can then respond to them. The vocalizations of the females can be received both by her own eggs and by the incubator eggs.

Two preliminary tests using both cooling and vocal interaction between a female on the nest and young in the laboratory incubator have been conducted so far. In both cases, all eggs in the incubator hatched within a period of 4 hours. Since the parent-young vocalization, together with daily cooling, apparently effected hatching synchronism in these

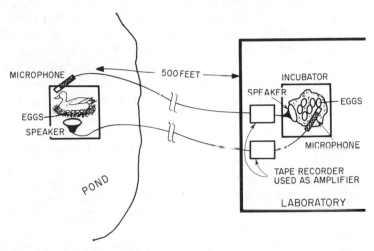

Figure 8–7 An experimental method of studying the effects of parent-young auditory communication upon hatching time and synchrony. In the current phase of this experiment, the nests are approximately 500 feet from the laboratory building housing the incubator with the eggs.

incubator eggs, we must be open to the possibility that parent-young vocal interaction before hatching may contribute less to the formation of the parent-young social bond than to the facilitation of hatching synchronism. Our current research is investigating this question. In any event, it certainly appears possible that the daily coolings serve to broadly synchronize the developmental progress of the duck embryos, while the parent-young vocal interactions before hatching provide the finer synchrony resulting in the observed 3 to 8-hour hatching synchronism observed in nature.

In the meantime, we have made further detailed studies upon the nature of the female mallard's vocalizations to her eggs. Specific observations of naturally incubating females and their eggs have shown that normally ducklings move into the air space within the egg some 24 hours before actual pipping begins. None of the observations made before ducklings move into the air space has revealed any incidence of spontaneous female vocalization to the eggs, although this finding may well be due to limited sampling. During the approximately 72-hour interval between the ducklings' entrance into the air space and the actual nest exodus, the female mallard's vocalizations have been found to have certain characteristics. When ducklings have entered into the air space, and until pipping occurs, the female mallard typically vocalizes at the rate of approximately 1 to 4 times within 1-minute intervals. When pipping occurs, which is approximately 48 hours before the nest exodus, the female vocalizes at the rate of 10 to 15 times within 1-minute intervals. Then there is a long period of time in which the female mallard's vocalization rate returns to the pre-pipping rate. In our observations, we have found that this long period of time, however, is interrupted periodically by 1- or 2-minute bursts of vocalization during which the rate can rise to a level of 45 to 68 per minute. Where we were able to check, this was always found to coincide with the hatching of one of the eggs in the clutch—that is, the actual exit of a duckling from its shell. After hatching, the vocalization rate returns to the low level, to be interrupted again by another burst coinciding with another young duckling hatching, and so on.

A typical vocalization rate pattern is illustrated by Figure 8–8, which is a record of a wild ground-nesting female mallard during the hour around the hatching of a duckling. This figure shows the maximum vocalization rate reached at the time of a duckling's exit from its egg. As can be seen, there were numerous 1-minute intervals in which this female made no vocalizations.

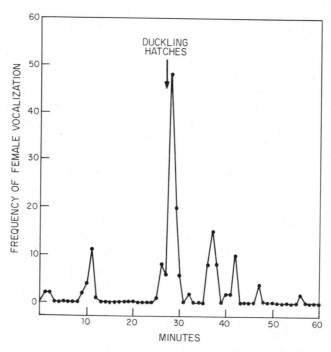

Figure 8–8 The vocalization record of a wild ground-nesting female mallard during the hour of hatching. The total numbers of clucks emitted during each minute are depicted by the points.

After all ducklings have hatched, the female mallard is generally relatively quiet for a number of hours. Bjarväll (1968) has reported similar observations. At the beginning of the nest exodus, the female vocalizes at a low rate, but this quickly builds up to a crescendo, not exceeding, at least in our observations, the rate of 40 to 65 per 1-minute interval. On the basis of these data, it becomes evident that there are two events during which vocalizations are emitted at the maximum rate. The first is whenever a duckling hatches; the second is during the nest exodus, when the female leads the hatchlings off the nest. The high vocalization rate during exodus continues for a longer or shorter time period, depending partly on how quickly the young follow the female mallard as she moves away from the nest.

We have made vocalization pattern records by transmitting the output of the taped recording of the females' vocalization through a Motorola Model MDA92,0-7 full-wave rectifier and then using the output from the full-wave rectifier to activate a chart recorder. The vocalizations of 12 wild female mallards during the nest exodus were studied through high-speed chart recording. Four of these females were ground-nesters, and 8 were elevated box-nesters. Their records showed that the normal vocalization rate of female mallards during exodus is between 3 and $3\frac{1}{2}$ per second during the bursts of vocalization (also called call clusters). Each individual vocalization typically has a duration of approximately 150 milliseconds, and the silent duration between the individual vocalizations is approximately 150 to 180 milliseconds. Other sounds, described later, are also made by the female mallard. Their duration can be from 300 to 500 milliseconds.

The 3 to $3\frac{1}{2}$ per second emission rate of vocalizations during the call clusters would, if prorated to an entire minute, be equivalent to a maximum of 210 per minute. However, such a figure would not give an accurate description of exodus vocalizations, since the 12 females studied were found to emit their individual vocalization at a total rate of 40 to 65 clucks per 1-minute interval during their nest exodus. Since Bjarväll (1968) has reported that females vocalize at the rate of 66 to 200 clucks per minute, it appears that such data are based upon prorating call rates on the basis of call clusters rather than on the basis of entire 1-minute intervals.

As these pages are being completed in June 1972, we have found a ground-nesting female which emitted 93 calls during the minute of exodus. This is the only duck of the many we have observed that has exceeded the 40 to 65 calls per minute rate.

The observations of wild female mallards have also revealed that there are clear and consistent individual differences between individual female mallards in their vocalization patterns. Figure 8–9 shows the vocaliza-

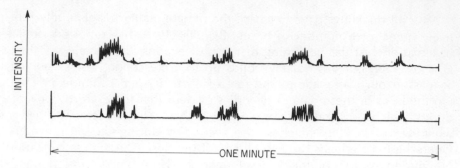

Figure 8–9 One-minute recordings of the vocalizations of 2 different female mallards to the stimulus tape of a hatching duckling. Each upward movement of the recording pen represents a single cluck, with the height of the upward stroke depicting the loudness of the cluck. Comparison of the patterns in the two records reveals some of the kinds of consistent individual differences in vocalization that occur among individual female mallards as well as the agreement between cluck clusters at those times when duckling sounds were emitted by the stimulus tape.

tion responses that were made by 2 different wild females to the 1-minute stimulus tape of a hatching duckling. Each vocalization emitted by the females is represented by one upward stroke of the recorder pen, and the amplitude of that stroke indicates the intensity of the vocalization. While individual differences in vocalizations are apparent for the 2 females, it is also evident that both records are vocalizations in response to the same 1-minute stimulus tape recording of hatching duckling sounds. The Lake Cove observations have shown that each female mallard has her own typical vocalization pattern. Some females make individual clucks spaced out in intervals of seconds. Others emit call clusters that consist of cluck triples or cluck quadruples. Still others may regularly vary in the number of clucks they emit within each call cluster, with the result that their call clusters are unequal. A few females emit many more clucks in their call clusters than do other females in the same situation. Despite their long call clusters, they still emit fewer than 70 clucks per 1-minute interval.

Investigations are continuing to determine whether these individual differences in vocalization patterns persist in successive breeding years, and whether there are effects of early experience upon characteristic vocalization patterns, such as was suggested by the observed differences between human-imprinted and field mallards. At the present time, we have data on 2 ducks over a period of 3 years. The calls, while different *between* the 2 ducks, are almost indistinguishable from one year to the next for the *same* ducks.

Wide-band sound spectrograms have been made of the vocalizations of female mallards at different stages of incubation, hatching, post-hatching, up to exodus, and through the nest exodus itself. For this purpose, a Kay Sona-Graph Model 6061B was employed. We used the frequency range of 85 to 8,000 Hz. Four of these wide-band sound spectrograms, all made from the same female mallard, are shown in Figure 8–10. This is the same female from which the bottom record in Figure 8–9 was obtained. These four sound spectrograms show the kinds of changes that occur in the pitch, duration, and rate of emissions of a female mallard's clucks during the progression of events from incubation through the nest exodus. Figure 8–10a is a sound spectrogram of one of the clusters shown in the bottom record of Figure 8–9. As may be recalled, these vocalizations were made in response to the taped sounds of a hatching duckling. Each cluck lasted about 150 milliseconds, and emission was at the rate of 3 per second. All the other sound spectrograms shown in Figure 8–10, however, are this female's vocal responses to her own newly hatched young. Figure 8–10b shows the female's vocal responses to the call of her own hatched ducklings. The clucks are softer and higher in pitch than in (a). They are also slightly shorter in duration, about 130 milliseconds, but have a similar emission rate. Figure 8–10c depicts the "groan"-like vocal responses of the female to the distress calls of her own young. They have a much longer duration than those in (a) and (b), with their latter components lasting approximately 300 milliseconds. They are emitted at a rate of approximately once every 1½ to 2 seconds. The cessation of the ducklings' distress calls and the onset of their contentment tones are almost immediate. Figure 8–10d depicts an almost quack-like vocal response made by the female mallard to the distress calls of her hatchlings. This call has a duration of approximately 450 milliseconds, and is emitted approximately once every 2 seconds. The distress calls of the ducklings stop immediately.

These typical records shown in Figure 8–10 thus demonstrate that the vocalizations of individual female mallards change both qualitatively and quantitatively during the progression of events from late incubation through nest exodus.

These studies on maternal-offspring vocalizations show that the relationship between the female mallard and the young may develop during the incubation period. As soon as the unhatched ducklings move into the air space within the eggshell prior to pipping, the female mallard vocalizes in response to sounds made by the ducklings. Since the movement into the air space occurs approximately 2 days before the actual hatching, ducklings may experience a great deal of communication with the female through these vocalizations. There is, in fact, an intensive communication and interaction between the female mallard and her offspring well before and during hatching. The pre-hatching communication may possibly set the stage for a very strong imprinting to the

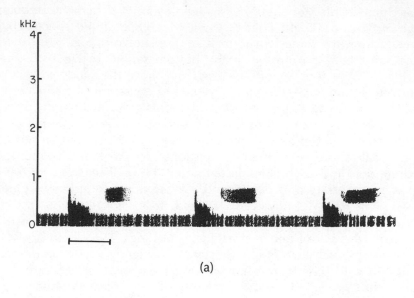

(a)

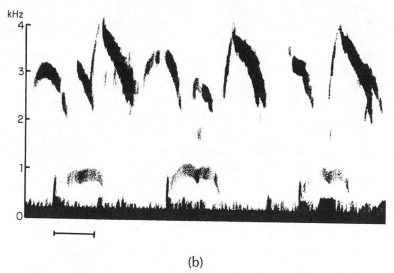

(b)

Figure 8–10 Sound spectrograms of vocalizations made by the same female mallard. (a) Cluster of vocal responses made by the female to a taped recording of hatching duckling sounds when her own eggs were 4 days before hatching. This cluster is one of those emitted in the vocalizations shown in the bottom record of Figure 8–9. Each cluck lasted about 150 milliseconds, and were emitted at the rate of approximately 3 per second. (b) The female's vocal responses to the call of her own hatched ducklings. The clucks are softer and higher in pitch than are the ones shown in (a). They are also slightly shorter in duration, about 130 milliseconds, but have a similar emission rate.

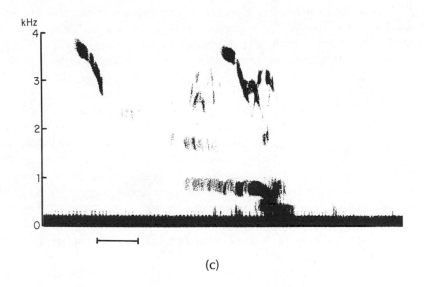

(c)

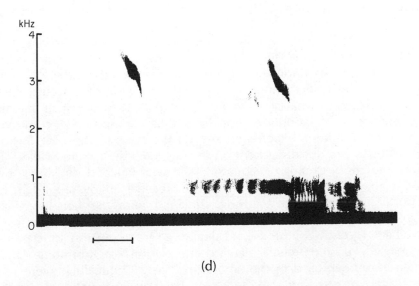

(d)

(c) "Groan"-like vocal responses of the female to the distress calls of her own young. They have a much longer duration, with their latter components lasting approximately 300 milliseconds. Their emission rate is approximately 1 every 1½ to 2 seconds. The cessation of the ducklings' distress calls and the onset of their contentment tones are almost immediate. (d) An almost quack-like vocal response made by the female mallard to the distress calls of her hatchlings. This call has a duration of approximately 450 milliseconds, and is emitted approximately once every 2 seconds. The distress calls of the ducklings stop immediately.

female mallard, in spite of the fact that the young duckling in the egg certainly cannot follow the parent object. In addition, the duckling remains with the female for a period of about 24 hours before the nest exodus occurs, and further vocal interactions occur during this period. While this might appear to constitute evidence against the law of effort (Hess, 1957), determined for laboratory imprinting, there is no reason to assume that there is not a tremendous effort that is performed by young ducklings in the nest as the female mallard moves about in the nest. Furthermore, wild female mallards often have been seen to push their ducklings about, step on them, scratch them with their sharp toes, and squeeze them. Casual observations, through binoculars and motion picture film, on several ground nests have revealed that a large amount of effort—in fact, probably painful effort—may be exerted by hatchling ducklings in the home nest situation. These observations, of course, should be supported with more objective data, but they do fit well with the laboratory findings of Kovach and Hess (1963) that electric shocks enhanced imprintability in critical age chicks.

Hence, it is clear that the experience of ducklings from the time of hatching until the nest exodus a day later is in many ways utterly different from that of ducklings hatched in a laboratory incubator and kept in darkness in social isolation until the time of the laboratory imprinting experience. It is also completely different from the experience of a laboratory-hatched duckling that is immediately placed in a laboratory imprinting experience in which it receives auditory and visual stimulation from the artificial imprinting stimulus, whether it is a duck decoy, a human being, or whatever. Even at the age of 16 hours since hatching, the experience of laboratory ducklings thus exposed to a continuous laboratory imprinting experience are not the same as those of 16-hour-old wild-hatched ducklings kept on the nest with the female mallard. The two experiences cannot be equated. The wild-hatched ducklings, even though they do not follow the mother, receive an overabundance of opportunity to develop a strong affiliation with the female mallard.

This fact is demonstrated by some of the several experiments that have been recently conducted at Lake Cove for the purpose of examining the efficacy of the female mallard in relation to imprinting objects which have been used in the laboratory. First, 20 ducklings were taken out of nest boxes, after they had been hatched by females, removed at the age of 16 hours, well before the nest exodus, and when they were past the peak critical period sensitivity demonstrated for laboratory imprinting. None of these ducklings responded to any sort of laboratory imprinting procedure, despite the fact that they had had no previous opportunity to follow the female, since she had been on the nest with them all during the time prior to their removal. The behavior of these ducklings was unvaried: they either "froze," ran to the nearest hiding place, or ran about with loud distress calls. However, we have found subsequently that in some cases it is possible to have such young follow in an apparatus. In these cases, the ducklings were ones that were removed from the nest box in the middle of the night—2 or 3 A.M.—and they followed a decoy if it emitted the call of a female mallard.

Hence, it is evident that the experiences in the nest with the female mallard for a period of approximately 16 hours, together with the 2 days or so of pre-hatch auditory communication between parent and young, result in an extremely complete imprinting. However, it is also true that the natural female on the nest is biologically the most appropriate imprinting object for a hatchling duckling. Therefore, it may be asked why ducklings ever make any responses at all to the imprinting object. While, at the beginning of this chapter, the notion that this might occur through sensory bombardment with inappropriate stimuli was discussed, the possibility of action through stimulus generalization should not be excluded. If stimulus generalization is involved in laboratory imprinting, there should be a gradient of responsiveness on the part of ducklings with respect to an array of different imprinting objects. Furthermore, such responsiveness to these objects should be quantifiable. One way of determining this is by placing some young animals for a brief time in the natural imprinting situation—that is, with the female mallard on the nest—for a short time period and then finding out how much longer other young animals of the same prior experience and age must be exposed to an artificial situation involving either a decoy, which has been the usual laboratory imprinting object, or a human being, in order to achieve the same degree of parent-young attachment. Such research has been only begun, but so far preliminary findings show that more than 100 minutes of concentrated following experience with an inappropriate imprinting object or a human being is required to approach the effect of 10 minutes experience with the natural imprinting object. This is concordant with the Hess and Hess (1969) finding that ducklings thoroughly imprinted for 3 weeks to a human being did not go to their imprinting object in a choice test as quickly as did those thoroughly imprinted for 3 weeks upon a decoy, even though *all* ducklings chose the correct object.

Still other work has been done with respect to the comparison of natural and artificial imprinting conditions. Twelve ducklings, in groups of 3 each, that had been hatched in the laboratory incubator and then kept visually and socially isolated in a light-proof box were than marked and placed at the age of 15 hours for a period of 10 minutes in the nest of a female that had young of about the same age. Then the young were removed and taken back into the laboratory. In every one of the cases in which this was done, the young animal subsequently chose a simulated female model in preference to an artificial imprinting object or human being when a later test was conducted. The simulated female was a decoy covered with the real skin and feathers of a female mallard, and it emitted the normal cluck-brooding sounds of a female mallard. The artificial imprinting object was the usual male mallard decoy with the standard gock sound (described in Hess, 1957) for half of the animals, and a human being for the other half.

It is clear, then, that the natural stimulus—the female mallard on the nest at the time of the hatching of young—is the most potent imprinting stimulus that can now be used. All other objects that have been used for laboratory imprinting—*even a simulated female model*—fail to approach the effectiveness of the real female mallard that has just incubated and hatched eggs. The imprinted attachment to a real female mallard is formed immediately and irreversibly, while with any other object, irreversible attachment is not immediate, and ducklings require a *considerably larger* amount of experience with these objects to form irreversible attachments. In fact, Schutz and Lorenz (Schutz, 1964, 1965) found that *weeks* of experience were necessary for sexual imprinting to take place.

In addition to these experiments, we have also conducted a series of exploratory studies involving rather small numbers of animals. The results from these, however, were so clear and consistent that they may well be regarded as also indicative of the nature of the natural imprinting process, in addition to giving information as to how further experiments should be conducted. For example, 3 ducklings between 6 and 8 hours of age that had been hatched in an incubator were imprinted for 10 minutes on a human being. Then they were placed in the nest of a female mallard at 10 A.M. shortly before the female's exodus from the nest with her young was to take place. This female had 8 young which she had hatched, and the 3 individually marked incubator-hatched young were added to her brood. She left the nest with *all* 11 young at 11:30 the same morning, so that the incubator-hatched and human-imprinted ducklings had been in the nest with her for 90 minutes before the occurrence of the nest exodus. Even though the thorough and intensive laboratory imprinting experience involved having the hatchlings follow the human being for a distance of at least 50 feet during the 10-minute imprinting period, the results of placing the ducklings with the female before the nest exodus was essentially the same as those of the previous experiment in that the real female mallard proved to be a superior imprinting object. Furthermore, this experiment was repeated with an additional 5 incubator-hatched ducklings similarly imprinted on a human being and then put into a female mallard's nest prior to the nest exodus: all 5 ducklings went with the female for the exodus and stayed with her.

Subsequently, 3 incubator-hatched ducklings that had been imprinted at the age of 15 hours to a human being were placed into a nest when the female mallard was *already outside* the nest calling for the nest exodus and when all her own young were still inside the nest. That is, she had gone down the ramp leading from the nest box into the water and was calling, but none of her own young had yet begun to follow her. Thus, the experimental ducklings had no experience with the female mallard inside the nest at the time the nest exodus was to begin. The 3 experimental ducklings, which had been individually marked, were placed with the female's own 7 young by the experimenters. The experimenters' approach caused the female to swim off to a distance of about 50 feet. After the experimenters had left, she returned to the foot of the nest and began calling. Her own young came down the ramp, one after the other, but the experimental ones did not. The female swam off with her own offspring, and the 3 experimental ducklings had to be retrieved from the nest after a period of time.

The same procedure was tried again with another 3 incubator-hatched, human-imprinted ducklings with another female mallard. The results were exactly the same, except that the experimental ducklings were not removed from the nest. This was done to find if the ducklings' distress calls might cause the female mallard to come back and get them. She did not, and all 3 experimental young were found dead in the nest the next day. This experiment and the previous one thus indicate that human-imprinted ducklings without experience with the female mallard in her nest cannot be imprinted to her, nor do they respond to her by leaving for the nest exodus. In contrast, ducklings that have had nest experience with the female are completely imprinted on her and respond to her by leaving for the nest exodus.

Perhaps it could be argued that a 10-minute laboratory experience, by reason of its temporal shortness, cannot be equivalent to the 24 to 26-hour experience normally had by wild-hatched ducklings in the nest before the exodus, particularly if a small amount of subsequent experience with the female mallard on the nest before the nest exodus can cause them to follow her. While such an argument does not take into account the fact that naïve ducklings that have been exposed for only 10 minutes to a real female mallard have already become irreversibly attached to her, an attempt was made to provide laboratory-hatched ducklings with a prolonged laboratory imprinting experience. Thus 5 laboratory-incubated ducklings were highly imprinted to a human being for a period of 20 hours. During this 20-hour marathon, the ducklings were touched, talked to, kept with the human experimenter, allowed to follow a bit, and handled affectionately. In short, these animals were maximally attended to during these 20 hours. At the end of this time, they were individually marked and placed in a nest with a female at 8 P.M. This female's own young had hatched during the day, and the nest exodus had not yet taken place. The following morning at 9 A.M., or 13 hours later, she left for the nest exodus. Both her own young and the marked experimental ducklings went with her for the exodus. Through observation with binoculars, the marked young were found to be still with the female at least a week later. As far as is known, these young grew up in the natural environment to be no different from the ducklings which the female had raised since hatching.

The converse of these experiments has also been performed. Eight ducklings, all of which had spent about 20 hours in the nest with the female mallard, were removed from the nest before she began the nest exodus. They were then hand-raised, and the experimenters made diligent attempts to imprint the ducklings to themselves. The ducklings were handled by the experimenters continually and were kept in the laboratory for 2 months, on every day of which lengthy attempts were made to socialize the ducklings and make contact with them. At the end of this period, however, these 8 ducklings were still indistinguishable from wild mallards. They continued to flee and act panic-stricken whenever a human being approached them. They never became, in any respect, human-imprinted ducks. At the end of the 2-month handling period, they were banded and released to the duck pond area. The following year, during the spring of 1971, and after the hunting season was over, there were still 5 of them left. In the next year, observations were begun to determine the nature of the nesting and parental behaviors of these ducks.

These pilot experiments, in totality, unambiguously indicate that during the period the ducklings are in the nest with the mallard female from the time of hatching and up to the nest exodus, an extremely strong social bond is formed between the ducklings and the female mallard, despite the fact that the young do not obviously follow her. Of course, they do have a considerable degree of sensory experience during that time, and can exert considerable effort in relation to the female as she moves about the nest, pushing them, stepping on them, squeezing them, or scratching them. *No amount of subsequent experience or handling by human beings appears able to break the attachment bond that is formed during this period.* On the other hand, an equal length of time spent with human beings fails to result in the formation of such an irreversible bond, as subsequent experience with a female mallard in the nest before the nest exodus *completely erases* the effects of the experience with human beings. Such ducklings come to resemble wild-hatched and wild-reared animals. Thus, the conclusion is inescapable that the real female mallard is by far the best and the most potent imprinting object available.

While these are not formal experiments, in the sense that they cannot be dealt with by means of conventional statistical manipulations, they do show what can and should be done in order to investigate imprinting as a real phenomenon rather than in relation to human-constructed laboratory artifacts. It is possible to investigate actual events and natural settings, not only for themselves but also so that they serve as the indispensable yardstick by which the effects of any experimental manipulation are to be judged. In fact, all the questions that have been raised by earlier published results of laboratory imprinting experimentation can also be examined by utilizing the normal, natural imprinting object and the feral setting. Such questions include those involving the critical period, the primacy versus recency effects, the effects of certain kinds of drugs, the effects of punishment, and the effects of massed versus spaced practice or experience.

The methodological significance of this research with the process of actual imprinting is that it represents a definite step in the direction away from the deprivation experience methodology which has characterized the laboratory study of imprinting for two decades. Deprivation methodology has been used in other areas of psychological research, and many investigators in the field of early experience effects have adopted it. Deprivation experiments can be very valuable in giving information regarding the nature of the processes involved in a specific phenomenon, but it is well to be aware of the potential pitfalls in relying upon them exclusively.

On the other hand, it is certainly possible to make mistakes and arrive at erroneous conclusions on the basis of the study of imprinting in its actual setting. In fact, there are already some good examples of this in the work of Gottlieb (1963c, 1965a, b, c). Gottlieb's (1963c, 1965a, b) work dealing with the importance of auditory cues in imprinting initiated the study of imprinting through the use of sophisticated recording techniques. Gottlieb is one of the few researchers who has done any of the necessary investigations to find out what actually goes on in natural imprinting. He has, in addition, studied aspects of events occurring before hatching in relation to imprinting (Gottlieb, 1961; with Klopfer, 1962; 1963b, 1965a, b, c; 1966, 1968). Regrettably, however, some of his finding have not been substantiated by data obtained at Lake Cove and elsewhere (e.g., Bjärvall, 1968).

For example, Gottlieb (1965a) has described the vocalizations made by female mallards during the periods of egg pipping, hatching, and exodus. He stated that there is no qualitative change in the mallard maternal vocalizations at any stage of incubation and hatching through exodus. As is apparent from our investigations at Lake Cove, this statement is inaccurate. In fact, the vocalizations of the incubating female begin as clucks and subsequently change into variations of quack-like sounds. Not only has spectrogram analysis (Figure 8–10) shown that they are qualitatively different, but subjective evaluations indicate that these vocalizations are, indeed, different. Furthermore, Gottlieb (1965a, p. 16) has presented a graph depicting the nature of the female mallard's vocalizations during the 22-hour period before the occurrence of the nest exodus. According to the graphic presentation of his data, Gottlieb has stated that the female mallard's initial vocalization rate is less than 2 per minute, and then rises constantly to reach a level of more than 240 per minute during the nest exodus. Such a rate, however, seems impossible, even on the basis of prorating from the maximum vocalization rate during call clusters, which does not exceed 3½ per second. A female mallard does not emit anywhere near 240 clucks per minute, at least not among the population resident at Lake Cove. Among the many females we have studied, only one has ever emitted more than 70 clucks during a single minute, and even a rate of 70 calls per minute is relatively unusual. It does not seem likely that female mallards in another wild population would emit 240 clucks per minute during the nest exodus. Bjärvall (1968) has also made note of inaccuracies in Gottlieb's (1965a) description of female mallard vocalizations. While Gottlieb (1965a) stated that female mallards begin vocalizing after hatching, and continue to do so until and through the time of the nest exodus, with the call rate increasing during the whole time, Bjarväll (1968) observed that after hatching there are several long periods of silence, until the occurrence of the nest exodus. We also have found this to be the case at Lake Cove. Bjarväll's own report of a female vocalization rate of 66 to 200 clucks per minute is obviously based upon proration from call clusters and falls within the maximum cluster rate of 3½ per second, since this, if prorated, would be 210 clucks per second. Therefore, Gottlieb's (1965a) report on female mallard vocalization appears to be erroneous in its description of call rates as well as in stating that there are no qualitative changes in the vocalizations. Gottlieb's report on female mallard vocalization obviously cannot be used as a basis for further research, as was also pointed out by Bjärvall (1968).

Still another of the several instances in which Gottlieb's data have not been corroborated occurs in his report (1965a) that the mallards investigated did not use elevated nest boxes. In contrast, Hess (1964), Burger (1964), and Bjärvall (1970) all have observed that mallards will use elevated nest boxes. In Chapter 5, we have dealt with our data regarding the use of nest boxes by mallards. In recent years, conservationists (e.g., Burger, 1964; Bjärvall, 1970) have become interested in promoting the use of elevated nest boxes by wild mallards because of the decreased destruction of eggs and offspring by ground predators. Hence, it appears that Gottlieb's (1965a) finding that none of the mallards in his study used elevated nest boxes must be interpreted in the light of evidence obtained at other places. Furthermore, as shown in Chapter 5, it is also necessary to investigate the factors disposing mallards to use elevated nest boxes.

Hence, it is obvious that, just because imprinting is studied in its natural setting, there is no guarantee that an experimenter will be able to avoid making errors. Strict attention must be paid to all factors present in the entire context in which imprinting occurs.

While the study of natural imprinting is still in its beginning, several important factors regarding the natural imprinting phenomenon have been revealed. For example, the fact (as already noted by Bjärvall, 1967, 1968) that the hatched ducklings stay in the nest with the female mallard well past the 13 to 16-hour critical period for imprinting in the laboratory situation has several consequences. First, the attachment between an actual parent and duckling is not based solely upon visual characteristics but upon the auditory modality as well. As may be recalled, Ramsay and Hess (1954) early demonstrated that auditory factors are important in eliciting following and attachment in laboratory imprinting, and Gottlieb (1963a, b, c; 1965a, b, c; 1966) has indicated that both auditory factors and prenatal experiences are important in the filial-parent attachment process. Second, all young, even the late hatchers, appear to be fully imprinted to the female mallard when the nest exodus occurs. The completion of the imprinting process can thus occur within the nest when each individual duckling is maturationally ready, and the fact that all ducklings immediately follow the female mallard at the nest exodus is the consequence of that imprinting. Third, the completion of the imprinting process *before* the occurrence of the nest exodus is advantageous to the survival of the young, since the nest exodus can thus be delayed an additional day if weather conditions are unfavorable without resulting in harmful effects upon the parent-young relationship.

There are certainly many factors in addition to the ones touched upon in this report, and they all require investigation in relation to parent-young interaction in the natural setting. It is very important, for example, to determine the effect of semi-domestication upon the observed behavior. Much of the literature has demonstrated that behavior often can reflect particular adaptations to specific ecological situations. Of importance is not only the specific ecological context but also the effects of early experience upon later behavior. For this reason, it is necessary, to take but one example, to be cautious in making generalizations to wild mallards on the basis of data obtained from semi-wild mallards.

A great deal more work remains to be done in the study of imprinting in the natural situation, particularly in the light of the fact that it is so very different from laboratory imprinting in having such definite, immediate, and permanent effects upon the hatchling—a fact that makes us aware that we do not yet know very much about the natural imprinting process. There are already others who have begun necessary work in this direction. Gottlieb (1963a, c; 1965a) has pioneered in the naturalistic observation of actual events in imprinting by his study of wood ducklings in the nest before the nest exodus. He showed that wood ducklings, which are members of a hole-nesting species, are very different from mallard ducklings, which are members of a ground-nesting species. Wood ducklings are highly resspsonsive to auditory stimuli alone whereas mallard ducklings are very much more responsive when there are both visual and auditory stimuli in the imprinting situation. Graves (1970) has also conducted comparative field and laboratory studies of imprinting in wild turkeys, jungle fowl, and domestic chickens. These studies have demonstrated still further the relationship between the ecological setting of the particular species and the factors to which hatchlings are responsive. Graves, in studying the parent-young relationship in these three species during and after the nest exodus, noted strikingly different ways in which the parent-young communication is conducted. Graves observed that Ossabaw Island wild turkeys live in relatively open forest and that the females lead their young quietly from place to place. Under such conditions the young are highly dependent upon visual stimuli to maintain contact with their parent. Jungle fowl, on the other hand, live in dense forests, and the hen clucks constantly to maintain contact with her offspring. Graves also studied the imprinting responses of these species in laboratory situations and found that while turkey poults formed stable imprinting bonds toward visual stimuli, jungle fowl chicks evidenced less stable bonds with visual stimuli. These chicks were found to exhibit appetitive behavior toward broody hen clucks and to recognize objects to which early exposure had occurred only if these objects emitted clucks emitted at the biologically appropriate rate.

These studies, which are within the compass of ecology, population biology, and evolution, together with those which we have been conducting indicate the trend which must be followed in the future in order to ascertain the actual imprinting processes occurring in nature. Once we have learned more about the dynamics of actual imprinting processes, we should be in a position to discover some aspects of their neurophysiological and macromolecular bases. Several researchers have begun such investigation in the area of laboratory imprinting. In our own laboratories, we have done some preliminary work involving developmentally scheduled macromolecular events during the first day of life. So far, it does appear possible that through such research, particularly when applied to actual imprinting, we will be able to find out just what it is that imprinting *does* to the animal and what structured mechanisms react to imprinting events, record them and the pathways that then influence the subsequent development and expression of later behaviors.

It has become evident that, in order to investigate reality, behavior research must not only utilize the best techniques that the laboratory has to offer but must also employ them in the actual setting in which the behavior in question naturally occurs. In the case of imprinting, biologically appropriate objects must be used in relation to each other, in order for the relevant variables to be adequately investigated. It has become important to understand that all findings and data generated by the scientific investigation of behavior must be interpreted and explained in terms of actual reality. This means that the "control" in imprinting research is the actual imprinting experience between the female mallard and young in the feral setting. That is, the actual imprinting experience must not only be studied but also must serve as the yardstick for measuring the effects of any experimental manipulation.

Up to this time, it has not been the normal procedure to do research outdoors. But it may be that the time has come to realize that, in at least some respects, laboratory research has a real potentiality of leading to a sterile and dead end, in which the behavior being investigated bears no relation at all to what actually occurs in nature. Therefore, in conclusion, it appears that the possibilities of utilizing the natural world, instead of the "highly controlled" laboratory situation, may become the way of the future as far as research in imprinting, ethology in general, and many areas of psychological research in behavior are concerned.

REFERENCES

BJÄRVALL, ANDERS. The critical period and the interval between hatching and exodus in mallard ducklings. *Behaviour,* 1967, **28,** 141–148.

BJÄRVALL, ANDERS. The hatching and nest-exodus behaviour of mallards. *Wildfowl,* 1968, **19,** 70–80.

BJÄRVALL, ANDERS. Nest-site selection by the mallard *(Anas platyrhynchos):* A questionnaire with special reference to the significance of artificial nests. *Viltrevy Swedish Wildlife,* 1970, **7,** 151–182.

BURGER, G. V. Experiments with nest boxes for mallard ducks at Remington Farms. *Transactions of the Northeast Fish and Wildlife Conference.* Hartford, Conn., 1964. 12 pp, mimeographed.

GOTTLIEB, GILBERT. Developmental age as a baseline for determination of the critical period in imprinting. *Journal of Comparative and Physiological Psychology*, 1961, **54,** 422–427.

GOTTLIEB, GILBERT. A naturalistic study of imprinting in wood ducklings *(Aix Sponsa)*. *Journal of Comparative and Physiological Psychology*, 1963, **56,** 86–91. (a).

GOTTLIEB, GILBERT. The facilitatory effect of the parental exodus call on the following response of ducklings: One test of the self-stimulation hypothesis. *American Zoologist*, 1963, **3,** 518. (Abstract). (b).

GOTTLIEB, GILBERT. "Imprinting" in nature. *Science*, 1963, **139,** 497–498. (c).

GOTTLIEB, GILBERT. Refrigerating eggs prior to incubation as a way of reducing error in calculating developmental age in imprinting experiments. *Animal Behaviour*, 1963, **11,** 290–292. (d).

GOTTLIEB, GILBERT. Components of recognition in ducks. *Natural History*, February 1965, **25,** 12–19. (a).

GOTTLIEB, GILBERT. Imprinting in relation to parental and species identification by avian neonates. *Journal of Comparative and Physiological Psychology*, 1965, **59,** 345–356. (b).

GOTTLIEB, GILBERT. Prenatal auditory sensitivity in chickens and ducks. *Science*, 1965, **147,** 1596–1598. (c).

GOTTLIEB, GILBERT. Species identification by avian neonates: Contributory effect of perinatal auditory stimulation. *Animal Behaviour*, 1966, **14,** 282–290.

GOTTLIEB, GILBERT. Species recognition in ground-nesting and hole-nesting ducklings. *Ecology*, 1968, **49,** 87–95.

GOTTLIEB, GILBERT, and KLOPFER, PETER H. The relation of developmental age to auditory and visual imprinting. *Journal of Comparative and Physiological Psychology*, 1962, **55,** 821–826.

GRAVES, HANNON B. Comparative ethology of imprinting: Field and laboratory studies of wild turkeys, jungle fowl, and domestic fowl. *American Zoologist*, 1970, **10,** 483. (Abstract).

HESS, ECKHARD H. Effects of meprobamate on imprinting in waterfowl. *Annals of the New York Academy of Sciences*, 1957, **67,** 724–733.

HESS, ECKHARD H. Imprinting. *Science*, 1959, **130,** 133–141.

HESS, ECKHARD H. Imprinting in birds. *Science*, 1964, **146,** 1128–1139.

HESS, ECKHARD H. The natural history of imprinting. *Annals of the New York Academy of Sciences*, 1972, **193,** 124–136.

HESS, ECKHARD H. "Imprinting" in a natural laboratory. *Scientific American*, 1972, **227,** No. 2, 24–31.

HESS, ECKHARD H. Incubation duration and hatching synchronism. In preparation.

HESS, ECKHARD H., and HESS, DORLÉ B. Innate factors in imprinting. *Psychonomic Science*, 1969, **14,** 129–130.

HESS, ECKHARD H., and PETROVICH, SLOBODAN B. The early development of parent-young interaction in nature. In: H. W. Reese and J. R. Nesselroade, editors, *Life-Span Developmental Psychology: Methodological Issues*. In press, 1973.

KLOPFER, PETER H. Is imprinting a Cheshire cat? *Behavioral Science*, 1967, **12,** 122–129.

KOVACH, JOSEPH K., and HESS, E. H. Imprinting: Effects of painful stimulation upon the following response. *Journal of Comparative and Physiological Psychology*, 1963, **56,** 461–464.

KOVACH, JOSEPH K., PADEN, PHILIP, and WILSON, GREGORY. Stimulus variables in the elicitation and short-range reversibility of early approach and following responses. *Journal of Comparative and Physiological Psychology,* 1968, **66,** 175–178.

LORENZ, KONRAD Z. Der Kumpan in der Umwelt des Vogels. Die Artgenosse als auslösende Moment sozialer Verhaltungswiesen. *Journal für Ornithologie,* 1935, **83,** 137–213, 289–413.

RAMSAY, A. OGDEN, and HESS, ECKHARD H. A laboratory approach to the study of imprinting. *Wilson Bulletin,* 1954, **66,** 196–206.

SCHUTZ, FRIEDRICH. Über geschlechtlich unterschiedliche Objektfixierung sexualler Reaktionen bei Enten im Zusammenhang mit dem Prachtkleid des Männchens. *Verhandlungen Deutsche Zoologischen Gesellschaft in München,* 1963. Leipzig: Akademische Verlagsgesellschafts Geest & Portig, K.-G., 1964. 282–287.

SCHUTZ, FRIEDRICH. Sexuelle Prägung bei Anatiden. *Zeitschrift für Tierpsychologie,* 1965, **22,** 50–103.

VINCE, MARGARET A. Social facilitation of hatching in the bobwhite quail. *Animal Behaviour,* 1964, **12,** 531–534.

VINCE, MARGARET A. Artificial acceleration of hatching in quail embryos. *Animal Behaviour,* 1966, **14,** 389–394. (a).

VINCE, MARGARET A. Potential stimulation produced by avian embryos. *Animal Behaviour,* 1966, **14,** 34–40. (b).

VINCE, MARGARET A. The effect of rate of stimulation on hatching time in the Japanese quail. *British Poultry Science,* 1968, **9,** 87–91. (a).

VINCE, MARGARET A. Retardation as a factor in the synchronization of hatching. *Animal Behaviour,* 1968, **16,** 332–335. (b).

VINCE, MARGARET A., and CHENG, R. The retardation of hatching in Japanese quail. *Animal Behaviour,* 1970, **18,** 210–214.

WILLIAMS, JOHN T., Jr., Developmental age and the critical period for imprinting. *Psychonomic Science,* 1972, **27,** 167–168.

Author Index

Subject Index